WARREN COUNTY, TENNESSEE

MARRIAGES

1900–1950

Robert A. C. Hillis, Jr.

Heritage Books
2024

WARREN COUNTY MARRIAGES - Continuation BOOK 7 - Jan 1900 to Oct 1900

Jacob C. MITCHELL to Lida JONES Issued 4 Jan 1900 Rites 7 Jan 1900
W. H. Hammer, J. P

Willie WINNETT to Eliza HOLDER Issued 4 Jan 1900 Rites 7 Jan 1900
D. C. Oliver, J. P.

Jesse EVANS (Col) to Martha BROWN (Col) Issued 3 Jan 1900 Rites 7 Jan 1900
Geo. Lee Neely, M. G.

I. G. REED to to Tobithey TEDER (?) Issued 5 Jan 1900 Rites7 Jan 1900
W. H. Hammer, J. P.

Huse LYNN to E. R. ROGERS Issued 8 Jan 1900 Rites 8 Jan 1900
J. L. Thaxton, J. P.

Chas. F. PUTERBAUGH to Eugenia MONTGOMERY Issued 8 Jan 1900 Rites 8 Jan 1900
J. E,. Jones, J. P.

J. M. McGREGOR to Belle CHASTAIN Issued 9 Jan 1900 Rites 10 Jan 1900
George L. Beech, J. P.

I, R. STARKMAN to S. R. CRAWFORD Issued 11 JAN 1900 Rites 14 Jan 1900
C. T. Kell, J. P.

R. E. SUMMERS to Eva M. COMBS Issued 12 Jan 1900 Rites 14 Jan 1900
O. H. Wood, J. P.

Thomas SMALLMAN to Della WORTHINGTON Issued 13 Jan 1900 Rites 14 Jan 1900
G. W. Looper, M. G.

Tom CURTIS to Lou ROBERTS Issued 20 Jan 1900 Rites 25 Jan 1900
I. W. Roberts, M. G.

Robert A. HERNDON to Mary E. HOLT Issued 20 Jan 1900 Rites 21 Jan 1900
J. W. Lance, J. P.

Louis STILES to Ada S. HENCH Issued 27 Jan 1900 NOt Executed

W. M. BOREN to Randy SIMMONS Issued 27 Jan 1900 Rites 28 Jan 1900
L. P. Sanders, J. P.

Charles MULLICAN to Kitie BARRETT Issued 30 Jan 1900 Rites 1 Feb 1900
S. V. Vanhooser, J. P.

Robt. C. HAWKINS to Ruby Lillian PARIS Issued 3 Feb 1900 Rites 3 Feb 1900
W. H. Sutton, M. G.

James P. MULLICAN to Lillie NEWBY Issued 3 Feb 1900 Rites 4 Feb 1900
S. V. Vanhooser, J. P.

Jasper COPE (Col) to Vesta PATTERSON (Col) Issued 10 Feb 1900 Rites 10 Feb 1900
W. P. Parker, M. G.

Grant IRVIN (Col) to Hessie WOODLEE (Col) Issued 10 Feb 1900 Not Executed

Thomas BYARS to Ella COTTON Issued 10 Feb 1900 Not Executed

John MARBURY (Col) to Eliza GRAYSON (Col) Issued 10 Feb 1900 Rites 10 Feb 1900
Geo. L. Beech, J. P.

Charles M. HAMBY to Estie May NUNLEY Issued 14 Feb 1900 Rites 18 Feb 1900
E. N. Yager, J. P.

William GENTRY, Jr. to Ida ARLEDGE Issued 15 Feb 1900 Rites 18 Feb. 1900
David H. Cordell, M. G.

T. J. RAMSEY (Col) to Challie RICHARDS (Col) Issued 19 Feb 1900 Rites 20 Feb 1900
O. H. Wood, J. P.

John GREEN to Belle LYTLE Issued 20 Feb 1900 Rites 20 Feb. 1900
Ernest Christian, M. G.

Huey YORK to Bettie BELL Issued 20 Feb. 1900 Rites 25 Feb 1900
J. A. Lance, J. P.

William KEESEY to Nora McGREGOR Issued 27 Feb 1900 Rites 4 Mar 1900
Geo. L. Beech, J. P.

W. J. CARDWELL to Georgia ETTER Issued 28 Feb. 1900 Rites 28 Feb. 1900
J. R. Stubblefield, M. G.

Hugh JONES to Stella WOMACK Issued 5 Mar 1900 Rites 5 Mar 1900
Sam V. Vanhooser, J. P.

Eugene JACO to Lena UPCHURCH Issued 8 Mar 1900 Rites 11 Mar 1900
L. P. Sanders, J. P.

J. F. YOUNGBLOOD to Daise L. CAMPBELL Issued 10 Mat 1900 Rites 11 Mar 1900
D.C. Oliver, J. P.

Willie GRIZZLE to Hattie NEWBY Issued 10 Mar 1900 Rites 11 Mar 1900
D. C. Oliver, J. P.

Isaac BLACK to A. Clara WEBSTER Issued 12 Mar 1900 Rites 12 Mar 1900
J. E. Jones, J. P.

Dock MARLER to Nora PALMER Issued 12 Mar 1900 Rites 14 Mar 1900
W. H. Hammer, J. P.

S. C. TYREE to Sudie HARWELL Issued 14 Mar 1900 Rites 14 Mar 1900
W. Weakley, M. G.

Frank BRATCHER to Maggie PRIEST Issued 16 Mar 1900 Rites 16 Mar 1900
W. M. Mason, J. P.

A. W. SINGLETON to Nellie May COATS Issued 16 Mar 1900 Rites 16 Mar 1900
J. E. Jones, J. F.

M. A. BONNER to Lula CROUCH Issued 17 Mar 1900 Rites 18 Mar 1900 H. A. Cunningham. M. G.

Jmaes TURNER to Hallie WHITMAN Issued 17 Mar 1900 Rites 17 Mar 1900 W. H. Stewart, M. G.

Henry LOCKHART to Cleo ETTER Issued 17 Mar 1900 Rites 17 Mar 1900 H. L. Walling, M. G.

J. B. GRISSOM to Louisa D. WEBB Issued 20 Mar 1900 Rites 25 Mar 1900 L. P. Potter, M. G.

T. B. WILSON to Maggie SMARTT Issued 23 Mar 1900 Rites 23 Mar 1900 J. C. Keathley, M. G.

James MELTON to Sidney HAMMER Issued 28 Mar 1900 Rites 28 Mar 1900 J. A. Lance, J. P.

Dave HOBBS to Allie CROUCH Issued 31 Mar 1900 Rites 1 Apr 1900 T. M. Carroll, J. P.

Emery CROWE to Martha MONTGOMERY Issued 31 Mar 1900 Rites 1 Apr 1900 Edward C. Boaz, Presby. Minister

Sam BYARS to Lizzie ROMANS Issued 7 Apr 1900 Rites 8 Apr 1900 L. P. Sanders, J. P.

Lusty FUGITT (Col) to Viola MARTIN (Col) Issued 12 Apr 1900 Not Executed

Alex PLEASANT (Col) to Piney GRIBBLE (Col) Issued 11 Apr 1900 Rites 15 Apr 1900 G. W. Looper, M. G.

E. P. SANDERS to Mary Ann MARLER Issued 14 Apr 1900 Rites 15 Apr 1900 W. H. Hammer, J. P.

Vance LUSK to Florence CARDWELL Issued 17 Apr 1900 Rites 18 Apr. 1900 J. C. Keathley, M. G.

Will LEVAN to Belle PEPPER Issued 17 Apr 1900 Rites 18 Apr 1900 W. B. Holmes, M. G.

Walker C. CASE to Lucinda PEDEN Issued 17 Apr 1900 Rites 18 Apr 1900 J. R. Stubblefield, M. G.

John H. TURNER to LAura BROWN Issued 18 Apr 1900 Rites 18 Apr 1900 I. M. Carroll, J. P.

Henry BESHEARS to Mary Ann BARNES Issued 19 Apr 1900 Rites Not Executed

Arch WILCHER to Jessie REYNOLDS Issued 23 Apr 1900 Rites 26 Apr 1900 W. E. Garner, M. G.

Sol HILLIS to Jessie D. WISEMAN Issued 30 Apr 1900 Returned Unsigned

Colley JOHNSON to Violet RUTLEDGE Issued 5 May 1900 Rites 6 May 1900 Jacob Stipe, M. G.

Allie HENNESSEE (Col) to Elnora GIPSON (Col) Issued 5 May 1900 Not Executed

Youree GARMON to Hattie CULLEN Issued 10 May 1900 Rites 11 May 1900 J. E. Jones, J. P.

Robert ZWINGLE to Blanchie MULLICAN Issued 10 May 1900 Rites 13 May 1900 Elisha Webb, M. G.

Moses BOLIN to Elizabeth MACKELHANEY Issued 12 May 1900 Rites 13 May 1900 E. F. Cunningham, J. P.

Samuel Parker WEBB to Lucinda GREEN Issued 17 May 1900 Rites 17 May 1900 Jno. C. Keathley, M. G.

Charlie TALLEY to Laura DARLING Issued 19 May 1900 Rites 28 May 1900 W. B. Holmes, M. G.

Stokley D. ROMAN (Col) to Jennie HIGGINBOTHAM (Col) Issued 4 June 1900 Rites 6/6/06 W. B. Holmes, M. G.

Henry CRUTCHER (Col) to Addie SEITZ (Col) Issued 7 June 1900 Rites 7 June 1900 Thomas W. Johnson, Col. M. G.

Johnnie DAY to Mazey TURNER Issued 13 June 1900 Rites 15 June 1900 J. A. Sluder, J. P.

Buck BOLIN to Janie JOHNSON Issued 16 June 1900 Rites 17 June 1900 E. F. Cunningham, J. P.

George W. SMITH to Clara LOWRY Issued 18 June 1900 Rites 25 June 1900 W. B. Holmes, M. G.

John W. GARTNER to Jessie Wanda GRIBBLE Issued 19 June 1900 Rites 20 June 1900 W. B. Holmes, M. G.

Chas. Calvin GILBERT to Alma Eliz. BRADFORD Issued 20 June 1900 Rites 20 June 1900 W. B. Holmes, M. G.

Sam DUNCAN (Col) to Carrie WILSON (Col) Issued 23 June 1900 Rites 24 June 1900 Thomas W. Johnson, Col. M. G.

Charles P. NEWMAN to Fairy LOCKE Issued 26 June 1900 Rites 27 June 1900 J. L. Thaxron, J. P.

Frank VAUGHN to Bertie Jane McDOWELL Issued 27 June 1900 Rites 1 July 1900 W. S. Grissom, J. P.

Reuben ROBINSON (Col) to Maria BRUSTER (Col) Issued 28 June 1906 Not Executed

James BLAIR to Willie SINGLETON Issued 30 June 1900 Rites 30 June 1900 J. E. Jones, J. P.

Buck DeBERRY to Minnie MOSS Issued 3 July 1900 Rites 4 Jumy 1900 Geo. W. Stroud, J. P.

Claudus ROGERS to Mary Edna EDWARDS Issued 4 July 1900 Rites 5 July 1900 Wm. H. Stewart, M. G.

Claud PEARSALL to Ada HAMILY Issued 4 July 1900 Rites 4 July 1900 W. B. Holmes, M. G.

Bill HAMMOND to Mary CANTRELL Issued 9 July 1900 Rites 9 July 1900 E. N. Yager, J. P.

J. D. SPAIN to Mimnie REEDER Issued 14 July 1900 Rites 14 July 1900 Jno. C. Keathley, M. G.

John FUSTON (Col) to Cora MASEY (Col) Issued 14 July 1900 Not Executed

A. S. ALLEN to Dovie LOCKE Issued 21 July 1900 Rites 22 July 1900 P. G. Potter, M. G.

Jack REEDER to Ada ADCOCK Issued 25 July 1900 Rites 26 July 1900 H. L. Walling, M. G.

A. C. GUTHRIE to Maud MALONE Issued 28 July 1900 Rites 29 July 1900 P. G. Potter, M. G.

Jeff WILLIAMS to Nancy HALL Issued 30 July 1900 Rites 30 July 1900 J. E. Jones, J. P.

W. M. ROLLER to Lizzie TROUPE Issued 1 Aug 1900 Rites 5 Aug 1900 J. A. Sluder, J. P.

F. B. NAFE to Mollie COLE Issued 1 Aug 1900 Rites 1 Aug 1900 Jno. C. Keathley, M. G.

P. G. COTTON to B. A. CHISAM Issued 3 Aug 1900 Rites 5 Aug 1900 L. Vanhooser, J. P.

George L. GILBERT to Mallie ELAM Issued 4 Aug 1900 Rites 12 Aug 1900 S. F. Harrie, M. G.

Billy PARKER to Armor HOOVER Issued 7 Aug 1900 Rites 9 Aug 1900 O. H. Wood, J. P.

G. E. MAHER to Beulah MADDUX Issued 8 Aug 1900 Rites 8 Aug 1900 E. N. Yager, J. P.

John L. LAAGER to Fannie Bell OGLE Issued 11 Aug 1900 Rites 12 Aug 1900 E. E. Ingram, M. G.

E. D. NUNLEY to Hanah DAWSON Issued 11 Aug 1900 Not Executed

William SUMMERHILL to Zora JETT Issued 11 Aug 1900 Rites 12 Aug 1900 E. N. Yager, J. P.

G. W. SHANNON to Nancy A. HULLETT Issued 14 Aug 1900 Rites 15 Aug 1900 I. M. Carroll, J. P.

W. Jasper MULLICAN to Emma CHISAM Issued 14 Aug 1900 Rites 19 Aug 1900 E. W. Mitchell, J. P.

Mortimer Augustine DOTY to Leona PARIS Issued 15 Aug 1900 Rites 15 Aug 1900 W. B. Holmes, M. G.

Alfred DUNCAN (Col) to Eliza SPURLOCK (Col) Issued 16 Aug 1900 Rites 16 Aug 1900 S. M. Keathley, M. G.

Lawrence HOBBS to Dessie TIPTON Issued 18 Aug 1900 Rites 19 Aug 1900 Fred Stepp, J. P.

John KIRBY to Martha MILLER Issued 18 Aug 1900 Rites 19 Aug 1900 E. M. Mitchell, J. P.

John F. HORNE to Della Mae DRAKE Issued 18 Aug 1900 Not Executed

Dallas SAVAGE (Col) to Lou KING (Col) Issued 21 Aug 1900 Rites 23 Aug 1900 A. W. Settles, M. G.

George STOKES to Lizzie JACOBS Issued 25 Aug 1900 Rites 26 Aug 1900 P. G. Potter, M. G.

Henry O'KELLEY to Lillie MYERS Issued 28 Aug 1900 Rites 2 Sep 1900 I. M. Carroll, J. P.

James GIBSON (Col) to Maggie MARTIN (Col) Issued 30 Aug 1900 Not Executed

Verheyden ALLEY to Dee HENDRIX Issued 1 Sept 1900 Rites 2 Sep 1900 E. N. Yager, J. P.

Mac BARNES to Lillie BOYD Issued 1 Sep 1900 Rites 1 Sep 1900 Ernest Christian, M. G.

Marshall H. MARKUM to Emma ALLISON Issued 1 Sep 1900 Rites 2 Sep 1900 J. L. Thaxton, J. P.

Sampson Vanhooser to Dora LORAN Issued 3 Sep 1900 Rites 3 Sep 1900 J. J. Womack, J. P.

Thomas MARTIN (Col) to Alice LANE (Col) Issued 3 Sep 1900 Not Executed

Noah ADCOCK to Lizzie BOULDIN Issued 3 Sep 1900 Rites 5 Sep 1900 I. G. Webb, J. P.

John W. PINEGAR to Ella BOULDIN Issued 3 Sep 1900 Rites 5 Sep 1900 I. G. Webb, M. G.

Lee MERCER (Col) to Edna BROWN (Col) Issued 4 Sep 1900 Rites 5 Sep 1900 A. W. Settles, M. G.

James ALLEN to Emma D. OWEN Issued 4 Sep 1900 Rites 5 Sep 1900
O. H. Wood, J. P.

Elmon BELL to Mollie MATHEWS Issued 7 Sep 1900 Rites 9 Sep 1900
D. C. Oliver, J. P.

Berry MITCHELL to Nancy YOUNG Issued 7 Sep 1900 Rites 9 Sep 1900
O. H. Wood, J. P.

E. S. CAGLE to Mollie ROGERS Issued 10 Sep 1900 Rites 12 Sep 1900
J. J. Meadows, J. P.

R. A. CULLEN to Hattie GANNON Issued 12 Sep 1900 Rites 12 Sep 1900
J. J. Womack, J. P.

Charles ROBERSON to Kizzie JOHNSON Issued 12 Sep 1900 Rites 12 Sep 1900
J. J. Womack, J. P.

Milton MOORE to Hallie ARGO Issued 15 Sep 1900 Rites 16 Sep 1900
O. H. Wood, J. P.

Elsie BONNER (Col) to Jessie WILBURN (Col) Issued 15 Sep 1900 Rites 17 Sep 1900

Jasper MILSTEAD to Maude MELTON Issued 15 Sep 1900 Rites 16 Sep 1900
S. M. Keathley, M.G.

Ernest ROBERTS (Col) to Lizzie COPE (Col) Issued 15 Sep 1900 Rites 16 Sep 1900
A. J. Hutchings, M. G.

Melburn POWELL to Sallie M. HENNESSEE Issued 15 Sep 1900 Rites 16 Sep 1900
Geo. L. Beech, J. P.

George GREEN to Maggie JONES Issued 15 Sep 1900 Rites 16 Sep 1900
L. P. Sanders, J. P.

J. M. LORANCE to Minnie May DeBERRY Issued 24 Sep 1900 Rites 21 Sep 1900
W. H. Stroud, M. G.

H. J. GREEN to Myrtle LYTLE Issued 22 Sep 1900 Rites 23 Sep 1900
Ernest Christian, M. G.

T. W. DAVIDSON to Della Blanche ARNOLD Issued 25 Sep 1900 Rites 26 Sep 1900
W. B. Holmes, M. G,

J. P. DAVENPORT to Susie TENPENNY Issued 28 Sep 1900 Rites 30 Sep 1900
R. H. Davenport, M. G.

B. M. ANDERSON to Thenie MARTIN Issued 28 Sep 1900 Rites 30 Sep 1900
I. G. Webb, M. G.

Sam LUSK to Maggie SAFLEY Issued 3 Oct 1900 Rites 3 Oct 1900
Jno. C. Keathley, M. G.

Thomas FOWLER to J. P. MACLIN Issued 4 Oct 1900 Rites 5 Oct 1900
A. H. Duncan, M. G.

J. F. WALLING to Ida KIRBY Issued 8 Oct 1900 Rites 10 Oct 1900
Jacob Stipe, M. G.

Furm JOHNSON to Demie HILLIS Issued 10 Oct 1900 Rites 10 Oct 1900
Geo. L. Beech, J. P.

John DAVIS to Roberts BIGGS Issued 11 Oct 1900 Rites 11 Oct 1900
J. J. Womack, J. P.

James DAVENPORT to Lizzie KIRBY Issued 11 Oct 1900 Rites 14 Oct 1900
M. J. Jones, J. P.

Joe RAMSEY to Myrtle DODD Issued 15 Oct 1900 Rites 19 Oct 1900
J. R. Stubblefield, M. G.

C. M. HUNTER to Ladye Lon WHEELER Issued 20 Oct 1900 Rites 21 Oct 1900
J. T. Martin, L. C.

Thomas YORK (Col) to Malisa WOOD (Col) Issued 20 Oct 1900 Rites 21 Oct 1900
C. T. Kell, J. P.

MARRIAGE RECORDS VOLUME 8 - Oct. 1900 - March 1904

Amos BILES to Cindy LINN Issued 28 Oct 1900 Rites 31 Oct 1900
J. L. Thaxton, J. P.

Horace PERRY to Cordelia JORDAN Issued 30 Oct 1900 Rites 1 Nov 1900
E. L. Moffitt, J. P.

Cal CAMPBELL to Annie SMITH Issued 1 Nov 1900 Rites 4 Nov 1900 (Record 4 Oct)?
D. C. Oliver, J. P.

Isaac JONES to Della KIRBY Issued 2 Nov 1900 Rites 4 Nov 1900
P. G. Potter, M. G.

Fate CROUCH to Nora MITCHELL Issued 3 Nov 1900 Rites 4 Nov 1900
O. H. Wood, J. P.

J. M. DAVENPORT to Ea-lie REED Issued 7 Nov 1900 Rites 11 Nov 1900
I. W. Vanhooser, J. P.

W. J. HULLETT to Paree FORD Issued 10 Nov 1900 Rites 11 Nov 1900
H. A. Cunningham, M. G.

W. R. OOLEY to Maggie ETTER Rites 10 Nov 1900 Rites 11 Nov 1900
J. E. Givins, L. E.

GRIBBLE
Granville/(Col) to Lina LOOPER (Col) Issued 13 Nov 1900 Rites 17 Nov 1900
J. D. Hash, J. P.

W. T. McAFEE to Bettie ARLEDGE Issued 15 Nov 1900 Rites 18 Nov 1900
O. H. Wood, J. P.

Henry FRENCH to Loula MARTIN Issued 17 Nov 1900 Rites 18 Nov 1900
F. W. Sunister (?) M. G.

S. F. HARRIS to Hesper CAMPBELL Issued 17 Nov 1900 Rites 18 Nov 1900
D. C. Oliver, J. P.

Henry PERRY to Blanche McCONNELL Issued 17 Nov 1900 Rites 18 Nov 1900
L. V. Scott, J. P.

James HOBBS to Margaret BILES Issued 19 Nov 1900 Rites 19 Nov 1900
J. L. Thaxton, J. P.

C. J. PEAK to Elvy BUCHAN Issued 19 Nov 1900 Rites 19 Nov 1900
J. J. Meadows, J. P.

S. C. REED to Bettie EARLS Issued 20 Nov 1900 Rites 20 Nov 1900
I. W. VAnhooser, J. P.

M. H. HANKINS to Maud Lee WALLING Issued 21 Nov 1900 Rites 22 Nov 1900
H. L. Walling, M. G.

Van MARTIN (Col) to Loula HUDDLESTON (Col) Issued 22 Nov 1900 Rites 22 Nov 1900
Thos W. Johnson

W. H. WOODLEE (Col) to Bell ARMSTRONG (Col) Issued 24 Nov 1900 Rites 29 Nov 1900
Thomas W. Johnson

J. T. MULLICAN to Eva CHISAM Issued 1 Dec 1900 Rites 25 Dec 1900
P. G. Potter, M. G.

Thomas R. PETTIT to May RUST Issued 1 Dec 1900 Rites 2 Dec 1900
Jacob Stipe, M. G.

Joe CHENAULT to Annie WALLING Issued 3 Dec 1900 Rites 3 Dec 1900
F. W. Smith, M. G.

Silas HASTINGS to Sallie HOOVER Issued 4 Dec 1900 Rites 6 Dec 1900
C. R. Wade, M. G.

Riley WEBB to Josie BYARS Issued Issued 5 Dec 1900 Rites 6 Dec 1900
S. W. Williams, J. P.

Andy STARKEY to Minnie DAVIS Issued 8 Dec 1900 Rites 9 Dec 1900
W. P. Faulkner, Sr.,M. G.

J. M. DUNCAN to Beatrice POPE Issued 10 Dec 1900 Rites 12 Dec 1900
Jacob Stipe, M. G.

F. M. WINNETT to Mary VAUGHN Issued 12 Dec 1900 Rites 13 Dec 1900
L. B. Sanders, J. P.

John STEMBRIDGE to Margaret J. YOUNGBLOOD Issued 13 Dec 1900 Rites 14 Dec 1900
G. W. Haley, J. P.

J. S. GOFF to Nannie BYNUM Issued 14 Dec 1900 Rites 16 Dec 1900
W. E. Martin, J. P.

Shady GREEN to Cannie ALLEN Issued 15 Dec 1900 Rites 16 Dec 1900
S. M. Keathley, M. G.

Lum HOLDER to Nora TITTLE Issued 18 Dec 1900 Rites 19 Dec 1900
Geo. T. Riggs, J. P.

Firm CUNNINGHAM to Jackie POTTER Issued 19 Dec 1900 Rites 23 Dec 1900
G. P. Potter, M. G.

W. E. FOSTER to L. E. BROWN Issued 22 Dec 1900 Rites 23 dec 1900
L. P. Sanders, J. P.

J.B. GREEN to F. L. CANTRELL Issued 22 Dec 1900 Rites 23 Dec 1900
P. G. Potter, M. G.

E. H. GREEN, Jr. to Dovie HENNESSEE Issued 22 Dec 1900 Rites 23 dec 1900
P. G. Potter, M. G.

Cert. #36 and #37 Blank

John MATHER to Perrie BROWN Issued 22 Dec 1900 Rites 23 Dec 1900
H. A. Cunningham, M. G.

Joe GRIBBLE to Recie TEETERS Issued 24 Dec 1900 Rites 23 Dec 1900
W. B. Holmes, M. G.

Irving FUGITT (Col) to Mary EWING (Col) Issued 24 Dec 1900 Rites 24 Dec 1900
D. C. Warren

W. P. BOTTOMS to Rachael McVEY Issued 24 Dec 1900 Rites 25 Dec 1900
S. H. Templeton, J. P.

DAn HENDERSON to Annie COACH Issued 24 Dec 1900 Rites 25 Dec 1900
J. L. Thaxton, J. P.

William LUSK (Col) to Minnie MARTIN (Col) Issued 24 Dec 1900 Rites 25 Dec 1900
I. T. Hillis, J. P.

S. H. NEWBY to Berthie NEWBY Issued 25 Dec 1900 Rites 25 Dec 1900
H. E. Marler, J. P.

Fred E. WOODARD to Emma YORK Issued 25 Dec 1900 Rites 26 Dec 1900
W. Weakley, M. G.

44 and #45 duplicates of the two above

Charles CORDELL to Lula HARMON Issued 26 Dec 1900 Not Executed

Charles PRICE (Col) to Mamie SAVAGE (Col) Issued 26 Dec 1900 Rites 27 Deec 1900
A. H. Duncan, M. G.

Mack GRAYSON (Col) to Susie RAMSEY (Col) Issued 26 Dec 1900 Rites 26 Dec 1900
W. A. PArker, M. G.

George S. STROUD to Ellie G. WOMACK Issued 26 Dec 1900 Rites 27 Dec 1900
W. B. Holmes, M. G.

Marvin PARKER to Ettie ROWAN Issued 27 Dec 1900 Rites 27 Dec 1900
B. T. Smotherman, M. G.

James STUBBLEFIELD (Col) to Tennie SMITH (Col) Issued 27 Dec 1900 Not Executed

William SMITH to Tennie LOCKE Issued 29 Dec 1900 Rites 30 Dec 1900
L. P. Sanders, J. P.

John G. ROWLAND to Jennie FERRELL Issued 29 Dec 1900 Rites 2 JAn 1901
J. G. Goff, J. P.

Lee BROWN (Col) to Mandy WOODARD (Col) Issued 30 Dec 1900 Rites 30 Dec 1900
O. H. Wood, J. P.

Frank LIVELY to Hattie DAUGHTERY Issued 29 Dec 1900 Rites 30 Dec 1900
P. G. Potter, M. G.

John BATES (Col) to Bell BRADFORD (Col) Issued 29 Dec 1900 Rites 29 Dec 1900
W. M. Ready, M. G.

Wm. F. ELKINS to Maggie BLUE Issued 29 Dec 1900 Rites 30 Dec 1900
W. B. Holmes, M. G.

Palfus KING (Col) to Dilcie ARMSTRONG (Col) Issued 31 Dec 1900 Rites 30 Dec 1900
A. W. Settle, M. G.

W. A. CONNELL to Josie EVANS Issued 1 JAn 1901 Rites 1 JAn 1901
W. Weakley, M. G.

T. C. WEBB to Loura YOUNG Issued 2 Jan 1901 Rites 3 JAn 1901
L. P. Sanders, J. P.

Sam SHERRILL to Roxie MARTIN Issued 5 JAn 1901 Rites 6 Jan 1901
J. D. Hash, J. P.

I. L. HILL to Sallie KEESEY Issued 7 JAn 1901 Rites 8 Jan 1901
J. C. Safley, J. P.

Dea BOYD to Drusie TANNER Issued 8 JAn 1901 Rites 9 JAn 1901
A. C. Myers, J. P.

F. L. LEEPER to Hallie M. COFFEE Issued 8 Jan 1901 Rites 8 JAn 1901
Alex Cowan, M. G.,

H. T. KING to Nancy GREEN Issued 8 JAn 1901 Rites 9 Jan 1901
S. M. Keathley, M. G.

Marion TAYLOR to Maggie BESS Issued 10 Jan 1901 Rites 13 Jan 1901
E. L. Moffitt, J. P.

George PATTERSON to Cora MULLICAN Issued 13 Jan 1901 Rites 16 Jan 1901
B. S. Tanner, M. G.

Chas. B. HAMRICK to Flora Jenettie GROVE Issued 12 Jan 1901 Rites 13 Jan1901
J. W. Cooley, M. G.

J. M. STIPE to Martha WALKER Issued 14 JAn 1901 Rites 16 Jan 1901
L. Safley, M. G.

W. H. GREEN to Maggie NUNLEY Issied 14 June 1901 Rites 17 Jan 1901
S. M. Keathley, M. G.

C. C. BELL to Hallie BILES Issued 16 JAn 1901 Rites 16 Jan 1901
H. W. Walling, M. G.

William JOHNSON to Randy McCORKLE Issued 17 Jan 1901 Rites 18 Jan 1901
L. Safley, M. G.

John WILLIS (Col) to Lillie GUEST (Col) Issued 19 Jan 1901 Rites 20 Jan 1901
J. R. Ramsey, J. P.

Chas. ROBERSON (Col) to Bell COPE (Col) Issued 19 Jan 1901 Rites 27 Jan 1901
J. J. Meadows, J. P.

Robert F. SMITH to Ora DAVIS Issued 19 Jan 1901 Rites 20 Jan 1901
W. Weakley, M. G.

Oliver WRIGHT to Helen ERWIN Issued 21 Jan 1901 Rites 22 Jan 1901
J. J. Mullican, J. P.

William KLIEN to R. Z. WOOD Issued 28 Jan 1901 Rites 31 Jan 1901
J. F. Martin, M. G.

Sterling STARKS (Col) to Mericy EDGE (Col) Issued 2 Feb 1901 Rites 2 Feb 1901
F. B. Bishop, M. G.

John H. SIMPSON to Lula RHEAY Issued 6 Feb 1901 Rites 7 Feb 1901
B. T. Smotherman

Alpha YOUNG (Col) to Hattie LEFTRICK (Col) Issued 11 Feb 1901 Rites 11 Feb 1901
T. W. Johnson

Jim ZWINGLE to Loula CUMMINGS Issued 14 Feb 1901 Rites 17 Feb 1901
I. G. Webb, M. G.

J. S. CUMMINGS to Bernice COCKS Issued 15 Feb 1901 Rites 17 Feb 1901
W. E. Marler, J. P.

J. W. OLIVER to Thursie LANCE Issued 23 Feb 1901 Rites 24 feb 1901
I. W. Vanhooser, J. P.

Wallace STEWMAN to Maud RICHARDSON Issued 1 Mar 1901 Rites 7 Mar 1901
J. P. Bowman, J. P.

William McGREGOR to Nancy JONES Issued 4 Mar 1901 Rites 5 Mar 1901
S. H. Templeton, J. P.

Terry HUSSEY to Mary HIBDON Issued 6 Mar 1901 Rites 6 Mar 1901
F. L. Leeper

Walter A. ROBINSON to Jessie May WEBB Issued 12 Mar 1901 Rites 12 Mar 1901
T. W. Smith, M. G.

Georeg BLACK to Mollie MEDLEY Issued 20 Mar 1901 Rites 20 Mar 1901
N. B. Hempbrey, J. P.

H. P. KEESEY to Maggie SMARTT Issued 23 MAR !()! Rites 24 Mar 1901
J. J. Meadows, J. P.

George HOLLINGSWORTH to Joe MITCHELL Issued 23 Mar 1901 Rites 23 Mar 1901
E. N. Yager, J. P.

William GLENN to Zora PERRY Issued 25 Mar 1901 Rites 28 Mar 1901
J. J. Mullican, J. P.

James Lusk ROSS to Jodie BLACK Issued 2 Apr 1901 Rites 3 Apr 1901
W. B. Holmes, M. G.

Wm. Davis LIVELY to Julia Quiggie CANTRELL Issued 3 Apr 1901 Rites 3 Apr 1901
S. T. Harrie, M. G.

Tom LEFTWICK (Col) to Ann RAINES (Col) Issued 6 Apr 1901 Rites 7 Apr 1901
J. C. Safley, J. P.

Lemuel SPAIN to Mandy CARR Issued 6 Apr 1901 Rites 7 Apr 1901
S, M. Keathley, M. G.

Hnery SHORES (Col) to Belle GRANNISON (Col) Issued 6 Apr 1901 Not Executed

John BRYANT to Sibbie BRIXEY Issued 15 Apr 1901 Rites 15 Apr 1901
J. J. Womack, J. P.

Howard BELL to Minnie HATFIELD Issued 15 Apr 1901 Rites 16 Apr 1901
J. J. Meadows, J. P.

James MARCRUM to Tildie STROUD Issued 16 Apr 1901 Rites 16 Apr 1901
P. G. Potter, M. G.

H. J. WILSON to Mary PENNINGTON Issued 17 Apr 1901 Rites 18 Apr 1901
J. A. Cunningham, M. G.

C. GRIBBLE to Phebe DRAKE Issued 25 Apr 1901 Rites 28 Apr 1901
I. T. Hillis, J. P.

Rutherford HICKS to Bertha M. HOLT Issued 27 Apr 1901 Rites 28 Apr 1901
Geo. T. Riggs, J. P.

Robert REYNOLDS to Pearl MITCHELL Issued 27 Apr 1901 Rites 25 Apr 1901
E. N. Yager, J. P.

William WORLEY to Francis RICHARDSON Issued 27 Apr 1901 Rites 27 Apr 1901
J. W. Cooley, .. G.

Alfred COTTON to Thelie SPARKMAN Issued 29 Apr 1901 Rites 16 May 1901
G. L. Ma---------, M. G.

Wilford PENNINGTON to Bertha BROWN Issued 1 May 1901 Rites 2 May 1901
J. A. Cunningham, M. G.

Sam RAMSEY to Maud PAYNTER Issued 3 May 1901 Rites 5 May 1901
J. R. Stubblefield, M. G.

Henry SPENCER to Jennie BAILEY Issued 11 May 1901 Rites 12 May 1901
E. N. Yager, J. P.

John L. COMER to Nevada PARKER Issued 13 May 1901 Rites 14 May 1901
B. T. Smotherman, M. G.,

John BROWN to Nancy Ann PIGG Issued 13 May 1901 Rites 15 May 1901
W. H. Stewart, M. G.

James PARISH to S. I. F. FERRELL Issued 25 June 1901 Rites 26 June 1901
I. G. Gribble, J. P.

Herbert WILLIAMS to Ruby SMITH Issued 26 June 1901 Rites 26 June 1901
R. W. Zamby, M. G.

G. R. HOLLAND to Leona JOHNSON Issued 1 July 1901 Rites 7 July 1901
I. W. Vanhooser, J. P.

James H. GREEN to Emma L. MELTON Issued 3 July 1901 Rites 4 July 1901
Sol Williams, J. P.

Charles JACOBS to Jimmie A. EDWARDS Issued 4 July 1901 Rites 4 July 1901
H. A. Cunningham, M. G.

Mac STEPP to Mable KIRBY Issued 5 July 1901 Rites 7 July 1901
L. V. Scott, J. P.

Will SMARTT (Col) to Minnie BRADFORD (Col) Issued 9 July 1901 Rites 9 July 1901
J. S. Rucker, M. G.

J. S. KIRBY to Lula RUCKER Issued 10 July 1901 Rites 11 July 1901
P. G. Potter, M. G.

Thos. BURKS (Col) to Layer BROWN (Col) Issued 11 July 1901 Rites 14 July 1901
A. H. Duncan, M. G.

R. F. BELCHER to Maud WINTON Issued 15 July 1901 Rites 17 July 1901
C. R. Wade, M. G.

John H. MAYFIELD to Nancy FARLESS Issued 19 July 1901 Rites 14 July 1901 (?)
S. H. Templeton, J. P.

Timothy JONES to Hesentine KIRBY Issued 20 July 1901 Rites 21 July 1901
G. W. Haley, J. P.

M. W. COWAN to Gertrude HARRIS Issued 7 Aug 1901 Rites 7 Aug 1901
J. R. Harrie, M. G.

S. V. GREEN to Nova REEDER Issued 10 Aug 1901 Rites 11 Aug 1901
W. H. Sutton, M. G.

George GROVE to Flora WATSON Issued 10 Aug 1901 Rites 11 Aug 1901
J. C. Safley, J. P.

Hiram HILDRETH to Harriett SAIN Issued 10 Aug 1901 Rites 18 Aug 1901
J. R. Ramsey, J. P.

Anderson NORTHCUTT to Ida WORLEY Issued 14 Aug 1901 Rites 18 Aug 1901
H. W. Stroud, J. P.

Will DAVIS to Octa STROUD Issued 21 Aug 1901 Rites 25 Aug 1901
O. H. Wood, J. P.

Albert M. ROSS to Nesiah H. REILLY Issued 14 May 1901 Rites 15 May 1901
W. Weakley, M. G.

Lewis ROWAN (Col) to Maggie IRVING (Col) Issued 23 May 1901 Rites 23 May 1901
Thomas W. Johnson, M. G.

Arthue SPENCER to Tennie HAILEY Issued 21 May 1901 Rites 22 May 1901
I. G. Gribble, J. P.

B. W. D. HILL to Sarah CARTWRIGHT Issued 25 May 1901 Rites 28 May 1901
E. L. Moffitt, J. P.

Joseph BURK ({Col) to Clenta HEARD (Col) Issued 25 MAY !()! Rites 26 May 1901
E. N. Yager, J. P.

Hugh W. FRED to Ruby WALLACE Issued 3 June 1901 Rites 4 June 1901
Edgar E. Folk, M. G.

Newt WILLIAMS to Beulah TEMPLETON Issued 3 June 1901 Rites 3 June 1901
E. N. Yager, J. P.

William HARDY to Fannie SLATEN Issued 4 June 1901 Rites 4 June 1901
I. G. Gribble, J. P.

R. P. BILES to Ida BELSHER Issued 6 June 1901 Rites 7 June 1901
B. T. Smotherman, M. G.

B. F. GOLDEN to Charlotte BYARS Issued 6 June 1901 Rites 7 June 1901
L. P. Sanders, J. P.

Sam RAMSEY (Col) to Susie SAVAGE (Col) Issued 8 June 1901 Rites 9 June 1901
J. S. Rucker

Willie SIMS to Flora McCORKLE Issued 9 June 1901 Rites 9 June 1901
W. S. Grissom, J. P.

Frank PATENT to Ida HARDCASTLE Issued 10 June 1901 Rites 13 June 1901
A. J. Crane, M. G.

John L. WILLIS to Mattie BURROUGHS Issued 11 June 1901 Rites 11 June 1901
A. C. Coury, M. G.

A. E. BANKS to Bettie ROGERS Issued 18 June 1901 Rites 18 June 1901
O. H. Wood, M. G.

William CURTIS to Martha PERRY Issued 19 June 1901 Rites 23 June 1901
E. L. Moffiee, J. P.

C. L. CUNNINGHAM to Florence ARGO Issued 20 June 1901 Rites 20 June 1901
W. Weakley, M. G.

Chas. D. COPE to Dora MULLICAN Issued 22 June 1901 Rites 23 June 1901
W. Weakley, M. G.

Tom DAVIS to Daisy CROUCH Issued 21 Aug 1901 Rites 25 Aug 1901
I. N. B. Humphrey, J. P.

G. W. CRAWLEY to Mrs. Rosie Ann EDWARDS Issued 21 Aug 1901 Rites 23 Aug 1901
J. E. Jones, J. P.

Johnn SMARTT (Col) to Mary CARPENTER (Col) Issued 24 Aug 1901 Rites 25 Aug 1901
J. S. Rucker, M. G.

J. H. COUCH to Lou MELTON Issued 24 Aug 1901 Rites 25 Aug 1901
N. B. Humphrey, J. P.

Robert POWELL to Rachael HENNESSEE Issued 24 Aug 1901 Rites 25 Aug 1901
Geo. L. Beech, J. P.

W. A. FULTS to Alice CRISP Issued 25 Aug 1901 Rites 27 Aug 1901
B. F. Smithson, M. G.

Colonel FUSTON to Ellen GRIBBLE Issued 28 Aug 1901 Rites 29 Aug 1901
P. G. Potter, M., G.

Lee VICKERS to Lucy Ann BRENCELOY (?) Issued 29 Aug 1901 Rites 29 Aug 1901
D. C. Oliver, J. P.

J. L. HOOVER to Nannie DeBERRY Issued 31 Aug 1901 Rites 1 Sep 1901
H. A. Cunningham, M. G.

Saint GUEST (Col) to Lena BROWN (Col) Issued 2 Sep 1901 Rites 2 Sep 1901
G. W. Stroud, J. P.

Henry WEBB (Col) to Alice ROGERS (Col) Issued 5 Sep 1901 Not Executed

Emanuel McBRIDE to Daisy SAVAGE Issued 5 Sept 1901 Rites 6 Sep 1901
I. G. Webb, J. P.

Doctor KEELE (Col) to Mollie COPE (Col) Issued 7 Sep 1901 Rites 7 Sep 1901

Thomas CANTRELL to Annie PEARSON Issued 8 Sep 1901 Rites 8 Sep 1901
Ernest Christian, M. G.

Cleveland SMITH to Fannie COPEHART Issued 10 Sep 1901 Rites 10 Sep 1901
M. J. Jones, J. P.

Jesse HOLT to Jane HENNESSEE Issued 9 Sep 1901 Rites 18 Sep 1901
G. W. Haley, J. P.

Page #168 duplicate of Smith & Copehart above

Will B. HENDERSON to Lizzie BROWN Issued 11 Sept 1901 Rites 11 Sep 1901
G. W. Haley, J. P.

Frank HARRISON to Violet SNYDER Issued 13 Sep 1901 Rites 13 Sep 1901
W. H. Stewart, M. G.

E. D. CAMPBELL to Lizzie MOSS Issued 13 Sept 1901 Rites 15 Sept 1901
I. G. Gribble, J. P.

P. F. WOMACK to Mrs. Allie MASON Issued 14 Sep 1901 Rites 15 Sep 1901
J. J. Womack, J. P.

Joe BURGER (Col) to Lucy HAMMONDS (Col) Issued 15 Sep 1901 Not Executed

Lafayette WILSON to SARAH MITCHELL Issued 18 Sep 1901 Rites 18 Sep 1901
E. N. Yager, J. P.

George STUBBLEFIELD to Belle WARE Issued 21 Sep 1901 Rites 23 Sep 1901
J. C. Safley, J. P.

Jack GREEN (Col) to Maria HILL (Col) Issued 25 Sep 1901 Rites 26 Sep 1901
Thomas W. Johnson, M. G.

John R. THOMAS to Callie FANN Issued 27 Sep 1901 Rites 29 Sep 1901
J. G. Goff, J. P.

James M. FREED to Matilda C. DRAKE Issued 28 Sep 1901 Rites 29 Sep 1901
G. T. Riggs, J. P.

J. B. WEBSTER to Bertha PARIS Issued 28 Sep 1901 Rites 29 Sep 1901
E. N. Yager, J. P.

Norman WILLIAMS to Jane HOLT Issued 30 Sep 1901 Rites 30 Sep 1901
D. C. Oliver, J. P.

Callie TUBB to Nellie WILSON Issued 30 Sep 1901 Rites 2 Oct 1901
G. T. Riggs, J. P.

W. L. MALONE to Ella GUTHRIE Issued 9 Oct 1901 Rites 9 Oct 1901
I. G. Grizzle, J. P.

J. M. PRATER to Adeline SMITH Issued 12 Oct 1901 Rites 13 Oct 1901
D. C. Oliver, J. P.

W. H. McWHIRTER to Cornelia ROBERTS Issued 12 Oct 1901 Rites 12 Oct 1901
C. T. Kell, J. P.

Marshall ROBERSON (Col) to Parlee CALIS- Issued 12 Oct 1901 Rites 17 Oct 1901

George T. MEDLEY to Sallie J. FREED Issued 12 Oct 1901 Rites 13 Oct 1901
G. T. Riggs, J. P.

Jacob H. FORDYEE to Altie D. FREED Issued 12 Oct 1901 Rites 13 Oct 1901
G. T. Riggs, J. P.

James BUTCHER to Leona FARLESS Issued 16 Oct 1901 Rites 17 Oct 1901
S. H. Templeton, J. P.

James WOODLEE (Col) to Ann MASEY (Col) Issued 18 Oct 1901 Rites 19 Oct 1901
S. Curry, M. G.

Andrew McCORKLE to Blanche MILLER Issued 19 Oct 1901 Rites 20 Oct 1901
E. N. Yager, J. P.

Frank A. RUTLEDGE to Lula F. FAULKNER Issued 22 Oct 1901 Rites 22 Oct 1901
E. N. Yager, J. P.

Walter Clark McAFEE to Nell Bibb HUMPHREY Issued 23 Oct 1901 Rites 24 Oct1901
W. Weakley, M. G.

J. T. McGREGOR to Mollie MARTIN Issued 25 Oct 1901 Rites 27 Oct 1901
W. S. Grissom, J. P.

Frank LAWSON (Col) to Rosa BARTLETT Issued 28 Oct 1901 Rites 28 Oct 1901
J. D. Hash, J. P.

Tom SMARTT (Col) to Gussie WEIDNUM (?) Issued 1 Nov 1901 Rites 1 Nov 1901
J. E. Reynolds, J. P.

John T. GREEN to Ocie CRIM Issued 9 Nov 1901 Rites 10 Nov 1901
O. C. Crain, J. P.

J. Manson BELL to Mary JORDEN Issued 9 Nov 1901 Rites 10 Nov 1901
G. W. Haley, J. P.

Sam B. JONES to Clora JONES Issued 14 Nov 1901 Rites 17 Nov 1901
B. T. Woosley, M. G.

Wm Pitt HICKERSON to Daisy Sanders FAULKNER Issued 20 Nov 1901 Rites 20 Nov 1901
R. W. Binkley, M. G,

James T. MARTIN to Emma FINGER Issued 20 Nov 1901 Rites 20 Nov 1901
W. R. Keathley, M. G.

Polk SMITH (Col) to Beulah DODSON (Col) Issued 20 Nov 1901 Rites 21 Nov 1901
J. L. Thaxton, J. P.

David W. DIAL to Bettie Florence PARKER Issued 20 Nov 1901 Rites 20 Nov 1901
R. W. Binkley, M. G.

George W. PENN to Mrs. Fannie STORRS Issued 27 Nov 1901 Rites
P. G. Potter, M. G.

Jesse BRIXEY to Della CRISP Issued 28 Nov 1901 Rites 28 Nov 1901
O. H. Wood, J. P.

George DURHAM to DAisy FREEMAN Issued 29 Nov 1901 Rites 30 Nov 1901
I. G. Webb, J. P.

Albert ORRICK to Leathie SMITHSON Issued 30 Nov 1901 Rites 2 Dec 1901
G. W. Haley, J. P.

L. D. HOLLANDSWORTH to Agnes T. OLIVER Issued 2 Dec 1901 Rites 3 Dec 1901
I. W. Vanhooser, J. P.

Harvey CLENDENEN to Alice JENNINGS Issued 3 Dec 1901 Rites 5 Dec 1901
J. C. Safley, J. P.

J. T. HENEGAR to Ada GARNER Issued 4 Dec 1901 Rites 5 Dec 1901
O. H. Wood, J. P.

James HUNTER to Randy HILLIS Issued 7 Dec 1901 Rites 8 Dec 1901
O. C. Crain, J. P.

Ed BLANKS to Ella RICHARDSON Issued 7 Dec 1901 Rites 8 Dec 1901
L. P. SANDERS, J. P.

Tom HENEGAR (C) to Nora RAMSEY (C) Issued 7 Dec 1901 Rites 8 Dec 1901
E. N. YAger, J. P.

John H. COLLIER to Mrs. Sallie ROBINSON Issued 11 Dec 1901 Rites 12 Dec 1901
G. T. Riggs, J. P.

Wm. Henry MADEWELL to Etta Florence GOLDTRAP Issued 14 Dec 1901 Rites 15 Dec
G. W. Keathley, M. G.

U. S. KNIGHT to Ella BYARS Issued 14 Dec 1901 Rites 15 Dec 1901
J. K. P. Wjitlock, J. P|

L. P. DAVIS to Era TURNER Issued 14 dec 1901 Rites 15 Dec 1901
S. M. Keathley, M. G.

D. H. MILLER to MAUDE ROWLAND Issued 18 Dec 1901 Rites 22 Dec 1901
I. T. Hillis, J. P.

M. C. TALLEY to Flora I. PARKER Issued 19 Dec 1901 Rites 22 Dec 1901
W. R. Keathely, M. G.

T. L. PEARSALL to Eliza POWELL Issued 20 Dec 1901 Rites 22 Dec 1901
S. T. Harris, M. G.

W. C. GARRETSON to Lillie LUSK Issued 21 Dec 1901   Not Executed

G. TIDDWELL (C) to Lula MERCER (C) Issued 21 dec 1901 Rites 22 Dec
Thos. W. Johnson, M. G.

Thomas C. CRAVEN to May COOPER Issued 21 Dec 1901 Rites 24 Dec 1901
N. B. Humphrey, J. P.

Charles LOCKE to Ella WAGNER Issued 23 Dec 1901 Rites 23 Dec 1901
J. L. Thaxton, J. P.

Lum WOOD to Sallie WOOD Issued 23 Dec 1901 Rites 24 Dec 1901
H. A. Cunninghma, M. G.

Firm HOLDER to Sylvaney RITCHEY Issued 23 Dec 1901 Rites 23 Dec 1901
J. G. Goff, J. P.

Isham EWTON to Jerry May McGEE Issued 24 Dec 1901 Rites 25 Dec 1901
L. P. Sanders, J. P.

Fred TILLETT to Evie NORTHCUTT Issued 24 Dec 1901 Rites 25 Dec 1901
R. W. Binkley, M. G.

R. PATTERSON to Genevie GREEN Issued 24 Dec 1901 Rites 25 Dec 1901
O. C. Crain, J. P.

John LOWE to Natie SISSOM Issued 24 Dec 1901 Rites 24 Dec 1901
E. N. Yager, J. P.

James GRIZZLE to Myrtle REYNOLDS Issued 25 Dec 1901 Rites 25 Dec 1901
W. Weakley, M. G.

Samuel GRIBBLE to Mary J. HENNESSEE Issued 25 Dec 1901 Rites 25 Dec 1901
J. C. Safley, J. P.

Dr. J. A. COUCH to Dovie LOGUE Issued 23 Dec 1901 Rites 25 Dec 1901
F. W. Smith, M. G.

Alex SCOTT (Col) to Ella KING (Col) Issued 25 Dec 1901 Rites 27 Dec 1901
N. B. Humphrey, J. P.

C. J. LAWRENCE to Maud ETTER Issued 28 Dec 1901 Rites 1 Jan 1902
W. H. Sutton, M. G.

Paul HERD (Col) to Evie SCOTT (Col) Issued 28 Dec 1901 Rites 29 Dec 1901
J. L. Thaxton, J. P.

Etter DYKES to Junie STOTTS Issued 28 Dec 1901 Rites 29 Dec 1901
D. H. Cordell

Robert MOON to Ada HODGE Issued 28 Dec 1901 Rites 29 Dec 1901
E. N. Yager, J. P.

Dave SMITH (Col) to Evia PRICHETT (Col) Issued 1 JAn 1902 Rites 1 Jan 1902
Thos. W. Johnson, M. G.

Cantrell VICKERS to Callie GIBBS Issued 1 Jan 1902 Rites 1 Jan 1902
J. G. Gribble, J. P.

Guller MYERS to Nannie GROVE Issued 3 Jan 1902 Rites 3 Jan 1902
J. R. Stubblefield, J. P.

J. O. ALTER to Ora MOON Issued 6 Jan 1902 Rites 9 Jan 1902
S. T. Harris, M. G.

W. H. PINEGAR to Eva PACK Issued 6 Jan 1902 Rites 8 Jan 1902
S. M. Keathley, M. G.

J. E. EVANS to Della FARLESS Issued 6 Jan 1902 Rites 6 Jan 1902
J. W. Cooley, M. G.

Alfred SMITH to Mattie CHASTAIN Issued 8 Jan 1902 Rites 9 Jan 1902
S. H. Templeton, J. P.

James SAVAGE (Col) to Evie SMITH (Col) Issued 9 Jan 1902 Rites 9 Jan 1902
A. H. Duncan, J. P.

John JACO to Della BARRETT Issued 10 Jan 1902 Rites 11 Jan 1902
G. W. Haley, J. P.

Eli McVEY to Ora COLLIER Issued 11 Jan 1902 Rites 12 Jan 1902
O. C. Crain, J. P.

B. F. GODDARD to Callista C. SNIPES Issued 14 Jan 1902 Rites 14 Jan 1902
S. M. Keathley, M. G.

Bob BELL to Tansey GIBBS Issued 15 June 1902 Rites 15 Jan 1902
M. J. Jones, J. P.

Chas. M. LUSK to Mattie BROWN Issued 15 Jan 1902 Rites 16 Jan 1902
S. M. Keathley, M. G.

Tolbert CROUCH to Rachael BROWN Issued 24 Jan 1902 Rites 26 Jan 1902
J. C. Safley, J. P.

Tom SMITH to Belle MUNCEY Issued 25 Jan 1902 Rites 26 JAn 1902
J. C. Safley, J. P.

Hackett EARLES to Maud HIGGINBOTHAM Issued 25 Jan 1902 Rites 26 Jan 1902
Ernest Christian, M. G.

Frank ANDERSON to Myra ROWLAND Issued 25 Jan 1902 Rites 26 jan 1902
P. G. Potter, M. G.

Tom PATTERSON (Col) to Josie HILL (Col) Issued 28 Jan 1902 Rites 28 Jan 1902
I. S. Rucker, M.G.

Charles MARTIN to Lizzie NORTON Issued 29 Jan 1902 Rites 30 Jan 1902
R. Keathley, M. G.

Hardy DAVENPORT to Mary MARTIN Issued 31 JAn 1902 Rites 31 Jan 1902
Elisha Webb, M. G.

E. J. ROACH to Carrie MYERS Issued 31 Jan 1902 Rites 2 Feb 1902
J. L. Thaxton, J. P.

Herbert LOWREY to Lula EARLES Issued 1 Feb 1902 Rites 2 Feb 1902
E. N. Yager, J. P.

Mervin D. GREEK to Nellie M. NAFE Issued 5 Feb 1902 Rites 5 Feb 1902
I. W. Weakley, M. G.

Victor POPE to Belle GRISSOM Issued 8 Feb 1902 Rites 8 Feb 1902
Jacob Stipe, M. G.

Byron CLENDENEN to Bertha SMARTT (Col) Issued 8 Feb 1902 Rites 25 Feb 1902
(col.)   N. B. Humphrey, M. G.

J. B. RAINS to Hattie LAWRENCE Issued 11 Feb 1902 Rites 11 Feb 1902
E. N. Yager, J. P.

Elijah BOMAR to Mrs. Mary HENEGAR Issued 19 Feb 1902 Rites 2^ Feb 1902
J. L. Thaxton, J. P.

A. M. PHILLIPS to Mrs. Octa EDWARDS Issued 19 Feb 1902 Rites 20 Feb 1902
J. L. Thaxton, J. P.

S. E. MOON to Frances RICE Issued 26 Feb 1902 Rites 26 Feb 1902
W. Weakley, M. G.

G. A. RUNDLES to Myrtle SHIRLEY Issued 1 Mar 1902 Rites 2 Mar 1902
H. A. CUnningham, M. G.

Henry HAMILTON to Bernice SCOTT Issued 1 Mar 1902 Rites 2 Mar 1902
G. W. Drake, M. G.

Wilburn SMARTT (Col) to Mandy WEBB (Col) Issued 3 MAR 1902 Rites 3 Mar 1902
James T. Broen, M. G.

George HILL (Col) to Rosa HILL (Col) Issued 12 Mar 1902 Rites 14 Mar 1902
J. J. Meadows, J. P.

Buck GLENN to Callie CANTRELL Issued 15 Mar 1902 Rites 16 Mar 1902
J. J. Mullican, J. P.

G. R. BONNER to Catherine SCOTT Issued 17 Mar 1902 Rites 23 Mar 1902
J. J. Meadows, J. P.

Clark BARTON to Pauline FAIRBANKS Issued 17 Mar 1902 Rites 18 Mar 1902
T. W. Smith, M. G.

C. P. MARTIN to Lyda FAULKNER Issued 17 Mar 1902 Rites 18 Mar 1902
T. W. Smith, M. G.

Christie MITCHELL to Alva CANTRELL Issued 25 Mar 1902 Rites 26 Mar 1902
H. L. Walling, M. G.

Ike NUNLEY to Luisa REEDER Issued 25 Mar 1902 Rites 26 Mar 1902
W. M. Milstead, M. G.

Charley C. SNIPES to Mrs. Mora SARTIN Issued 28 Mar 1902 Rites 30 Mar 1902
G. W. Stroud, J. P.

Sam L. BOYD to Frances HAYES Issued 29 Mar 1902 Not Executed

John W. AKEMAN to Thersia PETTITT Issued 2 Apr 1902 Rites 3 Apr 1902
S. H. Templeton, J. P.

R. H.DARNELL to Mary V. BROWN Issued 9 Apr 1902 Rites 10 Apr 1902
W. R. Keathley, M. G.

H. KIRBY (50) to Belle CANTRELL (30) Issued 10 Apr 1902 Rites 10 Apr 1902
E. N. Yager, J. P.

R. B. SIMRELL to Della BAILEY Issued 11 Apr 1902 Rites 11 Apr 1902
M. J. Jones, J. P.

E. W. HIGGINBOTHAM to Lula THATCH Issued 12 Apr 1902 Rites 13 Apr 1902
Ernest Christian, M. G.

Charley GLENN to Dovie SPENCER Issued 12 Apr 1902 Rites 13 April 1902
I. G. Gribble, J. P.

J. B. WEBB to Daisy ROWLAND Issued 12 Apr 1902 Rites 13 Apr 1902
L. P. Sanders, J. P.

Willie PATRICK to Millie GRIFFITH Issued 12 Apr 1902 Rites 13 Apr 1902
Ernest Christian, M. G.

Tom REYNOLDS to Daisy SLATTEN Issued 15 Apr 1902 Not Executed

Butler SMITH (Col) to Jennie SPURLOCK (Col) Issued 16 Apr 1902 Rites 16 Apr 1902
E. N. Yager, J. P.

George ROBERTS to Della JONES Issued 17 Apr 1902 Rites 25 Apr 1902
J. C. Safley, J. P.

P. M. GRIFFITH to Josie BRYANT Issued 19 Apr 1902 Rites 23 Apr 1902
P. G. Potter, M. G.

T. D. GREEN to Hettie Ann BARRETT Issued 22 Apr 1902 Rites 23 Apr 1902
L. P. SAnders, J. P.

J. B. COTTON to Flossie DAVIS Issued 27 Apr 1902 Rites 27 Apr 1902
J. J. Mullican, J. P.

Walter Anderson HOLMES to Belle WILSON Issued 22 Apr 1902 Rites 23 Apr 1902
W. B. Holmes, M. G.

Jesse WINNETT to Alica HOLDER Issued 24 Apr 1902 Rites 27 Apr 1902
D. C. Oliver, J. P.

George RAMSEY (Col) to Mattie SMARTT (col) Issued 24 Apr 1902 Not Executed

L. P. SANDERS to Ida TURNER Issued 26 Apr 1902 Rites 27 Apr 1902
S. M. Keathley, M. G.

F. H. PATRICK to Halie TUCK Issued 30 Apr 1902 Rites 30 Apr 1902
R. W.Binkley, M. G.

E. B. FINNEY to Mrs. Bettie C. ELTON Issued 9 May 1902 Rites 11 1902
J. R. Stubblefield, J. P.

Wm. WALKER to Docia WILSON Issued 10 May 1902 Rites 10 May 1902
J. E. Givans, M. G.

Noah BASHAM to Dora FULLER Issued 13 May 1902 Rites 15 May 1902
J. L. Thaxton, MJ. P.

James BOST to Catherine PARKER Issued 17 May 1902 Rites 18 May 1902
E. N. Yager, J. P.

Andrew STARKEY to Jocie BONNER Issued 17 May 1902 Not Executed

J. E. SMITH to Ella MASSIE Issued 19 May 1902 Rites 21 May 1902
J. W. Cooley, G.

James M. GOODNIGHT to Jennie Lee JONES Issued 22 May 1902 Rites 22 June 1902
W. Weakley, M. G.

Chas. HUDDLESTON (Col) to Dora SLATTEN (Col) Issued 28 May 1902 Rites 28 May /02
J. T. Brown, M. G.

George R. SPURLOCK to Margaret SIMPSON Issued 31 May 1902 Rites 1 June 1902
C. C. Harris, M. G.

Haskell RIGSBY to Bettie SMITH Issued 31 May 1902 Rites 31 May 1902
E. N. Yager, J. P.

James BROWN (Col) to Anna SMOOT (Col) Issued 1 Jun 1902 Rites 1 Jun 1902
C. C. Bright, M. G.

Will SMOOT (Col) to Elnora TIDWELL (Col) Issued 11 June 1902 Rites 11 Jun 1902
C. C. Bright, M. G.

Jcoac SAFLEY to Angie JACO Issued 14 Junc 1902 Not Executed

J. W. LOWE to Susie HILL Issued 14 Jun 1902 Rites 22 Jun 1902
P. H. Wood, J. P.

Jonathan SWANCUTT to Mary BRAXTON Issued 14 Jun 1902 Rites 15 Jun 1902
J. M. Denton, M. G.

Alford MARTIN (Col) to Maggie PHELPS (Col) Issued 17 Jun 1902 Rites 19 Jun 1902
J. J. Womack, J. P.

Wm. L. MANPIN to Elnora FERRELL Issued 22 June 1902 Rites 22 Jun 1902
Thomas W. Johnson, M. G.

Oscar SMITH to Lena SMITH Issued 23 Jun 1902 Rites 29 Jun 1902
L. P. Sanders, J. P.

William ROBERTS to Margaret BOULDIN Issued 28 JUN 1902 Rites 29 Jun 1902
J. W. Roberts, M. G.

Harvey SILLAWAY to Etta WILLIAMS Issued 1 July 1902 Rites 3 July 1902
S. M. Keathley, M. G.

John Y. TURNER to Ida C. STROUD Issued 3 July 1902 Rites 3 July 1902
W. H. Stewart, M. G.

G. H. STROUD to Ellen TURNER Issued 3 July 1902 Rites 3 July 1902
W. H. Stewart, M. G.

O. Z. MULLICAN to Eva PATTERSON Issued 5 Jul 1902 Rites 6 July1902
M. J. Jones, M. G.

Horace GANNON to Tisba HENDERSON Issued 10 July 1902 Not Executed

B. A. CAWTHON to Mary WORLEY Issued 12 Jul 1902 Rites 17 Jul 1902
D. C. Oliver, J. P.

G. C. KELL to Ellen ROMLAND Issued 17 Jul 1902 Rites 20 Jul 1902
J. D. Hash, J. P.

George CRAWLEY to Flora Belle EDWARDS Issued 19 Jul 1902 Rites 20 Jul 1902
O. H. Wood, J. P.

John CONLEY to Cynthia NEWBY Issued 22 Jul 1902 Rites 23 Jul 1902
W. E. Marler, J. P.

Ceaser BARNES (Col) to Jessie SNODGRASS (Col) Issued 23 Jul 1902 Rites 23Jul 1902
C. C. Bright, M. G.

W. A. SMITH to Mattie O. UNDERHILL Issued 26 July 1902 Rites 29 Jul.1902
G. W. Haley, J. P.

Geo. HUTCHENS (Col) to HAttie FERRELL (Col) Issued 29 July 1902 Rites 29 Jul 1902
Thomas W. Johnson, M. G.

T. R. JONES to Nezzie CAMPBELL Issued 2 Aug 1902 Rites 3 Aug 1902
P. G. Potter, M. G.

Joe MAYO to Ollie RICHARDSON Issued 2 Aug 1902 Rites 3 Aug 1902
J. W. Roberts, M. G.

Ernest JONES to Annie May FARLESS Issued 2 Aug 1902 Rites 3 Aug 1902
J. W. Cooley, M. G.

Briney SMARTT (Col) to Mattie GILES (Col) Issued 2 Aug 1902 Rites 3 Aug 1902
Thomas W. Johnson, M. G.

A. J. WOMACK to Martha J. SNIPES Issued 5 Aug 1902 Rites 10 Aug 1902
S. M. Keathley, M. G.

Eugene H. FLETCHER to Lizzie WOMACK Issued 6 Aug 1902 Rites 6 Aug 1902
R. W. Binkley, M. G.

J. P. EDWARDS to Mollie WOOD Issued 6 Aug 1902 Rites 7 Aug 1902
J. F. Martin, M. G.

G. C. DENTON to Martha E. FOSTER Issued 11 Aug 1902 Rites 17 Aug 1902
Robert Keaton, M. G.

S. W. GREEN to Mary JENKINS Issued 11 Aug 1902 Rites 11 Aug 1902
J. G. Goff, J. P.

Milton ARLEDGE to Ollie BESS Issued 12 Aug 1902 Rites 13 Aug 1902
C. S. CAmpbell, M. G.

Jo WALLING (Col) to Oscia COPPINGER (Col) Issued 15 Aug 1902 Rites 16 Aug1902
W. P. Parker, M. G.

D. C. SEARSEY LAWRENCE to Delia JONES Issued 20 Aug 1902 Rites 21 Aug 1902
A. A. Flanders,

F. F. MYERS (Col) to Martha CARR (Col) Issued 20 Aug 1902 Rites 21 Aug 1902
A. C. Myers, J. P.

Ed PARSLEY to Mollie HULETT Issued 22 Aug 1902 Rites 23 Aug 1902
Wm. H. Stroud, M. G.

Albert TANNER to Phebe TURNER Issued 27 Aug 1902 Rites 27 Aug 1902
W. Weakley, M. G.

Rowland MARTIN (Col) to Violet WORTHINGTON (Col) Issued 29 Aug 1902 Rites 29 Aug 1902
G. W. Looper, M. G.

C. R. WOMACK to Cora YOUNG Issued 30 Aug 1902 Rites 31 Aug 1902
W. E. Marler, J. P.

Joe SMITH to Odie BOYD Issued 2 Sep 1902 Rites 3 Sep 1903
J. D. Templeton, J. P.

W. E. GRIBBLE to Hallie JUSTICE Issued 10 Sep 1902 Rites 10 Sep 1902
S. M. Keathley, M. G.

J. A. GREEN to Octa BRYANT Issued 20 Sep 1902 Rites 21 Sep 1902
P. G. Potter, M. G.

J. L. McPEAK to S. E. WOMACK Issued 20 Sep 1902 Rites 21 Sep 1902
J. Mullican, M. G.

Charles BURKS to Margye HULETT Issued 27 Sep 1902 Rites 28 Sep 1902
O. H. Wood, J. P.

T. L. TEMPLETON to Lena SWINDLE Issued 27 Sep 1902 Not Executed

Lewis STILES to FAnnie DAVIS Issued 29 Sep 1902 Rites 29 Sep 1902
E. H. Yankey

Eugene E. HAWKINS to Bertha BLUE Issued 7 Oct 1902 Rites 7 Oct 1902
W. Weakley, M. G.

Arnold SMARTT to Olive SMARTT Issued 8 Oct 1902 Rites 11 Oct 1902
L. V. Scott, J. P.

H. P. MAXWELL to Lizzie CANTRELL Issued 9 Oct 1902 Rites 9 Oct 1902
H. L. Walling, M. G.

Wesley MARTIN (Col) to Mandy ROACH (Col) Issued 11 Oct 1902 Rites 12 Oct 1902
N. B. Humphrey, J. P.

John COLLIER to Sadie McGEE Issued 11 Oct 1902 Rites 12 Oct 1902
O. C. Crain, J. P.

Adam McBROOM to Willie DODD Issued 13 Oct 1902 Rites 15 Oct 1902
W. C. Haston, Judge

Polk ROBERSON to Malinda PEDEN Issued 14 Oct 1902 Rites 15 Oct 1902
A. C. Myers, J. P.

John McBRIDE to Jessie Belle CARTHRON Issued 14 Oct 1902 Rites 14 Oct 1902

Houston GIST (Col) to Maggie WORTHINGTON (Col) Issued 15 Oct 1902 Rites 18 Oct 1902
J. D. Hash, J. P.

Jesse D. HENNESSEE to Josie HARMON Issued 18 Oct 1902 Rites 18 Oct 1902
J. C. Safley, J. P.

Harris MILSTEAD to Ada TURNER Issued 24 Oct 1902 Not Executed

Martin KEEL to Elizabeth McCORKLE Issued 26 Oct 1902 Rites 26 Oct 1902
J. C. Safley, J. P.

E. H. WILEY to Mattie WILSON Issued 30 Oct 1902 Rites 30 Oct 1902
E. C. Preston, M. G.

G. D. DRAKE to Annie PANTER Issued 1 Nov 1902 Rites 2 Nov 1902
J. C. Safley, M. G.

J. B. McAFEE to Emma LISTER Issued 1 Nov 1902 Rites 2 Nov 1902
N. B. Humphrey, M. G.

E. Z. ANDERSON to Laura E. MORROW Issued 6 Nov 1902 Rites 6 Nov 1902
J. F. Martin

Clarence E. GOLLADAY to Palena E. CARR Issued 8 Nov 1902 Not Executed

Robert ARGO to Ella GRIFFITH Issued 8 Nov 1902 Rites 11 Nov 1902
O. H. Wood, J. P.

Lee WALKER to Della PARIS Issued 8 Nov 1902 Rites 9 Nov 1902
J. E. Goff, J. P.

S. T. JAKES to Bettie RAINS Issued 10 Nov 1902 Rites 11 Nov 1902
O. H. Wood, J. P.

J. G. ELROD to Lizzie BURKETT Rites 16 Nov 1902 (Permit attached for Burkett)
W. E. Martin, J. P.

Tolbert PATTERSON to Ethel RUSSELL Issued 19 Nov 1902 Rites 23 Nov 1902
W. E. Marler, J. P.

J. GUM ELROD to Lizzie BURKETT Issued 13 Nov 1902 Rites 16 Nov 1902
W. E. Marler, J. P.
(See 2nd one above)

Charley WILLIAMS to Lola BARRETT Issued 20 Nov 1902 Rites 20 Nov 1902
S. M. Keathley, M. G.

Hiley LOOPER (Col) to Annie BATES (Col) Issued 22 Nov 1902 Rites 23 Nov 1902

Brince POWELL to Katie LARSON Issued 22 Nov 1902 Not Executed

Dillard MADEWELL to Nannie WANNAMAKER Issued 22 Nov 1902 Rites 22 Nov 1902
L. V. Scott, J. P.

D. B. SMITH to Herma (?) Slatten Issued 24 Nov 1902 Rites 26 Nov 1902
C. T. Kell, J. P.

Cornelius SAVAGE (Col) to Cricket RAMSEY (Col) Issued 27 Nov 1902 Rites 27 Nov 1902

Columbus TALLEY to Mattie GREEN Issued 28 Nov 1902 Rites 30 Nov 1902
H. L. Walling, M. G.

Will FINNEY to Mattie CHANDLER Issued 29 Nov 1902 Rites 29 Nov 1902
J. D. Hash, J. P.

Charley TURNER to Effie TENPENNY Issued 29 Nov 1902 Rites 30 Nov 1902
M. J. Jones, J. P.

J. L. DULANEY to Bettie TALLEY Issued 29 Nov 1902 Rites 30 Nov 1902
J. L. Thaxton, J. P.

E. G. MEAD to Mary A. PAINE Issued 1 Dec 1902 Rites 2 Dec 1902
F. L. Leeper, M. G.

Will DUGAN to Leila SUMMERS Issued 2 Dec 1902 Rites 4 Dec 1902
M. J. Jones, J. P.

John McDOWELL to Clara CANTRELL Issued 5 Dec 1902 Rites 7 Dec 1902
Sol Williams, J. P.

Charlie STILES to Purnia BYARS Issued 6 Dec 1902 Rites 7 Dec 1902
Sol Williams, J. P.

Claud DAVIS to Myrtle COATES Issued 15 Dec 1902 Rites 15 Dec 1902
J. E. Jones, J. P.

Thomas O. BURGER to Hallie L. BELLAMY Issued 17 Dec 1902 Rites 17 Dec 1902
W. H. Cotton, M. G.

Pope BYARS to Octa GRIBBLE Issued 19 Dec 1902 Rites 21 Dec 1902
L. P. Potter, M. G.

Monroe CASH to Maggie SMITH Issued 20 Dec 1902 Rites 21 Dec 1902
E, N. Yager, J. P.

Larry RUSSELL to Olie SAFLEY Issued 20 Dec 1902 Rites 21 Dec 1902
W. E. Marler, J. P.

A. E. THOMASON to Sophia SMITH Issued 22 Dec 1902 Rites 24 Dec 1902
O. C. Crain, J. P.

James TITTLE to Paralee RUSSELL Issued 22 Dec 1902 Rites 24 Dec 1902
J. Carroll Stark, M. G.

Warren BETCHEL to Stella COLLIER Issued 23 Dec 1902 Rites 24 Dec 1902
S. M. Keathley, M. G.

Jesse L. GILBERT to Effie HUSSEY Issued 22 Dec 1902 Rites 24 Dec 1902
C. C. Hines

Owen M. WHITE to Katie HUDGENS Issued 24 Dec 1902 Rites 24 Dec 1902
M. P. Woods

Harold BYARS to Hassie GLENN Issued 24 Dec 1902 Rites Dec 1902
Sol Williams, J. P.

W. S. MARTIN to Mary FINGER Issued 24 Dec 1902 Rites 25 Dec 1902
W. R. Keathely, M. G.

Hugh PATTON to Fannie SMITH Issued 24 Dec 1902 Rites 25 Dec 1902
J. J. Mullican, J. P.

R. L. MONTANDON to Bertha ROMANS Issued 24 Dec 1902 Rites 25 Dec 1902
J. D. Hash, J. P.

N.J.H.VanMETER (Col) to Alica ARMSTRONG (Col) Issued 28 Dec 1902 Rites 28 Dec 1902
A. E. Martin

Imery RAMSEY (Col) to Martha MARTIN (Col) Issued 30 Dec 1902 Rites 31 Dec1902
J. L. Thaxton, J. P.

Ed ROWAN (Col) to Sarah NORTHCUTT (Col) Issued 31 Dec 1902 Rites 31 Dec 1902
A. H. Duncan, M. G.

Tom SMITH to Mrs. Melvina HILL Issued 31 Dec 1902 Rites 1 Jan 1903
G. L. Beech, J. P.

Jack MUNSEY to Mary RIGSBY Issued 6 Jan 1903 Rites 7 JAn 1903
J. L. Thaxton, J. P.

Richard MATHEWS to Sallie MEDLEY Issued 7 Jan 1903 Rites 11 Jan 1903
G. W. Haley, J. P.

S. T. BYARS to Hattie HAWKINS Issued 10 Jan 1903 Rites 11 Jan 1903
J. G. Goff, J. P.

John B. SHIRLEY to Mattie LOWE Issued 19 Jan 1903 Rites 19 Jan 1903
J. E. Jones, J. P.

Walter A. HILL to Shellie G. ETTER Issued 20 Jan 1903 Rites 25 Jan 1903
J. J. Meadows, J. P.

Frank BELL to Jennie OWENS Issued 21 Jan 1903 Rites 21 Jan 1903
S. M. Keathley, M. G.

Sam HIGGINBOTHAM to Martha DODSON Issued 24 Jan 1903 Rites 25 Jan 1903
G. L. Beech, J. P.

S. D. COCK to Ellen HOLDER Issued 24 JAn 1903 Rites 24 Jan 1903
W. E. Marler, J. P.

W. A. PARKER to Laura HENDERSON Issued 27 Jan 1903 Rites 29 Jan 1903
W. R. Keathley, M. G.

Walter MOSS to Nellie WILLETT Issued 31 Jan 1903 Rites 1 Feb 1903
L. P. Sanders, J. P.

Jonas VICK to Bettie McGREGOR Issued 5 Feb 1903 Rites 5 Feb 1903
A. J. Brien, M. G.

Charley BRADY to Lizzie WISEMAN Issued 7 Feb 1903 Rites 9 Feb 1903
S. H. Templeton, J. P.

Geo. LEEPER (Col) to Daisy COOPER (Col) Issued 13 Jan 1903 Rites 14 Feb 1903
G. W. Looper, M. G.

W. J. HUMBLE to Maggie WILLIS Issued 17 Feb 1903 Rites 18 Feb 1903
J. L. Thaxton, J. P.

W. J. TAYLOR to S. Etter EMERY Issued 19 Feb 1903 Rites 22 Feb 1903
J. J. Mullican, J. P.

Rice CLENDENON to Nancy B. CURTIS Issued 19 Feb 1903 Rites 22 Feb 1903
E. L. Moffitt, J. P.

J. C. GRISSOM to Maxey HENNESSEE Issued 20 Feb 1903 Rites 21 Feb 1903
J. C. Safley, J. P.

G. F. BILBREY to Emaline ST. JOHN Issued 28 Feb 1903 Rites 1 Mar 1903
S. M. Keathley, M. G.

James J. DARNELL to Arie BRIXEY Issued 4 Mar 1903 Rites 5 Mar 1903
J. R. Stubblefield, J. P.

Robert BARNES to Lizzie HAYES Issued 7 Mar 1903 Rites 10 Mar 1903
S. H. Templeton, J. P.

William TURNER to Susie JONES Issued 4 Feb 1903 Rites 5 Feb 1903
J. R. Stubblefield, J. P.

J. H. SMOOT to Mollie BREWER Issued 4 Apr 1903 Rites 5 Apr 1903
O. H. Wood, J. P.

Charley MILLER (Col) to Georgia WILLIAMS (Col) Issued 9 Apr 1903 Rites 11 Apr 1903
S. M. Keathley, M. G.

Lester JONES to Nancy BARNES Issued 21 Apr 1903 Rites 22 Apr 1903
G. L. Beech, J. P.

R. W. WILLIS to Lena ROSS Issued 22 Apr 1903 Rites 22 Apr 1903
W. H. Cotton, M. G.

Monroe DAVIS to Sallie ROMANS Issued 22 Apr 1903 Rites 26 Apr 1903
L. P. Sanders, J. P.

Tom LEFTWICH (Col) to Lula MILLER (Col) Issued 22 Apr 1903 Rites 22 Apr 1903
S. M. Keathley, M. G.

H. C. HOWARD to Rebeca WEBB Issued 25 Apr 1903 Rites 26 Apr 1903
H. L. Walling, M. G.

E. W. WEBB to Lou WEBB Issued 29 Apr 1903 Rites 29 Feb 1903
P. G. Potter, M. G.

Frank P. HILLIS to Amanda WANNAMAKER Issued 1 May 1903 Rites 3 May 1903
L. V. Scott, J. P.

John RIGGSBY to Martie BASHAM Issued 2 May 1903 Rites 2 May 1903
J. L. Thaxton, J. P.

Ellie McCANLIS to Dove WALKER Issued 2 May 1903 Rites 2 May 1903
J., E. Gr---- , M. G.

A. B. DAVIS to Lizzie GIVENS Issued 2 May 1903 Rites 3 May 1903
S. M. Keathley, M. G.

John COPE to Daisy HUDGENS Issued 5 May 1903 Rites 6 May 1903
S. M. Keathley, M. G.

D. C. MASON to Annie JACO Issued 6 May 1903 Rites 7 May 1903
S. M. Keathley, M. G.

W. C. ROACH to C. A. BROWN Issued 8 May 1903 Rites 8 May 1903
G. W. Stroud,

John HAWKINS to Clopie MORROW Issued 9 May 1903 Rites 10 May 1903
L. P. Sanders, J. P.

John DAVIS (Col) to Jennie ROACH (Col) Issued 14 May 1903 Rites 14 May 1903

James BOLIN to Della COPE Issued 23 May 1903 Rites 24 May 1903
J. L. Thaxton, J. P.

Isaac GRAYSON (Col) to Nannie COPE (Col) Issued 23 May 1903 Rites 23 May 1903
L. P. SAnders, J. P.

Geo. W. THOMPSON to Daisy O. KING Issued 28 May 1903 Rites 28 May 1903
W. R. Keathley, M. G.

Archie J. NELSON to Mary Etta CRADDOCK Issued 28 May 1903 Rites 31 May 1903
A. J. Brien, M. G.

Press ADCOCK to Rachael GOODWIN Issued 30 May 1903 Rites 31 May 1903
S. M. Keathley, M. G.

P. W. KING to Susie ST. JOHN Issued 2 June 1903 Rites 3 June 1903
W. H. Sutton, M. G.

James RAYBURN to Annie G. SMARTT Issued 3 June 1903 Rites 3 June 1903
L. A. Wiggington, M. G.

Thomas J. KING to Jessie WOODLEE Issued 5 Jun 1903 Rites 7 Jun 1903
S. S. Patterson

Sam M. LYNCH to Jessie JONES Issued 9 Jun 1903 Rites 9 Jun 1903
H. L. Walling, M. G.

Thomas EWTON to Flora LAWRENCE Issued 27 Jul 1903 Rites 29 Jul 1903
S. M. Keathley, M. G.

Erastus M. JONES to Mrs. Tennie JONES Issued 29 Jul 1903 Rites 29 Jul 1903
W. T. Tracy

Edward CARTWRIGHT to Mattie SMITH Issued 1 Aug 1903 Rites 2 Aug 1903
G. L. Beech, J. P.

R. E. FITZGERALD to Octa McAFEE Issued 4 Aug 1903 Rites 4 Aug 1903
G. W. Stroud, J. P.

William NORRIS to Hoida MILLER Issued 8 Aug 1903 Rites 23 Aug 1903
J. D. Hash, J. P.

Will GRISSOM to Sallie HANKINS Issued 15 Apr 1903 Rites 23 Apr 1903
Jacob Stipe, M. G.

Frank MICHAEL to Matilda LANCE Issued 17 Aug 1903 Rites 23 Aug 1903
H. A. Cunningham, M. G.

Dud CARR to Allie HOBBS Issued 18 Aug 1903 Rites 19 Aug 1903
J. L. Thaxton, J. P.

Alton HERNDON to Lula BURGH Issued 19 Aug 1903 Rites 20 Aug 1903
J. L. Thaxton, J. P.

Charles DAVIS to Lillie MAY Issued 20 Aug 1903 Rites 21 Aug 1903
L. P. Sanders, J. P.

Charles BRIGHT to Maggie MAY Issued 20 Aug 1903 Rites 21 Aug 1903
L. P. Sanders, J. P.

Lucius YORK to Mattie D_____ Issued 22 Aug 1903   Not Executed

Murphy DRAKE to Lou CANTRELL Issued 24 Aug 1903   Not Executed

Ira L. HENNESSEE to Ora RANDOLPH Issued 26 Aug 1903 Rites 26 Aug 1903
H. L. WAlling, M. G.

B. L. DUNLAP to Zanie GREEN Issued 26 Aug 1903 Not Executed

D. M. JORDAN to Josie SIMPSON Issued 28 Aug 1903 Rites 6 Sep 1903
G. W. Haley, J. P.

H. C. THACH to Edith MASON Issued 31 Aug 1903 Rites 31 Aug 1903
W, H. Cotton, M. G.

John E. WEBB to Mary GREEN Issued 1 Sep 1903 Rites 1 Sep 1903
J. M. Duton, M. G.

Walter B. SANDERS to Belva L. NORRIS Issued 2 Sep 1903 Rites 2 Sep 1903
L. P. Sanders, J. P.

I. M. QUICK to Rebecca JONES Issued 10 Jun 1903 Rites 11 Jun 1903
G. L. Beech, J. P.

H. A. FINGER to Elsie May STANLEY Issued 13 Jun 1903   Not Executed

Howard BELL (C) to Tina WOODLEE (C) Issued 13 Jun 1903 Rites 14 Jun 1903
J. J. Meadows, J. P.

John MASEY to Villa McLAUGHLIN Issued 13 Jun 1903 Rites 14 Jun 1903
W. R. Keathley, M. G.

Mose TIDWELL (C) to Lizzie B. HANDLEY (C) Issued 13 Jun 1903 Rites 14 Jun
Sam Curry, M. G.

B. F. WOODLEE to Ersie MYERS Issued 17 Jun 1903 Rites 17 Jun 1903
H. L. WAlling, M. G.

E. L. NEWMAN to Sallie SMARTT Issued 27 Jun 1903 Rites 28 Jun 1903
C. C. Hines, M. G.

Walter S. NORRIS to Elizabeth GRIBBLE Issued 1 Jul 1903 Rites 1 Jul 1903
R. W. Binkley, M. G.

Robert T. MULLICAN to Nance Lee GILLEY Issued 4 Jul 1903 Rites 5 Jul 1903
J. L. Thaxton, J. P.

Thomas LOWE to Willie REYNOLDS Issued 6 Jul 1903 Rites 7 Jul 1903
E. N. Yager, J. P.

Walter JORDAN to Nannie WILLIAMSON Issued 8 Jul 1903 Rites 15 Jul 1903
G. W. HAley, J. P.

C. W. INGLIS to Sarah McKNOGHT Issued 10 Jul 1903 Rites 12 Jul 1903
S. M. KEATHLEY, M. G.

A. T. NEWBY to Allie MULLIGAN Issued 16 Jul 1903 Rites 17 Jul 1903
W. E. Marler, J. P.

Marion MARTIN to Suella SIMONS Issued 18 Jul 1903 Rites 19 Jul 1903
L. Safley, M. G.

Jerry P. CATEN to Amy THIMISON Issued 22 Jul 1903 Rites 22 Jul 1903
J. E. Jones, J. P.

Granville LOOPER (C) to Cinda GRIBBLE (C) Issued 24 Jul 1903   Not Returned

Lodie ROMINE to Josephine DUKE Issued 24 Jul 1903 Rites 26 Jul 1903
H. A. Cunningham, M. G.

Ben MAYFIELD to Susan AUSTIN Issued 25 Jul 1903 Rites 26 Jul 1903
L. Safley, M. G.

Tom G. GARMON to Nettie JONES Issued 25 Jul 1903 Rites 26 Jul 1903
L. P. Sanders, J. P.

Willie MASON to Maude DODD Issued 25 Jul 1903 Rites 26 Jul 1903
P. G. Potter, M. G.

John TUCKER to Dorotha YOUNG Issued 5 Sep 1903 Rites 6 Sep 1903
H. A. Cunningham, M. G.

Hughey SUMMERS to Callie FOSTER Issued 6 Sep 1903 Rites 6 Sep 1903
M. J. Jones, J. P.

H. SLATTON to Louisa GRIBBLE Issued 8 Sep 1903 Rites 1 Oct 1903
I. G. Gribble, J. P.

Joe MARTIN (Col) to Florence DURLEY (Col) Issued 8 Sep 1903 Rites 8 Sep 1903
I. S. Rucker, M. G.

Will CARR (Col) to Dora MARTIN (Col) Issued 9 Sep 1903 Rites 11 Sep 1903
J. D. Hash, J. P.

J. W. EATON to Ida MURPHEY Issued 9 Sep 1903 Rites 9 Sep 1903
H. L. Walling, M. G.

J. E. ORICK to Hassie TALLEY Issued 11 Sep 1903 Rites 13 Sep 1903
O. H. Wood, J. P.

Charley TENPENNY to Belle STROUD Issued 12 Sep 1903 Rites 12 Sep 1903
M. J. Jones, J. P.

Polk BONNER (Col) to Lou DUNCAN (Col) Issued 17 Sep 1903 Rites 17 Sep 1903
S. M. _____, M. G.

J. L. CANTRELL to Jessie MORROW Issued 19 Sep 1903 Rites 20 Sep 1903
E. N. Yager, J. P.

Lee WILSON to Mary BASHAM Issued 19 Sep 1903 Rites 19 Sep 1903
J. L. Thaxton, J. P.

John C. CAMPBELL to Vesta CAMPBELL Issued 25 Sep 1903 Rites 27 Sep 1903
J. W. Gross, M. G.

Pink WOMACK to Nettie SIMMONS Issued 2 Oct 1903 Rites 4 Oct 1903
A. J. Brien, M. G.

Edward COPE to Josie BLUHM Issued 3 Oct 1903 Rites 4 Oct 1903
S. M. Keathley, M. G.

J. L. JACO to Lillian SIMONS Issued 3 Oct 1903 Rites 4 Oct 1903
JAcob Stipe, M. G.

Dan CUMMINGS to MAude MARTIN Issued 5 Oct 1903 Rites 6 Oct 1903
S. M. Keathley, M. G.

Isham G. WALKER to archir K. ROBERTS Issued 9 Oct 1903 Rites 15 Oct 1903
J. W. Gross, M. G.

W. H. BYARS to Mimmie BARNES Issued 22 Oct 1903 Rites 25 Oct 1903
S. H. Templeton, J. P.

Cann MASINGILL to Bettie SCOTT Issued 23 Oct 1903 Rites 26 Oct 1903
J. J. Meadows, J. P.

A,. R. FOSTER to H. M. REEDER Issued 24 Oct 1903 Rites 25 Oct 1903
Robert Keaton, M. G.

Walter THATCH to Maud PEARSON Issued 24 Oct 1903 Rites 25 Oct 1903
Granville Lipscomb, V. D. M.

Daniel T. SMOOT to Myrtle HINKLEY Issued 24 Oct 1903 Rites 25 Oct 1903
E. N. Yager, J. P.

Rance DURHAM to Jane FREEMAN Issued 24 Oct 1903 Not Executed

marion WEBB to Vesta ALLEN Issued 24 Oct 1903 Rites 25 Oct 1903

John PEAK to Sallie PERKINS Issued 27 Oct 1903 Rites 27 Oct 1903
J. J. Womack, J. P.

Ernest McGEE to Mary PATTERSON Issued 1 Nov 1903 Rites 1 Nov 1903
J. D. Templeton, J. P.

George W. COMER to Florence L. ANDERSON Issued 30 Oct 1903 Rites 1 Nov 1903
T. E. Alford, M. G.

G. A. KELL to I. A. MOFFITT Issued 3 Nov 1903 Rites 8 Nov 1903
E. J. Garner, M. G.

M. A. STANLEY to Ellennora WHEELER Issued 5 Nov 1903 Rites 5 Nov 1903
J. F. Martin, M. G.

Will WALKER to Sallie COTTON Issued 7 Nov 1903 Rites 8 Nov 1903
I. G. Webb, J. P.

Albert HALEY to May FERRELL Issued 7 Nov 1903 Rites 8 Nov 1903
I. G. Gribble, J. P.

Levander TEMPLETON to Lena SWINDELL Issued 10 Nov 1903 Rites 10 Nov 1903
E. N. YAGER, J. P.

Winfield McCORMICK to Bettie QUICK Issued 11 Nov 1903 Rites 12 Nov 1903
J. D. Templeton, J. P.

Thomas JENNINGS to Sarah Adeline TAYLOR Issued 14 Nov 1903 Rites 17 Nov 1903
O. C. Crain, J. P.

Walter HILLIS to Maud MYERS Issued 14 Nov 1903 Rites 14 Nov 1903
W. S. Grissom, J. P.

Girty DRAKE (Col) to Ada JOHNSON (Col) Issued 14 Nov 1903 Rites 15 Nov 1903
S. M. _____, M. G.

Horace F. HARWELL to Eleanor Grace MERCER Issued 16 Nov 1903 Rites 17 Nov 1903
W. H. Cotton, M. G.

Chas. A. FULLARD to Sarah Alice CARR Issued 21 Nov 1903 Rites 22 Nov 1903
E. J. GArner, M. G.

Thomas SMITH to Cora DAWSON Issued 21 Nov 1903 Cancelled - Improperly Issued

John HILLIS to Nettie HOODENPYLE Issued 24 Nov 1903 Rites 25 Nov 1903
W. R. PAine, M. G.

G. B. GREEN to Annie ALLEN Issued 28 Nov 1903 Rites 29 Nov 1903
Sol Mullican, J. P.

Harvey MACON to Beulah COPE Issued 30 Nov 1903 Rites 1 Dec 1903
B. T. Smotherman

L. Howard ROBERTSON to Myrtle TAYLOR Issued 8 Dec 1903 Rites 9 Dec 1903
O. H. Wood, J. P.

Charles COPEHART to Maud GOGGINS Issued 12 Dec 1903 Rites 13 Dec 1903
M. J. Jones, J. P.

Henry TIDWELL to Annie BROWN Issued 12 Dec 1903 Rites 13 Ded 1903
N. W. Ware, M. G.

Jesse L. LANCE to Della WILSON Issued 17 Dec 1903 Rites 19 Dec 1903
D. C. Oliver, J. P.

Samuel HALE to DELLA HARRISON Issued 19 Dec 1903 Rites 20 Dec 1903
I. T. Hillis, J. P.

J. W. DENTON to Flora CLARK Issued 19 Dec 1903 Rites 20 Dec 1903
J. M. Denton, M. G.

Andy ACUFF to Hannah HASH Issued 22 Dec 1903 Rites 27 Dec 1903
J. D. Hash, J. P.

A. M. BROWN to Fermette GOLLADAY Issued 22 Dec 1903 Rites 24 Dec 1903
F. E. Alford, M. G.

Arthue SAVAGE (Col) to FAnnie ISBELL (Col) Issued 24 Dec 1903 Rites 26 Dec 1903
A. H. Duncan, M. G.

O. E. CROWE to FAnnie SPARKMAN Issued 24 Dec 1903 Rites 31 Dec 1903
P. G. Potter, M. G.

A. H. BLANKENSHIP to Evie COLLIER Issued 24 Dec 1903 Rites 3 JAn 1904
J. J. Mullican, J. P.

Jesse P. BRYAN to Ella Lee JACOBS Issued 25 Dec 1903 Rites 27 Dec 1903
J. F. Martin, M. G.

James B. McMAHAN to Bettie Lee SMOOT Issued 26 Dec 1903 Rites 27 Dec 1903
W. N. Kell, J. P.

J. L. SMITH to Minnie WEBB Issued 26 Dec 1903 Rites 27 Dec 1903
Sol Mullican, J. P.

A. C. STILES to Sallie ROWLAND Issued 26 Dec 1903 Rites 27 Dec 1903
Sol Williams, J. P.

L. B. RICHARDSON to Mary E. McPHERSON Issued 26 Dec 1903 Rites 27 Dec 1903
A. C. Myers, J. P.

A. C. BROWN to Ruthie GREER Issued 26 Dec 1903 Rites 27 Dec 1903
J. W. Cooley, M. G.

George B. SHAWVER to Laura H. BLANKS Issued 26 Dec 1903 Rites 27 Dec 1903
R. W. Binkley, M. G.

M. V. McGEE to HAutie SAVAGE Issued 29 Dec 1903 Rites 14 Jan 1904
L. v. Scott, J. P.

Thomas MOORE to Bettie DAVIS Issued 30 Dec 1903 Not Executed

L. C. LANE to Lucy TROUP Issued 31 Dec 1903 Rites 3 JAn 1904
I. G. Webb, J. P.

James HUNT to Ella DODSON Issued 1 Jan 1904 Rites 3 JAn 1904
J. W. Cooley, M. G.

Jim SMARTT (Col) to DAisy HUNTER (Col) Issued 4 Jan 1904 Rites 7 JAn 1904
G. W. Dunham, J. P.

Jow WEBB to SAllie GREEN Issued 5 Jan 1904 Rites 5 Jan 1904
W. T. Coton, M. G.

Robert L.STONE to E. B. St. JOHn Issued 6 Jan 1904 Rites 7 Jan 1904
J. R. Stubblefield, M. G.

willie SIMONS to HAssie MILLER Issued 9 Jan 1904 Rites 10 Jan 1904
S. H. Templeton, J. P.

T. B. SPENCER (Col) to Minnie Louise JONES (Col) Issued 14 Jan 1904 Rites 14 JAn 1904
S. M. Utley, M. G.

James C. TURNER to Bettie THAXTON Issued 15 Jan 1904 Rites 17 JAn 1904
E. J. Garner, M. G.

Horace NORTHCUTT (Col) to MAry HUNT (Col) Issued 20 JAn 1904 Rites 21 JAn 1904
M. E. GArner, M. G,

Burr CHERRY to Mattir DOVE Issued 21 Jan 1904 Rites 24 JAn 1904
I. G. Webb, J. P.

Frank P. MITCHELL to Mary BROWN Issued 26 JAn 1904 Rites 26 Jan 1904
E. N. YAger, J. P.

C. F. CRAVEN to Lena ALLISON Issued 27 JAn 1904 Rites 27 JAn 1904
C. K. Carlock, M. G.

Joseph CURTIS to Mary KING Issued 5 Feb 1904 Rites 8 Feb 1905
E. L. Moffitt, J. P.

William KIRBY to SARAH RUTLEDGE Issued 8 Feb 1904 Rites 9 Feb 1904
W. S. Grissom, J. P.

Walter BYRD to Eva ALCORN Issued 13 Feb 1904 Rites 14 Feb 1904
J. J. Mullican, J. P.

D. TURNER to Ollie KESEY Issued 2 Apr 1904 Rites 3 Apr 1904
  J. C. Safley, J. P.

Lucian ROBERTS to Octa COPPINGER Issued 7 Apr 1904 Rites 7 Apr 1904
  E. L. Moffitt, J. P.

Cheatham WOODS to Ruthie Belle MADEWELL Issued 8 Apr 1904 Rites 8 Apr 1904
  L. V. Scott, J. P.

E. W. POTTER to Minnie SANDERS Issued 12 Apr 1904 Rites 12 Apr 1904
  W. H. Cotton, M. G.

I. H. HILLIS to Ollie COPPINGER Issued 15 Apr 1904 Rites 17 Apr 1904
  L. V. Scott, J. P.

James MUNSEY to Bettie DODD Issued 25 Apr 1904 Not Returned

Earl B. ST. JOHN to Bessie WEST Issued 25 Apr 1904 Rites 27 Apr 1904
  J. D. G----, M. G.

Carter LANDRUM to Lula SMARTT Issued 28 Apr 1904 Rites 28 Apr 1904
  R. W. Binkley, M. G.

Hilie WOODS to Mollie CASEY Issued 28 Apr 1904 Rites 1 May 1904
  A. H. Cunningham, M. G.

S. L. PHELPS to Mattie J. SMITH Issued 30 Apr 1904 Rites 1 May 1904
  W. H. Cotton, M. G.

Tull F. HASH to Lillie (Dollie) Holloway Issued 4 May 1904 Rites 8 May 1904
  J. D. Hash, J. P.

O. N. BIGELOW to Minnie COATS Issued 7 May 1904 Rites 8 May 1904
  W. H. Cotton, M. G.

Harley B. WEBB to Ida EARLS Issued 7 May 1904 Rites 8 May 1904
  J. E. Jones, J. P.

Arnold RIGGS to Novada B. PARKER Issued 14 May 1904 Rites 14 May 1904
  J. E. Jones, J. P.

Carlie DICKSON to Allie LISTER Issued 14 May 1904 Rites 15 May 1904
  B. L. Smotherman

J. G. MULLINAX to Bessie BOWEN Issued 17 May 1904 Rites 17 May 1904
  L. V. Scott, J. P.

Cas HOLLAND to Nancy DODD Issued 21 May 1904 Rites 22 May 1904
  J. L. Thaxton, J. P.

Ben ATNIPP to Mattie FISHER Issued 28 May 1904 Rites 28 May 1904
  E. N. Yager, J. P.

Fernando BOYD to Sarah MAXWELL Issued 2 June 1904 Rites 5 June 1904
  J. J. Meadows, J. P.

C. R. COLLINS to Ruby Jean SMARTT Issued 17 Feb 1904 Rites 17 Feb 1904
  R. W. Binkley, M. G.

I. B. FUGIT (Col)-to Mary FERRELL (Col) Issued 20 Feb 1904 Rites 21 Feb 1904
  G. W. Bowser, M. G.

Sam RHEAY to Carrie SMARTT Issued 26 Feb 1904 Rites 28 Feb 1904
  L. V. Scott, J. P.

William KENNEDY to Ida SWANN Issued 27 Feb 1904 Rites 28 Feb 1904
  O. H. Wood, J. P.

C. L. EDWARDS to Dultist PRESLY Issued 27 Feb 1904 Rites 27 Feb 1904
  E. N. Yager, J. P.

W. A. PRIEST to S. C. CRIM Issued 12 Mar 1904 Rites 14 Mar 1904
  I. T. Hillis, J. P.

John M. ROWLAND to Maude ADAIR Issued 12 Mar 1904 Rites 13 Mar 1904
  I. G. Webb, J. P.

E. A. VOEKEL to Mallie ARMSTRONG Issued 16 Mar 1904 Rites 16 Mar 1904

Gay. C. FEBRUARY to Frances BROWN Issued 18 Mar 1904 Rites 18 Mar 1904
  W. H. Cotton, M. G.

J. M. DODSON to Francis GLENN Issued 19 Mar 1904 -Not Executed

Charles BARNES to Vickey KEESEY Issued 22 Mar 1904 Rites 24 Mar 1904
  A. C. Myers, J. P.

Tivis LEWIS to Cora NUNLEY Issued 26 Mar 1904 Rites 27 Mar 1904
  F. E. Alford, M. G.

Ray H. CROWE to Lota LAWRENCE Issued 27 Mar 1904 Rites 29 Mar 1904
  E. N. Yager, K. P.

Roy ALLEN to Lena SMITH Issued 28 Mar 1904 Not Executed

Bill LOOPER (Col) to Prude MARTIN (Col) Issued 2 Jone 1904 Rites 4 June 104
W. S. Grissom, J. P.

George W. SNIPES to Loula LUTRELL Issued 3 June 1904 Rites 5 June 1904
H. A. Cunningham, M. G.

Jonathan HENDRIX to Rosa Belle PERKINS Issued 9 June 1904 Rites 9 June 1904
E. N. Yager, J. P.

L. B. PARKER to Vistoria F. PATY Issued 10 June 1904 Rites 14 June 1904
J. F. Martin

Will Munsey to Laura NUNLEY Issued 15 June 1904 Rites 15 June 1904

Hnery MARSHALL to Chanie SMARTT Issued 24 June 1904 Rites 25 June 1904
G. W. Dunham, J. P.

Huston ROMAN (Col) to Florence BOULDIN (Col) Issued 27 June 1904 Rites 2 July 1904
E. N. Yager, J. P.

J. P. TEMPLETON to Hettie HANKINS Issued 29 June 1904 Rites 3 July 1904
I. G. Webb, J. P.

Eliner BRYAN to Mary E. SISSOM Issued 2 July 1904 Rites 3 July 1904
H. A. Cunningham, M. G.

U. A. GIBBS to Elie CANTRELL Issued 2 July 1904 Rites 3 July 1904
L. P. Sanders, J. P.

B. MCBRIDE to Lynchia CHRISTIAN Iuused 9 July 1904 Rites 10 July 1904
J. C. Safley, J. P.

Lewis CLARK to Susie CAMPBELL Issued 12 July 1904 Rites 17 July 1904
G. W. Haley, J. P.

Thos, A. LEONARD to Octavia SMARTT Issued 13 July 1904 Rites 13 July 1904
R. W. Binkley, M. G.

V. B. GULLEY to Connie JONES Issued 15 July 1904 Rites 17 July 1904
W. T. Tracy

J. W. MARTIN to Margaret REESE Issued 16 July 1904 Rites 24 July 1904
S. H. Templeton, J. P.

John PARIS to Adaline SMITH Issued 18 July 1904 Rites 27 July 1904

A. T. PHILLIPS to Maud MILLICAN Issued 20 July 1904 Rites 21 July 1904
H. J. Boles, M. G.

W. T. GREEN to Minnie PATRICK Issued 21 July 1904 Rites 21 July 1904
J. K. Whitlock, J. P.

S. L. VANHOOSER to Mattie SAUNDERS Issued 23 July 1904 Rites 24 July 1904
W. E. Martin, J. P.

J. M. DAVENPORT to Rachael JOHNSON Issued 25 July 1904 Not Returned

John BARTON (Col) to Dovie MASON (Col) Issued 25 July 1904 Rites N. W. Ware, M. G.
N. G. Ware, M. G.

Alex THURMAN to Bell WALKER Issued 27 July 1904 Rites 27 July 1904
W. T. Tracy, M. G.

B. F. ANDREWS to Martha GREEN Issued 29 July 1904 Rites 31 July 1904
W. H. Cotton, M. G.

John BOREN to Bertie ROMANS Issued 6 August 1904 Rites 7 August 1904
L. P. Sanders, J. P.

Andrew MARTIN to George ANN McGee Issued 10 August 1904 Rites 11 August 1904
George L. Buck, J. P.

C. P. CANTRELL to Novie WALKER Issued 11 August 1904 Rites 14 August 1904
L. P. Sanders, J. P.

William BREWER to Novel YORK Issued 12 August 1904 Rites 14 August 1904
G. W. Haley, JI. P.

R. L. SHIRLEY to Gusta ARMSTRONG Issued 13 August 1904 Rites 14 August 1904
O. H. Wood, J. P.

Thomas R. WALKER to Meta BASHER Issued 18 August 1904 Rites 18 August 1904
E. N. Yager, J. P.

J. R. COPE to Vergia HUDGENS Issued 19 August 1904 Rites 21 August 1904
B. T. Smotherman, M. G.

W. T. WITT to Eva SLATTEN Issued 22 August 1904 Rites 24 August 1904
Jacob Stipe, M. G.

Lester SMARTT to Mary HILLIS Issued 24 August 1904 Rites 28 August 1904
L. V. Scott, J. P.

Forest MARTIN (Col) to Bulah LUSK (Col) Issued 27 August 1904 Not Returned

Lee BOREN to Ida DAVIS Issued 30 August 1904 Rites 4 Sept. 1904
Sol Williams, J. P.

Frank WOMACK to Zetta FORDYCE Issued 27 August 1904 Rites 27 August 1904
G. T. Riggs, J. P.

Arthue ROGERS to Manda LEWIS Issued 3 Sept. 1904 Rites 4 Sept. 1904
J. L. Thaxton, J. P.

W. H. PERRY to Myrtle CRITTENDON Issued 3 Sept. 1904 Rites 4 Sept. 1904
Sol Williams, J. P.

C. J. WILSON to Hattie MARTIN Issued 5 Sept. 1904 Rites 7 Sept. 1904
D. C. Oliver, J. P.

W. S. KING to Belle MCGREGOR Issued 6 Sept. 1904 Rites 6 Sept. 1904
A. J. Brien, M. G.

P. F. ELKINS to Lou NEAL Issued 7 Sept. 1904 Rites 7 Sept. 1904
C. K. Carlock, M. G.

J. M. HOBBS to Lucy COPE Issued 9 Sept. 1904 Not Returned

Jesse C. DAVENPORT to Mary MARCRUM Issued 10 Sept. 1904 Rites 13 Sept. 1904
O. H. Wood, J. P.

Jim VICKERS to Josie BRATCHER Issued 10 Sept. 1904 Not Returned

Wm. LORANCE to Mollie DEBERRY Issued 10 Sept. 1904 Rites 10 Sept. 1904
D. C. Oliver, J. P.

G. P. COPE to Edith JUDKINS Issued 14 Sept. 1904 Rites 18 Sept. 1904
W. G. COTTON, M. G.

W. B. Dodson to Sallie M. MITCHELL Issued 17 Sept. 1904 Rites 21 Sept. 1904
Jacob Stipe, M. G.

J. L. GREEN to Daisy E. MULLICAN Issued 17 Sept. 1904 Not Returned

Wm. HARPER to Emma DODD Issued 17 Sept. 1904 Rites 18 Sept. 1904
J. L. Thaxton, J. P.

W. T. McDANIEL to S. F. HOLDER Issued 22 Sept. 1904 Rites 22 Sept. 1904
E. N. Yager, J. P.

W. M. MITCHELL to Lucy BATES Issued 24 Sept. 1904 Rites 25 Sept. 1904
G. W. Haley, J. P.

Prate FULTS to Sarah LEWIS Issued 29 Sept. 1904 Not Returned

Charley ROACH (Col) to Maud MILLER (Col) Issued 1 Oct. 1904 Rites 1 Oct.1904
N. W. Ware, M. G.

James E. CARTWRIGHT to Jane L. BILES Issued 6 Ocr. 1904 Rites 6 Oct. 1904
W. H. Cotton, M. G.

Sam LAWSON to Docie KELL Issued 8 Oct. 1904 Rites 9 Oct. 1904
I. G. Webb, J. P.

J. E. NUNLEY to Lassie BARNES Issued 8 Oct. 1904 Rites 9 Oct. 1904
L. V. Scott, J. P.

Hugh SAVAGE (Col) to Laura SPURLOCK (Col) Issued 8 Oct. 1904 Rites 8 Oct. 1904
G. W. Dunham, J. P.

Press CRAWFORD to Mattie VICKERS Issued 12 Oct 1904 Rites 12 Oct. 1904
I. G. Webb, J. P.

R. L. FISHER to Martha SMITH Issued 14 Oct. 1904 Rites 16 Oct. 1904
Elisha Webb, M. G.

M. V. CRIM to Pearl FARLESS Issued 20 Oct. 1904 Rites 20 Oct. 1904
J. W. Cooley, M. G.

Will BROWN to Daisy DUNCAN Issued 22 Oct. 1904 Rites 22 Oct. 1904
J. E. Jones, J. P.

N. C. LEONARD to Susan BLACK Issued 25 Oct. 1904 Rites 25 Oct. 1904
R. W. Binkley, M. G.

Floyd L. HENNESSEE to Frankie HARMON Issued 29 Oct 1904 Rites 30 Oct. 1904
J. C. Safley, J. P.

T. M. BONNER to Maude HUDGENS Issued 29 Oct1904 Rites 30 Oct 1904
R. W. Binkley, M. G.

H. R. ROGERS to Minnie B. TOSH Issued 2 Nov. 1904 Rites 3 Nov. 1904
J. L. Thaxton, J. P.

J. J. ANDERSON to Amanda J. SNIPES Issued 8 Nov. 1904 Rites 9 Nov. 1904
L. P. Sanders, J. P.

Tom BONNER to Charity MADEWELL Issued 8 Nov. 1904 Rites 10 Nov. 1904
J. J. Meadows, J. P.

Will A. CANTRELL to Mary MONTANDON Issued 8 Nov. 1904 Rites 9 Nov. 1904
I. T. Hillis, J. P.

J. A. RANKIN to Annie MERRIMAN Issued 9 Nov. 1904 Rites 9 Nov. 1904
C. K. Carlock, M. G.

Dalton PASSONS to Isabelle VANCE Issued 10 Nov. 1904 Rites 11 Nov. 1904
J. D. Hash, J. P.

Arthur WILLIAMS (Col) to Sallie BROWN (Col) Issued 12 Nov. 1904 Rites 20 Nov. 1904
J. L. Thaxton, J. P.

George W. WEBB to Margaret MASON Issued 15 Nov. 1904 Rites 16 Nov. 1904
B. T. Smotherman, M. G.

G. T. AUTEN to Elvira PARISH Issued 16 Nov. 1904 Rites 17 Nov. 1904
J. G. Goff, J. P.

Floyd JETT to Ocie WEBB Issued 19 Nov. 1904 Rites 20 Nov. 1904
J. E. Jones, J. P.

J. L. FOSTER to Eula MULLICAN Issued 26 Nov. 1904 Rites 27 Nov. 1904
W. E. Marler, J. P.

Loren L. WILLIAMS to Mattie BARNETT Issued 26 Nov. 1904 Rites 27 Nov. 1904
J. T. Kelton, M. G.

Rueben TURNER to Katie HUGHES Issued 28 Nov. 1904 Rites 28 Nov. 1904
Wm. Milstead, M. G.

John BARNES to Etta TURNER Issued 10 Dec. 1904 Rites 18 Dec. 1904
J. J. Meadows, J. P.

O. T. CRAIN to Irene FINGER Issued 10 Dec. 1904 Rites 11 Dec. 1904
W. H. Cotton, M. G.

H. M. ROGERS to F. C. FULTS Issued 12 Dec. 1904 Rites 13 Dec. 1904
J. W. Swann

Abe SPURLOCK (Col) to Mauda HILL (col) Issued 12 Dec. 1904 Rites 12 Dec. 1904
E. N. Yager, J. P.

William WILLIAMS to Jamie DODSON Issued 15 Dec. 1904 Rites 14 Dec. 1904
J. R. Stubblefield

Jasper H. HUTCHINS to Eva Lee HENNESSEE Issued 14 Dec. 1904 Rites 14 Dec. 1904
R. W. Binkley, M. G.

John Romine JONES to Mela MARTIN Issued 18 Dec. 1904 Rites 18 Dec. 1904
J. D. Templeton, J. P.

R. A. MERRIMAN to Nettie WOOD Issued 18 Dec. 1904 Rites 18 Dec. 1904
C. K. Carlock, M. G.

Horace WOODS (Col) to Claudie PAGE (Col) Issued 18 Dec. 1904 Not Returned

William REYNOLDS to Elizabeth REED Issued 19 Dec. 1904 Rites 20 Dec. 1904
J. W. Swann

C. M. WOMACK to Lula F. LUTRELL Issued 20 Dec. 1904 Rites 25 Dec. 1904
E. M. Thompson

Jim HILL (Col) to Maude SOLOMON (Col) Issued 20 Dec. 1904 Rites 20 Dec. 1904
P. M. Paty

H. C. CURTIS to Mattie CARTWRIGHT Issued 21 Dec 1904 Rites 22 Dec. 1904
E. L. Moffitt, J. P.

J. J. POPE to Dovie PENDERGRASS Issued 21 Dec. 1904 Rites 25 Dec. 1904
Jacob Stipe, M. G.

Howard WRIGHT to Ella BRATCHER Issued 23 Dec. 1904 Rites 25 Dec. 1904
P. G. Potter, M. G.

G. D. WALKER to Mattie JONES Issued 23 Dec. 1904 Rites 23 Dec. 1904
Geo. L. Beech, J. P.

Frank BATES (Col) to Ella HOLLAND (Col) Issued 23 Dec. 1904 Rites 23 Dec. 1904
Samuel Curry, M. G.

Thomas CASEY to Mattie GILLEY Issued 23 Dec. 1904 Rites 25 Dec. 1904
J. A. Cunningham, M. G.

J. H. SNIPES to W. B. DEBERRY Issued 23 Dec. 1904 Rites 25 Dec. 1904
H. A. Cunningham, M. G.

A. J. GLENN to M. A. GREEN Issued 24 Dec. 1904 Rites 25 Dec. 1904
I. G. Webb, J. P.

T. M. SMOOT to Myrtle DOWNING Issued 24 Dec. 1904 Rites 25 Dec. 1904
H. A. Cunningham, M. G.

Melvin NUNLEY to Fannie MILLER Issued 24 Dec. 1904 Rites Dec. 25, 1904
E. N. Yager, J. P.

Robert HAMMONDS to Lena EDWARDS Issued Dec. 24, 1904 Rites Dec. 25, 1904
J. W. Swann

Charley BARNES (Col) to Birdie CRIPS (Col) Issued 24 Dec. 1904 Rites Dec. 25. 1904
Sam Curry, M. G.

G. W. CARAWAY to Milda CULVEYHOUSE Issued 26 Dec. 1904 Rites Dec. 26, 1904
George L. Beech, J. P.

Robert H. BONNER to Bertha RAMSEY Issued 26 Dec. 1904 Rites 27 Dec. 1904
J. D. Ginn, M. G.

John Everett MOORE to Allie BONNER Issued 27 Dec. 1904 Rites 28 Dec. 1904
W. H. Cotton, M. G.

Clee HILLIS to Lizzie PATRICK Issued 27 Dec. 1904 Not Returned

Jim BILES (Col) to Bessie BROWN (Col) Issued 27 Dec. 1904 Rites 28 Dec. 1904
Fred Anderson

B. F. LORING to Elizabeth Ann WRIGHTMAN Issued 31 Dec. 1904 Rites 1 Jan. 1905

George THAXTON to Myrtle CARR Issued 31 Dec. 1904 Rites 1 Jan. 1905
E. N. Yager, J. P.

Geo. W. PLYANT to Lillian MOORE Issued 2 Jan. 1905 Rites 4 Jan. 1905
Jno. S. Henley

James M. CRAWFORD to Alice C. MOON Issued 2 Jan. 1905 Rites 4 Jan. 1905
Jno. S. Henly

Will MCREYNOLDS (Col) to Mary MARBURY (Col) Issued 5 Jan. 1905 Rites 5 Jan. 1905
J. S. Nance, M. G.

Joe RAMSEY (col) to Leanard HAMMONDS (Col) Issued 7 Jan. 1905 Rites 8 Jan. 1905
J. L. Thaxton, J. P.

E. C. WHITLOCK to May SIMPSON Issued 7 JAn. 1905 Rites 8 Jan. 1905
J. K. P. Whitlock

L. A. MITCHELL to Blanche SMITH Issued 12 Jan. 1905 Rites 15 Jan. 1905
O. H. Wood, J. P.

H. T. DODSON to Clyo CHRISTIAN Issued 13 Jan. 1905 Rites 15 Jan. 1905
J. W. Cooley, M. G.

Loyd CAGLE to Nannie HOBBS Issued 16 Jan. 1905 Rites 16 Jan. 1905
J. J. Meadows, J. P.

Geo. W. MARTIN to Ella EATON Issued 29 Oct. 1904 Rites 31 Oct. 1904
J. W. Cooley, M. G.

Alex ROBERSON to Maggie PEDEN Issued 17 Jan. 1905 Rites 19 Jan. 1905
A. C. Myers, J. P.

George HAYES to Georgia MCGEE Issued 26 Jan. 1905 Rites 26 Jan. 1905
W. S. Grissom, J. P.

Key (2) CUMMINGS (Col) to Anna RAINS (Col) Issued 31 Jan 1905 Rites 31 Jan.1905
I. S. Binkley, M. G.

Eden WOODS (Col) to Harriett MILLER (Col) Issued 4 Feb. 1905 Rites 5 Feb. 1905
I. T. Hillis, J. P.

Robert SMITH to Minnie CANTRELL Issued 17 Feb. 1905 Rites 17 Feb. 1905
I. G. Webb, J. P.

Ernest MONTANDON to Ella ROWLAND Issued 17 Feb. 1905 Rites 19 Feb. 1905
C. T. Kell. J. P.

William ROGERS to Bell TOSH Issued 20 Feb. 1905 Rites 22 Feb. 1905
A. C. Tatum, M. G.

A. B. SUMMAR to Monie LaROSCHE Issued 21 Feb. 1905 Rites 22 Feb. 1905
J. W. Swann

Murphy DRAKE to Lou CANTRELL Issued 1 March 1905 Rites 1 Mar. 1905
Sol Williams, J. P.

J. B. MARTIN (Col) to Kate Lee SMITH (Col) Issued 1 Mar. 1905 Rites ?Mar. 1905
O. C. Crain, J. P.

H. J. HOLCOMB to Mattie SUTHERLAND Issued 2 Mar. 1905 Rites 5 Mar. 1905
W. E. Marler, J. P.

Leander SLAUGHTER to Mary COPPINGER Issued 3 Mar. 1905 Not Returned

G. W. BROWN (Col) to Annie McREYNOLDS (Col) Issued 4 Mar. 1905 Rites 6 Mar. 1905
J. S. Rucker.

Monroe KEATON to Elizabeth GREEN Issued 10 Mar. 1905 Rites 12 Mar. 1905
I. G. Webb, J. P.

Bob BRAGG (Col) to Ann MORFORD (COl) Issued 21 Mar. 1905 Rites 22 Mar. 1905
G. W. Dunham, J. P.

W. E. DUNHAM to Lena UPCHURCH Issued 21 Mar. 1905 Rites 24 Mar. 1905
I. G. Webb, J. P.

Willie HAWKINS to Ophie Lilliam WILSON Issued 23 Mar 1905 Rites 23 Mar. 1905
J. K. P. Whitlock, M. G.

E. H. ROBINSON to Bulah GRIBBLE Issued 25 Mar. 1905 Rites 26 Mar. 1905
P. G. Potter, M. G.

Ed FAULKNER (Col) to Agens BOLING (Col) Issued 1 Apr. 1905 Not Returned

W,. J. BENNETT to Ida RIGSBY Issued 5 Apr. 1905 Rites 5 Apr. 1905
D. C. Oliver, J. P.

Hershell JENNINGS to Belle COX Issued 8 Apr. 1905 Rites 9 Apr. 1905
J. J. Meadows, J. P.

John HIGGINBOTHAM (Col) to Kattie WEBB (Col) Issued 8 Apr. 1905 Rites 9 Apr 1905
L. P. Sanders, J. P.

Nathan STEWART to Francis CUMMINGS Issued 8 Apr 1905 Rites 9 Apr 1905
W. E. Marler, J. P.

Sam FOSTER (Col) to Katy COPE (Col) Issued 10 Apr 1905 Rites 10 Apr 1905
E. N. Yager, J. P.

Frank COWAN (Col) to Cindy PAGE (Col) Issued 15 Apr 1905 Rites 16 Apr 1905
N. W. Ware, M. G.

George RAMSEY (Col) to Mandy WARE (Col) Issued 21 Apr 1905 Rites 22 Apr 1905
N. W. Ware, M. G.

Willie BESS to Mary CURTIS Issued 21 Apr 1905 Rites 23 Apr 1905
I. W. Roberts, M. G.

Lucius GRIBBLE (Col) to Ida RAMSEY (Col) Issued 23 Apr. 1905 Rites 23 Apr 1905
I. T. Hillis, J. P.

Marion PANTER to Myrtle CHRISTIAN Issued 26 Apr 1905 Rites 27 Apr 1905
E. L. Moffitt, J. P.

Jmaes MUNSEY to Ev SMITH Issued 29 Apr 1905 Rites 30 Apr 1905
J. L. Thaxton, J. P.

Willie PRIEST to Leta CRIM Issued 3 May 1905 Rites 7 May 1905
W. S. Grissom, J. P.

Jesse H. BISHOP to Lela E. DODD Issued 4 May 1905 Rites 7 MAY 1905
J. K. P. Whitlock, M. G.

J. L. BISHOP to Cora POTERFIELD Issued 6 May 1905 Rites 7 May 1905
M. J. Jones, J. P.

Eron Fain TAYLOR to Clara Belle REYNOLDS Issued 8 May 1905 Rites 10 May 1905
Wm. M. Woodfin, M. G.

Will ROMANS to Mary MCDOWELL Issued 15 May 1905 Rites 20 May 1905
I. G. Gribble, J. P.

Gwyn MARTIN to Nannie MCVEY Issued 16 May 1905 Rites 18 May 1905
W. S. Grissom, J. P.

Lillard KEATON to Emma POLLARD Issued 17 May 1905 Rites 17 May 1905
P. G. Potter, M. G.

John COX to Lena SCOTT Issued 19 May 1905 Rites 19 May 1905
J. L. Thaxton, J. P.

Samuel B. BRITTIAN to Molly Black WALKER Issued 27 May 1905 Rites 29 May 1905
W. M. Taylor, M. G.

Henry CARR to Ella HOBBS Issued 3 June 1905 Rites 4 June 1905
W. N. Kell, J. P.

Charlie CUNNINGHAM to Hassie MOON Issued 8 June 1905 Rites 11 June 1905
J. W. Cooley, M. G.

Joe FISHER to Mollie PARSLEY Issued 9 June 1905 Rites 18 June 1905
J. D. Hash, J. P.

Josiah RAINS to Mina HARTER (?) Issued 10 June 1905 Rites 11 June 1905
J. L. Thaxton, J. P.

Sandy MARTIN (Col) to Mary RITCHEY (Col) Issued 10 June 1905 Rites 11 June 1905
S. M. Utley, M. G.

J, M, BAIN to Minnie ELAM Issued 13 June 1905   Rites --June 1905
R. W. Binkley, M. G.

Charles SPANGLER to Ada CANTRELL Issued 17 June 1905 Rites 18 June 1905
J. D. Guinn, M. G.

Hes BYNUM to Ella Stanley Issued 21 June 1905 Rites 22 June 1905
J. G. Goff, J. P.

Heorge W. HAYNES to Leta A. MITCHELL Issued 21 June 1905 Rites 21 June 1905
John S. Henley

J. R. GLENN to Annie MULLICAN Issued 24 June 1905 Rites 25 June 1905
W. S. Paine, M. G.

Will GRANDERSON (Col) to Bettie BONNER (Col) Issued 24 June 1905 Rites 24 June 1905
James T. Brown, M. G.

Bill BRATCHER to Minnie ELDRIDGE Issued 25 June 1905 Rites 25 June 1905
E. N. Yager, J. P.

Andrew J. STILES to Hattie Belle GREEN Issued 1 July 1905 Rites 2 July 1905
E. N. Yager, M. G.

Cleveland BESS to Gertie TURNER Issued 7 July 1905 Rites 9 July 1905
E. L. Moffitt, J. P.

John C. ROGERS to Addie ROBERTS Issued 14 July 1905 Rites 16 July 1905
M. H. Northcross

James W. WILSON to Bettie PATERSON (?) Issued 3 July 1905 Rites 3 July 1905
John S. Hendley

Firman MITCHELL to Ellen PACE Issued 3 July 1905 Rites 4 July 1905
John S. Hendley

Andrew ORICK to Lena BIRCH Issued 15 July 1905 Rites 16 July 1905
H. A. Cunningham, M. G.

H. P. SLAUGHTER to Emma KILLIAN Issued 21 July 1905 Not Returned

James S. BARTON to Mrs. Dora E. CLARK Issued 5 July 1905 Rites 5 July 1905
W. H. Cotton. M. G.

Dillard LOOPER (Col) to Visa MARBURY (Col) Issued 9 July 1905 Rites 9 July 1905
N. Ware, M. G.

E. H. ALLEN to Vernnie HUDSON Issued 25 July 1905 Rites 25 July 1905
I. G. Webb, J. P.

Nathan WHEELER to Holly YOUNG Issued 28 July 1905 Rites 30 July 1905
J. F. Martin, M. G.

Dock SCOTT to Ivrey FULTS Issued 5 Aug 1905 Rites 6 Aug 1905
J. L. Thaxton, J. P.

Fred CRITTENDEN to Eliza KIRBY Issued 5 Aug 1905 Rites 6 Aug 1905
E. N. Yager, J. P.

Zora DUKE to Emma SIMMONS Issued 5 Aug 1905 Rites 8 Aug 1905
O. H. Wood, J. P.

Charley OWEN to Love GIBBS Issued 7 Aug 1905 Rites 9 Aug 1905
W. S. Grissom, J. P.

Clarence HOBBS to Beulah HUNTLEY Issued 7 Aug 1905 Rites 9 Aug 1905
E. N. Yager, J. P.

W. D. CATES to Bettie BOTTOMS Issued 12 Aug 1905 Rites 13 August 1905
H. A. Cunningham. M. G.

Romulus DODSON to Tennie MOFFITT Issued 17 Aug 1905 Rites 17 Aug. 1905
W. M. McGregor, M. G.

Ross AKERS to Effie WALLING Issued 19 Aug 1905 Rites 20 Aug 1905
G. W. Haley, J. P.

William MULLICAN to Clara WOMACK Issued 22 Aug. 1905 Rites 22 Aug 1905
J. J. Mullican, J. P.

Robert L. ADCOCK to Dovie L. CANTRELL Issued 23 Aug 1905 Rites 23 Aug 1905
E. N. Yager, J. P.

Sydney HICKS (Col) to Julia MOON (Col) Issued 26 Aug 1905 Rites 26 Aug 1905
N. W. Ware, M. G.

William WILLIAMS to Margaret BURCH Issued 30 Aug 1905 Rites 2 Sept 1905
G. W. Dunham, J. P.

Peter ROBINSON (Col) to Bettie JENNINGS (Col) Issued 30 Aug 1905 Rites 30 Aug 1905
S. M. Utley, P. C.

C. S. ROBERTS to Lydia WITT Issued 31 Aug 1905 Rites 3 Aug 1905
J. G. Marcum

J. H. BONNER to Kate STROUD Issued 2 Sept 1905 Rites 3 Sept 1905
H. A. Cunningham, M. G.

Zack MILLER to Annie GRIFFITH Issued 2 Sept 1905 Rites 2 Sept. 1905
Geo. L. Buck, J. P.

Will RAMSEY (Col) to Phronie MCREYNOLDS Issued 4 Sept 1905 Rites 4 Sept 1905
E. N. Yager, J. P.

Jim CLAIBORNE to Lizzie TOSH Issued 4 Sept 1905 Rites 8 Sept 1905
J. R. Ramsey, J. P.

L. C. CHRISTIAN to Lizzie MEEKS Issued 4 Sept 1905 Rites 4 Sept 1905
L. V. Scott, J. P.

G. W. P. HAYNES to M. J. CRAIN Issued 7 Sept 1905 Rites 7 Sept 1905
L. P. Sanders, J. P.

Bob DAVIS to Adie CANTRELL Issued 16 Sept 1905 Rites 16 Sept 1905
E. N. Yager, J. P.

Horace DODD to Georgia TILLETT Issued 16 Sept 1905 Rites 18 Sept 1905
A. C. Tatum

John ROLLER to Lena MORGAN Issued 22 Sept 1905 Rites 24 Sept 1905
J. J. Mullican, J. P.

E. T. LAWRENCE to Hassie EITER Issued 23 Sept. 1905 Rites 24 Sept 1905
J. L. Thaxton, J. P.

N. B. SPURLOCK (Col) to Mamie WILSON (Col) Issued 23 Sept 1905 Rites 24 Sept 1905
G. W. Dunham, J. P.

Robert STILES to Winnie CROWE Issued 28 Sept 1905 Rites 28 Sept 1905
P. G. Potter, M. G.

James JOHNSON to Allie DODSON Issued 30 Sept 1905 Rites 1 Oct 1905
J. W. Cooley, M. G.

Rufe SWANN to Adeline WILLIAMS Issued 2 Oct 1905 Rites 3 Oct. 1905
H. A. Cunningham, M. G.

Edmund J. HARKNESS to Clara RICE Issued 11 Oct 1905 Rites 11 Oct 1905
W. H. Cotton, M.G.

Jnaes T. BOAZ to/PUTERBAUGH (?) Issued 13 Oct 1905 Rites 15 Oct 1905
Maud
E. C. Boaz, M. G.

Will MUNSEY to Pearl HENNESSEE Issued 14 Oct 1905 Rites 15 Oct 1905
G. W. Dunham, J. P.

William ROBERTS to Mrs. Margaret PERRY Issued 21 Oct 1905 Rites 22 Oct 1905
E. L. Moffitt, J. P.

Robert WHITLOCK to Minnie EARLS Issued 21 Oct 1905 Rites 22 Sept 1905
J. K. P. Whitlock

Charles GREEN to Martha MORTON Issued 23 Oct 1905 Rites 23 Oct 1905
E. N. Yager, J. P.

Ed NELSON to Alice ABBEY Issued 27 Oct 1905 Rites 28 Oct 1905
E. N. Yager, M. G.

Wash PRIEST to Dossie CRIM Issued 4 Nov. 1905 Rites 5 Nov. 1905
L. Safley, M. G.

John L. SMITH to Margie M. MONTANDON Issued 10 Nov 1905 Rites 12 Nov 1905
H. L. Cotton, M. G.

Ben LUSK to Ellen SCOTT Issued 11 Nov 1905 Rites 12 Nov 1905
W. E. Garner, M. G.

Wm. RICE (Col) to Callie WHITSON (Col) Issued 16 Nov 1905 Rites 16 Nov 1905
G. W. Dunham, J. P.

G. W. FINGER to Maude LANE Issued 18 Nov 1905 Rites 22 Nov 1905
R. W. Binkley, M. G.

Sam T. SMARTT to Jay HAYES Issued 25 Nov 1905 Rites 26 Nov 1905
C. K. Carlock, M. G.

Jim SMARTT (Col) to Nellie RICE (COl) Issued 25 Nov. 1905 Rites 26 Nov 1905
J. W. Sims

Mel YORK (Col) to Connie FISK (Col) Issued 1 Dec. 1905 Rites 3 Dec. 1905
James M. Crawford, M. G.

Oscar BONNER to Mary Het CATHCART Issued 1 Dec 1905 Rites 3 Dec 1905
L. V. Scott, J. P.

J. C. WARREN to Maude KIRBY Issued 14 Dec. 1905 Rites 14 Dec. 1905
P. G. Potter, M. G.

Dolley SMARTT(Col) to Mandy MARTIN (Col) Issued 16 Dec 1905 Rites 17 Dec. 1905
G. W. Dunham, J. P.

Jesse Lee GILBERT to Bertie MAYO Issued 16 Dec. 1905 Rites 17 Dec. 1905
R. W. Binkley, M. G.

J. C. CLARK to Mary Lee WOMACK Issued 20 Dec. 1905 Rites 20 Dec 1905
J. Stipe, M. G.

Kellie KING to Frances JUDKINS Issued 20 Dec. 1905 Not Returned

Robert WEBB to Beulah WEBB Issued 21 Dec 1905 Rites 25 Dec 1905
I. G. Webb, J. P.

W. B. COPE to Eva COUCH Issued 21 Dec 1905 Rites 25 Dec 1905
I. G. Webb, J. P.

Evander TROUP to Bettie DUNN Issued 22 Dec 1905 Rites 24 Dec. 1905
J. D. Nash, J. P.

Joe HALTERMAN to Maggie RHEA Issued 23 Dec. 1905 Rites 24 Dec. 1905
J. E. Clark, M. G.

Greenberry HAYES to Emma WHITEAKER Issued 23 Dec 1905 Rites 24 Dec. 1905
A. C. Myers, J. P.

Lawson MILSTEAD to Lucy ROGERS Issued 23 Dec 1905 Rites 24 Dec 1905
J. C. Safley, J. P.

Colonel BRATCHER to Sallie OWEN Issued 23 Dec 1905 Rites 24 Dec 1905
G. T. Riggs, J. P.

Zollie Vanhooser to Drusie CANTRELL Issued 23 Dec. 1905 Rites 24 Dec. 1905
I. G. Grizzle, J. P.

W. D. WISEMAN to Mrs. Lou HILLIS Issued 23 Dec. 1905 Rites 24 Dec. 1905
S. H. Templeton, J. P.

Martin WISEMAN to LIzzie CUTTS Issued 23 Dec. 1905 Rites 24 Dec 1905
E. N. Yager, J. P.

George SWANN to Pearl JACOBS Issued 23 Dec. 1905 Rites 27 Dec 1905
W. H. Stewart, M. G.

Frank PATTON to Alice GREEN Issued 23 Dec. 1905 Rites 24 Dec. 1905
L. P. Sanders, J. P.

J. P. PACE to Buzzie DAVIS Issued 23 Dec. 1905 Rites 24 Dec. 1905
E. N. Yager, J. P.

John PETEN to Ella TEMPLETON Issued 23 Dec 1905 Rites 24 Dec 1905
J. W. Cooley, M. G.

Arthur MARTIN (Col) to Caroline YORK (Col) Issued 23 Dec 1905 Rites 25 Dec1905
I. T. Hillis, J. P.

Albert PATRICK to Mattie E. HOLDER Issued 23 Dec. 1905 Rites 24 Dec. 1905
G. W. Haley, M. G.

William ADAIR to Ellen MCAFEE Issued 23 Dec 1905 Rites 24 Dec 1905
H. A. Cunningham, M. G.

Arthur DAVENPORT to Bettie CERTAIN Issued 26 Dec. 1905 Rites 26 Dec 1905
L. P. Potter, M. G.

Burr BLUE (Col) to Eldora STARKEY (Col) Issued 27 Dec 1905 Rites 28 Dec 1905
G. P. Prasier, J. P.

Isaac ROBERTS to Willie CARTER Issued 27 Dec 1905 Rites 28 Dec 1905
J. C. Safley, J. P.

Hnery UNDERHILL to Mandy PARSLEY Issued 28 Dec 1905 Rites 31 Dec 1905
J. G. Goff, J. P.

John C. DUNCAN to Lucy R. CARR Issued 4 Jan 1906 Rites 7 Jan 1906
H. A. Cunningham, M. G.

Nollie MARCUM to Mary Ann EDGE Issued 5 Jan 1906 Rites 7 Jan 1906
D. C. Oliver, J. P.

Linus BLANKS to Elie MERRIMAN Issued 6 Jan 1906 Rites 7 Jan 1906
C. K. Carlock, M. G.

H. B. MOFFITT to Mary ELKINS Issued 6 Jan 1906 Rites 7 JAn 1906
I. T. Hillis, J. P.

M. D. MCDOWELL to Alice M. RITCHIE Issued 9 JAn 1906 Rites 10 Jan 1906
J. K. P. Whitlock, M. G.

J. W. BRYAN to Pennie BRYAN Issued 12 Jan 1906 Rites 15 Jan 1906
W. N. Kell, J. P.

George DUNHAM to Cleo BROWN Issued 13 Jan 1906 Rites 14 Jan 1906
W. N. Kell, J. P.

John GIBBS to Dora PRIEST Issued 29 Jan 1906 Rites 19 Jan 1906
C. L. Kell, J. P.

Luster GANAN to Nannie BONNER Issued 23 Jan 1906 Rites 24 Jan 1906
O. H. Wood, J. P.

Frank SMITH (Col) to Ada SUTTLES (Col) Issued 24 Jan 1906 Rites 24 Jan 1906
A. H. Duncan, M. G.

Jess L. PORTERFIELD to Olie SUMMERS Issued 25 Jan 1906 Rites 28 Jan 1906
W. P. Davis, J. P.

Henry P. RITZINS to Julia M. HUNERWADEL Issued 26 Jan 1906 Rites 26 Jan 1906
R. W. Binkley, M. G.

Albert LANCE to Bettie A. CARR Issued 26 Jan 1906 Rites 28 Jan 1906
D. C. Oliver, J. P.

Everett CRAIN to Jennie COLLIER Issued 29 Jan 1906 Rites 29 Jan 1906
I. T. Hillis, J. P.

J. L. THAXTON to Bell COPE Issued 30 JAn 1906 Rites 1 Feb 1906
W. T. S. Cook, M. G.

J. M. AUSTIN to Nancy LIVELY Issued 31 Jan 1906 Rites 31 Jan 1906
J. D. Guinn, M. G.

Jim MARTIN to Ada GREEN Issued 31 Jan 1906 Rites 4 Feb 1906
J. J. Mullican, J. P.

Bynum B. KING to De MADEWell Issued 1 Feb 1906 Rites 3 Feb 1906
E. L. Moffitt, J. P.

Claud GLENN to Hattie DENTON Issued 1 Feb 1906 Rites 4 Feb 1906
I. D. Womack, M. G.

John GLENN to Bitha DENTON Issued 3 Feb 1906 Rites 4 Feb 1906
I. D. Womack, M. G.

James L. WOOD to Joannah WATSON Issued 8 Feb 1906 Rites 11 Feb 1906
B. F. Wood, M. G.

M. P. ROBERTS to Bertha ROGERS Issued 13 Feb 1906 Rites 16 Feb 1906
J. C. Safley, J. P.

Thoma s TURNER to Myrtle REEDER Issued 16 Feb 1906 Rites 16 Feb 1906
H. J. Boles, M. G.

O. L. GRANSTAFF to Laura ELAM Issued 17 Feb 1906 Rites 18 Feb 1906
H. A. Cunningham, M. G.

Howard MARTIN (Col) to Lizzie Belle MARBURY (Col) Issued 17 Feb 1906 Rites 18 Feb
I. T. Hillis, J. P.

G. V. DENTON to Pearl JOHNSON Issued 20 Feb 1906 Rites 22 feb 1906
Sol Williams, J. P.

Jos. Stewart RAMSEY to Va. Eliz. HUGHES Issued 23 Feb 1906 Rites 28 Feb 1906
J. D. Guinn, M. G.

Will HOLMAN (Col) to Lula BRITTON (COl) Issued 1 Mar 1906 Rites 1 Mar 1906
J. M. Lytle, M. G.

Norman NUNLEY to Nora TRAVIS Issued 5 Mar 1906 Rites 5 Mar 1906
J. J. Meadows, J. P.

James W. TURNER to Eula THAXTON Issued 5 Mar 1906 Rites 6 Mar 1906
W. P. Davis, J. P.

Eston DOYL to Eva WEBB Issued 7 Mar 1906 Rites 7 Mar 1906
G. T. Riggs, J. P.

William TOSH to Jeiie LYNN Issued 9 Mar 1906 Rites 11 Mar 1906
J. L. Thaxton, J. P.

Charles SANDERS to Della HERNDON Issued 10 Mar 1906 Rites 10 Mar 1906
J. W. Sims, M. G.

Charley ELROD to Bertha WATSON Issued 10 Mar 1906 Rites 11 Mar 1906
W. E. Martin, J. P.

Levi RUTLEDGE to Thula HENNESSEE Issued 16 Mar 1906 Rites 18 Mar 1906
J. W. Roberts, M. G.

Alf REYNOLDS to Mary SHIRLEY Issued 17 Mar 1906 Rites 18 Mar 1906
C. S. Campbell, M. G.

Elliott PANTER to Lillie SCOTT Issued 17 Mar 1906 Rites 19 Mar 1906
E. L. Moffitt, J. P.

Wm. Huddleston (Col) to Lou EVANS (Col) Issued 19 Mar 1906 Rites 15 Apr 1906
G. W. Dunham, J. P.

Alex SHIELDS to Louie Bell COOPER Issued 21 Mar 1906 Rites 22 Mar 1906
G. W. Dunham, J. P.

Fletcher MARTIN (Col) to Mamie WOOTEN (Col) Issued 21 Mar 1906 Rites 30 Apr 1906
N. W. Ware, M. G.

Alf JUDKINS to Ada GIBBS Issued 24 Mar 1906 Rites 25 Mar 1906
Sol Williams, J. P.

Luster PEYTON to Essie GRAVES Issued 26 Mar 1906 Rites 29 Mar 1906
W. P. Davis, J. P.

G. D. OLIVER to Lela WOMACK Issued 4 Aug 1906 Rites 5 Aug 1906
W. P. Davis, J. P.

Charley STUBBLEFIELD (Col) to Janie SWAFFORD (Col) Issued 14 Juen 1906 R 15/6/06
N. W. Ware, M. G.

Sam DOYLE to Nola LITTLE Issued 31 Mar 1906 Rites 1 Apr 1906
E. N. Yager, J. P.

Kenneth MADEWELL to Minnie HILL Issued 31 Mar 1906 Rites 1 Apr 1906
J. J. Meadvos, J. P.

Tennessee BAIN to Clarrisa TANNER Issued 3 Apr 1906 Rites 3 Apr 1906
J. E. Jones, J. P.

Roy SHERLEN to Cora DICKSON Issued 5 Apr 1906 Rites 6 Apr 1906
E. N. Yager, J. P.

Poley WATSON to Lou MCBRIDE Issued 18 Apr 1906 Rites 22 Apr 1906
J. W. Roberts, M. G.

William JOSSIE to Leta Belle COLLIER Issued 18 Apr 1906 Rites 18 Apr 1906
E. N. Yager, J. P.

Thomas SMARTT to Maggie JENNINGS Issued 19 Apr 1906 Rites 19 Apr 1906
J. S. Safley, J. P.

R. M. STEPP to Martha CHRISTIAN Issued 21 Apr 1906 Rites 2 May 1906
L. V. Scott, J. P.

Charles GREEN to Willie Belle PLYANT Issued 25 Apr 1906 Rites 29 Apr 1906
Jacob Stipe, M. G.

Sam STUBBLEFIELD to Sallie PARKER Issued 25 Apr 1906 Not Returned

L. B. SIMMONS to Etta YORK Issued 2 May 1906 Rites 2 May 1906
Allen Miller

Hnery ROSE to Polly MCBRIDE Issued 5 May 1906 Rites 6 May 1906
J. W. Roberts, M. G.

Walter H. KIRBY to Paralee HOLDER Issued 5 May 1906 Rites 6 May 1906
E. N. Yager, J. P.

R. L. DURHAM to Margie MATHEWS Issued 5 May 1906 Rites 6 May 1906
E. N. Yager, J. P.

Tullie TOSH to Mollie MCBRIDE Issued 7 May 1906 Rites 7 May 1906
J. L. Thaxton, J. P.

J. N. PEDEN to Mary DODSON Issued 12 May 1906 Not Returned

Joe SPRINGS (Col) to Daisy LOOPER (Col) Issued 14 May 1906 Rites 14 May 1906
Sam Ourry

Dock HOLDER to Grace BOAZ Issued 16 May 1906 Rites 16 May 1906
Allen Miller

Cooper SCOTT to Adel SLAUGHTER Issued 18 May 1906 Rites 18 May 1906
E. N. Yager, J. P.

Robert D. LEASON to Mary Lee BOSTICK Issued 18 May 1906 Rites 18 May 1906
Spurgeon Wingo, M. G.

E. T. PACE to Mollie FISHER   Issued 18 May 1906 Rites 18 May 1906
Surgeon Wingo, M. G.

Alexander KING to Francis JUDKINS   Issued 19 May 1906 Rites 20 May 1906
L. V. Scott, J. P.

Forest MARTIN (Col) to Bulah LUSK (Col) Issued 22 May 1906 Not Executed

Smart Cope LIVINGSTON (C) to Bertha Loretta MORFORD Issued 23 May 1906 Rites 23/5/06
J. M. Lyte, M. G.

K. D. MULLICAN to Jennie BLANKENSHIP Issued 24 May 1906 Rites 27 May 1906
I. D. Womack

Dalton BOULDIN to PEarl CHRISTIAN Issued 2 June 1906 Rites 11 June 1906
E. L. Moffitt, J. P.

W. D. SPENCER to Alica Ann THOMAS Issued 11 June 1906 Rites 12 June 1906
W. P. Davis, J. P.

James M. BURCH to Elizabeth WOOD   Issued 11 June 1906 Rites 11 June 1906
J. W. Sims, M. G.

Willie SANDERS to Lila CANTRELL   Issued 16 June 1906 Rites 16 June 1906
E. N. Yager, J. P.

Tom PATTERSON to Annie CRITTENDEN Issued 16 June 1906 Rites 16 June 1906
E. N. Yager, J. P.

Oliver BESS to Beada MADEWELL Issued 22 June 1906 Rites 23 June 1906
E. L. Moffitt, J. P.

G. W. HINKLEY to Libby MEISER Issued 25 June 1906 Rites 27 June 1906
H. Leo Boles, M. G.

George NUNLEY to Fannie LEWIS   Issued 26 June 1906   Rites 26 June 1906
H. A. Cunningham, M. G.

John T. COOPER to Lena ARNOLD   Issued 30 June 1906 Rites 1 July 1906
JAMES M. Crawford, M. G.

Murf DODSON to Maud MCGREGOR Issued 3 July 1906 Rites 4 July 1906
L. H. Templeton, J. P.

James EARLS to Maggie McCORKLE   Issued 3 July 1906 Not Returned

James RUTLEDGE to Mary RUTLEDGE   Issued 6 July 1906 Not Returned

Frank GLENN to Alice SPARKMAN   Issued 7 July 1906 Rites 8 July 1906
L. P. Sanders, J. P.

C. C. TODD to Ida TALLEY   Issued 7 July 1906 Rites 8 July 1906
H. A. Cunningham, M. G.

A. J. BESS to Ida WILLIAMS   Issued 10 July 1906 Rites 10 July 1906
L. V. Scott, J. P.

Frank TURNER to Martha SMARTT   Issued 14 July 1906 Not Returned

J. L. WOMACK to A. L. LORING   Issued 16 July 1906 Rites 16 July 1906
M. J. Jones, J. P.

Mack WARREN to Mary ATNIP   Issued 21 July 1906   Rites 22 July 1906
I. G. Gribble, J. P.

Jesse BOND to Myrtle PATRICK   Issued 25 July 1906 Rites 29 July 1906
L. V. Scott, J. P.

Scipis ROBERTS (Col) to Polly STONE (Col) Issued 25 July 1906 Rites 25 July 1906
G. V. Speons, M. G.

Arthur D. RICE to Lottie NORRIS Issued 1 Aug 1906 Rites 1 Aug 1906
J. D. Guim, M. G.

Dave PRIEST to Clara BRATCHER   Issued 3 Aug 1906 Rites 4 Aug 1906
I. G. Webb, J. P.

John T. HENDERSON to Rachael BRADFORD Issued 4 Aug 1906 Rites 4 Aug 1906
R. W. Binkley, M. G.

Chas. GRISWOLD (Col) to Mary Lee SPURLOCK (Col) Issued 4 Aug 1906 Rites 5 Aug '06
J. B. Bradford, M. G.

S. B. VINSON to Ada STANLEY   Issued 11 Aug 1906 Rites 12 Aug 1906
B. F. Woods, M. G.

D. W. KING to Lillie Mae MOORE Issued 14 Aug 1906 Rites 14 Aug 1906
J. D. Guim, M. G.

T. E. ADAMSON to Martha CHISOM Issued 14 Aug 1906 Rites 18 Aug 1906
M. J. Jones, J. P.

Talbert L. BURKETT to Minnie ELROD   Issued 18 Aug 1906 Rites 19 Aug 1906
W. E. Marler, J. P.

George AKEMAN to Bettie GILLENTINE   Issued 18 Aug 1906 Rites 19 Aug 1906
L. H. Templeton

O. D. WALKER to Paralee CATON Issued 16 Aug 1906 Rites 16 1906
J. M. Denton, M. G.

Cleve TIPPET to Birch MORROW Issued 18 Aug 1906 Rites 19 Aug 1906
I. G. Webb, J. P.

A. C. McGIBONEY to Lou MARTIN Issued 18 Aug 1906 Rites 19 Aug 1906
J. M. Crawford, M. G.

Sam GOFF to Nora NEWDY   Issued 24 Aug 1906 Rites 26 Aug 1906
W. E. Marler, J. P.

John MADEWELL to Nannie CURTIS   Issued 25 Aug 1906 Not Returned

Marvin FINGER to Rutha JACOBS   Issued 25 Aug 1906 Rites 26 Aug 1906
J. F. Martin, M. G.

John MILLER to Laura GRISSOM Issued 19 Dec 1905 Rites 24 Dec 1905
I. T. Hillis, J. P.

Haskell SMITH to Mamie GRIZZLE Issued 1 Jan 1906 Rites Not Executed Ret'd 5/24/06

A. J. NEWBY to Lina EARLS Issued 13 Jan 1906 Rites 14 Jan 1906
Geo. T. Riggs, J. P.

J. H. COPE to Emma PATTERSON Issued 3 Feb 1906 Rites 4 Feb. 1906
E. N. Yager, J. P.

Quill BURDEN (Col) to Minnie WOOTEN Issued 1 Mar 1906 Rites 1 Mar 1906
(Col)
J. M. Lytle, M. G.

R. S. AUSTIN to Mattie Mai RANKHORN Issued 29 Mar 1906 Not Returned

Jack Harry A. MILLER (Col) to Bobbie PRICHETT (Col) Issued 28 May 1906
Rites 28 May 1906 G. L. Speaker, M. G.

Hugh SLAUGHTER to Victoria SCOTT Issued 4 June 1906 Rites 6 June 1906
E. L. Moffitt, J. P.

Lawrence P. HUDDLESTON to Gracy Neal NEWMAN Issued 22 June 1906 Rites 23 June 1906
A. M. Trawick, Jr.

W. F. OUTLAW to Cora Bell SMOOT Issued 2 July 1906 Rites 2 July 1906
E. N. Yager, J. P.

A. J. OGLE to Ollie PEPPER Issued 3 July 1906 Rites 4 July 1906
G. W. Dunham, J. P.

Billoat BROWN to Rena M. HUGHES Issued 17 July 1906 Rites 17 July 1906
A. M. Trawick, M. G.

Claud SIMONS to Ellen BUTCHER Issued 18 Aug 1906 Rites 19 Aug 1906
S. H. Templeton, J. P.

O. D. STUBBLEFIELD to Lucy WHITLOCK Issued 13 Oct 1906 Rites 21 Nov 1906
J. A. Cunningham, M. G.

Beecher SIMONS to Annie MARTIN Issued 13 Oct 1906 Not Returned

Jessie KING to Dora PERRY Issued 20 Oct 1906 Rites 21 Oct 1906
L. V. Scott,. J. P.

Fred DAVEY to Jossie MASON Issued 20 Oct 1906 Rites 21 Oct 1906
E. N. Yager, J. P.

Martin THURMAN to Esty WILSON Issued 27 Oct 1906 Rites 27 Oct 1906
B. W. D. Barnes, J. P.

W. P. BOTTOMS to Brunette HAYES Issued 27 Oct 1906 Rites 28 Oct 1906
J. W. Cooley, M. G.

John ABBOT to Mattie CUMMINGS Issued 30 Oct 1906 Rites 1 Nov 1906
J. W. Cooley, M. G.

Lonnie FOSTER to Edna BARNES Issued 20 Aug 1906 Rites 29 Aug 1906
E. H. Hoover, M. G.

Lellon CANTRELL to Delia CANTRELL Issued 25 Aug 1906 Rites 27 Aug 1906
Sol Williams, J. P.

Walter KELLEY to Sallie HOLLANDSWORTH Issued 25 Aug 1906 Rites 26 Aug 1906
G. H. Atnip, M. G.

Will GRIFFITH to Gertie BOLES Issued 30 Aug 1906 Rites 2 Sept 1906
P. G. Potter, M. G.

Obia WISEMAN to Rozetta HAYES Issued 1 Sept 1906 Rites 1 Sept 1906
S. H. Templeton, J. P.

A. J. GREEN to A. J. BRUCE Issued 1 Sept 1906 Not Returned

Will WALKER to Mary DELANEY Issued 3 Sept 1906 Rites 3 Sept 1906
J. D. Quick

Lee ADAMS (Col) to Mamie SMARTT (Col) Issued 5 Sept 1906 Rites 5 Sept 1906
B. W. D. Barnes, J. P.

Dave MITCHELL to Bertha ARLEDGE Issued 8 Sept 1906 Rites 9 Sept 1906
G. W. Haley, J. P.

John R. RIGSBY to Mary Susie CARR Issued 14 Sept 1906 Rites 16 Sept 1906
G. W. Haley, J. P.

Robert CANTRELL to Sallie EARLS Issued 14 Sept 1906 Rites 14 Sept 1906
E. N. Yager, J. P.

Charles BARNES to Bertha MYERS Issued 18 Sept 1906 Rites 18 Sept 1906
E. L. Moffitt, J. P.

Leo BOLES to Ida MEISER Issued 22 Sept 1906 Rites 23 Sept 1906
P. G. Potter, M. G.

J. J. MITCHELL to Ellen Lucille DOUGLAS Issued 26 Sept 1906 Rites 26 Sep 1906
R. W. Binkley, M. G.

J. R. ELAM (Col) to Georgie GROSS (Col) Issued 29 Sept 1906 Rites 30 Sep 1906
Sam Curry, M. G.

W. A. WARREN to Delma CANTRELL Issued 12 Nov 1906 Rites 18 Nov 1906
J. G. Goff, J. P.

James FORD to Bessie SAIN Issued 26 Jan 1907 Rites 30 Jan 1907
J. R. Stubblefield

W. P. DICKSON to Fannie STACY Issued 29 Sept 1906 Rites 30 Sep 1906
Wm A Bell, J. P.

E. M. ROGERS to Pearl MOFFITT Issued 1 Oct 1906 Rites 10 Oct 1906
C. K. Carlock, M. G.

John M. TATE to Rebeca VAUGHAN Issued 9 Oct 1906 Rites 9 Oct 1906
D. T. Burch, M. G.

Cleveland NEWBY to Tommie STANLEY Issued 31 Oct 1906 Rites 4 Nov 1906 J. G. Goff, J. P.

Tommie JORDON to Bertha LANCE Issued 9 Nov 1906 Rites 11 Nov 1906 G. W. Haley, J. P.

Snoden McBRIDE to Mitty VICKORS Issued 10 Nov 1906 Rites 11 Nov 1906 J. L. Thaxton, J. P.

Lawson HOBBS (Col) to Eva JOHNSON (Col) Issued 15 Nov 1906 Rites 15 Nov 1906 H. W. Hawkins, M. G.

James L. COLVERT to Margeritte PAGE Issued 19 Nov 1906 Rites 20 Nov 1906 Jacob Stipe, M. G.

Toney PARKER to Lucy Della HOBBS Issued 26 Nov 1906 Rites 28 Nov 1906 W. N. Kell, J. P.

Mack SWANN to Etta BLAIR Issued 26 Nov 1906 Rites 28 Nov 1906 Harvey W Seay, M. G.

G. T. SCHMITZ to Minnie May RICE Issued 28 Nov 1906 Rites 28 Nov 1906 R. W. Binkley, M. G.

J, S. GRISSOM to Julia THOMISON Issued 30 Nov 1906 Rites 2 Dec 1906 J. M. Duncan, J. P.

Will PHILLIPS to Sallie BYARS Issued 8 Dec 1906 Rites 9 Dec 1906 J. K. P. Whitlock

M. A. WILSON to Etta HULETT Issued 11 Dec. 1906 Rites 13 Dec 1906 J. A. Cunningham, M. G.

I. W. SMITH to Corbin GILBERT Issued 11 Dec 1906 Rites 16 1906 J. E. Jones, J. P.

Robert WILSON to Myrtle BURKS Issued 14 Dec 1906 Rites 14 Dec 1906

Elijah.ROBERTS to Mary COPPINGER Issued 14 Dec 1906 Rites 6 Jan 1907 J. V. Scott, J. P.

Bee YORK to Mattie HULETT Issued 15 Dec 1906 Rites 16 Dec 1906 W. N. Kell, M. G.

William JENNINGS to Fannie McGREGOR Issued 15 Dec 1906 Rites 16 Dec 1906 H. T. McGregor, J. P.

James L. McAFEE to Mamie SIMS Issued 24 Dec 1906 Rites 24 Dec 1906 J. A. Cunningham, M. G.

Richard MARTIN to Martha MYERS Issued 21 Dec 1906 Rites 26 Dec 1906 J. W. Cooley, M. G.

W. W. SUMMERS to I. B. GILLEY Issued 21 Dec 1906 Rites 23 Dec 1906 J. C. Martin, M. G.

Alvin TRAVIS to Alice GILLEY Issued 22 Dec 1906 Rites 25 Dec 1906 H. W. Seay, M. G.

Charles GREER to Eliza KEATHLEY Issued 22 Dec 1906 Rites 23 Dec 1906 Allen Miller, M. G.

J. W. HARDCASTLE to Myrtle YORK Issued 22 Dec 1906 Rites 25 Dec 1906 R. W. Binkley, M. G.

Lawrence KEATON to Millie LITTLE Issued 22 Dec 1906 Rites 25 Dec 1906 P. G. Potter, M. G.

Mort GRIBBLE (Col) to Syothy YORK (Col) Issued 26 Dec 1906 Rites 27 Dec 1906 J. M. Duncan, J. P.

C. N. WRIGHT to Nellie DUNHAM Issued 26 Dec 1906 Rites 26 Dec 1906 J. W. Cooley, M. G.

Frank McPHERSON to Cora TURNER Issued 24 Dec 1906 Rites 29 Dec 1906 E. L. Moffitt, J. P.

Charles ASKEW to Hassie KING Issued 24 Dec 1906 Rites 24 Dec 1906 J. R. Stubblefield

Henry SCOTT to W. (Not finished) Page #440

W. C. BOGLE to Della CAMPBELL Issued 27 Dec 1906 Rites 30 Dec 1906 Samuel Byars, J. P.

Jess HENNESSEE to Allie LUTRELL Issued 28 Dec 1906 Rites 29 Dec 1906 W. W. Locke, J. P.

J. T. PRATER to S. R. WOMACK Issued 29 Dec 1906 Rites 30 Dec 1906 G. W. Haley, J. P.

Charlie DAVIS to Allie SMITH Issued 29 Dec 1906 Rites 31 Dec 1906 B. W. D. Barnes, J. P.

T. W. SMITH to Ida GREEN Issued 29 Dec 1906 Rites 30 Dec 1906 J. M. Green, J. P.

Osborn BIGELOW to Myrtle EDGE Issued 29 Dec 1906 Rites 30 Dec 1906 R. W. Binkley, M. G.

Frank SMITH (Col) to Novella LUSK (Col) Issued 29 Dec 1906 Rites 30 Dec 1906 Wm. Thurman,

Jess OWEN to Pearl HOLT Issued 31 Dec 1906 Rites 1 Jan 1907 G. W. Haley, J. P.

Walter M. BETZ to Nannie CUMMINGS Issued 1 JAn 1907 Rites 2 JAn 1907 J. A. Knight, J. P.

Charlie MARTIN to Ocie NASH Issued 1 Jan 1907 Rites 6 Jan 1907 Jas. Crawford, M. G.

C. R. ETTER to Lee HAYES Issued 5 Jan 1907 Rites 6 Jan 1907
J. Barnes, J. P.

Charles MASON to Susie BENNETT Issued 5 Jan 1907 Rites 6 Jan 1907
J. A. Knight, J. P.

JAmes WOOD (Col) to Ida PAGE (Col) Issued 14 Jan 1907 Rites 14 Jan 1907
J. M. Duncan, J. P.

H. M. GALLAGHER to Josephine TEMPLES Issued 19 Jan 1907 Rites 20 Jan 1907
B. A. Pendleton, M. G.

Jack WOODLEE (Col) to Georgie TIDWELL (Col) Issued 20 Jan 1907 Rites 20 Jan 1907
A---- Johnson/G T Spears

Knox CARR to Opha LANCE Issued 22 Jan 1907 Rites 27 Jan 1907
G. W. Haley, J. P.

John THORNS (Col) to Matilda HENEGAR (Col) Issued 22 Jan 1907 Rites 24 Jan 1907
J. E. Jones, J. P.

Chas. PENNINGTON to Jossie WOOD Issued 25 Jan 1907 Rites 27 Jan 1907
J. A. Cunningham, M. G.

G. T. DODSON to Parriet TURNER Issued 26 Jan 1907 Rites 27 Jan 1907
J. W. Cooley, M. G.

R. M. GROSS to Ella Mai NELSON Issued 2 Feb 1907 Rites 2 Feb 1907
R. W. Binkley, M. G.

Wiley COPPINGER to Lucy SMARTT Issued 7 Feb. 1907 Rites 10 Feb 1907
L. V. Scott, J. P.

Isaac GRIZZLE to Julia SANDERS Issued 9 Feb 1907 Rites 10 Feb. 1907
Allen Miller, M. G.

Harve JARRELL to Bertha MORRISON Issued 12 Feb 1907 Rites 13 Feb 1907
J. S. Mason, M. G.

A. M. JERNIGAN to L. M. BOWMAN Issued 13 Feb 1907 Not Returned

J. W. PATRICK to Laura SLAUGHTER Issued 15 Feb. 1907 Rites 17 Feb 1907
L. V. Scott, J. P.

George MEISER to Blanche JUSTICE Issued 18 Feb 1907 Rites 19 Feb 1907
Allen Miller, M. G.

I. P. GOGGINS to Ella FERRELL Issued 18 Feb 1907 Rites 24 Feb 1907
J. T. Turner, J. P.

I. A. GILLEY to Minnie Mai THOMAS Issued 22 Feb. 1907 Rites 24 Feb 1907
H. W. Seay, M. G.

Arthur M. WESTPHAL to Emma L. BIRT Issued 27 Feb 1907 Rites 13 Feb. 1907
C. G. Howell

Frank CAWN (Col) to Beulah CROCKETT Issued 28 Feb 1907 Rites 28 Feb 1907
G. T. Speaks, M. G.

J. D. CANTRELL to Delia Ann MOSS Issued 2 Mar 1907 Rites 3 Mar 1907
R. H. Mason, J. P.

John WOODARD (Col) to Daisy ROACH (Col) Issued 2 Mar 1907 Rites 3 Mar 1907
M. B. Newsom

Chas. B. PORTERFIELD to Hassie VANHOOSER Issued 9 Mar 1907 Rites 9 Mar 1907
J. W. Cooley, M. G.

R. H. FRENCH to Mollie GWYN Issued 9 Mar 1907 Rites 9 Mar 1907
(Col) D. T. Burch, M., G.

O. L. ROWLAND to Lissie BRIGHT Issued 14 Mar 1907 Rites 17 Mar 1907
J. B. Gribble, M. G.

O. L. FOSTER to Sarah D. YORK Issued 23 Mar 1907 Rites 24 Mar 1907
J. M. McGiboney, J. P.

Henry PEDEN to Cora NUNEMAKER Issued 29 Mar 1907 Rites 29 Mar 1907
C. G. Howell, Daylight Th

James SIMONS to Hassie HILLIS Issued 30 Mar 1907 Rites 2 Apr 1907
L. Safley, M. G.

Joe ETTER (Col) to Ada RITCHEY (Col) Issued 30 Mar 1907 Rites 31 Mar 1907
G. S. Speaks, M. G.

Robert HARDING (Col) to Carlie SMARTT (Col) Issued 30 Mar 1907 Rites 30 Mar 1907
D. T. Burch, M. G.

Jim BILES (Col) to Beulah ALEXANDER (Col) Issued 13 Apr 1907 Rites 13 Apr 1907
G. T. Speeks

H. VANHOOSER to Nannie GREEN Issued 16 Apr 1907 Rites 16 Apr 1907
J. J. Meadows, J. P.

W. J. MAXWELL to Jennie CLARK Issued 22 Apr 1907 Rites 25 Apr 1907

J. H. McCORMACK to Ina HALEY Issued 25 Apr 1907 Rites 28 Apr 1907
S. T. Byars, J. P.

Porter BROWN to Eva MARTIN Issued 28 Apr 1907 Rites 29 Apr 1907
G T Speaks, M. G.

Cal MATHEWS to Jimmie LAWSON Issued 29 Apr 1907 Rites 29 Apr 1907
R. H. Mason, J. P.

Ralph SMITH to Lilly VICKERS Issued 3 May 1907 Rites 5 May 1907
J. L. Thaxton, J. P.

Wm L. STILES to Hattie CHRISTIAN Issued 10 May 1907 Rites 11 May 1907
E. N. Yager, J. P.

Albert WOMACK to Annie Maud KELL Issued 11 May 1907 Rites 10 May 1907
I. G. Webb

Tim COPEHART to Sarah INGRIM Issued 11 May 1907 Rites 12 May 1907
J. T. Turner, J. P.

Alva WHITAKER to Lena DENTON Issued 11 May 1907 Rites 12 May 1907
P. G. Potter, M. G.

Tom CHRISTIAN to Inez BRADY Issued 11 May 1907 Rites 13 May 1907
J. J. Meadows, J. P.

Joe BILES (Col) to Mary SAVAGE (Col) Issued 15 May 1907 Rites 19 May 1907
W. L. Hunt, M. G.

Oscar WILLIAMSON to Eliza GREEN Issued 11 May 1907 Rites 19 May 1907
E. N. Yager, J. P.

T. F. DENTON to Josie LOCKE Issued 17 May 1907 Rites 19 May 1907
P. G. Potter, M. G.

John R. PARIS to Mary SMARTT Issued 20 May 1907 Rites 22 May 1907
H. W. Seay, M. G.

Wm. L. YORK to Hassie ROBINSON Issued 21 May 1907 Rites 22 May 1907
J. D. Northcutt

John PELHAM to Mary BASHAM Issued 24 May 1907 Rites 24 May 1907
H. W. Seay, M. G.

James SMITH to Goldie CROUCH Issued 25 May 1907 Rites 26 May 1907
J. W. Sims, M. G.

D. C. BARLOW to Maud SPAKES Issued 1 June 1907 Rites 2 June 1907
J. D. Hart

J. W. GRISSOM to Mollie WILCHER Issued 7 June 1907 Rites 9 June 1907
J. D. Hash

Jessie WILLIAMS to Lizzie BURTON Issued 10 June 1907 Rites 23 June 1907
George Brasier, J. P.

H. L. COMER to Viola SUMMERS Issued 12 June 1907 Rites 13 June 1907
H. W. Seay. M. G.

Peter R. CHRISTOPHEL to Juliah A. MARTIN Issued 14 June 1907 Rites 16 June 1907
W. J. Collier, M. G.

Jessie YORK to Fannie PARSLEY Issued 15 June 1907 Rites 16 June 1907
J. A. Cunningham. M. G.

Walter HILL to Sallie WOODS Issued 15 June 1907 Rites 16 June 1907
J. W. Sims, M. G.

P. ALLISON to Berniece SPARKMAN Issued 18 June 1907 Rites 18 June 1907
C. K. Carlock, M. G.

Willie RIDDLE to Martha BROWN Issued 24 June 1907 Rites 26 June 1907
George Brasier, J. P.

Wm. T. ARGO to Rosa Mai COTHERN Issued 26 June 1907 Rites 30 June 1907
J. W. Sims, M. G.

Ernest K. BONNER to Emma Lee CRAVEN Issued 28 June 1907 Rites 7 July 1907
J. R. Stubblefield

George HODGE to Maud PUGH Issued 29 June 1907 Rites 29 June 1907
E. N. Yager, J. P.

W. M. ANDERSON (Col) to Queen Payne (Col) Issued 3 July 1907 Rites 3 July 1907
D. T. Burch. M. G.

George BRADFORD to Mary TANNER Issued 3 July 1907 Rites 27 July 1907
J. L. Thaxton, J. P.

Will TEMPLETON to Rachel BARLOW Issued 6 July 1907 Rites 11 July 1907
J. D. Hash, J. P.

J. L. WHITAKER to Jane CANTRELL Issued 6 July 1907 Rites 6 July 1907
E. N. Yager, J. P.

Dock LOOPER to Mary MASON Issued 13 July 1907 Rites 13 July 1907
Sam Curry

W. A. PATRICK to Sophia CHRISTIAN Issued 16 July 1907 Rites 16 July 1907
L. V. Scott, J. P.

O. L. MITCHELL to Hallie FOSTER Issued 20 July 1907 Rites 21 July 1907
J. M. McGiboney,

Hiley WOOD to Zonic BURCH Issued 20 July 1907 Rites 21 July 1907
J. A. Cunningham, M. G.

John HASH to Rosia PENDERGRASS Issued 26 July 1907 Rites 28 July 1907
J. D. Quick, J. P.

Bud ROMANS to Dollie McCORMACK Issued 20 July 1907 Rites 28 July 1908
J. D. Quick, J. P.

Vach LANKFORD to Minnie BOULDIN Issued 27 July 1907 Rites 4 Aug 1907
E. L. Moffitt, J. P.

Hillery LOOPER to Flora MARTIN Issued 2 Aug 1907 Rites 3 Aug 1907
N. W. Ware, M. G.

John HIGGINS (Col) to Myrtle MARTIN (Col) Issued 10 Aug 1907 Rites 11 Aug. 1907
M. Jackson, M. G.

Lewis WILSON to Pearl COMER Issued 15 Aug 1907 Rites 15 Aug 1907
H. W. Seay, M. G.

C. M. COLLIER to Josephine DOUGLAS Issued 17 Aug 1907 Rites 20 Aug 1907
R. W. Binkley, M. G.

A. A. O. MALLEY to Eva TOWNES Issued 20 Aug 1907 Rites 21 Aug 1907
R. W. Binkley, M. G.

Frank CLENDENEN to Oshia CHRISTIAN Issued 23 Aug 1907 Rites 25 Aug 1907
L. V. Scott. M. G.

B. H. PRATER to Millie E. YOUNGBLOOD Issued 29 Aug 1907 Rites 1 Sept 1907
G. W. Haley, J. P.

Daniel R. BIZE to Mary A. HARRISON Issued 3 Sep 1907 Rites 3 Sep 1907
B. A. Pendleton

Frank RITCHEY to Josie SMITH Issued 6 Sept 1907 Not Returned

Clarence TALLEY to Hallie PAYNE Issued 7 Sep 1907 Rites 8 Sep 1907
W. S. Grissom, J. P.

Samuel Thos. BRATCHER to Ocie MASEY Issued 7 Sep 1907 Rites 8 Sep 1907
J. B. Vinson, J. P.

Claude TALLEY to Maude THOMSON Issued 11 Sept 1907 Rites 13 Sep 1907
W. S. Grissom, J. P.

John W. NELMS to Hallie WANNAMAKER Issued 12 Dep 1907 Rites 15 Sep 1907
L. V. Scott, J. P.

Alfred McGREGOR to Amie CHASTEEN Issued 13 Sept 1907 Rites 15 Sep 1907
J. W. Cooley, M. G.

Hubert THOMAS (Col) to Ada JOHNSON (Col) Issued 13 Sep 1907 Rites 13 Sep 1907
N. P. Gregge

Ben MYERS to Lizzie PERRY Issued 14 Sep 1907 Rites 15 Sep 1907
W. J. Cullium, M. G.

JAMES W. GRIZZLE to Nora JACO Issued 14 Sep 1907 Rites 15 Sep 1907
I. G. Welch, J. P.

E. E. BARNETT to Sallie SHERRILL Issued 14 Sep 1907 Rites 17 Sep 1907
Allen Miller

Sam ALEXANDER to Nettie Jane DAVIS Issued 19 Sep 1907 Rites 25 Sep 1907
P. G. Potter, M. G.

W. R. LANE to Nannie Bell COOPER Issued 20 Sep 1907 Rites 20 Sep 1907
W. N. Kell, J. P.

Jmaes CLARK to Ada BARNES Issued 21 Sep 1907 Rites 22 Sept 1907
L. Safley, M. G.

W. H. HAMILTON to Dora LISTER Issued 21 Sep 1907 Rites 22 Sep 1907
J. M. Green, J. P.

Elijah ROBERTS to Florence McBRIDE Issued 21 Sep 1907 Rites 24 Sept 1907
L. V. Scott, J. P.

Frank WARREN to Pauline CANTRELL Issued 21 Sep 1907 Rites 22 Sep 1907
E. N. Yager, J. P.

James Preston MALONE (Col) to Sadie M. WHITE (Col) Iss'd 26 Sep 1907 Rites 9/26/07
G. T. Speaks, M. G.

Thomas BRATCHER to Dona GRIBBLE Issued 26 Sep 1907 Rites 31(?) Sep 1907
J. B. Gribble, M. G.

Jackson MUNSEY to Rosa WARE Issued 28 Sept 1907 Rites 28 Sep 1907
E. N. Yager, J. P.

J. S. HARRISON to Jessie Miles SPURLOCK Issued 8 Oct 1907 Rites 8 Oct 1907
R. W. Binkley, M. G.

Joe PATTON to Ann BRATCHER Issued 9 Oct 1907 Rites 11 Oct 1907
J. G. Goff, J. P.

Hervey BOULDIN to Florida RICHARDSON Issued 11 Oct 1907 Rites 11 Oct 1907
J. W. Cooley, M. G.

Moses HARRIMAN to Fannie DAVENPORT Issued 12 Oct 1907 Rites 13 Oct 1907
I. McGregor, J. P.

John SMARTT to Hallie GREEN Issued 19 OCT 1907 Rites 20 Oct 1907
J. Barnes, J. P.

Robert ROLLINS to Mary JONES Issued 19 Oct 1907 Rites 20 Oct 1907
H. S. McGregor, J. P.

Lee PARSLEY to Anna May WHITLOCK Issued 19 Oct 1907 Rites 20 Oct 1907
J. L. Mason

Everett SMITH to Ella MARTIN Issued 19 Oct 1907 Rites 20 Oct 1907
N. P. Greggs

Isham G. H. EWTON to Bertie Victoria McGEE Issued 19 Oct 1907 Rites 19 Oct 1907
J. S. Lawrence, J. P.

Arthur BROWN (Col) to Sarah Martin (Col) Issued 19 Oct 1907 Rites 19 Oct 1907
N. P. Greggs

T. D. CUMMINGS to Jennie HAMILTON Issued 22 Oct 1907 Rites 22 Oct 1907
J. E. Jones, J. P.

Alfred S. LADD to Hallie PHILLIPS Issued 22 Oct 1907 Rites 27 Oct 1907
S. T. Byars, J. P.,.

D. H. PORTERFIELD to Callie HOLDER Issued 28 Oct 1907 Rites 28 Oct 1907
J. G. Goff, J. P.

Walter DUDLEY to Erie SMITH Issued 29 Oct 1907 Rites 29 Oct 1907
D, T. Burch, M. G.

Jos. Albert BLAKE to Will Austin MASON Issued 29 Oct 1907 Rites 29 Oct 1907
R. W. Binkley, M. G.

N. P. GREGGS to Bessie T. VAUGHN Issued 30 Oct 1907 Rites 30 Oct 1907
H. W. Rucker (Col) Minister

S. H. BYARS to Ebby ADCOCK Issued 7 Nov 1907 Rites 7 Nov 1907
W. T. Coten, M. G.

Aron MARBERRY to Ethel GARDNER Issued 18 Nov 1907 Rites 18 Nov 1907
H. W. Rucker, (Col) Minister

Earnest EARLS to Ora GIBBS Issued 20 Nov 1907 Rites 20 Nov. 1907
    E. N. Yager, J. P.

Clarence HUNTER to Effie WOODS Issued 23 Nov 1907 Not Returned

Willis GRIBBLE to Octa WOODS Issued 23 Nov 1907 Rites 11 Feb 1908
    W. S. Grissom. J. P.

Manard MASEY (Col) to Bertha RICE (Col) Issued 23 Nov 1907 Rites 23 Nov 1907
    Samuel Curry

Sidney MADEWELL to Laura KING Issued 25 Nov 1907 Rites 6 Dec 1907
    E. L. Moffitt, J. P.

Lee HILL to Edith COMER Issued 28 Nov 1907 Rites 1 Dec 1907
    J. F. Martin, M. G.

W. E. HIGGINBOTHAM to Minnie EARLS Issued 29 Nov 1907 Rites 1 Dec 1907
    Samuel Byars, M. G.

Victor MARTIN to Sarah SMITH Issued 30 Nov 1907 Rites 30 Nov 1907
    W. P. Parker

Hillie STILES to Maggie THOMASON Issued 30 Nov 1907 Rites 17 Dec 1907
    J. M. Green, J. P.

Henry BARLOW to Dossie SPAKES Issued 10 Dec 1907 Rites 11 Dec 1907
    J. D. Quick, J. P.

Book #10 - Warren County Marriages - Dec. 5, 1907 to Aug. 7, 1911

J. W. MOSS to Bernie MASIE Issued 5 Dec 1907 Rites 8 Dec 1907
    J. G. Goff, J. P.

C. L. JONES to Ola JONES Issued 10 Dec 1907 Rites 12 Dec 1907
    P. G. Potter, M. G.

George DOVE to Dovie McDOWELL Issued 14 Dec 1907 Rites 13 Dec 1907
    I. G. Webb

John MITCHELL to Jane CASEY Issued 17 Dec 1907 Rites 23 Dec 1907
    J. A. Cunningham, M. G.

Frank J. WINTON to Roberta BROWN Issued 17 Dec 1907 Rites 18 Dec 1907
    D. B. Coleman, M. G.

Claud WOODLEE to Ocie HUGHES Issued 18 Dec 1907 Rites 22 Dec 1907
    J. Barnes, J. P.

A. A. TURNER to Beula BLAIR Issued 18 Dec 1907 Rites 19 Dec 1907
    E. N. Yager, J. P.

Emmett CURTIS to Marilda CURTIS Issued 19 Dec 1907 Rites29 Dec 1907
    E. L. Moffitt, J. P.

W. W. MULLICAN to Lelia DUNLAP Issued 20 Dec 1907 Rites 19 Dec 1907 (Error)
    I. G. Webb

Clarence J. CLARK to Virgie E. HAYES Issued 20 Dec 1907 Rites 22 Dec 1907
    Jacob Stipe, M. G.

Hayes PARKER to Pearl BELCHER Issued 21 Dec 1907 Rites 22 dec 1907
    John A. Ramsey, Eld. ME Ch

Jesse SIMPSON to Ida JORDAN Issued 21 Dec 1907 Rites 24 Dec 1907
    G. M. Haley, J. P.

C. E. ROACH to Ellen ANDERSON Issued 23 dec 1907 Rites 23 Dec 1907
    A. A. Flanders, M. G.

Stokley ETTER to Sallie A. LOCKE Issued 23 Dec 1907 Rites 24 Dec 1907
    C. K. Carlock, M. G.

M. A. BONNER to Hallie WOODS Issued 24 dec 1907 Rites 25 Dec 1907
    J. A. Cunningham, M. G.

Grover DRAKE to Annie WEST Issued 24 Dec 1907 Rites 25 dec 1907
    J. C. Smoot, J. P.

James HODGE to May HAMILTON Issued 24 Dec 1907 Rites 27 Dec 1907
    J. L. Mason

C. J. STANLEY to Maggie PEARSON Issued 24 dec 1907 Rites 24 Dec 1907
    R. L. Peoples
    (Note attached - J. S. Stanley)

Joe ROBERTSON to Beta Clara LIVELY Issued 25 Dec 1907 Rites 26 Dec 1907
    E. C. Preston, M. G.

A. J. CRIM to Myrtle McBRIDE Issued26 Dec 1907 Rites 27 Dec 1907
                                        J. S. Lawrence, J. P.

Walter M. WATSON to Daisie MYERS Issued 27 Dec 1907 Rites 29 Dec 1907
                                        J. N. Elkins, J. P.

Burks SAVAGE to Belle MORFORD Issued 28 Dec 1907 Rites 29 Dec 1907
                                        Samuel KING

U. Y. DRAKE to Lillie Belle YAGER Issued 31 Dec 1907 Rites 1 Jan 1908
                                        A. W. Trawick, J. P.

Lusk C. STUBBLEFIELD to Susue BARNES Issued 3 JAn 1908 Rites 5 Jan 1908
                                        J. T. Thaxton, J. P.

J. T. HOLDER to Jennie NEWBY Issued 4 JAn 1908 Rites 5 Jan 1908
                                        W. N. Rhody, M. G.

James ROGERS to Minnie LUTRELL Issued 7 Jan 1908 Rites 7 Jan 1908
                                        R. W. Brinkley,M. G.

I. R. RAINS toZenobia BOYD Issued 9 JAn 1908 Rites 9 JAn 1908
                                        J. W. Cooley, M. G.

B. T. CANTRELL to C. E. COPE Issued 9 JAn 1908 Rites 12 Jan 1908
                                        J. M. Green, J. P.

C. J. POTTER to Mary Belmont MORFORD Issued 15 Jan 1908 Rites 15 Jan 1908
                                        R. W. Brinkley, M. G.

Sam JONES to Jonia GREEN Issued 16 Jan 1908 Not Executed

J. E. CANTRELL to Ella BYARS Issued 25 Jan 1908 Rites 26 Jan 1908
                                        E. N. Yager, J. P.

Ntahan GREEN to Sadie BUCKNER Issued 25 Jan 1908 Rites 26 Jan 1908
                                        Wm. A. Bell, J. P.

Hubert Leslie TOBITT to Mary Lucinda PEDEN Issued 25 Jan 1908 Rites 29 Jan 1908
                                        Sam Byars, J. P.

John WALKER to Annie WOODS Issued 25 Jan 1908 Rites 25 Jan 1908
                                        G. T. Speaks, M. G.

James PATTERSON to Canzada COPPINGER Issued 28 Jan 1908 Rites 28 Jan 1908
                                        H. W. Rucker, M. G.

G. W. UNDERHILL to Hassie DAVIS Issued 1 Feb 1908 Rites 2 Feb 1908
                                        E. N. Yager, J. P.

Robert T. JUDKINS to Effie COPE Issued 1 Feb 1908 Rites 2 Feb. 1908
                                        J. M. Green, J. P.

C. J. BRYAN to Allie May FAULKNER Issued 4 Feb 1908 Rites 5 Feb 1908
                                        R. L. Peiples, M. G.

Irvin McGEE to Mary BUTCHER Issued 8 Feb. 1908 Rites 9 Feb 1908
                                        J. W. Cooley, M. G.

J. M. GLENN to Ida LOGUE Issued 8 Feb 1908 Rites 9 Feb. 1908
                                        C. K. Carlock, M. G.

Ed BARNES to Lula NUNLEY Issued 11 Feb 1908 Rites 16 Feb 1908
                                        J. L. Thaxton, J. P.

J. Luther NEWBY to Eulah JONES Issued 13 Feb 1908 Rites 16 Feb 1908
                                        J. T. Turner, J. P.

Firm BOREN to Pearl IRVIN Issued 15 Feb 1908 Rites 16 Feb 1908
                                        I. G. Webb, J. P.

Clarence CRAWLEY to Ora MATTISON Issued 17 Feb 1908 Rites 23 Feb 1908
                                        J. W. Sims, M. G.

Tom SAVAGE (Col) to Ida MARTIN (Col) Issued 25 Feb 1908 Rites 25 Feb 1908
                                        G. Martin,. M. G.

Cleveland McGEE to Erma GRISSOM Issued 28 Feb 1908 Rites 1 Mar 1908
                                        J. N. ElkiNs, J. P.

Venus DODSON to Mariah CHASTEEN Issued 29 Feb 1908 Rites 1 Mar 1908
                                        J. W. Cooley, M. G.

Robert DONNAHUE to Lennie BONNER Issued 3 Mar 1908 Rites 15 Mar 1908
                                        B. B. Turner, M. G.

Ballard HUNTLEY to Clara HILLIS Issued 13 Mar 1908 Rites 13 Mar 1908
                                        L. V. Scott, J. P.

Norman COONROD to Sallie THOMAS Issued 17 Mar 1908 Rites 17 Mar 1908
                                        W. N. Kell, J. P.

George Inglis to Lucy ALLEN Issued 19 Mar 1908 Rites 19 Mar 1908
                                        J. L. MASON

Henry CHASTEEN to Hassie FARLESS Issued 21 Mar 1908 Rites 22 Mar 1908
                                        J. W. Cooley, M. G.

H. L. KILLIAN to Vina BROWN Issued 27 Mar 1908 Rites 29 Mar 1908
                                        L. V. Scott, J. P.

L. H. TURNER to Delia TURNER Issued 28 Mar 1908 Rites 29 Mar 1908
                                        H. T. McGregor, J. P.

Alex COPPINGER to Lillie PERRY Issued 28 Mar 1908 Rites 5 Apr 1908
                                        E. L. Moffitt, J. P.

L. R. RICE to Ella Lorene SMARTT Issued 1 Apr 1908 Rites 2 Apr 1908
                                        A. M. Trawick, Jr.

Dillard HOLT to Effie McCORMICK Issued 3 Apr 1908 Rites 5 Apr 1908
                                        J. C. Smoot, J. P.

William B. LeVALLEY to Flora B. TOPP Issued 4 Apr 1908 Rites 4 Apr 1908
                                        John B. Cowden, M. G.

Joe TUCK to Nellie BOST Issued 9 Jun 1908 Rites 9 Jun 1908
E. N. Yager, J. P.

Avery C. SMITH to Lela ARLEDGE Issued 9 Jun 1908 Rites 9 Jun 1908
John B. Crowder

Edman RICHARDSON to Gerthie DUKE Issued 13 Jun 1908 Rites 7 Jul 1908
J. C. Smoot, J. P.

Levander SLAUGHTER to Francis CHRISTIAN Issued 15 Jun 1908 Rites 15 Jun 1908
E. L. Moffitt, J. P.

John R. FORD to Myrtle Virgil GOODWIN Issued 17 Jun 1908 Rites 21 Jun 1908
E. N. Yager, J. P.

James BROWN to Laura BARNES Issued 17 Jun 1908 Not Returned

Waymon MITCHELL to DAisy MULLICAN Issued 18 Jun 1908 Rites 18 Jun 1908
E. N. Yager, J. P.

Everett HILL to Ophelia COPPINGER Issued 25 Jun 1908 Rites 25 Jun 1908
H. W. Rucker, M. G.

John WOMACK to Julia JUSTICE Issued 28 June 1908 Not Returned

William James MULLINS to Julia L. JUSTICE Issued 29 Jun 1908 Not Returned

Isaac ROMANS to Allie McDOWELL Issued 3 July 1908 Rites 5 Jul 1908
J. M. Green, J. P.

I. H. WEBB to Eva GIBBS Issued 3 Jul 1908 Rites 4 Jul 1908
E. N. Yager, J. P.

J. W. CASPER to Mattie Florence Edge Issued 8 Jul 1908 Rites 8 Jul 1908
G. Martin, M. G.

A. ROBERTS to Francis NUNLEY Issued 11 Jul 1908 Rites 12 Jul 1908
I. W. Roberts, M. G.

George CUNNINGHAM to Octa BUTCHER Issued 11 Jul 1908 Rites 12 Jul 1908
J. W. Cooley, M. G.

Thomas M. McCagg to Estella GIBBS Issued 11 Jul 1908 Rites 12 Jul 1908
E. N. Yager, J. P.

F. L. CROUCH to Jennie BROWN Issued 17 Jul 1908 Rites 17 July 1908
E. L. Moffitt, J. P.

John MARTIN to Mary TITTLE Issued 18 Jul 1908 Rites 19 Jul 1908
J. A. Knight, j. P.

F. N. COLLIER (Col) to Maude E. JOHNSON (Col) Issued 21 Jul 1908 Rites 21 Jul 1908
W. R. Smith, M. G.

Tim VINSON to Josie YOUNGBLOOD Issued 21 Jul 1908 Rites 22 Jul 1908
G. W. HALey,_J. P.

George EITER to Clara WARE Issued 22 Jul 1908 Rites 22 Jul 1908
C. G. Martin, M. G.

Charles COUCH to Lou Ann CHERRY Issued 7 Apr 1908 Not Returned

A. Y. PHILLIPS to Ricie HAMILTON Issued 11 Apr 1908 Rites 12 Apr 1908
J. W. Sims, M. G.,.

George SMITH to Bina HILLIS Issued17 Apr 1908 Rites 19 Apr 1908
H. T. McGregor, J. P.

John SMARTT (Col) to Nora MILLER (Col) Issued 18 Apr. 1908 Rites 19 Apr 1908
G. Martin, M. G.

B. F. LORING to Maude PARKER Issued 20 Apr 1908 Rites 21 Apr 1908
John B. Cowden, M. G.

J. C. GRIBBLE to Jennie Ann ARGO Issued 25 Apr 1908 Rites 26 Apr 1908
E. N. Yager, J. P.

J. W. SHERRELL to Lou HUNTER Issued 25 Apr 1908 Rites 27 Apr 1908
W. S. Grissom, J. P.

Frank NEAL (Col) to Annie JENNINGS (Col) Issued 27 Apr 1908 Rites 26 Apr 1908
Sam Curry

Albert H. WHITE to Leelia C. WEBB Issued 27 Apr 1908 Rites 28 Apr 1908
John B. Crowder, M. G.

W. T. POWELL to Vester WALLING Issued 28 Apr 1908 Rites 29 Apr 1908
Jacob Stipe, M. G.

S. D. GOODSON to Lissie KIDWELL Issued 29 Apr 1908 Rites 30 Apr 1908
I. G. Welch, J. P.

J. N. CHISHOLM to Lora Bell NEECE Issued 2 May 1908 Rites 2 May 1908
A. M. Trawick, J. P.

J. B. BROWN to Narnie HOLDER Issued 2 May 1908 Rites 3 May 1908
J.A. Knight, J. P.

Oscar FULTON to Ida GRIBBLE Issued 3 May 1908 Not Rteurned

Jessie A. STOTTS to Orbin MYERS Issued 4 MAy 1908 Rites 4 May 1908
E. N. Yager, J. P.

J. C. BOTTOMS to Minnie WHITAKER Issued9 May 1908 Rites 10 May 1908
J. W. Cooley, M. G.

S. L. EDWARDS to Laura J. YOUNG Issued 12 May 1908 Not Returned

John L. PENNINGTON to Carrie SMITH Issued 22 May 1908 Rites 22 May 1908
A. M. TrAWICK, Jr.

Rona CUNNINGHAM to Myrtle TODD Issued 23 May 1908 Rites 24 May 1908
J. W. Cooley, M. G.

T. L. LANCE to Lula EARLS Issued 30 May 1908 Rites 30 May 1908
John B. Crowder

Sam FOSTER (Col) to Mary Ann HUDDLESTON (Col) Issued 4 Jun 1908 Rites 4 Jun 1908

Will SCOTT to Georgia TURNER Issued 23 Jul 1908 Rites 23 Jul 1908
J. L. Thaxton, J. P.

W. D. KING to Leila PERRY Issued 25 Jul 1908 Rites 26 Jul 1908
L. V. Scott, J. P.

Thomas HOLLAND to Jennie HOLLAND Issued 25 Jul 1908 Rites 25 Jul 1908
E. N. Yager, J. P.

John A. GADDIS to Ethel HOODENPYLE Issued 29 Jul 1908 Rites 29 Jul 1908
A. M. Trawick, Jr.

JAmes PERRY to Carrie BILBREY Issued 1 Aug 1908 Rites 7 Aug 1908
E. N. Yager, J. P.

Tom SPURLOCK to Lou SMARTT Issued 1 Aug 1908 Rites 2 Aug 1908
W. W. Locke, J. P.

R. M. GREEN to Vina KENMER Issued 1 Aug 1908 Rites 2 Aug 1908
R. E. Wright, M. G.

J. S. WALLING to Hattie G. GRIBBLE Issued 1 Aug 1908 Rites 2 Aug 1908
J. M. Crawford, M. G.

Eugene MORFORD to Maggie ALEXANDER Issued 1 Aug 1908 Rites 1 Aug 1908
D. T. Burch, M. G.

John ALLISON to NAnnie MORRISON Issued 3 Aug 1908 Rites 3 Aug 1908
W. N. Kell, J. P.

Albert A. FLANDERS to Mary Lou MATHEWS Issued 3 Aug 1908 Rites 6 Aug 1908
J. M. Denton, M. G.

Walter M. HOWARD to Bertha Mai PIPKIN Issued 5 Aug 1908 Rites 5 Aug 1908
R. W. Binkley, M. G.

Monroe SMITH to Martha ROBERTS Issued 6 Aug 1908 Rites 7 Aug 1908
G. W. Haley, J. P.

Howard D. BURNS to Leona A. PARKER Issued 6 Aug 1908 Rites 6 Aug 1908
W. N. Kell, J. P.

Vinson BUSH to Dollie WILLIAMS Issued 7 Aug 1908 Rites 17 Aug 1908
J. C. Smoot, J. P.

Calhoun BOST to Josie BUTCHER Issued 8 Aug 1908 Rites 9 Aug 1908
J. W. Cooley, M. G.

Charley HENNESSEE to Maggie Mai SMITH Issued 8 Aug 1908 Rites 9 Aug 1908
A. C. Myers, J. P.

C. J. CUMMINGS to Hassie Pearl CRAIN Issued 8 Aug 1908 Rites 10 Aug 1908
R. W. Binkley, M. G.

George CHILDRESS to Nannie PISTOL Issued 11 Aug 1908 Rites 12 Aug 1908
D. T. Burch, M. G.

Robert COOPER to Nora HOLDER Issued 15 Aug 1908 Rites 16 Aug 1908
R. S. Kirby, J. P.

Orla PRICE to Sitha Bell CARR Issued 18 Aug 1908 Rites 18 Aug 1908
E. N. Yager, J. P.

Fred MOORE to Daisy STILES Issued 19 Aug 1908 Rites 19 Aug 1908
E. N. Yager, J. P.

John WARE to Edna BRADY Issued 22 Aug 1908 Rites 25 Aug 1908
E. N. Yager, J. P.

C. S. OLIVER to Silla GREEN Issued 25 Aug 1908 Rites 26 Aug 1908
Wm. A. Bell, J. P.

Ira GROSS to Bertha BRADY Issued 1 Sep 1908 Rites 2 Sep 1908
John B. Cowden, M. G.

Haskel SMITH to Aggie WOMACK Issued 3 Sep 1908 Rites 6 Sep 1908
Harvey W. Seay, M. G.

Haward BELL to Zephy BROWN Issued 3 Sep 1908 Rites 6 Sep 1908
W. E. Garner, M. G.

Noah BASHAM to Tennie HENDERSON Issued 5 Aug 1908 Rites 5 Aug 1908
W. W. Locke, J. P.

H. W. DOUGLAS to Laura Lee MARTIN Issued 5 Sep 1908 Not Returned

Denis BRAZELTON to Laura Ann WOOTEN Issued 6 Sep 1908 Rites 6 Sep 1908
G. T. Spears, M. G.

I. F. TURNER to India SAVAGE Issued 7 Sep 1908 Rites 19 Sep 1908
E. L. Moffitt, J. P.

James ROWLAND to Delia CANTRELL Issued 12 Sep 1908 Rites 13 Sep 1908
J. B. Gribble, M. G.

Milton McBRIDE to Demie FULTS Issued 12 Sep 1908 Rites 13 Sep 1908
J. L. Thaxton, J. P.

William T. TAYLOR to Callie MAYES Issued 25 Sep 1908 Rites 28 Sep 1908
E. L. Moffitt, J. P.

DAniel WEBSTER to Adline WILLIAMS Issued 25 Sep 1908 Rites 26 Sep 1908
E. N. Yager, J. P.

Isaac Leonard SPARKMAN to Adaline Louise CRAIN Issued 26 Sep 1908 Rites 28 Sep 1908
John B. Crowder, M. G.

Everett GILBERT to Josie Ella GASSAWAY Issued 28 Sep 1908 Rites 28 Sep 1908
John B. Crowder, M. G.

Henry GILBERT to Birdie JONES Issued 3 Oct 1908 Rites 4 Oct 1908
A. M. Trawicj, Jr.

Andrew WRIGHT to Bettie RODDY Issued 6 Oct 1908 Not Returned

Jack WARREN to Lela JONES Issued 6 Oct 1908 Rites 6 Oct 1908
Joe Pennington, J. P.

G. G. MABRY to Beulah A. SAIN Issued 15 Oct 1908 Rites 21 Oct 1908
D. B. Coleman, M,G.

Walter WOODARD (Col) to Annie WOODLEE (Col) Issued 19 Oct 1908 Rites 19 Oct 1908
Sam Curry, M. G.

John Luther AUSTIN to Bessie GARNETT Issued 20 Oct 1908 Rites 21 Oct 1908
A. M. Trawick, Jr.

Henry M. STREET to Mary W. PALMER Issued 24 Oct 1908 Rites 25 Oct 1908
E. N. Yager, J. P.

Eldridge ISIBELL (Col) to Lyda SMITH (Col) Issued 24 Oct 1908 Rites 24 Oct 1908
N. B. Morton

James FAULKNER (Col) to Perlie MATTERSON (Col) Issued 26 Oct 1908 Rites 26 Oct 1908
S, M. Curry, M. G.

R. G. GRISSOM to Rhoda Lee STIPE Issued 29 Oct 1908 Rites 1 Nov 1908
Jacob Stipe, M. G.

Vinson LANCE to Ollie JONES Issued 3 Nov 1908 Rites 4 Nov. 1908
G. W. Haley, M. G.

A. T. NEWRY to Rachel A. GAZAWAY Issued 4 Nov 1908 Rites 8 Nov 1908
J. D. Green, M. G.

Shelah ADAMS to Allie EDGE Issued 7 Nov 1908 Rites 8 Nov 1908
E. N. Yager, J. P.

Horace ROGERS to Vina COLLINS Issued 13 Nov 1908 Rites 15 Nov 1908
J. F. MARTIN, M. G.

A. E. THOMISON to Lou MILLRANEY Issued 20 Nov 1908   Not Returned

Milton BARNES to Emma MAYFIELD Issued 21 Nov 1908 Rites 22 Nov 1908
L. Safley, M. G.

James MILLRANEY to Dorcus McCAGG Issued 21 Nov 1908 Rites 21 Nov 1908
E. N. Yager, J. P.

Narve MOFFITT to Margie MEADOWS Issued 24 Nov 1908 Rites 24 Nov 1908
John B. Crowder, M. G.

Burt ROBERTS to Dora ROMAN Issued 24 Nov 1908 Rites 24 Nov 1908
G. T. SPeaks, M. G.

J. B. MASON to Curtie NUNNLEY Issued 27 Nov 1908 Rites 29 Nov 1908
W. M. Milstead, M. G.

Harve MOORE to May MASON Issued 28 Nov 1908 Rites 28 Nov 1908
E. N. Yager, J. P.

Lavada RUTLEDGE to Litta Belle PRIEST Issued 28 Nov 1908 Rites 29 Nov 1908
L. Safley, M. G.

S. M. SMOOT to Alta BICKEL Issued 30 Nov 1908 Rites 30 Nov 1908
Thomas R. Curtis, M. G.

M. R. BONNER to Flowry BELL Issued 2 Dec 1908 Rites 2 dec 1908
J. C. Smoot, J. P.

J. H. ETTER to Lucy F. ROMAN Issued 2 Dec 1908 Rites 2 Dec 1908
John B. Crowder, M. G.

Rev. Elijah WEAVER to Lena Pearl McCOLLUM Issued 5 Dec 1908 Rites 5 Dec 1908
T. B. Dean, M. G.

Warren CUMMINGS to Retta BIGELOW Issued 5 Dec 1908 Rites 6 Dec 1908
Samuel Byars, M. G.

George C. WOMACK to Carrie WAGONER Issued 5 Dec 1908 Rites 5 Dec 1908
Samuel Byars, M. G.

James B. UPCHURCH to Mollie CANTRELL Issued 5 Dec 1908 Rites 8 Dec 1908
J. B. Gribble, M. G.

Morris M. SAIN to Jessie B. MANSFIELD Issued 5 Dec 1908 Rites 10 Dec 1908
J. R. Stubblefield

F. R. SMITHSON to Aarmie May LORANCE Issued 11 Dec 1908 Rites 13 Dec 1908
J. C. Smoot, J. P.

Loyd CHRISTIAN to Genie CURTIS Issued 15 Dec 1908 Rites 20 Dec 1908
E. L. Moffitt, J. P.

J. W. WEBB to Mary E. GREEN Issued 16 Dec 1908 Rites 16 dec 1908
Wm. A. Bell, J. P.

Creed GRISSOM to Flossie MARTIN Issued 16 Dec 1908 Rites 20 Dec 1908
I. G. Welch

George PATTERSON to Calostie I. EVANS Issued 17 Dec 1908 Rites 20 Dec 1908
C. G. Potter, M. G.

Ira L. SPARKMAN to Mattir L. TURNER Issued 19 Dec 1908 Rites 20 Dec 1908
SAmuel Byars, M. G.

F. R. HAMMER to Della FARLS Issued 19 Dec 1908 Rites 20 dec 1908
John B. Crowder, M. G.

D. L. BOYD to Hattie HANKINS Issued 21 Dec 1908 Rites 25 dec 1908
J. D. Quick, J. P.

John BOULDIN to Lucy CANTRELL Issued 22 Dec 1908 Rites 22 Dec 1908
John B. Crowder, M. G.

Herschel WOMACK to Bernice CHERRY Issued 22 Dec 1908 Rites 29 Dec 1908
I. G. Webb, J. P.

J. E. DAVENPORT to Florence LANCE Issued 23 Dec 1908 Rites 24 Dec 1908
FraNK Michael, J. P.

George GOTHARD to Brady GILLEY Issued 23 Dec 1908 Rites 24 Dec 1908
R. W. Jernigan, M. G.

Bryan CLARK to Euna MARTIN Issued 23 Dec 1908 Rites 24 Dec 1908
J. B. Gribble, M. G.

T. G. CANTRELL to Thena GREEN Issued 25 dec 1908 Rites 25 dec 1908
Wm. A. Bell, J.|P.

Clifford MANSFIELD to Ella PARKER Issued 26 Dec 1908 Rites 28 Dec 1908
T. A. MAthews

Charley BRIGHT to Carlie McCORMACK Issued 26 dec 1908 Rites 27 Dec 1908
J. B. Gribble, M. G.

James E. HANES to Virgie May JONES Issued 26 dec 1908 Rites 26 Dec 1908
E. N. Yager, J. P.

J. H. MELTON to Callie COUCH Issued 26 dec 1908 Rites 27 dec 1908
H. T. McGregor, J. P.

Willie BRATCHER to Geneva MAZEY Issued 26 Dec 1908 Rites 27 Dec 1908
J. T. Vinson, J. P.

Gordon E. REYNOLDS to Octa E. ALLISON Issued 28 Dec 1908 Rites 30 dec 1908
Samuel Byars, M. G.

P. A. COPELAND to Vera TITTSWORTH Issued 30 dec 1908 Rites 30 dec 1908
J. E. Jones, J. P.

Hiram SMITH to rachel GILLENTINE Issued 30 dec 1908 Rites 3 JAn 1909
J. C. Smoot, J., P.

Dalton HOBBS to Sallie NUNNLEY Issued 31 Dec 1908 Rites 3 Jan 1909
Sam Byars, M. G.

Charles BROWN to Burt BARNES Issued 1 JAn 1909 Rites 3 Jan 1909
W. I. Hunt

Jess McDOWELL to Minnie CURBY Issued 2 Ajn 1909 Rites 3 Jan 1909
J. M. Green, J. P.

Zollie HANKINS to Nettie PLUMLEE Issued 4 Jan 1909 Rites 10 Jan 1909
J. D. Quick, J. P.

John AINIP to Fannie CHRISTIAN Issued 5 Jan 1909 Rites 6 Jan 1909
P. G. Potter, M. G.

Lee MULLIGAN to Nolie LANCE Issued 6 jan 1909 Rites 6 JAn 1909
E. N. Yager, J. P.

Mabus RUSSELL to Lula EVANS Issued 8 JAn 1909 Rites 8 JAn 1909
H. W. Rucker, M. G. (Col)

Frank TURNER to Gurtie ELLISON Issued 16 JAn 1909 Rites 17 JAn 1909
J. L. Thaxton, J. P.

Norman BYARS to Ella CALDWELL Issued 16 JAn 1909 Rites 17 Jan 1909
E. N. Yager, J. P.

Wm. M. DOYLE to Mabel LORING Issued 16 Jan 1909 Rites 16 Jan 1909
John B. Crowder, M. G.

Sam McBRIDE to Birdie MUNSEY Issued 21 JAn 1909 Rites 26 JAn 1909
W. W. Locke, J.|P.

J. F. GREEN to Stella WEBB Issued 23 Jan 1909 Rites 23 Jan 1909
Thos. R. Curtis, M. G.

harris FULTS to Mary BESS Issued 25 Jan 1909 Rites 26 JAn 1909
E. L. Moffitt, J. P.

M. J. GREEN to Lillie RIDDLE Issued 26 Jan 1909 Rites 27 Jan 1909
T. A. Mathews, M. G.

Luther BILES to Minnie RHEA Issued 27 Jan 1909 Rites 27 Jan 1909
T. A. Mathews, M. G.

Benjamin BATES to Velma HALEY Issued 28 Jan 1909 Rites 31 Jan 1909
Frank Michael, J. P.

J. J. WOMACK to Mary PHILLIPS Issued 8 Feb 1909 Rites 8 Feb 1909
Jow Pennington, J. P.

Oscar RAINS to Mary ELAM Issued 8 Feb 1909 Rites 28 Feb. 1909
J. C. Smoot, J. P.

Roy WOMACK to Edna PINEGAR Issued 11 Feb 1909 Rites 14 Feb 1909
E. N. Yager, J. P.

Terrie BROWN to Lou BONNER Issued 12 Feb 1909 Rites 14 Feb 1909
J. L. Thaxton, J. P.

Claud McREYNOLDS to Martha SCOTT Issued 13 Feb 1909 Rites 13 Feb 1909
S. M. Curry, M. G.

Will ROWLAND to Clara CANTRELL Issued 17 Feb 1909 Rites 21 Feb 1909
J. B. Gribble

Ross GIBBS to Dessie PATTERSON Issued 19 Feb 1909 Rites 20 Feb 1909
H. W. Seay, M. G.

Richard McDOWELL to Nervie WORTHINGTON Issued 22 Feb 1909 Rites 27 Feb 1909
J. B. Gribble

Elijah SAUNDERS to Leona MARLER Issued 23 Feb 1909 Rites 3 Mar 1909
B. F. Woods, M. G.

Newton HILL to Lenzie TURNER Issued 23 Feb 1909 Rites 13 Mar 1909
E. L. Moffitt, J. P.

J. C. PERRY to Edna GARMON Issued 27 Feb 1909 Rites 27 Feb 1907
E. N. Yager, J. P.

RAlph BROOKS to Edna ROBERSON Issued 2 Mar 1909 Rites 2 Mar 1909
J. E. Jones, J. P.

Thomas BROWN to Susie PEDEN Issued 6 Mar 1909 Rites 6 Mar 1909
G. W. Peden, J. P.

Eugene CRAWFORD to Bessie KELLEY Issued 1 May 1909 Rites 9 May 1909
J. M. McGiboney, J. P.

J. B. BYARS to Nellie Mae WHITTAKER Issued 1 May 1909 Rites 5 May 1909
P. G. Potter, M. G.

Luke FAULKNER to Dovie Belle RAMSEY Issued 1 May 1909 Rites 2 May 1909
T. O. Crisp, M. G.

S. TINDALE to Addie LANSFORD Issued 5 May 1909 Rites 5 May 1909
E. N. Yager, J. P.

Claud SCOTT to Emmer FULTZ Issued 7 May 1909 Rites 16 May 1909
I. W. Roberts, M. G.

Norris ROMLAND to Lena CANTRELL Issued 8 May 1909 Rites 9 May 1909
J. M. McGiboney, J. P.

John SAFLEY to Minnie MELTON Issued 8 May 1909 Rites 9 May 1909
H. T. McGregor, J. P.

Clarence MYERS to Maggie ELKINS Issued 15 May 1909 Rites 16 May 1909
W. S. Grissom, J. P.

W. Dall PRATER to Barbry DAVENPORT Issued 22 May 1909 Rites 23 May 1909
G. W. Haley, J. P.

George B. BEAVER to Susie Barnett MASON Issued 24 May 1909 Rites 25 May 1909
Thos. R. Curtis, M. G.

W. S. COTHRAN to Myrtle S. POCUS Issued 28 May 1909 Rites 28 May 1909
E. N. Yager, J. P.

L. B. MOFFITT to Mary LOCKE Issued 29 May 1909 Rites 30 May 1909
Samuel Byars, M.G.

Livy WINFREY to Sallie GREEN Issued 1 Jun 1909 Rites 2 Jun 1909
Harvey W. Seay, M. G.

J. A. DUGAN to Nettie HOLLANDSWORTH Issued 5 Jun 1909 Rites 6 Jun 1909
W. P. Davis, J. P.

Brewer DAVENPORT to Lowe TENPENNY Issued 5 June 1909 Rites 5 June 1909
J. M. McGiboney, J. P.

Lynn REDMON to Ella HARDCASTLE Issued 5 Jun 1909 Rites 15 Jun 1909
P. G. Potter, M. G.

A. E. B. RODNER to Louise WALKER Issued 9 Jun 1909 Rites 9 Jun 1909
John B. Crowder, M. G.

Alvin Fat HARLOW to Dora SHOCKLEY Issued 10 Jun 1909 Rites 10 Jun 1909
E. Allen Van Nuys

John HIGGINBOTHAM to Ernie MARBERRY Issued 12 Jun 1909 Rites 17 Jun 1909
Jno. H. Ellis, M. G.

H. C. TURNER to Myrtle DODD Issued 12 Jun 1909 Rites 13 Jun 1909
Joe Pennington, J. P.

J. L. MAYO to Nettie FERRELL Issued 6 Mar 1909 Rites 7 Mar 1909
E. N. Yager, J. P.

Will CARTER to Mollie McGREGOR Issued 11 Mar 1909 Rites 14 Mar 1909
A. C. Myers, J. P.

Byrd WEBSTER to Rachel DENTON Issued 12 Mar 1909 Rites 12 Mar 1909
J. J. Meadows, J. P.

Jim WILSON (Col) to Mat Mattison (Col) Issued 17 Mar 1909 Rites 17 Mar 1909
Joe Pennington, J. P.

Ben HILL to Minnie CLENDENON Issued 20 Mar 1909 Rites 21 Mar 1909
L. V. Scott, J. P.

Davis COPE to Sallie MITCHELL Issued 20 Mar 1909 Rites 21 Mar 1909
L. F. Daugherty, M. G.

Walter PERRY to Julia BOYDE Issued 3 Apr 1909 Rites 7 Apr 1909
E. L. Moffitt, J. P.

Arthur GOODWIN to Cora CROUCH Issued 3 Apr 1909 Rites 8 Apr 1909
J. L. Thaxton, J. P.

H. M. DOYLE to Winnie Dee LORING Issued 3 Apr 1909 Rites 3 Apr 1909
John B. Crowder, M. G.

John B. SHIRLEY to Autie AKERS Issued 10 Apr 1909 Rites 11 Apr 1909
J. C. Smoot, J. P.

John CULLEN to Rillie PENNINGTON Issued 10 Apr 1909 Rites 11 Apr 1909
Harvey Seay, M. G.

Ed PEDEN to Bettie BUSIE Issued 10 Apr 1909 Rites 11 Apr 1909
J. G. Goff, J. P.

Hiram WOODLEE (Col) to Nettie RANKINS (Col) Issued 12 Apr 1909 Rites 12 Apr 1909
S. M. Curry, M. G.

Arthur BAILEY to Ella ROBERTS Issued 15 Apr 1909 Rites 18 Apr 1909
J. T. Vinson, J. P.

Walter HILL to Jennie CRAWLEY Issued 27 Apr 1909 Rites 27 Apr 1909
J. T. Casey, M. G.

Walter HOLLAND to Macy GRACY Issued 28 Apr 1909 Rites 28 Apr 1909
W. P. Parker, M. G.

Floyd MARTIN to Genie TURNER Issued 28 Apr 1909 Rites 29 Apr 1909
H. T. McGregor, J. P.

James GESSLER to Alice ZWINGLE Issued 28 Apr 1909 Rites 29 Apr 1909
S. M. Keathley, M. G.

George SNIPES to Cecil McCLAIN Issued 1 May 1909 Rites 2 May 1909
J. R. Stubblefield

Willie C. DUKE to Florence L. BREWER Issued 12 Jun 1909 Rites 15 Jun 1909
R. W. Jernigan, M. G.

Charley DOVE to Annie McDOWELL Issued 17 Jun 1909 Rites 18 Jun 1909
I. G. Webb, J. P.

Josh WILSON to Florence LANCE Issued 19 June 1909 Rites 23 June 1909
G. W. Haley, J. P.

Forest S. WOMACK to Cordelia Irene PHELPS Issued 25 Jun 1909 Rites 27 June 1909
J. R. Ramsey, J. P.

William Thomas HENNESSEE to America GREEN Issued 25 Jun 1909 Rites 27 Jun 1909
H. T. McGregor, J. P.

Thomas A. BREWER to Bessie DARNELL Issued 26 Jun 1909 Rites 27 Jun 1909
G. P. Brasier, J. P.

Henry BARNES to Elnora GIBSON Issued 26 Jun 1909 Rites 26 Jun 1909
J. E. Jones, J. P.

Ulysses GARNER to Linie VANOVER Issued 1 Jul 1909 Rites 4 Jul 1909
W. E. Garner, M. G.

George GOWAN to Letha HARRELL Issued 3 Jul 1909 Rites 4 Jul 1909
W. N. Kell, J. P.

Charles COTTON to Mary Lou WOMACK Issued 3 Jul 1909 Rites 31 Jul 1909
I. G. Webb, J. P.

Arvel PEGG to Florence STONE Issued 3 July 1909 Rites 3 July 1909
W. N. Kell, J. P.

Leonard VanHOOSER to Mebel LISTER Issued 2 Jul 1909 Rites 4 Jul 1909
J. M. Green, J. P.

Vessie DUNLAP to Elua BOREN Issued 3 July 1909 Rites 4 Jul 1909
W. T. Caero, M. G.

James R. BOYD to Josie CUNNINGHAM Issued 3 Jul 1909 Rites 4 Jul 1909
H. T. McGregor, M. G.

Irving MARBURY to Maude RAMSEY Issued 6 Jul 1909 Rites 7 Jul 1909
J. H. Ellis, M. G.

Logan BETTS to Dovie HARDCASTLE Issued 10 Jul 1909 Rites 11 Jul 1909
R. S. Kirby, J. P.

Henry MARTIN to Nora LOOPER Issued 10 Jul 1909 Not Returned

Sam JONES to Johnnie GREEN Issued 15 Jul 1909 Rites 15 Jul 1909
W. A. Bell, J. P.

Elam SMITH to Laura SHAW Issued 15 Jul 1909 Rites 15 Jul 1909
E. N. Yager, J. P.

Newman MARLER to Jimmie MULLICAN Issued 16 July 1909 Rites 17 Jul 1909
W. P. Davis, J. P.

John HOLLOWAY to Pearl THOMAS Issued 17 July 1909 Rites 17 July 1909
S. M. Curry, M. G.

J. H. HIGGINBOTHAM to Catherine Bonner SCOTT Issued 17 Jul 1909 Rites 17 Jul 1909
J. E. Jones, J. P.

Charles H. RIDDLE to Rachel L. MALONE Issued 23 Jul 1909 Rites 4 Auh 1909
J. R. Stubblefield, M. G.

Jack MARBERRY to Flora MARTIN Issued 24 Jul 1909 Rites 25 Jul 1909
N. B. Morton, M. G.

Francis Marion GREEN to Flora Josephine GRIBBLE Issued 31 Jul 1909 Rites 1 Aug 1909
M. H. Northcross, M. G.

W. L. BARNES to Laura WALKER Issued 31 Jul 1909 Rites 1 Aug 1909
H. T. McGregor, J. P.

Bob SPARKMAN to Hattie SCOTT Issied 31 July 1909 Rites 1 Aug 1909
J. G. Goff, J. P.

Colonel PENDLETON to Lisie Ann PELHAM Issued 3 Aug 1909 Rites 3 Aug 1909
W. N. Kell, J. P.

J. W. GULLEY to Maud DAVIS Issued 7 Aug 1909 Rites 8 Aug 1909
W. T. CATON, M. G.

W. C. HERNDON to May BROWN Issued 8 Aug 1909 Rites 12 Aug 1909
J. C. Smoot, J. P.

Joe H. ADAMS to Hallie MAYO Issued 11 Aug 1909 Rites 11 Aug 1909
John B, Cowden, M. G.

Henry McPHERSON to Charity DANIEL Issued 16 Aug 1909 Rites 16 Aug 1909
A. C. Myers, J. P.

Carroll JONES to Anna E. JONES Issued 16 Aug 1909 Rites 18 Aug 1909
W. P. Davis, J. P.

Henry DOBBS to Eliza LEMMONS Issued 27 Aug 1909 Rites 27 Sug 1909
Frank Michael, J. P.

Fred GILBERT to Lena FENNELL Issued 30 Aug 1909 Rites 30 Aug 1909
Wm. A. Bell, J. P.

Harrison BILES to Josie May LOCKE Issued 30 Aug 1909 Rites 30 Aug 1909
E. N. Yager, J. P.

J. D. SLAUGHTER to Hallie BARNES Issued 4 Sep 1909 Rites 4 Sep 1909
E. N. Yager, J. P.

Bob SLIGER to Rosha WEBSTER Issued 7 Sep 1909 Rites 7 Sep 1909
E. N. YAGER, J. P.

W. H. FISHER to Audie GREEN Issued 9 Sep 1909 Rites 10 Sep 1909
J. D. Hash, J. P.

D. T. WILLIAMS to Mary ROACH Issued 11 Sep 1909 Rites 12 Sep 1909
J. F. Martin, L. E.

Mitch SMITH (Col) to Cynthia COPE (Col) Issued 11 Sep 1909 Rites 13 Sep 1909
N. B. Morton, M. G.

Joe COUCH to May WEBB Issued 14 Sep 1909 Rites 19 Sep 1909
I. G. Webb, J. P.

C. N. JOHNSON to Maude WEBB Issued 15 Sep 1909 Rites 16 Sep 1909
John B. Cowden, M. G.

G. C. BENNETT to Cora BLACKBURN Issued 15 Sep 1909 Rites 19 Sep 1909
J. P. Brasier, J. P.

Clarence MORGAN to Nannie WOMACK Issued15 Sep 1909 Rites 16 Sep 1909
W. T. Coton, M. G.

O. A. (Elex) WINNETT to MARGARET PATTEN Issued 17 Sep 1909 Rites 19 Sep 1909
J. T. Vinson, J. P.

Joe SMITH to Lizzie KIRBY Issued 17 Sep 1909 Rites 19 Sep 1909
G. W. Haley, J. P.

Arthur LAFEVER to Mattir GILBERT Issued 25 Sep 1909 Rites 26 Sep 1909
E. N. Yager, J. P.

William VICKERS to Hilda WALKER Issued 30 Sep. 1909 Rites 3 Oct 1909
L. V. Scott, J. P.

Claud VINSON to Maude STROUD Issued 1 Oct 1909 Rites 2 Oct 1909
Wm. A. Bell, J. P.

Floyd LUSK (Col) to Georgia GRIBBLE (Col) Issued 2 Oct 1909 Rites 2 Oct 1909
W. S. Grissom, J. P.

Abner LORANCE to Olga TODD Issued 4 Oct 1909 Rites 5 Oct 1909
G. P. Brasier, J. P.

H. B. MASTERSON to Mattie CHISM Issued 8 Oct 1909 Rites 10 Oct 1909
J. D. Hash, J. P.

Gentry Guy FISHER to Eula WEST Issued 9 Oct 1909 Rites 14 Oct 1909
P. G. Potter, M., G..

Shady M. GREEN to Dicy GOLDEN Issued 15 Oct 1909 Rites 17 Oct 1909
P. G. Potter, M, G.,

Ben ROACH to Ella FOSTER Issued 16 Oct 1909 Rites 17 Oct 1909
J. C. Smoot, J. P.

Virgil HENNESSEE to Julia McGREGOR Issued 16 Oct 1909 Rites 20 Oct 1909
E. N. Yager, J. P.

Huburn CANTRELL to Josie GLENN Issued 20 Oct 1909 Rites 24 Oct 1909
L. F. Daugherty, M. G.

E. L. YOUNG to Margaret WILLIAMSON Issued 20 Oct 1909 Rites 24 Oct 1909
G. W. Haley, J. P.

George PARSLEY to Martha DOCKREY Issued 23 Oct 1909 Rites 24 Oct 1909
J. T. Vinson, J. P.

J. T. WOMACK to Ninnie SMOOT Issued 23 Oct 1909   Not Returned

Billie FULTS to Mary JENNINGS Issued 25 Oct 1909 Rites 27 Oct 1909
L. V. Scott, J. P.

Leslie MORFORD (Col) to Lucinda Page (Col) Issued 27 Oct 1909 Rites 28 Oct 1909
N. B. Morton

George FULTS to Pearl EDWARDS Issued 27 Oct 1909 Rites 31 Oct 1909
J. C. Smoot, J. P.

Manuel PATTON to Sallie Florence DENTON Issued 30 Oct 1909 Not Returned

Harry ALLEN to Lola FOSTER Issued 6 Nov 1909 Rites 7 Nov 1909
E. N. Yager, J. P.

Murphy EVANS to Ada GROVE Issued 6 Nov 1909 Rites 6 Nov 1909
H. T. McGregor, J. P.

George McGEE to Lee HENNESSEE Issued 13 Nov 1909 Rites 18 Nov 1909
H. T. McGregor, J. P.

Horace NORTHCUTT (Col) to Esther COONROD (Col) Issued 18 Nov 1909 Rites 19 Nov 190
W. E. Garner, M. G.

George Gates THURMAN to Dollis VAn WOODY Issued 23 Nov 1909 Rites 23 Nov 1909
John B. Cowden, M. G.

E. A. BROWN to Emma ALLISON Issued 23 Nov 1909 Rites 24 Nov 1909
Sam T. Byars, M. G.

Bige GRIBBLE to Mary BRATCHER Issued 23 Nov 1909 Rites 28 Nov 1909
J. D. Quick, J. P.

J. C. BLACKBURN to Lizzie STROUD Issued 27 Nov 1909 Rites 27 Nov 1909
G. P. Brasier, J. P.

J. H. GREEN to I. D. CUNNINGHAM Issued 29 Nov 1909 Rites 29 Nov 1909
J. C. Smoot, J. P.

Tom MORRISON to Jessie McAFEE Issued 3 Dec 1909 Rites 3 Dec 1909
W. N. Kell, J. P.

J. C. ROBERTS to Sdella CHISAM Issued 6 Dec 1909 Rites 8 Dec 1909
J. C. Clark, M. G.

Tom BOWLEN to Laura TURNER Issued 8 Dec 1909 Rites 9 Dec 1909
E. N. Yager, J. P.

Milan OAKLEY (Col) to Callie RICE (Col) Issued 8 Dec 1909 Rites 8 Dec 1909
D. S. Ransaw

Jesse HALEY to Eva WILSON Issued 10 Dec 1909 Rites 10 Dec 1909
Frank Michael, J. P.

Cannon MASON to Beulah WOMACK Issued 11 Dec 1909 Rites 12 Dec 1909
Joe Pennington, J. P.

Cleveland NEWBY to Lizzie ASKEW Issued 12 Dec 1909 Rites 12 Dec 1909
J. M. Green, J. P.

JAmes THOMAS (Col) to Hattie BRYANT (Col) Issued 13 Dec 1909 Rites Rites 13 Dec
E. N. Yager, J. P.

Asa DAVIS to Ines HALE Issued 18 Dec 1909 Rites 19 Dec 1909
W. W. Locke, J. P.

Alton BISHOP to Ellen WILSON Issued 18 Dec 1909 Rites 19 Dec 1909
G. W. Haley, J. P.

Marcus WRIGHT to Girtie COUCH Issued 22 dec 1909 Rites 26 Dec 1909
L. F. Daugherty, M. G.

Oscar ROGERS to Hattie NORTHCUTT Issued 22 Dec 1909 Rites 24 dec 1909
Sam T. Byars, M. G.

Firm DOUGLAS to Hattie BARRETT Issued 22 dec 1909 Rites 26 Dec 1909
J. R. Stubblefield, M. G.

Jim DAVIS to Ethel GARMAN Issued 23 Dec 1909 Rites 23 Dec 1909
John B. Cowden, M. G.

Carson NEWBY to Martha JORDEN Issued 23 Dec 1909 Rites 26 Dec 1909
G. W. HAley, J. P.

Loyd BROWN to Vera CANTRELL Issued 23 Dec 1909 Rites26 Dec 1909
Sam T. Byars, M. G.

Charles HOLLANDSWORTH to Rosa HALEY Issued 23 Dec 1909 Rites 26 Dec 1909
J. M. McGiboney, J. P.

Rupert DURHAM to Willie POINTER Issued 24 Dec 1909 Rites 26 Dec 1909
J. R. Stubblefield, M. G.

Arthur NUNLEY to Allie STONE Issued 24 Dec 1909 Rites 25 Dec 1909
L. V. Scott, J. P.

Frank MOORE to Lula RANDOLPH Issued 24 Dec 1909 Rites 25 dec 1909
J. A. Page, M. G.

R. B. GILBERT to Bertha JONES Issued 25 Dec 1909 Rites 24 Dec 1909 (?)
Sam T. Byars, M. G.

Frank TURNER to Odie BILBREY Issued 28 Dec 1909
L. R. Hogan

Walter DUNCAN to Cleo ROGERS Issued 29 Dec 1909 Rites 29 Dec 1909
W. N. Kell, J. P.

J. B. MITCHELL to Beulah Benton CANTRELL Issued 29 Dec 1909 Not Returned

J. G. PEELER to Grace WEBB Issued 29 Dec 1909 Rites 29 Dec 1909
Wm. Thurman, Elder, C of C

W. D. WHITLOCK to Mabel LUTRELL Issued 30 Dec 1909 Rites 2 Jan 1910
J. T. Casey, M. G.

George THOMAS to Enda COPE Issued 1 Jan 1910 Rites 2 Jan 1910
J. L. Thaxton. J. P.

Thomas HIGGINBOTHAM to Girtrice RUCKER Issued 1 Jan 1910 Rites 1 JAn 1910
R. L. Nelson, M. G.

Charles CURL to Matilda DAUGHERTY Issued 5 Jan 1910
J. R. Stubblefield, M. G.

Robert T. PARKER to Beulah STROUD Issued 8 Jan 1910 Rites 9 JAn 1910

Ed MARTIN to Myrtle Templeton Issued 8 JAn 1910 Rites 8 Jan 1910
H. T. McGregor, J. P.

Isham ALEXANDER to Willis DAVIS Issued 10 JAn 1910 Rites 10 Jan 1910
P. G. Potter, M. G.

G. A. LANCE to Vena HALEY Issued 11 Jan 1910 Rites 12 Jan 1910
Frank Michael, J. P.

Clyde STOTTS to Blanche MORTON Issued 13 Jan 1910 Rites 25 Jan 1910
L. V. Scott, J. P.

Frank T. LAWRENCE to Irene TALIAFERRO Issued 15 Jan 1910 Rites 18 JAn 1910
John B. Cowden, M. G.

W. C. REEDER to Delma HUTSON Issued 29 JAn 1910 Rites 30 JAn 1910
J. M. Green, J. P.

Harvey DODD to Nettie WILSON Issued 29 Jan 1910 Rites 30 Jan 1910
Frank Michael

D. P. MYERS to Hattie Belle MADEWELL Issued29 JAn 1910 Not Executed

R. B. STUBBLEFIELD to Blanche GIBBS Issued 31 Jan 1910 Rites 3 Feb 1910
A. C. Myers, J. P.

Everet GROVE to Callie MCGREGOR Issued 2 Feb 1910 Rites3 Feb 1910
A. C. Myers, J. P.

Jesse ELAM to Annie CUNNINGHAM Issued 2 Feb 1910 Rites 6 Feb 1910
J. C. Smoot, J. P.

Charles KILLIAN to Maud CARTER Issued 4 Feb 1910 Rites 6 Feb 1910
L. V. Scott, J. P.

William SELLARS to Amanda HOLDER Issued 7 Feb 1910 Rites 10 Feb 1910
W. P. Davis, J. P.

Wm. A. RICHARDSON to Margaret F. PEPPER Issued 14 Feb 1910 Rites 15 Feb 1910
Sam T. Byars, M. G.

Philip GRISSOM to Melia SAFLEY Issued 16 Feb 1910   Not Returned

Will GREEN (Col) tp Callie DURLEY (Col) Issued 17 Feb 1910 Rites 17 Feb 1910
J. W. Richmond, M. G.

Horace ALLMON to Hattie BREWER Isseud 9 Apr 1910 Rites 10 Apr 1910
J. C. Snoot, J. P.

Olice HUNTER (Col) to Mary ROWAN (Col) Issued 11 Apr 1910 Rites 11 Apr 1910
Sam Curry, M. G.

Oliver Thurman STILES to Ida Everline GRIBBLE Issued 16 Apr 1910 Rites 16 Apr
J. B. Gribble, J. P.

Willia PAGE to Rocksie PARSLEY Issued 23 Apr 1910 Rites 24 Apr 1910
G. W. HAley, J. P.

Hiram BARRETT to Calie DAVIS Issued23 Apr 1910 Rites 23 Apr 1910
S. T. Byars, M. G.

J. C. NENWORTH to Eva J. WRIGHT Issued 26 Apr 1910 Rites 26 Apr 1910
W. N. Kell, J. P.

William Clay GREEN to Graty Florence SPARKMAN Issued 30 Apr 1910 Rites 1 May 1910
J. B. Gribble, J. P.

Melvin Rowan (Col) to Allene NEWBY (Col) Issued 30 Apr 1910 Rites 1 May 1910
Joe Pennington, J. P.

Wilson NEWBY to Emma REDMON Issued 3 May 1910 Rites 8 May 1910
J. T. Turner, J. P.

Oscar SELLARS to Cleo WOMACK Issued 7 May 1910 Rites 0 May 1910
J. M. McGiboney, J. P.

G. C. RICH to Betha BAIN Issued 16 May 1910 Rites 4 July 1910
G. W. Haley, J. P.

W. M. HENNESSEE to Carry Ruth CAMPBELL Issued 23 May 1910 Rites 23 May 1910
J. C. Snoot, J. P.

Merrell EITER (Col) to Nettie GILLEY (Col) Issued 4 Jun 1910 Rites 4 Jun 1910
E. N. YAGER, J. P.

Leslie WINDOM (Col) to Lou Lilliam HILL (Col) Issued 4 Jun 1910 Rites 5 Jun 1910
J. W. Richmond, M. G.

William GREEN to Eva GREEN Issued 6 Jun 1910 Rites 6 Jun 1910
H. C. Hudson, J. P.

Walter AMES to Maggie WISEMAN Issued 6 Jun 1910 Rites 8 Jun 1910
B. W. D. Barnes, J. P.

Chester SAUNDERS to Bessie STONE Issued 7 Jun 1910 Rites 7 Jun 1910
Thos R. Curtis, M. G.

Ed HENDERSON (Col) to Julia ROACH (Col) Issued 8 Jun 1910 Rites 8 Jun 1910
Fred R. Anderson, M. G.

G. W. BROWN (Col) to Agness PARKER (Col) Issued 9 Jun 1910 Rites 12 Jun 1910
J. R. Richmond, M. C.

Jesse DUKE to Ova WEBB Issued 11 Jun 1910 Rites 19 Jun 1910
J. C. Snoot, J. P.

Tom DUKE to Annie ELAM Issued 19 Feb 1910 Rites 20 Feb 1910
J. C. Snoot, J. P.

Herman PELHAM to Clara E. WRIGHT Issued 19 Feb 1910 Rites 19 Feb 1910
E. N. Yager, J. P.

Charles ROGERS to Nannie SCOTT Issued 21 Feb 1910 Rites 22 Feb 1910
J. Barnes, J. P.

Joe TATE to Nervie GREEN Issued 22 Feb 1910 Rites 13 Mar 1910
E. L. Moffitt, J. P.

Newt McKNIGHT to Hassie PARIS Issued 26 Feb 1910 Rites 27 Feb 1910
G. W. Haley, J. P.

P. E. HENNESSEE to Carrie BILBREY Issued 26 Feb 1910 Rites 27 Feb 1910
H. T. McGregor, J. P.

Melvin A. G. FELTY to Nealy McGEE Issued 2 Mar 1910 Rites 2 Mar 1910
L. R. Hogan

Scheely HILL (Col) to Mattir BURKS (Col) Issued 3 Mar 1910 Rites 3 Mar 1910
J. W. Richmond, M. G.

Elmer BELL to Annie May HIGGINBOTHAM Issued 6 Mar 1910   Not Returned

Nathan CLARK to Arkie BARNES Issued 12 Mar 1910 Rites 12 Mar 1910
A. C. Myers, J. P.

Ben YOUNG (Col) to Julia CARTER (Col) Issued 14 Mar 1910 Rites 15 MAR !(!)
E. N. Yager, J. P.

C. R. LOWRY to Bertha L. NEWBY Issued 14 Mar 1910 Rites 15 Mar 1910
P. G. Potter, M. G.

J. M. CRISP to Beulah Benton LOCKE Issued 21 Mar 1910 Rites 24 1910
S. T. Byars, M. G.

Lock WEEMS to Ada GILBERT Issued 22 Mar 1910 Rites 23 Mar 1910
Thos R. Curtis, M. G.

John O'NEAL to Ada JONES Issued 26 Mar 1910 Rites 26 Mar 1910
Wm. Thurman, Elder c of C

Charlie POTTER to Jenire ASKEW Issued 26 Mar 1910 Rites 27 Mar 1910
J. M. Green, J. P.

W. W. BLAIR to Myrtle May PARIS Issued 1 Apr 1910 Rites 3 Apr 1910
Thos R Curtis, M. G.

Geoege BYARS to Eva MISER Issued 1 Apr 1910 Rites 3 Apr 1910
P. G. Potter, M. G.

Finley BRUSTER (Col) to Martha ROBERTS (Col) Issued 2 Apr 1910 Rites 2 Apr 1910
E. N. Yager, J. P.

Thomas J. BARNES to Willie Belle PHELPS Issued 8 Apr 1910 Rites 10 Apr 1910
Wm. Thurman, Elder, C of C

R. P. WEBB to Etta GREEN Issued 15 Jun 1910 Rites 16 Jun 1910
L. F. Daugherty, M. G.

Hubert BROWN (Col) to Amie FRENCH (Col) Issued 18 Jun 1910 Rites 20 Jun 1910
G. T. Speaks, M. G.

Ed MEARS to Nora MEARS Issued 23 Jun 1910 Rites 23 Jun 1910
John B. Cowden, M. G.

Silas Marberry (Col) to Cora Wilson (Col) Issued 25 Jun 1910 Rites 26 Jun 1910
J. W. Richmond, M. G.

Will MAYES to Octa DANIELS Issued 27 Jun 1910 Rites 27 Jun 1910
A. C. Myers, J. P.

John RIDDLE to Mai SMOOT Issued 29 Jun 1910 Rites 3 Jul 1910
Rouchen Horton, M. G.

John LOCKE to Belle MERRIMAN Issued 1 July 1910 Rites 3 Jul 1910
S. T. Byars, M. G.

Groce ALLEN to Grace WEBB Issued 2 Jul 1910 Rites 3 Jul 1910
J. M. McGiboney, J. P.

Joe FREED to Elsie CROSSEN Issued 2 Jul 1910 Rites 4 Jul 1910
Wm. A. Bell, J. P.

J. J. HOOD to Della WEST Issued 6 Jul 1910 Rites 6 Jul 1910
John B. Cowden, M. G.

Grover MERRITT to Maggie PARKER Issued 6 Jul 1910 Rites 6 Jul 1910
Wm. A. Bell, J. P.

L. C. WALKER to Maggie ZWINGLE Issued 8 Jul 1910 Rites 8 Jul 1910
W. R. Wilson, M. G.

Virgil HUNTER (Col) Issued 9 Jul 1910 Not Returned

Robert PARSLEY to Lula BROWN Issued 9 Jul 1910 Rites 10 Jul 1910
J. T. CASEY, M. G.

Claud JONES to Velma HOLDER Issued 22 Jul 1910 Rites 23 Jul 1910
J. L. Jones, M. G.

Ada ROBERTS to Lillie PERRY Issued 23 July 1910 Rites 24 Jul 1910
L. V. Scott, J. P.

Lonnie BOGLE to Alica CAMPBELL Issued 30 Jul 1910 Rites 30 Jul 1910
Frank Michael, J. P.

Henderson SMITH to Maye HODGE Issued 5 Aug 1910 Rites 6 Aug 1910
J. M. Green, M. G.

Hassell ARLEDGE to Willie BARNES Issued 5 Aug 1910 Rites 7 Aug 1910
J. N. Darnell

Joseph J. OLIVER to Myrtle H. BIGGS Issued 6 Aug 1910 Rites 7 Aug 1910
J. T. Casey, M. G.

Will COLWELL to Minnie HENDERSON Issued 6 Aug 1910 Rites 7 Aug 1910
W. W. Locke

Leonard LEBO (Col) to Mattie HERD (Col) Issued 13 Aug 1910 Rites 14 Aug 1910
D. S. Ransaw

John DRIVER to Edna E. FRENCH Issued 13 Aug 1910 Rites 14 Aug 1910
John B. Cowden, M. G.

Bob SLIGER to Rosha WEBSTER Issued 13 Aug 1910 Rites 14 Aug 1910
S. A. Owen, M. G.

Russ FULTS to Nannie HILLIS Issued 16 Aug 1910 Rites 16 Aug 1910
H. T. McGregor, J. P.

H. B. SUMMERS to Octa MITCHELL Issued 18 Aug 1910 Rites 18 Aug 1910
G. H. Atnip, M. G.

John HILLIS to Manerva McGEE Issued 19 Aug 1910 Rites 20 Aug 1910
W. S. Grissom, J. P.

Fred BASHAM to Lillie JENNINGS Issued 26 Aug 1910 Rites 28 Aug 1910
Frank Michael, J. P.

Lee NORTHCUTT to Angie JENNINGS Issued 27 Aug 1910 Rites 28 Aug 1910
Frank Michael, J. P.

Sam GARNER to Bertha HOLMES Issued 30 Aug 1910 Rites 31 Aug 1910
S. T. Byars, M. G.

G. F. BILBREY to Sallie MILLER Issued 1 Sep 1910 Rites 1 Sep 1910
E. N. Yager, J. P.

W. M. SIMPSON to Sarah JONES Issued 2 Sep 1910 Rites 4 Sep 1910
J. C. Smoot, J. P.

Burr WILSON to Lizzie AKERS Issued 10 Sep 1910 Rites 11 Sep 1910
G. W. Haley, J. P.

G. D. TURNER to Lena SAVAGE Issued 17 Sep 1910 Rites 18 Sep 1910
H. T. McGregor, J. P.

Harrison PRATER to Della ROBERTS Issued 24 Sep 1910 Rites 25 Sep 1910
G. W. Haley, J. P.

Smith LIVELY to Gae FELTY   Issued 24 Sep 1910 Rites 25 Sep 1910
Wm. Thurman, Elder, C of C

Bon MARTIN (Col) to Lula EVANS (Col) Issued 24 Sep 1910 Rites 25 Sep 1910
D. S. Kansaw

Harris COUCH to Florence CROUCH Issued 27 Sep 1910 Rites 2 Oct 1910
J. C. C. Smoot, J. P.

Claud MILSTEAD to Lena CUNNINGHAM Issued 28 Sep 1910 Rites 28 Sep 1910
Wm. Thurman, Elder C of C

J. B. EARLS to Annie RANKIN Issued 29 Sep 1910 Rites 29 Sep 1910
S. T. Byars, M. G.

JAmes BROWN to Jane WILSON Issued 30 Sep 1910 Rites 9 Oct 1910
J. W. Sims, M. G.

H. J. WILLIAMSON to Lillie L. HERNDON Issued 4 Oct 1910 rites 9 oct 1910
G. W. Haley, J. P.

Calvin PAGE (Col) to Tessa MARTIN (Col) Issued 6 Oct 1910 Rites 7 Oct 1910
W. S. Grissom, J. P.

H. C. WILSON to Eliza RIGSBY Issued 7 Oct 1910 Rites 9 Oct 1910
G. W. Haley, J. P.

Will WOODS (Col) to Featy LOCKE (Col) Issued 7 Oct 1910 Rites 8 Oct 1910
J. C. Odum, M. G.

J. L. PHILLIPS to Leafie DEBERRY Issued 10 Oct 1910 Returned - Not Solemnized

Jim ROWAN (Col) to Lonnie OAKLEY (Col) Issued 12 Oct 1910 Rites 12 Oct 1910
E. N. Yager, J. P.

Jesse EVANS to Josie PATRICK Issued 15 Oct 1910 Rites 15 Oct 1910
J. Barnes, J. P.

Parks SAIN to Reta EATON Issued 15 Oct 1910 Rites 19 Oct 1910
J. R. Stubblefirld, M. G.

S. V. GREEN to Mrs. Callie CARTER Issued 15 Oct 1910 Rites 15 Oct 1910
R. E. Wright, M. G.

Curg FERRELL to Julia Lee FERRELL Issued 19 Oct 1910 Rites 19 Oct 1910
E. N. Yager, J. P.

J. L. FINGER to Maggie COPE Issued 19 Oct 1910 Rites 20 Oct 1910
Not Signed

Tracy DEWEY to Dovie KIRBY Issued 24 Oct 1910 Rites 25 Oct 1910
L. R. Hogan

Oscar J. RANKIN (Col) to Lexie V. COPE (Col) Issued 26 Oct 1910 Rites 26 Oct 1910

F. R. HOOVER to Sallie FULTS Issued 26 Oct 1910 Rites 27 Oct 1910
J. A. CUnningham. M. G.

Robert HOBBS to Maud NUNLEY Issued 29 Oct 1910 Rites 30 Oct 1910
J. Barnes, J. P.

Noah BOST to Katie RUTTER Issued 29 Oct 1910 Rites 29 Oct 1910
R. H. Mason, J. P.

L. F. PATRICK to Mandy PEARSON Issued 31 Oct 1910 Rites 11 May 1911
J. Barnes, J. P.

Charles WEBSTER to Ada MATHIS Issued 1 Nov 1910 Rites 1 Nov 1910
E. N. Yager, J. P.

JAmes Argo to Lillie ROGERS Issued 2 Nov 1910 Rites 2 Nov 1910
B. W. D. Barnes, J. P.

Robert CAMPBELL to Eliza CAMPBELL Issued 3 Nov 1910 Rites 6 Nov 1910
Frank Michael, J. P.

Crit RAINS to Annie MARTIN Issued 11 Nov 1910 Rites 3 Nov 1910
J. C. Smoot, J. P.

Wm. Marvin CAMPEN to Beulah WOMACK Issued 11 Nov 1910 Rites 12 Nov 1910
T. A. Wiggington, M. G.

John Paul FINGER to Jimmie TILLETT Issued 15 Nov 1910 Rites 15 Nov 1910
D. E. Hinkle, M. G.

C. S. KYLE to Isa EDGE Issued 17 Nov 1910 Rites 17 Nov 1910
W. P. davis, J. P.

Felix WOMACK to Flossie GRIBBLE Issued 18 Nov 1910 Rites 20 Nov 1910
J. M. Green, J. P.

Victor E. SEMONES to Julia TALIAFERRO Issued18 Nov 1910 Rites 18 Nov 1910
D. E. Hinkle, M. G.

Bernard BANBACK to Lillie DAUGHERTY Issued 25 Nov 1910 Rites 27 Nov 1910
J. C. Smoot, J. P.

Clee HILLIS to Pearl FULTS Issued 28 Nov 1910 Rites 29 Nov 1910
L. V. Scott, J. P.

Bob LYLES to Pearl CARROLL 29 Nov 1910 Rites 29 Nov 1910
Joe Pennington, J. P.

John COLLINS to Rillie PENNINGTON Issued 29 Nov 1910 Rites 29 Nov 1910
E. N. Yager, J. P.

William CRAWLEY to Eliza WILLIAMS Issued 3 Dec 1910 Rites 4 Dec 1910
J. C. Smoot, J. P.

THomas Benton POTTER to Lisle COLLINS Issued 5 Dec 1910 Rites 6 Dec 1910
John B. Cowden, M. G.

John F. YERGAN to FAnnie STEWART Issued 7 Dec 1910 Rites 8 Dec 1910
G. Hainie, J. P.

Jim LIST (Col) to Maggie MITCHELL (Col) Issued 8 Dec 1910 Rites 11 Dec 1910
I. H. Hunt, M. G.

Floyd BOREN to Annie ROWLAND Issued 12 Dec 1910 Rites 18 Dec 1910
J. M. Green, J. P.

Claud VICKERS to Edith GRISSOM Issued 13 Dec 1910 Rites 14 Dec 1910
J. D. Quick, J. P.

J. A. McBRIDE to Osie CHRISTIAN Issued 13 Dec 1910 Rites 14 Dec 1910
P. G. Potter, M. G.

George HENNESSEE to Mollie BIRD Issued 13 Dec 1910 Rites 13 Dec 1910
E. N. Yager, J. P.

Ed NUNNLEY to Ada MILSTEAD Issued 30 Dec 1910 Rites 1 Jan 1911
J. Barnes, J. P.

J. L. BARNES to Mary L. HILL Issued 2 JAn 1911 Rites 3 Jan 1911
E. L. Moffitt, J. P.

J. B. DUGAN to Cleo STANLEY Issued 2 JAn 1911 Rites 8 JAn 1911
J. T. Vinson, J. P.

Ed CRAIN to Wilma HENNESSEE Issued 3 Jan 1910 Rites 4 Jan 1911
John B. Cowden, M. G.

F. M. SMARTT to Ellen NUNLEY Issued 4 Jan 1911 Rites 5 JAn 1911
J. Barnes, J. P.

Homer C. BAKER to Mai OUTLAW Issued 6 Jan 1911 Rites 6 Jan 1911
J. E. Jones,. J. P.

H. P. PIKE to Emmaline CAWTHRON Issued 10 JAn 1911 Rites 10 Jan 1911
J. C. Smoot, J. P.

Sam T. COMER to Ethel FINGER Issued 10 Jan 1910 Rites 12 Dec 1910
W. A. Stroud, P. G.

John A. HENDRIXSON to Ella MULLICAN Issued 12 Jan 1911 Rites 12 Jan 1911
D. E. Hinkle, M. G.

Robert STANLEY to Myrtle REED Issued 16 JAn 1911 Rites 17 Jan 1911
W. P. Davis, J. P.

A. R. PEPPER to Rosa ROGERS Issued 21 Jan 1911 Rites 22 Jan 1911
S. T. Byars, JM. G.

Raful WYANT to Odie KELL Issued 23 JAn 1911 Rites 29 JAn 1911
G. P. Brasier, J. P.

Carl NORTH to Annie Mai JONES Issued 26 Jan 1911 Rites 26 Jan 1911
D. E. Hinkle, M. G.

W. A. MOSS to Louisie CANTRELL Issued 28 JAn 1911 Rites 29 Jan 1911
J. F. Turner, J. P.

Quill HOWARD to Hattie ADCOCK Issued 28 Jan 1911 Rites 29 Jan 1911
P. G. Moore, J. P.

Stephen CANTRELL to Martha MATTISON Issued 28 Jan 1911 Rites 29 Jan 1911
S. T. Byars, M. G.

J. F. PRATT to Esther ARGO Issued 2 Feb 1911 Rites 2 Feb 1911
J. R. Stubblefield, M. G.

Charlie WOODLEE to Lelia CURTIS Issued 3 Feb 1911 Rites 5 Feb 1911
L. V. Scott, J. P.

Colonel PENNINGTON to Ada COUCH Issued 4 Feb 1911 Rites 5 Feb 1911
J. C. Smoot, J. P.

Walter HILLIS to Ersie DODSON Issued 16 Dec 1910 Rites 18 Dec 1910
L. Safley, M. G.

S. L. BATY to J. B. DOBBS Issued 17 Dec 1910 Rites 18 Dec 1910
J. L. Thaxton, J. P.

J. E. HUDSON to Lula CANTRELL Issued 21 Dec 1910 Rites 22 Dec 1910
J. B. Gribble, M. G.

Walter HOLT to Mary GAN Issued 21 Dec 1910 Rites 23 Dec 1910
J. C. Smoot, J. P.

W. Paris CARR to Ethel VANOVER Issued 21 Dec 1910 Rites 21 Dec 1910
G. P. Brasier, J. P.

Ronnal Bruce JONES to Blanche BOLT Issued 21 Dec 1910 Rites 25 Dec 1910
S. T. Byars, M. G.

Forest MARTIN (Col) to Lillie WOODS (Col) Issued 22 Dec 1910 Not Returned

Joe HENNESSEE to Jessie TUCK Issued 22 Dec 1910 Rites 22 Dec 1910
L. R. Hogan

Alton YOUNGBLOOD to Bettie DAVENPORT Issued 24 Dec 1910 Rites 25 Dec 1910
Frank Michael, J. P.

Algernon LOWERY to Arrah ROGERS Issued 24 Dec 1910 Rites 25 Dec 1910
W. N. Kell, J. P.

Eather FULTS to Martha PATRICK Issued 24 Dec 1910 Rites 24 Dec 1910
L. V. Scott, J. P.

Rheuby SAFLEY to Leona COPE Issued 24 Dec 1910 Rites 25 Dec 1910
J. M. Green, J. P.

Ernest B. PRATER to Fannie JONES Issued 24 Dec 1910 Rites 25 Dec 1910
G. W. Haley, J. P.

Warren COPE to Etta GLENN Issued 24 Dec 1910 Rites 25 Dec 1910
L. F. DAUGHERTY, M. G.

Will HENEGAR to Austie HAMMONS Issued 24 Dec 1910 Rites 25 Dec 1910
J. C. Smoot, J. P.

Bruce ARGO to Nellie RHEAY Issued 24 Dec 1910 Rites 25 Dec 1910
J. Barnes, J. P.

Ores W. MOOR to Octa E. TURPIN Issued 27 Dec 1910 Rites 27 Dec 1910
D. E. Hinkle, M. G.

JAmes Lewis McDANIEL to Saddie SMARTT Issued 27 Dec 1910 Rites 27 Dec 1910
D. E. Hinkle, M. G.

Abe DRAKE to Mollie CRANE Issued 28 Dec 1910 Not Returned

Jim FARLESS to Nora GRIMES Issued 28 Dec 1910 Rites 29 Dec 1910
J. E. Jones, J. P.

Mack BROWN to Annie TOSH Issued 6 Feb 1911 Rites 19 Feb 1911
G. P. BraSIER, J. P.

Oscar MAYES to Mary PEARSON Issued 7 Feb 1911 Rites 8 Feb 1911
E. L. Moffitt, J. P.

James ELMON (Col) to Laura PARIS (Col) Issued 18 Feb 1911 Rites 18 Feb 1911
D. S. Ransaw

Vernon L. NORTHCUTT to Joy NORTHCUTT Issued 28 Feb 1911 Rites 8 Mar 1911
J. R. Stubblefield, M. G.

C. C. TALLEY to Nealie NEESMITH Issued 1 Mar 1911 Rites 1 Mar 1911
E. N. YAGER, J. P.

Jesse E. GARNER to Lou NORTHCUTT Issued 6 Mar 1911 Rites 8 Mar 1911
J. R. Stubblefield, M. G.

George R. McDANIEL to SARAH ISABELL WADE Issued 9 May 1911 Rites 9 Mar 1911
W. N. Kell, J. P.

Joe KIRBY to Cartance HOLDER Issued 11 Mar 1911 Rites 12 Mar 1911
G. W. Haley, J. P.

Allen F. SIMS to Mary CRAWLEY Issued 13 Mar 1911 Rites 13 Mar 1911
W. N. Kell, J. P.

W. T. OUTLAW to Ninnie SMOOT Issued 15 MAR !(!! Rites 15 Mar 1911
J. J. Meadows, J. P.

G. R. JONES to Nannie O'NEAL Issued 18 Mar 1911 Rites 19 Mar 1911
W. S. Grissom, J. P.

John OLIVER to Eula WOMACK Issued 18 Mar 1911 Rites 18 Mar 1911
W. P. Davis, J. P.

Elzy CROUCH to Willie De BERRY Issued 22 MAR !(!! Rites 26 Mar 1911
J. T. Vinson, J. P.

Willie WRIGHT to Lena FOWLER Issued 23 Mar 1911 Rites 23 Mar 1911
E. N. Yager, J. P.

Nathan BRATCHER to Maude WILSON Issued 24 Mar 1911 Rites 24 Mar 1911
J. T. Vinson, J. P.

Will SCOTT (Col) to Lou SPURLOCK Issued 24 Mar 1911 Rites 26 Mar 1911
W. W. Locke, J. P.

J. C. SMARTT to Viola DYER Issued 1 Apr 1911 Rites 2 Apr 1911
Frank Michael, J. P.

Martin McGEE to Celia HILLIS Issued 3 Apr 1911 Rites 4 Apr 1911
W. S. Grissom, J. P.

R. D. PENDLETON to Willie BELL Issued 8 Apr 1911 Rites 9 Apr 1911
S. T. Byars, JM. G.

Elmer ELKINS to Lucy BOYD Issued 14 Apr 1911 Rites 15 Apr 1911
W. S. Grissom, J¦ P.

Sam EDWARDS (Col) to Sallie TIDWELL (Col) Issued 17 Apr 1911 Rites 17 Apr 1911
J. W. Richmond, M. G.

Bon DONIHUE (Col) to Bessie COPE (Col) Issued 18 Apr 1911 Rites 23 Apr 1911
J. L. Thaxton, J. P,

Newt PRATER to Grace ST. JOHN Issued 21 Apr 1911 Rites 23 Apr 1911
G. W. Haley, M. G.

J. R. BLANKENSHIP to S. N. KIDWELL Issued 26 Apr 1911 Rites 30 Apr 1911
P. G. Moore, J. P.

D. M. BASELER to B. A. ELKINS Issued 8 May 1911 Rites 8 May 1911
John B. Cowden, M. G.

Elijah R. LEE to Sarah Frances BONNER Issued 9 May 1911 Rites 10 May 1911
D. E. Hinkle, M. G.

Jim POWELL to Ella FARLESS Issued 10 May 1911 Rites 14 May 1911
E. N. Yager, J. P.

Joe FEDIN to Lillie O'NEAL Issued 11 May 1911 Rites 14 May 1911
B. W. D. Barnes, J. P.

Ed McGREGOR to Hassie NORTHCUTT Issued 16 May 1911 Rites 21 May 1911
J. R. Stubblefield, M. G.

Zack SMARTT (Col) to Marie WEBB (Col) Issued 20 May 1911 Not Returned

A. J. SPARKMAN to Lou CRAWLEY Issued 25 May 1911 Rites 25 May 1911
S. T. Byars, M. G.

John GRIFFITH to Mollie JACKSON Issued 3 Jun 1911 Rites 4 Jun 1911
W. A. Bell, J. P:

J. E. DUGGIN to Nora CLARK Issued 13 June 1911 Rites 14 Jun 1911
P. G. Potter, M. G.

J. B. RONEY to Mecia E. EARL Issued 14 Jun 1911 Rites 14 Jun 1911
L. R. Hogan, M. G.

Joseph Sumner CUMMINGS to Mary Cynthia RAMSEY Issued 17 Jun 1911 Rites 17 Jun 1911
L. R. Hogan, M. G.

Will PHELPS to Lela LORANCE Issued 22 Jun 1911 Rites 22 Jun 1911
G. W. Haley, J. P.

Grover McVEY to Ada KELL Issued 27 Jun 1911 Rites 29 Jun 1911
Jacob Stipe, M. G.

John BAINES (Col) to Lizzie MARTIN (Col) Issued 29 Jun 1911 Rites 29 JUN 1911
J. W. Richmond, M. G.

Harve CLENDENON to Tasker MADEWELL Issued 8 Jul 1911 Rites 9 Jul 1911
L. V. Scott, J. P.

Stokes HUDELSTON (Col) to JAnie ROACH (Col) Issued 8 Jul 1911 Rites 8 Jul 1911
J. W. Richmond, M. G.

W. M. CRUSE to Mary JACO Issued 12 July 1911 Rites 23 Jul 1911
J. D. Quick, J. P.

W. L. SWALLOWS to Mattie HUTCHESON Issued 13 Jul 1911 Rites 13 Jul 1911
B. A. Pendleton

Fletcher SMOTHERMAN to Pauline WEST 13 July 1911 Rites 13 Jul 1911
P. G. Potter, M. G.

C. M. GRIBBLE to Flora WILSON Issued 15 July 1911   Not Returned

Jesse MARTIN to Georgia MELTON Issued 18 Jul 1911 Rites 19 Jul 1911
Chas. L. Talley, M. G.

Isaac W. FOSTER to Lou LANCE Issued 18 Jul 1911 Rites 19 Jul 1911
Frank Michael, J. P.

J. W. COURTNEY to Emma B. WILLIAMS Issued 19 Jul 1911 Rites 19 Jul 1911
E. N. Yager, J. P.

Willie THOMISON to Josie McVEY Issued 20 Jul 1911 Rites 23 Jul 1911
J. N. Elkins, J. P.

George STEEDLEY to Mary SWANCUTT Issued 22 Jul 1911 Rites 23 Jul 1911
E. N. Yager, J. P.

Eb CHRISTIAN to Ella MYERS Issued 22 Jul 1911 Rites 24 Jul 1911
H. T. McGregor, J. P.

Will PARKER to Neil FAULKNER Issued 22 Jul 1911 Rites 24 Jul 1911
John J. Ransom, M. G.

Willie HOLT to to Rebecca VAUGHN Issued 26 Jul 1911   Not Returned

W. C. WIMBERLY to Lizzie GREEN Issued 28 Jul 1911 Rites 25 Jul 1911
L. V. Scott, J. P.

C. M. TALLEY to Lillie PEPPER Issued 29 Jul 1911 Rites 30 Jul 1911
Wm. A. Bell, J. P.

Jim SMITH to Lina MUNCEY Issued 2 Aug 1911 Rites 2 Aug 1911
J. L. Thaxton, J. P.

Joe JENKINS to Fluella BROWN Issued 5 Aug 1911 Rites 6 Aug 1911
E. L. Moffitt, J. P.

Escal CURTIS to Vickie BALES Issued 5 Aug 1911 Rites 6 Aug 1911
H. T. McGregor, J. P.

Joe FOWLER to Lou WRIGHT Issued 7 Aug 1911 Rites 7 Aug 1911
E. N. Yager, l.l. P.

Book 11 - Warren County Marriages - Aug. 9, 1911 to May 8, 1915

Aaron Burr BROWN to Theona McCURDY Issued 9 Aug 1911 Rites 9 Aug 1911
S. A. Owen

WA. A. FISHER to Ella WOMACK Issued 15 Aug 1911 Rites 16 Aug 1911
P. G. Moore, J. P.

Floyd HILLIS to Selmer DAVENPORT Issues 17 Aug 1911 Rites 18 Aug 1911
J. W. Cooley, M. G.

John FUGITT to Daisy PRATER Issued 17 Aug 1911 Rites 18 Aug 1911
Frank Michael, J. P.

E. R. HOLDER to May WEBB Issued 19 Aug 1911 Rites 27 Aug 1911
G. W. Haley, J. P.

Claude BOREN to Annie TEMPLETON Issued 26 Aug 1911 Rites 27 Aug 1911
J. W. Cooley, M. G.

T. U. CURTIS to Mrs. Lou ROBERTS Issued 26 Aug 1911 Rites 10 Sep 1911
W. S. Grisso, J. P.

W. M. ADCOCK to Belle NEWBY Issued 28 Aug 1911 Rites 28 Aug 1911
P. G. Moore, J. P.

William CRISP to Ethel WILLIAMS Issued 2 Sep 1911 Rites 2 Sep 1911
J. C. Smoot, J. P.

Arthur David ALCOTT to Agnes McGUIRE Issued 9 Dep 1911 Rites 9 Sep 1911
L. R. Hogan, M. G.

Martin JENKINS to Emma CURTIS Issued 9 Sep 1911 Rites 10 Sep 1911
E. L. Moffitt, J. P.

Harris BARNES to Lucille McGREGOR Issued 9 Sep 1911 Rites 10 Sep 1911
Rites J. J. Meadows, J. P.

Isaac ROBERTS to Rachel SMARTT Issued 14 Sep 1911 Rites 8 May 1912
J. J. Meadows, J. P.

Frank MINOGUE to Lena WALKER Issued 15 Sep 1911 Rites 15 Sep 1911
S. A. Owen

Ed SMITH to Lillie PHILLIPS Issued 15 Sep 1911 Rites 17 Sep 1911
G. W. Haley, J. P.

Palo McVEY to Martha THOMISON Issued 16 Sep 1911 Rites 17 Sep 1911
H. T. McGregor, J. P.

James E. BAKER to Maggie L. LEWIS Issued 18 Sep 1911 Rites 19 Sep 1911
L. R. Hogan, M. G.

R. BROWN (Col) to Sarah GWYNN (Col) Issued 20 Sep 1911 Rites 20 Sep 1911
I. W. Hunt, M. G.

Oscar FRENCH (Col) to Mary RICHARDS (Col) Issued 21 Sep 1911 Rites 21 Sep 1911
D. S. Ransaw, M. G.

A. J. CANTRELL to Artimishi BLANKS Issued 23 Sep 1911 Rites 24 Sep 1911
S. T. Byars, M. G.

Andy GREEN to Mandy MARTIN Issued 28 Oct 1911 Rites 28 Oct 1911
E. N. Yager, J. P.

Anson LANCE to Ethel FLEMONS Issued 28 Oct 1911 Rites 31 Oct 1911
J. C. Smoot, J. P.

B. F. SHAVER to Josie ARGO Issued 1 Nov 1911 Rites 1 Nov 1911
Wm. Thurman

Murphy WALLACE to Ocie McBRIDE Issued 6 Nov 1911 Rites 12 Nov 1912
W. W. Locke, J. P.

Hackett PARIS to Mary DONNELL Issued 7 Nov 1911 Rites 8 Nov 1911
S. T. Byars, M. G.

Grover HALEY to Hassie CAMPBELL Issued 10 Nov 1911 Rites 12 Nov 1911
Frank Michael, J. P.

Math PASSONS to Essie AUSTIN Issued 10 Nov 1911 Rites 12 Nov 1911
W. S. Grissom, J. P.

Oscar MARTIN to Maude DODSON Issued 11 Nov 1911 Rites 12 Nov 1911
J. W. Cooley, M. G.

Murphy GRIBBLE (Col) to Belle LUSK (Col) Issued 20 Nov 1911 Not Returned

James K. BRANTLEY to Avis WILSON Issued 22 Nov 1911 Rites 23 Nov 1911
L. R. Hogan, M. G.

Jim FRANKS to Ila RASCOE Issued 28 Nov 1911 Rites 28 Nov 1911
E. N. Yager, J. P.

E. W. WALLING to Lula E. BLUE Issued 29 Nov 1911 Rites 30 Nov. 1911
John B. Cowden, M. G.

F. H. HOWARD to Winnie G. BLUE Issued 29 Nov 1911 Rites 30 Nov 1911
John B. Cowden, M. G.

Wiley YORK (Col) to Martha MARTIN (Col) Issued 1 Dec 1911 Rites 2 Dec 1911
W. S. Grissom, J. P.

G. R. DeFORD to Bernice SALTZ Issued 4 Dec 1911 Rites 4 Dec 1911
T. W. Noland, M. G.

JAmes E. RIFFEL to Sue Ella MARTIN Issued 6 Dec 1911 Rites 7 Dec 1911
John B. Cowden, M. G.

Ernold YOUNGBLOOD to Nora DAVENPORT Issued 7 Dec 1911 Rites 7 Dec 1911
G. W. Haley, J. P.

Andrew COPPINGER to Minnie KILLIAN Issued 9 Dec 1911 Rites 9 Dec 1911
E. N. Yager, J. P.

Arthur SMITH to Lela SHOCKLEY Issued 9 Dec 1911 Rites 10 Dec 1911
J. C. Smoot, J. P.

Albert RAY to Beatrice TOSH Issued 15 Dec 1911 Rites 17 Dec 1911
G. P. Brasier, J. P.

N. F. F. TITTSWORTH to Hattie MULLICAN Issued 15 Dec 1911 Rites 17 Dec 1911
P. G. Moore, J. P,

Henry SPURLOCK to Belle HENDERSON Issued 23 Sep 1911 Rites 23 Sep 1911
E. N. Yager, J. P.

Ernest RIGSBY to Lena DUNCAN Issued 29 Sep 1911 Rites 4 Oct 1911
W. N. Kell, J. P.

Harrison COPE (Col) to Mary MASEY (Col) Issued 30 Sep 1911 Rites 1 Oct 1911
J. Barnes, J. P.

France FULTS to Nannie RAY Issued 2 Oct 1911 Rites 3 Oct 1911
E. L. Moffitt, J. P.

B. B. JONES to Deedie NORTHCUTT Issued 2 Oct 1911 Rites 4 Oct 1911
G. W. Haley, J. P.

General SOLOMON (Col) to Ida PAGE (Col) Issued 4 Oct 1911 Rites 4 Oct 1911
D. S. Rensaw, M. G.

Charley REEDER to Maggie NUNLEY Issued 6 Oct 1911 Rites 8 Oct 1911
J. L. Thaxton, J. P.

Frank BOST to Elba BOREN Issued 7 Oct 1911 Rites 8 Oct 1911
J. M. Green, J. P.

Dillard CHILTON to Binnie BRACKNEY Issued 11 Oct 1911 Rites 11 Oct 1911
S. T. Byars, M. G.

Jim BROWN to Lizzie WIMBERLY Issued 12 Oct 1911 Rites 13 Oct 1911
J. L. Thaxton, J. P.

Jack LOCKE to Marcie Lee SPARKMAN Issued 13 Oct 1911 Rites 15 Oct 1911
J. M. McGiboney, J. P.

Charley S. McGREGOR to Castella KEATHLEY Issued 13 Oct 1911 Rites 15 Oct 1911
J. M. McGIBONEY, J. P.

Isaac COOPER to Bertha ANDERSON Issued 14 Oct 1911 Rites 15 Oct 1911
J. C. Smoot, J. P.

Ed NEWBY to Lurley EARLES Issued 14 Oct 1911 Rites 15 Oct 1911
W. P. Davis, J. P.

I. D. WEBB to Mandy HODGE Issued 14 Oct 1911 Rites 14 Oct 1911
J. E. Jones, J. P.

E. P. HANKINS to Nettie Mai COTTEN Issued 21 Oct 1911 Rites 22 Oct 1911
J. B. Gribble, M. G.

Eashful HARRIS (Col) to Emma HUDDLESTON (Col) Issued 21 Oct 1911 Rites 23 Oct 1911
C. H. Gardner, M. G.

Sam MARTIN to Ella MILLRANEY Issued 27 Oct 1911 Rites 29 Oct 1911
W. S. Grissom, J. P.

Will BLANKS to Louise SANDERS Issued 28 Oct 1911 Rites 29 Oct 1911
Joe Pennington, J. P.

Vance CRIM to Ella BYARS Issued 28 Oct 1911 Rites 29 Oct 1911
E. N. Yager, J. P.

J. C. GREEN to Ethel STILES Issued 16 Dec 1911 Rites 17 dec 1911
                                              Joe Pennington, J. P.

G. W. SNIPES to Ethel BREWER Issued 16 Dec 1911 Rites 17 dec 1911
                                              T. J. Pentecost, M. G.

John LUSK (Col) to Missie BARTLEY (Col) Issued 16 dec 1911   Not Returned

John WEBB to Hessie WILSON Issued 16 Dec 1911 Rites 17 Dec 1911
                                              G. W. Haley, J. P.

Feliz E. MALONE to Jessie M. RHEA Issued 18 Dec 1911 Rites 24 Dec 1911
                                              Rouchen Horton, M. G.

Hershell NEWBY to Carlie BISHOP Issued 19 Dec 1911 Rites 20 Dec 1911
                                              S. T. Byars, M. G.

John BARNES to Janie BALES Issued 20 Dec 1911 Rites 24 Dec 1911
                                              E. L. Moffitt, J. P.

Lee SMITH to Minnie FARLESS Issued20 Dec 1911 Rites 22 Dec 1911
                                              T. J. Pentecoct, M. G.

Charlie PARKER to Alica KELL Issued21 Dec 1911 Rites 24 Dec 1911
                                              J. L. Thaxton, J. P.

R. H. SMITH to Mary WALKER Issued 21 Dec 1911 Rites 24 Dec 1911
                                              J. L. Jones, M. G.

S. G. PENDERGRASS to Julia JOHNSON Issued 22 Dec 1911 Rites 24 Dec 1911
                                              J. D. Quick, J. P.

John CROUCH to Rachel QUALLS Issued 22 Dec 1911 Ret'd. not Solemnized

J. S. TEMPLETON to Hassie BOST Issued 23 Dec 1911 Rites 24 Dec 1911
                                              H. T. McGregor, J. P.

John CROUCH to Lou HILLIS Issued 23 Dec 1911 Rites 24 Dec 1911
                                              J. L. Thaxton, J. P.

Levi CRIM to Cora EPPERSON Issued 23 dec 1911 Rites 24 Dec 1911
                                              S. T. Byars, M. G.

H. B. MOFFITT to Janie MEADOWS Issued 26 Dec 1911 Rites 27 Dec 1911
                                              S. T. Byars, M. G.

Jim CROUCH to Maggie NEWBY Issued 26 Dec 1911 Rites 27 Dec 1911
                                              Wm. A. Bell, J. P.

Walter GREEN to Lillian WEBB Issued 30 dec 1911 Rites 21 dec 1911
                                              J. S. Lawrence, J. P.

Joseph BONNER to Myrtle HUNTLEY Issued 2 Jan 1912 Rites 18 Jan 1912
                                              J. L. Thaxton, J. P.

Burley VANATTA to Pearl LUSK Issued 17 JAn 1912 Rites 21 JAn 1911
                                              J. L. Thaxton, J. P.

Joel PAYNE to MArtha TAYLOR Issued 22 Jan 1912 Rites 25 JAn 1912
                                              W. T. Caten, M. G.

G. A. SMOOT to Cora BROWN Issued 23 Jan 1912 Rites 28 JAn 1912
                                              J. C. Smoot, J. P.

Frank BARRY to Alma DARNELL Issued 26 Jan 1912 Rites 28 Jan 1912
                                              Rouchen Horton, M. G.

W. E. MARTIN to Georgia B. TILLETT Issued 27 JAn 1912 Rites 28 Jan 1912
                                              S. T. Byars, M. G.

Bob OWENS to Isabelle MASON Issued 3 Feb 1912 Rites 4 Feb. 1912
                                              S. T. Byars, M. G.

Isaac GRIZZLE to Fannie KING Issued 7 Feb 1912 Rites 7 Feb 1912
                                              S. T. Byars, A. G.

W. N. KELL to Martha J. KELL Issued 10 Feb 1912 Rites 11 Feb 1912
                                              J. L. Thaxton, J. P.

Marcus LYTLE to Lizzie PERRY Issued 12 Feb 1912   Not Solemized

William BYRD to Mattie ASMUS Issued 13 Feb 1912 Rites 14 Feb 1912
                                              S. T. Byars, M. G.

W. H. JONES to Mattie MARTIN Issued 16 Feb 1912 Rites 18 Feb 1912
                                              L. Safley, M. G.

Charles ALLEN to Annie COOK Issued 17 Feb 1912 Rites 20 Feb. 1912
                                              E. N. Yager, J. P.

Edwin GOLLADAY to Bonnie PARKER Issued 17 Feb 1912 Rites 25 Feb 1912
                                              C. M. Epps

Charlie HOBBS to Malinda DUKE Issued 17 Feb 1912 Rites 25 Feb 1912
                                              G. P. Brasier, J. P.

H. Rowan ETTER to Jadie H. WILLIAMS Issued 24 Feb 1912 Rites 25 Feb 1912
                                              R. L. Whitlock, M. G.

H. L. ELAM to Cora SWOAP Issued 1 Mar 1912 Rites 3 Mar 1912
                                              J. C. Smoot, J. P.

Frank DAVIS to Minnie ROGERS Issued 2 Mar 1912 Rites 3 Mar 1912
                                              Wm. A. Bell, J. P.

Harrison GILBERT to Della PARIS Issued 9 Mar 1912 Rites 10 Mar 1912
                                              S. T. Byars, M. G.

Floyd SLAUGHTER to Myra BOYD Issued 16 Mar 1912 Rites 20 Mar 1912
                                              J. Barnes, J. P.

Andrew ORICK to Mary AUSTIN Issued 21 Mar 1912 Rites 23 Mar 1912
                                              W. S. Grissom, J. P.

Syrus HASTON to Ella Mai SAFLEY Issued 22 Mar 1912 Rites 24 Mar 1912
                                              Jacob Stipe, M. G.

Joe HANKINS to Lucile FINGER Issued 23 Mar 1912 Rites 24 Mar 1912
C. M. Epps

Marcus LYTLE to Nancy TATE Issued 30 Mar 1912   Not Returned

W. M. BROWN to America HERNDON Issued8 Apr 1912 Rites 8 Apr 1912
J. E. Jones, J. P.

John H. MOORE (Col) to Nettie JOHNSON (Col) Issued 9 Apr 1912 Rites 9 Apr 1902
W. A. Rogers, M. G.

S. C. STUBBLEFIELD to Octa WHITLOCK Issued 13 Apr 1912 Rites 13 Apr 1912
E. N. Yager, J. P.

T. P. BRAGG to Rubie FOSTER Issued 19 Apr 1912 Rites 28 Apr 1912
Jow Pennington, J. P.

Charles R. WOMACK to Clara Belle SMITH Issued 20 Apr 1912 Rites 20 Apr 1912
L. R. Hogan, M. G.

Dixie CALHOUN to Lou Harris BONDS Issued 23 Apr 1912 Rites 28 Apr 1912
S. T. Byars, M. G.

A. W. McMAHAN to Amanda GILLENTINE Issued 26 Apr 1912 Rites 28 Apr 1912
J. C. Smoot, J. P.

Earn PEPPER to Lillie Belle ROACH Issued 27 Apr 1912 Rites 27 Apr 1912
Wm. A. Bell, J. P.

Robert SHIELDS to Dora Mai BURCH Issued 27 Apr 1912 Rites 28 Apr 1912
J. C. Smoot, J. P.

Ernest TAYLOR to Mandy PASSONS Issued 30 Apr 1912 Rites 3 May 1912
W. P. Davis, J. P.

V. W. HALL to Ruth SMITH Issued 1 May 1912 Rites 2 May 1912
S. A. Owen, M. G.

Sam FULTS to Maggie McBRIDE Issued 4 May 1912 Rites 5 May 1912
J. L. Thaxton, J. P.

E. B. HILL to Kate TURNER Issued 6 May 1912 Rites 12 May 1912
H. T. McGregor, J. P.

James DODSON to Pearl MARTIN Issued 11 May 1912 Rites 12 May 1912
J. W. Cooley, M. G.

Willie Fisk (Col) to Mattie Williams (Col) Issued 18 May 1912 Rites 20 May 1912
W. S. Grissom, J. P.

JAmes O'NEAL to Nettie SIMONS Issued 24 May 1912 Rites 26 May 1912
H. T. McGregor, J. P.

Herbert LANCE to Mary CATES Issued 24 May 1912   Ret'd. not solommized

Frank TAYLOR to Bertha TAYLOR Issued 27 May 1912 Rites 27 May 1912
E. L. Moffitt, J. P.

Eddie WOMACK to Tabitha HASH Issued 29 May 1912 Rites 1 Jun 1912
Elisha Webb, M. G.

Joe GROVE to Maud DEWEESE Issued 1 Jun 1912 Rites 23 Jun 1912
W. S. Grissom, J. P.

Herbert LANCE to Mary CATES Issued 5 JUN 1912 Rites 6 JUN 1912
Frank Michael, J. P.
(See Page 105)

Vernel PAGE to Etta JONES Issued 8 Jun 1912 Rites 24 Jun 1912
J. D. Parsley, M. G.

W. R. BYFORD to Idella SISSOM Issued 8 Jun 1912 Rites 9 Jun 1912
J. W. Cooley, M. G.

Elvin ELKINS to Mamie Cooper LIVELY Issued 10 Jun 1912 Rites 11 Jun 1912
L. R. Hogan. M. G.

Norman TAYLOR to Nan TURNER Issued10 Jun 1912 Rites 10 Jun 1912
J. J. L. Jones, M. G.

W. N. MASON to Beatrice M. ROBINSON Issued 11 Jun 1912 Rites 11 Jun 1912
J. D. Gunn, M. G.

G. W. TEETERS to Adie FAIRBANKS Issued 15 Jun 1912 Rites 16 Jun 1912
H. T. McGregor, J. P.

Rufus DURLEY (Col) to Chaney SMARTT (Col) Issued 15 Jun 1912 Rites 1 Jul 1912
J. C. Smoot, J. P.

Henry HERNDON to Bessie MEDLEY Issued 15 Jun 1912 Rites 16 Jun 1912
G. W. Haley, J. P.

Henry STANLEY to Novella BRASWELL Issued 17 Jun 1912 Rites 23 Jun 1912
J. T. Turner

Charles Hansel FAULKNER to Ada Belle WILSON Issued 26 Jun 1912 Rites 27 Jun 1912
L. R. Hogan, M. G.

Tom BROWN (Col) to Harriett SPURLOCK (Col) Issued 29 Jun 1912 Rites 30 Jun 1912
G. F. Brasier, J. P.

Will GARDNER to Lillie SPANGLER Issued 29 Jun 1912 Rites 30 Jun 1912
L. V. Scott, J. P.

D. W. RUSSELL to Ethel TURNER Issued 3 Jul 1912 Rites 3 Jul 1912
H. L. Walling, M. G.

Will MARTIN to Vinnie ELKINS Issued 12 Jul 1912 Rites 13 Jul 1912
W. S. Grissom, J. P.

Ben ROBERTS to Lela COPPINGER Issued 13 Jul 1912 Rites 13 Jul 1912
E. L. Moffitt, J. P.

W. B. PARTON to Eliza EDGE Issued 13 Jul 1912 Rites 14 Jul 1912
R. E. Wright, M. G.

B. F. SHELTON to Pressie A. RAINS Issued 13 Jul 1912 Rites 14 Jul 1912
J. C. Smoot, J. P.

John TUBB to Florence MAGNESS Issued 17 Jul 1912 Rites 17 Jul 1912
R. S. Kirby, J. P.

Jess HOLT to Myrtle PAGE Issued 20 Jul 1912 Rites 21 Jul 1912
Geo. W. Snipes, M. G.

L. E. NORROD to Minnie GIBBS Issued 27 Jul 1912 Rites 27 Jul 1912
J. M. Green, J. P.

Oscar FOSTER to Hattie DENTON Issued 27 Jul 1912 Rites 28 Jul 1912
J. M. McGiboney, J. P.

Jesse Bonner (Col) to Jennie Belle RAMSEY (Col) Issued 27 Jul 1912 Rites 28 Jul1912
W. W. Locke, J. P.

W. A. WOODLEE to Charity WANNAMAKER Issued 27 Jul 1912 Rites 28 Jul 1912
L. V. scott, J. P.

A. B. AUSTIN to Sopha McGREGOR Issued 30 Jul 1912 Rites 31 Jul 1912
W. S. Grissom. J. P.

Wilson ALLEN to Maggie EPPERSON Issued 31 Jul 1912 Rites 1 Aug 1912
S. T. Byars, M. G.

Thurman REDMON to Callie TITISWORTH Issued 1 Aug 1912 Rites 4 Aug 1912
P. G. Moore, J. P.

Andrew St. JOHN to Ida VANCE Issued 3 Aug 1912 Rites 4 Aug 1912
J. D. Hash, J. P.

Charlie BOUNDS to Annie ADCOCK Issued 3 Aug 1912 Rites 4 Aug 1912
P. G. Potter, M. G.

Walter BROWN to Lottie CROUCH Issued 8 Aug 1912 Rites 8 Aug 1912
W. N. Kell, J. P.

John THATCH to Vera DAVIS Issued 10 Aug 1912 Rites 11 Aug 1912
Geo. H. Gilbert, M. G.

Frank ELKINS to Violet JOHNSON Issued 10 Aug 1912 Rites 15 Aug 1912
Frank Michael, J. P.

John RIGSBY to Bettie Mary Ethel DYER Issued 13 Aug 1912 Rites 18 Aug 1912
Frank Michael, J. P.

R. C. CUNNINGHAM to Fronia PASSONS Issued 16 Aug 1912 Rites 18 Aug 1912
J. W. Cooley, M. G.

Roy NORTHCUTT to Cleo MORROW Issued 17 Aug 1912 Rites 18 Aug 1912
J. L. Thaxton, J. P.

Charley TRUSTY to Velma ROSS Issued 21 Aug 1912 Rites 27 Aug 1912
J. T. Turner

Clarence KIRBY to Jennie GIBBS Issued 21 Aug 1912 Rites 25 Aug 1912
W. P. Davis, J. P.

John W. McGREGOR to Bertha WOMACK Issued 22 Aug 1912 Rites 28 Aug 1912
Joe Pennington, J. P.

T. A. BOTTOMS to Leta CRAIN Issued 27 Aug 1912 Rites 28 Aug 1912
H. T. McGregor, J. P.

Robert McBEE to Ethel SWEARENGEN Issued 30 Aug 1912 Rites 1 Sep 1912
J. L. Thaxton, J. P.

Jack MARBERRY (Col) to Della LIST (Col) Issued 31 Aug 1912 Rites 1 Sep 1912
S. J. Beasley, M. G.

Jim MITCHELL to Ella WOMACK Issued 31 Aug 1912 Rites 1 Sep 1912
Wm. A. Bell, J. P.

Ed DRIVER to Mattie BENNETT issued 2 Sep 1912 Rites 3 Sep 1912
Geo. L. Beech, J. P.

Wm. M. CUMMINGS to Mrs. Aggie SNIPES Issued 2 Sep 1912 Rites 4 Sep 1912
J. W. Cooley, M. G.

J. S. PORTER to Laura Agness OLIVER Issued 3 Sep 1912 Rites 4 Sep 1912
W. P. Davis, J. P.

A. B. F. MURRAY (Col) to Blanche WOODLEE (Col) Issued 3 Sep 1912 Rites 3 Sep 1912
W. A. Rogers, M. G.

Forrest PHIFER to Mary L. BOYD Issued 4 Sep 1912 Rites 4 Sep. 1912
A. J. McBride, M. G.

V. H. HOPKINS (Col) to Vira BAKER (Col) Issued 7 Sep 1912 Rites 7 Sep 1912
S. J. Bensley, M. G.

SAm HENNESSEE to Alyenne SIMPSON Issued 12 Sep 1912 Rites 12 Sep 1912
D. E. Hinkle, M. G.

Aaron DYER to Josie ORRICK Issued 13 Sep 1912 Rites 15 Sep 1912
A. Z. Holder, J. P.

Tom UNDERWOOD to Jessie MANNING Issued 20 Sep 1912 Rites 20 Sep 1912
J. B. Brown, J. P.

Jett MASEY to Dollie BAILEY issued 20 Sep 1912 Not Returned

Willie HOLLAND (Col) to Blanche MARTIN (Col) Issued 21 Sep 1912 Rites 21 Sep 1912
G. L. Burch, J. P.

Enoch SMITH to Mollie FUSTON Issued 22 Sep 1912 Rites 22 Sep 1912
G. L. Beech, J. P.

William DELONG to Winnie Caroline WHITE Issued 27 Sep 1912 Not Returned

E. D. BENNETT to Della JARRELL Issued 3 Oct 1912 Rites 6 Oct 1912
O. H. Wood, J. P.

John PATRICK to Mrs. HAttie PATRICK Issued 6 Oct 1912 Rites 6 Oct 1912
J. B. Brown, J. P.

J. F. MELTON to Sallie E. GRIBBLE Issued 9 Oct 1912 Rites 9 Oct 1912
L. R. Hogan, M. G.

Ebb DUNCAN to Ida WILLIAMSON Issued 10 Oct 1912 Rites 13 Oct 1912
A. Z. Holder, J. P.

Henry DUNCAN (Col) to Florence DURLEY (Col) Issued 14 Oct 1912 Rites 16 Oct 1912
J. S. Nance

D. H. LEDBETTER to Rachel QUALLS Issued 18 Oct 1912 Rites 27 Oct 1912
J. B., Dobbs, J. P.

R. H. HALE to Flora KELLEY Issued 19 Oct 1912 Rites 23 Oct 1912
Lonnie Cubbins, M,. G.

E. F. CUNNINGHAM to Jane MITCHELL Issued 25 Oct 1912 Rites 27 Oct 1912
J. W. Cooley, M. G.

Dewitt SMITH to Gertie DEBERRY Issued 25 Oct 1912 Rites 27 Oct 1912
W. C. Lorance, J. P.

James BAKER to Ather MCGIBBONEY Issued 26 Oct 1912 Rites 29 Oct 1912
J. D. Quick, J. P.

Cheatam REEDER to R. Vena Elizabeth KEATON Issued 1 Nov 1912 Rites 3 Nov 1912
J. W. Cooley, M. G.

W. G. PARSLEY to Pearl WILSON Issued 2 Nov 1912 Rites 3 Nov 1912
A. Z. Holder, J. P.

William COLWELL to Alice JONES Issued 6 Nov 1912 Rites 9 Nov 1912
P. G. Potter, M. G.

Charlie BRIGHT to Carrie COPE Issued 8 Nov 1912 Rites 8 Nov 1912
J. L.Smith, J. P.

Denton MOONEYHAM to MAggie SAFLEY Issued 9 Nov 1912 Rites 10 Nov 1912
J. D. Hash, J. P.

Ralph McCULLOCH to Jessie WOOTEN Issued 9 Nov 1912 Rites 12 Nov 1912
John B. Cowden, M. G.

Jim RUTLEDGE to Maude TRAWICK Issued 12 Nov 1912 Rites 14 Nov 1912
J. D. Hash, J. P.

SAm PASSONS to Sallie PAYNE Issued 16 Nov 1912 Rites 17 Nov 1912
C. M. Collier, J. P.

Edward BONNER (Col) to Bessie SMARTT (Col) Issued 16 Nov 1912 Rites 16 Nov 1912
J. B. Dobbs, J. P.

Frank CROUCH to Gracie BASHAM Issued 23 Nov 1912 Rites 24 Nov. 1912
G. P. Brasier, J. P.

R. E. MARTIN to Kate ARNATTE Issued 27 Nov 1912 Rites 27 Nov 1912
T. W. Noland, M. G.

Stanley WILLIAMS to Jessie PATTON Issued 27 Nov 1912 Rites 3 Dec 1912
J. L. Jones, M. G.

Landy TEMPLETON to Beulah SAFLEY Issued 30 Nov 1912 Rites 1 Dec 1912
J. D. Hash, J. P.

Clarence McGEE to Earsie BOTTOMS Issued 30 Nov 1912 Rites 1 dec 1912
A. C. Myers, J. P.

R. L. COMER to Octa WOMACK Issued 2 Dec 1912 Rites 2 dec 1912
J. C. Odum

I. F. McPEAK to Florence WOMACK Issued 3 dec 1912 Rites 5 dec 1912
Jeremiah Mullican, M. G.

Frank L. KIRBY to Mary Belle CHASTAIN Issued 7 Dec 1912 Rites 8 dec 1912
J. W. Cooley, M. G.

W. V. DUNLAP to Ophia COPE Issued 10 dec 1912 Rites 25 Dec 1912
P. G. Moore, M. G.

W. H. MILRANEY to Matilda BOULDIN Issued 14 Dec 1912 Rites 15 Dec 1912
C. M. Collier, J. P.

Roy MITCHELL to Annie FARLESS Issued 14 Dec 1912 Rites 15 Dec 1912
L. G. Patrick, J. P.

Clayborn TAYLOR (Col) to Parlee MARBERRY (Col) issued 18 Dec 1912 Rites 18 dec 1912
S. J. Beasley, M. G.

Charlie HARDIN to Mattir TROGLIN Issued 21 Dec 1912 Rites 21 Dec 1912
G. L. Beech, J. P.

Elihue ELAM to Beulah TODD Issued 21 Dec 1912 Rites 25 dec 1912
J. C. Smoot, J. P.

Farmer J. WILLIS to Lillie May TAYLOR Issued 21 Dec 1912 Rites 24 Dec 1912
C. M. Epps

W. C. DAVIS to Venie SHELTON Issued 24 Dec 1912 Rites 25 Dec 1912
L. G. Patrick, J. P.

Bob CUNNINGHAM to Ethel FARLESS Issued 24 Dec 1912 Rites 25 dec 1912
H. T. McGregor, J. P.

W. T. MULLICAN to Gracie Pearl CLARK Issued 24 Dec 1912 Rites 25 Dec 1912
John B. Cowden. M. G.

Charlie MUNCY to Barshie NUNLEY Issued 24 Dec 1912 Rites 25 Dec 1912
J. L. Thaxton, J. P.

Elsie MARTIN (Col) to Ethel MARTIN (Col) Issued 24 Dec 1912 Rites 24 Dec 1912
J. B. Dobbs, J. P.

W. A. GRIBBLE (Col) to Queen Ester WINTON (Col) Issued 26 Dec 1912 Rites 27 Dec1912
C. M. Epps

Arthur J. SHADOW to Annie E. WOOTEN Issued 3 Feb 1913 Rites 4 Feb 1913
L. B. Jones, M. G.

M. A. BONNER to Minnie BLACKBURN Issued 6 Feb 1913 Rites 6 Feb 1913
L. G. Patrick, J. P.

J. Edward KIDD to Gladys ARGO Issued 5 Feb 1913 Rites 9 FEB !(!#
Rouchen Horton, M. G.

Kelley MITCHELL to Malvina GANN Issued 6 Feb 1913 Rites6 Feb 1913
L. G. Patrick, J. P.

Beecher WANNAMAKER to Ollie COPPINGER Issued 14 Feb 1913 Rites 16 Feb 1913
Taylor Perry, J. P.

Claud MEEKS to Savannah BONNER Issued 18 Feb 1913 Rites 27 Feb 1913
W. T. Barnes, J. P.

Luke FAULKNER to Beulah MARTIN Issued 18 Feb 1913 Rites 18 Feb 1913
J. S. NAnce

T. J. TAYLOR to Ida JOHNSON Issued 22 Feb 1913 Rites 23 Feb 1913
A. C. Myers, J. P.

F. M. GARNER to Maggie GREEN Issued 27 Feb 1913 Rites 28 Feb 1913
P. G. Moore, J. P.

E. H. WEBB to Ethel BOYD Issued 28 Feb 1913 Rites 2 MAr 1913
L. C. Lane, J. P.

Joe MASON to Vesta SHUSTER Issued 11 MAr 1913   Not Returned

Roy SMITH to Belle CROUCH Issued 12 Mar 1913 Rites 12 Mar 1912
O. H. Wood, J. P.

J. H. GRIBBLE to Clara PRIEST Issued 12 Mar 1913 Rites 13 MAr 1913
C. M. Collier, J. P.

H. M. CAGLE to Millie TURNER issued 15 Mar 1913 Rites 16 Mar 1913
Taylor Perry, J. P.

Charles SENEKER to Alice STROUD Issued 19 Mar 1913 Rites 20 MAr 1913
J. R. Stubblefield, M. G.

George TURNER to Laura TURNER Issued 20 Mar 1913 Rites 20 Mar 1913
J. F. Martin, J. P.

J. E. RAYBURN to Clyda BLACKBURN Issued 22 Mar 1913 Rites 22 Mar 1913
L. G. Patrick, J. P.

Robert ORRICK (ART) to Nettie McVEY Issued 29 Mar 1913 Rites 30 Mar 1913
W. S. Grissom, J. P.

Frank C. GARNER to Minnie CALLAHAN Issued 27 MAr 1913 Rites 30 Mar 1913
C. M. Epps

Leslie RAMSEY (Col) to Carrie RICE (Col) Issued 30 Mar 1913 Rites 30 Mar 1913
H. L. Walling, M. G.

Rance MARTIN to Etta JONES Issued 26 Dec 1912 Rites 29 dec 1912
W. S. Grissom, J. P.

B. M. DOWNING to Lizzie SWOAP Issue 28 dec 1912 Rites 31 Dec 1912
J. T. CaSET, M. G.

Rufus RAINS to Dovie YOUNG Issued 28 Sep. 1912 Rites 1 Jan 1913
J. A. Cunningham, M. G.

Leslie H. JUSTICE to Effie TAYLOR Issued 28 Dec 1912 Rites 1 JAn 1913
John B. Cowden. M. G.

A. M. SCOTT to Emma HALEY Issued 31 Dec 1912 Rites 5 Jan 1913
A. Z. Holder, J. P.

J. W. YOUNG to Vester DEBERRY Issued 6 JAn 1913 Rites 12 JAn 1913
W. C. Lorance, J. P.

Hartwell TURNER to Becca SWINDLE Issued 10 Jan 1913 Rites 12 Jan 1913
J. L. Jones, M. G.

J. M. CANTRELL to Zena MARTIN Issued 10 JAn 1913 Rites 12 Jan 1913
J. L. Smith, J. P.

Rush MATLOCK (Col) to Catherine ADCOCK (Col) Issued 15 JAn 1913 Rites 15 Jan 19913
S. J. Beasley, M. G.

Warner BOYD to Clellie GREEN Issued 16 JAn 1913 Rites 19 JAn 1913
L. C. Lane, J. P.

A. D. BENNETT to Annie Mai MANSFIELD Issued 16 Jan 1913 Rites 17 JAn 1913
J. R. Stubblefeirld, M. G.

Frank TATE to GENIE ROGERS Issued 17 JAn 1913 Rites 19 JAn 1913
Taylor Perry, J. P.

Norman MOORE (Col) to Belle Dora FAULKNER (Col) Issued 17 JAn 1913 Rites 17 JAN
J. S. Nance

Isaac KEITH to Nancy RAYMOND Issued 23 JAn 1913 Rites 26 JAn 1913
W. A. Tramel, M. G.

Errie GLENN to Vistoria ASKEW Issued 23 JAn 1913 Rites 24 JAn 1913
J. M. Green, J. P.

John GARNER to Leva KIRBY Issued 25 JAn 1913 Rites 25 JAn 1913
R. L. Whitlock, M. G.

Will BRATCHER to Lula NEWBY Issued 25 JAn 1913 Rites 26 JAn 1913
J. T. Vinson, J. P.

James SAVAGE to Samantha JONES Issued 25 JAn 1913 Rites 25 JAn 1913
F. Bell, M. G.

H. C. BARKER to Edna WIMBERLY Issued 28 JAn 1913 Rites9 Feb 1913
J. W. Cooley, M. G.

O. B. SMITH to Vernie HALE Issued 28 JAn 1913 Rites 2 Feb 1913
Chas. T. Cates, M. G.

J. I. WALKER to Willia PASSON Issued 19 Jun 1913 Rites 22 Jun 1913
H. L. Jones, J. P.

J. L. PHILLIPS to Onie TURNER Issued 21 Jun 1913 Rites 7 Jun 1913
J. T. Vinson

Pete SCOTT (Col) to Harriet ADCOCK (Col) Issued 21 Jun 1913 Rites 21 Jun 1913
S. J. Beasley, M. G.

Luther BAKER (Col) to Ruby HIGGINBOTHAM (Col) Issued 22 Jun 1913 Rites 22 Jun 1913
S. J. Beasley, M. G.

George C. CARTER to May Burnam JONES Issued 30 Jun 1913 Rites 30 Jun 1913
T. W. Noland, M. G.

Thomas McGREGOR to Amanda BURKETT Issued 3 Jul 1913 Rites 4 Jul 1913
A. Z. Holder, J. P.

Robert HENDRIXSON to Tennie STILES Issued 5 Jul 1913 Rites 6 Jul 1913
J. M. Green, J. P.

Luther NUNLEY to Mary JAne JENNINGS Issued 5 Jul 1913 Rites 6 Jul 1913
TAylor Perry, J. P.

B. T. MARTIN (Col) to Lcla HUNTER (Col) Issued 5 Jul 1913 Rites 6 Jul 1913
S. J. Beasley, M. G.

W. P. CANTRELL to Mary BYARS Issued 15 Jul 1913 Rites 20 Jul 1913
P. G. Potter, M. G.

J. R. TRAMEL to Ada CANTRELL Issued 17 Jul 1913 Rites 20 Jul 1913
P. G. Moore, J. P.

Bob RHEA to Corlee SMARTT Issued 19 Jul 1913 Rites 19 Jul 1913
W. T. Barnes, J. P.

Erman VICKERS to Hassie SMITH Issued 19 Jul 1913 Rites 20 Jul 1913
J. P. Hughes, J. P.

Isaiah DURHAM to Martha GRAHAM Issued 19 Jul 1913 Rites 20 Jul 1913
J. B. Gribble, M. G.

I. R. RAINS to Minnie GRAHAM Issued 21 Jul 1913 Rites 21 Jul 1913
J. T. casey, M. G.

Lee BANKS to Jane NELSON Issued 24 Jul 1913 Rites 27 Jul 1913
L. G. patrick, J. P.

J. A. MADEWELL to Ethel McBRIDE Issued 21 Jul 1913 Rites 30 Jul 1913
J. L. Thaxton, J. P.

H. C. OVERTURFF to Edna COPPINGER Issued 26 Jul 1913 Rites 27 Jul 1913
L. G. Patrick, J. P.

Larkin PRIEST to Nannie GEORGE Issued 29 Jul 1913 Rites 4 Oct 1913
J. D. Quick, J. P.

J. M. CRAIN to Josie BOST Issued 11 Apr 1913 Rites 13 Mar 1913
J. S. Lawrence, J. P.

O. L. CUNNINGHAM to Jessie CRAWFORD Issued 12 Apr 1913 Rites 13 Apr 1913
J. B. Gribble

D. Matt CARR to Izora WOOD Issued 26 Apr 1913 Rites 27 Apr 1913
G. P. Brasier, J. P.

Jesse MADEWELL to Cleo CATHCART Issued 29 Apr 1913 Rites 30 Apr 1913
Taylor Perry, J. P.

Sandy JONES to Ellen BRADY Issued 30 Apr 1913 Rites 4 May 1913
H. L. Jones, J. P.

Joe M. COLLIER to Jennie RUST Issued 30 Apr 1913 Rites 3 May 1913
T. W. Noland, M. G.

Alfred MATHEWS to Willie YORK Issued 3 May 1913 Rites 11 May 1913
R. R. Tucker, M. G.

Harrison GANN to Mandy PARSLEY Issued 3 May 1913 Rites 3 May 1913
A. Z. Holder, J. P.

Herbert BAKER to Sarah TERRY Issued 10 May 1913 Rites 10 May 1913
J. H. Hillsman, M. G.

T. L. PEARSALL to Ada KIRBY Issued 17 May 1913 Rites 18 May 1913
E. G. Sewell, M. G.

Clelon BOREN to Osia MALONE Issued 17 May 1913 Rites 18 May 1913
J. M. Green, J. P.

E. D. NEWBY to Minnie PERKIN Issued 17 May 1913 Rites 18 May 1913
J. B. Dobbs, J. P.

James Armstrong LEEPER, Jr. to Virginia FAULKNER Issued 21 May 1913 Rites 22 May
L. R. Hogan, M. G.

Will ELKINS to Flora REEDER Issued 24 May 1913 Rites 25 May 1913
L. G. Patrick, J. P.

J. T. FISHER to Alta JUDKINS Issued 28 May 1913 Rites 29 May 1913
J. B. Dobbs, J. P.

J. E. WATSON to Belle BRADY Issued 30 MAy 1913 Rites 1 Jun 1913
H. L. Jones, J. P.

Luther MARSHALL (Col) to Lillie Mai SAIN (Col) Issued 3 Jun 1913 Rites 3 JUN 1913
S. J. Beasley, M. G.

Phillip BON DREAU to Abbie ELKNIS Issued 5 Jun 1913 Rites 5 Jun 1913
L. G. Patrick, J. P.

A. E. MASON to Lou JONES Issued 14 Jun 1913 Rites 16 Jun 1913
H. T. McGregor, J. P.

John ELKINS to Georgia CONLIN Issued 16 Jun 1913 Rites 16 Jun 1913
L. G. Patrick, J. P.

Joe WALLING (Col) to Hallie McREYNOLDS (Col) Issued 2 Aug 1913 Rites 3 Aug 1913
J. B. Booth, M. G.

Zollie SAFLEY to Ethel JACKSON Issued 2 Aug 1913 Rites 3 Aug 1913
J. M. Green, J. P.

Everett JONES (Col) to Fannie May BAKER (Col) Issued 3 Aug 1913 Rites 3 Aug 1913
S. J. Beasley, M. G.

F. H. KEITH to Georgia REEVES Issued 5 Aug 1913 Rites 5 Aug 1913
L. G. Patrick, J. P.

W. S. HILL to Alene MITCHELL Issued 8 Aug 1913 Rites 9 Aug 1913
O. E. Tallman, B. A.

Harvey ARNOLD to Mai YOUNG Issued 9 Aug 1913 Rites 10 Aug 1913
J. L. Smith, J. P.

George HILL to Audie COUCH Issued 9 Aug 1913 Rites 10 Aug 1913
P. G. Moore, J. P.

Dillar GWYNN (Col) to Ada BROWN (Col) Issued 9 Aug 1913 Rites 16 Aug 1913
J. L. Thaxton, J. P.

sam SMITH (Col) to Ora RICE (Col) Issued 9 Aug 1913 Rites 10 Aug 1910
J. B. Booth, M. G.

Will BROWN to Carrie WOODLEE Issued 12 Aug 1913 Rites 17 Aug 1913
A. P. Hill, J. P.

Newt RAINS to Florence CANTRELL Issued 14 Aug 1913 Rites 17 Aug 1913
J. A. Cunningham. M. G.

George RIGSBY to Martha PAGE Issued 15 Aug 1913 Rites 17 Aug 1917
A. Z. Holder, J. P.

George S, SIMONS to Victoria O'NEAL Issued 16 Aug 1913 Rites 17 Aug 1913
H. T. McGregor, J. P.

Bob PENNINGTON to Eunice REDMON Issued 16 Aug 1913 Rites 16 Aug 1913
J. B. Brown, J. P.

H. H. MARTIN to M. C. ADAMSON Issued 19 Aug 1913 Rites 20 Aug 1913
J. L. Jones, M. G.

Walter HENDERSON (Col) to Notie WOOD (Col) Issued 23 Aug 1913 Rites 24 Aug 1913
C. M. Collier, J. P.

Irving ROBERTS to Ethel QUICK Issued 23 Aug 1913 Rites 24 Aug 1913
J. D. Templeton, J. P.

John L. OFFICER (Col) to Florence J. LEE (Col) Issued 23 Aug 1913 Rites 24 Aug 1913
S. J. Beasley, M. G.

S. A. HALEY to Helen SPURLOCK Issued 27 Aug 1913 Rites 28 Aug 1913
W. P. davis, J. P.

Clyde PHILLIPS to Lela WOMACK Issued 30 Aug 1913 Rites 31 Aug 1913
P. G. Potter, M. G.

H. A. ARGO to Jessie FIFER Issued 30 Aug 1913 Rites 29 Aug 1913 ?
H. T. McGregor, J. P.

John WOODARD (Col) to Ada Belle SAVAGE (Col) Issued 31 Aug 1913 Rites 31 Aug 1913
S. J. Beasley, M. G.

J. C. NEWBY to A. M. WARREN Issued 4 Sep 1913 Rites 7 Sep 1913
P. G. Potter,

Enoch SAFLEY to Maggie ISREAL Issued 10 Sep 1913 Rites 11 Sep 1913
W. T. Barnes, J. P.

Jack DURHAM to Ella SIMONS Issued13 Sep 1913 Rites 14 Sep 1913
H. T. McGregor, J. P.

John Anderson MAYO to Cora Mai BURBAGE Issued 13 Sep 1913 Rites 14 Sep 1913
Geo. W. Gilbert, M. G.

Earnest WILSON to Dillie HOLDER Issued 13 Sep 1913 Rites 14 Sep 1913
W. C. Lorance, J. P.

Simpson DUNLAP to Bettie ADAIR Issued 16 Sep 1913 Rites 17 Sep 1913
T. A. MAthews

H. D. WILSON to Dochie WALKER Issued 20 Sep 1913 Rites 21 Sep 1913
J. A. Booher

W. P. LUSK to Elizabeth GRIZZLE Issued 20 Sep 1913 Rites 21 Sep 1913
T. W. Noland, M. G.

H. P. STUBBLEFIELD to Nora Belle HENNESSEE Issued 20 Sep 1913 Rites 21 Sep 1913
Price Billingsley, M. G.

J. A. MULLICAN to Lizzie McGREGOR Issued 22 Sep 1913 Rites 22 Sep 1913
L. G. Patrick, J. P.

C. P. BOTTOMS to Adelle GARDNER Issued 24 Sep 1913 Rites 25 Sep 1913
S. T. Byars, M. G.

Will CARR (Col) to Beulah LUSK (Col) Issued 30 Sep 1913 Rites 5 Oct 1913
C. M. Collier, J. P.

Fletcher MARTIN (Col) to Ada RITCHEY (Col) Issued 30 Sep 1913 Rites 30 Sep 1913
G. L. Beech, J. P.

Walter Raymond DANIELSON to Eliz. Evaston MELTON Issued 11 Oct 1913 Rites 12 Oct 19
S. T. Byars, M. G.

C. S. BARNES to Hilmer MARTIN Issued 13 Oct 1913 Rites 15 Oct 1913
W. C. Lorance, J. P.

I. E. CAMPBELL to Annia CAMPBELL Issued 15 Oct 1913 Rites 16 Oct 1913
J. T. Vinson, J. P.

Roy HARDCASTLE to Vela May VAN HOOSER Issued 16 Oct 1913 Rites 19 Oct 1913
C. M. Gleaves

Thurman STILES to Josephine GRIBBLE Issued 20 Dec 1913 Rites 21 Dec 1913
J. B. Gribble, M. G.

Joe RAINS to Dena YOUNG Issued 23 dec 1913 Rites 24 Dec 1913
J. A. Cunningham, M. G.

J. J. CANTRELL to Pearl GARNER Issued 23 dec 1913 Rites 25 Dec 1913
P. G. Moore, J. P.

John Cooper TUNE to Mai Winsett BUMPAS Issued 23 Dec 1913 Rites 24 dec 1913
L. B. Jamison, M. G.

F. V. BROWN to Ova MARLER Issued 24 dec 1913 Rites 25 dec 1913
S. T. Byars, M. G.

B. F. MYERS to Manerva PATTON Issued 24 dec 1913 Rites 24 Dec 1913
L. G. Patrick, J. P.

W. C. BURBAGE to Delia BYRD Issued 24 Dec 1913 Rites 25 dec 1913
J. C. Odum, M. G.

Oscar BOYD to Mary LYTLE Issued 24 Dec 1913 Rites 24 Dec 1913
E. L. Moffitt, J. P.

W. F. WELLS to Pearl MARTIN Issued 24 dec 1913 Rites 25 dec 1913
H. L. Jones, J. P.

Roy LUTRELL to Minnie HOLLANDSWORTH Issued 26 Dec 1913 Rites 26 Dec 1913
A. Z. Holder, J. P.

Walter HUGHES to Polly BRYANT Issued 26 Dec 1913 Rites 28 Dec 1913
W. P. dAVIS, J. P.

SAm NORTHCUTT to Zelma TIPTON Issued 27 dec 1913 Rites 27 dec 1913
A. P. Hill, J. P.

Jim GRIBBLE to Jennie COLLIER Issued 27 Dec 1913 Rites 27 Dec 1913
T. W. Noland, M. G.

Claude BREWER to Emma CATES Issued29 Dec 1913 Rites 29 Dec 1913
J. C. Smoot, J. P.

G. T. ODINEAL to Dala HENDRICKS Issued 1 JAn 1914 Rites 1 Jan 1914
G. L. Beech, J. P.

E. L. CANTRELL to Nannie CANTRELL Issued 17 JAn 1914 Rites 18 Jan 1914
P. G. Moore, J. P.

Clay GREEN to Florence TAYLOR Issued 17 JAn 1914 Rites 18 Jan 1914
J. R. Stubblefield, M. G.

Hugh SAIN to Ocie ODELL Issued 19 JAn 1914 Rites 19 JAn 1914
J. F. Martin, L. E.

Sam CONLIN to Lillie BOST Issued 20 Jan 1914 Rites 20 JAn 1914
L. G. Patrick, J. P.

Huston Grey PHILLIPS to Jennie LAFEVERS Issued 21 Jan 1914 Rites 21 Jan 1914
W. C. Lorance, J. P.

Tom REYNOLDS to Belle LOWE Issued 18 Oct 1913 Rites 18 Oct 1913
L. G. Patrick, J. P.

Nathan TROUPE to Maggie HUDSON Issued 4 Nov 1913 Rites 9 Nov 1913
L. C. Lane, J. P.

O. B. WOODARD to Willie E. WOMACK Issued 8 Nov 1913 Rites 8 Nov 1913
T. W. Noland, M. G.

G. Herman MOORE to Ulzo DUNLAP Issued 10 Nov 1913 Rites 10 Nov 1913
J. D. Hash, J. P.

J. H. MATHIS to Belle MULLIGAN Issued 12 Nov 1913 Rites.16 Nov 1913
H. L. Jones, J. P.

Dave RAMSEY (Col) to Fannie SCOTT (COL) Issued 14 Nov 1913 Rites 15 Nov 1913
G. P. Brasier, J. P.

Hugh WINTON (Col) to Walsie MERCER (COL) Issued 17 Nov 1913 Rites 17 Nov 1913
George Lee

Jesse CHRISTIAN to Nettie RHEA Issued 17 Nov 1913 Rites 23 Nov 1913
E. L. Moffitt, J. P.

Franklin Potter BLUE to Phronia Ida WILLIAMS Issued 20 Nov 1913 Rites 20 Nov 1913
F. H. Harlan, M,. G.

Elijah McCORMICK to Cora SLAUGHTER Issued 22 Nov 1913 Rites 30 Nov 1913
E. L. Moffitt, J. P.

Edd WOOTEN (Col) to Ethel McGEHEE (Col) Issued 24 Nov 1913 Rites 27 Nov 1913
George Lee

Wade WOOTEN (Col) to Ester BLUE (Col) Issued 29 Nov 1913 Rites 11 Dec 1913
J. S. Nance, M. G.

Herbert LOCKE (Col) to Bettie BLUE (Col) Issued 29 Nov 1913 Rites 29 Nov 1913
S. J. Busey

Aubry YOUNG to Vera WOMACK Issued 4 Dec 1913 Rites 12 Dec 1913
J. L. Smith, J. P.

Otie CUMMINGS to Eva TITTSWORTH Issued 9 Dec 1913 Rites 14 dec 1913
P. G. Moore, J. P.

Hervey BROWN (Col) to Allie SAVAGE (Col) Issued 13 Dec 1913 Rites 14 Dec 1913
W. C. Lorance, J. P.

Hartford MATHERLY to Ida BENNETT Issued 15 Dec 1913 Rites 15 Dec 1913
J. B. Dobbs, J. P.

G.T. BRIGHT to Mattie BLANKENSHIP Issued 16 Dec 1913 Rites 17 Dec 1913
J. L. Smith, J. P.

G. R. LOCKE to Mattie Belle ROWLAND Issued 20 Dec 1913 Rites 20 Dec 1913
J. L. Smith, J. P.

Richard SIMMONS to Tennie BREWER Issued 21 Jan 1914 Rites 22 Jan 1914
W. C. Lorance, J. P.

G. D. ROMANS to May CUNNINGHAM Issued 23 JAn 1914 Rites 25 JAn 1914
I. W. Parish

Howell Madison CARNEY to Althea Fay HUGHES Issued 27 JAn 1914 Rites 29 JAn 1914
T. W. Noland, M. G.

Hugh WOOD to Stella COPPINGER Issued 31 Jan 1914 Rites 1 Feb 1914
J. F. Martin, L. E.

M. C. GREEN to Nora PARKER Issued 5 Feb 1914 Rites 5 Feb 1914
J. B. Dobbs, J. P.

Obey TURNER to Malissie MORTON Issued 6 Feb 1914 Rites 6 Feb 1914
J. B. Dobbs, J. P.

Arren YORK to Delia TEMPLES Issued 7 Feb 1914 Rites 8 Feb 1914
J. A. Cunningham, M. G.

Ben BATES to Pearl WOODLEE Issued 7 Feb 1914 Not Returned

H. J. STANLEY to Sarah WALKER Issued 11 Feb 1914 Rites 11 Feb 1914
H. L. Jones, J. P.

A. W. GRISSOM to Leslie GREEN Issued 14 feb 1914 Rites 15 Feb 1914
A. P. Hill, J. P.

Royce HOBBS to Leta Mai EARLS Issued 16 Feb 1914 Rites 16 Feb 1914
G. L. Beech, J. P.

Guy TAYLOR toCarrie HUTCHINGS Issued 16 Feb 1914 Rites 16 Feb 1914
J. A. Booher, J. P.

Charlie DAVIS ro Mellie BRIGHT Issued 16 Feb 1914 Rites 18 Feb 1914
J. M. Green, J. P.

J. F. WILLIAMS to Blackston Orgen NORTON Issued 25 Feb 1914 Rites 1 Mar 1914
P. G. Potter, J. P.

A. CURTIS to Catherine TAYLOR Issued 27 Feb 1914 Rites 28 Feb 1914
E. L. Moffitt, J. P.

Evan LANE to Minnie COTTON Issued 28 Feb 1914 Rites 1 Mar 1914
L. C. Lane, J. P.

J. J. WOODLEE to Esther MARTIN Issued 2 Mar 1914 Rites 3 Mar 1914
A. P. Hill, J. P.

Rollie WOOTEN to Lee BANKS Issued 6 Mar 1914 Rites 8 Mar 1914
J. P. Hughes, J. P.

J. M. TAYLOR to Buelah QUALLS Issued 10 Mar 1914 Rites 12 Mar 1914
J. P. Hughes

Tullie TOSH to Lillie PEPPER Issued 14 Mar 1914 Rites not solemnized

R. D. RUSSELL (Col) to Laura MARBERRY (Col) Issued 16 Mar 1914 Rites 16 Mar 1914
J. S. Nance, M. G.

Frank COATS to Clara HOBBS Issued 16 Mar 1914 Rites 18 Mar 1914
J. L. Thaxton, J. P.

Marshall FOWLER to Hester COPPINGER Issued 21 Mar 1914 Rites 22 Mar 1914
A. P. Hill, J. P

Henry Spurgeon VAN DEREN to Josephine LIVELY Issued 24 Mar 1914 Rites 24 Mar 1914
R. W. Binkley, M. G.

Joe W.DEAKINS to Eunice BROWN Issued 24 Mar 1914 Rites 25 Mar 1914
Cliff M. Epps

John SMITH to Mattie EDGE Issued 25 Mar 1914 Rites 29 Mar 1914
J. M. Green, J. P.

Leon McGREGOR to Annie Lee GRIBBLE Issued 31 Mar 1914 Rites 31 Mar 1914
L. G. Patrick, J. P.

W. A. SMITH to Lucy J. SMITH Issued 1 Apr 1914 Rites 1 Apr 1914
G. L. Beech, J. P.

Minus HENDRICKS to Clara GRIMES Issued 8 Apr 1914 Rites 8 Apr 1914
Truman L. Pearsall

Will MILLER (Col) to Ras STONE (Col) Issued 8 Apr 1914 Rites 8 Apr 1914
J. S. Nance, M. G.

Theodore WILLIAMS to Emma JONES Issued 11 Apr 1914 Rites 15 Apr 1915
W. P. Davis, J. P.

Levi BARNES to Josie JONES Issued 11 Apr 1914 Rites 12 Apr 1914
Price Billingsley, M. G.

Henry JOHNSON to Della ELKINS Issued 11 Apr 1914 Rites 12 Apr 1914

J. M. FREED to Geneva SNIPES Issued 17 Apr 1914 Rites 21 Apr 1914
G. W. Snipes, M. G.

Roy WOOD to Wavie MYERS Issued 18 Apr 1914 Rites 19 Apr 1914
H. T. McGregor, J. P.

Robert REDMON to Ovie SUMMERS Issued 28 Apr 1914 Rites 5 May 1914
P. G. Potter, M. G.

Jim WEBB to Bessie McCORMACK Issued 2 May 1914 Not Returned

Alfred BOYD to Willie JENNINGS Issued 2 May 1914 Rites 3 May 1914
E. L. Moffitt, J. P.

Will HUNTLEY to Winnie BONNER Issued 5 MAY !(!$ Rites 12 May 1914
J. L. Thaxton, J. P.

James M. MARTIN to Fannie WHEELER Issued 6 May 1914 Rites 7 May 1914
J. F. Martin, L. E.

T. R. COLWELL to Tillie PEDEN Issued 7 May 1914 Rites 10 May 1914
J. T. Vinson, J J P.

A. B. MOFFITT to Ida KELL Issued 7 May 1914 Rites10 May 1914
S. T. Byars, M. G.

George DAVIS to Octa McBRIDE Issued 9 May 1914 Rites 10 May 1914
Claud Myers, M. G.

S. A. SHIPP to Bessie CRAIN Issued 9 May 1914 Rites 10 May 1914
S. F. Sims, M. G.

Fred M. TURNEY (TIERNEY) to Florence JONES Issued 14 May 1914 Rites 14 May 1914
L. R. Hogan, M. G.

Miles MUNCY to Martha GREEN Issued 16 May 1914 Rites 17 May 1914
J. L. Thaxton, J. P.

Cass Collier to Florence M. SMITH Issued 16 May 1914 Rites 17 May 1914
W. S. Grissom, J. P.

Jewell MULLICAN to Maud WARE Issued 3 Jun 1914 Rites 3 Jun 1914
J. B. Dobbs, J. P.

Ransom Burks (Col) to Mollie MARTIN (Col) Issued 3 Jun 1914 Rites 3 Jun 1914
J. T. Turner, J. P.

Arthur CROUCH to Emma HILLIS Issued 6 Jun 1914 Rites 7 Jun 1914
G. P. Brasier, J. P.

Elia BROWN to Mary GIBBS Issued 6 Jun 1914 Rites 7 Jun 1914
J. J. Meadows, J. P.

Charles Higginbotham to Ada Mai Farless Issued 8 Jun 1914 rites 13 jun 1914
T. L. Pearsall

W. M. HOWLAND (Col) to Ella Mai ROACH (Col) Issued 13 Jun 1914 Rites 14 Jun 1914
G. W. Dunham, J. P.

Brack MALONE to Lula BYARS Issued 13 Jun 1914 Rites 14 Jun 1914
T. L. Pearsall

W. T. EUBANK to Margarette MULLICAN Issued 13 Jun 1914 Rites 14 Jun 1914
S. F. sims, M. G.

Henry RICHARDSON (Col) to Ada MASEY (Col) Issued 20 Jun 19014 Rites 21 Jun 1914
F. M. Story, M. G.

J. E. SMITH ot Katie KILIAN Issued 26 Jun 1914 Rites 28 Jun 1914
J. W. Gross, M. G.

H. M. FENNELL to Belle ROACH Issued 27 Jun 1914 Rites 28 Jun 1914
J. W. Cooley, M. G.

Ewing GREEN to Amanda GEORGE Issued 27 Jun 1914 Rites 28 Jun 1914
A. J. McBride, M. G.

C. W. NAYLOR to Sallie Joe LORING Issued 29 Jun 1914 Rites 30 Jun 1914
P. G. Potter, J. P.

Claud GREEN to Linniw MORROW Issued 30 Jun 1914 Rites 2 Jul 1914
A. P. Hilli, J. P.

Ross WINSTON (Col) to Hattie MARBERRY (Col) Issued 2 JUL 1914 Rites 2 JUL 1914
F. M. Story, M. G.

Sam FARLEY to MATTIE WHITE Issued3 Jul 1914 Rites 4 Jul 1914
L. Safley, M. G.

Dan BEATY to Louisa SLATTON Issued 4 Jul 1914 Rites 4 Jul 1914
J. F. Turner, J. P.

Horace DODD to Lou GAMBLE Issued4 Jul 1914 Rites 5 Jul 1914
G. W. Snipes, M. G.

James Lee MITCHELL to Rosa GLENN Issued 10 Jul 1014 Rites 12 Jul 1914
P. G. Moorc, J. P.

George HENNESSEE to Mallie GREEN Issued 10 Jul 1914 Rites 11 Jul 1914
A. P. Hill, J. P.

H. C. WHITEAKER to Dona STAFFORD Issued 11 Jul 1914 Rites 12 Jul 1914
J. A. Booher, J. P.

Joe JONES to Cass CATON Issued 16 JUL 1914 Rites 16 Jul 1914
J. L. Smith, J. P.

Dee BUSEY to Cynthia HOLDER Issued 16 Jul 1914 Rites 17 Jul 1914
H. L. Jones, J. P.

Grady MSRTIN to Nola Belle NEWBY Issued 25 Jul 1914 Rites 26 Jul 1914
G. H. Atnip, M. G.

H. F. COPE to Myrtle PHELPS Issued 25 Jul 1914 Rites 26 Jul 1914
H. T. McGregor, J. P.

Earnest MILLER to Aggie Belle BOST Issued 25 Jul 1914 Rites 27 Jul 1914
J. B. Dobbs, J. P.

Joe ANDERSON to Willie CATES Issued 25 Jul 1914 Rites 26 Jul 1914
J. C. Smoot, J. P.

Hardie COPE (Col) to Jessie MASEY (Col) Issued 25 Jul 1914 Rites 4 Oct 1914
A. P. Hill, J. P.

S. T. GIBBS to Hilda GREEN Issued 31 Jul 1914 Rites 1 Aug 1914
I. D. Walker, .. G.

Byron MITCHELL to Winnie COOLEY Issued 1 Aug 1914 Rites 2 Aug 1914
J. T. Cacoy, M. C.

Frank BOTTOMS to Mary GRISSOM Issued 1 Aug 1914 Rites 2 Aug 1914
H. L. McGregor, J. P.

O. D. STUBBLEFIELD to Laura Lee JUSTICE Issued 8 Aug 1914 Rites 9 Aug 1914
J. F. Martin, LJ E.

Mack STUBBLEFIELD to Annie BARNES Issued 15 Aug 1914 Rites 15 Aug 1915 H. T. McGregor, J. P.

T. C. NEWBY to Letha DEBERRY Issued 15 Aug 1914 Rites 16 Aug 1914 J. T. Vinson

Rufus WOMACK (Col) to Susie SPURLOCK (Col) Issued 15 Aug 1914 Rites 16 Aug 1914 Geo. T. Boldin, M. G.

R. B. HENDRICKSON to Sarah SIMPSON Issued 22 Aug 1914 Rites 22 Aug 1914 J. B. Dobbs, J. P.

Joe HENNESSEE to SALLIE WEBB Issued 22 Aug 1914 Rites 23 Aug 1914 S. T. Byars, M. G.

James BASHAM to G. Noby BASHAM Issued 29 Aug 1914 Rites 30 Aug 1914 J. L. Thaxton, J. P.

Harry McCLAIN to Bertie MERRIMAN Issued 29 Aug 1914 Rites 2 Sep 1914 J. ... Stubblefield, M. G.

A. O. WOODS to Bertha ELROD Issued 29 Aug 1914 Rites 30 Aug 1914 J. T. Turner, J. P.

Oscar BOREN to Tennie GIBBS Issued 1 Sep 1914 Rites 2 Sep 1914 J. L. Smith, J. P.

Horace HALE to Vernice CUBBINS Issued 4 Sep 1914 Rites 6 Sep 1914 J. D. Quick, J. P.

Robert ELLIOT to Martha BOYD Issued 5 Sep 1914 Rites 6 Sep 1914 J. J. Meadows, J. P.

Oris Mai BROWN to Willie May DEAKINS Issued 5 Sep 1914 Rites 6 Sep 1914 Price Billingsley, M. G.

Henry ANDERSON to Maggie SMOOT Issued 5 Sep 1914 Rites 6 Sep 1914 J. C. Smoot, J. P.

H. H. POTTER to Prudie THOMPKINS Issued 5 Sep 1914 Rites 6 Sep 1914 J. M. Green, J. P.

Tom MARTIN (Col) to Mart MARTIN (Col) Issued 5 Sep 1914 Rites 5 Sep 1914 J. S. Nance, M. G.

Will SNIPES to Lydia TAYLOR Issued 11 Sep 1914 Rites 13 Sep 1914 J. C. Odum, M. G.

Albert TEMPLETON to Annis MARTIN Issued 12 Sep 1911 Rites 13 Sep 1914 J. W. Cooley, M. G.

A. V. PACK to Lizzie DURHAM Issued 13 Sep 1914 Rites 13 Sep 1914 J. B. Gribble, M. G.

Bill DAVIS to Hassie PATTON Issued 19 Sep 1914 Rites 19 Sep 1914 L. G. Patrick, J. P.

Lee WOODS (Col) to Lillie SCOTT (Col) Issued 19 Sep 1914 Rites 20 Sep 1914 G. P. Brasier. J. P.

Wallace BARNES to Lee HILL Issued 15 Sep 1914 Rites 27 Sep 1914 A. P. Hilli, J. P.

Henry CANTRELL to Ella REDMON Issued 25 Sep 1914 Rites 27 Sep 1914 P. G. Moore, J. P.

Jodie PATRICK to Cora ROGERS Issued 26 Sep 1914 Rites 27 Sep 1914 L. G. Patrick, J. P.

Jeff GARNER to Sarah ROGERS Issued 2 Oct 1914 Rites 4 Oct 1914 J. C. Duncan, M. G.

John BLAIR to Elizabeth SMITH Issued 2 Oct 1914 Rites 4 Oct 1914 W. H. Hammer, J. P.

W. Hozie JULIAN to Jessie Christian PRESTON Issued 2 Oct 1914 Rites 4 Oct 1914 I. W. Parish

Bob McBRIDE to Flora WIMBERLY Issued 3 Oct 1914 Rites 4 Oct 1914 J. L. Thaxton, J. P.

Charlie CUNNINGHAM to Josie Lena QUICK Issued 3 Oct 1914 Rites 4 Oct 1914 B. S. McCollum, J. P.

Roy JORDAN to Ethel WILLIAMSON Issued 10 Oct 1914 Rites 19 Oct 1914 S. T. Byars, M. G.

Bob CRAWLEY to Elithe BONNER Issued 10 Oct 1914 Rites 11 Oct 1914 J. C. Smoot, J. P.

Jim HOLDER to Attie CRAIN Issued 10 Oct 1914 Rites 11 Oct 1914 J. M. Green, J. P.

J. B. WOMACK to Pearl AMENT Issued 12 Oct 1914 Rites 20 Oct 1914 L. C. Lane, J. P.

John C. PAGE to Katherine Mering BOSTICK Issued 15 Oct 1914 Rites 15 Oct 1914 T. W. Noland, M. G.

W. T. ROBINGSON to Effie CRIPP Issued 16 Oct 1914 Rites 23 Oct 1914 H. L. Jones, J. P.

Horace ARGO to Shellie NORTHCUTT Issued 16 Oct 1914 Rites 25 Oct 1914 W. T. Barnes, J. P.

Jonah NUNNELLY to Ethel TURNER Issued 16 Oct 1914 Returned - Not Solemnized

C. W. MOONEYHAM to Annie MULLICAN Issued 17 Oct 1914 Rites 18 Oct 1914 L. C. Lane, J. P.

Cooper FERRELL to Etta ANDERSON Issued 17 Oct 1914 Rites 17 Oct 1914 W. H. Hammer, J. P.

Johnson HILL to Alma FINGER Issued 5 Dec 1914 Rites 6th Dec 1914
T. W. Noland, M. G.

W. A. THAXTON to Nannie Lee BELL Issued 5 Dec 1914 Rites 13 Dec 1914
S. T. Byars, M. G

B. F. TRAWICK to Ella JARRELL Issued6 Dec 1914 Rites 12 Dec 1914
J. F. Martin, M. G.

Byran KEEK to Rena JARRELL Issued 7 Dec 1914 Rites 7 Dec 1914
L. G. Potter, J. P.

Elijah SIMS to Susan GARNER Issued 8 Dec 1914 Rites 10 Dec 1914
J. A. Cunningham, M. G.

Jesse TURNER to Estelle Lee GREEN Issued 11 Dec 1914 Rites 11 Dec 1914
H. T. McGregor, J. P.

W. C. TURNER to Delia MARKUM Issued 12 Dec 1914 Rites 13 Dec 1914
W. H. Hammer, J. P.

Will LYNCH to Mabel STOTTS Issued 18 Dec 1914 Rites 20 Dec 1914
G. P. Brasier, J. P.

W. T. GILLENTINE to Vera BREWER Issued 19 Dec 1914 Rites 20 Dec 1914
J. C. Smoot, J. P.

Shelie ISBELL (Col) to Nora PINKERTON (Col) Issued19 Dec 1914 Rites 20 Dec 1914
W. A. Johnson, M. G.

Martin WISEMAN to Mary MAXWELL Issued 22 Dec 1914 Rites 30 Dec 1914
A. P. Hill, J. P.

James GILLEY to Allie CUNNINGHAM Issued22 Dec 1914 Rites 22 Dec 1914
J. C. Duncan, M. G.

F. C. HORNER to Mary TYREE Issued 22 Dec 1914 Rites 23 Dec 1914
Price Billingsley, M. G.

W. F. YORK to Lurah Pearl MURPHY Issued 23 DEC !(!$ Rites 23 Dec 1914
Jno. B. Cowden, M. G.

Basil CLARK to Lina WOMACK Issued 24 Dec 1914 Rites 24 Dec 1914
J. C. Calhoun, M. G.

Herman COLLIER to Nola CLARK Issued 24 Dec 1914 Rites 24 Dec 1914
J. C.

W. F. WILSON to Robie SMITH Issued 25 Dec 1914 Rites 25 Dec 1915
J. C. Calhoun, M. G.

W. F. ELLEDGE to Nannie MARTIN Issued 26 Dec 1914 Rites 26 Dec 1914
S. F. Sims

Charles Hardie MOORE to Constance Maxine SEDBERRY Issued 26 Dec 1914 Rites28 Dec
F. W. Muse, M. G.

Henry HAMILTON (c) to Laura Wilson (Col) Issued 17 Oct 1914 Rites 18 Oct 1914
G. W. Dunham, J. P.

EL. L. WOOD to Cora MOORE Issued 17 Oct 1914 Rites 18 Oct 1914
J. R. Stubblefield, M. G.

James T. ALLEN to Rubie HOLDER Issued 17 Oct 1914 Rites 18 Oct 1914
W. H. Hammer, J. P.

Cleve DENTON to Metie KELLEY Issued19 Oct 1914 Rites 25 Oct 1914
G. H. Atnip, J. P.

W. B. SPURLOCK to Mollie KNIGHT Issued 23 Oct 1914 Rites 23 Oct 1914
L. G. Patrick, J. P.

Luther SMITH to Myrtle PATTERSON Issued 24 Oct 1914 Rites 25 Oct 1914
J. M. Green, J. P.

Lin WOOD (Col) to Mattie Joe BONNER (Col) Issued 24 Oct 1914 Rites 25 Oct 1914
G. P. Brasier, J. P.

Isham DENTON to Nannie MITCHELL Issued 7 Nov 1914 Rites 8 Nov 1914
W. L. Keaton, M. G.

Monroe BROWN to Hassie VANHOOSER Issued 7 Nov 1914 Rites 8 Nov 1914
W. P. Davis, J. P.

#503 in Marriage Book completely obliterated with blue ink pen. All clerk entries in book are of black.

Lester W. RIZOR to Charlotte WEBB Issued 13 Nov 1914 Rites 14 Nov. 1914
H. L. Walling, M. G.

Floyd Dodson ROBINSON to Bessie May STEWART Issued 20 Nov 1914 Rites 21 Nov 1914
S. T. Byars, M. G.

Houston PARTON to Luke ADAMSON Issued 24 Nov 1914 Rites 29 Nov 1914
W. H. Hammer, J. P.

G. W. ELAM to Cora BREWER Issued 25 Nov 1914 Rites 26 Nov 1914
J. W. Cooley, M. G.

Dennie YOUNG to Hallie SMITH Issued 26 Nov 1914 Rites 26 Nov 1914
J. W. Cooley, M. G.

William CRAVEN to Ethel MOULDER Issued 27 Nov 1914 Rites 27 Nov 1914
J. A. Cunningham, M. G.

Dan ROBERTS to Maggie AUSTIN Issued 28 Nov 1914 Rites 29 Nov 1914
W. S. Grissom, J. P.

Joe WALKER to Allene CANTRELL Issued 2 Dec 1914 Rites 6 Dec 1914
P. G, Moore, J. P.
(50 cent stamp affixed)

P. G. BYARS, JR. to Jennie FUGGITT Issued 4 Dec 1914 Rites 9 Dec 1914
P. G. Potter, M. G.

Dock PEDIGO to Nettie SMITH Issued 26 Dec 1914 Rites 27 Dec 1914
L. G. Patrick, J. P

Floyd FREEMAN to Fannie SIMONS Issued 26 Dec 1914 Rites 27 Dec 1914
J. B. Dobb, J. P.

Tom BESS to Hailey PANTER Issued 27 Dec 1914 Rites 3 Jan 1915
E. L. Moffitt, J. P.

H. B. ADAMS to Flora BEATY Issued 2 Jan 1915 Rites 3 Jan 1915
J. L. Thaxton, J. P.

Sol MULLICAN to Mary AVERY Issued 3 Jan 1915 Rites 3 Jan 1915
P. G. Moore, J. P.

J. W. WILLIAMSON to Anna LANCE Issued 2 Jan 1915 Rites 3 Jan 1915
A. Z. Holder, J. P.

Mose MARTIN to Susan MARTIN Issued 4 Jan 1915 Rites 7 Jan 1915
J. D. Hash, J. P.

Venus YORK to Alice MITCHELL Issued 4 Jan 1915 Rites 5 JAn 1915
J. D. Quick, J. P.

Wm. Thomas DEAKINS to Grace Lee SAIN Issued 5 Jan 1915 Rites 6 Jan 1915
C. M. Epps, M. G.

W. N. WOODS to Myrtle WILSON Issued 5 Jan 1915 Rites 10, JAn 1915
J. C. Odum

George ELKINS to Mary LUCAS Issued 7 JAn 1915 Rites 17 Jan 1915
J. T. CaSEY, M. G.

Floyd BOYD to Bertha FISHER Issued 8 Jan 1915 Rites 10 JAn 1915
L. C. Lane, J. P.

Letter from IRS - stating marriage bond nor marriage license is
subject to tax stamp of 50 cents charged since Nov 13, 1914,
dated January 7, 1915.

M. M. SMARTT to Bertie MAXWELL Issued 9 JAn 1915 Rites 17 Jan 1915
A. P. Hill, J. P.

R. B. SPURLOCK to Sallie SMITH Issued 11 Jan 1915 Rites 11 Jan 1915
George L. Burch

J. W. McDOWELL to Josie DAVIS Issued 11 Jan 1915 Rites 11 Jan 1915
A. Z. Holder, J. P.

Tom BAILEY to Tennie PEDEN Issued 16 JAn 1915 Rites 19 JAn 1915
J. T. Vinson, J. P.

David M. LOGUE to Mrs. E. M. CANTRELL Issued 19 Jan 1915 Rites 19 Jan 1915
J. D. Hash, J. P.

Lee ALLEN to Alice WOMACK Issued 20 Jan 1915 Rites 21 JAn 1915
P. G. Potter, M. G.

Ernest HUGHES to Beulah WHITLOCK Issued 23 JAn 1915 Rites 24 Jan 1915
W. H. Hammer, J. P.

EArl THOMAS to Druvicie WALKER Issued 23 JAn 1915 Rites 24 JAn 1915
W. P. Davis, J. P.

Sewell WOODLEE to Annie BESS Issued 26 JAn 1915 Rites 27 Jan 1915
T. L. Pearsall

Harvey BATEY to Bettie PINEGAR Issued 29 JAn 1915 Rites 31 JAn 1915
G. N. Atnip, J. P.

Hershell MARLER to Ella CANTRELL Issued 30 JAn 1915 Rites 31 Jan 1915
G. N. Atnip, J. P.

Blanton WILLIS to Dena SAIN Issued 30 JAn 1915 Rites 31 Jan 1915
C. M. Epps, M. G.

Henry BRATCHER to Ethel TAYLOR Issued 12 Feb 1915 Rites 14 Feb 1915
J. T. Vinson, J. P.

E. C. BETCHEL to M. B. LYLES Issued 13 Feb 1915 Rites 13 Feb 1915
W. H. Hammer, J. P.

George WRIGHT to Ida Lee STEMBRIDGE Issued 18 Feb 1915 Rites 18 Feb 1915
P. G. Potter, M. G.

Roy BOST to Lou ROLLER Issued 20 Feb 1915 Rites 21 Feb 1915
T. L. Pearsall

D. C. BAIN to Mrs. Ida GLENN Issued 22 Feb 1915 Rites 23 Feb 1915
P. G. Moore, M. G.

Fulton McBRIDE to Lou Ella BOLT Issued 27 Feb 1915 Rites 28 Feb 1915
S. T. Byars, M. G.

Willie MILLER (Col) to Lillian HILL (Col) Issued 1 Mar 1915 Rites16 Mar 1915
G. L. Beech, J. P.

Luther BOST to Gladdis BAIN Issued 2 Mar 1915 Rites 7 Mar 1915
J. D. Templeton, J. P.

J. W. DAVIS to Lou BOREN Issued 9 Mar 1915 Not Returned

Joe SMITH to Thula RUTLEDGE Issued 10 Mar 1915 Rites 10 Mar 1915
J. J. Meadows, J. P.

Clyde NEWBY to Etta MELTON Issued 12 Mar 1915 Rites 21 Mar 1915
J. T. Vinson, J. P.

John DICKSON to Mai GAINES Issued 13 Mar 1915 Rites 14 Mar 1915
T. L. Pearsall

Frank LANE to Edith MORTON Issued 13 Mar 1915 Rites 13 Mar 1915
T. W. Noland, M. G.

Jonah NUNLEY to Ethel TURNER Issued 18 Mar 1195 Rites 27 Mar 1915
W. W. Milstead, M. G.

C. M. WOMACK to Mary HANCOCK 18 Mar 1915 Rites 21 Mar 1915
G. H. Atnip, J. P.

Lewis WOMACK (Col) to Bertha Mae MASON (Col) Issued 20 Mar 1915 Rites 20 Mar 1915
J. B. Booth, M. G.

W. F. ASKEW to Nannie GIBBS Issued 20 Mar 1915 Rites 20 Mar 1915
J. B. Dobbs, J. P.

R. M. Hurtt to Fern STALEY Issued 25 Mar 1915 Rites 27 Mar 1915
F. W. Muse, M. G.

R. L. STUBBLEFIELD to Bettie HARRISON Issued 31 Mar 1915 Rites 4 Apr 1915
J. A. Cunningham, M. G.

Charlie GREER to Rhoda BLANKS Issued 1 Apr 1915 Rites 4 Apr 1915
J. B. Gribble, M. G.

C. E. GRAVES to Martha E. SHIELDS Issued 5 Apr 1915 Rites 11 Apr 1915
W. H. Hammer, J. P.

T. A. CHAPMAN to Laura MOORE Issued 7 Apr 1915 Rites 7 Apr 1915
L. R. Hogan, M. G.

Lucian H. CORDELL to Frances TALLIAFERRO Issued 7 Apr 1915 Rites 15 Apr 1915
T. W. Noland, M. C.

Jim CRAWFORD to Ella R. KEATON Issued 10 Apr 1915 Rites 10 Apr 1915
J. B. Gribble, M. G.

E. W. LYNN to Bertha STOTTS Issued 15 Apr 1915 Rites 18 Apr 1915
L. B. Williams, M. G.

Jim BROWN (Col) to Cora BROWN (Col) Issued 17 Apr 1915 Rites 18 Apr 1915
George Lee

Bob BARNES to Fannie BROWN (Col) Issued 17 Apr 1915 Rites 18 Apr 1915
George Lee

A. J. SPARKMAN to Sally TALLEY Issued 21 Apr 1915 Rites 21 Apr 1915
S. T. Byars, M. G.

H. L. ERWIN to Flora FULTS Issued 23 Apr 1915 Rites 26 Apr 1915
J. C. Smoot, J. P.

Will CLAYBORNE to Mary HOBBS Issued 1 May 1915 Rites 2 May 1915
I. H. Argo, M. G.

Hampton WOMACK to Samantha WOMACK Issued 6 May 1915 Rites 8 May 1915
P. G. Moore, J. P.

William COLLIER to Wavie McGEE Issued 8 May 1915 Rites 9 May 1915
B. S. McCollum, J. P.

Shelie MULLICAN to Belle BOUNDS Issued 8 May 1915 Rites 9 May 1915
J. T. Turner, J. P.

Book 12 - Warren County Marriages - May 8, 1915 to Oct. 30, 1918

Hewey GREEN to Grace PHELPS Issued 8 May 1915 Rites 9 May 1915
L. G. Patrick, J. P.

Sam HIGGINBOTHAM to Lettie SCOTT Issued 8 May 1915 Rites 9 May 1915
H. T. McGregor, J. P.

Logan DAVIS to Callie MELTON Issued 8 May 1915 Rites 9 May 1915
L. G. Patrick, J. P.

John C. RANKIN to Malissia HUTCHINGS Issued 12 May 1915 Rites 12 May 1915
Price Billingsley, M. G.

A. C. SUMMERS to Mrs. Annie SPENCER Issued 12 May 1915 Rites 12 May 1915
W. P. Davis, J. P.

W. F. TYREE to Eliza HYDER Issued 15 May 1915 Rites 16 May 1915
J. C. Smith, J. P.

Ruddie CANTRELL to Ola PINEGAR Issued 22 May 1915 Rites 22 May 1915
L. F. Daugherty, M. G.

Feliz GLENN to Myrtle PINEGAR Issued 22 May 1915 Rites 23 May 1915
P. G. Moore, J. P.

S. F. BRATCHER to Jimmie AKERS Issued 22 May 1915 Rites 23 May 1915
P. G. Moore, J. P.

Paul DUNHAM to Willie JORDAN Issued 22 May 1915 Rites 23 May 1915
T. W. Noland, M. G.

John Lytle COLVILLE to Bessie Clark SMITH Issued 1 Jun 1915 Rites 1 Jun 1915
John B. Cowden, M. G.

Paul ZWINGLE to Avis Marie PITT Issued 2 Jun 1915 Rites 2 Jun 1915
C. M. Zwingle, M. G.

Isaac DENTON to Matilda SMOOT Issued 6 Jun 1915 Rites 5 Jun 1915
J. C. Smoot, J. P.

Oda PEDIGO to Oza RAINS Issued 5 Jun 1915 Rites 5 Jun 1915
J. B. Dobbs, J. P.

Alton HENEGAR to Lettie SPURLOCK Issued 12 Jun 1915 Rites 12 Jun 1915
O. H. Wood, J. P.

M. BRADLEY to Mattie FERRELL Issued 12 Jun 1915 Rites 12 Jun 1915
T. W. Noland, M. G.

E. E. GRANDEY to Mary Ethel GOLDEN Issued 14 Jun 1915 Rites 14 Jun 1915
W. S. Long, M. G.

Elgar Leland ROGERS to Irene MYERS Issued 16 Jun 1915 Rites 17 Jun 1917
Price Billingsley, M. G.

Perry GREEN to Margie DUNLAP Issued 18 Jun 1915 Rites 20 Jun 1915
P. G. Moore, J. P.

Claud GROVE to Minnie O'NEAL Issued 19 Jun 1915 Rites 20 Jun 1915
W. S. Grissom, J. P.

Elmer JONES to Vena HUDSON Issued 19 Jun 1915 Rites 20 Jun 1915
W. P. Davis, J. P.

Elbert PATRICK to Ethel SWEARENGAN Issued 20 Jun 1915 Rites 20 Jun 1915
J. B. Dobbs, J. P.

H. C. HAWKINS to Rose TALLIAFERRO Issued 21 Jun 1915 Rites 22 Jun 1915
T. W. Noland, M. G.

Nathan BRASWELL to Cynthia GREEN Issued 26 Jun 1915 Rites 27 Jun 1915
W. H. Hammer, J. P.

Frank UNDERHILL to Lula PAGE Issued 3 Jul 1915 Rites 4 Jul 1915
A. Z. Holder, J. P.

A. A. VASBURG to Susie HOLDER Issued 12 Jul 1915 Rites 14 Jul 1915
H. J. Jones, J. P.

Horace BRASWELL to Daisy BENNETT Issued 17 Jul 1915 Not Returned

Lemuel CRIPS to Lela BRASWELL Issued 25 Jul 1915 Rites 4 Aug 1915
J. T. Turner, J. P.

G. B. FLETCHER to Sophie MOOREHEAD Issued 27 Jul 1915 Rites 27 Jul 1915
T. W. Noland, M. G.

Foster BOYD to Ida Lee CLARK Issued 31 Jul 1915 Rites 1 Aug 1915
J. D. Northcutt

Frank BATES (Col) to Lou DUNCAN Issued 31 Jul 195 Rites 7 Aug 1915

M. F. NORTHCUTT to Bettie Lou ROGERS Issued 7 Aug 1915 Rites 8 Aug 1915
G. P. Brasier, J. P.

C. L. CHERRY to Beatrice JONES Issued 12 Aug 1915 Rites 15 Jul 1915
L. C. Lane, J. P.

Luther PACK to Jennie Pedigo Issued 12 Aug 1915 Rites 22 Aug 1915
A. A. Flanders, M. G.

William PASSONS to Bertha BRATCHER Issued 13 Aug 1915 Rites 14 Aug 1915
L. SAFLEY, M. G.

T. A. McCAGG to Willie T. EARLES Issued 14 Aug 1915 Rites 14 Aug 1915
L. G. Patrick, J. P.

L. R. MANSFIELD to Lillie May BILES Issued 14 Aug 1915 Rites 15 Aug 1915
J. Barnes, J. P.

Tullus GRISSOM to Lula PAINE Issued 14 Aug 1915 Rites 17 Aug 1915
J. D. Quick, J. P.

Louis BAILEY to Edith JONES Issued 16 Aug 1915 Rites 16 Aug 1915
J. T. Vinson, J. P.

Hubert SIMMS to Hester SWANN Issued 16 Aug 1915 Rites 17 Aug 1915
E. F. Cunningham, J. P.

Charley MOORE to Nellie BLAIR Issued 19 Aug 1915 Rites 21 Aug 1915
S. T. Byars, M. G.

Ernest ALLEN to FANNIE FERGUSON Issued 19 Aug 1915 Rites 19 Aug 1915
J. B. Dobbs, J. P.

E. M. WOMACK to Alica BRADY Issued 21 Aug 1915 Rites 29 Aug 1915
J. T. Vinson, J. P.

R. K. SHIELDS to Hassie C. GILBERT Issued 21 Aug 1915 Rites 22 Aug 1915
J. W. Colley, M. G.

Tom NORTHCUTT (Col) to Lou Ann MASEY (Col) Issued 21 Aug 1915 Rites 22 Aug 1915
W. I. Hunt, M. G.

Temple SPARKMAN to Herma SMITH Issued 21 Aug 1915 Rites 25 Aug 1915
Jacob Stipe, M. G.

Marvin Thurman ROYSTER to Eliz. Corrine KENNEDY Issued 25 Aug 1915 Rites 26 Aug
T. W. Noland, M. G.

Chatham C. MORFORD to Jessie Lee RANDOLPH Issued 25 Aug 1915 Rites 26 Aug 1915
L. R. Hogan, M. G.

B. S. WEESNER to Nina BURCH Issued 30 Aug 1915 Rites 2 Sep 1915
J. F. Marks

E. T. SIMMONS to Dora JOHNSON Issued 2 Sep 1915 Rites 5 Sep 1915
T. M. Eaton,

Venis GLENN to Myrtle Irene MAYFIELD Issued 2 Sep 1915 Rites 5 Sep 1915
J. L. Smith, J. P.

Richard DAVIS to Bartha SHELTON Issued 4 Sep 1915 Rites 5 Sep 1915
L. G. Patrick, J. P.

Clarence BREWER to Marilda L. MALONE Issued 11 Sep 1915 Rites 12 Sep 1915
C. M. Pullive (?) M. G.

William A. WRIGHT to Mrs. Josie LYNCH Issued 11 Sep 1915 Rites 19 Sep. 1915
G. P. Brasier, J. P.

John L. BROWN to Grace JONES Issued 11 Sep 1915 Rites 12 Sep 1915
S. T. Byars, M. G.

Henry CLARK (Col) to Lou McGREGOR (Col) Issued 11 Sep 1915 Rites 12 Sep 1915
S. M. King, M. G.

O. E. CARR to Nola BRATCHER Issued 11 Sep 1915 Rites 12 Sep 1915
W. C. Lorance J. P.

Hervey J. ALLISON to Willie CLARK Issued 15 Sep 1915 Rites 15 Sep 1915
J. C. CALhoun, M. G.

Levi RUTLEDGE to Ruby HARTT Issued 15 Sep 1915 Rites 15 Sep 1915
J. D. Quick, J. P.

James A. KING (Col) to Martha MASTERS (Col) Issued 18 Sep 1915 Rites 18 Sep 1915
J. B. Booth, M. G.

Albert YORK (Col) to Lina WOOD (Col) Issued 21 Sep 1915 Rites 26 Sep 1915
C. M. Collier, J. P.

Bige GRIBBLE to Emma TALLANT Issued 22 Sep 1915 Rites 6 Oct 1915
J. B. Bratcher, M. G.

Spurgeon MOORE to Elsie BLAIR Issued 23 Sep 1915 Rites 26 Sep 1915
J. B. Dobbs, J. P.

Denna RITCHEY to Etta SMITH Issued 23 Sep 1915 Rites 26 Sep 1915
J. T. Vinson, J. P.

Luther ROGERS to Bess HENSLEY Issued 25 Sep 1915 Rites 26 Sep 1915
C. M. Epps, M. G.

Chas. B. McCROSKY to Laura B. MOFFITT Issued 25 Sep 1915 Rites 26 Sep 1915
S. T. Byars, M. G.

W. T. FARLESS to Della O'NEAL Issued 2 Oct 1915 Rites 3 Oct 1915
E. L. Moffitt, J. P.

M. D. DAVIS to Vernon CLARK Issued2 Oct 1915 Rites 4 Oct 1915
W. G. Adcock, M. G.

Vealter CLARK to Motie WARD Issued 5 Oct 1915 Rites 6 Oct 1915
G. H. Atnip, J. P.

Tom WOOD to Lizzie BYARS Issued 5 Oct 1915 Rites 5 Oct 1915
L. G. Patrick, J. P.

Corbett BLANKENSHIP to Cloie FISHER Issued 7 Oct 1915 Rites 15 Oct 1915
L. C. Lane, J. P.

Vernon M. CAMPBELL to Stella GOFF Issued 9 Oct 1915 Rites 10 Oct 1915
J. T. Vinson, J. P.

Lawrence Larry KELLER to Emma Irene MEADOWS Issued 11 Oct 1915 Rites 12 Oct 1915
S. T. Byars, M. G.

Robert Lee DOSSETT to Myrtle Carroll PATTERSON Issued 13 Oct 1915 Rites 14 Oct
L. R. Hogan, M. G.

Forest H. CANTRELL to Mary Eliz. CLARK Issued 16 Oct 1915 Rites 16 Oct 1915
L. R. Hogan, M. G.

Alton B. LOCKE to Hallie CANTRELL Issued 27 Oct 1915 Rites 27 Oct 1915
S. T. Byars, M. G.

J. B. BENSON to Dossie CRIM Issued 29 Oct 1915 Rites 30 Oct 1915
J. B. Gribble, M. G.

S. H. McCORMACK to Sarah Lee BAKER Issued 2 Nov 1915 Rites 3 Nov 1915
J. D. Quick, J. P.

Dent McGREGOR to Addie TEETERS Issued 4 Nov 1915 Returned - Not Solemnized

Zora HAMRICK to Eula SHERRELL Issued 9 Nov 1915 Rites 12 Nov 1915
C. M. Collier, J. P.

W. T. WARREN to Willie SANDERS Issued 10 Nov 1915 Rites 12 Nov 1915
B. F. Woods, M. G.

Irvin REED to Stacy GRIFFIN Issued 17 Nov 1915 Rites 18 Nov 1915
G. H. atnip, J. P.

Oscar DELONG to Lena WOOD Issued 18 Nov 1915 Rites 21 Nov 1915
Jacob Stipe, M. G.

Robert MITCHELL to May CUBBINS Issued 20 Nov 1915 Rites 21 Nov 1915
J. W. Cooley, M. G.

George AUTEN to Elvira AUTEN Issued 20 Nov 1915 Rites 21 Nov 1915
H. L. Jones, J. P.

G. R. ETTER to Erma Lee WOODLEE Issued 22 Nov 1915 Rites 24 Nov 1915
S. T. Byars, JM. G.

L. M. WINFREE to Hattie FUSTON Issued 25 Nov 1915 Rites 2. Nov 1915
Geo. L. Peach, J. P.

John ALLISON to Alice HOBBS Issued 27 Nov 1915 Rites 28 Nov 1915
O. H. Woods, J. P.

Ernest POTTER to Lou BOREN Issued 2 Dec 1915 Rites 5 Dec 1915
J. M. Green, J. P.

W. I. ROBERTS to Daisy SMARTT Issued 2 Dec 1915 Rites 3 Dec 1915
A. P. Hill, J. P.

J. Fred MURPHY to Ella McGREGOR Issued 4 Dec 1915 Rites 5 Dec 1915
W. P. Davis, J. P.

John Everett TUBB (Col) to Ruby MERCER (col) Issued 7 Dec 1915 Rites 7 Dec 1915
George Lee, M. G.

Floyd MARTIN to Emma BARNES Issued 10 Dec 1915 Rites 12 Dec 1915
L. Safley, M. G.

Will H. SMOOT to Sarah Eliz. ROACH Issued 11 Dec 1915 Rites 19 Dec 1915
G. W. Stroud, J. P.

Thos. Moody ALLISON to Jessie May MITCHELL Issued 14 Dec 1915 Rites 14 Dec 1915
J. H. Settle, M. G.

Houston KILLIAN to Minnie CATHCART Issued 17 Dec 1915 Rites 17 Dec 1915
J. W. Gross, M. G.

W. E. MOSS to Taudye SLATTON Issued 17 Dec 1915 Rites 19 Dec 1915
P. G. Potter, M. G.

John C. MULLICAN to Mary Lou ROGERS Issued 18 Dec 1915 Rites 18 Dec 1915
T. M. Eaton, J. P.

Willie FRAZIER to Mediae TEMPLES Issued 18 Dec 1915 Rites 19 Dec 1915
J. C. Duncan, M. G.

W. G. BOST to to Ethel ROGERS Issued 18 Dec 1915 Rites 24 Dec 1915
J. W. Cooley, M. G.

Willie JORDAN to Ethel LANCE Issued 18 dec 1915 Rites 19 dec 1915
A. Z. Holder, J. P.

Sheley JONES to Hattie MILLER Issued 20 Dec 1915 Rites 25 dec 1915
J. B. Dobbs, J. P.

Toy TAYLOR to Lena May MARTIN Issued 20 Dec 1915 Rites 20 Dec 1915
J. H. Settle, M. G.

Dallas HOLDER to Mabel VASBURG Issued 20 Dec 1915 Rites 22 Dec 1915
W. P. Davis, J. P.

D. O. CANTRELL to Paralee HOLDER Issued 22 dec 1915 Rites 24 Dec 1915
P. G. Potter, M. G.

Irving BOYD to Leila TEMPLETON Issued 23 Dec 1915 Rites 25 Dec 1915
J. D. Quick, J. P.

J. D. Odum to Myrtle May PERRY Issued 23 dec 1915 Rites 23 Dec 1915
S.T. Byars, M. G.

J. S. ROWE to Della Mae GROSS Issued 23 Dec 1915 Rites 23 dec 1915
A. J. Morgan, M. G.

Thomas PELHAM to May WILSON Issued 24 Dec 1915 Rites 25 Dec 1915
O. H. Wood, J. P.

Lonnie SHOAL to Maud JORDAN Issued 24 Dec 1915 Rites 25 Dec 1915
G. P. Brasier, J. P.
(License signed - Lonnie Jordan)

H. H. ROWLAND to Ella McCORMACK Issued 24 Dec 1915 Rites 25 Dec 1915
J. D. Quick, J. P.

William WOMACK (Col) to Lizzie Lee PRICE (Col) Issued 24 Dec 1915 Rites 30 Dec 1915
Geo. T. Bolden, M. G.

Rufus SWAFORD (Col) to Hattie RICHARDSON (Col) Issued 24 Dec 1915 Rites 24 Dec
A. K. Kennedy, M. G.

Jewell PARSLEY to Esther DODD Issued 25 Dec 1915 Rites 26 Dec 1915
A. Z. Holder, J. P.

Luther BARRETT to Patsy WINFREE Issued 25 dec 1915 Rites 25 Dec 1915
Wm. V. Whitson, JDG.

Sterling TURNER to Vadie TURNER Issued 25 dec 1915 Rites 25 Dec 1915
J.B. Dobbs, J. P.

Frank P. MITCHELL to Della POWELL Issued 25 dec 1915 Rites 26 Dec 1915
S. T. Byars, M. G.

J. D. TUCKER to Eula PAGE Issued 25 Dec 1915 Rites 25 dec 1915
John H. Settle, M. G.

William GWYN to Ona BERRY Issued 25 dec 1915 Rites 27 dec 1915
T. M. Eaton, J. P.

M. H. GRIMMETT to Willie WRAY MAUZY Issued 27 Dec 1915 Rites 28 Dec 1915
L. R. Hogan, M. G.

Pink WOMACK to Nettie WALLING Issued 28 Dec 1915 Rites1 JAn 1916
A. H. Byars

Amon BESS to Mollie MARTIN Issued29 Dec 1915 Rites 2 JAn 1916
P. G. Moore, J. P.

Korman EDGE to Lillie May JORDAN Issued 30 dec 1915 Rites 2 JAn 1916
A. Z. Holder, J. P.

Jesse CUNNINGHAM to Bertha UNDERWOOD 1 JAn 1916 Rites 2 JAn 1916
J. C. Odum, M. G.

Willie ADCOCK to Vesta BOUNDS Issued 1 JAn 1916 Rites 1 JAn 1916
L. G. Patrick, J. P.

J. F. PUGH to HAllie CANTRELL Issued 1 JAn 1916 Rites 2 JAn 1916
J. B. Dobbs, J. P.

Harry E. HOUSE to Wineford H. YOUNG Issued 3 JAn 1916 Rites 5 JAn 1916
J. H. Settle, M. G.

Grover WOODLEE to SArah Jane JENNINGS Issued 5 JAn 1916 Rites 6 JAn 1916
A. P. Hill, J. P.

Dreadman ROBERTS to Beulah MADEWELL Issued 5 JAn 1916 Rites 9 Jan 1916
W. T. Barnes, J. P.

Ovie CAMPBELL to Vester MASEY Issued 7 Jan 1916 Rites 9 Jan 1916
J. T. Vinson, J. P.

J. E. BAILEY to Lizzie GOFF Issued 7 Jan 1916 Rites 9 JAn 1916
J. T. Vinson, J. P.

Jim BOULDIN to Susie ROGERS Issued 8 JAn 1916 Rites 16 Jan 1916
A. P. Hill, J. P.

V. G. BURKS to Mary Etta YOUNG Issued 12 Jan 1916 Rites 16 JAn 1916
J. T. Casey, M. G.

Wash SPARKMAN to Martha NEWBY Issued 18 JAn 1916 Rites 20 Jan 1916
J. T. Vinson, J. P.

Venus ISREAL to Pearl WALKER Issued 22 Jan 1916 Rites 22 Jan 1916
J. J. Meadows, J. P.

W. S. DODSON to Ellen VOGEL Issued 24 Jan 1916 Rites 26 Jan 1916
J. B. Brown, J. P.

Zeb MARTIN to HAttie Pearl MASON Issued 25 JAn 1916 Rites 26 JAn 1916
J. T. Vinson, J. P.

Lowry RUSSELL to Ella BYARS Issued28 JAn 1916 Rites 28 Jan 1916
J. B. Dobbs, J. P.

R. C. CAMP to Addie TEETERS Issued 2 Feb 1916 Rites 3 Feb 1916
A. P. Hill, J. P.

H. J. BOST to Prudie BARRETT Issued 3 feb 1916 Rites 3 Feb 1916
J. B. Dobbs, J. P.

W. B. SAFLEY to Ella BLUHM Issued 4 Feb 1916 Rites 5 Feb 1916
J. M. Green, J. P.

I. H. GREEN to Mary SMOOT Issued 5 Feb 1916 Rites 6 Feb 1916
J. M. Green, J. P.

Robert C. PIRTLE to Mary Lou CHISAM Issued 5 Feb 1916 Rites 5 Feb 1916
Price Billingsley, M. G.

Martin CURTIS to Ethel CURTIS Issued 8 Feb 1916 Rites 10 Feb 1916
E. L. Moffitt, J. P.

D. W. ADAMS to Nancy TEETERS Issued 10 Feb 1916 Rites 10 Feb 1916
L. G. Patrick, J. P.

Floyd MILLER to Beulah SPURLOCK Issued 12 Feb 1916 Rites 13 Feb 1916
J. A. Booher, J. P.

Jesse BUTCHER to Lena PINEGAR Issued 12 Feb 1916 Rites 13 Feb 1916
P. G. Potter, M. G.

Irving FARLESS to Lila GREEK Issued 16 Feb 1916 Rites 16 Feb 1916
J. B. Broen, J. P.

H. W. ROGERS to Nannie ROGERS Issued 19 Feb 1916 Rites 20 Feb 1916
S. T. Byars, M. G.

C. L. HASH to Mammie LOWRY Issued 23 Feb 1916 Rites 1 Mar 1916
J. D. Hash, J. P.

George Head SMITH to Lilly James WALLING Issued 23 Feb 1916 Rites 24 Feb 1916
L. R. Hogan, J. P.

C. W. CONLIN to Ella May HIGGINBOTHAM Issued 4 Mar 1916 Rites 4 Mar 1916
J. B. Dobbs, J. P.

Dock LOOPER (Col) to Mary LOOPER (Col) Issued 4 Mar 1916 Rites 4 Mar 1916
J. B. Booth, M. G.

Hugh BEADEN to Mae ROGERS Issued 8 Mar 1916 Rites 9 Mar 1916
A. L. Hodge, M. G.

W. B. BOREN to Myrtle SCHROCK Issued 11 Mar 1916 Rites 12 Mar 1916
J. L. Smith, J. P.

G. W. FERGUSON (Col) to Dee BRYMER (Col) Issued 16 Mar 1916 Rites 16 Mar 1916
J. D. Hash, J. P.

N. T. WALL to M. M. MULLICAN Issued 24 Mar 1916 Rites 24 Mar 1916
Lonnie Cubbins

Charles EVANS to Bessie BURCH Issued 25 Dec 1916 Rites 26 dec 1916
S. T. Byars, M. G.

John A. ROBINSON to Dollie CROUCH Issued 17 Mar 1916 Rites 29 Mar 1916
O. H. Wood, J. P.

George MULLICAN to Bettie LONG Issued 27 Mar 1916 Rites 28 Mar 1916
Lonnie Cubbins

Zollie GOODSON to Cora JERNIGAN Issued 27 Mar 1916 Rites 27 Mar 1916
W. V. Whitson, Jdg.

Asa MARTIN (Col) Rites Octa WOODS (Col) Issued 28 Mar 1916 Rites 28 Mar 1916
W. S. Grissom, J. P.

W. C. WHITLOCK to Minnie COOPER Issued 1 Apr 1916 Rites 2 Apr 1916
J. T. Casey, M. G.

Emmett SMITH (Col) to Doshia Bell SPURLOCK (Col) Issued 2 Apr 1916 Rites 2 Apr
W. L. Denton, M. G.

F. C. DUGGIN to Alice LANCE Issued 8 Apr 1916 Rites 9 Apr 1916
J. H. Murrell, M. G.

Andy McGOWAN to Elizabeth ANDERSON Issued 10 Apr 1916 Rites 13 Apr 1916
G. P. Brasier, J. P.

Grade TAYLOR to Etta MULLICAN Issued 10 Apr 1916 Rites 11 Apr 1916
J. T. Vinson, J. P.

J. M. WOMACK to Sina ENGLISH Issued 12 Apr 1916 Rites 12 Apr 1916
J. B. Dobbs, J. P.

W. G. MOORE to Myrtle Lee DUNLAP Issued 20 Apr 1916 Rites 20 Apr 1920
J. L. Smith, J. P.

Roy WEBB (Col) to Georgia WILLIAMS Issued 21 Apr 1916 Rites 23 Apr 1916
J. M. Green, J. P.

Earnest HOLDER to Josie VANATTA Issued 29 Apr 1916 Rites 29 Apr 1916
L. G. Patrick, J. P.

John M. HARTT to Florence CRIM Issued 29 Apr 1916 Rites 30 Apr 1916
J. J. Meadows, J. P.

Minnie WILSHER to Mary WISEMAN Issued 29 Apr 1916 Rites 29 Apr 1916
C. L. Webster

Felix W. MUSE to Johnnie D. FAULKNER Issued q Mau 1916 Rites 1 May 1916
F. N. Butler

Severina GIOVANNOLI to Lucille Va. McCURLEY Issued 1 May 1916 Rites 2 May 1916
A. J. Morgan, M. G.

Chester KELL to Lula ROGERS Issued 3 May 1916 Rites 7 May 1916
A. J. McBRIDE, M. G.

Phillip MITCHELL (col) to Nettie BROWN (Col) Issued 5 May 1916 Rites 5 May 1916
J. T. Casey, M. G.

Jarvis STARKEY to Hallie SUMMERS Issued 5 May 1916 Rites 7 May 1916
H. L. Walling, M. G.

Robert Dudley BURCH to Cora DAVIS Issued 6 May 1916 Rites 7 May 1916
L. G. Patrick, J. P.

W. L. ROBINSON to Lena FOSTER Issued 12 May 1916 Rites 12 May 1916
L. G. Patrick, J. P.

R. L. STUBBLEFIELD to Dollie HOLDER Issued 12 May 1916 Rites 14 May 1916
Price Billingsley, M. G.

Orian SCOTT to Vera Mae FREEZE Issued 13 May 1916 Rites 14 May 1916
O. H. Wood, MJ. P.

George HALEY to Bertie CANTRELL Issued 18 May 1916 Rites 21 May 1916
J. L. Smith, J. P.

Firm CUNNINGHAM to Lera BURKS Issued 20 May 1916 Rites 21 May 1916
J. T. Casey, M. G.

Nelson JOHNSON (Col) to Clara Belle KING (Col) Issued 26 May 1916 Rites 28 May
A. Z. Holder, J. P.

DAniel WEBSTER to Susan E. MATHIS Issued 27 May 1916 Rites 29 May 1916
J. B. Dobbs, J. P.

Herbert ROBINSON to Sarah FREEMAN Issued 27 May 1916 Rites 27 May 1916
J. B. Brown, J. P.

Frank M. JARRELL to Stella ROGERS Issued 3 Jun 1916 Rites 4 Jun 1916
O. H. Woods, J. P.

Hpward STROUD to Willie JUSTICE Issued 8 Jun 1916 Rites 8 Jun 1916
G. P. Brasier, J. P.

Fred C. WILSON to Eva HARDIN Issued 10 Jun 1916 Rites 11 Jun 1916
J. A. Booher, J. P.

W. W. LOCKE, Jr. to Sophia WILLIAMS Issued 10 Jun 1916 Rites 11 Jun 1916
S. T. Byars, M. G.

Otis L. HAMMER to Mamie REYNOLDS Issued 10 Jun 1916 Rites 11 Jun 1916
P. G. Potter, J. P.

Wallace S. WOOTEN to Nellie S. MASON Issued 21 Jun 1916 Rites 22 Jun 1916
A. J. Morgan, M. G.

Alton H. DAVENPORT to Ruby AKERS Issued 24 Jun 1916 Rites 25 Jun 1916
W. C. Lorance, J. P.

William SELLS to Maude GREEN Issued 24 Jun 1916 Rites 25 Jun 1916
John W. Settle, M. G.

Austin McQUEEN (Col) to Ressie HOLLAND Issued 27 Jun 1916 Rites 26 Jun 1916
W. V. Whitson, Jdg.

J. H. COPE to Sallie COPE Issued 27 Jun 1916 Rites 29 Jun 1916
P. G. Moore, J. P.

Will H. YOUNG to LASSIE May KIRBY Issued 29 Jun 1916 Rites 31 Jun 1916
S. T. Byars, M. G.

Frank PARKER to Bessie BONNIE Issued 30 Jun 1916 Rites 2 Jul 1916
J. C. Duncan, M. G.

Livy TAYLOR to Beatrice LYTLE Issued 1 Jul 1916 Rites 3 Jul 1916
E. L. Moffitt, J. P.

Elisha TOSH to Lizzie May TATE Issued 1 Jul 1916 Rites 2 Jul 1916
J. P. Stubblefield, M. G.

I. W. WARE to Ethel MUNCEY Issued 1 Jul 1916 Rites 2 Jul 1916
H. T. McGregor, J. P

Newt CHISAM to Mary SPARKMAN Issued 3 Jul 1916 Rites 3 Jul 1916
W. V. Whitson, Jdg.

T. A. GLENN to Nannie TITTSWORTH Issued 5 Jul 1916 Rites 6 Jul 1916
P. G. Moore, J. P.

Joe MASSINGILL to Lula MUNCEY Issued 6 Jul 1916 Rites 22 Jul 1916
Wm. Milstead, M. G.

Lusius York (Col) to Jessie WORTHINGTON (Col) Issued 11 Jul 1916 Rites 12 Jul
W. S. Grissom, J. P.

Sam TAYLOR to Pauline PATTON Issued 21 Jul 1916 Rites 21 Jul 1916
J. T. Vinson, J. P.

Charley HALE to Maude RUTLEGE Issued 21 Jul 1916 Not Retuened

W. C. TALBERT to Maggie ORRICK Issued 22 Jul 1916 Rites 23 jul 1916
J. A. Cunningham, M. G.

Bernice CANTRELL to Loreta NEWBY Issued 23 jul 1916 Rites 23 Jul 1916
P. G. Potter, M. G.

J. O. GROSS to Mrs. Dora COPE Issued 24 Jul 1916 Rites 24 Jul 1916
A. J. Morgan, M. G.

J. S. NORRIS (Col) to Hattie MARTIN (Col) Issued 24 Jul 1916 Rites 24 Jul 1916
L. G. Patrick, J. P.

JAmes Wm. McGEE to Lula McGEE Issued 29 Jul 1916 Rites 29 Jul 1916
Price Billingsley, M. G.

Willia HALE to Axie COOLEY Issued 1 Aug 1916 Rites 6 Aug 1916
J. T. Casey, M. G.

Ike SWANN to Bessie MILLER Issued 2 Aug 1916 Rites 22 Aug 1916
J. W. eaton, Jdg.

Jesse GILLENTINE to Sylva LASSITER Issued 3 Aug 1916 Rites 6 Aug 1916
J. W. Cooley, M. G.

Charles BRIEN to Carrie BEAN Issued 3 Aug 1916 Rites 3 Aug 1916
Chas. T. Cates

P. M. ATNIP to Maggie PARKS Issued 5 Aug 1916 Rites 6 Aug 1916
L. F. Daugherty, M. G.

Jacob CURTIS to Malissie LYTLE Issued 11 Aug 1916 Rites 13 Aug 1916
F. L. Wallace, M. G.

C. A. HILL to Ona Louise NORROD Issued 12 Aug 1916 Rites 13 Aug 1916
L. R. Hogan, M. G.

Lodis YOUNG to Cennia BYARS Issued 12 Aug 1916 Rites 13 Aug 1916
L.F. Daugherty, M. G.

B. M. DAVIS to Maggie FISHER Issued 12 Aug 1916 Rites 13 Aug 1916
S. T. Byars, M. G.

Clarence CRAWFORD to Lucy CAPSHAW Issued 15 Aug 1916 Rites 15 Aug 1916
S. W. D. Green

Thomas EARLES to Lillie ABLE Issued 22 Aug 1916 Rites 22 Aug 1916
J. B. Dobbs, J. P.

HArry LOCKE (Col) to Hattie May KING (Col) Issued 26 Aug 1916 Rites 3 Sep 1916
W. C. Lorance, J. P.

Aus DAVIS to Beulah GRIBBLE Issued 1 Sep 1916 Rites 3 Sep 1916
L. C. Lane, J. P.

Erb LOCKE (Col) to Susie May BROCK (Col) Issued 2 Sep 1916 Rites 11 Sep 1916
W. C. Lorance, J. P.

Joe GROVE to Grace MARTIN Issued 2 Sep 1916 Rites 3 Sep 1916
J. T. Casey, M. G.

Calvin LANE (Col) to Mary Lee SPURLOCK (Col) Issued 2 Sep 1916 Rites 3 Sep 1916
Wm. Caswell, M. G.

Robert M. SEAL to Mabel Clara JONES Issued 2 Sep 1916 Rites 3 Sep 1916
J. T. Vinson, J. P.

William CROUCH to Bertha RICH Issued 2 Sep 1916 Rites 3 Sep 1916
H. H. Leach, M. G.

G. V. DENTON to Bessie BREWER Issued 7 Sep 1916 Rites 7 Sep 1917
J. B. Dobbs, J. P.

Ray FANN to Martha LAFEVERS Issued 8 Sep 1916   Not Returned

G. P. COPE to Lon SAFLEY Issued 9 Sep 1916 Rites 9 Sep 1916
J. B. Dobbs, J. P.

A. S. COPPINGER to Mamie WALKER Issued 9 Sep 1916 Rites 10 Sep 1916
A. P. Hill, J. P.

Arthur S. COPPINGER to Mable BARNES Issued 9 Sep 1916 Rites 10 Sep 1916
A. P. Hill, J. P.

G. M. D. GROVES to Minnie WHITE Issued 9 Sep 1916 Rites 24 Sep 1916
C. M. Collier, J. P.

Bill ALLISON to Minnie CUNNINGHAM Issued 9 Sep 1916 Rites 12 Sep 1916
O.H. Wood, J. P.

Gilliam WOAMCK to Rosa HALEY Issued 11 Sep 1916 Rites14 Sep 1916
J. B. Gribble, M. G.

A. J. INGLE to Martha Eliz. WILSON Issued 14 Sep 1916 Rites 14 Sep 1916
L. R. Hogan, M. G.

JAmes P. SANDERS to Ella May LUSK Issued 14 Sep 1916 Rites 16 Sep 1916
J. H. Settle, M. G.

Willie WHITTENBURG to Mary Ruth DAVIDSON Issued 16 Sep 1916 Rites 16 Sep 1916
Price Billingsley, M. G.

Hubert HOLDER to Ella WILLIAMSON Issued 16 Sep 1916 Rites 17 Sep 1916
A. Z. Holder, J. P.

Robert MELTON to Bertha FOSTER Issued 16 Sep 1916 Rites 19 Sep 1916
J. B. Dobbs, J. P.

Hillis SAVAGE (Col) to Belle LOCKE (Col) Issued 18 Sep 1916 Rites 18 Sep 1916
Rem. Caswell, M. G.

Cecil JOHNIGAN (Col) to Ella HIGGINBOTHAM (Col) Issued 18 Sep 1916 Rites 18 Sep
L. G. Patrick, J. P.

J. R. GRAMLING to Ruby C. MANSFIELD Issued 19 Sep 1916 Rites 20 Sep 1916
Price Billingsley, M. G.

Livy H. WILLIAMS to Bettie STOTTS Issued 19 Sep 1916 Rites 21 Sep 1916
S. T. Byars, M. G.

John C. CANTRELL to Mary Lou CATON Issued 19 Sep 1916 Rites 22 Sep 1916
I. G. Webb, J. P.

E. F. HERD (Col) to Hillie May YORK (Col) Issued 19 Sep 1916 Rites 19 Sep 1916
G. W. Wych, M. G.

W. E. WARD to Winnie JONES Issued 22 Sep 1916 Rites 24 Sep 1916
G. H. Atnip, M. G.

G. A. J. MITCHELL to Martha HALE Issued 22 Sep 1916 Rites 24 Sep 1916
J. W. Cooley, M. G.

Lofton GRIFFIN to Margie WOMACK Issued 23 Sep 1916 Rites 24 Sep 1916
G.H.Atnip, M. G.

Bill ROGERS to Vesta JOHNSON Issued 23 Sep 1916 Rites 23 Sep 1916
C. M. Collier, J. P.

C. G. WHITEAKER to Susie POTTER Issued 23 Sep 1916 Rites 24 Sep 1916
J. A. Booher, J. P.

Alex PATRICK to Octa WOMACK Issued 23 Sep 1916 Rites 24 Sep 1916
L. G. Patrick, J. P.

Bill COTTON to Flossie MULLICAN Issued 27 Sep 1916 Rites 27 1916
J. B. Dobbs, J. P.

Jennings PATTON to Grace DELANEY Issued 27 Sep 1916 Rites 27 Sep 1916
J. M. Green, J. P.

B. B. WILSON to Pearl KEITH Issued 30 Sep 1916 Rites 8 Oct 1916
P. G. Potter, M. G.

W. F. FRASIER to Mrs. Beulah MITCHELL Issued 5 Oct 1916 Rites 5 Oct 1915
John H. Settle, M. G.

Axum BOREN to Kinie GLENN Issued 7 Oct 1916 Rites 8 Oct 1916
J. L. Smith, J. P.

Oscar SAVAGE to Susan STOTTS Issued 7 Oct 1916 Rites 8 Oct 1916
H. T. McGregor, J. P.

J. M. HUGHES to Ruby J. COLLINS Issued 9 Oct 1916 Rites 11 Oct 1916
L. R. Hogan, M. G.

B. G. MOORE to Ada BLANKS Issued 13 Oct 1916 Rites 15 Oct 1916
L. R. Hogan, M. G.

Herman WILSON to Vera HOLDER Issued 14 Oct 1916 Rites 15 Oct 1916
A. Z. Holder, J.,P.

Arsa GROSS to Wallie BALES Issued 14 Oct 1916 Rites 15 Oct 1916
J. J. Meadows, J. P.

Harvey GREEN to Mollie SAFLEY Issued 17 Oct 1916 Rites 18 Oct 1916
Frank B. Shepherd

J. R. STROUD to Jettie MARTIN Issued 20 Oct 1916 Rites 21 Oct 1916
T. B. Clark, M. G.

Knox CARR to Stella CARRICK Issued 21 Oct 1916 Rites 24 Oct 1916
W. C. Lorance, J. P.

Harold EVANS to Nannie McGEE Issued 21 Oct 1916 Rites 22 Oct 1916
J. W. Cooley, M. G.

James M. MEDLEY to Pheobe CRAVEN Issued 23 Oct 1916 Rites 23 Oct 1916
L. G. PATRICK, J. P.

SAm MULLICAN to Nellie JONES Issued 25 Oct 1916 Rites 25 Oct 1916
W. H. Hammer, J. P.

Arthur WEBB (Col) to Pearl THOMAS (Col) Issued 28 Oct 1916 Rites 28 Oct 1916
P. G. Summers, M. G.

Orville JONES to Loti Mae WARD Issued 1 Nov 1916 Rites 2 Nov 1916
W. P. DAvis, J. P.

Dan PERRY to CAroline KING Issued 3 Nov 1916 Rites 4 Nov 1916
W. T. Barnes, J. P.

Jesse CHRISTIAN to Frank COPPINGER Issued 4 Nov 1916 Not Returned

Robert WILINSON to Mary POTTER Issued 4 Nov 1916 Rites 5 Nov 1916
J. M. Green, J.P.

C. C. JONES to Jemmie HILLIS Issued 8 Nov 1916 Rites 11 Nov 1916
F. W. Muse, M. G.

F. H. MARTIN to Alta MORRIS Issued 8 Nov 1916 Rites 9 Nov 1916
G. P. Brasier, J. P.

W. J. WAGNER to Minnie WHITTENBURG Issued 10 Nov 1916 Rites 10 Nov 1916
T. B. Clark, M. G.

Windell BARNES to Thelia BOYD Issued 11 Nov 1916 Rites 12 Nov 1916
W. T. Barnes, J. P.

Herschell SMITH to Lillie PEDEN Issued 13 Nov 1916 Rites 14 Nov 1916
A. Z. Holder, J. P.

John OWEN to Mary TODD Issued 21 Nov 1916 Rites 24 Nov 1916
W. C. Lorance, J. P.

Joseph C. COATS to Ada Belle WRIGHT Issued 22 Nov 1916 Rites 27 Nov 1916
J. Barnes, J. P.

S. A. MITCHELL to MArtha Jean MYERS Issued 23 Nov 1916 Rites 23 Nov 1916
Price Billingsley, M. G.

Shelie MARKIM to Lona MUNCY Issued 25 Nov 1916 Rites 26 Nov 1916
A. Z. Holder, J. P.

Albert BROWN (Col) to Annie TALLEY (Col) Issued 29 Nov 1916 Rites 29 Nov 1916
G. P. Summers, M. G.

Will SPURLOCK (Col) to Jessie LADD (Col) Issued 29 Nov 1916 Not Returned

Charlie McGEE to Manda Alice McGEE Issued 2 Dec 1916 Rites 3 Dec 1916
H. T. McGregor, J. P.

EArl CONROD (col) to Nettie Ann RAMSEY (Col) Issued 5 Dec 1916 Rites 6 Dec 1916
O. H. Wood, J. P.

Fred TITTSWORTH to Offie JONES Issued 9 Dec 1916 Rites 10 Dec 1916
P. G. Moore, J. P.

Thomas CHASTAIN to Myra SMOOT Issued 9 Dec 1916 Rites 10 Dec 1916
J. W. Cooley, M. G.

Arthue MASON to Mandy HOLDER Issued 11 Dec 1916 Rites 11 Dec 1916
Price Billingsley, M. G.

B. M. SANDERS to Maggie MARTIN Issued 29 Dec 1916 Rites 31 Dec 1916
P. G. Moore, J. P.

Wm. Calvin LOONEY to Flora Myrtle MEDLEY Issued 30 Dec 1916 Rites 30 Dec 1916
John H. Settle, M. G.

Charles RITCHEY to Lula JONES Issued 3 JAn 1917 Rites 7 Jan 1917
S. T. Byars, M. G.

James D. WOMACK to Nannie CHILTON Issued4 JAn 1917 Rites 4 Jan 1917
L. G. Patrick, J. P.

Orian WOMACK to Ollie GLENN Issued 5 Jan 1917 Rites 7 AJn 1917
J. L. Smith, J. P.

Thurman McGEE to Nettie HILLIS Issued 12 Jan 1917 Rites14 Jan 1917
H. T. McGregor, J. P.

J. L. EVANS to Helen BRADY Issued 13 JAn 1917 Rites 14 Jan 1917
J. W. Cooley, M. G.

Jim BROWN (Col) to Pearl SPURLOCK (Col) Issued17 Jan 1917 Rites 28 Jan 1917
T. H. Busby

Marshall COUCH to Ethel NEAL Issued 19 Jan 1917 Rites 21 Jan 1917
W. R. Keaton, M. G.

L. K. GIBBS to MAe GRIMES Issued 20 Jan 1917 Rites 21 JAn 1917
L. G. Patrick, J. P.

Eugene SMITH to Marcus YORK Issued 23 Jan 1917 Rites 23 jan 1917
A. J. Morgan, M. G.

Robert Lee JONES to Elizabeth LIVELY Issued 23 Jan 1917 Rites 24 Jan 1917
Price Billingsley, M. G.

Jesse CHRISTIAN to Thela LYTLE Issued 31 Jan 1917 Rites 2 Feb 1917
E. L. Moffitt, J. P.

G. W. QUICK to Martha BLACKWELL Issued 3 Feb 1917 Rites 4 Feb 1917
J. L. Smith, J. P.

M. T. GRIBBLE to Ora GREEN Issued10 Feb 1917 Rites 11 Feb 1917
B. S. McCollum, J. P.

Callie JONES to Lillian ADAMSON Issued 12 Feb 1917 Rites 18 Feb1917
H. L. Jones, J. P.

W. A. BALES to Pearl HOBBS Issued 16 Feb 1917 Rites 21 Feb 1917
R. L. Stubblefield, M. G.

Charlie HAMMER to Messie EARLS RONEY Issued 22 Feb 1917 Rites 27 Feb 1917
S. T. Byars, M. G.

Chas. T. SMITHSON to Theresa LOGAN Issued 24 Feb 1917 Rites 24 Feb 1917
C. H. Smithson, M. G.

R. E. WOMACK to Nancy CHASTAIN Issued 1 Dec 1916 Rites 11 Dec 1916
J. W. Cooley, M. G.

Perry A. GRIBBLE to Onie B. GLENN Issued 11 Dec 1916 Rites 17 Dec 1916
J. M. Green, J.P.

Charlie CLARK to Evie JONES Issued 16 Dec 1916 Rites 21 Dec 1916
H. T. McGregor, J. P.

JOHN PASSONS to MAttie ROBERTS Issued 18 Dec 1916 Rites 21 Dec 1916
J. D. Quick, J. P.

J. C. TEELERS to Ida TURNER Issued 21 Dec 1916 Rites 25 Dec 1916
J. F. Martin, M. G.

Elijah DOAK to Flossie McBRIDE Issued 21 Dec 1916 Rites 24 Dec 1916
J. J. Meadows, J. P.

G. A. WOMACK to Vertie Mae KELLEY Issued 21 Dec 1916 Rites 24 dec 1916
G. H. Atnip, M. G.

Emmett McGREGOR to MAndy HILLIS Issued 22 Dec 1916 Rites 24 Dec 1916
E. D. McBRIDE, M. G.

George JENNINGS to Edna WEBB Issued 22 Dec 1916 Rites 24 Dec 1916
L. C. Lane, J. P.

S.A. DRAKE to Wavie Lee HASH Issued 22 Dec 1916 Rites 24 dec 1916
J. D. Quick, J. P.

C. KNOWLES to Eliza MOUSLEY Issued 23 Dec 1916 Rites 24 Dec 1916
W. S. Grissom, J. P.

Foster MARTIN (col) to Thula LOOPER (Col) Issued 23 Dec 1916 Rites 24 Dec 1916
J. A. W. Moore

Charlie GILLENTINE to Rhoda SAFLEY Issued 23 Dec 1916 Rites 24 Dec 1916
H. T. McGregor, J. P.

Dalton O'NEAL to Oma HILL Issued23 Dec 1916 Rites 24 Dec 1916
E. L. Moffitt, J. P.

W. N. CRAIN to Lizzie EWTON Issued 23 Dec 1916 Rites 24 Dec 1916
B. S. McCollum, J. P.

L. R. CAPSHAW to Lela PAGE Issued 23 Dec 1916 Rites 23 Dec 1916
J. B. Dobbs, J. P.

Vernon CRIM to Maude STUBBLEFIELD Issued 23 Dec 1916 Rites 24 Dec 1916
J. B. Dobbs, J. P.

Ollie YOUNG to Myrtle ADCOCK Issued 25 Dec 1916 Rites 28 Dec 1916
L. F. Daugherty, M. G.

Will LINCY (Col) to Maggie HAMMONS Issued 26 Dec 1916 Rites 28 Dec 1916
A. J. Morgan, M. G.

Edgar BREEDLOVE to Minnie HALE Issued 1 Mar 1917 Rites 1 Mar 1917 A. H. Byars

JAmes RHODES (Col) to Zelma SWAFFORD (Col) Issued 7 Mar 1917 Rites 7 Mar 1917 J. A. Moore

Thomas BARNES to Ocie SCOTT Issued 7 Mar 1917 Rites 8 Mar 1917 E. L. Moffitt, J. P.

Gillam CARR to Anna Lou VICKERS Issued 10 Mar 1917 Rites 11 Mar 1917 J. Barnes, J. P.

Willie WALKER to Beulah HOLDER issued 10 Mar 1917 Rites 11 Mar 1917 J. T. Vinson, J. P.

Patrick HENNESSEE to Lena ROGERS Issued 10 Mar 1917 Rites 11 Mar 1917 J. J. Meadows, J. P.

Roy NORTHCUTT to Sallie JENKINS Issued 15 Mar 1917 Rites 15 Mar 1917 S. T. Byars, M. G.

Ross MAYO to Adell CARVER issued 17 Mar 1917 Rites 18 Mar 1917 T. B. Clark, M. G.

C. R. WOMACK to Mollie SMITH Issued 17 Mar 1917 Rites 18 Mar 1917 T. B. Clark, M. G.

Ransom SWINDELL to Bernice WATSON Issued 20 Mar 1917 Not Returned

H. L. WALLING to Mrs. SAllie COPE Issued 24 Mar 1917 Rites25 Mar 1917 P. G. Potter, M. G.

Claud VINSON to Florence WILSON Issued 24 Mar 1917 Not Retuened

J. L. McGEE to Dora HILLIS Issued 28 Mar 1917 Rites 28 Mar 1917 J. B. Dobbs, J. P.

Howard S. RAMSEY to Elizabeth Mae BONNER Issued 28 Mar 1917 Rites 29 Mar 1917 Price Billingsley, M. G.

J. M. WOOD to Mrs. Dovie JONES Issued 29 Mar 1917 Rites 30 Mar 1917 H. L. Jones, J. P.

E. N. DELZELL to Alma BURKS Issued 7 Apr 1917 Rites7 Apr 1917 J. T. Casey, M. G.

Henry NEWCOME to May SMITH Issued7 Apr 1917 Rites 7 Apr 1917 L. G. Patrick, J. P.

E. C. HALTERMAN to Lillian GRIBBLE issued 10 Apr 1917 Not Returned

John SMITH to Tennie May BULLARD Issued 10 Apr 1917 Rites 12 Apr 1917 J. T. Vinson, J. P.

Charles DAVIS to Bettie HENNESSEE Issued 11 Apr 1917 Rites 11 Apr 1917 L. G. Patrick, J. P.

Walter GREEN to MAttie DONNELL Issued 16 Apr 1917 Rites 16 Apr 1916 B. S. McCollum, J. P.

Lytle WINTON (CO to Allie May SCOTT (Col) Issued 17 Apr 1917 Rites Apr 17 1917 T. M. Eaton, J. P.

Harmen ENSBERGER to Lillie May DeGROAT Issued 18 Apr 1917 Rites 18 Apr 1917 AL. Hodge, M. G.

Magness COPE to Josie ZWINGLE Issued18 Apr 1917 Rites 18 Apr 1917 H. L. Walling, M. G.

Colonel FRAZIER to Ophie EDWARDS Issued 21 Apr 1917 Rites 22 Apr 1917 J. A. Brixey, J. P.

Darius BOYD to May COPPINGER Issued 24 Apr 1917 Rites 26 Apr 1917 J. J. Meadows, J. P.

Tom SNELLING (Col) to Hattie SANFORD (Col) Issued 25 Apr 1917 Rites 25 Apr 1917 J. S. Nance, M. G.

Robert T. HASH to Inez Margarette DUNCAN Issued 28 Apr 1917 Not Returned

Henry C. PRYOR to Martha GOLDEN Issued 2 May 1917 Rites 2 May 1917 John H. Settle, M. G.

Livie FAIRBANKS to Ermie BOTTOMS Issued 5 May 1917 Returned - Not Solemnized

J. L. WARREN to Mary Jane PURSER Issued 8 May 1917 Rites 3 Jun 1917 H. L. Jones, M. G.

John BOYD to Alice STEPP Issued 11 May 1917 Rites 13 May 1917 C. T. Webster, M. G.

John B. WALKER to Laura WOMACK Issued11 May 1917 Rites 11 May 1917 J. W. Eaton, Jdg.

O. C. CHRISTIAN to Della TAYLOR Issued 12 May 1917 Rites 13 May 1917 J. W. Gross, M. G.

Arzy CURTIS to Alda BOYD Issued 12 May 1917 Rites 13 May 1917 J. W. Gross, M. G.

Enoch NORTHCUTT (Col) to Lillie WINTON (Col) Issued 12 May 1917 Rites 13 May 1917 T. M. Eaton, J. P.

Abe CURTIS to Bettie GROVE Issued 12 May 1917 Rites 13 May 1917 H. T. McGregor, J. P.

W. L. PATTERSON to Alice Lee Emma DAVIS Issued 19 May 1917 Rites 20 May 1917 J. M. Green, J. P.

Jesse HIGGINBOTHAM to Eliza SCOTT Issued 26 May 1917 Rites 17 May 1917 J. D. Templeton, J. P.

Levie F IRBANKS to Delia BARNES Issued 26 May 1917 Rites 26 May 1917 H. T. McGregor, J. P.

Sidney MADEWELL to Thelia KUHN Issued 29 May 1917 Rites 30 May 1917 E. L. Moffitt, J. P.

J. T. STROUD to Edna HUDSON Issued 7 Aug 1917 Rites 7 Aug 1917
J. G. Patrick, J. P.

E. L. SMITH to Myrtle KING Issued 9 Aug 1917 Rites 9 Aug 1917
J. W. Cooley, M. G.

Howard S. YORK to Alma DODSON Issued 9 Aug 1917 Rites 12 Aug 1917
J. D. Quick, J. P.

Martin FARLESS to Omagh OVERALL Issued 11 Aug 1917 Rites 12 Aug 1917
A. J. Morgan, M. G.

O. D. McGREGOR to Lizzie PERRY Issued 13 Aug 1917 Rites 13 Aug 1917
L. G. Patrick, J.P.

Jim WITT to Dora MARTIN Issued 14 Aug 1917 Rites 17 Aug 1917
J. E. Will, M. G.

Benton ROGERS to Georgia KELL Issued 17 Aug 1917 Rites 18 Aug 1918
W. S. Grisson, J. P.

Mack Rhea to Myrtle WALKER Issued 20 Aug 1917 Rites 22 Aug 1917
F. C. Boyd, J. P.

Ernest WOMACK (Col) to Lucille SMITH (Col) Issued 20 Aug 1917 Rites 20 Aug 1917
J. M. Green, J. P.

Joe BOTTOMS to Wavie CRAIN Issued 25 Aug 1917 Rites 26 Aug 1917
H. T. McGregor, J. P.

Everett DAVIS to Hassie SAUNDERS Issued 30 Aug 1917 Rites 30 Aug 1917
P. G. Potter, M. G.

John B. WASHBURN to Wave OWEN Issued 1 Sep 1917 Rites 2 Sep 1917
P. G. Potter, M. G.

Robert H. CANTRELL to Emma May PENNINGTON Issued8 Sep 1917 Rites 8 Sep 1917
J. H. Settle, M. G.

Howard STANLEY to Inex TURNER Issued 8 Sep 1917 Rites 9 Sep 1917
J. T. Vinson, J. P.

Algie CARTWRIGHT to Amanda GREEN Issued 11 Sep 1917 Rites 11 Sep 1917
J. H. Settle, M. G.

W. E. MERRITT to Nannie GREEN Issued 14 Sep 1917 Rites 16 Sep 1917
J. H. Settle, M. G.

F. M. MARTIN (Col) to Pearl FISK (Col) Issued 20 Sep 1917 Rites 20 Sep 1917
J. D. HaSH, J. P.

Henry W. REDMON to Rowena Eliz. PENNINGTON Issued 20 Sep 1917 Rites 20 Sep

Jesse POWELL to Grace KILLIAN Issued 21 Sep 1917 Rites 21 Sep 1917
H. T. McGregor, J. P,

Wade H. JONES to Ada FUSTON Issued 21 Sep 1917 Rites 22 Sep 1917
H. J. Boles, M. G.

Tom MITCHELL (Col) to Ernie MARBERRY (Col) Issued 30 May 1917 Rites 30 May 1917
J. S. Nance, M. G.

H. S. WILSON to Jessie Belle WILCOX Issued 1 Jun 1917 Rites1 Jun 1917
Frank B. Shepherd, M. G.

Fred SAIN to Ruby STUBBLEFIELD Issued1 Jun 1917 Rites 1 Jun 1917
T. B. Clark, M. G.

Jesse L. NUNLEY to Fannie Belle NEWMAN Issued 2 Jun 1917 Rites 2 Jun 1917
Frank B. Shepherd, M. G,

Frank WARREN to Isabel JONES Issued 2 Jun 1917 Rites 10 Jun 1917
P. G. Potter, M. G.

L. D. GOLDEN to Ozella MABE Issued 2 Jun 1917 Rites 2 Jun 1917
G. L. Beech, J. P.

W. M. FUSTON to Edith GRIBBLE Issued 8 Jun 1917 Rites 10 Jun 1917
J. M. Green, J. P.

Joseph Kelly MARTIN to Bessie BOOHER Issued 15 Jun 1917 Rites 16 Jun 1917
S. T. Byars, M. G.

Thos. Claud THUNDERBURK to Ulzo Louise BOLES Issued 16 Jun 1917 Rites 17 Jun 1917.
P. G. Totter, M. G.

Floyd KEATON to Barba DAVENPORT Issued 16 Jun 1917 Rites 17 Jun 1917
A. Z. Holder, J. P.

W. J. WILLAIMS to Lelie G. NEARN Issued 20 Jun 1917 Rites 20 Jun 1917
J. D. Northcutt

Claudie HOLLAND to Jewell WALKER issued 23 Jun 1917 Rites24 Jun 1917
L. G. Patrick, J. P.

Frank MOORE to Grace RIGGS Issued 3 Jul 1917 Rites 4 Jul 1917
L. R. Hogan, M. G.

Hascal CUNNINGHAM to Martha HENNESSEE Issued 7 Jul 1917 Rites 8 Jul 1917
H. T. McGregor, . P.

E. W. LANCE to Annon GILLEY Issued 9 Jul 1917 Rites 12 Jul 1917
Price Billingsley, M. G.

J. Ray SAFLEY to Sarah HASH Issued 27 Jul 1917 Rites 27 Jul 1917
J. D. Hash, J. P.

Lee LOCKE (col) to Laura PENINGTON (Col) Issued 28 Jul 1917 Rites 29 Jul 1917
L. G. Patrick, J. P.

J. L. MARTIN to Maude CURTIS Issued4 Aug 1917 Rites 5 Aug 1917
H. T. McGregor, J. P.

Warren McMAHAN to Mary Louise ADKINS Issued 4 Aug 1917 Rites 5 Aug 1917
O. H. Wood, J. P.

Walter HILL to Alene MITCHELL Issued 7 Aug 1917 Rites7 Aug 1917
F. C. Boyd, J. P.

Virgil Kiah HORTON to Cora JAne DODSON Issued 26 Sep 1917 Rites 27 Sep 1917
A. L. Hodge, M. G.

Lonnie HILLIS to Ollie FULTS Issued 28 Sep 1917 Rites 30 Sep 1917
J. J. Meadows, J. P.

W. D. DAVIS to Flossie EMERY Issued 29 Sep 1917 Rites 6 Oct 1917
W. C. Lorance, J. P

Bill HALE to Mary HILLIS Issued 1 Oct 1917 Rites 1 Oct 1917
J. D. Quick, J. P.

O. B. PAYNE to Catherine McGIBONEY Issued 1 Oct 1917 Rites 3 Oct 1917
J. D. HASH, J. P.

Alva YORK to Edna GALLADAY Issued 5 Oct 1917 Rites 7 Oct 1917
A. L. Hodge, M.G.

Berry HUDDLESTON (Col) to Sue FOSTER (Col) Issued 6 Oct 1917 Rites 6 Oct 1917
J. B. Brown, J. P.

Albert MOORE to Pearl WILLIAMS Issued 6 Oct 1917 Rites 7 Oct 1917
J. A. Brixey, J. P.

John L. HALLUM to Hattie Belle FENNELL Issued 12 Oct 1917 Rites 12 Oct 1917
L. R. Hogan, M. G.

Richard WEST to Margie WILSON Issued 13 Oct 1917 Rites 13 Oct 1917
W. W. Locke, J. P.

Charlie WOOD (Col) to Gertrude SPURLOCK (Col) Issued 13 Oct 1917 Rites 14 Oct 1917
W. W. Locke, J. P.

John MASEY to Ola STIPES Issued 13 Oct 1917 Rites 14 Oct 1917
J. M. Green, J. P.

Bate FRENCH (Col) to Rosa Bell RAMSEY (Col) Issued 15 Oct 1917 Rites 15 Oct 1917
W. W. Locke, J. P.

Enoch J. RAMSEY to Edna Wave SMARTT Issued 18 Oct 1917 Rites 18 Oct 1917
L. R. Hogan, M. G.

DAn BEATY to Emma HESSELTINE Issued 19 Oct 1917 Rites 19 Oct 1917
P. G. Potter, M. G.

Jim HALE to Shelie DODSON Issued 20 Oct 1917 Rites 20 Oct 1917
J. B. Dobbs, J. P.

Tim MARKEM to Mollie MARKEM Issued 20 Oct 1917 Rites 25 Oct 1917
J. T. Vinson, J. P.

Tom COOPER to Wilda TRUITT Issued 27 Oct 1917 Rites 28 Oct 1917
(Court order - name change Bk 27 Pg 229)   J. A. Brixey, J. P.

Marles WOODS to Roberta PINKLIN Issued 27 Oct 1917 Rites 28 Oct 1917
L. G. Patrick, J. P.

Henry Thos. BARRETT to Lella Etherl McCORKLE Issued 2 Nov 1917 Rites 3 Nov 1917
L. R. Hogan, M. G.

John C. HAMMER to Mollie WHEELER Issued 3 Nov 1917 Rites 4 Nov 1917
S. T. Byars, M. G.

Horace B. JULIAN to Johnye R. BRYSON Issued 3 Nov 1917 Rites 4 Sep 1917
J. M. Green, J. P.

L. J. MILLER to S. A. CRAIN Issued 5 Nov 1917 Rites 5 Nov 1917
J. W. Eaton, Jdg.

JAmes T. SIMS to Sadie MERCER issued 7 Nov 1917 Rites 7 Nov 1917
A. J. Morgan, M. G.

D. M. CLARK to Ollie PASSONS Issued 8 Nov 1917 Retuened - Not SOLOMNIZED

George SAVAGE (Col) to Sallie TIDWELL (Col), Issued 8 Nov 1917 Rites 10 Nov 1917
J. B. Dobbs, J. P.

Lee HARRIS to Nettie SELLARS Issued 9 Nov 1917 Rites 10 Nov 1917
L. G. Patrick, J. P.

Jacob J. COPPLE to Alberta M. BAKER Issued 13 Nov 1917 Rites 14 Nov 1917
J. T. Parsons, M. G.

Eston Taylor RICHARDS to Georgia BLACK Issued 13 Nov 1917 Rites 14 Nov 1917
A. J. Morgan, M. G.

Parker BOULDIN to Nannie MARTIN Issued 14 Nov 1917 Rites 18 Nov 1917
C. M. Collier, J. P.

Jesse GREEN to Mary SIMMONS Issued 17 Nov 1917 Rites 18 Nov 1917
J. L. Smith, J. P.

Jim YORK (Col) to Octa WOODS (Col) Issued 17 Nov 1917 Rites 17 Nov 1917
C. M. Collier, J. P.

Alton HALTERMAN to Novella PATTON Issued 21 Nov 1917 Rites 22 Nov 1917
J. D. Quick, J. P.

E. C. MILLER to Lois KEYTON Issued 21 Nov 1917 Rites 29 Nov 1917
H. E. Baker, M. G.

Phillip SMITH (Col) to Ruby SPURLOCK (Col) Issued 24 Nov 1917 Rites 24 nov
J. B. Hobbs, J. P.

J. B. HOLDER to Glisson TAYLOR Issued 28 Nov 1917 Rites 29 Nov 1917
P. G. Potter, M. G.

James ROGERS to Kate NEMAN Issued 1 Dec 1917 Rites 2 Dec 1917
Byrd Phillips, M. G.

W. W. TURNER to Anna CLARK Issued 1 dec 1917 Rites 2 Dec 1917
W. W. Locke, J. P.

Wm Bruce SAVAGE to Ermie Lee BOTTOMS Issued 8 Dec 1917 Rites 10 Dec 1917
L. G. Patrick, J. P.

Robert I. GRIZZLE to Fannie D. MASSIE Issued 2 Jan 1918 Rites 3 Jan 1918
A. J. Morgan, M. G.

Lonie BATES (Col) to Beatrice HUNTER (Col) Issued 2 Jan 1918 Rites 2 JAn 1918
J. S. Nance, M. G.

C. R. REED to Ophie HUDSON Issued 5 Jan 1918 Rites 6 Jan 1918
John Davis, J. P.

J. M. CUMMINGS to Ocie SWINDELL Issued 8 JAn 1918 Rites 8 JAn 1918
J. T. Vinson, J. P.

Avery EVANS to Girtie McGREGOR Issued 12 Jan 1918 Rites 13 Jan 1918
H. T. McGregor, J. P.

Borwn OLIVER to Maud E. MEISER Issued 19 Jan 1918 Rites 20 Jan 1918
Price Billingsley, M. G.

John BOULDIN to Willie MORTON Issued 21 Jan 1918 Rites 21 Jan 1918
J. B. Dobbs, J. P.

Oren TEMPLETON to Shrilda GLENN Issued 22 Jan 1918 Rites 27 Jan 1918
B. G. Moore, J. P.

Dave St. JOHN to Lena REYNOLDS Issued 24 Jan 1918 Rites 27 Jan 1918
W. S. Reynolds, J. P.

Jim RAMSEY (Col) to Pearl THOMASON (Col) Issued 24 Jan 1918 Rites 24 Jan 1918
J. S. Nance, M. G.

Willie CRIM to Gay STIPE Issued 2 Feb 1918 Rites 3 Feb 1918
J. M. Green, J. P.

Charlie BRIGHT to Mary REYNOLDS Issued 4 Feb 1918 Rites 5 Feb 1918
J. W. Cooley, M. G.

Will CURTIS to Ict GREEN Issued 5 Feb 1918 Rites 5 Feb 1918
F. C. Boyd, J. P.

Schuyler BAILEY to Stella BRATCHER uisued 8 Feb 1918 Rites 10 Feb 1918
J. T. Vinson, J. P.

Edward D. HOTCHKISS to Willett EArl Issued 14 Feb 1918 Rites 14 Feb 1918
Price Billingsley, M. G.

Bill FANN to Fannie MARTIN Issued 15 Feb 1918 Rites 15 Feb 1918
J. W. EAton, J. P.

D. G. ORICK to Lou JOHNSON Issued 19 Feb 1918 Rites 20 Feb 1918
C. M. Collier, J. P.

J.D. SWINDELL to Gladys HOWARD Issued 20 Feb 1918 Rites 27 Feb 1918
J. L. McPeak, M. G.

William RICH to Musie PARIS Issued 21 feb 1918 Rites 24 Feb 1918
L. R. Hogan, M. G.

Hiram DAVIS to Martha McGREGOR Issued8 Dec 1917 returned - Not Solemnized

Amonell ROGERS to Emma HALE Issued 13 Dec 1917 Rites 14 Dec 1917
W. S. Grissom, J. P.

J. G. ROBERTSON to Julia SMITH Issued 18 Dec 1917 Rites 19 Dec 1917
F. W. Muse, M. C,

Charles MORGAN to Lela BROWN Issued 18 Dec 1917 Rites 25 Dec 1917
P. G. Moore, J. P.

Tom WALKER to Anna WALKER Issued 19 Dec 1917 Rites 19 Dec 1917
L.G. Patrick

Claud DEBERRY to Bettie WILSON Issued 19 Dec 1917 Rites 23 Dec 1923
A. Z. Holder, J. P.

Arzie HILLIS to Alethia OWEN Issued 19 Dec 1917 Rites 23 Dec 1917
J. A. Cunningham, M. G.

Monroe DODD to Minnie MILLER Issued 19 Dec 1917 Rites 22 Dec 1917
A. Z. Holder, J. P.

Bill LEWIS to Hettie FULTS Issued 20 Dec 1917 Rites 21 Dec 1917
A. L. Hodge, M. G.

C. H. MOONEYHAM to Ophia Irene WEBB Issued 22 Dec 1917 Rites 27 Dec 1917
L. C. Lane, J. P.

Everett O. WEBB to Hettie Bell WOMACK Issued 22 Dec 1917 Rites 25 Dec 1917
J. L. Smith, J. P.

George CUNNINGHAM to Alice SIMMONS Issued 22 Dec 1917 Rites 25 Dec 1917
A. L. Hodge, M. G.

A. C. WOODS to Annie VERNON (Col) Issued 24 Dec 1917 Rites 24 Dec 1917
(Col) J. N. Washington, M. G.

Birt ROBERTS (Col) to Bertha RICE (Col) Issued 25 dec 1917 Rites Dec 25 |(17
J. A. W. Moore, M. G.

G. D. CASEY to Levada BOWMAN Issued Dec 26 1917 Rites 27 Dec 1917
J. A. Cunningham, M. G.

J. S. CRANE, Jr. to Martha REDMON Issued 26 Dec 1917 Rites 28 Dec 1917
W. S. Grissom, J. P.

Hamp D. CATEN to Mae REYNOLDS Issued 27 dec 1917 Not Returned

T. M. JACKSON to Dellie POLLARD issued 28 Dec 1917 Rites 30 Dec 1917
J. B. Brown, J. P.

H. L. McGEE to Burton BOST Issued 30 Dec 1917 Rites 30 Dec 1917
B. S. McCollum, J. P.

Almond MARTIN (Col) to Minnie HUNTER (Col) Issued31 Dec 1917 Rites 31 Dec 1917
J. S. Nance, M. G.

A. B. FORD to Willie SPARKMAN Issued 22 Feb 1918 Rites 22 Feb 1918
J. W. Eaton, Jdg.

Thurman LANCE to Mimmie Mae GRIFFITH issued 22 Feb 1918 Rites 24 feb 1918
A. Z. Holder, J. P.

Bryan MOORE to Docie GREEN Issued 28 Feb 1918 Rites 2 Mar 1918
L. R. Hogan, M. G.

Harry E. BETCHEL ro Elnora WILCHER Issued 2 Mar 1918 Rites 2 Mar 1918
J. B. Dobbs, J. P.

G. D. GREEN to Mary McCORMACK Issued 2 Mar 1918 Rites 3 MAr 1918
J. B. Dobbs, J. P.

W. W. GROSS to Rosa Lee HOBBS Issued 2 Mar 1918 Rites 3 Mar 1918
J. W. Cooley, M. G.

Thurman CLARK to Ina ALLEN Issued 9 MAr 1918 Rites 16 Mar 1918
A. J. Morgan, M. G.

G. W. TEMPLETON to Pauline ELKINS Issued16 Mar 1918 Rites 16 Mar 1918
J. B. Dobbs, J. P.

Edward HILL to Linnie Pearl WHITTENBURG Issued18 Mar 1918 Rites 18 Mar 1918
G. C. Boyd, J. P.

James H. KIRBY to Mattie KIRBY Issued 18 Mar 1918 Rites 18 Mar 1918
J. B. Dobbs, J. P.

Jonah E. BROWN to Anna Bell WILCHER Issued 20 Mar 1918 Rites 18 Mar 1918
F. S. Womack, J. P.

JAmes WOMACK (Col) to Matilda Ann THORN (Col) Isseud 22 Mar 1918 Rites 22 Mar
J. S. NANCE, M. G.

L. M. HITT to Martha POTTER Issued 27 Mar 1918 Rites 27 Mar 1918
S. T. Byars, M. G.

Alaska GOLDEN to Estelle PRYOR Issued 30 Mar 1918 Rites 31 Mar 1918
H. E. Baker, M. G.

Dion ROGERS to Eliza Irene BONNER Issued 6 Apr 1918 Rites 14 Apr 1918
F. C. Boyd, J. P.

Gladys BONNER to Estelle ROGERS Issued 10 Apr 1918 Rites 11 apr 1918
J. T. Parsons, M. G.

Ed MARTIN to Pearl TURNER Issued 11 Apr 1918 Rites 12 Apr 1918
H. T. McGregor, J. P.

Grundy WEBB to Lettie EARLS Issued 13 Apr 1918 Rites 13 Apr 1918
J. B. Dobbs, J. P.

Joe KINES (Col) to Alice FRENCH (Col) Issued 15 Apr 1918 Rites 15 Apr 1918
J. S. NANCE, M. G.

Polk WHITLOCK to Ethel LASSITER Issued 17 Apr 1918 Rites 21 apr 1918
J.A. Cunningham, M. G.

Mikey BRIGHT to Clistie GRIBBLE Issued 20 Apr 1918 Rites 21 Apr 1918
J. M. Green, J. P.

Ira ROGERS to Nora SMITH Issued 20 Apr 1918 Rites 26 Apr 1918
F. C. Boyd, J. P.

Graves JOHNSON to Dora NUNLEY Issued 22 Apr 1918 Rites 22 Apr 1918
F. C. Boyd, J. P.

Reeder RAMSEY to Belle MYERS Issued 27 Apr 1918 Rites 28 Apr 1918
O. H. Wood, J. P.

Harris HOBBS to Jessie FARLESS Issued 27 Apr 1918 Rites 28 Apr 1918
G. L. Beech, J. P.

Howard W. PERSINGER to Madgie Mai FISHER Issued 2 May 1918 Rites 2 May 1918
A. J. Morgan, M. G.

P. L. DENNIS to Effie WHITMAN Issued 2 May 1918 Rites 3 May 1918
J. T. Vinson, J. P.

Bouldin LAWRENCE (Col) to Maud SPURLOCK (Col) Issued 6 May 1918 Rites 6 May 1918
W. W. Locke, J. P.

Harry A. WATT to Opal Irene LEE Issued 9 May 1918 Rites 14 May 1918
C. G. Howell, M. G.

Miller HUNTER to Mary Ellen MARTIN Issued 11 May 1918 Rites 12 May 1918
J. L. McPeak, M. G.

A. S. HILL to Mary Etta BARNES Issued 11 May 1918 Rites 13 May 1918
A. J. Morgan, M. G.

J. R. HENDERSON to Mrs. Parlee KIRBY Issued 15 May 1918 Rites 16 May 1918
E. R. Little, M. G.

J. P. BLAIR to Leona SCOTT Issued 16 May 1918 Rites 16 May 1918
L. G. Patrick, J. P.

Lucious DUNLAP to Lena BRYANT Issued 18 May 1918 Rites 21 May 1918
J. D. Quick, J. P.

Rupert BAKER to Elizabeth DAVIS Issued 24 May 1918 Rites 26 May 1918
H. E. Baker, M. G.

Auborn H. GRAY to MAry Velma HUGHES Issued 25 May 1918 Rites 25 May 1918
G. C. Brewer, M. G.

Joe O'NEAL to Addie BARNES Issued 25 May 1918 Rites 26 May 1918
H. T. McGregor, J. P.

W. L. CUNNINGHAM to Rebecca HAMMONS Issued 29 May 1918 Rites 29 May 1918
J. T. Casey, M. G.

J. H. FERRELL to Susie DRIVER Issued 27 May 1918 Rites 29 May 1918
J. B. Dobbs, J. P.

Willie S. ALLEN to Bessie ADAMSON Issued 1 Jun 1918 Rites 2 Jun 1918
J. T. CAsey, M. G.

George WORLEY to Bernice HULBERT Issued1 Jun 1918 Rites 2 Jun 1918
Byrd Phillips, M. G.

Bryan GREEK to Harriet FISHER Issued 8 Jun 1918 Rites 9 Jun 1918
H. T. McGregor

DAniel W. NELSON to Lillie Mae GIBBS Issued 15 Jun 1918 Rites 15 Jun 1918
L. G. Patrick, J. P.

BAsil H. COOK to Novella MERRITT Issued 15 Jun 1918 Rites 16 Jun 1918
H. E. Baker, M. G.

Hobart COPE (Col) to Mimmie ROBINSON (Col) Issued 15 Jun 1918 Not Returned

John Thos. MULLICAN to Virgie Maud STROUD Issued 16 Jun 1918 Rites 16 Jun 1918
G. L. Beech, I. P.

Virgil St. JOHN to Tisie RICHARDSON Issued 22 Jun 1918 Rites 22 Jun 1918
W. S. Grissom. J. P.

Mose Lee WALLER to Margretta WHITSON Issued 25 Jun 1918 Rites25 Jun 1918
L.R. Hogan, M. G.

Joseph Allen BRYANT to Florence Morford ROGERS Issued 26 Jun 1918 Rites 26 Jun
L. R. Hogan, M. G.

Charles PEPPER to Pheoba EARLS Issued 4 Jul 1918 Rites 4 Jul 1918
Byrd Phillips, M. G.

John BARNES to Isabell GILLEY Issued 6 Jul 1918 Rites 7 Jul 1918
J. T. CAsey, M. G.

J. O. REDMON to Madgie CANTRELL Issued 6 Jul 1918 Rites 12 Jul 1918
P. G. Potter, M. G.

Richard RUCKER, Jr. (Col) to Nannie JETT (Col) Issued 12 Jul 1918 Rites 12 Jul
L. G. Patrick, J. P.

C. Marvin JONES to Lizzie May OAKS Issued 19 Jul 1918 Rites 21 Jul 1918
A. Z. Holder, J. P.

Ed B. JOHNSON to JAmie BETHEL Issued 25 Jul 1918 Rites 25 Jul 1918
G. L. Beech, J. P.

D. P. GREEN to Alma DELONG Issued 27 Jul 1918 Rites 6 Aug 1918
I. G. Webb, J. P.

Wm. Brown SPURLOCK to Willie PEELER Issued 27 Jul 1918 Rites 28 Jul 1918
H. L. Jones, J. P.

Robert L. GARNER to Sallie WINTON Issued 30 Jul 1918 Rites 31 Jul 1918
J. T. Casey, M. G.

Elmer LAWRENCE to Ruth HAYES Issued 1 Aug 1918 Rites 1 Aug 1918
A. J. Morgan, M. G.

Dillard GWYNN (Col) to Dora DONAHUE (Col) Issued 5 Aug 1918 Rites 7 Aug 1918
I. W. Hunt

Ray LAWS to Nora SCALF Issued 6 Aug 1918 Rites 6 Aug 1918
J. W. Cooley, M. G.

Adam MARKUM to Fannie YOUNGBLOOD Issued 12 Aug 1918 Rites 14 Aug 1918
A. Z. Holder, J. P.

Harry G. PHILLIPS to Martha E. ILHERAN Issued 19 Aug 1918 Rite 19 Aug 1918
J. W. Eaton, Jdg.

Hugh ARNOLD to Ora GREEN Issued 20 Aug 1918 Rites 26 Aug 1918
J. L. McPeak, M. G.

John GREEN to Ilene BRYEN Issued 20 Aug 1918 Rites 25 Aug 1918
H. E. BAker, M. G.

Haburn TURNER to Elmar TURNER Issued 21 Aug 1918 Rites 22 Aug 1918
P. G. Moore, J. P.

Isham RAOCH to Maggie TURNER Issued 22 Aug 1918 Rites 22 Aug 1918
G. P. Brasier, J. P.

Herbert BOND to Bessie DAVENPORT Issued 22 Aug 1918 Rites 25 Aug 1918
G. H. Atulp, M. G.

Paty GWYNN (Col) to Arline BONNER (Col) Issued 24 Aug 1918 Rites 25 Aug 1918
O. H. wood, J. P.

W. T. HENNESSEE to Zoe SWINDELL Issued 24 Mar 1918 Rites 25 Mar 1918
A. J. Morgan, M. G.

John FARRAR to Zora WEST Issued 28 Aug 1918 Rites 29 Aug 1918
J. W. Eaton, Jdg.

Jess Tom TURNER to Mary Etta WASHBURN Issued 4 Sep 1918 Rites 4 Sep 1918
A. J. Morgan, M. G.

Cock LOOPER (Col) to Maude ROACH (Col) Issued 5 Sep 1918 Rites 5 Sep 1918
J. S. Nance, M. G.

Livy McCORMACK to Bessie WOOD Issued 7 Sep 1918 Rites 8 Sep 1918
P. N. Moffitt, J. P.

R. L. ESTES to Etta PUCKETT Issued 11 Sep 1918 Rites 11 Sep 1918
G. B. Beaver, J. P.

Roy Martin to Arvie SHUSTER Issued 12 Sep 1918 Rites 13 Sep 1918
W. V. D. Miller, J. P.

Charlie RIDDLE to Mary YORK Issued 21 Sep 1918 Rites 22 Sep 1918
J. D. Northcutt

Andrew BARNES to Eliza Jane BOYD Issued 24 Sep 1918 Rites 26 Sep 1918
P. N. Moffitt, J. P.

Nixon HENDRICKS to Ocie JONES Issued 24 Sep 1918 Rites 25 Sep 1918
Price Billingsley, M. G.

J. T. Whitlock to Mary Etta GRIFFITH Issued 26 Sep 1918 Rites 26 Sep 1918
J. T. Casey, M. G.

E. L. BARNES to Nellie SHIRLEY Issued 27 Sep 1918 Rites 29 Sep 1918
J.A. Cunningham, M. G.

I. P. GREEN to Nannie KELLER Issued 28 Sep 1918 Rites 28 Sep 1918
J. T. Casey, M. G.

W. N. LANCE to Nancy Emmaline WINNETT Issued 4 Oct 1918 Rites 6 Oct 1918
A. C. Lorance, J. P.

Barnum MARTIN (Col) to Hassie BARTLEY (Col) Issued4 Oct 1918 Rites 5 Oct 1918
J. D. Hash, J. P.

J. E. DUNLAP to RAye HALTERMAN Issued 5 Oct 1918 Rites 26 Dec 1918
W. V. D. Miller, J. P.

Bruce CURTIS to Bessie GILLENTINE Issued 9 Oct 1918 Rites 9 Oct 1918
E. Christian, M. G.

Minor GARDNER (Col) to Lizzie THOMPSON (Col) Issued 9 Oct 1918 Rites 10 Oct 1918
J. A. W. Moore, M. G.

Jesse TAYLOR to Maude MOFFITT Issued 11 Oct 1918 Rites 13 Oct 1918
FAte WAlker, J. P.

Chas. PENDLETON to Mary TURNER Issued 12 Oct 1918 Rites 12 Oct 1918
O. H. Wood, J. P.

Isaiah ROBERTS to Lou BARNES Issued 14 Oct 1918 Rites 14 Oct 1918
J. C. knight, M. G.

J. W. SANDERS to Susie DOVE Issued 16 Oct 1918 Rites 17 Oct 1918
L. C. Lane, J. P.

Capel Ernest JACKSON (Col) to Nora B. MARTIN (Col) Issued18 Oct 1918 Not Returned

Lusk ROGERS to Pearl RICHARDSON Issued 21 Oct 1918 Rites 25 Oct 1918
L. B. Moffitt, J. P.

Forrest B. KEITH to Margarett Lucille HUTCHINS Issued 26 Oct 1918 Rites 26 Oct
A. J. Morgan, M. G.

Charlie HARDING to Maude Eliz. NEWBY Issued 30 Oct 1918 Rites 31 Oct 1918
G. H. Atnip, M. G.

586 Marriages in this book

Book 13 - Warren County Marriages - Nov. 1, 1918 to Feb 7, 1922

Roy GRIFFITH to Effie FUSTON Issued 1 Nov 1918 Rites 1 Non 1918
Geo. B. Beaver, J. P.

W. H. KEELE to Pearl HURTT Issued 6 Nov 1918 Rites 6 Nov 1918
L. G. Patrick, J.P.

J. S. DYER to Lodus DULANEY Issued 9 Nov 1918 Rites 9 Nov 1918

Worth JONES to Nora O'NEAL Issued 9 Nov 1918 Rites 10 Nov 1918
L. G. Patrick, J. P.

Sam GREEN to Flora WHITE Issued 16 Nov 1918 Rites 17 Nov 1918
H. E. Baker, M. G.

Earl P. CAMPBELL to Marion Cornelia GRAY Issued 16 Nov 1918   Not Returned

Marshall McGEEHEE (Col) to Lizzie THOMAS (Col) Issued 19 Nov 1918 Rites 20 Nov

O. H. LOGAN to George Ella SIMPSON Issued 20 Nov 1918 Rites 20 Nov 1920
E. C. Leeper, M. G.

Robert Wm. DEMESEE to Ella Pearl BILBREY Issued 20 Nov 1918 Not Returned

Eill MARTIN (Col) to Lizzie EDMONDSON (Col) Issued 23 Nov 1918 Rites 24 Nov 1918

Logan WATLEY to Jennie SMOOT Issued 23 Nov 1918 Rites 24 Nov 1918
B. S. McCollum, J. P.

J. F. CUNNINGHAM to Lula DAVENPORT Issued30 Nov 1918 Rites 1 Dec 1918
W. C. Lorance, J. P.

Clark DAVENPORT to Flora HILLIS Issued 20 Dec 1918 Rites 22 Dec 1918
A. Z. Holder, J. P.

Philip MAYFIELD to Ova McBRIDE Issued 21 Dec 1918 Rites 22 Dec 1918
W. V. D. Miller, J. P.

A. H. MOFFITT to Annie Ruth STUBBLEFIELD Issued 21 Dec 1918 Rites 22 Dec 1918
Byrd Phillips, M. G.

Arch COPE (Col) to Birtie BARNES (Col) Issued 21 Dec 1918 Rites 22 Dec 1918
Sam King, M. G.

John FISHER to Sarah Belle GREEN Issued 21 Dec 1918 Rites 22 Dec 1918
L. C. Lane, J. P.

Claud CRAWFORD to Clara CUNNINGHAM Issued 21 Nov 1918 Rites 21 Nov 1918
A. J. Morgan, M. G.

J. M. HASH to Lola YATES Issued 23 Dec 1918 Rites 24 Dec 1918
E. J. Bachmen, M. G.

Andrew SIMONS to Gladys AUGHINBAUGH Issued 23 Dec 1918 Rites 24 Dec 1918
Fate Walker, J. P.

Jesse J. O'CONNOR to Minnie SWEARINGIN Rites 23 Dec 1918 Rites 23 Dec 1918
J. W. Eaton, Jdg.

S. W. HILLIS to Grace SIMONS Issued 21 Feb 1919 Rites 23 Feb 1919
A. Z. Holder, J. P.

John FORD to Mattie SPARKMAN Issued 25 Feb 1919 Rites 25 Feb 1919
A. J. Morgan, M. G.

James SHUGARS (Col) to Shumpen TALLEY (Col) Issued 10 Mar 1919 Rites 10 Mar
J. S. NAnce

F. C. STONE to Effie FOSTER Issued 14 Mar 1919 Rites 14 1919
O. H. Woods, J. P.

C. T. PENNINGTON to Annie CANTRELL Issued 15 Mar 1919 Rites 16 Mar 1919
J. A. Brixey, J. P.

Franklin H. COUCH to Lilliam THAXTON Issued 20 Mar 1919 Rites 20 1919
A. J. Morgan, M. G.

E. L. STANFORD to Ada BELCHER Issued 22 Mar 1919 Rites 22 Mar 1919
J. M. Eaton, Jdg.

John W. GOODSON to Vida E. GRIBBLE Issued 26 Mar 1919 Rites 27 Mar 1919
P. G. Patten, M. G.

Lee R. WINNARD to Louise Francis CARRICK Issued 28 Mar 1919 Rites 30 Mar 1919
W. C. Lorance, J. P.

Bethel McGINNIS to Alline GREEN Issued 28 Mar 1919 Rites 30 Mar 1919
L. F. DAugherty, M. G.

J. D. HERNDON to Hassie MEDLEY Issued 29 Mar 1919 Rites 1919
W. C. Lorance, J. P.

Zara ALLEN to Lou RAMSEY Issued 20 Mar 1919 Rites 31 Mar 1919
J. B. DAvis, J. P.

J. C. SHANNON to Alice FULLER Issued 5 Apr 1919 Rites 13 Apr 1919
G. P. Brasier, J. P.

Will McCORMACK to Pheoba HALE Issued 8 Apr 1919 Rites 13 Apr 1919
J. D. HAsh, J. P.

SAm SIMS (Col) to Josie HUNTER (Col) Issued 9 Apr 1919 Rites 9 Apr 1919
J. S. Nance, M. G.

William J. BLANKS to MaGGIE F. PATTERSON Issued 12 Apr 1919 Rites 13 Apr 1919
B. S. McCollum, J. P.

William Thos. RAMSEY to Lucille Zena ROGERS Issued 12 Apr 1919 Rites 15 Apr 1919
J. T. Parson, M. G.

George STOKES (Col) to Sallie MARTIN (Col) Issued 14 Apr 1919 Rites 14 Apr 1919
W. W. Locke, J. P.

Martin HIGGINBOTHAM (C) to Mattie Belle SIMS (C) Issued 17 Apr 1919 Rites 1919
L. G. Patrick, J. P.

Christie DODSON to Alice COUCH Issued 26 Dec 1918 Rites 26 Dec 1918
L. P. Sanders, J. P.

Lilburn ELAM to Nora FARLESS Issued 27 Dec 1918 Rites 27 Dec 1918
J. W. Cooley, M. G.

Charles E. ENGLISH to Anna GANNAWAY Issued 28 Dec 1918 Rites 30 Dec 1918
R. D. Hill, M. G.

W. V. CANTRELL to Minnie Bell BROWN Issued 1 JAn 1919 Rites 1 JAn 1919
L. G. Patrick, J. P.

Vernon ADAMSON to Minnie FOSTER Issued 3 JAn 1919 Not Returned

John H. GESSLER to Hilda BRAGG Issued 16 JAn 1919 Rites 17 JAn 1919
Price Billingsley, M. G.

William G. SNEAD to Susie Lydia ASHLEY Issued 20 JAn 1919 Rites 21 JAn 1919
A. J. Morgan, M. G.

Wm. O. HAMMONS to Lela WILSON Issued 20 Jan 1919 Rites 22 Jan 1919
J. A. Brixey

Jim LANE to Ida Omelia LOCKE Issued 25 JAn 1919 Rites 26 Jan 1919
P. G. Moore, J. P.

Clyde EATON to Ruby JUSTICE Issued 29 JAn 1919 Rites 2 Feb 1919
J. R. Stubblefield, M. G.

DAvid McPHERSON to Mary HILLIS Issued 1 Feb 1919 Rites 16 June 1919
L. G. Patrick, J. P.

Levi MADDUX (Col) to Etta RICE (Col) Issued 1 Feb 1919 Rites 2 Feb 1919
S. T. Lytton, M. G.

Odus ADCOCK to Bessie YOUNG Issued 3 Feb 1919 Not Returned

John Burr PENDLETON to Mary Louise McGUIRE Issued4 Feb 1919 Rites 4 Feb 1199
G. P. Brasier, J. P.

James M. SAPP to Myrtle SMARTT Issued8 Feb 1919 Rites 8 Feb 1919
L. G. Patrick, J. P.

P. G. COUCH to Florence HIGGINBOTHAM Issued 8 Feb 1919 Rites 9 Feb 1919
B. S. McCollum, J. P.

Samuel Walter FITTS to Ethel Rosetta JOHNSON Issued 11 Feb 1919 Rites 16 Feb
J. G. Goff, J. P.

JAmes HODGE to Maggie ROGERS Issued 14 Feb 1919 Returned - Not Solemnized

Agige HUMPHREY to Josie STULTS Issued 14 Feb 1919 Rites 9 Apr 1919
R. W. Smartt, Jdg.

Jeff MEARS to Hallie MOORE Issued 19 Feb 1919 Rites 21 Feb 1919
J. G. Goff, J. P.

M. H. BYLES to Mrs. Belle STUBBLEFIELD Issued 21 Feb 1919 Rites 22 Feb 1919
R. D. Hill, M. G.

Roosevelt BOULDIN (Col) to Manda EVANS (Col) Issued 19 Apr 1919 Rites 19 Apr 1919
J. S. Nance, M. G.

F. M. HILL to Amanda McGREGOR Issued 19 Apr 1919 Rites 20 Apr 1919
G. A. Wilson, J. P.

Charlie SPURLOCK (Col) to Minnie BROWN (Col) Issued 19 Apr 1919 Rites 22 Apr 1919
W. W. Locke, J. P.

Emmett TODD to Bertha YORK Issued 1 May 1919 Rites 4 May 1919
J. A. Cunningham, M. G.

Elijah Franklin WALKER to Lella Lee BARNES Issued 2 May 1919 Rites 8 May 1919
L. V. Scott, J. P.

John TURNER to Erma WOMACK Issued 3 May 1919 Rites 25 May 1919
J. B. Davis, J. P.

J. L. STANLEY to Allie McCORMACK Issued 7 May 1919 Rites 9 May 1919
L. G. Patrick, J. P.

Levi COPPINGER to Bessie WOOD Issued 8 May 1919 Rites 11 May 1919
G. P. Brasier, J. P.

Fred McGEEHEE (Col) to Julia HILL (Col) Issued 9 May 1919 Rites 9 May 1919
Jared O. Dixon

Elisha ROBERTS to Maggie WALLING Issued 9 May 1919 Rites 9 May 1919
L. G. Patrick, J. P.

Walter HIGGINBOTHAM to May Bell McGEE Issued 9 May 1919 Rites 11 May 1919
B. S. McCollum, J. P.

Lester TAYLOR to Maud JONES Issued 10 May 1919 Rites 11 May 1919
A. P. Robinson, J. P.

Leslie Bruce STOTTS to Alice Lee HENNESSEE Issued 10 May 1919 Rites 11 May 1919
P. N. Moffitt, J. P.

J. W. WOODLEE to Tennie WANNAMAKER Issued 10 May 1919 Returned - Not Solemnized

Ed DAvis LEE (Col) to ConnY May WILLAIMS (Col) Issued 13 May 1919 Rites 13 May 919
Jared O. Dixon

Bertrand HENNESSEE to Winnie JOHNSON Issued 17 May 1919 Rites 18 May 1919
P. N. Moffitt, J. P.

Roy PATTON to Minnie HALE Issued 20 May 1919 Returned - Not Solemnized

Waymon McGEE to Eunice McVEY Issued 21 May 1919 Rites 21 May 1919
L. G. Patrick, J. P.

BACLE HORTON to Cassie DODSON Issued 23 May 1919 Rites 24 May 1919
A. J. Morgan, M. G.

Euge F. PEARSALL to Maude SMARTT Issued 24 May 1919 Rites 25 May 1919
L. G. Patrick, J. P.

Lon WHITE to Julia JENNINGS Issued 24 May 24 1919 Rites 25 May 1919
S. H. Templeton, J. P.

Ernest OSMENT to Jennie BARRETT Issued 28 May 1919 Rites 1 Jun 1919
H. L. Jones, J. P.

Sam D. WILSON to Carrie B. ROBINSON Issued 30 May 1919 Rites 31 May 1919
A. J. Morgan, M. G.

Jim Emery SHOCKLEY (Col) to Octa YORK (Col) Issued 31 May 1919 Rites 3 Jun 1919
J. O. Dixon

Bryan BARNES to Mary Lou STUBBLEFIELD Issued 31 May 1919 Rites 1 Jun 1919
J. L. Barnes, J. P.

Lawrence COPE (Col) to Marinda BILBREY (Col) Issued 31 May 1919 Rites 31 May 1919
J. O. Dixon

I. W. FINLEY to Allie FISHER Issued 3 Jun 1919 Rites 4 Jun 1919
P. G. Potter, M. G.

William SIMS to Vrigie Lee COOPER Issued 5 Jun 1919 Rites 5 Jun 1919
J. A. Brixey, J. P.

P. N. HUDSON to Susie MEADOWS Issued 12 Jun 1919 Rites 12 Jun 1919
E. J. Bonham, M. G.

C. C. ZWINGLE to Mamie Jean MULLICAN Issued 14 Jun 1919 Rites 14 Jun 1919
L. G. Patrick, J. P.

Jas. Arthur MULLICAN to Bessie Lee DAVIS Issued 18 Jun 1919 Rites 18 Jun 1919
A. J. Morgan, JM. G.

Johnnie BOST to Randa BOTTOMS Issued 18 Jun 1919 Rites 22 Jun 1919
B. S. McCollum, J. P.

Ernest RICH to Birdie TURNER Issued 21 Jun 1919 Rites 23 Jun 1919
G. H. Atnip, J. P.

Will Lusk (Col) to Viola JONES (Col) Issued 21 Jun 1919 Rites 22 Jun 1919
W. H. Boddie

Roy W. ROGERS to Nancy MOFFITT Issued 26 Jun 1919 Rites 26 Jun 1919
Roland C. Elzey

Thomas J. WAGNER to Susie McAFEE Issued 28 Jun 1919 Rites 2 Jul 1919
Price Billingsley, M. G.

B. P. EVANS to Lucy Haden CLOUD Issued 1 Jul 1919 Rites 1 Jul 1919
E. C. Leeper, M. G.

Tom KING (Col) to Mattie DURLEY (Col) Issued 1 Jul 1919 Rites 3 Jul 1919
J. A. Brixey, J. P.

Wm. R. BALDWIN to Nellis Winton CARDWELL Issued 3 Jul 1919 Rites 3 Jul 1919
Price Billingsley, M. G.

Hugh GRAYSON (Col) to Minnie L. JETT (Col) Issued 3 Jul 1919 Rites 4 Jul 1919
W. H. Boddie, M. G.

Jess JENNINGS to Lillie CAGLE Issued 4 Jul 1919 Returned - Not SOLEMNIZED

Ernest ADAMS to Effie ROLLER Issued 5 Jul 1919 Rites 6 Jul 1919
J. G. Goff, J. P.

Davis EDGE to Nell TAYLOR Issued 12 Jul 1919 Rites 13 Jul 1919
H. E. BAker, M. G.

Newt SADLER to Serena FERRELL Issued 17 Jul 1919 Rites 19 Jul 1991
J. G. Goff, J. P.

James C. GOODLOE, Jr. to Mary E. REAMS Issued 18 Jul 1919 Rites 19 Jul 1919
F. L. Leeper, M. G.

Amos LANCE to Opal SCOTT Issued 18 Jul 1919 Rites 20 Jul 1919
W. C. Lorance, J. P.

D. L. SMITH to Lela MITCHELL Issued 19 Jul 1919 Rites 19 Jul 1919
Geo. L. Beech, J. P.

Willie GREEN to Ada B. MILLRANEY Issued 19 Jul 1919 Rites 19 Jul 1919
W. P. Davis, J. P.

Neal SMITH to Dora JOHNSON Issued 22 July 1919   Not Returned

Oliver WARREN to Bernice WATSON Issued 23 Jul 1919 Rites 27 Jul 1919
H. L. Jones, J. P.

J. T. McDOWELL to Ether WALLING Issued 30 Jul 1919 Rites 30 Jul 1919
L. G. Patrick, J. P.

Oscar B. WOMACK to Ida Lee GREEN Issued 31 Jul 1919 Rites 31 Jul 1919
Price Billingsley, M. G.

Hershell PATTON to Addie PATTON Issued 31 Jul 1919 Rites 3 Aug 1919
L. G. PATRICK, J. P.

Robert FAIRBANKS to Ora May OAKWOOD Issued 2 Aug 1919 Returned - Not Solemnized

Claud PENNINGTON to Mattie Belle ALLEY Issued 2 Aug 1919 Rites 3 Aug 1919
L. P. Sanders, J. P.

Geo. H. HENEGAR to Eugenia HIDER Issued 4 Aug 1919 Rites 6 Aug 1919
E. C. Leeper, M. G.

Arthue PANTER to Alma CLENDENON Issued 8 Aug 1919 Rites 8 Aug 1919
G. H. O'Neal, M. G.

John CRIM to HAllie GREEN Issued 9 Aug 1919   Not Returned

Herman P. STUBBLEFIELD to Mamie HALL Issued 9 Aug 1919 Rites 10 Aug 1919
E. A. Elam, M. G.

Ernest O'NEAL to Estele WEBSTER Issued 9 Aug 1919 Rites 10 Aug 1919
J. W. Cooley, M. G.

Jesse TODD to Lizzie NUNLEY Issued 9 Aug 1919 Rites 9 Aug 1919
Price Billingsley, M.G.

Obey Hill (Col) to Julia Ann SPURLOCK (Col) Issued 9 Aug 1919 Rites 10 Aug 1919
G. L. Beech, J. P.

Joe MILRANEY to Lou Eva HILLIS Issued 9 Aug 1919 Rites 16 Aug 1919
Fate Walker, J. P.

Floyd BROWN to Violet CARTER Issued 9 Aug 1919 Rites 9 Aug 1919
Price Billingsley, M. G.

E. M. HOLT to Lola DAVENPORT. Issued 9 Aug 1919 Rites 9 Aug 1919
H. E. Baker, M. G.

Will THOMASON to Dovie SUMMERS Issued 9 Aug 1919 returned - Not SOLemnized
(Certificate attached stating she was 14 yrs 2 mos old 9/1/1919)

Yance MALONE to Janie DIXON Issued 11 Aug 1919 Rites 11 Aug 1919
L. G. Patrick, J. P.

Waymon MAYFIELD to Eva HIGGINBOTHAM Issued 12 Aug 1919 Rites 12 Aug 1919
J. W. Cooley, M. G.

JAmes C. WILSON to FAnnie YOUNG Issued 13 Aug 1919 Rites 13 Aug 1919
W. P. Davis, J. P.

G. W. BARNES to Nora CUNNINGHAM Issued 13 Aug 1919 Rites 17 Aug 1919
J. A. Cunningham, M. G.

Walter WEBB to Lula DRAKE Issued 14 Aug 1919 Rites 14 Aug 1919
L. P. Sanders, J. P.

Frank HOBBS to Vivian SMARTT Issued16 Aug 1919 Rites 30 Aug 1919
P. N. Moffitt, J. P.

R. L. WOOD to Mrs. Myrtle WOOD Issued 16 Aug 1919 Rites 17 Aug 1919
E. C. Leeper, M. G.

Albert WOMACK to Vera HENDRIX Issued 18 Aug 1919 Rites 20 Aug 1919
P. G. Moore, J. P.

Tommie L. BRATTEN to Clara SELF Issued 19 Aug 1919 Rites 21 Aug 1919
H. L. Jones, J. P.

Joe EDWARDS to Sydney A. SMARTT Issued 19Aug 1919 Rites 20 Aug 1919
JAmes Rayburn, M. G.

Alfred STILES to Mrs. M. E. ALLISON Issued 21 Aug 1919 Rites 21 Aug 1919
H. L. Walling, M. G.

Robert ROLLER to Nellie COPE Issued 22 Aug 1919 Rites 14 Sep 1919
J. G. Goff, J. P.

Clarence CUNNINGHAM to BeuLah Mae BAIN Issued 23 Aug 1919 Rites 24 Aug 1919
J. W. Cooley, M. G.

O. W. OAKLEY to Etta SAIN Issued 25 Aug 1919 Rites 26 Aug 1919
R. T. Skinner, M. G.

Charlie MOORE to Lela BENNETT Issued 26 Aug 1919 Rites 27 Aug 1919
G. L. Beech, J. P.

Alex JOHNSON to Belle GRISSOM Issued 27 Aug 1919 Rites 27 Aug 1919
J. D. Hash, J. P.

Henry Perry to Hettie PEDIGO Issued 1 Sep 1919 Rites 1 Sep 1919
L. G. Patrick, J. P.

Floyd SAPP to Irene HIGGINBOTHAM Issued 2 Sep 1919 Rites 2 Sep 1919
Geo. B. Beaver, J. P.

J. R. HALE to Mary FORD Issued 5 Sep 1919 Rites 7 Apr 1919
H. L. Jones, J. P.

W. M. ADCOCK to Ada DUNCAN Issued 6 Sep 1919 Rites 7 Sep 1919
G. L. Beech, J. P.

Tom HELTON to Lillie RINER Issued 6 Sep 1919 Rites 7 Sep 1919
M. G. Nelson, M. G.

Tom McCORMACK to Ophia WOMACK Issued 11 Sep 1919 Rites 14 Sep 1919
L. G. Patrick, J. P.

James K. POTTER to Mira WEBB Issued 13 Sep 1919 Rites 14 Sep 1919
L. P. Sanders, J. P.

John B. TUBB to Ruby E. WOMACK Issued 15 Sep 1919 Rites 15 Sep 1919
Price Billingsley, M.G.

W. H. TENPENNY to Emma Bell McGREGOR Issued 15 Sep 1919 Rites 15 Sep 1919
L. G. Patrick, J. P.

A. A. PRICE to Ethel PINEGAR Issued 15 Sep 1919 Rites 15 Sep 1919
R. W. Smartt, Jdg.

Bernard HENEGAR to Sarah STROUD Issued 23 Sep 1919 Rites 24 Sep 1919
Price Billingsley, M. G.

Everett R. SHOCKLEY (Col) to Lela B. MARTIN (Col) Issued 25 Sep 1919 Rites 25 Sep
J. S. Nance, M. G.

Otto SMITH to Collie WALKER Issued 25 Sep 1919 Rites 25 Sep 1919
L. G. PATRICK, J. P.

Lonnie GILLEY to Minnie Belle CUNNINGHAM Issued 25 Sep 1919 Rites 27 Sep 1919
J. C. Clark, M. G.

T. H. GRISSOM to Jennie HERNDON Issued 26 Sep 1919 Rites 27 Sep 1919
J. W. Cooley, M. G.

Noah SUMMERS to Elva YOUNGBLOOD Issued 27 Sep 1919 Rites 28 Sep 1919
A. Z. Holder, J. P.

A. O. LOCKE to Willie WOMACK Issued 1 Oct 1919 Rites 1 Oct 1919
L. C. Lane, J. P.

D. W. LOCKE to Mazell SELLARS Issued 1 Oct 1919 Rites 1 Oct 1919
L. C. Lane, J. P.

James A. BROWN to Florence JULIAN Issued 2 Oct 1919 Rites 2 Oct 1919
R. T. Skinner, M. G.

Roy BLANKENSHIP to Sallie McDOWELL Issued 2 Oct 1919 Rites 3 Oct 1919
L. C. Lane, J. P.

Charles WILLIAMS to Ida BROWN Issued 3 Oct 1919   Not Returned

John Wm. PEREN to Sallie Belle FUSTON Issued 4 Oct 1919 Rites 4 Oct 1919
Price Billingsley, M. G.

Tilman TITTLE to Carlie Mae HARDEN Issued 7 Oct 1919 Rites 8 Oct 1919
G. A. Wilson, J. P.

Haston MARTIN to Sallie LOCKE Issued 8 Oct 1919 Rites 9 Oct 1919
L. C. Lane, J. P.

L. Frank MASON to Maude GENTRY Issued 11 Oct 1919 Rites 12 Oct 1919
J. R. Stubblefield, M. G.

J. L. HARDING to Rebecca SPURLOCK Issued 11 Oct 1919 Rites 11 Oct 1919
G.A. WIlson, J. P.

H. L. SIMMONS to Eva Lou CUMMINGS Issued 14 Oct 1919 Rites 23 Oct 1919
Fate Walker, J. P.

C. W. PERRY to Ida STROUD Issued 14 Oct 1919 Rites 14 Oct 1919
L. G. Patrick, J. P.

John DIXON to Dora PENNINGTON Issued 17 Oct 1919 Rites 19 Oct 1919
J. A. Brixey, J. P.

Clyde GOODSON to Beulah GRIBBLE Issued 17 Oct 1919 Rites 18 Oct 1919
G. W. Hinkley, J. P.

M. F. BROWN to Rosa LYNN Issued 18 Oct 1919 Rites 19 Oct 1919
L. B. Moffitt, J. P.

Bob McBRIDE to Mary FULTS Issued 18 Oct 1919 Rites 19 Oct 1919
L. B. Moffitt, J. P.

J. R. CRAIN to Effie GRISSOM Issued 20 Oct 1919 Rites 21 Oct 1919
J. E. Witt, M. G.

Jesse CASEY to Mary Neil HARRISON Issued 25 Oct 1919 Rites 26 Oct 1919
J. E. Clark, M. G.

J. W. WARNER, Jr. to Kate BADGER Issued 25 Oct 1919 Rites 25 Oct 1919
E. C. Leeper, M. G.

Jesse JENNINGS to Lillie CAGLE Issued 25 Oct 1919 Rites 26 Nov 1919
W. M. Milstead, M. G.

Virgil HOPKINS (Col) to Doshie Bell SPURLOCK (C) Issued 29 Oct 1919 Rites 29 Oct
J. S. NAnce, M. G.

Kelton JOINES to Maude McGREGOR Issued 31 Oct 1919 Rites 2 Nov 1919
G. A. Wilson, J. P.

Floice ARGO to Ethel MAXWELL Issued 1 Nov 1919 Rites 1 Nov 1919
Thos J. Wagner, M. G.

Wiley GREEN to Maud HOLT Issued 1 Nov 1919 Rites 2 Nov 1919
P. G. Potter, M. G.

Elie MULLICAN to Posey GRIBBLE Issued 1 Nov 1919 Rites 16 Nov 1919
P. G. Potter, M. G.

Thos. Nelson SHIELDS to Myrtle Mai DAVIS Issued 1 Nov 1919 Rites 1 Nov 1919
J. W. EAton, Jdg

T. W. SPARKMAN to Flora SMITH Issued 4 Nov 1919 Rites 5 Nov 1919
A. J. Cantrell, J. P.

George L. BOYD to Carrie LATHAN Issued 7 Nov 1919 Rites 7 Nov 1919
E. C. Leeper, M. G.

Charlie PENDLETON to Ella PELHAM Issued 8 Nov 1919 Rites 8 Nov 1919
L. G. Patrick, J. P.

Ernest COCK to Lula TURNER Issued8 Nov 1919 Rites 9 Nov 1919
G. H. atnip, M. G.

Lee CARTWRIGHT to Lillie Belle McGEE Issued 8 Nov 1919 Rites 9 Nov 1919
A. P. Roberson, J. P.

Haston ROGERS to Bessie SMOOT Issued 14 Nov 1919 Rites 16 Nov 1919
J. A. Cunningham, M. G.

Alton O. BLAIR to Florence DAVIS Issued 15 Nov 1919 Rites 15 Nov 1919
L. G. Patrick, J. P.

John R. LEWIS to Mary Lee ROWLAND Issued 15 Nov 1919 Rites 16 Nov 1919
J. C. Elkins, M.G.

Tom LILLARD (Col) to Pheobe BLACK (Col) Issued 16 Nov 1919 Rites 16 Nov 1919
E. S. Bedford,

E. A. CLOUD to Avo BOLES Issued 20 Nov 1919 Rites 20 Nov 1919
Price BILLINGSLEY, M. G.

C. Z. EDGE to Bettie CRAVEN Issued 20 Nov 1919 Rites 20 Nov 1919
E. C. Leeper, M. G.

E. L. BOST to Ellen TEMPLETON Issued 22 Nov 1919 Rites 23 Nov 1919
A. P. Toberson, J. P.

J. K. SPARKMAN to Ollive DENTON Issued 22 Nov 1919 Rites 23 Nov 1919
A. J. Cantrell, J. P.

Joe H. MARTIN to Merica MARTIN Issued 25 Nov 1919 Rites 25 Nov 1919
L. G. Patrick, J. P.

Robert T. CRAGG to Edna Mae McCORMACK Issued 5 Dec 1919 Rites 6 Dec 1919
J. D. Hash, J. P.

J. E. FULTS to Ophia Eliz. LOCKE Issued 6 Dec 1919 Rites 9 Dec 1919
J. R. Goodpasture, M. G.

Jesse H. DENHAM to Maggie MARTIN Issued 6 Dec 1919 Rites 7 Dec 1919
E. C. Leeper, M. G.

W. M. POLLARD to Ercie GREEN Issued 9 Dec 1919 Rites 9 Dec 1919
J. T. Casey, M. G.

S. E. EVANS to Corrine McMULLEN Issued 12 Dec 1919 Rites 14 Dec 1919
A. Z. Holder, M. G.

R. B. DEAN (Col) to Georgia BRAGG (Col) Issued 12 Dec 1919 Rites 12 Dec 1919
J. S. NAnce, M. G.

Burgess ALLEN to Alma MASEY Issued 13 Dec 1919 Rites 14 Dec 1919
W. P. Davis, J. P.

Army BOTTOMS to Flora BUTCHER Issued 13 Dec 1919 Rites 15 Dec 1919
S. H. Templeton, J. P.

J. E. WIMBERLY to Mamie COPPINGER Issued 15 Dec 1919 Rites 16 Dec 1919
E. C. Leeper. M. G.

S. M. MOFFITT to Pearl PHIFER Issued 17 DEC 1919 Rites 17 Dec 1919
N. M. Hill, J. P.

P. B. STROUD to Annie Mai ARLEDGE Issued 18 Dec 1919 Rites 18 Dec 1919
Price Billingsley, M. G.

M. E. KELL to Ova SIMMONS Issued19 Dec 1919 Rites 19 Dec 1919
Fate WAlker, J. P.

R. J. BOYD to Ora McGREGOR Issued 20 Dec 1919 Rites 21 Dec 1919
A. P. Roberson, J. P.

Joe BRATCHER to Nan SADDLER Issued 20 Dec 1919 Rites 21 Dec 1919
J. G. Goff, J. P.

John A. REEDER to Ora Belle CANTRELL issued 23 Dec 1919 Rites 25 Dec 1919
P. G. Potter, M. G.

Charlie McVEY to Estelle BOST Issued 23 Dec 1919 Rites 24 Dec 1919
J. D. Templeton, J. P.

A. L. McBRIDE to Lillie May LYNN Issued 23 Dec 1919 Rites 25 Dec 1919
L. B. Moffitt, J. P.

A. L. BONNER to Dora JOHNSON Issued 24 Dec 1919 Rites 24 Dec 1919
L.G. Patrick, J. P.

A. C. SCOTT to Ora Mai OAKWOOD Issued 24 dec 1919 Rites 24 dec 1919
A. P. Roberson, J. P.

Robert Bryan SCRUGGS to Sadie Lee WOODLEE Issued 25 Dec 1919 Rites 25 Dec 1119 Price Billingsley, M. G.

Alvin JORDAN to Edith WALKER Issued 25 Dec 1919 Rites 25 Dec 1919 J. E. Clark, M. G.

Cecil YORK (Col) to Beatrice SMARTT (Col) Issued 25 Dec 1919 Rites 25 Dec 1919 W. W. Locke, J. P.

Clarence T. ROWAN (Col) to Marion TURNER (Col) Issued 25 Dec 1919 Rites 25 Dec J. O. Dixon, M. G.

Hiram PRATHER to Orie Belle GREEN Issued 26 Dec 1919 Rites 26 Dec 1919 J. B. Bryan, J. P.

Wm. Howard LYNN to Mecca Lee COPE Issued 27 Dec 1919 Rites 28 Dec 1919 L. B. Moffitt, J. P.

D. W. MOON to Pearl McMAHAN Issued29 Dec 1919 Rites 1 Jan 1920 H. T. King, M. G.

Elbert JENNINGS to Fannie WILSON Issued 30 Dec 1919 Rites 30 Dec 1919 F. W. Muse, M. G.

Tom PELHAM to Lou PENDLETON Issued 31 Dec 1919 Rites 31 Dec 1919 O. H. Wood, J. P.

Jim WOODLEE to Ocie WANNAMAKER Issued 2 JAn 1919 Rites 4 Jan 1919 L. V. Scott, J. P.

Livy WOODLEE to Velma HOBBS Issued 2 JAn 1920 Rites 4 Jan 1920 J. L. Barnes, J. P.

A. T. MULLICAN to Delia WALKER Issued 5 Jan 1920 Rites 5 JAn 1920 J. G. Goff, J. P,

Calvin McMILLEN to Rachel MOONEYHAM Issued 5 JAn 1920 Rites 5 JAn 1920 G. A. Wilson, J. P.

Otis ADCOCK to Bessie YOUNG Issued 7 Jan 1920 Rites 11 Jan 1920 P. G. Potter, M. G.

Charles P. LORING to Martha KENNEDY Issued 7 JAn 1920 Rites 7 Jan 1920 J. M. Horn, M. G.

Gent TODD to Cleo ELKINS Issued 9 JAn 1920 Rites 9 Jan 1920 H. T. King, M. G.

H. A. McMAHAN to Helen CARLSON Issued 9 JAn 1920 Rites 11 JAn 1920 G. A. Wilson, J. P.

Hollis BROWN (col) to Willie MERCER (Col) Issued 13 JAn 1920 Rites 14 Jan 1920 F. S. Womack, J. P.

W. M. MILSTEAD to Allie NUNLEY Issued 14 Jan 1920 Rites 14 Jan 1920 P. N. Moffitt, J. P.

Jesse ROBERTS to Grover WOODLEE Issued 17 JAn 1920 Rites 18 Jan 1920 J. L. Barnes, J. P.

W. A. COTTON to Virgil O. COUCH Issued 17 Jan 1920 Rites 18 Jan 1920 L. C. Lane, J. P.

A. A. STANLEY to Maud ANDERSON Issued 17 Jan 1920 Rites 19 Jan 1920 J. M. Horn, M. G.

Rufus SWAFORD (Col) to Vicie LOOPER (Col) Issued 24 Jan 1920 Rites 24 Jan 1920 J. O. Dixon, M. G.

W. R. MASTERS to Effie HOLT Issued 26 JAn 1920 Rites 29 Jan 1920 J. R. Goodpasture, M. G.

JAmes WOODLEE (Col) to Jessie MILLS (Col) Issued 2 Feb 1920 Rites 2 Feb 1920 (Returns supplied by order of court 5/17/47) C. H. Talley, M. G.

J. H. HOBBS to Flossie MARTIN Issued 6 Feb 1920 Rites 8 Feb 1920 A. P. Roberson, J. P.

Albert GIBBS to Lillie CUTTS Issued 6 Feb 1920 Rites 6 Feb 1920 L. G. Patrick, J. P.

Virgil HOBBS to Octa WANNAMAKER Issued 12 Feb 1920 Rites 15 Feb 1920 L. V. Scott, J. P.

Bob PENNINGTON to GAy CRIM Issyed 14 Feb 1920 Rites 15 Feb 1920 J. C. Elkins, M. G.

Eford BOST to Etta McBRIDE Issued 19 Feb 1920 Rites 22 Feb 1920 J. A. Templeton, J. P.

Lucian ROBERTS to Lizzie PERRY Issued 21 Feb 1920 Rites 26 Feb. 1920 M. M. Hill, J. P.

George JONES to Bell NEWBY issued 23 Feb 1920 Rites 23 Feb 1920 W. P. Davis, J. P.

Grady BRADSHAW to Maggie ROGERS Issued 25 Feb 1920 Rites 26 Feb 1920 R. C. Crosslin, M. G.

Gordon LORING to Nelle BOOHER Issued 25 Feb 1920 Rites 25 Feb 1920 J. M. Horn, M. G.

George T. MARTIN to Elizabeth DENBY Issued 8 Mar 1920 Rites 9 Mar 1920 Price Billingsley, M. G.

T. E. VADEN to Mary CORDER Issued 18 Mar 1920 Rites 18 Mar 1920 E. C. Leeper, M. G.

Jimmie JONES to Quixie HAYES Issued 15 MAr 1920 Rites 16 Mar 1920 P. G. Potter, M. G.

Charles LIST (Col) to Clara FAULKNER (Col) Issued 18 MAr 1920 Rites 18 Mar 1920 J. S. NAnce, M. G.

Joe M. ROBINSON to Hassie BAIN Issued 18 MAr 1920 Rites 18 MAr 1920 H. T. king, M. G.

R. H. WEBB to Maude CRUISE Issued 19 Mar 1920 Rites 21 Mar 1920
L. C. Lane, J. P.

Bill GIPSON to Myrtle GRIMES Issued 20 Mar 1920 Rites 20 Mar 1920
L. G. Patrick, J. P.

Jim EDGE (Col) to Louise WHITE (Col) Issued 20 Mar 1920 Rites 20 Mar 1920
J. S. Nance, M. G.

J. M. PEDEN to Emma STANLEY Issued 22 Mar 1920 Rites 22 Mar 1920
A. Z. Holder, J. P.

Milton SMARTT to Loma ROGERS Issued 24 Mar 1920 Rites 25 Mar 1920
J. L. Barnes, J. P.

Howard MASEY to Etta SCOTT Issued 25 Mar 1920 Rites 28 MAr 1920
W. C. Lorance, J. P.

C. Haskell ADCOCK to Macon YOUNG Issued 26 Mar 1920 Rites 26 Mar 1920
P. G. Potter, M. G.

Jasper E. JUSTICE to Pearl BLAIR Issued 26 Mar 1920 Rites 28 Mar 1920
L. B. Moffitt, J. P.

J. C. CARTER to Nora CASE Issued 27 Mar 1920 Rites 28 Mar 1920
J. L. Barnes, J. P.

Alton HOOVER to Cora CRAWLEY Issued 2 Apr 1920 Rites 4 Apr 1920
J. A. Brixey, J. P.

Hazen E. SEIP to Pauline CLARK Issued 5 Apr 1920 Rites 5 Apr 1920
Price Billingsley, M. G.

WAlter Edwin LEE to Marie MOFFITT Issued 7 Apr 1920 Rites 8 Apr 1920
J. B. Broen, J. P.

E. Z. McVEY to Minnie CRAIN Issued 10 Apr 1920 Rites 10 Apr 1920
J. B. Brown, J. P.

Jim TANNER to Mollie MARTIN Issued 10 Apr 1920 Rites 11 Apr 1920
A. Z. Holder, J. P.

S. E. SPAULDING to Mabel E. ARMSTRONG Issued 14 Apr 1920 Returned-Not Solemnized
(Clerk wrote went to M'boro Th. and married there)

R. B. JUSTICE to Allene DAVIS Issued 15 Apr 1920 Rites 18 Apr 1920
O. H. Wood, J. P.

Marion CLENDENON to Mrs. Parriet CURTIS Issued 16 Apr 1920 Rites 17 Apr 1920
M. M. Hill, J. P.

Arsey RHEA to Lillie FULTS Issued 20 Apr 1920 Rites 25 Apr 1920
P. N. Moffitt, J. P.

R. C. STUART to Sue RUCKER issued 21 Apr 1920 Rites 21 Apr 1920
J. D. Templeton, J. P.

Haskell MADEWELL to Belle BONNER Issued 24 Apr 1920 Rites 25 Apr 1920
L. V. Scott, J. P.

Wash MAYFIELD to Lena BOST Issued 28 Apr 1920 Rites 29 Apr 1920
W. V. D. Miller, J. P.

Eugene JACO to NORA SIMMONS Issued 29 Apr 1920 Rites 2 May 1920
L. C. Lane, J. P.

Roy PATTON to Mamie CRAWFORD Issued 30 Apr 1920 Rites 1 May 1920
J. D. Hash, J. P.

Elmer COLE to Nannie JENNINGS Issued1 May 1920 Rites 1 May 1920
S. H. Templeton, J. P.

George W. MARTIN to Willie O'NEAL Issued 4 May 1920 Rites 5 May 1920
J. T. Casey, M. G.

L. A. RIDLEY to Nancy E. RAMSEY Issued 8 May 1920 Rites 8 May 1920
H. T. King, M. G.

George DAVIS to Belle TENPENNY Issued 8 May 1920 Rites 9 May 1920
O. H. Wood, J. P.

Robert THOMPSON to Flora ROBINSON Issued 13 May 1920 Rites 14 May 1920
Price Billingsley, M. G.

J. H. DODD to Mary E. FUSTON Issued 15 May 1920 Rites 16 May 1920
A. Z. Holder, J. P.

JAmes MASON to MAy HUTCHINGS Issued 15 May 1920 Rites 16 May 1920
Price Billignsley, M. G.

john HARGIS to Ova MELTON Issued 15 May 1920 Rites 15 May 1920
G. L. Beech, J. P.

Floyd WHITWORTH to Josie MAYFIELD Issued 19 May 1920 Rites 20 May 1920
W. V. D. Miller, J. P.

E. S. BEDFORD (Col) to SArah BREWINGTON (Col) Issued 21 May 1920 Rites 23 May
C. M. Lawrence, M. G.

Renzo TANNER to Maggie SMARTT Issued22 May 1920 Rites 24 May 1920
J. L.Barnes, J. P.

T. L. BYRD to Daisy CARDWELL Issied 26 May 1920 Rites 26 May 1920
R. T. Skinner, M. G.

Lee KNOX (Col) to Susie May MARTIN (Col) Issued 29 MAy 1920 Rites 29 May 1920
E. S. Bedford, M. G.

Smith WHITEAKER to Gertie PERRY Issued 29 May 1920 Rites 29 May 1920
S. H. Templeton, J. P.

Wilson JACKSON to Lizzie BOST Issued 29 May 1920 Not Returned

Charles H. MEADOWS to Clara Josephine DARNELL Issued 31 MAy 1920 Rites 1 Jun 1920
J. T. Pearsall, M. G..

C. H. SPENCER (Col) to Qweeter DUNNIEHUE (Col) Issued 1 Jun 1920 Rites 1 Jun 1920
E. R. Stokes, M. G.

Charlie E. BOWERMAN to Hallie Jeane ADAIR Issued 3 Jun 1920 Rites 3 Jun 1920
J. T. Casey, M. G.

A. W. HILL . to Reggie EITER Issued 3 Jun 1920 Rites 6 Jun 1920
Thos. J. Wagner, M. G.

Van MARTIN (Col) to Alice BATES (col) Issued 4 Jun 1920 Rites 4 Jun 1920
J. S. NANCE, M. G.

Nathan SMARTT (col) to Martha SPURLOCK (Col) Issued 7 Jun 1920 Not Returned

J. T. VINSON to Olive WILLIAMS Issued 12 Jun 1920 Rites 13 Jun 1920
H. L. Jones, J. P.

Joe McGREGOR (Col) to Eva HOBBS (Col) Issued 14 Jun 1920 Rites 14 Jun 1920
J. H. Talley, M. G.

Charels H. FUDGE to Beulah Jane MARTIN Issued 15 June 1920 Rites 15 Jun 1920
H. T. King, M. G.

Melvin ROWAN (Col) to Annie Mae BELL (Col) Issued 16 Jun 1920 Rites 16 Jun 1920
E. S. Bedford, M. G.

Newton RUTLEDGE to Mollie CUMMINGS Issued 19 Jun 1920 Rites 20 Jun 1920
Fate Walker, J. P.

John WALKER (Col) to Ova MARTIN (Col) Issued 19 Jun 1920 Rites 19 Jun 1920
J. S. Nance, M. G.

George C. PUCKETT to Mary Victoria ROBINSON Issued 23 Jun 1920 Rites 23 Jun 1920
J. W. Eaton, Jdg

Oscar GRIBBLE to Rosa FIELDS Issued 26 June 1920 Rites 27 Jun 1920
J. D. HASH, J. P.

Charles L. PHELPS to Anna Mae MARTIN Issued 26 Jun 1920 Rites 26 Jun 1920
E. C. Leeper, M. G.

Wm. R. SMITH to Artie Mildred GRIFFITH Issued 26 Jun 1920 Rites 26 Jun 1920
H. L. Walling, M. G.

Thomas C. FISHER to Maude BOYD Issued 30 Jun 1920 Rites 4 Jul 1920
L. C. Lane, J. P.

M. M. MORRISON to Rebecca WHITSON Issued 30 Jun 1920 Rites 30 Jun 1920
E. C. Leeper, M. G.

Walden PARKER to Daisy CUNNINGHAM Issued 2 Jul 1920 Rites 4 Jul 1920
J. A. Brixey, J. P.

W. B. DRAKE to Mary HILLIS Issued 3 Jul 1920 Rites 4 Jul 1920
J. E. Witt, M. G.

R. F. BRATCHER to Edith Mae DAVIS Issued 3 Jul 1920 Rites 4 Jul 1920
E. C. Leeper, M. G.

Lonnie PEDEN to Mamie PORTERFIELD Issued 17 Jul 1920 Rites 18 Jul 1920
J. G. Goff, J. P.

Isaac B. SMITH to Flora JONES Issued 17 Jul 1920 Rites 18 Jul 1920
J. M. Horn, M. G.

Hervey HOBBS to Tennie WANNAMAKER Issued 17 Jul 1920 Rites 18 Jul 1920
J. L. Barnes, J. P.

Thurman ROBERTS to Fannie ELKINS Issued 19 Jul 1920 Rites 19 Jul 1920
E. C. Leeper, M. G.

Willie BARNES to Gertha JONES Issued 24 Jul 1920 Rites 25 Jul 1920
L. G. Patrick, J. P.

Marshall H. MARKUM to Velma Alice WOOTEN Issued 26 Jul 1920 Rites 27 Jul 1920
F. S. Womack, J. P.

Johnson HAMMONS to Nellie Gray SCOTT Issued 31 Jul 1920 Rites 1 Aug 1920
J. H. Talley, M. G.

E. L. NOBLE to Blanche LIVELY Issued 4 Aug 1920 Rites 5 Aug 1920
H. T. King, M. G.

J. D. VANATTA to Ida Belle PARKER Issued 10 Aug 1920 Rites 11 Aug 1920
J. C. Elkins, M. G.

Marion MARTIN to Rosa HIGGINS Issued 13 Aug 1920 Rites 15 Aug 1920
J. E. Clark, M. G.

Logan GILLENTINE to Mattie LEE STROUD Issued 14 Aug 1920 Rites 14 Aug 1920
P. G. Potter, M. G.

Ben PRATER (Col) to Lucinda FOSTER (Col) Issued 16 Aug 1920 Rites 16 Aug 1920
J. S. Nance, M. G.

G. W. ELAM to Eva CROUCH Issued 21 Aug 1920 Rites 22 Aug 1920
W. C. Lorance, J. P.

Rice S. BARNES to Willie Marie MARTIN Issued 21 Aug 1920 Rites 22 Aug 1920
J. L. Barnes, J. P.

Willie HOUSE to Beulah SMITHSON Issued 22 Aug 1920 Rites 23 Aug 1920
J. W. Eaton, Jdg.

A. J. WEBB, Jr. to Shellie E. CANTRELL Issued 23 Aug 1920 Rites 28 Aug 1920
L. P. Sanders, J. P.

Neal SMITH to Willie Lee MILSTEAD Issued 3 Sep 1920 Rites 7 Sep 1920
J. L. Barnes, J. P.

J. H. GRIFFIN to Gertrude Ellen DOTSON Issued 4 Sep 1920 Rites 4 Sep 1920
Price Billingsley, M. G.

Claud CUNNINGHAM to Hallie ROGERS Issued 4 Sep 1920 Rites 10 Sep 1920
Price Billingsley, M. G.

Connie HARRIS to Eunice BUTCHER Issued 16 Oct 1920 Rites 17 Oct 1920
W. P. Davis, J. P.

Bertha HENNESSEE to Emma GRISSOM Issued 23 Oct 1920 Rites 24 Oct 1920
J. B. Brown, J. P.

Iron H. PENNINGTON to Cleo GOOD Issued 25 Oct 1920 Rites 26 Oct 1920
J. A. Cunningham. M. G.

Walter TERRY (Col) to Belle SPURLOCK (Col) Issued 26 Oct 1920 Rites 26 Oct 1920
Geo. B. Beaver, J. P.

Wm. Jarve STARKEY to Bessie May Bell Issued 28 Oct 1920 Rites 31 Oct 1920
J. A. Brixey, J. P.

Will CUNNINGHAM to Lillie C. COPE Issued 30 Oct 1920 Rites 31 Oct 1920
R. A. Skelton, M. G.

Laton BRIXEY to Minnie Lee HOOVER Issued 30 Oct 1920 Rites 31 Oct 1920
O. H. Wood, J. P.

Martin GRIBBLE to Allie Swann MASON Issued 4 Nov 1920 Rites 4 Nov 1920
J. M. Horn, M. G.

Ernest A. GRIFFIN to Vera JONES Issued 4 Nov 1920 Rites 4 Nov 1920
J. W. Eaton, Jdg.

Clinton DURHAM to Maud GRAY Issued 6 Nov 1920 Rites 7 Nov 1920
J. M. Horn, M. G.

Harvey BOST to Ova HILL Issued 6 Nov 1920 Rites 7 Nov 1920
B. S. McCollum, J. P.

Rance H. MABRY to Mary Ada MOSER Issued 6 Nov 1920 Rites 7 Nov 1920
R. A. Skelton, M. G.

Hervie O'NEAL to Mabel RIDDLE Issued 12 Nov 1920 Rites 12 Nov 1920
Price Billingsley, M. G.

J. F. DENTON to Berchie SPARKMAN Issued 12 Nov 1920 Rites 13 Nov 1920
L. P. Sanders, J. P.

Walter S. McDOWELL to Bessie L.JONES Issued 13 Nov 1920 Rites 25 Nov 1920
W. P. Davis, J. P.

Hampton WOMACK to Bessie BLANKENSHIP Issued 13 Nov 1920 Rites 16 Nov 1920
L. F. Daugherty, M. G.

Louis WALKER to Martha WELCH Issued 22 Nov 1920 Rites 22 Nov. 1920
R. W. Snartt, Jdg.

A. G. RITCHEY to Pauline VINSON Issued 23 Nov 1920 Rites 25 Nov 1920
Price Billingsley, M. G.

Eugene MOULDER to Mary RAINS Issued 27 Nov 1920 Rites 28 Nov 1920
J. A. Brixey, J. P.

Eugene CLARK (Col) to Viola GUEST (Col) Issued 10 Sep 1920 Rites 10 Sep 1920
B. S. McCollum, J. P.

Orphus GARRISON to Myrtle ROGERS Issued 18 Sep 1920 Rites 19 Sep 1920
L. B. Moffitt, J. P.

L. H. DENTON to Lula KING Issued 22 Sep 1920 Rites 23 Sep 1920
L. P. Sanders, J. P.

Roy DAVENPORT to Hassie Cleo BAIN Issued 22 Sep 1920 Rites 26 Sep 1920
P. G. Potter, M. G.

Arthur MAY to Mabel WINSTEAD Issued 23 Sep 1920 Rites 26 Sep 1920
O. H. Wood, J. P.

Frank SPURLOCK (Col) to Tessa MARTIN (Col) Issued 25 Sep 1920 Rites 26 Sep 1920
G. A. Johnson

H. B. ELROD to Sadie BARRETT Issued 27 Sep 1920 Rites 29 Sep 1920
P. G. Potter, M. G.

Arzy BOYD to Josie MAXWELL Issued 29 Sep 1920 Rites 30 Sep 1920
P. N. Moffitt, J. P.

Elom CREEN to Amanda CARTWRIGHT Issued 1 Oct 1920 Rites 1 Oct 1920
L. F. Daugherty, M. G.

J. O. COOPER to Lela HOOVER Issued 1 Oct 1920 Rites 1 Oct 1920
Price Billingsley, M. G.

Claud CATHCART to Annie CRAIN Issued 1 Oct 1920 Rites 4 Oct 1920
L. P. Sanders, J. P.

James S. CUMMINGS to Dovie JONES Issued 2 Oct 1920 Rites 2 Oct 1920
W. P. Davis, J. P.

J. H. POTTER to May BARRETT Issued 2 Oct 1920 Rites 2 Oct 1920
E. C. Leeper, M. G.

Arthur VICKERS to May ROBERSON Issued 7 Oct 1920 Rites 15 Oct 1920
H. L. Jones, J. P.

J. F. ROGERS to Lila Belle CUNNINGHAM Issued 9 Oct 1920 Rites 9 Oct 1920
A. P. Roberson, J. P.

Worth MILLER to Dora SCOTT Issued 9 Oct 1920 Rites 9 Oct 1920
L. B. Moffitt

John French BRANTLEY to Mary Graham WILSON Issued 12 Oct 1920 Rites 12 Oct 1920
J. R. Goodpasture, M. G.

Pascal ODOM to Maude GILREATH Issued 13 Oct 1920 Rites 15 Oct 1920
H. L. Jones, J. P.

Jake FAULKNER (Col) to Estella MARTIN (Col) Issued 14 Oct 1920 Rites 14 Oct 1920
J. S. Nance, M. G.

Tom CHISAM to Nannie WEBB Issued 16 Oct 1920 Rites 17 Oct 1920
J. W. Eaton, Jdg.

Tom BAILEY to May LEDMAN Issued 30 Nov 1920 Rites 30 Nov 1920
A. B. Moffitt

Roland SHIRLEY to Ruby May WILSON Issued 3 Dec 1920 Rites 5 Dec 1920
J. A. Brixey, J. P.

Emmett CLARK to Lela PEARSON Issued 4 Dec 1920   Returned - Not Solemnized

J. E. BYARS to Ella Mae BLANKS Issued 4 Dec 1920 Rites 4 Dec 1920
E. C. Leeper, M. G.

Tommie TURNER to Mary MORTON Issued 4 Dec 1920 Rites 4 Dec 1920
J. W. Cooley, M. G.

John Roy BRAGG to Chloe ADCOCK Issued 7 Dec 1920   Not Returned

H. J. WILSON to Eva LEMONS Issued 9 Dec 1930 Rites 26 Dec 1920
O. H. Wood, J. P.

Will SIMONS to Ella MAYO Issued 11 Dec 1920 Rites 12 Dec 1920
G.,L. Beech, J. P.

Davis JONES to Alma TEMPLETON Issued 21 Dec 1920 Rites 29 Dec 1920
L. F. Daugherty, M. G.

James P. TODD to Madge KELL Issued 21 Dec 1920 Rites 22 Dec 1920
A. B. Moffitt

Vester HENDERSON to Ida MILRANEY Issued 23 Dec 1920 Rites 24 Dec 1920
H. E. Ramsey, J. P.

J. W. ROLLER to Gracie COPE Issued 23 Dec 1920 Rites 26 Dec 1920
H. L. Jones, J. P.

P. G. DAVIS to Martha CANTRELL issued 23 Dec 1920 Rites 26 Dec 1920
L. F. Daugherty, M. G.

James Elmer VICKERS to Linnie FULTS Issued 23 Dec 1920 Rites 24 Dec 1920
L. B. Moffitt, J. P.

Jake STARKEY to Irene MITCHELL Issued 23 Dec 1920 Rites 24 Dec 1920
H. M. Horn, M. G.

Willie Lee GRAYSON (Col) to Susie HUDDLESTON (Col)   24 Dec 1920 Rites 24 Dec
J. S. NAnce, M. G.

Martin Mc GEE to Lela DIXON Issued 24 Dec 1920 Rites 24 Dec 1920
J. W. Eaton, Jdg.

E. F. ALLMAN to Bettie ROACH Issued 24 Dec 1920 Rites 25 Dec 1920
J. A. Brixey, J. P.

James RHODES (Col) to MATTIE FINGER (Col) Issued 24 Dec 1920 Rites 26 Dec 1920
M. B. Newsom

Frank C. SAFLEY to Nannie L. STROUD Issued 25 Dec 1920 Rites 25 Dec 1920
H. T. King, M. G.

Frank WOODLEE (Col) to Lourena LEE (Col) 26 Dec 1920 Rites 26 Dec 1920
E. S. Bedford, M. G.

Herman CUTTS to Lizzie CALDWELL Issued 27 Dec 1920 Rites 29 Dec 1920
W. P. Davis, J. P.

Charlie PHILLIPS to Helen CANTRELL Issued 30 Dec 1920 Rites 2 Jan 1921
W. P. Davis, J. P.

Willie FRAZIER to Emma HOBBS Issued 31 Dec 1920 Rites 2 Jan 1921
O. H. Woods, J. P.

T. V. McMAHAN to Annie Mai DUNCAN Issued 31 Dec 1920 Rites 1 Jan 1921
A. Z. Holder, J. P.

Floyd GARRISON to Etta ROGERS Issued 31 Dec 1920 Rites 2 Jan 1921
L. B. Moffitt, J. P.

Monroe GREEN to Etta CANTRELL Issued 31 Dec 1920 Rites 2 JAn 1921
P. G. Moore, J. P.

Fred ANDES to Nellie YORK Issued 1 Jan 1921 Rites 1 Jan 1921
Price Billingsley, M. G.

Louis MONTANDON to Esther COOK Issued 1 JAn 1921 Rites 1 Jan 1921
H. T. King, M. G.

L. L. SCOTT to Rubie Lee MARTIN Issued 6 JAn 1921 Rites 9 Jan 1921
P. N. Moffitt, J. P.

William Percy MARTIN to Augusta WALLING issued 6 Jan 1921 Rites 25 Jan 1921
R. T. Skinner, M. G.

George W. McGREGOR to Ida CURTIS Issued 8 JAn 1921 Rites 9 Jan 1921
P. N. Moffitt, J. P.

John JONES to MArgie SELLARS Issued 18 Jan 1921 Rites 23 Jan 1921
H. L. Jones, J. P.

Thomas·L. HOGWOOD to Ella Pearl BILBREY Issued 22 JAn 1921 Rites 22 Jan 1921

Pete MARTIN (Col) to Pearl FOSTER (Col) Issued 22 Jan 1921 Rites 21 Jan 1921
J. S. Nance, M. G.

Herbert BROWN to CARRIE HOBBS Issued 24 Jan 1921 Rites 25 Jan 1921
O. H. Wood, J. P.

Elsia FULTS to Doshia SMARTT Issued 24 Jan 1921 Rites 10 Mar 1921
Thos. J. Wagner, M. G.

Andy BROWN to Docie COPPINGER Issued 29 Jan 1921 Rites 31 Jan 1921
G. P. Brasier, J. P.

R. D. CROWE to Ila Mai ALLISON Issued 31 JAn 1921 Rites 31 Jan 1921
J. M. Horn, M. G.

Tom DAVIS to Jessie DODD Issued 25 Mar 1921 Rites 26 Mar 1921
A. Z. Holder, J. P.

Frank C. HILLIS to Tennie DAVIS Issued 26 Mar 1921 Rites 27 Mar 1921
R. L. Barnett, J. P.

Ernest MARTIN (Col) to Hattie MARTIN (Col) Issued 26 Mar 1921 Rites 27 Mar 1921
J. H. Talley, M. G.

Robert MOORE to Viola BOYD Issued 26 Mar 1921 Rites 26 Mar 1921
E. S. Bedford, M. G.

Bob MITCHELL to Harriet HAYES issued 30 Mar 1921 Rites 30 Mar 1921
H. T. King, M. G.

Roy BLACK to Alma SMITH Issued 1 Apr 1921 Rites 1 Apr 1921
W. P. Davis, J. P.

Foster FERRELL to Aubrey SMITHSON Issued 9 Apr 1921 Rites 17 Apr 1921
J. A. Brixey, J. P.

G. W. DAVIS to Josie WEBB Issued 9 Apr 1921 Rites 10 Apr 1921
L. P. Sanders, J. P.

Herbert BATES to Lela TURNER Issued 9 Apr 1921 Rites 10 Apr 1921
T. R. Clark, J. P.

James LYONS to Ida BENNETT Issued 13 Apr 1921 Rites 14 Apr 1921
W. P. Davis, J. P.

J. A. FOSTER to Mary Lou COUCH issued 18 Apr 1921 Rites 18 Apr 1921
H. T. King, M. G.

Robert LAFEVER to Lillie HITTSON Issued 18 Apr 1921 Rites 18 Apr 1921
H. E. Ramsey, J. P.

Andrew BROWN (Col) to Beulah ALLEN (Col) Issued 19 Apr 1921 Rites 21 Apr 1921
I. N. Smoot, J. P.

Floyd VICKERS to Onie Lee SMITHSON Issued 20 Apr 1921 Rites 28 JAn 1921
H. L. Jones, J. P.

Marvin M. BILES to Rena M. BRIXEY Issued 21 Apr 1921 Rites 24 Apr 1921
G. P. Brasier, J. P.

Petway McCALEB to Birtie ANDERSON Issued 22 Apr 1921 Rites 22 Apr 1921
T. A. Craddock, J. P.

J. W. MARTIN to Louise HILLIS Issued 22 Apr 1921 Rites 23 Apr 1921
R. L. Barnett, J. P.

Marrion JONES to Hilda DAVENPORT Issued 23 Apr 1921 Rites 23 Apr 1921
R. L. Whitlock, M. G.

Willie GORDON to Nancy SANDERS Issued 23 Apr 1921 Rites 24 Apr 1921
J. R. Stubblefield, M. G.

N. J. H. VANMETER (Col) to Mary SMITH (Col) Issued 24 Apr 1921 Rites 24 Apr 1921
J. H. Talley, M. G.

W. R. WRIGHT to America NUNLEY Issued 3 Feb 1921 Rites 3 Feb 1921
H. T. King

Dave WANFORD to Maggie NEAL Issued 3 Feb 1921 Rites 3 Feb 1921
R. T. Skinner, M. G.

Grover PELHAM to Nellie TURNER Issued 12 Feb 1921 Rites 11 Feb. 1921
J. M. Horn, M. G.

Lee BANKS to Anna REDMON Issued 12 Feb 1921 Rites 12 Feb 1921
W. P. Davis, J. P.

Vance PELHAM to Lela SIMMONS Issued 16 Feb 1921 Rites 16 Feb 1921
Price Billingsley, M. G.

E. A. PHILPOT to Ethel DAVIS Issued 16 Feb 1921 Returned - Not Solemnized

Jim PINEGAR to Martha PINEGAR Issued 24 Feb 1921 Rites 25 Feb 1921
J. R. Goodpasture, M. G.

Jerry R. KILLIAN to Lela KIRKPATRICK Issued 25 Feb 1921 Rites 26 Feb 1921
G. L. Beech, J. P.

W. S. LIVELY to Ethel COOK Issued 25 Feb 1921 Rites 26 Feb 1921
H. T. King, M. G.

M. L. AKIN to Maud BONNER Issued 26 Feb 1921 Rites 27 Feb 1921
A. J. McBRIDE, M. G.

Isaac RHEA to Frankie SMARTT issued 4 Mar 1921 Rites 5 Mar 1921
P. N. Moffitt, J. P.

Marshall BOYD to Charlotte GROSS Issued 7 Mar 1921 Rites 8 Mar 1921
Thos. J. Wagner, M. G.

J. S. WARREN to Clara NEWBY Issued 10 Mar 1921 Rites 17 Mar 1921
H. L. Jones, J. P.

John WEBB (Col) to Nora B. MARTIN (Col) Issued 15 Mar 1921 Rites 15 Mar 1921
J. S. Nance, M. G.

D. H. KING to Mary Laura BELL Issued 16 Mar 1921 Rites 17 Mar 1921
R. T. Skinner, M. G.

Roy CROUCH to Clarisa KENNEDY Issued 19 Mar 1921 Rites 27 Mar 1921
H. E. Ramsey, J. P.

Ralph EARLS to Minnie SMARTT Issued19 Mar 1921 Rites 20 Mar 1921
R. T. Skinner, M. G.

Guy LaVaughn ROBERTS to Lydia Maude WHITE Issued 19 Mar 1921 Rites 20 Mar 1921
J. M. Horn, M. G.

Charlie KENNEDY to Flora CROUCH Issued 24 Mar 1921 Rites 27 Mar 1921
H. E. Ramsey, J. P.

Doyle ORICK to Agnes SWANGAR Issued 30 Apr 1921 Rites 1 May 1921
J. A. Cunningham, M. G.

George ROLLER to Connie R. DAVIS Issued 30 Apr 1921   Not Returned

T. J. CARRICK to Mabel LANCE Issued 30 Apr 1921 Rites 1 May 1921
W. C. Lorance, J. P.

W. C. SINGLETON to Walker BONNER Issued 2 May 1921 Rites 4 May 1921
J. W. Eaton, Jdg.

L. B. FOSTER to Florence KEMPER Issued 6 May 1921 Rites 6 May 1921
Price Billingsley, M. G.

Jones M. GREER to Othala KELL Issued 6 May 1921 Rites 12 May 1921
E. C. Leeper, M. G.

Rufus UNDERWOOD to Lena PENNINGTON Issued 6 May 1921 Rites 6 May 1921
J. W. Eaton, Jdg.

Wince BARNES to Ruby WARE Issued 6 May 1921 Rites 8 May 1921
P. N. Moffitt, J. P.

W. J. CHRISTIAN to Eva HOOVER Issued 7 May 1921 Rites 8 May 1921
J. A. Brixey, J. P.

W. N. HANNAH to Alberta LEWIS Issued 12 May 1921 Rites 12 May 1921
H. T. King, M. G.

Henry HENDERSON to Hallie TALLEY Issued 21 May 1921 Rites 21 May 1921
C. L. Webster

Henry JONES to Martha POWELL Issued 21 May 1921 Rites 21 May 1921
H. T. King, M. G.

Arcie HENNESSEE to Icy NUNLEY Issued 21 MAY 1921 Rites 21 May 1921
H. T. King, M. G.

I. H. GREEN to Mai GREEN Issued 21 May 1921 Rites 22 May 1921
P. G. Moore, J. P.

L. B. SPARMAN to Sudie TURNER Issued 21 May 1921 Rites 22 May 1921
W. E. Higginbotham

Carl W. PEARSALL to MArgie JOHNSON Issued 25 May 1921 Rites 25 May 1921
T. R. Clark, J. P.

Andrew BROWN to Minnie BOTTOMS Issued 30 May 1921 Rites 30 May 1921
E. C. Leeper, M. G.

William Jesse CORE (?) to Hettie Rose GOODPASTURE issued 31 May 1921 Rites 1 Jun
J. R. Goodpasture, M. G.

F. C. CURTIS to Lillie RHEA Issued 1 Jun 1921 Rites 1 Jun 1921
W. P. Davis, J. P.

C. SAVAGE (Col) to Ophelia CARPENTER (Col) Issued 1 Jun 1921 Rites 1 Jun 1921
J. H. Talley

Robert L. BOTTOMS to Georgia PARKER Issued 2 Jun 1921 Rites 3 Jun 1921
J. W. Hall, M. G.

Wm. A. STEEL to Virginia MULLICAN Issued 3 Jun 1921 Rites 3 Jun 1921
G. L. Beech, J. P.

T. D. OWENS to Emma PRIEST Issued 4 Jun 1921 Rites 4 jun 1921
J. D. Hash, J. P.

Houston WILSON to Brina JONES Issued 4 Jun 1921 Rites 5 Jun 1921
T. A. Craddock, J. P.

Grady MULLICAN to Oleta BOLES Issued 5 Jun 1921 Rites 5 Jun1921
H. T. King, M. G.

Worth L. BRYAN to Nelle H. LIVELY Issued 7 Jun 1921 Rites 8 Jun 1921
H. T. King, M. G.

John KENNEDY to Lora HUTCHINS Issued 11 June 1921 Rites 12 May 1921
H. E. Ramsey, J. P.

Marshall CROUCH to Laura ROGERS Issued 11 Jun 1921 Rites 28 Jan 1922
J. A. Brixey, J. P.

L. K. GRISSOM to Reatha JONES Issued 11 Jun 1921 Rites 19 Jun 1921
L. F. Daugherty, M. G.

James PACK to Lucille BUCKNER Issued 12 Jun 1921 Rites 13 jun 1921
P. G. Potter, M. G.

L. J. BONNER to Willie BRAWLEY Issued 17 jun 1921 Rites 18 Jun 1921
H. T. King, M. G.

Eden M. LANE to Ethelda G. WILLIAMS Issued 18 Jun 1921 Rites 19 jun 1921
J. M. Horn, M. G.

Axom BOREN to Eunice BLANKENSHIP Issued 18 Jun 1921 Rites 26 Jun 1921
L. F. Daugherty. M. G.

Chas. T. POWELL to Magnolia GOLDEN Issued 24 Jun 1921 Rites 12 Jun 1921
David M. Hamilton, Elder

Sam EMERY to Lena THURMAN Issued 25 jun 1921 Rites 25 Jun 1921
A. Z. Holder, J.. P.

J. E. McCLOWN to George NICHOLS Issued 27 Jun 1921 Rites 28 Jun 1921
R. N. Brown, M. G.

Wiley W. HASH to Henrietta E. MARTIN Issued 29 Jun 1921   Not Returned

J. Jeff CURTIS to Mattie L. McGEE Issued 1 July 1921 Rites 3 Jul 1921
A. P. Roberson, J. P.

Reuben R. TILGHMAN to Blanche HIGGINBOTHAM Issued 3 Jul 1921 Rites 14 Jul 1921
J. M. Horn, M.!G.

W. F. CANTRELL to Georgia MALONE Issued 4 July 1921 Rites 5 Jul 1921
W. P. Davis, J. P.

Elmon SMITH to Edith McBRIDE issued 5 Jul 1921 Rites 10 Jul 1921
J. L. Barnes, J. P.

Elza GRISSOM to Hassie REEDER Issued 9 Jul 1921 Rites 10 Jul 1921
W. W. Locke, J. P.

Benton CLARK to Chloe ALLEN issued 11 Jul 1921 Rites 11 Jul 1921
W. P. Davis, J. P.

G. L. HALEY to Fannie FREEMAN Issued 16 Jul 1921 Rites 17 Jul 1921
T. A. Craddock, J. P.

Oziah STEMBRIDGE to Theo JONES Issued 16 Jul 1921 Rites 12 Jul 1921
P. G. Potter, M. G.

William F. STEPP to Nora Mai NORTHCUTT issued 20 Jul 1921 Rites 20 Jul 1921
R. S. McCollum, J. P.

Andy MITCHELL to Nannie REYNOLDS Issued 25 Jul 1921 Rites 25 Jul 1921
J. M. Horn, M. G.

Alvis SIUNE to Edna VICKERS Issued 26 Jul 1921 Rites 26 Jul 1921
W. P. Davis, J. P.

Luther HUGHES to Etta WHITLOCK Issued 30 Jul 1921 Rites 31 Jul 1921
T. A. Craddock, J. P.

A. E. MARTIN to Hattie DIXON Issued 1 Aug 1921 Rites 1 Aug 1921
H. T. King, M. G.

Carl DUNLAP to Palastine CANTRELL issued 3 Aug 1921 Rites 7 Aug 1921
L. F. Daugherty. M. G.

Carl H. WERBER to Jessie L. THROWER Issued 6 Aug 1921 Rites 6 Aug 1921
H. T. King, M. G.

W. M. JOHNSON to Garce MORROW issued 6 Aug 1921 Rites 6 Aug 1921
H. T. King, M. G.

J. C. BARNES to Pauline PEDIGO Issued 9 Aug 1921 Rites 14 Aug 1921
W. C. Lorance, J. P.

Chas. C. GALLOWAY to Belle McBRIDE Issued 16 Aug 1921 Rites 25 Aug 1921
G. W. Angel. M. G.

J. F. SIMPSON to Sarah B. DODD Issued 18 Aug 1921 Rites 18 Aug 1921
W. P. Davis, J. P.

Russ FULTS to Georgia CURTIS Issued 22 Aug 1921 Rites 22 Aug 1921
S. M. Smartt, M. G.

J. W. CHISAM to Smaantha WOMACK Issued 26 Aug 1921 Rites 28 Aug 1921
L. C. Lane, J. P.

Andy SMARTT to Nettie BRAXTON Issued 27 Aug 1921 Rites 31 Aug 1921
J. L. Barnes, J. P.

Earl G. GILBERT to Bessie Lee ROBISON Issued 30 Aug 1921 Rites 4 Sep 1921
W. P. Davis, J. P.

E. B. HARRIS to Allie EVANS Issued 30 Aug 1921 Rites 31 Aug 1921
Fred T. Evans, M. G.

B. S. DODSON to Lela Mai FARLESS Issued 30 Aug 1921 Rites 31 Aug 1921
J. W. Cooley, M. G.

Willie GLENN to Annie May CHISAM Issued 1 Sep 1921 Rites 4 Sep 1921
L. H. Daugherty, M. G.

Wm. E. BLOCHER to Mrs. Molloe WORLEY issued 7 Sep 1921 Rites 7 Sep 1921
H. T. King, M. G.

Bob T. PHILLIPS to Ressye ALLEN Issued 7 Sep 1921 Rites 8 Sep 1921
P. G. Potter, M. G.

Henry BYARS to Ella O'NEAL Issued 10 Sep 1921 Rites 11 Sep 1921
O. H. Wood, J. P.

Frank SAIN to Lila SMOOT Issued 10 Sep 1921 Rites 11 Sep 1921
R. A. Skelton, M. G.

Coy MORGAN to Lizzie DAVIS Issued 12 Sep 1921 Rites 18 Sep 1921
L. F. Daugherty, M. G.

Lessie Parker WOOD to Bertha Pauline ROACH issued 13 Sep 1921 Rites 18 Sep
F. L. Leeper, M. G.

G W. GOINES to Oder HARREL issued 17 Sep 1921 Rites 18 Sep 1921
J. T. Casey. M. G.

Tom CUTTS to Kittie BARRETT issued 17 Sep 1921 Rites 17 Sep 1921
W. P. Davis, M. G.

Chas. B. JULIAN to Mazell MASON Issued 17 Sep 1921 Rites 17 Sep 1921
H. T. King, M. G.

Lonnie ATNIP to Eliza Lee FOUCH Issued 17 Sep 1921 Rites 18 Sep 1921
P. G. Potter, M. G.

Willie THOMASON to Bettie DODD Issued 18 Sep 1921 Rites 18 Sep 1921
W. P. Davis, J. P.

John DEADMON to Katie TURNER issued 19 Sep 1921 Rites 19 Sep 1921
P. N. Moffitt, J. P.

Ed BARNES to Hassie McCLURE Issued 24 Sep 1921 Rites 24 Sep 1921
Fate Walker, J. P.

J. M. S. PARKER to Nolia WALLS Issued 29 Sep 1921 Rites 29 Sep 1921
J. B. Brown, J. P.

Walter KLee GOTHARD to Athon TAYLOR Not Returned

Emmett SCURLOCK to Effie RICHARDSON Issued 1 Dec 1921 Rites 2 Jan 1922
Fate WAlker, J. P.

Lessie BULLARD to Lydia McMILLEN Issued 3 Dec 1921 Rites 4 dec 1921
T. A. Craddock, J. P.

Earl KIMBALL to Ollie SHIRLEY Issued 8 Dec 1921 Rites 11 Dec 1921
J. A. Brixey, J. P.

E. C. WHEELER to Stella BROWN issued 9 dec 1921 Rites 11 Dec 1921
J. R. Goodpasture, M. G.

Haskel CURTIS to Ethel GREEN Issued 10 dec 1921 Rites 11 Dec 1921
N. M. Hill, J. P.

Walter BRATCHER to Stacy MILLER Issued 13 Dec 1921 Rites 18 Dec 1921
H. L. Jones, J. P.

Robert Seth McCALLEN to Mildred LENOIR BURROUGHS Issued 13 Dec 1921 Rites 14 Dec
B. T. Lannom. M. G.

Bernice CHISAM to Mollie RANKHORN issued 16 dec 1921 Rites 25 Dec 1921
L. C. Lane, J. P.

Isaac RACKLEY to Rosa Lee JOHNSON Issued 17 Dec 1921 Rites 20 Dec 1921
T. M. Eaton, J. P.

George Daniel TAYLOR to Isabelle MULLICAN Issued 17 Dec 1921 Rites 18 Dec 1921
G. L. Beech. J. P.

Eugene B. CRAWFORD to Nancy Ellen HASH Issued 23 dec 1921 Rites 23 dec 1921
M. V. D. Miller, J. P.

Chas. F. GROVE, Jr. to Ella Mai McGEE Issued 24 Dec 1921 Rites 25 dec 1921
J. W. Cooley, M. G.

Joe WOMACK to May ELLIOTT Issued 24 dec 1921 Rites 24 dec 1921
W. P. Davis, J. P.

Oscar J. HARRIS to Lola TAYLOR issued 24 Dec 1921 Rites 25 Dec 1921
J. W. Cooley, M. G.

Tracy WOMACK to Cleo FOSTER issued 26 Dec 1921 Rites 27 dec 1921
T.A. Craddock, J. P.

I. F. PHELPS to Ethel SMITH Issued 28 dec 1921 Rites 28 dec 1921
Geo. B. Beaver, J. P.

Jim E. CANTRELL to Maggie TEMPLETON Issued 28 Dec 1921 Rites 28 dec 1921
W. P. Davis, J. P.

Henry BOND to Willie WHITLOCK issued 31 Dec 1921 Rites 1 Jan 1922
T. A. Craddock, J. P.

Leslie G. HULETT to Peggie HAMMONDS Issued 31 Dec 1921 Rites 1 Jan 1922
J.A. Brixey, J. P.

Vernon JONES to Daisy JONES Issued 1 Oct 1921 Rites 2 Oct 1921
G. A. Wilson, J. P.

Bill SMITH (Col) to Norena GWYNN (Col) Issued 1 Oct 1921 Rites 1 Oct 1921
E. S. Bedford, M. G.

G. T. MARTIN to Recie HAMMONS Issued 3 Oct 1921 Rites 3 Oct 1921
E. L. Moffitt, J. P.

T. C. SMARTT to Mary BROWN Issued 3 Oct 1921 Rites 4 Oct 1921
F. L. Leeper, M. G.

Lloyd Leon MOONEYHAM to Retta PATTON Issued 8 Oct 1921 Rites 8 Oct 1921
H. T. King, M. G.

Roy GWYN (Col) to Willie Ester MARTIN (Col) Issued 8 Oct 1921 Rites 9 Oct 1921
H. E. Ramsey, J. P.

Robert SMARTT(Col) to Mattie KING (Col) Issued 13 Oct 1921 Rites 15 Oct 1921
J. A. Brixey, J. P.

Claud TURNER to Emma TAYLOR Issued 17 Oct 1921 Rites 18 Oct 1921
W. E. Higginbotham

VAnce LOWERY to Virginia HEFNER Issued 19 Oct 1921 Rites 23 Oct 1921
Earnest C. Love

Marlin HITCHCOCK to Laura GEORGE Issued 1 Nov 1921 Rites 1 Nov 1921
J. D. HAsh, J. P.

Carl EVANS to Dora HILLIS Issued 2 Nov 1921 Rites 5 Nov 1921
J. T. Casey, M. G.

Joe M. COMER to Zella Irene MYERS Issued 2 Nov 1921 Rites 2 Nov 1921
R. A. Skelton, M. G.

Elmer DAVIS to Myrtle DAVIS Issued 3 Nov 1921 Rites 1 Dec 1921
L. F. Daugherty, M. G.

Horace ADCOCK (Col) to Lula FOSTER (Col) Issued 3 Nov 1921 Rites 5 Nov 1921
W. P. Davis, J. P.

A. D. HILLIS to Cleo BESS Issued 5 Nov 1921 Not Returned

Luther E. GRIBBLE to Clara MARTIN Issued 19 Nov 1921 Rites 20 Nov 1921
L. C. Lane, J. P.

Timmie PRIEST to Nettie GROVE issued 23 Nov 1921 Rites 27 Nov 1921
R. L. Barnett, J. P.

J. L. HARDING to Clara Belle DUNCAN Issued 26 Nov 1921 Rites 26 Nov 1921
B. S. McCollum, J. P.

J. F. CARROLL to Cora STROUD Issued 30 Nov 1921 Rites 1 Dec 1921
G. P. Brasier, J. P.

Dudley LEWIS to Willie Mai HASTON Issued 31 Dec 1921 Rites 1 JAn 1921
L. B. Moffitt, J. P.

JAmes McGREGOR to Georgie Mai PRESTON Issued 31 Dec 1921 Rites 1 Jan 1921
J. B. Brown, J. P.

Hobert H. WILLIAMS to Ora LUSK Issued 3 Jan 1922 Rites 4 Jan 1922
R. A. Skelton, M. G.

Jas. William HAVRON to Oma Lee TURNER Issued 7 JAn 1922 Rites 7 Jan 1922
M. M. Hill, J. P.

Provine TUBBS (Col) to Bulah SMARTT (Col) Issued 7 JAn 1922 Rites 7 JAn 1922
W. W. Locke, J. P.

Dillard GRIFFITH to Lola BRATTEN Issued 10 JAn 1922 Rites 11 Jan 1922
G. H. Atnip, M. G.

A. T. WOOD to Mae CANTRELL issued 11 Jan 1922 Rites 15 JAn 1922
P. G. Potter, M. G.

Frank TURNER to Mattie CANTRELL Issued 11 Jan 1922 Rites 15 Jan 1922
P. G. Potter, M. G.

S. P. MARBURY (Col) to Mary Ann SMITH (Col) Issued 14 Jan 1922 Rites 15 Jan 1922
E. S. Bedford, M. G.

T. L. YOUNG to Vernie HALE Issued 17 JAn 1922 Rites 11 Jan 1922
E. H. Liles, M. G.

Wilburn T. FULTS to Nancy SANDERS Issued 20 JAn 1922 Rites 20 JAn 1922
R. A. Skelton, M. G.

FAte SIMS (Col) to Reece SETTLE (Col) Issued 23 Jan 1922 Rites 23 Jan 1922
J. S. Nance, M. G.

Isham ROACH to Mrs. Martha WALLS Issued 25 Jan 1922 Rites 25 jan 1922
B. T. Lannom, M. G.

Thomas O. HUDSON to Zona P. COPE issued 26 jan 1922 Rites 1 Feb 1922
L. C. Lane, J. P.

Oscar ANDES to Lula Mae ROGERS Issued 31 jan 1922 Rites 31 Jan 1922
A. B. Moffitt

Loring WILLIAMS to Nola DELONG Issued 31 Jan 1922 Rites 1 Feb 1922
T. A. Craddock, J. P.

J. C. SLATTON to Roena COPE Issued 2 Feb 1922 Not Returned

Horace C. HOGAN to Ewell CUNNINGHAM Issued 6 Feb 1922 Rites 16 Feb 1922
J. W. Cooley, M. G.

W. A. ALLISON to Selmer TALLEY Issued 7 Feb 1922 Rites 7 Feb 1922
J. W. Cooley, M. G.

Book 14 - Warren County Marriages - Feb 7, 1922 to Feb 18, 1925

Robert BARTLEY (Col) to Dollie HUNTER (Col) Issued 7 Feb 1922 Rites 17 Feb 1922
J. A. Huddleston

Jesse GRIBBLE (Col) to Reatha HUNTER (Col) Issued7 Feb 1922 Rites 8 Feb 1922
W. V. D. Miller, J. P.

Charles E. DODD to Mary Jane HOLDER Issued 10 Feb 1922 Rites 14 Feb 1922
G. H. Atnip, M. G.

S. A. DOUGLAS to Josie GROVE Issued 11 Feb 1922 Rites 12 Feb 1922
S. H. Templeton, J. P.

Charles M. HILLIS to Lee WAGNER Issued 16 Feb 1922 Rites 18 Feb 1922
Thos. J. Wagner, M. G.

Howard MELSER to Roberta WATKINS Issued 16 Feb 1922 Rites 16 Feb 1922
T. R. Clark, J. P.

Claud SIMONS to Martha BRATCHER Issued 18 Feb 1922 Rites28 Feb 1922
J. B. Brown, J. P.

Haskel NUNLEY to Nora BOULDIN Issued 20 Feb 1922 Not Returned

Nathan McREYNOLDS (Col) to Elnora GIPSON (Col) Issued 20 Feb 1922 Rites 20 Feb
E. S. Bedford, M. G.

Olie PHILLIPS to Maude WEBB Issued 21 Feb 1922 Rites 22 Feb 1922
P. G. Potter, M. G.

JAmes L. WOMACK to Lorena G. CHISHOLM Issued 24 Feb 1922 Rites 26 Feb 1922
W. V. D. Miller, J. P.

Orein EARLS to Florence PERRY Issued 25 Feb 1922 Rites 26 Feb 1922
J. T. Casey, M. G.

Floyd REDMON to Ethel HENDERSON Issued 25 Feb 1922 Rites 27 Feb 1922
L. B. Moffitt, J. P.

L. C. WHITE (col) to Mollie FRENCH (Col) Issued 26 Feb 1922 Rites 26 Feb 1922
W. G. Strickland

Armstead ANDERSON to Clatie Mai ROGERS Issued 27 Feb 1922 Rites 3 Mar 1922
B. T. Lannom, M. G.

J. B. NELSON to Myrtle FARLESS Issued1 Mar 1922 Rites 5 Mar 1922
J. W. Cooley, M. G.

Orville BELL to Willie JARRELL Issued 11 Mar 1922 Rites 12 Mar 1922
O. H.Wood, J. P.

Clifton HALE to Elvia CANTRELL Issued 11 Mar 1922 Rites 12 Mar 1922
W. P. Davis, J. P.

Robert D. BURCH to Maggie EARLS Issued 13 Mar 1922 Rites 19 Mar 1922
W. P. DAvis, J. P.

Shelia GILLEY to Mary FRAZIER Issued 15 Mar 1922 Rites 19 Mar 1922
J. A. Brixey, J. P.

C. T. MARSH to Hester MILSTEAD Issued 16 Mar 1922 Rites 16 Mar 1922
G. L. Beech, J. P.

C. L. TUBB to Allie HUGHES Issued 17 Mar 1922 Rites 17 Mar 1922
W. P. DAvis, J. P.

George ROLLER to Thelma LOCKE Issued 18 Mar 1922 Rites 19 Mar 1922
L. P. SAnders, J. P.

John Alfred BLAKELY to Mamie Etter BILES Issued 18 Mar 1922 Rites 23 Mar 1922
R. A. Skelton, M. G.

Albert FISHER to Willie HUTCHINS Issued 28 Mar 1922 Rites 3 Apr 1922
L. F. DAUGHERTY, M. G.

Furd BROWN (Col) to Mattie GUEST (Col) Issued 30 Mar 1922 Rites 4 Apr 1922
H. E. Ramsey, J. P.

Lester MONTANDAN to Zora BRYANT Issued 1 Apr 1922 Rites 1 Apr 1922
J. D. Hash, J. P.

John FOSTER (Col) to Lillian DURAHM (Col) Issued 8 Apr 1922 Rites 9 Apr 1922
J. S. NAnce, M. G.

Hiram ROBINSON to MAude COPEHART Issued 8 Apr 1922 Rites 9 Apr 1922
G. W. Hinkley, J. P.

Burnie WOODLEE to Kate EARLS Issued 12 Apr 1922 Rites 12 Apr 1922
J. T. Casey, M. G.

Erbie PATTON to Minnie MAy COUCH Issued 13 Apr 1922 Rites 15 Apr 1922
J. W. Cooley, M. G.

Tom BRADY to Fluella NEWBY Issued 15 Apr 1922 Rites 16 Apr 1922
T. A.Craddock, J. P.

Earl JONES to Robie Lee WINTON Issued 15 Apr 1922 Rites 15 Apr 1922
O. H. Wood, J. P.

Carbon REED to Ova CAMPBELL Issued 16 Apr 1922 Rites 16 Apr 1922
R. T. Skinner, M. G.

J. J. BOST to Alice MAYFIELD Issued 19 Apr 1922 Rites 19 Apr 1922
J. D. Templeton, J. P.

Brown Ramsey GARDNER to HAllie May CRAWFORD Issued 22 Apr 1922 Rites 22 Apr 1922
J. W. Cooley, M. G.

Edward Hatcher WILLIS to Eliz. Susanna BLUE Issued 24 Apr 1922 Rites 23 Apr 1922
Chas. R. Brewer

Frank K. BELL to Anna Lee CURTIS Issued 28 Apr 1922 Rites 12 MAy 1922
W. P. DAvis, J. P.

John A. RICE to Emma E. CUNNINGHAM Issued 29 Apr 1922 Rites 30 Apr 1922
R. T. Skinner, M. G.

HArtford MATHERLY to Louise LAWS Issued 1 May 1922 Not Returned

Richard ALLEN to HAzel ROBERTS Issued 4 May 1922 Rites 7 May 1922
L. F. DAugherty, M. G.

J. J. LYTLE to Pearl CLENDENEN Issued 5 May 1922 Not Returned

George WOODLEE to Ruby PARKS Issued 12 May 1922 Rites 14 May 1922
J. W. Cooley, M. G.

Schyler WINFREE to Helen GREEN Issued 13 May 1922 Rites 14 May 1922
L. P. Sanders, J. P.

Robert YOUNGBLOOD to CArr PRATER Issued 17 May 1922 Rites 17 May 1922
W. P. DAvis, J. P.

Clyde BANKS to Clara CANTRELL Issued 19 May 1922 Rites 22 May 1922
J. W. L. Sandusky, M. G.

Robert L. FINGER to Helen BENNETT Issued 22 May 1922 Rites 22 May 1922
J. W. Cooley, M. G.

H. B. STILES to Maggie Mae SPAIN Issued 27 MAy 1922 Rites 27 May 1922
J. W. eATON, Jdg.

W. E. MULLICAN to Rachel FARLESS Issued 27 May 1922 Rites 27 May 1922
G. L. Beech, J. P.

S. W. NOMLIN (Col) to Cynthia SMITH (Col) Issued 31 May 1922 Rites 1 Jun 1922
W. G. Strickland

Henry GREEN to Winnie BRATTEN Issued 2 Jun 1922 Rites 3 JUN 1922
B. T. LANNOM, M. G.

John A. MARSH to Susie MARSH Issued 5 Jun 1922 Rites 5 Jun 1922
E. H. Liles, M. G.

Robert OFFICER (Col) to Pauline PATTERSON (Col) Issued 7 Jun 1922 Rites 7 Jun 1922
W. G. Strickland

Ira SAFLEY to CArrie DUNLAP Issued 7 Jun 1922 Rites 11 Jun 1922
J. D. HAsh, J. P.

Dennie DUNLAP to Lena STIPE Issued 7 Jun 1922 Rites 24 Jun 1922
W. V. D. Miller, J. P.

John BALDWIN to Eula DELANEY Issued 8 Jun 1922 Rites 8 Jun 1922
B. T. Lannom, M. G.

Alvia CLENDENON to Nettie SIMONS Issued 10 Jun 1922 Rites 10 Jun 1922
P. N. Moffitt, J. P.

Charles DIXON to Mattie Mai BYRD Issued 10 Jun 1922 Rites 11 Jun 1922
J. W. Cooley, M. G.

Wm. Edward SMITH to Mary Amanda RUTHERFORD Issued 12 Jun 1922 Rites 14 Jun 1922
F. L. Leeper, M. G.

Mack PARTON to Verona TRAWEEK Issued 24 Jul 1922 Rites 22 Jul 1922
J. W. Cooley, M. G.

Elbert Lee NORRIS to Bessie Mae BEDWELL Issued 26 Jul 1922 Rites 30 Jul 1922
J. E. Clark, M. G.

John F. BLAIR to Essie SCOTT issued 28 Jul 1922 Rites 29 Jul 1922
J. T. Casey, M. G.

Sherman ROGERS to Alice WILLIAMSON Issued 4 Aug 1922 Rites 6 Aug 1922
J.A. Brixey, J. P.

William SMARTT (Col) to Leona WOODS (Col) Issued 5 Aug 1922 Rites 5 Aug 1922
W. W. Locke, J. P.

John Comer MASON to Carmon Grace VANADGRIFF Issued 5 Aug 1922 Rites 5 Aug 1922
T. A. Craddock, J. P.

Bryan McGEE to Gladys ROY Issued 5 Aug 1922 Rites 5 Aug 1922
W. P. Davis, J. P.

Edmund W. SEALS to Mabel McCRARY Issued9 Aug 1922 Rites 13 Aug 1922
F. L. Leeper, M. G.

FAte HILL to Katherine PARIS Issued 10 Aug 1922 Returned - Not Solemnized

Fate LYNN to JAnie SCOTT Issued 12 Aug 1922 Rites 13 Aug 1922
L. B. Moffitt, Jr. P.

Clyde SMITH to Annie PERRY Issued 16 Aug 1922 Not Returned

Marcus SHERRELL to Bessie ORICK Issued 18 Aug 1922 Rites 5 Sep. 1922
A. Z. Holder, J. P.

Emmett MYERS to Maggie EARL Issued 19 Aug 1922 Rites 25 Aug 1922
W. P. davis, J. P.

J. E. TURNER to Cecil SELF Issued 19 Aug 1922 Rites 25 Aug 1922
H. L. Jones, J. P.

Roy MALONE to Cora May DODSON Issued 21 Aug 1922 Rites 21 Aug 1922
B. T. Lannon, M. G

Ralph ARNOLD to Nettie HUBBARD Issued 24 Aug 1922 Rites 24 Aug 1922
W. P. Davis, J. P.

H. W. ROGERS to Nannie ROGERS Issued 24 Aug 1922 rItes 24 Aug 1922
B. S. McCollum, J. P.

Otis Monroe WHITLOCK to Lula BOND Issued 26 Aug 1922 Rites 6 Sep 1922
G. H. Atnip, J. P.

RAlph HAGII to Georgia TOWELL Issued 26 Aug 1922 Rites 27 Aug 1922
J. E. Clark, M. G.

John Thurman SMITH to Ruby Mai SMITHSON Issued 26 Aug 1922 Rites 28 Aug 1922
E. H. liles, M. G.

T. L. CURRY (Col) to Janie DAVIS (Col) Issued 15 Jun 1922 Rites 17 Jun 1922
Wm. T. E. Travis, M. G.

James A. SMITH to Rosa MATHIS Issued 16 Jun 1922 Rites 18 Jun 1922
W. P. Davis, J. P.

Clyde D. BARTLETT to Bettie Lou LORING Issued 17 jun 1922 Rites 17 Jun 1922
R. T. Skinner, M. G.

Rollie PEPPER (Col) to Nannie MARTIN (Col) Issued 17 Jun 1922 Rites 18 Jun 1922
Wm. T. E. Travis, M. G.

Clyde TURNER to Lowry NEWBY Issued 17 Jun 1922 Rites 18 Jun 1922
A. Z. Holder, J. P.

JAmes Dewey DARNELL to JoAnna Hazel McAFEE Issued 21 Jun 1922 Rites 22 Jun 1922
Thos. J. Wagner, M. G.

CArl H. OWENS to Mary LOU CANTRELL Issued 22 Jun 1922 Rites 22 Jun 1922
T. L. Leeper, M. G.

Bert C. JOHNSON to Marie GRISSOM Issued 24 Jun 1922 Rites 25 Jun 1922
L. SAfley, M. G.

Thomas J. CURTIS to Ella BURCH Issued 27 Jun 1922 Rites 27 Jun 1922
W. P. Davis, J. P.

W. M.CASS to Maude PRATER issued 1 Jul 1922 Rites 4 Jul 1922
W. H. Craven

H. A. CUNNINGHAM to Nettie GROVE Issued 1 Jul 1922 Rites 3 Jul 1922
A. B. Moffitt

Anderson KING (Col) to Lou BROWN (Col) Issued 1 Jul 1922 Rites 1 Jul 1922
G. P. Brasier, J. P.

John T. ROGERS to Maggie CUNNINGHAM Issued 1 Jul 1922 Rites 1 Jul 1922
J. L. Barnes, J. P.

E. W. DONNELL to Mevolyn RHEA Issued 2 Jul 1922 Rites 2 Jul 1922
R. T. Skinenr, M. G.

Thomas FULTS to Alka SCOTT Issued 4 Jul 1922 Rites 4 Jul 1922
W. P. Davis, J. P.

Irving CUNNINGHAM to Lela SHERRELL Issued 8 Jul 1922 Rites 9 Jul 1922
J. E. Clark, M. G.

Clyde S. JONES to Johnnie Ida GREEN Issued 8 Jul 1922 Rites 9 Jul 1922
G. P. Potter, M. G.

Willie TEMPLETON to Pina ROGERS Issued 22 Jul 1922 Rites 22 Jul 1922
J. W. Cooley, M. G.

Olaway WEBB (Col) to May RUSSELL (Col) Issued 22 Jul 1922 Rites 22 Jul 1922
J. S. Nance, M. G.

John E. BRATCHER to Abbie HOLDER Issued 28 Aug 1922 R.tes 28 Aug 1922
W. P. Davis, J. P.

H. R. SULLIVAN to Vella Mai LITTLE Issued 30 Aug 1922 Rites 30 Aug 1922
P. G. Potter, M. G.

Howard ELROD to Leatha WOOD Issued 30 Aug 1922 Rites 6 Sep 1922
P. G. Potter, M. G.

W. C. MOSS to Frankie Lee HENNESSEE Issued 31 Aug 1922 Rites 1 Sep 1922
L. P. Sanders, J. P.

W. I. HILLIS to Jennie TEMPLETON Issued 2 Sep 1922 Rites 2 Sep 1922
J. W. Cooley, M. G.

Walter A. MARTIN to Beatrice HILL Issued 4 Sep 1922 Rites 7 Sep 1922
E. S. Bedford, M. G.

Robert SIMONS to Clara Mae WEBSTER Issued 4 Sep 1922 Rites 5 Sep 1922
J. W. Cooley, M. G.

... 6 Sep 1922
J. ?. Casey, M. G.

JAmes A. CHAMBERS to Elizabeth BELL Issued 8 Sep 1922 Rites 10 Sep 1922
E. D. Martin, M. G.

Wade PARKER to Cora GUNN Issued 9 Sep 1922 Rites 10 Sep 1922
R. A. Skelton, M. G.

C. E. EVANS to Mary Myrtle FARLESS Issued 9 Sep 1922 Rites 10 Sep 1922
J. W. Cooley, M. G.

Harvey DODD to May HOLLAND Issued 14 Sep 1922 Rites 14 Sep 1922
W. C. Lorance, J. P.

Will KIRBY to Emma JOHNSON Issued 14 Sep 1922 Rites 16 Sep 1922
J. A. Brixey, J. P.

Herman STARKEY to Velma BALES Issued 16 Sep 1922 Rites 17 Sep 1922
Ed. Jones, J. P.

Henry BARNES to Addie JOHNSON Issued 16 Sep 1922 Rites 16 Sep 1922
J. S. Nance, M. G.

Eugene Brackett ESTES to Mary Eva HENDRIXSON Issued 20 Sep 1922 Rites 20 Sep
F. L. Leeper, M. G.

Chas. L. CARPENTER to Vear Canzada WARREN Issued 21 Sep 1922 Rites 21 Sep 1922
B. F. Lannom, M, G.

Herman KEATHLEY to Mary ROLLER Issued 22 Sep 1922 Rites 24 Sep 1922
L. F. DAugherty, M. G.

Jimmie COPE to Ruth COTTON Issued 23 Sep 1922 Rites 11 Oct 1922
M. Smoot, J. P.

Ivy Joe RAMSEY to Allie SPURLOCK Issued 25 Sep 1922 Rites 29 Sep 1922
(Col)
E. S. Bedford, M. G.

Eulis HALE to Ersie HALE Issued 29 Sep 1922 Rites 1 Oct 1922
J. W. Cooley, M. G.

Lawrence MARTIN to Fannie LEFTRICT Issued 29 Sep 1922 Rites 29 Sep 1922
(Col)
E. S. Bedford, M. G.

Arthur TURNER to Laura TAYLOR Issued 30 Sep 1922 Rites 1 Oct 1922
P. G. Pottre, M. G.

Clark CANTRELL to Nettie LOTHON Issued 30 Sep 1922 Rites 1 Oct 1922
P. G. Potter, M. G.

C. T. DUNCAN to Nellie REDMON Issued 4 Oct 1922 Rites 4 Oct 1922
W. P. Davis, J. P.

Hall Houston CANTRELL to Eula Mai HILL Issued 7 Oct 1922 Rites 8 Oct 1922
P. G. Moore, M. G.

Arthur SMITH to Virgia SIMONS Issued 7 Oct 1922 Rites 7 Oct 1922
W. K, Tidwell, M. G.

Jim HALE to Lee BURGESS Issued 7 Oct 1922 Rites 8 Oct 1922
J. W. Cooley, M. G.

Wm.THOMPSON (Col) to Gertrude DRAKE Issued 12 Oct 1922 Rites 12 Oct 1922
(Col)
R. Ed. Jones, J. P.

Byron WARREN to Susie HIGDON Issued 12 Oct 1922 Rites 12 Oct 1922
W. P. DAvis, J. P.

Erton DUNLAP to Carrie MOON Issued 13 Oct 1922 Rites 24 dec 1922
J. D. Hash, J. P.

Walter MELTON to Ethel HOLLANDSWORTH issued 14 Oct 1922 Rites 14 Oct 1922
Price Billingsley, M. G.

Gilbert GRAYSON (Col) to Elenor MORFORD (Col) Issued 14 Oct 1922 Rites 14 Oct
E. S. Bedford, M. G.

Walter LEE SAVAGE (Col) to Arbelle ROACH (Col) Issued 14 Oct 1922 Rites 14 Oct
E. S. Bedford, M. G.

William K. HARGETT to Velma WRIGHIMAN Issued 18 Oct 1922 Rites 18 Oct 1922
J. T. Casey, M. G.

George PERREN to Elizabeth CRAIN Issued 18 Oct 1922 Rites 18 Oct 1922
R. T. Skinner, M. G.

Elbert YATES to Ethel COLE Issued 20 Oct 1922 Rites 20 Oct 1922
W. P. Davis, J. P.

Fred BELL to Adele CURTIS Issued 20 Oct 1922 Rites 22 Oct 1922
J. R. Goodpasture, M. G.

Dewey SLATTON to Willie SANDERS Issued 21 Oct 1922 Rites 22 Oct 1922
P. G. Potter, M. G.

J. W. CLARK to Maude JONES Issued 24 Oct 1922 Rites 24 Oct 1922
J. A. Brixey, J. P.

Charles CANTRELL to Lula EATON Issued 27 Oct 1922 Rites 29 Oct 1922
P. G. Moore, J. P.

T. T. CRAWFORD to Clara COOPER issued 27 Oct 1922 Rites 28 Oct 1922
J. B. Brown, J. P.

Billie CAMPBELL to Jennie BLAIR Issued 28 Oct 1922   Not Returned

Arthue EDWARDS (Col) to Nancy ELLIOTT (Col) Issued 30 Oct 1922 Rites 30 Oct 1922
Wm. T. E. Travis, M. G.

Everett SANDERS to Lola TUBB Issued 2 Nov 1922 Rites 2 Nov 1922
R. ED. Jones, J. P.

W. C. RAY to Lillie MYERS Issued 4 Nov 1922 Rites 5 Nov 1922
J. L. Barnes, J. P.

Leon LUTRELL to Mollie HILLIS Issued8 Nov 1922 Rites 8 Nov 1922
W. T. Davis, J. P.

Luther McGIBONEY to Mildred WALLACE Issued 8 Nov 1922 Rites 12 Nov 1922
Fate Walker, J. P.

E. Will GUEST (Col) to Della ALLEN (Col) Issued 13 Nov 1922 Rites 13 Nov 1922
I. M. Smoot, J. P.

A. M. HENNESSEE to Mary JACOBS Issued 18 Nov 1922 Rites 18 Nov 1922
O. H. Wood, J. P.

W. E. BONNER to Laura JOHNSON Issued 18 Nov 1922 Rites 5 Dec 1922
J. L. Barnes, J. P.

Wallace WOMACK to Shelby SMITH Issued 18 Nov 1922 Rites 18 Nov 1922
L. F. Daugherty, M. G.

Eugene WHEELER to Lillie Francis HUGHES Issued 19 Nov 1922 Rites 19 Nov 1922
B. T. Lannom, M. G.

Roosevelt LUSK (Col) to Gertrude CUMMINGS (Col) Issued 20 Nov 1922 Rites 20 Nov
E. S. bedford, M. G.

Anthony HOPPE to Mollie KING Issued 22 Nov 1922 Rites 22 Nov 1922
E. Ed. Jones, J. P.

Walter ROGERS to Sue Ann MYERS Issued 24 Nov 1922 Rites 26 Nov 1922
J. L. Barnes, J. P.

J,. D. HUTCHESON to Goldie MARTIN Issued 25 Nov 1922 Rites 25 Nov 1922
R. L. Barnett, J. P.

Andrew ROACH to Mazel PELHAM Issued 25 Nov 1922 Rites 25 Nov 1922
O. H. Wood, J. P.

T. E. BASHAM to Ollie Belle SMITH Issued 25 Nov 1922 Rites 26 nov 1922
W. E. Garner, M. G.

Clyde YOUNG to Oma Mai ROMANS Issued 25 Nov 1922   Not Returned

Brown McBRIDE to Ocie Mai NUNLEY Issued 25 Nov 1922 Rites 26 Nov 1922
L. B. Moffitt, J. P.

Herman STEWART to Mary HIBDON Issued 27 Nov 1922 Rites 29 Nov 1922
L. P. SAnders, J. P.

Charles HALE to Sallie MOSS Issued 30'nov 1922 Rites 3 Dec 1922
L. P. Sanders, J. P.

Will CUMMINGS (Col) to Beulah GRAYSON (Col) Issued 2 dec 1922 Rites 2 dec 192?
J. S. Nance, M. G.

Miles MUNCY to Lillie LUTRELL Issued 5 Dec 1922 Rites 7 Dec 1922
P. N. Moffitt, J. P.

Abe Bonner CROWE to Avis Velma EVANS Issued 5 Dec 1922 Rites 10 Dec 1922
R. T. Skinner, M. G.

Wilson S. PHILLIPS to Charles Mai ROBERTS Issued6 Dec 1922 Rites 20 Dec 1922
R. T. Skinner, M. G.

C. F. DAVENPORT to Novella BAIN Issued 8 Dec 1922 Rites 17 Dec 1922
G. H. Atnip, J. P.

H. T. ATNIP to Florence CRIM Issued8 Dec 1922 Rites 9 Dec 1922
T. R. Clark, J. P.

Ivory BELL to Francis BISHOP issued 9 Dec 1922 Rites 10 Dec 1922
A. Z. Holder, J. P.

T. E. TALIAFERRO to Susie Lee NOFFITT Issued 11 dec 1922 Rites 27 Dec 1922
B. T. Lannom, M. G.

T. J. BRAGG to Ida Belle BRYANT Issued 12 Dec 1922 Rites 13 dec 1922
P. G. Potter, M. G.

Ben KEENER to Mary TAYLOR Issued 14 dec 1922 Rites 16 dec 1922
J. D. Hash, J. P.

Wm. Leo BILBREY to Ethel Lee McGEE Issued 14 Dec 1922 Rites 17 dec 1922
J. W. Cooley, M. G.

Jim PINEAGR to Martha PINEGAR Issued 16 dec 1922 Rites 17 dec 1922
E. Edd Jones, J. P.

H. S. McBRIDE to Anna NUNLEY Issued 16 dec 1922 Rites 24 dec 1922
L. B. Moffitt, J. P.

W. H. TURNER to Lillie BASHAM Issued 16 dec 1922 Rites 16 dec 1922
W. W. Locke, J. P.

Laymon POWELL to Flonie MOONEYHAM Issued 16 Dec 1922 Rites 17 dec 1922
J. D. Hash, J. P.

Thurman BUTCHER to Bessie WHITEAKER Issued 30 Dec 1922 Rites 30 dec 1922
A. P. Roberson, J. P.

Burger GREEN to Margie WALLER Issued 30 Dec 1922 Rites 31 Dec 1922
J. W. Cooley, M. G.

Curl GRISSOM to Katherine GREEN Issued 4 Jan 1923 rites 4 Jan 1923
L. P. Sanders, J. P.

Tom SMOOT to R. E. LASSITER Issued 5 JAn 1923 Rites 7 Jan 1923
J.A. Cunningham, M. G.

Walton LAWSON to VAdie FUSON Issued 6 Jan 1923 Rites 6 JAn 1923
P. G. Potter, M. G.

L. A. ARLEDGE to Ruby BRADY Issued 6 JAn 1923 Rites 6 JAn 1923
J. Paul Slayden, M. G.

John CLAXTON (Col) to Sadie BROWN (Col) Issued 18 JAn 1923 Rites 18 Jan 1923
R. Ed Jones, J. P.

Clyde DAVIS to Willie BELL Issued 20 Jan 1923 Rites 20 Feb 1923
J. Paul Slayden, M. G.

R. L. WHITLOCK to Oda TITTSWORTH Issued 20 Jan 1923 Rites 20 Jan 1923
J. A. Cunningham, M. G.

Arthur PIPPIN to Jennie Lee McDOWELL Issued 27 Jan 1923 Rites 29 Jan 1923
W. P. Davis, J. P.

W. T. GARDNER to Esther GROVES Issued 27 Jan 1923 Rites 27 jan 1923
W. V. D. Miller, J. P.

Owen Bethel SMITH to Vera Clay PEDIGO Issued 30 Jan 1923 Rites 30 jan 1923
W. P. Davis, J. P.

John HICKS to Lillian McCORMICK Issued 3 feb 1923 Rites 4 feb 1923
B. S. Collum, J. P.

Gentry COPE to Vestie COPE Issued 5 Feb 1923 Rites 5 Feb 1923
L. P. Sanders, J. P.

C. R. BYRD to Mary Lou BYARS Issued 6 feb 1923 rites 7 feb 1923
P. G. Potter, M. G.

Irvin Jones GRIZZELL to Hattie JERNIGAN Issued 9 Feb 1923 Rites 9 Feb 1923
B. T. LANNOM, M. G.

Bill BREEDLOVE to Agnes HALE Issued9 Feb 1923 Rites 19 feb 1923
W. P. Davis, J. P.

Jmes Womack GOODNIGHT to Lena D. TURNER Issued 9 Feb 1923 Rites 9 feb 1923
B. T. Lannom, M. G.

Arthur CATES to Elvina CATES Issued 10 feb 1923 Rites 11 Feb 1923
J. D. hash, J. P.

Lusk WEBB to Clara ADCOCK Issued 19 Dec 1922 Rites 21 dec 1922
P. G. Potter, M. G.

Frank DILLON to Sarah ASKEW Issued 23 Dec 1922 Rites 23 dec 1922
R. E. Jones, J. P.

John GROVE to Etta McGREGOR Issued 23 Dec 1922 Rites 25 dec 1922
J. W. Cooley, M. G.

Sam JOHNSON (Col) to Anna Mai LOCKE (Col) Issued 22 dec 1922 Rites 24 dec 1922
Sam King, M. G.

Raymond BROWN (Col) to Lucile SAVAGE (Col) Issued 24 dec 1922 Rites 26 dec 1922
J. S. NAnce, M. G.

Edgar BROWN to Jessie PEPPER issued 24 Dec 1922 Rites 20 May 1923
R. T. Skimer, M. G.

Leo TURNER to Jucy May HENDRICKS Issued 25 dec 1922 Rites 23 dec 1922
E. H. Liles, M. G.

HArold Eugene WOODLEE to Martha Alice JORDAN Issued 23 Dec 1922 Rites 24 dec
J. W. Cooley, M. G.

J. A. LAWRENCE to Ruby PARKER Issued 23 dec 1922 Rites 27 dec 1922
J. A. Brixey, J. P.

Elijah NEAL to Geneva BASS Issued 23 dec 1922 Rites 23 dec 1922
W. E. Bluhm, M. G.

Dewey CANTRELL to Bettie DONNELL Issued 23 dec 1922 Rites 24 dec 1922
W. P. Davis, J. P.

Robert HUDSON to Flora THOMPSON issued 24 dec 1922 Rites 24 dec 1922
R. edd Jones, J. P.

Bryant SEAMONS to Emma MILLER Issued 26 dec 1922 Rites 31 JAn 1923
W. V. D. Miller, J. P.

Herman SLATTON to Vesta SANDERS Issued 27 dec 1922 Rites 27 dec 1922
J. B. Brown, J. P.

C. M. BRYSON to Mimmie MULLICAN Issued 27 dec 1922 Rites 27 Dec 1922
J. B. Broen, J. P.

Claud DENTON to Ruth BARRETT Issued 29 dec 1922 Rites 30 dec 1922
E. Patton, Elder

Robert FAIRBANKS to Nannie BUTCHER issued 30 dec 1922 Rites 31 dec 1922
J. Paul Slayden, M. G.

Corbin MARTIN to Mary Ann KEATHLEY issued 30 dec 1922 Rites 31 Dec 1922
L. C. LAne, J. P.

Obie TAYLOR to Willie McCURDY Issued 30 dec 1922 Rites 31 dec 1922
J. W. Cooley, M. G.

Charles CLENDENEN to Anna BOULDIN Issued 30 Dec 1922 Rites 30 dec 1922
R. Ed Jones, J. P.

Wheeler PERRY to Lela BROWN Issued 10 Feb 1923 Rites 11 Feb 1923
M. M. Hill, J. P.

Tot TOLBERT to Leona ANDERSON Issued 10 Feb 1923 Rites 11 Feb 1923
G. H. Atnip, J. P.

Frank NORRIS to Lillie DAVIS issued 14 feb 1923 Rites 14 feb 1923
J. Paul Slayden, M. G.

Jim VanHOOSER to Fannie VAN HOOSER Issued 21 Feb 1923 Rites 21 feb 1923
W. P. Davis, J. P.

Henry TIDWELL (Col) to MAggie SMITH (Col) Issued 22 Jub 1923 Rites 22 Feb 1922
W. H. Craven, M. G.

Toney NEIGHBORS to Ola MORRIS Issued 23 Feb 1923 Rites 25 Feb 1923
Claude Myers, M. G.

Haskel NUNLEY to MAry Edith SMITH Issued 24 Feb 1923 Rites 4 Mar 1923
P. N. Moffitt, J. P.

James B. GAZZAWAY to Mabel E. BLANKENSHIP Issued 25 Feb 1923 Rites 25 Feb 1923
E. H. Liles, M. G.

John J. BELL to Minnie belle CHAMBERS Issued 28 Feb 1923 Rites 25 Mar 1923
R. Ed Jones, J. P.

S. R. ROGERS to L. L. SMARTT Issued 3 MAr 1923 Rites 4 Mar 1923
J. L. Barnes, J. P.

John MUNCY to Letha BASHAM Issued 3 Mar 1923 Rites 4 Mar 1923
W. W. Locke, J. P.

Fiem TURNER to Nora GRIFFY Issued 4 Mar 1923 Rites 4 Mar 1923
T. A. Craddock, J. P.

Wm. H. MERRITT to Bertha PRYOR Issued 5 MAr 1923 Rites 6 Mar 1923
A. C. Parker, M. G.

Rowland MARTIN (Col) to Bessie YORK (COl) Issued 10 Mar 1923 Rites 10 Mar 1923
J. S. NAnce, M. G.

Orian NUNLEY to Quixie May CARRICK issued 15 Mar 1923 Rites 25 Mar 1923
J. A. Cunningham, M. G.

Lindon L. REAMS to Hudie WOOTEN Issued 16 Mar 1923 Rites 16 Mar 1923
F. L. Leeper, M. G.

W. V. FARLESS to E. C. CURTIS Issued 20 Mar 1923 Rites 20 Mar 1923
A. P. Robertson. J. P.

Elmer JONES to Levada BLAIR Issued 21 Mar 1923 Rites 25 Mar 1923
A. Z. Holder, J. P.

Robert ORRICK to Elva SUMMERS Issued 29 Mar 1923 Rites 31 Mar 1923
J. A. Cunningham, M. G.

Guy W. COOPER to Anna Lorena MOONEYHAM Issued 30 Mar 1923 Rites 1 Apr 1923
F. L. Leeper, M. G.

Ben TAYLOR to Lela PEARSON Issued 31 Mar 1923 Rites 31 Mar 1923
W. V. D. Miller, J. P.

Jesse TURNER to Ethel TURNER Issued 31 Mar 1923 Rites 1 Apr 1923
J. W. Cooley, M. G.

Dudley TEMPLETON to Huhanna BAKER Issued 4 Apr 1923 Rites 14 Apr 1923
L. C. LAne, J. P.

Lee Otis GRIBBLE to Cleo Alma MOORE Issued 5 Apr 1923 Rites 6 Apr 1923
B. T. Lannom, M. G.

Homer JORDAN to Etta SIMONS Issued 6 Apr 1923 Rites 11 Apr 1923
A. B. Moffitt

R. L. TAYLOR to K. A. CLENDENON Issued 7 Apr 1923 Rites 7 Apr 1923
A. P. Robertson, J. P.

Ernest PEDIGO to Bessie GREEN Issued 13 Apr 1923 Rites 14 Apr 1923
R. Ed Jones, J. P.

L. O. GRIFFIN to Loreta Van HOOSER Issued 14 Apr 1923 Rites 15 Apr 1923
T. A. Craddock, J. P.

Horace AGILEY to Lela WALLACE Issued 14 Apr 1923 Rites 14 Apr 1923
B. T. Lannom, M. G.

Fred CASITY to Hallie HALE issued 16 Apr 1923   Not Returned

Charles FULTS to Edna OVERTURF Issued 18 Apr 1923 Rites 18 Apr 1923
B. T. Lannom. M. G.

Charles M. STROUD to Alma McLAUGHLIN Issued 21 Apr 1923 Rites 21 apr 1923
R. L. Wood, J. P.

Vernon GARNER to Sarah JAne WRIGHT issued 24 Apr 1923 Rites 29 Apr 1923
Calude Myers, M. G.

John PARKER to Frances BLOCK Issued 24 Apr 1923 - Not Returned

Luster BLANKS to Minnie Lee CAMPBELL Issued 24 Apr 1923 Rites 2 May 1923
J. R. Goodpasture, M. G.

Jim TAYLOR to MAry ANN GILBERT Issued 28 Apr 1923 Rites 29 Apr 1923
R. E. Jones, J. P.

Ewin LOCKE (Col) to Julia WILLIAMS (Col) Issued 28 Apr 1923   Not Returned

Robert SAVAGE (cOl) to Alice BELL (Col) Issued 3 May 1923 Rites 3 May 1923
N. J. H. VAnMeter, M. G.

Bargg YOUNG to Ruby Bell CONGER Issued 3 May 1923 Rites 3 May 1923
J. Paul Slayden, M. G.

Harley GROSS to Fannie SIMONS Issued 3 May 1923 Rites 3 May 1923
E. L. Moffitt, J. P.

Roy O. LEE to Ocie MULLICAN Issued 5 MAy 1923 Rites 5 MAy 1923
R. Ed Jones, J. P.

L. C. CAMPBELL to Georgia CRAWLEY issued 5 MAy 1923 Rites 6 MAy 1923
O. H. Wood, J. P.

C. W. WARE to Anna MAYNARD Issued 8 MAy 1923 Rites 12 May 1923
R. Ed Jones, J. P.

Madewell ALLISON to Minnie SIMONS Issued 11 MAy 1923 Rites 12 May 1923
W. C. Lorance, J. P.

Carroll JACKSON to MAi HOBSON Issued 12 May 1923 Rites 13 MAy 1923
R. Ed Jones, J. P.

Ed Lee to Roberta SMITH Issued 12 May 1923 Rites 12 May 1923
N. J. H. VAnMeter, M. G.

Allen Bryan WARE to Cleo CURTIS Issued 19 MAy 1923 Rites 20 MAy 1923
E. L. Moffitt, J. P.

Fred LESTER to MAry TURNER Issued 20 MAy 1923 Rites 20 MAy 1923
J. B. Brown, J. P.

Virgil SMITH to Ocie Pearl BELL Issued 25 MAy 1923 Rites 27 MAy 1923
W. C. Whitlock, J. P.

Paul SMARTT to Lyda STONER Issued 26 MAy 1923 Rites 3 Jun 1923
J. L. Barnes, J. P.

Ben F. SMITH to Ethel CHRISTIAN Issued 26 MAy 1923 Rites 27 MAy 1923
A. P. Roberson, J. P.

Bill GILBERT to Estella SCHROCK Issued 1 Jun 1923 Rites 3 jun 1923
L. F. Daugherty, M. G.

R. L. WRIGHT to Anna RAY Issued 2 jun 1923 Rites 2 Jun 1923
R. Ed Jones, J. P.

Bernard DAVIS to Erman COLE Issued 2 Jun 1923 Rites 2 jun 1923
Fate WAlker, J. P.

Wayman NORTHCUTT (COl) to Alice BONNER (Col) Issued 7 Jun 1923 Rites8 Jun
H. E. Ramsey, J. P.

Shelie MATHIS to Nellie CHILDRESS Issued 9 Jun 1923 Rites 9 Jun 1923
W. P. DAvis, J. P.

Pascal WRIGHT to Clara SMITHSON Issued9 Jun 1923 Rites 9 Jun 1923
R. Edd Jones, J. P.

Osmond C. WOODLEE to CArrie McGREGOR Issued 13 jun 1923 Rites 14 Jun 1923
A. P. Roberson, J. P.

EARL SMITH to Dixie CAPHART Issued 16 Jun 1923 Rites 16 jun 1923
R. T. Skinner, M. G.

Franklin Daekins REYNOLDS to MArgaret Frences CRICK Issued 16 Jun 1923 Rites 16 Jun
B. T. Lannom, M. G.

Wayman SMARTT to mattie Mai BESS Issued 16 Jun 1923 Rites 16 Jun 1923
J. W. Cooley, M. G.

Grady WOAMCK to Icie Mai HALEY Issued 16 Jun 1923 Rites 17 Jun 1923
J. W. Cooley, M. G.

Lewis SMITH (Col) to Corene MARSHALL (Col) Issued 18 Jun 1923 Rites 18 Jun 1923
R. Ed Jones, J. P.

A. L. ELROD to Roca BOGLE Issued 19 Jun 1923 Rites 20 Jun 1923
A. Z. Holder, J. P.

J. T. BELL to Nell Blanche SAIN Issued 19 Jun 1923 Rites 20 jun 1923
B. T. Lannom, M. G.

Andrew J. BOYD to Ethel Sallie WAGONER Issued 23 Jun 1923 Rites 25 jun 1923
A. P. Roberson, J. P.

John B. GLENN to Emma Lee KEATHLEY Issued 26 Jun 1923 rites 27 Jun 1923
P. G. Moore, J. P.

Walter BAIN to DAisy DAVENPORT Issued 26 Jun 1923 Rites 15 Jul 1923
T. A. Craddock, J. P.

E. P. HALEY to MAy WILLIAMS Issued 30 Jun 1923 Rites 30 Jun 1923
W. P. Davis, J. P.

Joe MEDLEY to Elsie HOLDER issued 30 Jun 1923 Rites 30 Jun 1923
J. W. Cooley, M. G.

Kellum CHILTON to Mattie CAMPBELL Issued 30 jun 1923 Returned - Not SOLEMNIZED

Eugene STARKEY to Ruby JAne HERNDON issued 7 Jul 1923 Rites 8 Jul 1923
J. A. Brixey, J. P.

Robert MAYFIELD to Shelie MARTIN Issued 14 Jul 1923 Rites 14 Jul 1923
L. C. Lane, J. P.

Talley FREED to Emma PATTERSON Issued 14 Jul 1923 rites 28 Jul 1923
H. L. Jones, J. P.

Joe Turney YOUNG to Nell Edwards SMOOT Issued 16 Jul 1923 Rites 16 jul 1923
E. H. Liles, M. G.

Cleve MAYFIELD to Lillian RAY Issued 19 jul 1923 Rites 22 jul 1923
L. F. Daugherty, M. G.

A. L. CHRISTIAN to Hallie Lee JENNINGS Issued 21 Jul 1923 Rites 28 Jul 1923
P. N. Moffitt, J. P.

Bub RAMSEY to Vira TURNER Issued 25 Jul 1923 Rites 29 jul 1923
W. C. Whitlock, J. P.

Arthur CRIPPS to Lula THREAT issued 25 Jul 1923 Rites 29 Jul 1923
W. C. Whitlock, J. P.

S. A. GRISSOM to Louise KELL Issued 28 Jul 1923 Rites 29 Jul 1923
R. T. Skinner, M. G.

Roy CHISAM to Virgie KELLEY issued 2 Aug 1923 Rites 11 Aug 1923
L. C. Lane, J. P.

Clifford HOLDER to Fannie DUNN Issued 2 Aug 1923 Rites 5 Aug 1923
W. C. Whitlock, J. P.

Jesse STEMBRIDGE to Ruby SULLENS Issued 2 Aug 1923 Rites 4 Aug 1923
W, C, Whitlock, J. P.

Troy WALLER to Dovie SUMMERS Issued 4 Aug 1923 Rites 5 Aug 1923
(date added by court order of 4/10/1961)   P.G. Potter, M. G.

John PAINTER to Cleo KEASY Issued 11 Aug 1923 Rites 12 Aug 1923
S. H. Templeton, J. P.

A. D. BROWN to Anna Francis SCOTT issued 13 Aug 1923 Rites 13 Aug 1923
J. Paul Slayden, M. G.

Clay GOLDEN to Bessie BIMBALOUGH issued 15 Aug 1923 Rites 16 Aug 1923
J. D. Hash, J. P.

John PATTERSON to Emma FUSTON Issued 17 Aug 1923 Rites 17 Aug 1923
W. P. Davis, J. P.

Sam PERRY to Odessa WIRES Issued 18 Aug 1923 Returned - not Solemnized

John W. UNDERHILL to MAttie Lee WINNETT issued 18 Aug 1923 Rites 18 Aug 1923
W. C. Whitlock, J. P.

Cecil BARNES to Nora McGREGOR Issued 20 Aug 1923 NOT Solemnized

H. Smith WHITE to FAye E. WARE Issued 22 Aug 1923 Rites 22 Aug 1923
E. D. Martin, M. G.

Earl MOODY to Effie HALE Issued 24 Aug 1923 Rites 24 Aug 1923
Fate Walker, J. P.

Jesse ADAMS to Mammie JONES Issued 24 Aug 1923 Rites 26 Aug 1923
W. C. Whitlock, J. P.

R. T. McDANIEL to Jennie GAFFIN Issued 25 Aug 1923 Rites 26 Aug 1923
R. T. Skinner, M. G.

D. P. WATSON to Dollie MULLICAN Issued 25 Aug 1923 Rites 26 Aug 1923
John T. Smithson, M. G.

Russell SPENCER (Col) to Gladys PAGE (Col) Issued 27 Aug 1923 Returned - Not Solemnized

Remus TERRY to Emma YORK Issued 27 Aug 1923 Rites 27 Aug 1923
R. Ed Jones, J. P.

Homer ANDERSON to Clara CANTRELL issued 1 Sep 1923 Rites 1 Sep 1923
J. W. Cooley, M. G.

John WARD to Lula HALE issued 4 Sep 1923 rites 4 Sep 1923
Fate Walker, J. P.

James P. GLASSCOCK to MAggie Lee CRAWLEY issued 6 Sep 1923 Rites 6 Sep 1923
R. T. Skinner, M. G.

R. A. MADEWELL to Noval WHEELER Issued 8 Sep 1923 Rites 9 Sep 1923
J. B. Brown, J. P.

Marcus STONER to Lucy Emma STEPP Issued 8 Sep 1923 Rites 8 Sep 1923
R. Ed Jones, J. P.

Less DENNIS to Rosa PEDEN Issued8 Sep 1923 Rites 9 Sep 1923
G. H. atnip, M. G.

Herman H. KIRBY to Nealy McGEE Issued 8 Sep 1923 Rites 9 Sep 1923
J. Paul Slayden, M. G.

Clarence WEBB to to Nora COUCH Issued 14 Sep 1923 Rites 14 Sep 1923
L. C. Lane, J. P.

George RAMSEY (col) to Eliz. KIRBY (COL) Issued 17 Sep 1923 Rites 17 Sep 1923
J. S. Nance, M. G.

Luther CROUCH to Irene WILLIAMS Issued 19 Sep 1923 Rites 19 Sep 1923
B. T. lannom, M. G.

Robert F. ADAMS to Mary Louise HENNESSEE Issued 20 Sep 1923 Rites 20 Sep 1923
B. T. LAnnom, M. G.

Toy PARSLEY to Ester McDOWELL Issued 21 Sep 1923 Rites 23 Sep 1923
G. H. atnip, M. G.

Albert TANNER to Alta JOINS Issued 21 Sep 1923
R. Ed Jones, J. P.

JACKSON TAYLOR to Anna BROWN Issued 22 Sep 1923
R. Ed Jones, J. P.

Lee CLEMONS to Nettie HOBBS Issued 22 Sep 1923 Rites 23 Sep 1923
P. N. Moffitt, J. P.

Ben ROACH (Col) to Eula BILES (Col) Issued 22 Sep 1923 Rites 23 sep 1923
R. L. Wood, J. P.

Elson ANDERSON to Lola PEPPER issued 22 Sep 1923 Rites 22 Sep 1923
R. Ed Jones, J. P.

Dewey CANTRELL to Eva SMITH Issued 25 Sep 1923   Not Returned

J. A. CANTRELL to MAndy WEST issued 27 Sep 1923 Rites 27 Sep 1923
W. P. davis, J. P.

E. D. MARTIN to Myrtle Hall CAIN Issued 27 Sep 1923 rites 30 Sep 1923
J. Paul Slayden, M. G.

Jesse POWELL to Mildred STEPP Issued 27 Sept 1923 Rites 28 Sep 1923
E. D. Martin, M. G.

Robert E. JOHNSON to Ella Mae FERRELL issued 27 Sep 1923 Rites 28 Sep 1923
J. G. Goff, J. P.

E. L. PASSON to Clara Lee HOLDER issued 29 Sep 1923 Rites 30 Sep 1923
A. Z. Holder, J. P.

Hubert WILLIAMS to Essie REED Issued 1 Oct 1923 Rites 1 Oct 1923
Boyd S. Fielder, M. G.

Estill R. FULTS to Julia Eliz TRAIL Issued 3 Oct 1923 Rites 4 Oct 1923
J. Paul Slayden, M. G.

A. M. YOUNG to MAndy DRIVER Issued 6 Oct 1923 Rites 6 Oct 1923
R. Ed Jones, J. P.

Alpha WOODLEE to Belle HAMMONS Issued 6 oct 1923 Rites 6 Oct 1923
J. L. Barnes, J. P.

Oscar NUNLEY to Iva COPPINGER issued 10 Oct 1923 Rites 14 Oct 1923
P. N. Moffitt, J. P.

Esher AVERY to HAzel ADOCOCK Issued 11 Oct 1923 Not Returned

Grady WRIGHT to Carrie B. DUTTON Issued 12 Oct 1923 Rites 21 Oct 1923
R. L. Wood, J. P.

Jerry TALLEY to Lula BELL issued 13 Oct 1923 Rites 14 Oct 1923
R. ed Jones, J. P.

Robert Isbell (Col) to Mabel DRAKE (col) Issued 23 Oct 1923 Rites 24 Oct 1923
J. S. Nance, M. G.

John PAINTER to Cora CHRISTIAN Issued 24 Oct 1923 Rites 26 Oct 1923
M. M. Hill, J. P.

Worthy H. CLOVIS to Lydia GILBERT Issued 27 Oct 1923 Rites 27 oct 1923
C. E. Hawkins, M. G.

W. J. RIZOR to Roberta MEISER Issued 1 Nov 1923 Rites 1 Nov 1923
E. H. Liles, M. G.

J. H. SCOTT to Laura SMARTT issued 1 Nov 1923 Rites 1 Nov 1923
A. J. McBRIDE, M. G.

J. D. DUNCAN to Sallie PETTIT Issued 3 Nov 1923 Rites 4 nov 1923
J. D. hash, J. P.

HArry SWAFFORD to Erline SCOTT Issued 3 Nov 1923 Rites 3 Nov 1923
D. L. Garrett, M. G.

W. E. WINSTEAD to FAnnie MOSLEY issued 8 Nov 1923 Rites 11 Nov 1923
C. E. Hawkins, M. G.

Will COOPER (Col) to Tennessee DEVINS (Col) Issued 12 Nov 1923 Rites 12 Nov
R. Ed Jones, J. P.

Jerry ROBERTS to Minnie ODEL Issued 13 Nov 1923 Not returned

Amon McCORMICK to Wavie PRIEST Issued 16 Nov 1923 Rites 16 nov 1923
W. V. D. Miller, J. P.

W. T. HAMMER to Elizabeth NEWMAN Issued 17 Nov 1923 Rites 18 nov 1923
E. H. Liles, M. G.

William HALE to Louise NEAL Issued 22 Nov 1923 Rites 24 Nov 1923
R. Ed Jones, J. P.

Wiley SIMMONS to MAry McBRIDE Issued 24 Nov 1923 Rites 26 Nov 1923
W. V. D. Miller, J. P.

Charles GRIFFITH to Ora Lee DODD issued 28 Nov 1923 Rites 28 nov 1923
W. P. davis, J. P.

JAck NELSON to Lora REYNOLDS Issued 1 Dec 1923 Rites 2 dec 1923
A. L. Cope, J. P.

Dick RITCHIE to Henry SANDERS Issued 8 dec 1923 Not Returned

Austin TURNER to Edna FREED Issued 13 Dec 1923 Rites 16 dec 1923
W. C. Whitlock, J. P.

G. W. NARRAMORE to Effie Mae BAILEY Issued 15 Dec 1923 Rites 16 dec 1923
C. E. Hawkins, M. G.

Houston BRATCHER to Minnie E. LASSITER Issued 15 dec 1923 Rites 16 dec 1923
H. L. Jones, J. P.

Noel FOSTER to Geneva GRIFFITH Issued 15 dec 1923 Rites 19 dec 1923
W. P. davis, J. P.

Albert GRIBBLE to Alma JUDKINS Issued 17 dec 1923 Rites 25 Dec 1923
L. F. DAugherty, M. G.

George McBRIDE to NAncy NUNLEY Issued 18 dec 1923 Rites 18 Dec 1923
A. L. Cope, J. P.

James BOGLE to SAllie BILBREY issued 19 dec 1923 Rites 19 dec 1923
R.Ed Jones, J. P.

Clarence HAYES to Novella BRYANT issued 20 dec 1923 rites 23 dec 1923
P. G. Potter, M. G.

JAmes BARRETT to Malinda GREEN Issued 20 dec 1923 Rites 20 dec 1923
A. J. McBRIDE, M. G.

Richard DODD to Mai HILL Issued 22 Dec1923 Rites 22 dec 1923
J. T. Casey, M. G.

Lawson HILL to Edna SIMONS Issued 22 Dec 1923 Rites 23 dec 1923
M. M. Hill, J. P.

Tom NORTHCUTT to Cora ALLISON Issued 22 Dec 1923 Rites 23 dec 1923
A. L. Cope, J. P.-

Charles C. GOLDEN to Gladys BARBEE Issued 24 dec 1923 Rites 24 dec 1923
R. Ed JONES, J.P.

Calvin HARRELL to Susie (Bing) FERRELL issued 24 Dec 1923 Rites 25 dec 1923
C. E. Hawkins, M. G.

John RIGGS to Hazel CHRISTIAN Issued 24 dec 1923 Rites 25 dec 1923
S. O. McAdoo

Alvin E. GREEN to Pauline ARGO issued 25 Dec 1923 Rites 25 dec 1923
C. E. Hawkins, M. G.

John LAWSON to Vera COTTON Issued 25 dec 1923 Rites 25 dec 1923
A. J. mcBride

John LUSK (Col) to Lena MARTIN (Col) Issued 28 dec 1923 Rites 28 dec 1923
W. V. D. Miller, J. P.

T. R. WOODS to MArtha BLANKS Issued 28 dec 1923 Rites 29 dec 1923
W. H. Craven, M. G.

Everett BOULDIN to Cleo KELL Issued 29 dec 1923 Rites 30 dec 1923
Fate Walker, J. P.

Clyde BLANKS to Gladys WALKER Issued 29 dec 1923 Rites 30 dec 1923
A. Z. Holder, J. P.

Harvey BATES to George BARNES Issued 29 Dec 1923 Rites 30 Dec 1923
J. Paul Slayden, M. G.

Jess JUDKINS to Eva LUNA Issued 2 JAn 1924 Rites 2 Jan 1924
J. B. Brown, J. P.

George MACON (Col) to Elmer HUNTER (Col) Issued 5 Jan 1924 rites 6 JAn 1924
J. S. NAnce, M. G.

W. H. MILLRANEY to Sophia COLE issued 5 Jan 1924 Rites 6 Jan 1924
Fate Walker, J. P.

Homer DENNIS to Lora DAVENPORT issued 7 Jan 1924 Rites 8 jan 1924
T. A. Craddock, J. P.

Ben McGEEHEE to Estene MASEY issued 13 Jan 1924 Rites 13 Jan 1924
D. L. Garrett, M. G.

W. B. C. CUNNINGHAM to Dollie BARNES Issued 18 Jan 1924 Rites 20 jan 1924
J. A. Cunningham, M. G.

Raymond STILES to Liivia GRIBBLE Issued 18 JAn 1924 rites 23 jan 1924
J. Paul Slayden, M. G.

Harry Sutton MOLLOY to Jocie Elaine MYERS Issued 19 jan 1924 Rites 25 Jan 1924
W. P. Willis

Charlie B. BROWN to Dollie MARTIN Issued 21 jan 1924 Rites 24 jan 1924
R. J. Tucker

W. V. PEDEN to Athelia Edna BARNES Issued 22 Jan 1924 rites 22 jan 1924
J. Paul Slayden, M. G.

M. C. McBRIDE to Dollie FINLEY Issued 26 Jan 1924 Rites 26 jan 1924
R. ed Jones, J. P.

Tom CRAWLEY to Virginia DONNELL Issued 2 Feb 1924 Rites 3 Feb 1924
R. L. Wood, J. P.

Henry CURTIS to Jessie Lee HENRY Issued 2 Feb 1924 Rites 4 feb 1924
J. B. Brown, J. P.

JAmes WRIGHT to JAnie SMITH Issued 6 Feb 1924 Rites 6 Feb 1924
T. R. Clark, J. P.

J. C. TRAVIS to D. S. CHRISTIAN Issued 10 feb 1924 Rites 10 feb 1924
R. Ed Jones, J. P.

Fred MYERS to Virgia KING issued 11 feb 1924 Rites 11 Feb 1924
R. Ed Jones, J. P.

Edd SMITH to NAnnie HOBBS Issued 12 Feb 1924 rites 13 feb 1924
T. N. Moffitt, J. P.

W. H. SMARTT to Lena BELL Issued 13 feb 1924 rites 13 feb 1924
S. O. McAdoo, M. G.

J. D. MONTGOMERY to Sarah HASH Issued 18 feb 1924 Rites 18 Feb 1924
J. D. HASh, J. P.

George WALKER to MAmie STARKEY Issued 23 feb 1924 Rites 24 Feb 1924
W. P. DAvis, J. P.

T. T. SPENCER to Ruby Lillian MARTIN Issued 25 Feb 1924 Rites 25 feb 1925
N. J. H. VAn Meter, M. G.

MArion BELL to Atla SELF Issued 27 feb 1924 rites 2 Mar 1924
Thomas CArter

Frank BOULDIN to Emma ROBERTS Issued 1 Mar 1924 Rites 3 Mar 1924
M. M. Hill, J. P.

Jack WOODLEE to Laura McGREGOR Issued 3 Mar 1924 Rites 3 Mar 1924
P.N. Moffitt, J. P.

William WOOD (Col) to Dina PLEASANT Issued 5 Mar 1924 Rites 5 Mar 1924
E. S. Bedford, M. G.

J. SAm GREEN to Nolen BOYD Issued 6 Mar 1924 Rites 6 Mar 1924
J. T. casey, M. G.

Hershel TURNER to Percie COPE Issued 13 Mar 1924 Rites 14 Mar 1924
L. F. ADugherty, M. G.

Ourg MORTON to Mattie B. TANNER Issued 14 Mar 1924 Rites 14 Mar 1924
W. P. Davis, J. P.

F. L. BENNETT to Louise BELL Issued 20 Mar 1924 Rites 21 Mar 1924
J. T. Casey, M. G.

Roy WILSON to Eula Pearl SHIRLEY Issued 22 Mar 1924 Rites 23 Mar 1923
J. A. Qunningham, M. G.

J. L. NORRIS to Alberta McCLANAHAN Issued 22 Mar 1924 Rites 22 Mar 1924
C. E. uawkins, M. G.

Frank HENNESSEE to Shelby EARLS Issued 30 MAr 1924 Rites 30 MAr 1924
A. E. Elam, M. G.

William EDWARDS to Loise GILLEY Issued 8 Apr 1924 Rites 9 Apr 1924
J. T. CAsey, M. G.

Charlie HENDERSON to Annie Mae HOBBS Issued 11 Apr 1924 Rites 11 Apr 1924
J. L. Barnes, J. P.

CAlvin NEAL to MAdge RIGGS Issued 11 Apr 1924 Rites 12 Apr 1924
J. R. Goodpasture, M. G.

C. D. PARSLEY to Flora HALEY Issued 11 Apr 1924 Rites 13 Apr 1924
J. W. HALL, M. G.

Jim BROWN (Col) to Velma COPE (Col) Issued 12 Apr 1924 Rites 15 Apr 1924.
R. L. Wood, J. P.

Ivory PATRICK to Hallie MILSTEAD Issued 12 Apr 1924 Rites 12 Apr 1924
P. N. Moffitt, J. P.

J. M. PEARSON to FAnnie BASSON Issued 17 Apr 1924 Not Returned

H. C. STIPE to Sallie May McGIBONEY Issued 18 Apr 1924 Rites 20 Apr 1924
W. V. D. Miller, J. P.

Millard E. L. RAY to MAry CORDELL Issued 18 Apr 1924 Rites 18 Apr 1924
R. Ed Jones, J. P.

Bob BALE to Martha TAYLOR Issued 18 Apr 19224 Rites 19 Apr 1924
W. P. DAVIS, J. P.

J. A. EDDINGTON to Josephine VAUGH Issued 19 Apr 1924 Rites 19 Apr 1924
J. Paul Slayden, M. G.

John LAWSON to Bell ROBINSON Issued 24 Apr 1924 Rites 25 Apr 1924
J. G. Goff, J. P.

Huston WEBB to SAdie BURTON Issued 25 Apr 1924 Rites 25 Apr 1924
E. H. Liles. M. G.

Clifford HILL to Lena STOTTS Issued 25 Apr 1924 Rites 29 Apr 1924
P. N. Moffitt, J. P.

Robert Lewis BARKSDALE to Willie CRAIN Issued 26 Apr 1924 Rites 26 Apr 1924
E. H. Liles, M. G.

W. P. HOGANS (Col) to Ida Lee FRENCH (Col) Issued 9 MAy 1924 Rites 9 MAy 1924
S. J. Beaskey, M. G.

E. B. KISER to Beulah Lee JACKSON Issued 10 May 1924 Rites 25 May 1924
C. E. HAwkins, M. G.

F. L. DAVIS to Virgia ROBINSON Issued 17 May 1924 Rites 17 May.1924
W. P. Davis, J. P.

Olney MOONEYHAM to Edda EVANS Issued 31 May 1924 rites 2 jun 1924
W. V. D. Miller, J. P.

J. M.PERRY to Audry Lee BARNES Issued 31 May 1924 Rites 1 Jun1924
P. N. Moffitt, J. P.

Robert DEARMAN to Serena Eliz. DARNELL Issued 1 Jun 1924 Rites 1 Jun 1924
J. D. GUNN, M. G.

Russell SPENCER (Col) to Gladys PAGE (Col) Issued 5 Jun 1924 Rites 5 Jun 1924
J. S. nance, M. G.

Willie MAYO to Cleo BESS Issued 6 Jun 1924 Rites 7 Jun 1924
P. N. Moffitt, J. P.

Cecil YORK (Col) to MAry Lou RAMSEY (Col) Issued 6 Jun 1924 Rites 6 Jun 1924
J. S. Nance, M. G.

Charlie MEDLEY to Essie BOLEY Issued 13 Jun 1924 Rites 15 Jun 1924
W. C. Lorance, J. P.

Felie PAGE to Dedie SMITHSON Issued 14 Jun 1924 Rites 14 Jun 1924
W. P. DAvis, J. P.

Oval PAGE to Clara Bell JONES Issued 14 Jun 1924 Rites 14 Jun 1924
W. P. davis, J. P.

Landy CLENDENON to Aline SIMONS Issued 14 Jun 1924 Rites 15 Jun 1924
A. P. Roberson, J. P.

RAnsom SMARTT (Col) to MAud MILLER (Col) Issued 14 Jun 1924 Rites 14 Jun 1924
J. S. Nance, M. G.

Kenneth KESEY to Willie Mai WARE Issued 14 Jun 1924 rites 15 Jun 1924
P. N. Moffitt, J. P.

Jim John DEARMAN to Virginia HAYES Issued 21 Jun 1924 Rites 22 Jun 1924
C. E. Hawkins, M. G.

Willie BARNHILL (Col) to Lula TERRY (Col) Issued 21 Jun 1924 Rites 21 Jun 1924
J. S. NAnce, M. G.

Landa MALONE to Ida CRAWFORD Issued 28 Jun 1924 Rites 29 Jun 1924
R. Ed Jones, J. P.

Levoy M. TILLETT to Ruby G. McAFEE Issued 28 Jun 1924 rites 29 Jun 1924
J. Pual Slayden, M. G.

DAn HENDERSON to Clara LEE MUNCEY Issued1 Jul 1924 Rites 1 Jul 1924
J. T. Casey, M. G.

Omus GARRISON to Reta WILCHER Issued 16 Aug 1924 Rites 16 Aug 1924 W. B. Snipes, M. G.

Ause DAVIS to Beulah DAVIS Issued 16 Aug 1924 Rites 16 Aug 1924 W. P. Davis, J. P.

Jim CASE to Bessie Lee BAIN Issued 16 Aug 1924 Rites 17 aug 1924 P. B. Stroud, CC Clerk

Leben EMERY to Esta THURMAN Issued 16 Aug 1924 Rites 23 Aug 1923 W. C. Whitlock, J. P.

Leslie P. WOOD to Margarette Ellen DAVIS Issued 19 Aug 1924 Rites 19 Aug 1924 F. L. Leeper, M. G.

Christman R. SWIFT to Ruby MOORE Issied 21 Aug 1924 Rites 31 Aug 1924 W. P. Davis, J. P.

W. T. HENNESSEE to Julia WHITE Issued 23 Aug 1923 Rites 23 Aug 1923 S. H. Templeton, J. P.

Porter HUGHES to Pearl Lee ELLIOTT Issued 30 Aug 1924 Rites 30 Aug 1924 C. E. Hawkins, M. G.

Ernest MAYO to Louise DAVIS Issued 30 Aug 1924 Rites 31 aug 1974 Chas. T. Powell, M. G.

W. J. BUTCHER to Maggie PRESTON Issued 30 Aug 1924 Rites 30 Aug 1924 L. P. Sanders, J. P.

Everett WALLING to Mattie MOONEYHAM Issued 30 Aug 1924 Rites 6 Sep 1924 W. V. D. Miller, J. P.

Pope REDMON to Bertha May FREED Issued 1 Sep 1924 Rites 20 Sep 1924 W. C. Whitlock, J. P.

H. C. TURNER to Willene MITCHELL Issued 1 Sep 1924 Returned - Not Solemnized

Shelah PRATER to Maurine CATES Issued 2 Sep 1924 Rites 4 Sep 1924 E. T. Brazzle, M. G.

M. C. PEARSALL to Alice EARLS Issued 6 Sep 1924 Rites 6 Sep 1924 G. H. O'NEAL, M. G.

George COONROD (Col) to Tennie FRANCE (Col) Issued 8 Sep 1924 Rites 8 Sep 1924 I. N. Smoot, J. P.

Sterling WALL to Hallie HUDSON Issued 8 Sep 1924 Rites 8 Sep 1924 L. C. Lane, J. P.

John REDMAN to Aubra ADAMSON Issued 9 Sep 1924 Rites 10 sep 1924 L.F. Daugherty, M. G.

Wayman M. ROBERTS to Martha GILLENTINE Issued 9 Sep 1924 Rites 9 Sep.1924 J. B. Dobbs, J. P.

Albert DEARMOND (Col) to Mandy NORTHCUTT (Col) Issued 13 Sep 1924 Rites 13 Sep J. W. Eaton, Jdg.

V. L. BURCH to Anna P. EARL Issued 3 Jun 1924 Rites 4 Jul 1924 S. C. McAdoo, M. G.

EJ. J. TUCK to Lillian GREER Issued 5 Jul 1924 Rites 5 Jul 1924 W. P. davis, J. P.

Elbert KELL to Mammie TUCKER issued 5 JUL 1924 Rites 6 JUL 1924 R. Ed Jones, J. P.

Alvin TURNER to MAude PENNINGTON Issued 7 Jul 1924 Rites 7 Jul 1924 W. P. DAvis, J. P.

Charles CUNNINGHAM to Nina May TURNER Issued 11 July 1924 Rites 11 Jul 1924 W. P. Davis, J. P.

Chas. McMAHAN to Lida Norene MOON Issued 12 Jul 1924 Rites 13 Jun 1924 J. D. Hash, J. P.

J. J. MEADOWS to Lena Pearl HILLIS Issued 14 Jul 1924 Rites 14 Jul 1924 R. El Jones, J. P.

Estie GRIFFIN to Vera HOLDER Issued 15 Jul 1924 Rites 16 Jul 1924 G. H. Atnip, M. G.

Raymons WILLIAMS to PAuline ROGERS Issued 18 Jul 1924 Rites 20 Jul 1924 Boyd S. Fields, M. G.

Roy LONG to Mammie TANNER issued 19 Jul 1924 Rites 20 Jul 1924 H. L. Jones, J. P.

Northcutt THROWER to Grace GRANDSTAFF Issued 19 Jul 1924 Rites 20 jul 1924 W. S. Marshall, M. G.

Jow S. BELL to Edna Grace KESEY Issued 19 Jul 1924 Rites 20 Jul 1920 W. S. Marshall, M. G.

P. S. BARNETTE to Lura COMER Issued 26 Jul 1924 Rites 27 jul 1924 C. E. Hawkins, M. G.

Ernest BOYD to Lora STEWART Issued 29 Jul 1924 Rites 30 Jul 1924 J. R. Goodpasture, M. G.

Huston MARTIN to Bennie GRIBBLE Issued 2 Aug 1924 Rites 3 Aug 1924 L. C. Lane, J. P.

Bill LOOPER (Col) to Anna Lee GIBSON (Col) Issued 2 Aug 1924 rites 2 Aug 1924 J. L. Long, M. G.

Bob LOCKE (Col) to WOODS (COL) Issued 11 Aug 1924 Rites 11 Aug 1911 N. J. H. VAnMeter, M. G.

Joe LORANCE to Flossie UNDERWOOD Issued 13 Aug 1924 Rites 16 Aug 1924 W. C. Lorance, J. P.

Wlmer Neal WALLING to MAi Belle STUBBLEFIELD Issued 14 Aug 1924 Rites 14 Aug 1924 C. E. Hawkins, M. G.

James FARLESS to Beckie QUICK Issued 15 Sep 1924 Rites 15 Sep 1924
J. B. Dobbs, J. P.

HArvey PATTERSON to Jessie BOLT Issued17 Sep 1924 Rites 18 Sep 1924
W. P. davis, J. P.

Jim FARLESS to MAy HILLIS Issued 17 Sep 1924 Rites17 Sep 1924
E. D. McBride, M. G.

Hosa HOWARD to Pearl EARLS Issued 20 Sep 1924 Rites 21 Sep 1924
J. B. Dobbs, J. P.

Floyd SCOTT to Fannie CRAWLEY Issued 20 Sep 1924 Rites 20 Sep 1924
J. W. Eaton, Jdg.

Ernest McBRIDE to Willie GREEN Issued 20 Sep 1924 Rites 20 Sep 1924
J. L. Barnes, J. P.

Robert BRYAN to Mattie CUTTS Issued 23 Sep 1924 Rites 23 sep 1924
C. G. Howell, M. G.

R. Bert HARRISON to DAisy Leta KING Issued 25 Sep 1924 Rites 26 Sep 1924
B. S. Fielder, M. G.

Livingston D. HILL to Edna HUNTER Issued 26 Sep 1924 Rites 27 Sep 1924
J. Paul Slayden, M. G.

Rob KEELE (Col) to Bertha RINE (Rowan ?) (Col) Issued 26 Sep 1924 Rites 28 Sep
J. S. Nance, M. G.

D. B. WAGONER to Ione WOOTEN Issued 22 MAr 1924 Rites 2 Mar 1924
W. P. DAvis, MJ. P.
#503 in book - #502 & #504 both Sep)

Charlie KELL to Lucille GOLLIDAY Issued 27 Sep 1924 Rites 29 Sep 1924
W. E. Garner, M. G.

Parmer SIMMONS to Nellie HASTINGS Issued 29 Sep 1924 Rites 30 Sep 1924
O. H. Wood, J. P.

Wheeler McGREGOR to Emma TURNER Issued 4 Oct 1924 Rites 4 Oct 1924
I. P. McGregor, J. P.

J. B. CRIPPS to Virgie CRIPPS Issued 7 Oct 1924 Rites 9 Oct 1924
P. Turner, J. P.

Charlie PEDEN to Novella SMITH Issued 9 Oct 1924 Rites 12 Oct 1924
W. C. Whitlock, J. P.

G. BLOOMBERG to Artie EVANS Issued 9 Oct 1924 Rites 9 Oct 1924
J. B. Dobbs, J. P.

Charles HIGHT to Ophia CARPENTER Issued 11 Oct 1924 Rites 11 Oct 1924
E. F. Douglas, M. G.

Arthue MARTIN (Col) to Myrtle DUNCAN (Col) Issued 13 Oct 1924 Rites 13 Oct 1924
N. J. H. VanMeter, M. G.

Ward DEMITT to Elizabeth SMITH Issued 14 Oct 1924 Rites 15 Oct 1924
F. L. Leeper, M. G.

George LEWIS to Laura BRATCHER Issued 16 Oct 1924 Rites 17 Oct 1924
J. L. Smith, J. P.

F. C. STEPHENS to Nannie MAYNARD Issued 20 Oct 1924 Rites 20 Oct 1924
A. Z. Holder, J. P.

W. C. PAINE to Nannie HILLIS Issued 22 Oct 1924 Rites 23 Oct 1924
Fate Walker, J. P.

Robert HOLT to Wavie HARPER issued 25 Oct 1924 Rites 26 Oct 1924
H. J. Wilson, J. P.

Toy LATHAM to Emma MAi GOOCH Issued 28 Oct 1924 Rites 28 Oct 1924
W. P. Davis, J. P.

Willie B. WITTY to Ollie Lee SUMMERS Issued 28 Oct 1924 Rites 1 Nov 1924
J. N. Wimmett, J. P.

Eston COPE to Vena COPE Issued 28 Oct 1924 Rites 2 Nov 1924
E. R. Little, M. G.

Charlie JOHNSON to Owah TRUSTY Issued 1 Nov 1924 Rites 9 Nov 1924
A. A. Flanders, M. G.

Vance LUSK to Ellen MARTIN Issued 1 Nov 1924 Rites 1 Nov 1924
J. B. Dobbs, J. P.

Everett BESS to Esta SCRUGGS Issued 1 Nov 1924 Rites 2 Nov 1924
P. N. Moffitt, J. P.

Floyd COPPINGER to Zada HILLIS Issued 1 Nov 1924 Rites 2 Nov 1924
P. N. Moffitt, J. P.

Herman TAYLOR to Augusta HOWARD Issued 5 Nov 1924 Rites 5 Nov 1924
W. P. davis, J. P.

Will FRAZIER to Ollie YORK Issued 8 Nov 1924 Rites 9 Nov 1924
O. H. Wood, J. P.

Willie CANTRELL to Louise HENNESSEE Issued 8 Nov 1924 Rites 9 Nov 1924
J. L.Smith, J. P.

Robert DRIVER to Delcemia BOLT Issued 8 Nov 1924 Rites 9 Nov 1924
W. P. Davis, J. P.

Kie NEAL to Clara FISHER Issued 8 Nov 1924 Rites 9 Nov 1924
W. P. DAvis, J. P.

Will FORD to Bettie HOLLY Issued 10 Nov 1924 Rites 16 Nov 1924
G. H. Atnip, M. G.

C. B. ADAMS to Ruby RAMSEY Issued 11 Nov 1924 Rites 11 Nov 1924
F. M. Dowell, M. G.

Clarence BURCH to Bertha Mai RAOCH issued 13 Nov 1924 Rites 13 Nov 1924
J. W. Eaton, Jdg.

Elijah STEPHENS to Mary T. MARTIN Issued 20 Dec 1924 Rites 21 Dec 1924
Price Billingsley, M. G.

Paul PARSON to Claudia AYLER Issued 21 Dec 1924 Rites 21 Dec 1924
C. E. Hawkins, M. G.

Sutton GRIBBLE to Dell PISTOLE Issued 22 Dec 1924 Rites 22 Dec 1924
W. P. DAvis, J. P.

Coleman DUGGIN to Susie HENDERSON Issued 13 Dec 1924 Rites 14 Dec 1924
J. N. Winnett, J. P.

Clarence HILL to Ida Mai CANTRELL Issued 15 Dec 1924 Rites 24 Dec 1924
W. P. Davis, J. P.

Everett RAY to Clata CHISAM Issued 22 Dec 1924 Rites 23 Dec 1923
P. G. Moore, J. P.

Jack MUNCEY to Bonnie McBRIDE Issued 23 Dec 1924 Rites 23 Dec 1924
J. R. Stubblefirle, M. G.

Fred BLAIR to Etna THOMPSON Issued 23 Dec 1924 Rites 25 Dec 1924
J. N. Winnett, J. P.

W. L. SULLIVAN to Cleo SANDERS Issued 23 dec 1924 Rites 31 Dec 1924
E. R. Little, M. G.

Troy SANDERS to Etoile MAYNARD Issued 23 Dec 1924 Rites 24 Dec 1924
E. R. Little, M. G.

John MARTIN to Lucy NEAL Issued 24 Dec 1924 Rites 27 Dec 1924
W. C. Whitlock, J. P.

Bethel JONES to Grady ANDERSON Issued 25 Dec 1924 Rites 25 Dec 1925
J. R. Goodpasture, M. G.

Clarence RAMSEY (Col) to Clara DUNNIHUE (Col) Issued 25 Dec 1924 Rites 25 Dec
J. S. Nance, M. G.

H. B. POWELL to Belle CAGLE Issued 26 Dec 1924 Rites 26 Dec 1924
J. B. Dobbs, J. P.

Henry RAMSEY (Col) to Hellen DURHAM (Col) Issued 26 Dec 1924 Rites 28 Dec 1924
J. S. Nance, M. G.

Chester GRIFFITH to Edith CANTRELL Issued27 Dec 1924 Rites 4 JAn 1925
I. G. Gribble, J. P.

Shelton SELF to SALLIE TURNER Issued 27 Dec 1924 Rites 28 Dec 1924
P. Turner, J. P.

HArley CLENDENEN to Martha RIGSBY Issued 27 Dec 1924 Rites 28 Dec 1928
J. B. Dobbs, J. P.

Hershell GIBBS to Rosalee WISEMAN Issued28 Dec 1924 Rites 28 Dec 1924
F. L. Leeper, M. G.

L. FISHER to Rosa WOMACK Issued 14 Nov 1924 Rites 16 nov 1924
G. H. Atnip, M. G.

Ewell BRATCHER to Clara EMELTON Issued 15 Nov 1924 Rites 15 Nov 1924
P. Turner, J. P.

D. L. THOMAS to Robbie Lee HILL Issued 15 Nov 1924 Rites 15 Nov 1924
W. P. Davis, J. P.

R. D. TITTLE to Malisa WOODS Issued 15 Nov 1924 Rites 16 nov 1924
J. N. Winnett, J. P.

Jim BROWN (Col) to Hallie WHITE (Col) Issued 19 Nov 1924 Rites 19 Nov 1924
R. Ed Jones, Recorder

Willie LYTLE to Lou KING Issued 22 Nov 1924 Returned - Not Solemnized

V. E. COPE to Anna Mary WOMACK Issued 26 Nov 1924 Rites 27 Nov 1924
J. Paul Slayden, M. G.

Emmett CLARK to Robie TALLANT Issued 28 Nov 1924 Rites 28 Nov 1924
W. V. D. Miller, J. P.

Elbert WOODS to Anna Lee WOODSIDE Issued 28 Nov 1924 Rites 30 Nov 1924
I. N. Smoot, J. P.

Mance SIMMONS to Dora BOYD Issued 29 Nov 1924 Rites 30 Nov 1924
G. P. Brasier, J. P

J. L. DODD to Delma WRIGHT Issued 2 Dec 1924 Rites 20 Dec 1924
W. P. Davis, J. P.

John TITTSMORTH to Julia Ellen HENDRIXSON Issued 9 Dec 1924 Rites 13 Dec 1924
I. G. Gribble, J. P.

Eber BEATY to Pauline RAY Isseud 9 Dec 1924 Rites 9 Dec 1924
I. G. Gribble, J. P.

Brown SEALS to Wilma FOSTER Issued 9 Dec 1924 Rites 10 Dec 1924
Price Billingsley, M. G.

Wesley BEATY to Inez RAY Issued 10 Dec 1924 Rites 13 Dec 1924
I. G. Gribble, J. P.

T. F. CARRICK to Emma CUNNINGHAM Issued 11 Dec 1924 Rites 11 Dec 1924
John Morton, M. G.

E. C. McBRIDE to CArrie HOBBS Issued 13 Dec 1924 Rites 13 Dec 1924
O. H. Wood, J. P.

Henry HOBBS to Kelly (Callie) GOOCH Issued 15 Dec 1924 Rites 25 Dec 1924
W. P. Davis, J. P.

F. E. SMITHSON to Eula HALEY Issued 20 Dec 1924 Rites 24 Dec 1924
J. N. Winnett, J. P.

Herbert GRAHAM to George Ann YOUNGBLOOD Issued 30 Dec 1924 Rites 1 JAn 1924
　　　　　　J. T. Casey, M. G.

O. H. WHITLOCK to Evelyn HANCOCK Issued 31 Dec 1924 Rites 31 Dec 1924
　　　　　　J. T. Casey, M. G.

Willie H. HOBBS (Col) to Ritha WOOTEN (Col) Issued1 Jan 1925 Rites 1 JAn 1925
　　　　　　J. S. NAnce, M. G.

Frank C. NEAL to Lizzie Mai BLANKS Issued 1 Jan 1925 Rites 4 Jan 1925
　　　　　　J. R. Goodpasture, M. G.

Ezra DYER to Pauline YOUNG Issued 3 Jan 1925 Returned - Not Solemnized

Farnk C. NEWBY to Emma CAGLE Issued 9 Jan 1925 Rites 9 JAn 1925
　　　　　　J. T. CaSEY, M. G.

Willie PERRY to Jewel REYNOLDS Issued 17 JAn 1925 Rites 17 JAn 1925
　　　　　　W. P. Davis, J. P.

Willie HASTON to Gladys WILCHER Issued 17 Jan 1925 Rites 18 Jan 1925
　　　　　　W. B. Snipes, M. G.

Rollie PATTON to Dollie Mai SEAMONS Issued 17 JAn 1925 Rites 25 JAn 1925
　　　　　　Fate Walker, J. P.

R. M. POE to Jennie SHERRELL Issued 21 Jan 1925 Rites 22 Feb 1925
　　　　　　W. V. D. Miller, J. P.

E. W. SUTHERLIN to Lola JARRELL Issued 21 Jan 1925 Rites 22 Jan 1925
　　　　　　L. C. Lane, J. P.

Ed SMITH to Lyda McGREGOR Issued 24 Jan 1925 Rites 24 Jan 1925
　　　　　　J. N. Wimnett, J. P.

Jim BROWN to Hallie WHITE Issued 22 Jan 1925 Not Returned

Joe TITTSWORTH to Ruth JENNINGS Issued 26 Jan 1925 Rites 28 Jan 1925
　　　　　　Llewellyn Lawrence, M. G.

J. B. BAIN to Julia VICKERS Issued 29 JAn 1925 Rites 29 JAn 1925
　　　　　　J. B. Dobbs, J. P.

Floyd SIMONS to Nettie PERRY Issued 4 Feb 1925 Rites 4 Feb 1925
　　　　　　F. L. Leeper, M. G.

WAllace NEELY to Elsie PATTON Issued 4 Feb 1925 Rites 8 Feb 1925
　　　　　　L. F. DAugherty, M. G.

Willie MOORE (Col) to NAncy E. MARTIN (Col) Issued 7 Feb 1925 Rites 13 Feb 1925
　　　　　　D. P. Myers, J. P.

Oscar MAYO to Ruby Lee GROVE Issued 7 Feb 1925 Rites 8 Feb 1925
　　　　　　J. Paul Slayden, M. G.

Hugh STILES to Elma NORROD Issued 7 Feb 1925 Rites 8 Feb 1925
　　　　　　J. B. Dobbs, J. P.

Cecil OVERTURFF to Martha KIBBLE Issued 7 Feb 1925 Rites 7 Feb 1925
　　　　　　VAn McGee, J. P.

Thomas BESHERSE to Nancy CLEMENS Issued 11 Feb 1925 Rites 11 Feb 1925
　　　　　　W. P. Davis, J. P.

O. S. WOODLEE to Georgia SCOTT Issued 13 Feb 1925 Rites 15 Feb 1925
　　　　　　J. L. Barnes, J. P.

Jim BYARS to Nannie HENNESSEE Issued 14 Feb 1925 Rites 24 feb 1925
　　　　　　J. B. Dobbs, J. P.

Robert BLANKS to Bethiah BELL Issued 14 Feb 1925 Rites 15 Feb 1925
　　　　　　J. R. Goodpasture, M. G.

Willie McREYNOLDS (Col) to Avo EVANS (Col) Issued 16 Feb 1925 Rites 16 Feb 1925
　　　　　　J. S. Nance, J. P.

Guy PATTERSON to Georgia Mai NEWBY Issued 17 Feb 1925 Rites 17 Feb 1925
　　　　　　J. B. Dobbs, J. P.

Johnnie MORTON to Maudie GULLEY Issued 18 Feb 1925 Rites 18 Feb 1918
　　　　　　W. P. Davis, J. P.

597 Marriages recorded in this book.

Book 15 - Warren County Marriages - Feb. 23 1925 to Jan. 7, 1928

Clarence WOMACK to Margie SANDERS Issued 23 Feb 1925 Rites 25 Feb 1925
E. R. Little, M. G.

Franck C. MITCHELL to Essie RIGSBY issed 25 Feb 1925 Rites 25 Feb 1925
J. W. Eaton, Jdg.

Ambros GRISSOM to Minnie JENNINGS Issued 27 Feb 1925 Rites 28 Feb 1928
E. L. Moffitt, J. P.

Thomas LEE (Col) to Bessie BILES (Col) Issued 28 Feb 1925 Returned - Not Solemnizd

Raymond L. BYRD to Clara H. VANHOOSER Issued4 Mar 1925 Rites 4 Mar 1925
J. B. Dobbs, J. P.

JAmes N. SMOOT to Hersie BOTTOMS Issued 7 Mar 1925 Rites 8 Mar 1925
O. H. Lane, M. G.

Tatum YOUNG to Nannie CUMMINGS Issued 7 Mar 1925 Rites 7 Mar 1925
H. J. Wilson, J. P.

Robert HUDGINS (Col) to Willie MILLER (Col) Issued 9 Mar 1925 Rites 10 Mar 1925
D. P. Myaores, J. P.

George BRADY to Grace HILLIS Issued 11 Mar 1925 Rites 11 MAr 1925
J. B. Dobbs, J. B.

R. E. KEATON to Mary FRZIER Issued 14 Mar 1925 Rites 14 Apr 1925
O. H. Wood, J. P.

Howard ADCOCK to Novella REEDER Issued 14 Mar 1925 Rites 15 Mar 1925
J. G. Gribble, J. P.

Dewey HERNDON to Elizabeth HORNNIE Issued 14 Mar 1925 Rites 14 MAR 1925
J. B. Dobbs, J. P.

Thomas O. BREMER to Isa Innes WATSON Issued 18 Mar 1925 Rites 18 Mar 1925
W. P. Davis, J. P.

John C. HILLIS to Annie FARLESS Issued 18 Mar 1925 Rites 18 Mar 1925
W. P. Davis, J. P.

Marvin L. HALL to Ruby Lee KELL Issued 21 Mar 1925 Rites 21 Mar 1925
W. P. Davis, J. P.

Charles WHITE (Col) to Minnie STARKEY (Col) Issued 23 Mar 1925 Rites 23 Mar 1925
W. P. Davis, J. P.

D. P. WOMACK to Malissa PATTERSON Issued 27 Mar 1925 Rites 29 Mar 1925
A. A. Flanders, M. G.

Randolph LOWERY to Mildred HUTCHINGS Issued 27 Mar 1925 Rites 28 Mar 1925
R. J. Tucker

Lawson HALL to Ruby DAVIS Issued 3 Apr 1925 Rites 3 Apr 1925
Fate Walker, J. P.

John PARKER to Frances BLACK Issued 3 Apr 1925 Rites 4 Apr 1925
F. M. Dowell, M. G.

Jesse SIMPSON to Edith DAVENPORT Issued 4 Apr 1925 Rites 5 Apr 1925
J. W. Winnett, J. P.

Tom ROMAN (col) to Johnnie BRADFORD (Col) Issued 10 Apr 1925 Rites 11 Apr 1925
J. S. Nance, M. G.

George DAVIS to Nena Grace CAPSHAW Issued 10 Apr 1925 Rites 12 Apr 1925
L. F. Daugherty, M. G.

Will DIXSON to Lillie HODGE Issued 11 Apr 1925 Rites 11 Apr 1925
J. B. Dobbs, J. P.

George DEHLE to Virginia HAYHURST Issued 13 Apr 1925 Rites 13 Apr 1925
W. P. DAvis, J. P.

G. A. REYNOLDS to Myrtle JARRELL Issued 17 Apr 1925 Rites 19 Apr 1925
O. H. Wood, J. P.

Ira HILL to Alta McVEY Issued 18 Apr 1925 Rites 18 Apr 1925
I. P. McGregor, J. P.

E. D. TURNER to Vicie CHRISTIAN Issued 24 Apr 1925 Rites 25 Apr 1925
E. L. Moffitt, J. F.

DeWitt AKERS to Ova GOFF Issued 25 Apr 1925 Rites 26 Apr 1925
P. Turner, J. P.

Huse ROMAN (Col) to Carrie SCOTT (Col) Issued 25 Apr 1925 Rites 25 Apr 1925
J. S. Nance, M. G.

Elda BONNER to Zora PEDIGO Issued 25 Apr 1925 Rites 26 Apr 1925
A. Z. Holder, J. P.

Frank FORD (Col) to Estella WHERRY (Col) Issued 27 Apr 1927 Rites 27 Apr 1927
D. L. Garrett, M. G.

Louis MAYFIELD to Cona ADCOCK Issued 27 Apr 1925 Rites 10 May 1925
L. F. Daugherty, M. G.

Willie CANTRELL to Dovie HAMILTON Issued 2 May 1925 Rites 6 May 1925
J. B. Dobbs, J. P.

Hubert ROBINSON to Hellen CARRICK Issued 3 May 1925 Rites 3 May 1925
J. S. Nance, M. G.

Jack ARGO to Stella MADEWELL Issued 4 May 1925 Rites 4 May 1925
J. B. Dobbs, J. P.

W. T. WARREN to Alta QUICK Issued 6 May 1925 Rites 24 May 1925
P. Turner, J. P.

Dalton HILLIS to Ora LORANCE Issued 5 Jun 1925 Rites 7 Jun 1925
H. J. Wilson, J. P.

Hollie WOODS to Delma REDMON Issued 6 Jun 1925 Rites 14 Jun 1925
W. H. Craven

Eddie Sylvester PATTERSON to Mary Bell CASS Issued 8 May 1925 Rites 9 MAy 1925
W. S. MArshall, M. G.

A. W. POWELL to Marshie CAGLE Issued 9 May 1925 Rites 9 May 1925
J. B. Dobbs, J.P.

J. R. GRIBBLE (Col) to Vannita SAVAGE (col) Issued 9 May 1925 Rites 9 May 1925
J. B. Dobbs, J. P.

L. B. PARKER to Maude RUTLEDGE Issued 11 May 1925 Rites 11 May 1925
J. T. Casey, M. G.

MAnfred HARDING to Lela HILL Issued 15 May 1925 Rites 16 May 1925
J. B. Dobbs, J. P.

Tom ARGO to Jennie BRAXTON Issued 16 MAy. 1925 Rites 17 May 1925
J. L. Barnes, J. P.

Loring FULTS to Charity OVERTURF Issued 21 May 1925 Rites 21 May 1925
Van McGee, J. P.

Woodford MILLINER to Bessie May ROGERS Issued 23 May 1925 Rites 23 May 1925
R. L. Woods, J. P.

George ELAM (Col) to Mattie THOMAS (Col) Issued 23 May 1925 Rites 23 May 1925
N. J. H. VAnMeter

John TROUTMAN (Col) to Orlene HUGGINS (Col) Issued 25 May 1925 Rites 25 MAy 1925
D. P. Myers, J. P.

Morgan ANDERSON (Col) to Willie LOOPER (Col) Issued 29 MAy 1925 Rites 30 May 1925
J. S. Nance, M. G.

Alva Hale RICH to Florence HOLCOMB Issued 30 May 1925 Rites 31 May 1925
R. C. Womack, J. P.

Cecil NELSON to Louise McGEE Issued 29 May 1925 Rites 30 May 1925
J. B. Dobbs, J. P.

Luther LEE (Col) to Velma SMARTT (Col) Issued 8 Jun 1925 Not Returned

L. L. SISK to Alberta GARRETT Issued 11 Jun 1925 Rites 11 Jun 1925
Albert S. Hale,

Erbie MOORE to Julia VAUGHN Issued 13 Jun 1925 Rites 17 Jun 1925
L. C. Lane, J. P.

Shelah BRASWELL to MAurine JOHNSON Issued 13 Jun 1925 Rites 13 Jun 1925
Name Chage - court order 12/22/60   W. P. Davis, J. P.

Alton B. LYNCH to Alta Mai BATES Issued 13 Jun 1925 Rites 13 Jun 1925
W. P. DAvis, J. P.

S. O. JOHNSON to SAllie Lee MITCHELL Issued 19 Jun 1925 Rites 21 Jun 1925
D. P. Myers, J. P.

Tom Mason McQUEEN to Josephine RAMSEY issued 20 Jun 1925 Rites 7 Jul 1925
C. E. Hawkins, M. G.

John H. STEMBRIDGE to Martha KIRBY Issued 20 Jun 1925 Rites 22 Jun 1925
J. N. Winnett, J. P.

Henry JORDAN to Hellen McLAUGHLIN Issued 20 Jun 1925 Returned - Not Solemnized

Calud M. CARUTHERS to Grace M. GAUZMAN Issued 20 Jun 1925 Rites 20 Jun 1925
J. R. Goodpasture, M. G.

Thomas MARTIN (col) to India HILL Issued 20 jun 1925 Rites 21 Jun 1925
N. J. H. VAnMeter, M. G.

H. H. GESSLER to MArgarette RHEA Issued 20 Jun 1925 Rites 20 Jun 1925
C. E. Hawkins

Buford WHITELOW (Col) to Agnes LOOPER (Col) Issued 20 Jun 9125 Rites 20 Jun 1925
J. S. Nance, M. G.

SAmuel H. HILTON to Winnie Mae WALKER issued 24 Jun 1925 Rites 1 Jul 1925
N. M. Hill, J. P.

Clarence TENPENNY to MAud KING Issued 1 Jul 1925 Rites 1 Jul 1925
John Morton, M. G.

Charlie COPE to Bettie POWELL Issued 3 Jul 1925 Rites 12 Jul 1925
J. B. Dobbs, J. P.

Sam MORGAN to Wylie HEARSE Issued 4 Jul 1925 Rites 5 Jul 1925
H. J. Wilson, J. P.

Dorsey RAMSEY (Col) to Sallie Mai LOCKE (Col) Issued 6 Jul 1925 Rites 6 Jul 1925
J. B. Dobbs, J. P.

Herman KELLEY to Nettie JOHNSON Issued 9 Jul 1925 Rites 9 Jul 1925
W. B. Snipes, M. G.

Charles PAYNE to Ethel LANE Issued 11 Jul 1925 Rites 12 Jul 1925
W. V. D. Miller, J. P.

McKinley HILL to Addie JACOBS Issued 13 Jul 1925 Rites 27 Jul 1925
N. J. H. VanMeter, M. G.

Lester McCORMICK to Cordia HAMILTON Issued 16 jul 1925 Rites 17 jul 1925
Irving Patton, J. P.

Hershell GUY to Ethel WRIGHT Issued 16 Jul 1925 Rites 17 Jul 1925
Irving Patton, J. P.

Lester SMARTT to Flossie HUTCHINS Issued 16 Jul 1925 Rites 19 jul 1925
W. B., Snipes, M. G.

Owen TURNER to Estelle SMITH Issued 17 jul 1925 Rites 18 Jul 1925
P. Turner, J. P.

Joe Cecil BAKER to Callie Agnes BRATCHER Issued 18 Jul 1925 Rites 18 Jul 1925
Irving Patton, J. P.

Lawrence PEARSON to Elizabeth SMITH Issued 18 Jul 1925 Rites 22 Jul 1925
J. L. Barnes, J. P.

Manson PACK to Norma REYNOLDS Issued 31 Jul 1925 Rites 31 Jul 1925 W. P. Davis, J. P.

Foster B. JOHNSON to Carrie HERON Issued 31 Jul 1925 Rites 31 Jul 1925 Walter Hindmore, M. G.

Alva JONES to Velma SCHROCK Issued 1 Aug 1925 Rites 2 Aug 1925 L. C. Lane, J. P.

George W. WIANDT Lura Mai GOLLIDAY Issued 1 Aug 1925 Rites 15 Aug 1925 Alvis J. Davis

Will HALE to PAuline COOLEY Issued 1 Aug 1925 Rites 1 Aug 1925 F. M. Dowell, M. G.

JAcob J. CHAPMAN to Beatrice WARREN Issued 5 Aug 1925 Rites 5 Aug 1925 F. M. Dowell, M. G.

Herman JONES to Ethel MAYFIELD issued 13 Aug 1925 Rites 15 Aug 1925 W. P. Davis, J. P.

Hershell MAYNARD to Lavada CRAIG Issued 14 Aug 1925 Rites 14 Aug 1925 Irving Patton, J. P.

A. E. McKENZIE to Edith Matthews JOHNSON Issued 17 Aug 1925 Rites 17 Aug 1925 C. E. Hawkins

Jim SMITH to May JONES Issued 21 Aug 1925 Rites 21 Aug 1925 P. G,. Moore, J. P.

Albert PATTERSON to Virgia ESTES Issued 23 Aug 1925 Rites 25 Aug 1925 I. G. Gribble, J. P.

Dozier ORRICK to Vester TODD Issued 24 Aug 1925 Rites 26 Aug 1925 H. J. Wilson, J. P.

Walter CHEERS to Carmine CLARK Issued 25 Aug 1925 Rites 25 Aug 1925 Llewellyn T. LAWRENCE, M. G.

Byron JONES to Maggie LOU BAIN Issued 26 Aug 1925 Rites 26 Aug 1925 W. P. Davis, J. P.

Jim C. ROGERS to Luvile BRYAN Issued 29 Aug 1925 Rites 30 Aug 1925 A. B. Moffitt

Joe SIMS to Erine MITCHELL Issued 2 Sep 1925 Rites 2 Sep 1925 N. J. H. VanMeter, M. G.

J. D. BURNETT to Artie Gay MONTANDON Issued 3 Sep 1925 Returned - Not SOLEMNIZED

Edgar R. BAIN to Martha R. NEWBY Issued 4 Sep 1925 Rites 17 Sep 1925 O. H. Lanc, J. P.

D. W. BRADFORD to Ruby WRIGHT Issued 5 Sep 1925 Rites 6 Sep 1925 W. G. Keyt, M. G.

Leonard HITCHCOCK to Julia HASH issued 5 Sep 1925 Rites 5 Sep 1925 W. P. Davis, J. P.

D. C. MURCHISON to Cecil MALONE Issued 5 Sep 1925 Rites 6 Sep 1925 R. E. L. Taylor, M. G.

S. J. McBRIDE to Lila JORDAN Issued 10 Sep 1925 Rites 11 Sep 1925 G. B. Wooten

Eldridge RUSSELL to Leona LOCKE Issued 12 Sep 1925 Rites 13 Sep 1925 J. Paul Slayden, M. G.

F. M. FISCHER to Ova Edna ROBINSON Issued 15 Sep 1925 Rites 17 Sep 1925 J. Paul Slayden, M. G.

HARRY W. JENNISON to Flora B. HOWARD Issued 16 Sep 1925 Rites 16 Sep 1925 J. B. Dobbs, J. P.

John H. TIDWELL (Col) to Mary LOOPER (Col) Issued 18 Sep 1925 Rites 18 1925 J. B. Dobbs, J. P.

Ezra DYER to Ruby CAMPBELL Issued 19 Sep 1925 Rites 20 Sep 1925 A. . Holder, J. P.

Charlie BOND to Minnie Lee HALEY issued 19 Sep 1925 Rites 27 Sep 1925 Stephen Robinson, M. G.

Vesta PERRY to Gladys WOOD Issued 26 Sep 1925 Rites 26 Sep 1925 F. . Dowell, M. G.

William WOODS (Col) to Florence MARTIN (Col) Issued 28 Sep 1925 Rites 28 Sep N. J. H. VanMeter. M. G.

HArvey YOUNG to Ruby FREEZE Issued 2 Oct 1925 Rites 4 Oct 1925 J. A. Cunningham, M. G.

Bethel GREEN to Florence BLANKENSHIP Issued 2 Oct 1925 Rites 4 Oct 1925 L. C. Lane, J. P.

Brackett TURNER to KAte PEDIGO Issued 12 Oct 1925 Rites 15 Oct 1925 A. Z. Holder, J. P.

Jere G. RUSSELL to Ruth MOORE Issued 14 Oct 1925 Rites 14 Oct 1925 F. L. Leeper, M. G.

Aubrey JONES to Lizzie McCORMICK Issued 17 Oct 1925 Rites 18 Oct 1925 Irving PATTON, J. P.

Winford KNOWLES to Emma PARIS Issued 19 Oct 1925 Rites 31 Oct 1925 I. G. Gribble, J. P.

Ed SCOTT (Col) to Cinda SPURLOCK (Col) Issued 20 Oct 1925 Not returned

Edward HAMILTON to Myrtle BROWN Issued 21 Oct 1925 Rites 21 Oct 1925 Robert S. Tinnon

J. C. ROBERTS to Thelma NEAL Issued 24 Oct 1925 Rites 24 Oct 1925 Fate Walker, J. P.

Lucian WOODS (Col) to Jennie CARR (col) Issued24 Oct 1925 Rites 24 oct 1925
D. P. Myers, J. P.

Shirley SPENCER to Maggie MARTIN Issued 7 Nov 1925 Rites 8 Nov 1925
J. B. Dobbs, J. P.

John Wm. BOYD to Ozell CHRISTIAN Issued 19 Nov 1925 Rites 19 nov 1925
J. Paul Slayden, M. G.

G. R. KIRBY to Mimmie Mai GLENN Issued20 Nov 1925 Rites 29 Nov 1925
S. W. D. Green

Finis RICH to Flora DUGGAN Issued 21 Nov 1925 Rites 21 Nov 1925
R. L. Whitwell, J. P.

George WILLIAMSON to Myrtle GATHER Issued 21 Nov 1925 Rites 22 Nov 1925
J. N. Winnett, J. P.

Lawrence LAWSON to Flossie ODEL Issued 27 Nov 1925 Rites 27 Nov 1925
J. W. Eaton, JDG.

Edgar NEAL to Hazel FUSTON Issued 4 dec 1925 Rites 9 Dec 1925
J. B. Dobbs, J. P.

Sylvester McBRIDE to Mattie PASSON issued 5 Dec 1925 Rites 5 Dec 1925
J. E. Clark, M. G.

Boyd DIXSON to Edna Grace BOULDIN Issued 5 dec 1925 Rites 5 Dec 1925
R. S. Tinnon, M. G.

R. L. STUBBLEFIELD to Ruth L. GIVENS Issued 10 dec 1925 Rites 12 dec 1925
J. Paul Slayden, M. G.

Hugh DILLEHAY to Louise PRITCHARD Issued 12 dec 1925 Rites 12 dec 1925
J. B. Dobbs, J. P.

C. A. TUCKER to Josephine COUCH Issued 12 dec 1925 Rites 13 dec 1925
F. M. Dowell, M. G.

Jesse WOOD to Eunice FERRELL Issued 12 dec 1925 Rites 13 Dec 1925
F. M. Dowell, M. G.

John PAINE (Col) to Mattir PRIME (Col) Issued 19 dec 1925 Rites 20 dec 1925
Irving Patton, J. P.

George MITCHELL, Jr. to Flora Bell DODD Issued 19 dec 1925 rites 24 dec 1925
L. P. Sanders, J. P.

George KING to Roberta LOCKE Issued 19 dec 1925 Rites 20 dec 1925
N. J. H. VanWeter, M. G.

E. S. WALLACE to Lillie JONES Issued 21 dec 1925 Rites 26 dec 1925
J. E. Clark, M.jG.

Vanna (?) SMITH to Lillie Mai PENNEGER Issued 21 dec 1925 Rites 23 dec 1925
W. C. Whitlock, J. P.

J. R. CASS to Agnes MOORE Issued 22 dec 1925 Rites 23 Dec 1925
Wm. Craven,

Almer TAYLOR to Roberta CAMPBELL Issued 23 dec 1925 Rites 24 dec 1925
Chas. T. POWELL

Clifton PATTON to Mary DUNCAN Issued 23 Dec 1925 Rites 24 dec 1925
J. E. Clark, M. G.

Mouey HENNESSEE to Mimmie McGEE Issued 23 Dec 1925 Rites 27 Dec 1925
I. P. McGregor, J. P.

L.C. JORDAN to Willie Roe DODSON Issued 24 Dec 1925 Rites 25 dec 1925
W. P. Davis, J. P.

G. W. SIMONS to Willie Mai ROWLAND Issued 24 Dec 1925 Rites 25 Dec 1925
W. G. Keyt, M. G.

R. K. HAMRICK to Maggie Belle WALLACE Issued 25 Dec 1925 Rites 26 Dec 1925
J. E. Calrk, M. G.

Brown FIELDS to Ova CANTRELL Issued 26 dec 1925 ites 26 dec 1925
W. V. D. Miller, J. P.

J. T. WARD to Jessie Lee NEWBY Issued 26 dec 1925 Rites 26 dec 1925
W. P. Davis, J. P.

Walter YOUNG to Lillie Mai ROGERS Issued 26 Dec 1925 Rites 27 dec 1925
W. B. Snipes, M. G.

C. E. MILLS to Vesta WALLING issued 1 Jan 1926 Rites 1 jan 1926
Irving Patton, J. P.

Hiram TODD to Lillie KIRBY Issued 2 jan 1926 Rites 29 Jan 1926
I. G. Gribble, J. P.

Wayne WOODLEE to Jewell CHAMBERS Issued 4 Jan 1926 Rites 5 Jan 1926
J. Paul Slayden, M. G.

Buck McKEE to Nodie ROGERS Issued 4 Jan 1926 Rites 4 Jan 1926
W. P. Davis, J. P.

Robert MITCHELL (Col) to Modie ROACH (Col) Issued 6 JAn 1926 Rites 6 Jan 1926
J. S. Nance, M. G.

Zera HILLIS to WAvie BOTTOMS Issued 9 JAn 1926 Rites 10 Jan 1926
I. P. McGregor, J. P.

Luther TURNER to Edna Lee McCORMICK Issued 17 JAn 1926 Rites 17 Jan 1926
P. N. Moffitt, J. P.

George WRIGHT to Emma TASH Issued 18 JAn 1926 Rites 18 JAn 1926
J. B. Dobbs, J. P.

Elbert Lee NORRIS to Mollie ROBERTS Issued 22 Jan 1926 Rites 29 Jan 1926
L. C. Lane, J. P.

Robert SEALS to Eunice HUDSON Issued 23 Jan 1926 Rites 24 Jan 1926
Irving Patton, J. P.

Joe ANDERSON (Col) to Emma JOHNSON (Col) Issued 26 Jan 1926 Rites 26 JAn 1926
J. S. Nance, M. G.

Willey BARRETT to Gladys STEMBRIDGE Issued 28 Jan 1926 Rites 29 Jan 1926
I. G. Gribble, J. P.

Joe YORK to Mary Belle TENPENNY Issued 28 Jan 1926 Rites 31 jan 1926
E. Patton

Ernest SMITH to Nannie Mc BRIDE issued 30 JAn 1926 Rites 2 Feb 1926
P. N. Moffitt, J. P.

G. E. BREEDLOVE to Margie PAINE Issued 30 Jan 1926 rites 30 Jan 1926
L. C. Lane. J. P.

H. T. ROGERS to Lassie SMARTT Issued 30 JAn 1926 Rites 7 JAn 1926
W. H. Byles, J. P.

BArney FUSTON to Hallie BRADY Issued 30 JAn 1926 Rites 31 jan 1926
W. T. Warren, J. P.

Lanus MILLIGAN to Augusta JONES Issued 30 JAn 1926 Rites 31 jan 1926
W. T. Warren, J. P.

Rose PATRICK to Mary E. BOREN Issued 5 Feb 1926 Rites 6 Feb 1926
W. V. D. Miller, J. P.

Ewen T. POWERS to Grace BENNETT Issued 6 Feb 1926 Rites 7 Feb 1926
W. P. Davis, J. P.

P. G. WEST to Etta Mai HUTCHINS Issued 3 dec 1925 Rites 3 Dec 1925
J. B. Dobbs, J. P.
(Out of Order)

Lonnie PARISH to Lou ARGO Issued 13 Feb 1926 Rites 13 Feb 1926
J. B. Dobbs, J. P.

Tom PELHAM to Ellen SIMONS Issued 18 Feb 1926 Rites 18 feb 1926
John Morton, M. G.

Paul HOBBS to Bessie GRAHAM Issued 19 Feb 1926 Rites 20 Feb 1926
O. H. Wood, J. P.

J. I. OVERHOLSER to Flossie Pearl CANTRELL Issued 24 Feb 1926 Rites 24 feb 1926
J. B. Dobbs, J. P.

Levy CLENDENEN to Emma Gladys TURNER Issued 25 feb 1926 Rites 26 feb 1926
P. N. Moffitt, J. P.

Grady LANCE to Bertha LORANCE Issued 25 Feb 1926 Rites 28 feb 1926
H. J. Wilson, J. P.

John BRATCHER to Mildred BYARS Issued 27 Feb 1926 Rites 27 Feb 1926
J. B. Gribble

A. A. JACOBS to Minnie HOLLIS Issued 27 Feb 1926 Rites 28 Feb 1926
W. B. Snipes, M. G.

A. P. TITITSWORTH to Mrs. M. L. CANTRELL Issued 1 Mar 1926 Rites 3 mar 1926
I. G. Gribble, J. P.

Basil E. SLOAN to Wilma P. CUNNINGHAM Issued 1 Mar 1926 Returned - Not Solemnized

W. M. RIDDLE to Sarah PENDLETON Issued 4 Mar 1926 Rites 4 Mar 1926
J. Paul Slayden, M. G.

Grady ANDERSON to Gertrude ROBERTS Issued 6 Mar 1926 Not Returned

Brown CROUCH to Mary KILGORE Issued6 Mar 1926 Returned - Not Solemnized

D. D. SMITHSON to Mrs. Ross DILLON Issued 6 Mar 1926 Rites 6 Mar 1926
W. P. Davis, J. P.

Virgil HUTCHINS to Eula Mai MITCHELL Issued 13 Mar 1926 Rites 14 Mar 1926
L. F. Daugherty, M. G.

Oliver PHILPOT to Eula Mai ROGERS Issued 13 Mar 1926 Rites 17 Mar 1926
W. P. Davis, J. P.

C. C. HILDRETH to Roberta COPE Issued 27 Mar 1926 Rites 28 Mar 1926
W. T. Warren, J. P.

Thurman JORDAN to Alta F. BAIN Issued 27 Mar 1926 Rites 1 Apr 1926
J. N. Winnett, J. P.

Herchell McCOLLUM to Leola HILLIS Issued 27 Mar 1926 Rites 29 Mar 1926
R. S. Tinnon, M. G.

Will SIMMONS to Gladys WALLING Issued 30 Mar 1926 Rites 4 Apr 1926
W. V. D. Miller, J. P.

Thomas HENNESSEE to Nora CAMPBELL Issued 31 Mar 1926 Rites 1 Apr 1926
E. Patton

George PATRICK to Reecie PRIEST Issued 1 Apr 1926 Rites 2 Apr 1926
L. C. Lane, J. P.

T. C. SELF to Martha ROLLER Issued 2 Apr 1926 Rites 4 Apr 1926
Richard Turner, M. G.

Robert BASHAM to May THAXTON Issued 3 Apr 1926 Rites 4 Apr 1926
W. B. Snipes, M. G.

Dewey HOLDER to Mattie Bell WILSON Issued 3 Apr 1926 Rites 10 Apr 1926
J. N. Winnett, J. P.

Crawford McGEE to Florence JUDKINS Issued 3 Apr 1926 Rites 4 Apr 1926
J. B. Dobbs, J. P.

BAskom CHANDLER to Jennie HASH Issued 6 Apr 1926 Rites 10 Apr 1926
W. V. D. Miller, J. P.

A. B. CRIPPS to Armelia MALONE Issued 6 Apr 1926 Rites 11 apr 1926
W. P. Davis, J. P.

Palo McVEY to Cecil HILLIS Issued 10 Apr 1926 Rites 10 Apr 1926
D. P. Myers, J. P.

Charles HERNDON to Mary KEATON Issued 12 Apr 1926 Rites 12 Apr 1926
E. Patton

Tom LEFTRICK to Belle SCOTT Issued 14 Apr 1926 Rites 14 Apr 1926
J. B. Dobbs, J. P.

Charles GULLICK to Ethel BARNES Issued 17 Apr 1926 Rites 18 Apr 1926
R. S. Tinnon, M. G.

Hubert GRIFFITH to Alta JOHNSON Isssed 17 Apr 1926 Rites 17 Apr 1926
D. P. Myers, J. P.

Orvil BOREN to Martha CANTRELL Issued 20 Apr 1926 Rites 21 Apr 1926
P. G. Woods, J. P.

Silas PRIEST to Willie E. TEMPLETON Issued 20 Apr 1926 Rites 20 Apr 1926
R. S. Tinnon, M. G.

Cecil GILLEY to Lodiline HAWKINS Issued 21 Apr 1926 Rites 21 Apr 1926
A. J. Davis, M. G.

Milford RICHARDSON to Novella PONDER Issued 22 Apr 1926 Rites 22 apr 1926
J. B. Dobbs, J. P.

Richard SMITH to Mary HOLLAND Issued 24 Sep 1926 Rites 24 Apr 1926
J. W. Cooley, M. G.

Henry CHRISTIAN to Vera PARKS Issued 24 Apr 1926 Rites 27 Apr 1926
G. H. O'NEAL, M. G.

Dillard RAMSEY to Alta FREED Issued 26 Apr 1926 Rites 29 Apr 1926
W. C. Whitclok, J. P.

Eb SCOTT to Rachel TURNER Issued 26 Apr 1926 Rites 28 Apr 1926
I. P. McGregor, J. P.

G. F. RAY to Druvicie THOMAS Issued 28 Apr 1926 Rites 29 Apr 1926
W. P. Davis, J. P.

George WOMACK to Mary F. ROWLAND Issued 14 May 1926 Rites 16 May 1926
Irving Patton, J. P.

Tom ROBINSON to Maud POWERS Issued 15 May 1926 Rites 15 May 1926
F. M. Dowell, M. G.

Preston McMAHAN to Violet GOFF Issued 18 May 1926 Rites 19 May 1926
W. T. Warren, J. P.

Comer SHERRELL to Ova FULLER Issued 20 May 1926 Rites 21 May 1926
Claud Myers

N. B. JONES to Ida McCORMICK Issued 20 May 1926 Rites 5 Jun 1926
J. L. Barnes, J. P.

Elza STONER to Cinda MASENGALL Issued 21 May 1926 Rites 23 May 1926
P. N. Moffitt, J. P.

J. M. REDDING to Ella HOWLEY Issued 22 May 1926 Rites 22 May 1926
C. L. Webster, M. G.

Joe JONES to Maye WILLIAMSON Issued 22 May 1926 Rites 22 May 1926
J. W. Eaton, JDg.

Robert GRIZZELL to Josephine MORRORD Issued 23 May 1926 Rites 23 May 1926
R. S. Tinnon, M. G.

George Francis WISEINER to Zella Estelle THOMPSON Issued 25 May 1926 Rites 28 May
J. Paul Slayden, M. G.

Hervey JONES to Flora HAMMONS Issued 27 May 1926 Rites 27 May 1926
W. P. Davis, J. P.

William N. PARIS to Carmine L. WOODSIDE Issued 2 Jun 1926 Rites 2 Jun 1926
F. M. Dowell, M. G.

Jas. Grant STUBBLEFIELD to Hazel Woodson KING Issued 2 Jun 1926 Rites 3 Jun 1926
J. Paul Slayden, M. G.

Toy PARSLEY to Georgia LAFEVERS Issued 5 Jun 1926 Rites 6 Jun 1926
W. C. Whitlock, J. P.

Tom DUNCAN to Etta McMAHAN Issued 5 jun 1926 Returned - Not Solemnized

E. BURKS to Thenia TENPENNY Issued 7 Jun 1926 Rites 7 Jun 1926
J. B. Dobbs, J. P.

Melton BAILEY to Hannah MAI SUMMERS Issued 11 Jun 1926 Rites 13 May 1926
J. R. Bailey, M. G.

J. B. HAWK to Gladys GRIBBLE Issued 16 Jun 1926 Rites 16 Jun 1926
I. G. Gribble,

Ben J. GLAZE to Nellie B. ARNOLD Issued 19 Jun 1926 Not Rteurned

Zeke NEWBY to Tula GOFF Issued 19 Jun 1926 Rites 21 Jun 1926
W. T. Warren, J. P.

Elkin LAnier RIPPY to Sallie Bell BINKLEY Issued 19 Jun 1926 Rites 19 Jun 1926
Tom L. Roberts, M. G.

John WHITEAKER to Eva WHITTAKER Issued 28 Aug 1926 Rites 29 Aug 1926
I. P. McGregor, J. P.

Grady MULLICAN to PAuline YOUNG Issued 21 Jun 1926 Returned - Not Solemized

E. M. DUNLAP to Lillie SHERRELL Issued 22 Jun 1926 Returned - Not Solemized

Jesse BRATCHER to Stella McMAHAN Issued 26 Jun 1926 Rites 27 Jun 1926
J. N. Winnett, J. P.

Andy GRIBBLE to Swan MOSS Issued 27 Jun 1926 Rites 27 Jun 1926
W. P. Davis, J. P.

F. R. STAFFORD to Etta MAi MAGNESS Issued 30 Jun 1926 Rites 30 Jun 1926
W. P. Davis, J. P.

C. H. MOONEYHAM to Mrs. Della COPE Issued 1 Jun 1926 Rites 1 Jul 1926
J. Paul Slayden, M. G.

Charlie JONES to Zula WARREN Issued 2 Jul 1926 Rites 2 Jul 1926
J. B. Dobbs, J. P.

Hobart EARLS to Nannie ROACH Issued 3 Jul 1926 Rites 3 Jul 1926
J. B. Dobbs, J. P.

McKinley JONES to Lona TURNER Issued 3 Jul 1926 Rites 9 Jul 1926
L. F. Daugherty, M. G.

D. L. RAMSEY,Jr. to Dorthy SIMPSON Issued 3 Jul 1926 Returned -.Not Solemnized

Charles JENNINGS to Maude BROUDON Issued 3 Jul 1926 Rites 3 Jul 1926
J. B. Dobbs, J. P.

E. L. MOFFITT to Anna NELSON Issued 5 Jul 1926 Rites 5 Jul 1926
J. B. Dobbs, J. P.

Homer DRIVER to Martha BAIN Issued 8 Jul 1926 Rites 8 Jul 1926
J. B. Dobbs, J. P.

M. B. LOCKE to Gertrude LAWS Issued 12 Jul 1926 Rites 12 Jul 1926
J.B. Dobbs, J. P.

Harry TAYLOR (Col) to Annia Mai RAMSEY Issued 17 Jul 1926 Rites 18 Jul 1926
J. S. NAnce, M. G.

Paul McBRIDE to Marie PERRIGEN Issued 17 Jul 1926 Rites 17 Jul 1926
W. P. Davis, J.P.

Millard HOBBS to Pearl ROGERS Issued 17 Jul 1926 Rites 18 Jul 1926
W. H. Byles, J. P.

HArvey WILSON to Rosa PELHAM Issued 17 Jul 1926 Rites 20 Jul 1926
W. H. Byles, J.|P.

Joe COLLINS to Alberta MAYO Issued 19 Jul 1926 Rites 19 Jul 1926
ChaS. T. Powell

Willie HICKS to Pearl CUTTS Issued 21 Jul 1926 Rites 21 Jul 1926
W. P. Davis, J. P.

W. E. MITCHELL to Virgie MAi BOREN Issued 22 Jul 1922 Rites 22 Jul 1926
L. F. DAugherty, M. G.

T. H. HARRISON, Jr. to Alyne R. NESBIT Issued 23 Jul 1926 Rites 23 Jul 1926
R. S. Tinnon, M. G.

Louie McBRIDE to Sophia Mai HERMAN Issued 23 Jul 1926 Rites 23 Jul 1926
O. H. Wood, J. P.

Horace CLENDENEN to Levesta LANKFORD Issued 24 Jul 1926 Rites 28 Jul 1926
E. L. Moffitt, J. P.

Jim SIMONS to Frankie COPPINGER Issued 24 Jul 1926 Rites 24 Jul 1926
J. W. Cooley, JM. G.

Byron CLENDENEN (Col) to Therly BLACK (Col) Issued 27 Jul 1926 Rites 2 Aug 1926
N. J. H. Van Meter, M. G.

Otis JONES to Olis MITCHELL Issued 31 Jul 1926 Rites 1 Aug 1926
J. B. Dobbs, J. P.

Seth Thos. WILLIAMS to Seawillow DENTON Issued 1 Aug 1926 Rites 1 Aug 1926
F. M. Dowell, M. G.

Thurman MARTIN to Mattie LEE DURHAM Issued 6 Aug 1926 Rites 8 Aug 1926
L. C. Lane, J. P.

Lawrence SMITH (Col) to Maye HILL (Col) issued 7 Aug 1926 Not Returned

John Bethel MAGNESS to Frances LOWRY Issued 9 Aug 1926 Rites 14 Aug 1926
A. J. Davis

Arsil ARGO to Ora FULTS Issued 1 Aug 1926 Rites 13 Aug 1926
J. L. Barnes, J. P.

Wiley GRIBBLE to Mai SIMMONS Issued 12 Aug 1926 Rites 15 Aug 1926
L. C. Lane, J. P.

Willard C. WHITTENBURG to Callie Pearson Issued 12 Aug 1926 Returned - Not Solemnize

Arthur Weir CROUCH to Druella STUBBLEFIELD Issued 13 Aug 1926 Rites 14 Aug 1926
Alvin Davis

Ernest PEPPER to MArgie KENNEDY Issued 14 Aug 1926   Returned - Not Solemnized

Elijah McGEE to Minnie JONES Issued 14 Aug 1926 Rites 18 Aug 1926
W. C. Whitlock, J. P.

C. F. EVANS to Dela UPCHURCH Issued 17 Aug 1926 Rites 17 Aug 1926
F. L. Leeper, M. G.

Alvah HILL to Catherine KING Issued 18 Aug 1926 Rites 18 Aug 1926
John T. Lewis

Shelah HARDING to Eula MASSEY Issued 19 Aug 1926 Rites 28 Aug 1926
W. T. Warren, J. P.

Oscar MEDLEY to Alina SHERRELL Issued 19 Aug 1926 Rites 22 Aug 1926
A. Z. Holder, J. P.

James C. STUBBLEFIELD to Addie JACOBS Issued 21 Aug 1926 Rites 22 Aug 1922
O. H. Lane

Clarence TILLETT to Winnie DARNELL Issued 21 Aug 1926 Rites 22 Aug 1926
O. H. Lane

George GREEN to RAchel NEAL Issued 21 Aug 1926 Rites 22 Aug 1926
L. P. SAnders, J. P.

L. P. LOONEY to Lola JONES Issued 23 Aug 1926 Rites 23 Aug 1926
W. P. Davis, J. P.

John H. DAVIS to Mary Lou DAVIS Issued 28 Aug 1926 Rites 29 Aug 1926
J. L. Smith, J. P.

W.A. GRISWOLD to Thelma Osborne SNIPES Issued 28 Aug 1926 Rites 28 Aug 1926
Alvis J. DAvis

Everett ROMANS to Bethsadie SMITH Issued 30 Aug 1926 Rites 30 Aug 1926
E. D. Martin, M. G.

Dallas CARRICK to Nittie LANCE Issued 31 Aug 1926 Rites 5 Sep 1926
J. N. Winnett, J. P.

Sam DARNELL to Jessie CRIM Issued 4 Sep 1926 Rites 4 Sep 1926
W. P. Davis, J. P.

Vester SCOTT (Col) to Ive Belle HILL (Col) Issued 7 Sep 1926 Rites 7 Sep 1926
J. S. Nance, M. G.

Joe RIGSBY to Beatrice FOSTER Issued 7 Sep 1926 Rites 9 Sep 1926
W. T. Warren, J. P.

Chas. Edmond FOSTER to Ettie Bell GREEN Issued 7 Sep 1926 Rites 9 Sep 1926
(Name chabge-court order 10/26/63)   J. S. Templeton, M. G.

RAlph DAVENPORT to Ora Lee SUMMERS Issued 9 Sep 1926 Rites 10 Sep 1926
H. J. Wilson, J. P.

Roy CARTWRIGHT to Irene MYERS Issued 10 Sep 1926 Rites 11 Sep 1926
I. P. McGregor, J. P.

Charles BYRD to Blanche COPE Issued 11 Sep 1926 Rites 11 Sep 1926
W. P. Davis, J. P.

Charles NEAL to Risha ESKEW Issued 11 Sep 1926 Rites 12 Sep 1926
L. P. Sanders, J. P.

J. C. McGIBONEY to Leotra HARTT Issued 11 Sep 1926 Rites 12 Sep 1926
W. V. D. Miller, J. P.

C. D. BRADY to Edith TURNER Issued 11 Sep 1926 Rites 11 Sep 1926
W. T. Warren, J. P.

J. B. LOCKE to Mourning C. BETCHEL Issued 11 Sep 1926 Rites 11 Sep 1926
Frank R. Davis, Jdg.

Chas. H. SMITH, Jr. to Mary U. GRISSOM Issued 14 Sep 1926 rites 19 Sep 1926
Chas. Hillis, J. P.

Furman RIVERS (col) to Jennie REED (Col) Issued 17 Sep 1926 Rites 17 Sep 1926
J. T. J. T. Potillo (?)

Asa BYARS to Ella HUDGINS Issued 18 Sep 1926 Rites 19 Sep 1926
J. L. Smith, J. P.

Warren HARRISON to Hattie Lee JOHNSON Issued 22 Sep 1926 Rites 22 Sep 1926
A. B. Moffitt, M. G.

Harold THURMAN to Lena SMITH Issued 25 Sep 1926 Rites 25 Sep 1926
J. B. Dobbs, J. P.

Robert CATES to Nora McGREGOR Issued 25 Sep 1926 Rites 25 Sept 1926
J. B. Dobbs, J. P.

Homer WOOD to Minda TURNER Issued 25 Sep 1926 Rites 25 Sep 1926
P. Turner, J. P.

T. L. NORTHCUTT to Georgia May REYNOLDS Issued 1 Oct 1926 Rites 1 Oct 1926
O. H. Wood, J. P.

S. H. BYARS to F. Z. GREEN Issued 4 Oct 1926 Rites 4 Oct 1926
J. E. Clark, M. G.

Herman ROGERS to Velma McCORKLE Issued 8 Oct 1926 Rites 9 Oct 1926
J. Paul Slayden, M. G.

Sam BRADY to Magnolia PURSER Issued 10 Oct 1926 Rites 10 Oct 1926
P. Turner, J. P.

George SPARKMAN to Mandie WRIGHT Issued 11 Oct 1926 Rites 12 Oct 1926
L. F. Daugherty, M. G.

Alton TURNEY to Maggie St. JOHN Issued 18 Oct 1926 Rites 18 Oct 1926
J. N. Winnett, J. P.

Curtis ADCOCK to ROsa FLANDERS Issued 23 Oct 1926 Rites 24 Oct 1926
P. G. moore, J. P.

Smith WALLING (Col) to Josephine McKINLEY (Col) Issued 23 Oct 1926 Rites 24 Oct
F. L. Kirby, J. P.

Anderson MAYO to Clora EMBERTON Issued 25 Oct 1926 Rites 25 Oct 1926
F. L. Leeper, M. G.

Roy SIMMONS to Bonnie HIGGINS Issued 26 Oct 1926 Rites 27 Oct 1926
A. Z. Holder, J. P.

Alfred STEMBRIDGE to Linnie KIRBY Issued 27 Oct 1926 Rites 31 Oct 1926
A. Z. Holder, J. P.

B. G. GOWAN to Ruby RIEVES Issued 29 Oct 1926 Rites 30 Oct 1926
J. B. Dobbs, J. P.

C. L. SIMMONS to Carl PATTERSON Issued 30 Oct 1926 Rites 31 Oct 1926
W. P. Davis, J. P.

R. O. PATTERSON to Queen BATES Issued 31 Oct 1926 Returned - Not Solemnized

Henry JORDAN to Evon BROCK Issued 5 Nov 1926 Rites 5 nov 1926
J. B. Dobbs, J. P.

William SCOTT to CLORA REEDER Issued 6 Nov 1926 Rites 6 Nov 1926
W. P. Davis, J. P.

Henry WARD to Clara LOWRY Issued 6 Nov 1926 Rites 6 Nov 1926
Ernest Ricj, M. G.

James W. GENTRY to Dorothy West DEWS Issued 8 Dec 1926 Rites 9 Dec 1926
Bruce L. Lyle, M. G.

J. A. BOWDOIN to Zona PARSLEY Issued 10 Dec 1926 Rites 10 Dec 1926
F. L. Leeper, M. G.

John E. BRASHER to Pauline Elua GREEN Issued 11 Dec 1926 Rites 11 Dec 1926
R. D. DAvis

R. O. PATTERSON to Queen BATES Issued 11 Dec 1926 Rites 11 Dec 1926
Isaac Grizzle, J. P.

Robie SCHROCK to Thelma MARTIN Issued 14 Dec 1926 Rites 14 Dec 1926
J. B. DObbs, J. P.

James WOODS to Mattie REDMON Issued 18 Dec 1926 Rites 18 Dec 1926
Isaac Grizzle, J. P.

W. N. CATHCART to Parthenia MILLER Issued 18 dec 1926   Not Returned

Ellis MOORE to Allie WOODLEE Issued 18 Dec 1926   Not Returned

Marion WILLIAMS to Goudie HUDSON Issued 19 dec 1926 Rites19 Dec 1926
J. Paul Slayden, M. G.

J. J. CANTRELL to Clara Mai HODGE Issued 22 dec 1926 Rites 24 dec 1926
J. E. Clark, M. G.

Joe H. TALLEY to Eliza Audie BLAIR Issued 22 Dec 1926 Rites 26 Dec 1926
Ernest Rich

Ezra BARNES to Ora Lee WILSON Issued 22 Dec 1926 Rites 1 Jan 1927
O. H. Wood, J. P.

Charles ROBERTS to Clara MAi GREEN Issued 23 Dec 1026 Rites 23 dec 1926
J. E. Clark, M. G.

Walter SIMONS to Anna LAWSON Issued 23 dec 1926 Rites 25 Dec 1926
W. V. D. Miller, J. P.

T. L. IIILLIS to Wardie BESS Issued 23 Dec 1926 Rites 25 dec 1926
J. T. Casey, M. G.

Hershel MEADOWS to Lottie McGEE Issued 23 dec 1926 Rites 23 dec 1926
W. P. Davis, J. P.

Eugene MARTIN to Helena PATTERSON Issued 24 dec 1926 Rites 24 dec 1926
W. P. Davis, J. P.

Sam SCOTT to Martha Lou BOTTOMS Issued 24 dec 1926 Rites 25 dec 1926
I. P. McGregor, J. P.

Mason McFERRIN to Rilla DAVENPORT issued 24 dec 1926 Rites 24 dec 1926
J. B. Dobbs, J. P.

Bill DRAKE to Odell WINDHAM Issued 24 dec 1926 Rites 25 dec 1926
E. R. Little, M. G.

S. E. SMITTIE to Laura Ruth GIBBS issued 11 Nov 1926 Rites 11 Nov 1926
Thos. J. Wagner, M. G.

Tom DUNCAN to Frances LAWS Issued 3 Nov 1926 rites 13 Nov 1926
J. B. Dobbs, J. P.

Aubry WANNAMAKER to Malissa SMARTT Issued 13 Nov 1926 Rites 14 Nov 1926
P. N. Moffitt, J. P.

Robert ISBEL (Col) to Mary COPE (Col) Issued 15 Nov 1926 Rites 13 Nov 1926
W. F. Bolton, M. G.

Henry HILL (Col) to Nora MARTIN (Col) Issued 18 Nov 1926 Rites 20 Nov 1926
E. S. Bedford, M. G.

William BOLES to Nobia MAYFIELD Issued 19 nov 1926 Rites 19 Nov 1926
J. B. Dobbs, J. P.

Clarence SIMMONS to Beulah HALE Issued 23 Nov 1926 Rites 28 Nov 1926
Irving Patton,. J. P.

R. O. DENTON to Grace BUTCHER Issued 23 Nov 1926 Rites 25 Nov 1926
R. S. Tinnon, M. G.

Richard MURRY to Lydia Pottie MOFFITT Issued 23 Nov 1926 rites 24 Nov 1926
F. L. Leeper, M. G.

Landy Davis RAMSEY to Maxine PAGE issued 24 Nov 1926 rites 25 Nov 1926
Alvis. J, Davis

Leonard BETCHEL to Alma McGEE Issued 27 Nov 1926 Rites 27 Nov 1926
W. P. Davis, J. P.

Elda SCOTT to Nellie Gray CLENDENEN Issued 27 Nov 1926 Rites 28 nov 1926
P. N. Moffitt, J. P.

Irvin BOTTOMS to Hazel CHASTAIN Issued 27 Nov 1926 Rites 28 Nov 1926
I. P. McGregor, J. P.

Richard SPURLOCK (Col) to Mariah WEBB (Col) Issued 27 Nov 1926 Rites 28 Nov 1926
E. S. Bedford, M. G.

Omer REYNOLDS to Lavisa STOTTS Issued 29 Nov 1926 Rites 29 nov 1926
J. L. Barnes, J. P.

John McCORMICK to Melvina DULANEY Issued 2 dec 1926 Rites 5 Dec 1926
Irving Patton, J. P.

Jesse HUTSON to Maye RAMSEY issued 3 Dec 1926 Rites 3 Dec 1926
W. P. Davis, J. P.

Valta BUTCHER to Elsie LAWSON Issued 4 dec 1926 Rites 4 Dec 1926
R. D. Davis, M. G.

W. L. BURCH to Lula HELEN Issued 4 Dec 1926 Rites 7 Dec 1926
A. B. Moffitt, M. G.

louis GREEN to Julia Va. WHITE Issued 25 Dec 1926 Not Returned

Merrel EITER (Col) to Mart MARTIN (Col) Issued 25 Dec 1926 Rites 25 Dec 1926
N. J. H. VanMeter, M. G.

Forrest B. CORLEY to Eliz. Dale WILSON Issued 27 Dec 1926 Rites 27 Dec 1926
D. Edgar Allen

I. N. TENPENNY to Mabel GRIBBLE Issued 27 Dec 1926 Rites 27 Dec 1926
Llewellyn T. LAWRENCE, M. G.

C. E. COLE to Virgin George JULIAN Issued 31 Dec 1926 Rites 1 JAN !(&
D. Edgar Allen

Arnold HOBBS to Mattie HICKS Issued 1 Jan 1927 Rites 2 Jan 1927
I. N. Smoot, J. P.

Finis SMITH to Lillie MILSTEAD Issued 15 Jab 1927 Rites 16 Jan 1927
J. L. Barnes, J. P.

C. C. LANE to Estelle MAYNARD Issued 15 Jan 1927 Rites 15 Jan 1927
J. L. Smith, J.P.

Hunter HUDSON to Ellen PAGE Issued 15 Jan 1927 Rites 16 Jan 1927
E. R. Little, M. G.

Elmer GROVES to Florence PRIEST Issued 22 JAn 1927 Not Returned

Frank ROLLER to Flora GRIBBLE Issued 22 Jan 1927 Rites 23 JAn 1927
E. R. Little, M. G.

Lennie BRATTEN to Lena HENDRICKS Issued 22 Jan 1927 Rites 23 Jan 1927
W. P. Davis, J. P.

Lester McBRIDE to Enzie HILLIS Issued 22 JAn 1927 Rites 22 Jan 1927
J. B. Dobbs, J. P.

Morris W. WOMACK to Margarette CROUCH Issued 28 JAn 1927 Rites 5 Feb 1928
Alvis J. Davis, M. G.

Moe GOLDBERG to Nell SAUNDERS Issued 7 Feb 1927 Rites 7 Feb 1927
W. P. Davis, J. P.

Harold ROGERS to Sarah ADCOCK Issued 10 Feb 1927 Rites 10 Feb 1927
J. B. Dobbs, J. P.

Hense STUBBLEFIELD to Josephine DAVIS Issued 10 Feb 1927 Rites 12 Feb 1927
Alvis J. Davis, M. G.

Jesse Walling ADAMSON to Annie LAura WARREN Issued 12 Feb 1927 Rites 12 Feb
J. Paul Slayden, M. G.

B. F. KELLEY to Susa STUBBLEFIELD Issued 12 Feb 1927 Rites 12 Feb 1927
W. P. Davis, J. P.

Clyde BOULDIN to Ida PERRY Issued 18 Feb 9127 Rites 20 Feb 1927
N. M. Hill, J. P.

Robert DAMRON to Brownie L. ADCOCK Issued 19 Feb 1927 Rites 20 Feb 1927
J. Paul Slayden, M. G.

Charles SIMMONS to Louise YORK Issued 19 Feb 1927 Rites 20 Feb 1927
W. V. D. Miller, J. P.

Clarence HOLT to Mary DENNIS Issued 19 Feb 1927 Rites 20 Feb 1927
R. O. WomaCK, J. P.

Will LIGGETT (Col) to Elvin ESKRIDGE (Col) Issued 17 Feb 1927 Rites 19 Feb 1927
Bruce L. Lyles, M. G.

Cornie DUTTON to Julia BURCH Issued 21 Feb 1927 Rites 22 Feb 1927
P. G. Brasier, J. P.

W. M. WEBB to Bertha HOLDER Issued 22 Feb 1927 Rites 23 Feb 1927
J. W. Cooley, M. G.

Polk ELDER to Beulah TURNER Rites 24 Feb 1927
I. N. Smoot, J. P.

I. C. MITNER to Jesse THAXTON Issued 26 Feb 1927 Rites 26 Feb 1927
L.L. Lawrence, M. G.

Wm. G. DENTON to Louise F. PEPPER Issued 26 Feb 1927 Rites 27 Feb 1927
D. Edgar Allen

Howard McCORMICK to Alta GRISSOM Issued 4 Mar 1927 Rites 6 Mar 1927
J. L. Barnes, J. P.

Anthony BAIN to Minnie RIGSBY issued 11 MAr 1927 Rites 11 Mar 1927
Frank R. Davis, Jdg.

Morton RAMSEY (Col) to Anna B. SPURLOCK (Col) Issued 11 Mar 1927 Rites 12 Mar 1927
W. P. DAvis, J. P.

George BARNES to Pauline SAVAGE Issued 12 May 1927 Rites 12 Mar 1927
P. N. Moffitt, J. P.

Bennie DAVIS to Maggie PINEGAR Issued 12 Mar 1927 Rites 15 Mar 1927
E. D. McBride, M. G.

Charles BROCK to Audrey Bell DONEY Issued 1 Mar 1927 Rites 12 Mar 1927
I. N. Smoot, J. P.

Joe MITCHELL to Hattie CANTRELL Issued 12 Mar 1927 Rites 13 Mar 1927
J. B. Dobbs, J. P.

Dean WHITMAN to Clara Lee MUNCEY Issued 10 Mar 1927 Rites 12 Mar 1927
(Name Change - Court order 6/18/69)   J. B. Dobbs, J. P.

Toy PITMAN to Hassie HANKINS Issued 19 Mar 1927 Rites 4 Apr 1927
W. V. D. Miller, J. P.

Hayden McCORMICK to MAry POPE issued 19 Mar 1927 Rites 4 Apr 1927
W. V. D. Millier, J. P.

F. M. SIMMONS to Bettie DELANEY Issued 26 Mar 1927 Rites 27 Mar 1927
Irving Patton, J. P.

Cleveland TAYLOR to Irene CURTIS Issued 22 Apr 1927 rites 24 Apr 1927
N. M. Hill, J. P.

Dennie McCORMICK to Sallie REED Issued 23 Apr 1927 Rites 23 Apr 1927
A. B. Moffitt, M. G.

Thurman CRISP (Col) to Erlina REYNOLDS (Col) Issued 25 Apr 1927 Rites 25 Apr
J. B. Dobbs, J. P.

W. S. LANCE to H. W. GRIFFITH Issued 29 Apr 1927 Rites 1 May 1927
A. Z. Holder, J. P.

A. C. HOLLAND to Clara Belle DUNCAN Issued 29 Apr 1927 Rites 30 Apr 1927
W. P. Davis, J. P.

Jim TODD to Lou ADAMS Issued 29 Apr 1927 Rites 30 Apr 1927
A. Z. Holder, J. P.

J. E. BOREN to Leta STILES Issued 30 Apr 1927 Rites 1 May 1927
E. R. Little, M. G.

R. L. McMAHAN to Gladys EDGE Issued 30 Apr 1927 Rites 1 May 1927
P. Turner, J. P.

George HALE to MAi OWENS Issued 2 May 1927 Rites 2 May 1927
V. D. Lusk, J. P.

C. L. GLENN to Lamon ADCOCK Issued 3 May 1927 Rites 4 May 1927
P. G. Moore, J. P.

Lively COPE to PAuline CANTRELL Issued 5 MAy 1927 Rites 8 May 1927
L. F. Daugherty, M. G.

T. T. SHAW (Col) to Vera M. LEAGUE (Col) Issued 6 May 1927 Rites 6 May 1927
W. P. Davis, J. P.

Oscar N. GRIBBLE to Dee Ida STOTTS Issued 6 May 1927 Rites 7 May 1927
J. Paul Slayden, M. G.

Willie PINEGAR to Nola Lee YOUNG Issued 7 May 1927 Rites 8 May 1927
Irving Patton, J. P.

J. T. HICKS to Lillie F. MATTHEWS Issued 7 MAy 1927 Rites 8 May 1927
R. D. DAvis, M. G.

Joe D. YOUNG to Jessie MAi WINNETT Issued 7 MAy 1927 Rites 8 May 1927
A. Z. Holder, J. P.

Martin COOLEY to Bettie FARLESS Issued 14 May 1927 Rites 14 May 1927
D. Edgar Allen

Dorsie LUTRELL to Beulah WARREN Issued 14 May 1927 Rites 14 May 1927
W. P. DAvis, J. P.

G. H. WIMBERLY to Sarah WALKER Issued 19 May 1927 Rites 19 May 1927
B. F. Killian

Robert B. POTTER to Margaret Allen TRAIL Issued 26 MAr 1927 Rites 26 Mar 1927
J. Paul Slayden, M. G.

Eston HATFIELD to Nettie Fern GOODWIN Issued 29 Mar 1927 Not Returned
Chas. T. Powell

Claudie WOODS to Katie MULLIGAN Issued 2 Apr 1927 Rites 3 Apr 1927
N. M. Hill, J. P.

Brentley WALKER to Maggie PANTER Issued 2 Apr 1927 Rites 3 Apr 1927
N. M. Hill, J. P.

Buford WOODLEE to Bertha BYRD Issued 2 Apr 1927 Rites 2 Apr 1927
J. Paul Slayden, M. G.

Robert HERNDON to Flora McCORMICK Issued 2 Apr 1927 Rites 3 Apr 1927
J. N. Winnett, J. P.

James DODD to Sylvia DAVENPORT Issued 3 Apr 1927 Rites 3 Apr 1927
W. P. DAvis, J. P.

Robert ROBINSON to Elizabeth OWENS Issued 6 Apr 1927 Rites 6 Apr 1927
I. G. Gribble, J. P.

Sterling WILSON to JAnie Mai PERRY Issued 7 Apr 1927 rites 16 apr 1927
J. N. Winnett, J. P.

Denton BARNES to MAry E. MOORE Issued 9 Apr 1927 Rites 9 Apr 1927
J. B. Dobbs, J. P.

Will ODELL to Muude RUTLEDGE Issued 9 Apr 1927 Rites 9 Apr 1927
J. E. Clark, M. G.

Walter FIELDS to Bessie TEMPLETON Issued 11 Apr 1927 rites 11 Apr 1927
J. E. Clark, M. G.

Bright OVERALL to Minnie BRATTEN Issued 15 Apr 1927 Rites 17 Apr 1927
J. N. Winnett, J. P.

SAm KING (Col) to Hattie Bell FAULKNER (Col) Issued 15 Apr 1927 Rites 16 feb
W. F. Bolton, M. G.

Reece ROBERTS to Berta SLATTON Issued 15 Apr 1927 Returned - Not Solemnized

L. L. ROSE to Martha Louise CARTER Issued 15 Apr 1927 rites 17 apr 1927
J. Paul Slayden, M. G.

Floyd McCOLLUM to Ollie ROBERTS Issued 16 Apr 1927 rites 17 Apr 1927
J. B. Dobbs, J. P.

S. H. BYARS to F. Z. GREEN Issued 19 Apr 1927 rites 19 Apr 1927
Irving PAtton, J. P.

Albert ELROD to Lucille DURHAM Issued 19 Apr 1927 Rites 24 Apr 1927
J. B. Dobbs, J. P.

Edgar BAIN to Jimmie NEWBY Issued 20 Apr 1927 Rites 21 apr 1927
W. P. Davis, J. P.

Edison Cox to Sallie ROGERS Issued 20 May 1927 Rites 22 May 1927
    W. H. Byles, J. P.

Edward CLENDENEN to Willie Mai PANTER issued 21 May 1927 Rites 24 May 1927
    J. L. Barnes, J. P.

W. E. SULLIVAN to Bessie BURCH Issued 21 May 1927 Rites 22 May 1927
    L. B. Moffitt, J. P.

P. R. BARTHOLOMEW to Eunice Lucille COPE Issued 22 May 1927 Rites 22 May 1927
    J. B. Dobbs, J. P.

Ray BRATTEN to Virginia STILES Issued 29 May 1927 Rites 30 May 1927
    D. Edgar Allen

Walter WOMACK to Thelma FISHER issued 31 May 1927 Rites 31 May 1927
    W. V. D. Miller, J. P.

Luther BROYLES to Pearl YOUNGBLOOD Issued 4 Jun 1927 Rites 5 Jun 1927
    J. W. Cooley, M. G.

Norman BEAN to Myrtle JUDD Issue 4 Jun 1927 Rites 5 Jun 1927
    L. T. Lawrence, M. G.

Roy HARDING to Nannie MILLER Issued 7 Jun 1927 Rites 12 JUN 1927
    Chas. T. Powell

Thurman M. WHITLOCK to Francis P. KELL Issued 11 Jun 1927 Rites 11 Jun 1927
    J. B. Dobbs, J. P.

Hugh GRAYSON (Col) to Catherine MARBERRY (Col) Issued 18 Jun 1927 Rites 18 Jun 1927
    Frank B. Davis, Jdg.

George HARPER to Lorena HOLT Issued 18 Jun 1927 Rites 18 Jun 1927
    W. P. Davis, J. P.

George H. JONES to Lou HENNESSEE issued 18 Jun 1927 Rites 18 Jun 1927
    J. E. Clark, M. G.

Walter Ray BRAGG to Louise M. POTTER Issued 23 Jun 1927 Rites 24 Jun 1927
    S. C. Sewell, M. G.

A. J. CRIM to Myrtle McBRIDE Issued 2 Aug 1927 Rites 4 Aug 1927
    D. P. Myers, J. P.

James ANDERSON to June PELHAM Issued 2 Aug 1927 Rites 2 Aug 1927.
    John Morton, M. G.

Ollie McGEE to Lela BAIN Issued 25 Jun 1925 Rites 3 Jul 1927
    J. N. Winnett, J. P.

Shelia PRATER to Lola Mai GOINS Issued 25 Jun 1927 Rites 25 Jun 1927
    W. P. DAvis, J. P.

John Newton HOOVER to Susie Grey MARLER Issued 29 Jun 1927 Rites 29 Jun 1927
    C. M. Oullias, M. G.

Bill MELTON to Daisy May STAGGS Issued 29 Jun 1927 Rites 29 Jun 1927
    J. B. Dobbs, J. P.

Bethel MULLICAN to VAndaley NORROD Issued 29 Jun 1927 Rites 29 Jun 1927
    J. B. Dobbs, J. P.

George R. WILSON to Mattie E. NEFF Issued 30 Jun 1927 Rites 5 Jun 1927
    C. G.Howell

Frank CASKEY to Dovie Pearl WALLACE Issued 2 Jul 1927 Rites 2 Jul 1927
    W. P. Davis, J. P.

Ernest HARRIS to Bertha BUSEY Issued 2 Jul 1927 Rites 3 Jul 1927
    J. N. Winnett, J. P.

Charlie ROGERS to Johnnie Mai BICKFORD Issued 2 Jul 1927 Rites 30 Jul 1927
    Irving Patton, J. P.

Ernest McBRIDE to Ella SCOTT Issued 2 Jul 1927 Rites 4 Jul 1927
    W. B. Snipes, M. G.

Richard HARRIS (Col) to Howard HUNTER (Col) Issued 2 Jul 1927 Rites 2 Jul 1927
    W. F. Bolton, M. G.

Homer DICKSON to Hassie NUNLEY Issued 4 Jul 1927 Rites 4 Jul 1927
    Irving Patton, J. P.

Eugene H. JACOBS to Odetta FULTS Issued 5 Jul 1927 Rites 9 Jul 1927
    Alvis J. Davis, M. G.

J. M. BROWN to Nonie WHEELING Issued 6 Jul 1927 Rites 10 Jul 1927
    W. H. Craven, M. G.

Thomas LEFTRICK (Col) to Louise MARTIN (Col) Issued 9 Jul 1927 Rites 18 Jul 1927
    W. F. Bolton, M. G.

Enoch BAIN to Delma ROMANS Issued 11 Jul 1927 Rites 16 Jul 1926
    J. L. Smith, J. P.

Troy VAUGHN to Audrey V. JONES Issued 14 Jul 1927 Rites 15 Jul 1927
    Irving Patton, J. P.

Hilary PARKER to Clara GILLEY Issued 15 Jul 1927 Rites 17 Jul 1927
    G. W. Baxter, M. G.

C. H. MARR to Lyda MOON Issued 15 Jul 1927 Rirtes 16 Jul 1927
    Irving Patton, J. P.

W. C. RANDOLPH to Josie EVANS Issued 16 Jul 1927 Rites 16 Jul 1927
    W. P. Davis, J. P.

Harrison BONNER (Col) to Francis MARTIN (Col) Issued 16 Jul 1927 Rites 16 Jul
    N. J. H. VanMeter, M. G.

John FISHER to Venna SPARKMAN Issued 18 Jun 1927 Rites 18 jul 1927
    Irving Patton, J. P.

(Page 244 missed in numbering)

BArton WARE to Beatrice GREEN Issued 19 Aug 1927 Rites 19 Aug 1927
Frank P. DAvis, Jdg.

C. P. HERRIMAN to Eppie MULLINS Issued 20 Aug 1927 Rites 21 Aug 1927
E. F. Cunningham, J. P.

Dexter NEAL to Hannah ADCOCK Issued 20 Aug 1927 Rites 8 Sep 1927
R. D. Davis

Frank L. PATRICK to Lilliam TURNER Issued 20 Jul 1927 Rites 23 Jul 1927
F. L. Leeper, M. G.

J. M. FISHER to Josie SANDERS Issued 26 Aug 1927 Rites 28 Aug 1927
J. B. Dobbs, J. P.

Haskell SAVAGE (Col) to Clara Lee BEAN (Col) Issued 27 Aug 1927 Rites 27 Aug
N. J. H. VanMeter, M. G.

W. B. BREWER to Hassie HERNDON Issued 31 Aug 1927 Rites 3 Sep 1927
D. Edgar Allen

R. E. KIMBOL to Laura TOLIVER Issued31 Aug 1927 Rites 4 Sep 1927
E. F. Cunningham, J. P.

Kenneth SLATTON to Violet McCOY Issued 1 Sep 1927 Rites 3 sep 1927
Irving Patton, J. P.

HArshel FAULKNER (Col) to Jennie L. LOOPER (Col) Issued 2 Sep 1927 Rites 2 Sep
W. F. Bolton, M. G.

Charles BROWN to Jessie STUBBLEFIELD Issued 3 Sep 1927 Rites 4 Sep 1927
Alvis DAvis, M. G.

J.A. ROLLER to Bessie Lou CANTRELL Issued3 Sep 1927 Rites 4 Sep 1927
E. R. Little, M. G.

F. Z. POTTER to MAggie WALKER issued 6 Sep 1927 Rites 7 Sep 1927
J. E. SAnders, J. P.

B. L. TURNER to Virgia NEWBY Issued 6 Sep 1927 Rites 6 Sep 1927
W. H. Byles, J. P.

Ace DAVIS to Hassie SMITH issued 6 Sep 1927 Rites 8 Sep 1927
W. P. Davis, J. P.

Robert WINDSOR to KAte JOHNSON Issued 8 Sep 1927 Rites 9 Sep 1927
J. Paul Slayden, M. G.

Frank PRESTON to Velma ELKINS Issued 9 Sep 1927 Rites 9 Sep 1927
J. B. Dobbs, J. P.

Joseph TAYLOR to Maud FULTS Issued 10 Sep 1927 Rites 10 Sep 1927
W. P. Davis, J. P.

Ernest HUSSEY to Naomi P. CANTRELL Issued 10 Sep 1927 Rites 11 Sep 1927
L. T. Lawrence, M. G.

M. F. JOHNSON to Sibbie J. VAUGHN Issued 16 Sep 1927 Rites 17 Sep 1927
E. Potter, M. G.

Jim B. CLARK to Cora BESS Issued 20 Jul 1927 Rites 20 Jul 1927
Fate Walker, J. P.

Firm LUSK to Mamie BEASLEY Issued 23 Jul 1927 Rites 24 Jul 1927
Chas. Hillis, J. P.

Medford PRATER to Oda BROYLES Issued 23 Jul 1927 Rites 24 Jul 1927
J. N. Winnett, J. P.

Dalton LAWRENCE to Mabel DUKE Issued 27 Jul 1927 Rites 28 jul 1927
J. N. Winnett, J. P.

Walter BRYSON to Hallie Mai DONNELL Issued 29 Jul 1927 Rites 30 Jul 1927
J. B. Dobbs, J. P.

Oscar JOHNSON to Bertha MARTIN Issued 29 Jul 1927 Rites 29 Jul 1927
W. P. DAvis, J. P.

Hoover DAVIS to Capola EARLS Issued 30 jul 1927 Rites 30 jul 1927
J. N. Winnett, J. P.

Jeese DAVENPORT to Lucy BARRETT Issued 1 Aug 1927 Rites 3 Aug 1927
E. A, Rich, M. G.

Elbert RIGSBY to Willie HUTCHINGS Issued 2 Aug 1927 Rites 2 Aug 1927
Frank R. Davis, Jdg.

JAmes B. BROWN to Mary BONNER Issued 2 Aug 1927 Rites 9 Sep 1927
E. L. Moffitt, J. P.

Gus MASON (Col) to Julia WHITE (Col) Issued 4 Aug 1927 Rites 4 Aug 1927
J. T. Potillo, P. C.

Marvin TALLEY to Jeannett ROACH Issued 4 Aug 1927 Rites 6 Aug 1927
W. H. Craven, M. G.

H. C. COPE (Col) to Bessie BILES (Col) Issued 4 Aug 1927 Rites 4 Aug 1927
J. B. Dobbs, J. P.

Owen TURNER to Mattie SMITH Issued 4 Aug 1927 Rites 5 Aug 1927
R. Turner, M. G.

Robert GARDNER to Avo GROVES Issued 8 Aug 1927 Rites 8 Aug 1927
D. P. Myers, J. P.

Sam STEMBRIDGE to Bertie DELONG Issued 12 Aug 1927 Rites 13 Aug 1927
I. G. Gribble, J. P.

Robert CLEMONS to Lucille DELONG Issued 13 Aug 1927 Rites 13 Aug 1927
I. G. Gribble, J, P.

Orval HUTCHENS to Cleo BLANKENSHIP Issued 15 Aug 1927 Rites 16 Aug 1927
J. L. Smith, J. P.

GArrett COPE (Col) to Jessie P. RAMSEY (Col) Issued 17 Aug 1927 Rites 27 Aug
W. F. Potter, M. G.

Staley ROBINSON to Gladys JORDAN Issued 18 Aug 1927 Rites 18 Aug 1927
W. E. Higginbotham

Will THOMAS (Col) to Lela NORTHCUTT (Col) Issued 20 Sep 1927 Rites 20 Sep 1927
W. I. Hunt

John I. LYLES to Velma PATTERSON Issued 24 Sep 1927 Rites 24 Sep 1927
W.F.Presley

(John LORISTER) John P. KOERTZ to Georgia WOODS Issued 24 Sep 1927 Rites 25 Sep
(Court change from Lorister to Koertz - 8/25/43) D. Edgar Allen

Arthur SHOWERS to Mildred PELHAM Issued 24 Sep 1927 rites 28 Sep 1927
W. P. Davis, J. P.

Orah WOMACK to Dora MASTERS Issued 1 Oct 1927 Rites 2 Oct 1927
R. W. Smartt, Jdg.

Murray T. DRAKE to Linnie MOORE Issued q Oct 1927 Rites 3 Oct 1927
F. L. Leeper, M. G.

Frank Kell to Grace KELLEY Issued 1 Oct 1927 Rites 2 Oct 1927
F. L. Leeper, M. G.

E. M. DUNLAP to Lillie SHERRELL Issued 1 Oct 1927 Rites 2 Oct 1927
W. V. Miller, J,. P.

Jesse SCOTT to Bertha MILLER Issued 8 Oct 1927 Rites 9 Oct 1927
J. N. Winnett, J. P.

Morris LENTZ to Mary Lou DOAK Issued 14 Oct 1927 Rites 14 Oct 1927
L. T. Lawrence, M. G.

Walter B. HAMMER to Jessie M. HARDING Issued 15 Oct 1927 Rites 15 Oct 1927
E. E. Grandey

J. C. MYERS to Irene BLANKS Issued 15 Oct 1927 Rites 16 Oct 1927
D. Edgar Allen

Wesley COLE to Bessie Mai McCORMICK Issued 17 Oct 1927 Rites 18 Oct 1927
J. E. Clark, M. G.

JAke FAULKNER (Col) to Ora ELMONE (Col) Issued 19 Oct 1927 Rites 19 Oct 1927
E. S. Bedford, M. G.

Toy CANTRELL to Virginia RIGGS Issued 20 Oct 1927 Rites 20 Oct 1927
W. H. Craven

A. P. ADCOCK to Mrs. Allean GREEN Issued 21 Oct 1927 Rites 22 Oct 1927
L. F. Daugherty, M. G.

George BURCH to Annie Mai FERRELL Issued 22 Oct 1927 Rites 23 Oct 1927
W. H. Craven

Horace ARGO to Maggie JENNINGS Issued 22 Oct 1927 Rites 22 Oct 1927
J. A. Cunningham

Newton RAINS to Mattie YOUNGBLOOD Issued 22 Oct 1927 Rites 27 Oct 1927
E. F. Cunningham

Almon PARSLEY to Pauline JONES Issued 25 Oct 1927 Rites 25 Oct 1927
F. L. Leeper, M. G.

H. P. WOMACK to MAry M. MOFFITT Issued 25 Oct 1927 Rites 1 Nov 1927
J. Paul Slayden, M. G.

Elbert L. ROWLAND to Flora Belle GREEN Issued 28 Oct 1927 Rites 29 Oct 1927
J. Paul Slayden, M. G,.

George CUNNINGHAM to Millie MYERS Issued 5 Nov 1927 Rites 6 Nov 1927
J. L. Barnes, J. P.

Arthur O. GLENN to Nannie Lee GREEN Issued 5 Nov 1927 Rites 5 Nov 1927
J. Paul Slayden, M. G.

Homer DENNIS to CAllie L. HILL Issued 10 Nov 1927 Rites 12 Nov 1927
W. C. Whitlock, J. P.

C. A. GLENN to Vera JONES Issued 10 Nov 1927 Rites 13 Nov 1927
L. F. Daugherty, M. G.

Pink DAVIS to Angie GREEN Issued 12 Nov 1927 Rites 13 Nov 1927
L. C. LAne, J. P.

Murphy DRAKE to Mrs. Hattie GLENN Issued 12 Nov 1927 Rites 12 Nov 1927
W. P. DAvis, J. P.

Ewin SPARKMAN to Mildred TALLEY Issued12 Nov 1927 Rites 12 Nov 1927
J. E. Clark, M. G.

Robert L. ANDERSON to Margaretta BROWN Issued 12 Nov 1927 Rites 12 Nov 1927
J. Paul Slayden, M. G.

Wallace McREYNOLDS (Col) to Rhoda GRAYSON (Col) Issued 13 Nov 1927 Rites 13 Nov
E. F. Carter

Isham J. PERRY to Edna Lee DODSON Issued 14 Nov 1927 Rites 14 Nov 1927
L. B. Moffitt

Heborn LANCE to Ruth SIMONS Issued 19 Nov 1927 Rites 19 Nov 1927
J. N. Winnett, J. P.

J. B. FULTS to Barbra CAMPBELL Issued 22 Nov 1927 Rites 23 Nov 1927
W. H. Byles, J. P.

Robert BARNES to Clara ROBERTS Issued 30 Nov 1927 Rites 15 Dec 1927
E. L. Moffitt, J. P.

Thurman DODSON to Emma FARLESS Issued 10 Dec 1927 Rites 10 Dec 1927
J. B. Dobbs, J. P.

W. Y. ROBINSON to Robbie PARKER Issued 10 Dec 1927 Rites 10 Dec 1927
W. P. DAvis, J. P.

Tim LOCKE (Col) to Cora SOLOMON (Col) Issued 11 Dec 1927 rites 11 Dec 1927
W. P. DAvis, J. P.

Paul PHIFER to Alma SPARKMAN Issued 15 Dec 1927 Rites 15 Dec 1927
D. P. Myers, J. P.

Jasper LYNN to Bernice TOSH Issued 16 Dec 1927 Rites 17 Dec 1927
W. H. Byles, J. P.

Alton TEMPLETON to Thelma BRANCH Issued 17 Dec 1927 Rites 18 Dec 1918
Irving Patton, J.

Greenie WILLIAMS to May VANDERPOOL Issued 17 Dec 1927 rites 25 Dec 1927
I. H. Gribble, J. P.

CAsto HARGIS to Rebecca BRATTEN (?) Issued 17 Dec 1927 Rites 25 Dec 1927
J. N. Winnett, J. P.

Jim DONNELL to Lucy WARE Issued 17 Dec 1927 Rites 24 Dec 1927
J. B. Dobbs, J. P.

H. S. FUSTON to Nellie MCDOWELL Issued 19 Dec 1927 Rites 25 Dec 1927
P. Turner, J. P.

JAmes PAINE to Eunice G. PARSONS Issued 20 Dec 1927 Rites 20 Dec 1927
W. V.D. Miller, J. P.

Waletr PARKHURST to Alta TAFT issued 20 Dec 1927 Rites 24 Dec 1927
W. T. WArren, J. P.

Lanis WOMACK to Hester PATTON Issued 20 Dec 1927 Rites 25 Dec 1927
L. F. Daugherty, M. G.

Lester DODSON to Irene MOONEYHAM Issued 21 Dec 1927 Rites 27 Dec 1927
D. Edgar Allen

Foster B. SHOCKLEY (Col) to Avo E. LUSK (Col) Issued 21 Dec 1927 Rites 21 Dec
H. E. Erwin, M. G.

William KIRNEY (Col) to Audrey BROWN (Col) Issued 22 Dec 1927 Not Returned

Will GRAVLSON (Col) to Gertrude THOMPSON (Col) Issued 22 Dec 1927 Not Returned

Jack RUST to Josie PATTERSON Issued 22 Dec 1927 Rites 25 Dec 1927
Bruce L. Lyle

Ira ANDERSON to Dellys McVEY Issued 22 Dec 1927 Rites 25 Dec 1927
Bruce L. Lyles

Noah COPPINGER to HAllie GRIFFIE Issued 22 Dec 1927 Rites 24 Dec 1927
A. Z. Holder, J. P.

Heo. Haywood HOLDER to Martha B. LANCE Ixssued 24 Dec 1927 Rites 25 Dec 1927
J. N. Winnett, J. P.

J. A. CRAIN to Lula TALLEY issued 24 Dec 1927 Rites 24 Dec 1927
J. B. Dobbs, J. P.

Frank D. BOSSON to Josie Gazaway NEWBY Issued 24 Dec 1927 Rites 25 Dec 1927
Irving Patton, J. P.

Shelia TUBBS to Ethel PERRY Issued 24 Dec 1927 Rites 25 Dec 1927
J. N. Winnett, J. P.

Wm. R. TATE, Jr. to Maria Lou HUTCHINS Issued 29 Dec '927 Rites 31 Dec 1927
J. Paul Slayden, M. G.

Andy HILLIS to Minnie Lee BOTTOMS Issued 29 Dec 1927 Rites 25 Dec 1927
W. P. Davis, J. P.

Mark W. MINOR to Lida Ruth BRADLEY Issued 31 Dec 1927 Rites 31 Dec 1927
D. Edgar Allen, J.

Frank HENEGAR to Lola MELTON Issued 31 Dec 1927 Rites 1 JAn 1928
P. Turner, J. P.

Marcus CLENDENEN to Reta CHAMBERS Issued 31 Dec 1927 rites 31 Dec 1927
I. P. McGregor, J. P.

James THOMAS to Susie Mai SMARTT issued 31 Dec 1927 Rites 1 JAN 1928
W. E. Garner, M. G.

Earl G. GILBERT to Bessie GREEN Issued 3 Jan 1928 Rites 3 JAn 1928
W. P. davis. J. P.

Willia ELAM (Col) to Bessie COPE (Col) Issued 3 Jan 1928 Rites 3 JAn 1928
E. F. Carter

581 Marriages in this book

Book 16 - Warren County Marriages - Jan 7 , 1928 to June 29 , 1929

Ova CLENDENON to Lassie COPPINGER Issued 7 JAn 1928   Returned - Not Solemnized

Paul HASTON to Octa ROACH Issued 7 Jan 1928 Rites 8 Jan 1928
W. B. Snipes, M. G.

Walterson EMERSON to Dora Mai NEWBY Issued 7 Jan 1928 Rites 8 Jan 1928
J. B. Dobbs, J. P.

JAmes Hillis HUNTER to Mary Margarette McCOY Issued 9 JAn 1928 Rites 10 JAn
J. PAul Slayden, M, G.

Tom COUCH to Cleo CUNNINGHAM Issued 11 JAn 1928 Rites 11 Jan 1928
J. B. Dobbs, J. P.

James SMITH to Ona BYARS Issued 14 JAn 1928 Rites 14 JIn 1928
J. L. BArnes, J. P.

George MARTIN (Col) to Stella SAVAGE (Col) Issued 14 Jan 1928 Rites 14 JAn
W. F. Bolton, M. G.

Henry PAGE to Wilsie CROWNOVER Issued 14 Jan 1928 Rites 14 JAn 1928
J. B. Dobbs, J. P.

Roy PHIFER to Eunice BARNETT Issued 14 Jan 1928 Rites 14 Jan 1928
W. V. D. Miller, J. P.

John B. GOLDEN to Della RANDOLPH Issued 16 Jan 1928 Rites 16 JAn 1928
J. B. Dobbs, J. P.

George WOOLARD to Myrtle WOOLARD Issued 20 JAn 1928 Rites 20 Jan 1928
Stokley Etter, J. P.

Robert L. DAVENPORT to Dixie PARKER Issued 21 JAn 1928 Rites 22 JAn 1928
W. P. Davis, J. P.

J. R. JONES to Nellie MOFFITT Issued 21 Jan 1928 Rites 22 Jan 1928
J. E. Witt, M. G.

C. H. COPE to JAne Tubb BUTLER Issued 24 JAn 1928 Rites 25 JAn 1928
D. Edgar Allen

Floyd McGREGOR to Artie BLOOMBERG Issued 27 JAn 1928 Rites 29 Jan 1928
J. W. Cooley, M. G.

Charles BROWN to Jessie THOMPSON Issued 3 Feb 1928 Returned - Not Solemnized

Lee SPARKMAN to Pheoba TALLEY Issued 4 Feb 1928   Not Returned

JAmes T. DAVIS to Lula RANKHORN Issued 6 Feb 1928 Rites 8 Feb 1928
J. L. Smith, J. P.

William SCOTT to Gladys JONES Issued 7 Feb 1928 Rites 8 Feb 1928
J. T. Casey, M. G.

Marshall SCOTT to Flora BOULDEN Issued 11 Feb 1928   Returned - Not Solemnized

J. B. KEATHLEY to Ollie Mai BRATCHER Issued 11 Feb 1928 Rites 12 Feb 1928
J. B. Gribble, M. G.

C. L. MAIDWELL to Charity GREEN Issued 11 Feb 1928 Rites 12 Feb 1928
N. M. Hill, J. P.

Qwin GILBERT to Otela GRISSOM Issued 11 Feb 1928 Rites 11 Feb 1928
J. B. Dobbs, J. P.

Gentry ALLEN to Jewell GOLDEN Issued 14 Feb 1928 Rites 14 Feb 1928
I. G. Gribble, J. P.

Herbert WILSON to Sarah BOULDIN Issued 18 Feb 1928 Rites 18 Feb 1928
J. B. Dobbs, J. P.

Freeman EVANS (Col) to Beatrice STUBBLEFIELD (C) Issued 18 Feb 1928
Rites 20 Feb 1928 H. E. Erwin, M. G.

John WOOD to Lila ELROD Issued 19 Feb 1928 Rites 19 Feb 1928
W. P. Davis, J. P.

H. L. TANNER to MAry Lee HENNESSEE Issued 20 Feb 1928 Rites 20 Feb 1928
F. L. Leeper, M. G.

Roy GROSS to Bessie GAMBLE Issued 20 Feb 1928 Rites 20 Feb 1928
L. T. Lawrence, M. G.

McKinley WILSON to CArrie Lee NEWBY Issued 24 Feb 1928 Rites 26 Feb 1928
J. B. Dobbs, J. P.

J. F. SPURLOCK (C) to Clara BELL RAMSEY (C) Issued 25 Feb 1928 Rites 25 Feb 1928
W. P. DAvis, J. P.

JAmes GRAYSON (C) to Virginia MARBERRY (C) Issued 26 Feb 1928 Rites 26 Feb 1928
E. F. Carter, M. G.

Isaac ANDERSON to Irene McBRIDE Issued 3 MAr 1928 Rites 3 Mar 1928
Claud Myers, M. G.

Roy YOUNG to Beatrice WALKER Issued 3 Mar 1928 Rites 17 MAr 1928
J. N. Winnett, J. P.

Terry HOOVER to Joe Francis HARPOLE Issued 12 Mar 1928   Returned - Not Solemnized

Walter ARGO to Hallie BONNER Issued 16 MAr 1928 Rites 18 Mar 1928
O. H. Wood, J. P.

James WILSON to Sallie TAYLOR Issued 16 MAr 1928 Rites 18 MAr 1928
J. T. Casey, M. G.

H. P. HULAN to Ruby ALLEN issued 16 MAt 1928 Rites 16 Mar 1928
J. L. Smith, J. P.

Charles SCOTT to Nannie MYERS Issued 17 Mar 1928 Rites 18 Mar 1928
J. Paul Slayden, M. G.

Will BURDEN (C) to Margie MARTIN (C) Issued 21 Mar 1928 Rites 21 mar 1928
H. E. Erwin, M. G.

Albert CROUCH to Hattie JONES Issued 22 Mar 1928 Rites 22 Mar 1928
G. P. Brasier, J. P.

William J. HAGWOOD to Bessie HOLT Issued 23 Mar 1928 Rites 24 Mar 1928 J. B. Dobbs, J. P.

Cloy MOODY to Mary E. KERR Issued 23 Mar 1928 Rites 25 Mar 1928 Irving Patton, J. P.

Truman RAMSEY (C) to Dora LOCKE (C) Issued 24 Mar 1928 Riets 24 Mar 1928 W. P. Davis, J. P.

Delbert CANTRELL to Cora MILLER Issued 31 Mar 1928 Rites 1 Apr 1928 J. B. Dobbs, J. P.

Huel MOORE to Lila Mai GREER Issued 31 Mar 1928 Rites 31 Mar 1928 W. P. Davis, J. P.

Leborn STEWART to Nannie Lee BRATCHER Issued 4 Apr 1928 Rites 4 Apr 1928 J. N. Winnett, J. P.

Sandy RHODES (C) to Ellen BLACK (C) Issued 9 Apr 1928 Rites 9 Apr 1928 E. S. Bedford, M. G.

Leonard THROWER (C) to Ina NORTHCUTT (C) Issued 16 Apr 1928 rites 16 apr 1928 A. J. Davis

Calud JONES to Ida TRAMBLE Issued 16 Apr 1928 Rites 17 Apr 1928 A. Z. Holder, J. P.

Venous DODSON to Lucy Emma ROSE Issued 18 Apr 1928 Rites 18 Apr 1928 Irving Patton, J. P.

J. Q. CLARK to Lydia SIMS Issued 21 Apr 1928 Rites 22 Apr 1928 Irving Patton, J. P

J. W. ROGERS to Jennie SMITH Issued 21 Apr 1928 Rites 5 May 1928 VAn McGee

Lewis ROBERTS to Tiny BOULDIN issued 28 Apr 1928 Rites 28 Apr 1928 E. L.Moffitt, J. P.

G. R. McGREGOR to Ollie Mai COLE Issued 2 MAy 1928 rites 2 May 1928 FAte Walker, J. P.

Homer MAXWELL to Loretta CROWE Issued 5 May 1928 Rites 5 May 1928 D. Edgar Allen

J. E. TINDLE to Minnie ODELL Issued 12 May 1928 Rites 12 Mar 1928 J. E. Clark, M. G.

Huston HAYES to Grady RICHMOND Issued 12 May 1928 Rites 12 MAy 1928 Bruce L. Lyles

Arthur STEPHENS to Octa GRIFFITH Issued 12 May 1928 Rites 7 May 1928 I. G. Gribble, J. P.

Tommie ROMANS to Carrie SMITH issued 12 MAy 1928 Rites 16 May 1928 J. E. Sanders, J. P.

Leland WALLER to Velma HOOVER Issued 17 May 1928 Rites 18 May 1928 Claud Myers, M. G.

Raymond ARGO to Ruby TASH Issued 18 May 1928 Rites 20 May 1928 O. H. Wood, J. P.

Bobby DICKEY (C) to Willie LEFTRIK (C) Issued 19 May 1928 Rites 19 May 1928 W. F. Bolton, M. G.

CArson NEWBY to Jennie TUCKER Issued 26 May 1928 Rites 2 Jun 1928 Chas. T. Powell

Cecil HANLEY to Anna FRAZIER Issued 26 May 1928 Rites 26 May 1928 J. B. Dobbs, J. P.

Ernest ROBERTS to Wavie HASH (DRAKE) Issued 2 Jun 1928 Rites 2 Jun 1928 D. P. Myers, J. P.

Jesse C. HILLIS to CAtherine BUTLER isseud 2 Jun 1928 Rites 2 Jun 1928 J. B. Dobbs, J. P.

Albert DICKSON Mottie Lee STARKEY Issued 26 May 1928 Rites 27 May 1928 J. B. Dobbs, J. P.

Ed EVANS (C) to Beulah BELL (C) Issued 2 Jun 1928 Rites 3 Jun 1928 E. F. Carter, M. G.

Clarence E. MULTOG to Avis (EVANS) CROWE Issued 2 Jun 1928 Rites 3 Jun 1928 D. Edgar ALLEN

L. D. MARTIN to MAry BLANKS Issued 6 Jun 1928 Rites 6 Jun 1928 J. B. Dobbs, J. P.

Herbert ROBERTS to Maggie ROMANS Issued 9 Jun 1928 Rites 9 Jun 1928 L. C. Lane, J. P.

Herbert PASSONS to Vassie MAi DAVIS Issued 7 Jun 1928 Rites 10 Jun 1928 J. N.,Winnett, U. P.

Everett PITMAN to Mary BAKER Issued 9 Jun 1928 Rites 10 Jun 1928 W. V. D. Miller, J. P.

Qurley MYERS to Christine MUNCEY Issued 14 Jun 1928 Rites 17 Jun 1928 J. B. Dobbs, J. P.

Risden D. DeFORD to CAtherine D. ELKINS Issued 15 Jun 1928 Rites 16 Jun 1928 L. T. Lawrence, M. G.

Joe BELL to Helen BENNETT Issued 16 Jun 1928 Rites 23 Jun 1928 J. B. Dobbs, J. P.

Hugh GIBBS to Lillie DENTIS Issued 19 Jun 1928 Rites 23 Jun 1928 J. B. Dobbs, J. P.

Jess GILBERT to Effie JONES Issued 19 Jun 1928 Rites 19 Jun 1928 J. B. Dobbs

Suell SMARTT to Linsey RHEAY Issued 21 Jun 1928 Rites 21 Jun 1928
P. N. Moffitt, J. P.

Phocion WRIGHT to Mary Lee PRIEST Issued 21 Jun 1928 Rites 21 jun 1928
Frank R. Davis, Jdg.

B. T. GROVE to Jeffie Marie ROGERS Issued 21 Jun 1928 Rites 21 jun 1928
D, Edgar Allen

Charley TEMPLETON to Earn BREEDLOVE Issued 22 Jun 1928 Rites 23 jun 1928
L. C. Lane, J. P.

Herman TAYLOR to Inez MASON Issued 24 Jun 1928 Rites 24 Jun 1928
J. Paul Slayden, M. G.

Lyell COTTON to Maggie L. DELONG Issued 27 Jun 1928 Rites 27 Jun 1928
W. P. Davis, J. P.

Walter RAY to Ocie RAY Issued 29 Jun 1928 Rites 29 Jun 1928
J. L. BArnes, J. P.

RAymond MULLINS to Carrie AUSTIN Issued 30 Jun 1928 Rites 39 Jun 1928
O. H.Wood, J. P.

Willie COPPINGER to Amy STONER Issued 2 Jul 1928 Rites 4 Jul 1928
E. D. Martin, M. G.

JOHN ENGLAND to Jewell SAYLORS Issued 3 Jul 1928 Rites 3 Jul 1928
J. T. Casey, J. P.

Rhea BROYLES to Lula BRADLEY issued 3 Jul 1928 Rates 3 Jul 1928
J. T. Casey, J. P.

George HUSSEY to Cora SILLOWAY Issued 7 Jul 1928 Rites 7 Jul 1928.
L. T. Lawrence, M. G.

JamesCOFFEE (C) to MArtha LEE (C) Issued 16 Jul 1928 Rites 16 Jul 1928
W. F. Bolton, M. G.

Joe LEE (G) to MArgaret SAVAGE (C) Issued 19 Jun 1928 Rites 19 Jun 1928
E. S. Bedford, M. G.

H. H. LANCE to PAuline CHISAM Issued 20 Jul 1928 Rites 20 Jul 1928
J. N. Winnett, J. P.

CAntrell MILLS to Mottie R. NORRIS Issued 21 Jul 1928 Rites 22 Jul 1928
Irving PAtton, J. P.

Ben RHEA to Gertrude HOBBS Issued 21 Jul 1928 Rites 21 Jul 1928
J. L. Barnes, J. P.

Harlam STUBBLEFIELD to Opal BOYD Issued 21 Jul 1928 Rites 21 Jul 1928
W. P. Davis, J.P.

Von MARTIN (C) to Mazel SPURLOCK (C) Rites 21 Jul 1928 Rites 21 jul 1928
W. P. DAvis, J. P.

Thurman BAKER to Enzie McCOY Issued 21 Jul 1928 Rites 22 Jul 1928
D. P. Myers, J. P.

Millard PADGETT to Dovie YOUNG Issued 21 Jul 1928 Rites 29 Jul 1928
L. B. Moffitt, J. P.

E. L. BATEY to MAbel MULLINAX issued 24 Jul 1928 Rites 24 Jul 1928
J. B. Dobbs, J. P.

Robert A. (BOB) Byars to Jessie PHELPS issued 25 Jul 1928 Rites 30 Jul 1928
F. L. Leeper, M. G.

Denton FULTS to Christine SCOTT Issued 30 Jul 1928 Rites 31 Jul 1928
J. R. STUBBLEFIELD, M. G.

John R. COX to MAggie BASHAM Issued 31 Jul 1928 Rites 4 Aug 1928
Stokley Eter, J. P.

Colonel BROYLES to Hester ROBERTS Issued 2 Aug 1928 Rites 2 Aug 1928
J. E. Sanders, J. P.

E. C. LOFTIS to Clara L. SULLENS Issued 2 Aug 1928 Rites 2 Aug 1928
W. T. WARren, J. P.

Brown CROUCH, Jr. to Jimmie Lee PRATER Issued 2 Aug 1928 Rites 3 Aug 1928
G.R. Briggs, J. P.

Charles NUNLEY to Eunice BRADY Issued 2 Aug 1928 Rites 2 Aug 1928
W. H. Byles, J. P.

Eugene RHEA to Emma RHEA Issued 3 Aug 1928 Rites 3 Aug 1928
J. L. Barnes, J. P.

Kelton BOULDIN to Grace MAi MOORE issued 4 Aug 1928 Rites 4 Aug 1928
J. B. Dobbs, J. P.

G. L. OWENS to Mai EARLS Issued 4 Aug 1928 Rites 4 Aug 1928
J. B. Dobbs, J. P.

Ira DULANEY to Flora LOCKE Issued 4 Aug 1928 Rites 5 Aug 1928
W. V. D. Miller, J. P.

M. B. MITCHELL to MAbel VICKERS Issued 6 Aug 1928 Rites 7 Aug 1928
W. H. Craven, M. G.

Estol DENTON to Alma CRAVEN Issued 7 Aug 1928 Rites 11 Aug 1928
J. W. Cooley, M. G.

Jimmie BYARS to Lina SMITH Issued 8 Aug 1928 Rites 8 Aug 1928
W. P. DAvis, J. P.

Audly PANTER to Etta NUNLEY Issued 9 Aug 1928 Rites 10 Aug 1928
J. L. Barnes, J. P.

Cecil CHRISTIAN to Nora Mai McGREGOR Issued 9 Aug 1928 Rites 9 Aug 1928
W. H. Craven, M. G.

Hubert GWYN to May Bell NORTHCUTT Issued 10 Aug 1928 Rites 12 Aug 1928
Alvis J. DAvis, M. G.

Grady H. WOMACK to Magdoline JUDKINS Issued 12 Aug 1928 Rites 12 Aug 1928
J. Paul Slayden, M. G.

Ernie McGLOTHEN to Prilla JOHNSON Issued 17 Aug 1928 Rites 17 Aug 1928
N. M. Hill, J. P.

PArker WOODLEE to Willie WOODLEE Issued 17 Aug 1928 Rites 19 Aug 1928
J. L. BArnes, J. P.

Wayne HILLIS to Jessie CARROLL Issued18 Aug 1928 Rites 22 Aug 1928
B. F. Killian

C. C. CARDWELL to Alice GROVE Issued 22 Aug 1928 Rites 26 Aug 1928
L. T. LAwrence, M. G.

Tom GRAHAM to Sadie MORTON Issued 22 Aug 1928 Rites 22 Aug 1928
John Morton, M. G.

lloyd TURNER to Quxie NEWBY Issued 25 Aug 1928 Rites 26 Aug 1928
W. T. Warren, J. P.

James LOOPER (C) to Mammie MARTIN (C) Issued 25 Aug 1928 Rites 31 Aug 1928
D. P. Myers, J. P.

Joseph B. PEPPER to Margarette SPANGLER Issued 25 Aug 1928 Not Returned

Nelia FISK (C) to Alta MARTIN (C) Issued 26 Aug 1928 Rites 26 Aug 1928
W. V. D. Miller, J. P.

Tim M. HANEY to Clara B. TILLER Isseud 27 Aug 1928 Rites 27 Aug 1928
P. G. Moore, J. P.

L. M. CANTRELL to MArie WOMACK Issued 29 Aug 1928 Rites 29 Aug 1928
E. D. Martin, M. G.

Henry HARGIS to Estelle TITTLE Issued 1 Sep 1928 Rites 2 Sep 1928
Bruce L. Lyle

DAllas ROBINSON to Jim NEWBY Issued 3 Sep 1928 Rites 3 Sep 1928
A. Z. Holder, J. P.

E. C. BUMBALOUGH to Maggie MOONEYHAM Issued 4 Sep 1928 Rites 4 Sep 1928
W. R. Thurman, M. G.

Seamon PRIEST to Osia HOBBS Issued 8 Sep 9182 Rites 9 Sep 1928
Reece H. Rogers, M. G.

Charles CANTRELL to Willie RAy STILES Issued 8 Sep 1928 Rites 8 Sep 1928
J. Paul Slayden, M. G.

W. C. WAGGONER to Una B. SAFRIET Issued 10 Sep 1928 Rites 10 Sep 1928
L. T. LAwrence, . M. G.

Willie JOE THROWER to Mabel Christian FUSTON Issued 14 Sep 1928 Rites 14 Sep 1928
Bruce L. Lyle

Earl TURNER to Willie E. HURT Issued 14 Sep 1928 Rites 15 Sep 1928
I. N. Smoot, J. P.

Charles WHITE (CO) to Novella BILES (C) Issued 15 Sep 1928 Rites 15 Sep 1928
J. B. Dobbs, J. P.

Johnnie DUTTON to Losta CRAVEN Issued 15 Sep 1928 Rites 15 Sep 15 1928
O. H. Wood, J. P.

Robert WATTS to Delzell KIRBY Issued 15 Sep 1928 Rites 15 Sep 1928
E. R. Little, M. G.

Charles OLIVER to Jessie Lucille COOK Issued 17 Sep 1928 Rites 17 Sep 1928
Bruce L. Lyle, M. G.

W. F. McCORMACK to Sophia AUSTIN Issued 18 Sep 1928 Rites 23 sep 1928
J. L. Walker, J. P.

Arch FULTS to Cora PICKETT Issued 22 Sep 1928 Rites 22 Sep 1928
J. L. BARNES, J. P.

Alton STEVENS to Lydia WOMACK Issued 22 Sep 1928 Rites 23 Sep 1928
I. G. Gribble, J. P.

J. N. LEWIS to Belle DOAK Issued 22 Sep 1928 Rites 24 Sep 1928
J. E. Sanders, J. P.

Lee HUSSEY to Mary D. CANTRELL Issued 27 Sep 1928 Rites 27 Sep 1928
L. T. Lawrence, M. G.

Vernon PICKETT to Lassie TAYLOR Issued29 Sep 1928 Rites 29 Sep 1928
E. L. Moffitt, J. P.

John T. SPARKMAN to Cora COPE Issued 29 Sep 1928 Rites 30 Sep 1928
W. V. D. Miller, J. P.

J. M. DURHAM to Laura BURKETT Issued 29 Sep 1928 Rites 30 Sep 1928
Bruce L. LYle

Barton SMITH to Louise WOMACK Issued 2 Oct 1928 Rites 6 Oct 1928
L. T. Lawrence, M. G.

Charels LORANCE to Estelle SUMMERS Issued 3 Oct 1928 Rites 4 Oct 1928
Bruce L. Lyles

Allen SMITH to Mina Belle BESS Issued 4 Oct 1928 Rites 4 Oct 1928
VAn McGee

Thou (?) JUDKINS to Estie WOODS Issued 5 Oct 1928 Rites 7 Oct 1928
J. N. Winnett, J. P.

J. G. HALEY to MAry E. SHIELDS Issued 6 Oct 1928 Rites 1 Nov 1928
E. F. Cunningham, J. P.

George H. NEWMAN to Susie STILES Issued 6 Oct 1928 Rites 7 Oct 1928
J. Paul Slayden, M. G.

Draydon DUGGIN to Clara Bell McNABB Issued 10 Oct 1928 Rites 11 Oct 1928
J. T. Lawrence, M. G.

Monrow Gist GREEN to LAura LOCKE Issued 12 Oct 1928 Rites 12 Oct 1928
J. B. Dobbs, J. P.

Zollie COTTON to Susie FISHER Issued 13 Oct 1928 Rites 13 Oct 1928
J. Paul Slayden, M. G.

J. R. STILES to Clisty BRIGHT Issued 13 Oct 1928 Rites 14 Oct 1928
E. R. Little, M. G.

Sutton Smoot to Lucille RAYBURN Issued 13 Oct 1928 Rites 14 Oct 1928
E. R. Little, M. G.

John W. CAMPBELL to Ada FERRELL Issued 22 Oct 1928 Rites 28 Oct 1928
J. R. BAiley, M. G.

Col C. JONES to Clara BROWN Issued 27 Oct 1928 Rites 28 Oct 1928
J. N. Winnett, J. P.

Henry SCOTT (C) to Bettie Lou HUGGENS (C) Issued 28 Oct 1928 Rites 11 Nov 1928
W. P. Davis, J. P.

J. M. CAMPBELL to Beulah CAMPBELL Issued 3 Nov 1928 Rites 11 Nov 1928
J. R. BAiley, M. G.

Clay WOODLEE to Lena SMARTT Rites 3 Nov 1928 Rites 4 Nov 1928
J. L. BArnes, J. P.

Richard Harold WOMACK to Vera Louise SCHROCK Issued 3 Nov 1928 Rites 3 Nov
W. V. D. Miller, J. P.

Thomas HOWARD to LAura CURTIS Issued 5 Nov 1928 Rites 5 Nov 1928
J. E. Witt, M. G.

H. C. WOODLEE to Cleo MILSTEAD Issued 8 Nov 1928 Rites 8 Nov 1928
W. B. Snipes, M. G.

W. H. MAYO to Minnie GRIFFIN Issued 8 Nov 1928 Rites 8 Nov 1928
J. B. Dobbs, J. P.

James Thos. KELL to Arty MAi ATNIP Issued 10 Nov 1928 Rites 8 Nov 1928
J. Paul Slayden, M. G.

J. S. CRAIN to Goldie BONNER Issued 13 Nov 1928 Rites 14 Nov 1928
F. L. Leeper, M. G.

Charles DUNCAN (C) to Bessie GIBBS (C) Issued14 dec 1928 Rites 14 Nov 1928
Frank R. Davis, Jdg,

EARL HUDGINS to Lucille HUSSEY Issued 16 Nov 1928 Rites 17 Nov 1928
L.T.Lawrence, M. G.

Roy Wallace HARRELL to Pearl Rice COLVILLE Issued 16 Nov 1928 Rites 17 Nov 1928
L. T. LAwrence, M. G.

Lee MERCER (C) to Josie MYERS (C) Issued 16 Nov 1928 Rites 17 Nov 1928
J. B. Dobbs, J. P.

Eugene WILLIAMSON to Clydia CRIM Issued 16 Nov 1928 Rites 17 Nov 1928
W. P. Davis, J. P.

George L. BROWN to Mary Emma BRATTON Issued 21 Nov 1928 Rites 21 Nov 1928
L. T. Lawrence, M. G.

Eston CLENDENEN to Ruby CASS Issued 24 Nov 1928 Rites 25 Nov 1928
W. H. Vraven, M. G.

Jesse CARR (C) to MAggie PLEASANT (C) Issued 24 Nov 1928 Rites 24 Nov 1928
D. P. Myers, J. P.

Plato CRABTREE to Velma BEASLEY Issued 24 Nov 1928 Rites 25 Nov 1928
P. A. Kirby, M. G.

John S. ROBERTS to Ione CALDWELL issued 25 Nov 1928 Rites 25 Nov 1928
Bruce L. Lyle, M. G.

Howard SCOTT to Vella McBRIDE Issued 27 Nov 1928 Rites 27 Nov 1928
W. H. Byles, J. P.

George TAYLOR to Letha DELONG Issued 27 Nov 1928 Rites 28 Nov 1928
W. V. D. Miller, J. P.

Powell MEASLES to YAnta VAUGHN issued 29 Nov 1928 Rites 2 Dec 1928
J. E. Clark, M. G.

Thomas MOORE to Lillie Mai WAGONER Issued 30 Nov 1928 Rites 14 Dec 1928
I. G. Gribble, J. P.

Pammle (?) LATHAN to Elizabeth HERWN Issued 1 Dec 1928 Rites 1 Dec 1928
J. B. Dobbs, J. P.

Silas HENNESSEE to Clara TURNER Issued 1 Dec 1928 Rites 2 Dec 1928
J. L Barnes, J.P.

Homer PERRY to Vassie CHRISTIAN Issued 1 Dec 1928 Rites 2 Dce 1928
J. B. Dobbs, J. P.

Milton ACUFF to Pearl CORNWELL Issued 1 Dec 1928 Rites 1 Dec 1928
J. Paul Slayden, M. G.

Albert LEWIS to Afton WILSON Issued 4 Dec 1928 Rites 4 Feb 1929.
J.W. Cooley, M. G.

EArl W. FINGER (C) to MAry E. MORROW (C) Issued 8 Dec 1928 Rites 9 Dec 1928
A. H. Huff, M. G.

Butler GRIBBLE to Bertie JUDKINS Issued 8 Dec 1928 Rites 8 Dec 1928
L. F. DAugherty, M. G.

Wils KNOWLES to Charlie SUMMERS Issued 13 Dec 1928 Rites 13 Dec 1928
J. B. Dobbs, J. P.

Lyman COUCH to Louise RAY Issued 14 Dec 1928 Rites 23 Dec 1928
P. G. Moore, J. P.

R. T. SAMRTT to SAmmie NORTHCUTT Issued 15 Dec 1928 Returned - Not Solemized

Ova CLENDENEN to Lassie COPPINGER Issued 15 Dec 1928 Rites 16 Dec 1928
P. N. Moffitt, J. P.

Noel JOHNSON to Louise TURNER issued 15 Dec 1928 Returned - Not SOLEMNIZED

Carl WALLING to Elizabeth CURTIS Issued 15 Dec 1928 Rites 16 Dec 1928
J. Paul Slayden, M. G.

W. Q. KEATHLEY to Lorinie WILLIAMSON Issued 15 Dec 1928 Rites 16 Dec 1928
L. C. Lane, J. P.

Winton CONASTER to Jessie LEE BAIN Issued 15 Dec 1928 Rites 15 Dec 1928
Van McGee

Almon ROBERTSON to Mae McCORD Issued 17 Dec 1928 Rites 23 Dec 1928
J. N. Winnett, J. P.

Hershell MILLS to Fowler CATES Issued 20 Dec 1928 Rites 22 Dec 1928
E. F. Cunningham, J. P.

Frank M. LESTER to Zola TURNER Issued 21 Dec 1928 Rites 23 Dec 1928
J. Paul Slayden, M. G.

Ollie MILLER (C) to Velva MARTIN (C) Issued 22 Dec 1928 Not Returned

Franklin GLENN to Mary Eliz. WOMACK Issued 22 dec 1928 Rites 25 Dec 1928
P. G. Moore, J. P.

Lee POWELL to Grace KING Issued 22 Dec 1928 Rites 22 Dec 1928
J. B. Dobbs, J. P.

Charles SPARKMAN to Hazel MONTANDON issued 22 Dec 1928 Rites 25 dec 1928
D. P. Myers, J. P.

Willie BArney MAYNARD to Flora BLACK Issued 22 Dec 1928 Rites 22 Dec 1928
J. B. Dobbs, J. P.

F. McLean CUTTS to Neta Crowe BLOUNT Issued 22 Dec 1928 Rites 22 Dec 1928
L. T. Lawrence, M. G.

JAck CUMMINGS to Evelyn GARMON Issued 22 Dec 1928 Rites 23 Dec 1928
J. PAul Slayden, M. G.

Jas. Patterson NEWBY to Rowena HASTON Issued 24 Dec 1928 Rites 25 Dec 1928
J. B. Dobbs, J. P.

Frank L. DODGE to CAroline A. CARLSON Issued 24 Dec 1928 Rites 24 Dec 1928
L. T. Lawrence, M. G.

Wm. Arthur MARTIN to Nannie Lee VANHOOSER Issued 25 Dec 1928 Rites 25 Dec 1928
A. H. Huff, M. G.

J. D. ELROD to Evelyn WOMACK Issued 25 Dec 1928 Rites 25 Dec 1928
J. Paul Slayden, M. G.

Nathan M. MCGHEE to Eula Mai WINTON Issued 26 Dec 1928 Rites 26 Dec 1928
W. E. GArner, M. G.

Alvie BRADFORD (C) to Mary Ann SMITH Issued 27 Dec 1928 Rites 27 Dec 1928
E. S. Bedford, M. G.

Smith DURHAM to Nancy ANDERSON Issued 29 Dec 1928 Rites 29 Dec 1928
Bruce L. Lyle

George YOUNG to Tennie OWENS Issued 29 Dec 1928 Rites Dec 1928
Bruce L. Lyle

Herman HARPER to Anna Lee McBRIDE Issued 29 Dec 1928 Rites 29 Dec 1928
J. L. BArnes, J. P.

Odel FUSTON to Grady TURNER Issued 31 Dec 1928 Rites 31 Dec 1928
I. G. Gribble, J. P.

Wilma C. BEAM to Wilma MARTIN Issued 2 Jan 1929 Rites 2 Jan 1929
D. P. Myers, J. P.

J. D. MORLEY to Mary HASTON Issued 8 Jan 1929 Rites 21 Jan 1929
Irving Patton, J. P.

John GANNON to Hallie BARNES issued 8 Jan 1929 Rites 8 JAn 1929
W. ll. Dyles, J. P.

Charley THURMAN to Ida ADAMSON ISsued 15 Jan 1929 Rites 15 Jan 1929
J. B. Dobbs, J. P.

JAmes JOHNSON to Lizzie MAYES Issued 21 jan 1929 Rites 25 Jan 1929
I. P. McGregor, J. P.

Lester SCOTT to Thelma KILLIAN Issued 26 Jan 1929 Rites 27 Jan 1929
P. N. Moffitt, J. P.

Horace N. PARKS to Mattie Lee McCORMACK Issued 26 Jan 1929 Rites 26 Jan 1929
A. H. Huff, M. G.

Comer ANDERSON to Cleora GARRISON Issued 29 Jan 1929 Rites 29 Jan 1929
Frank R. Davis, JDG.

RAy ASHBURN to Ocie KING Issued 30 JAn 1929 Rites 30 Jan 1929
J. B. Dobbs, J. P.

Newman KEMP to Pearline LYNCH Issued 4 Feb 1929 Rites 4 feb 1929
J. B. Dobbs, J. P.

JAmes FISK (C) to MAry GRAYSON (C) Issued 6 Feb 1929 Rites 7 Feb 9129
D. P. Myers, J. P.

Oscar KELL to Prudie Myrtle PRATER Issued 9 Feb 1929 Rites 10 Feb 1929
J. B. Dobbs, J. P.

Alton SHERRELL to Grace HOLLIS Issued 15 Feb 1929 Rites 17 Feb 1929
E. F. Cunningham, J. P.

Luther DOVE to Aline CANTRELL Issued 19 Feb 1929 Rites 22 Mar 1929
D. P. Myers, J. P.

Bill SMITH to Virgie ELROD Issued 23 Feb 1929 Rites 2 Mar 1929
J. B. Dobbs, J, P.

H.G. MOHONEY to Mary Morse McQUIDDY Issued 28 Feb 1929 Not Returned

Albert YORK (C) to Flora GRAYSON (C) Issued 28 Feb 1929 Rites 1 Mar 1929
D. P. Myers, J. P.

Arthur SIMONS to Rachel DAVENPORT Issued 2 Mar 1929 Rites 2 Mar 1929
J. B. Dobbs, J. P.

Lewis BARLOW to Erma MASON Issued 2 Mar 1929 Rites 17 Mar 1929
J. E. Clark, M. G.

Elvin S. SPANGLER to Lucinda BRYANT Issued 2 Mar 1929 Rites 3 Mar 1929
J. Paul Slayden, M. G.

J. J. HOWARD (CO to Bertha BROWN (C) Issued 2 Mar 1929 Rites 2 Mar 1929
J. R. Gray, M. G.

J. A. KING to Martha J. FULTS Issued 6 Mar 1929 Rites 7 Mar 1929
A. Z. Holder, J. P.

B. L. WALKER to Octa L. BLANKENSHIP Issued 9 Mar 1929 Rites 17 Mar 1929
L. F. Daugherty, M. G.

Harris Clark JACOBS to Nell Irene FULTS Issued 9 Mar 1929 Rites 17 Mar 1929
G. W. Baxter

Benjamin F. BOYD to Phela Louise ROBERSON Issued 29 Mar 1929 Rites 2 Jun 1929
J. Paul Slayden, M. G.

Henry ASKEW to Alice ROLLER Issued 9 Mar 1929 Rites 6 Apr 1929
P. A. Kirby, M. G.

A. C. OAKLEY to Ada CHAPMAN Issued 14 Mar 1929 Rites 17 Mar 1929
I. G. Gribble, J. P.

Elvie SIMMONS to Lucy NUNLEY Issued 15 Mar 1929 Rites 16 Mar 1929
E. F. Cunningham, J. P.

Lester BLUHM to Lulia CALDWELL Issued 15 Mar 1929 Rites 15 Mar 1929
W. P. Davis, J. P.

Eugene YORK (C) to Thola SMARTT Issued 15 Mar 1929 Returned - Not Solemnized

Frank ALLEN to Bonnie HILLIS Issued 16 Mar 1929 Rites 7 Apr 1929
D. P. Myers, J. P.

William MARTIN (C) to Pearlie FOSTER (C) Issued 21 Mar 1929 Rites 21 Mar 1929
E. F. Foster, M. G.

Lemuel WOOD (C) to Jessie Lee FISK (C) Issued 23 Mar 1929 Rites 23 Mar 1929
D. P. Myers, J. P.

Arlie MAYNARD to Bessie SMITH Issued 23 Mar 1929 Rites 7 Apr 1929
J. B. Dobbs, J. P.

Elmore SNIDER to Augusta BURKS Issued 27 Mar 1929 Rites 28 Mar 1929
Fate Walker, J. P.

I. M. DAVIS to Zola FRANKS Issued 28 Mar 1929 Rites 30 Mar 1929
L. F. Daugherty, M. G.

James BREWER to FANNIE BELCHER Issued 27 Mar 1929 Rites 28 Mar 1929
Bruce L. Lyle, M. G.

W. R. ALLISON to Louise THAXTON Issued 3 Apr 1929 Rites 4 Apr 1929
Bruce L. Lyle, M. G.

J. M. TITTSWORTH to Lula ADCOCK Issued 9 Apr 1929 Rites 10 Apr 1929
P. A. Kirby, M. G.

Ira SAFLEY to Alverne RHEINHART Issued 12 Apr 1929 Rites 12 Apr 1929
D. P. Myers, J. P.

Willie ALSUP to HAzel NORTHCUTT Issued 13 Apr 1929 Rites 13 Apr 1929
Frank R. Davis, Jdg.

Robert McCORKLE to Georgia Lee FARLESS Issued 17 Apr 1929 Rites 17 Apr 1929
J. B. Dobbs, J. P.

Emmett GOFF to Bobbie STANLEY Issued 20 Apr 1929 Rites 28 Apr 1929
P. Turner, J. P.

J. R. PHILLIPS to Belle ROWLAND Issued 22 Aug 1929 Rites 22 Apr 1929
J. B. Dobbs, J. P.

Herbert CLINE (C) to Allie BARTLEY (C) Issued 23 Apr 1929 Rites 24 Apr 1929
D. P. Myers, J. P.

F. J. CANTRELL to M. B. LOCKE Issued 24 Apr 1929 Rites 24 Apr 1929
J. Paul Slayden, M. G.

Eugene BILES (C) to Catherine SPURLOCK (C) Isseud 24 Apr 1929 Rites 24 Apr 1929
J. B. Dobbs, J. P.

Fred HALE to Mary AUSTIN Issued 25 Apr 1929 Rites 25 Apr 1929
P. N. Moffitt, J. P.

Arnold BREWER to Frances Marion SCOTT Issued 27 Apr 1929 Rites 28 Apr 1929
Reese H. Rogers, M. G.

L. D. SPARKMAN to Elva PARKER Issued 27 Apr 1929 Rites 5 May 1929
John Clark, M. G.

Eugene NUNLEY to Bettie DIXSON Issued 3 May 1929 Rites 3 May 1929
W. H. Byles, J. P.

George C. TRAIL to Nova Lee REEDER Issued 11 May 1929 Rites 12 May 1929
E. D. Martin, M. G.

Clarence BLANKS to Alice DUTTON Issued 11 May 1929 Rites 11 May 1929
J. B. Dobbs, J. P.

H. Vivian STEWART to Pauline JONES Issued 3 May 1929 Rites 5 May 1929
J. Paul Slayden, M. G.

H. Vivian STEWART to Jessie Mai MOBLEY Issued 4 MAy 1929 Rites 5 May 1929
O. H. Wood, J. P.

Charles PENNINGTON to Martha McGOWAN Issued 8 MAy 1929 Rites 9 May 1929
E. F. Cunningham, J. P.

Tom RAMSEY (c) to Annie MARTIN (C) Issued 11 May 1929 Rites 11 May 1929
W. P. Davis, J. P.

Malcomb R. NEWBY to Dovie PHILLIPS Issued 13 May 1929 Rites 13 May 1929
Frank P. Davis, Jdg.

Dillard JUDKINS to Georgia ROGERS Issued 16 May 1929 Rites 19 May 1929
J. B. Dobbs, J. P.

Robert DAVIS to Vesta FIELDS Issued 17 May 1929   Retuened - Not Solemnized

Murphy DODSON to Mottie HELTON Issued 17 May 1929 Rites 18 May 1929
D. P. Myers, J. P.

Eula AKERS to Grace WEST Issued 18 May 1929 Rites 18 May 1929
A. Z. Holder, J. P.

J. GRIFFITH to Goldie PRATER issued 18 MAy 1929 Rites 18 May 1929
A. Z. Holder, J. P.

Tom MAYFIELD to CharliE ELKINS Issued 23 May 1929 Rites 23 May 1929
J. B. Dobbs, J. P.

W. J. CROSSLIN to Lourine THROWER Issued 23 May 1929 Rites 23 May 1929
A. H. Huff, M. G.

Ben McMAHAN to Pearl DENNIS Issued 25 MAy 1929 Rites 26 May 1929
W. C. Whitlock, J. P.

Clarence HAWKINS to Emma Brown DODD Issued 25 May 1929 Rites 2 Jun 1929
J. N. Winnett, J. P.

William MARTIN to Laura ARGO Issued 25 May 1929 Rites 26 May 1929
O. H. Wood, J. P.

J. E. WALKER to Mary Frances McDEARMAN Issued 26 MAy 1929 Rites 31 May 1929
Bruce L. Lyle, M. G.

Charles PISTOLE to Catherine BLANKS Issued 31 May 1929 Rites 1 Jun 1929
R. S. LAmb, M. G.

R. T. SMARTT to Fay NORTHCUTT Issued 1 Jun 1929 Rites 1 Jun 1929
J. L. Barnes, J. P.

Wm. Alonzo Stewart, Jr. to Ruth Woodward CROWE Issued 1 Jun 1929 Rites 8 Jun 1929
A. H. Huff, M. G.

Ed SPARKMAN to Estelle SPECK Issued 1 Jun 1929 Rites 2 Jun 1929
D. P. Myers, J. P.

Ivory HILLIS to Ivis BAIN Issued 4 Jun 1929 Rites 4 Jun 1929
W. V. D. Miller, J. P.

Willie Lee McKINGHT to Verna WINNETT Issued 5 Jun 1929 Rites 9 Jun 1928
A. Z. Holder, J. P.

Alex Wilson, Jr. to Bessie WALKER issued 6 Jun 1929   Returned - Not Solemnized

Jesse DAVIS to Grace STUBBLEFIELD Issued 8 Jun 1929 Rites 8 Jun 1929
J. B. Dobbs, J. P.

Clyde HUNTER to N. M. MARTIN Issued 8 Jun 1929 Rites 9 Jun 1929
J. R. Gray, M. G.

S. M. FORD to Maggie COUCH Issued 8 Jun 1929 Rites 8 Jun 1929
W. P. Davis, J. P.

V. E. STONER to Beatrice HOBBS Issued 14 Jun 1929 Rites 15 Jun 1929
E. D. Martin, M. G,

Gilbert MADEWELL to Eula LOCKE Issued 14 Jun 1929 Rites 20 Jun 1929
W. V. D. Miller, M. G.

Willie MULLICAN to Inez BARNES Issued 15 June 1929 Rites 20 Jun 1929
P. Turner, J. P.

Dave HALE to Nellie FORD Issued 18 Jun 1929 Rites 18 Jun 1929
D. P. Myers, J. P.

Kermit DODSON to Delma FORD Issued 18 Jun 1929 Rites 18 Jun 1929
D. P. Myers, J. P.

C. R. WOMACK to Sallie Lee CARVER Issued 19 Jun 1929 Rites 19 Jun 1929
J. Petty Ezell, M. G.

Hazel MARBERRY (C) to Frankie May SIMPSON (C) Issued 20 Jun 1929 Rites 23 Jun
R. W. Scott

Hobart GRIFFITH to Nora ELROD Issued 20 Jun 1929 Rites 20 Jun 1929
W. P. Davis, J. P.

Marvin WILSON to Ona FREEZE Issued 21 Jun 1929 Rites 24 Jun 1929
O. H. Wood, J. P.

Gwynn SUMMERS to Jollene SHIRLEY Issued 22 Jun 1929 Rites 23 Jun 1929
E. F. Cunningham, J. P.

JAmes BLANKS to Bernie BREWER Issued 22 Jun 1929 Rites 23 Jun1929
E. F. Cunningham, J. P.

Plummer CRUSE to Lula McCORMICK Issued 24 Jun 1929 Rites 17 Jul 1929
D. P. Myers, J. P.

Charles ROSS to Ova Lee CRAWFORD Issued 28 Jun 1929 Rites 28 Jun 1929
John Morton, M.G.

A. F. MASON to Ruth WELCH Issued 28 Jun 1929 Rites 30 Jun 1928
J. Paul Slayden, M. G.

J. B. LACK to Lucille HICKEY Issued 3 Jul 1929 Rites 3 Jul 1929
                                          J. B. Dobbs, J. P.

Eston COP to Susie REDMOND Issued 6 Jul 1929 Rites 7 Jul 1929
                                          L. F. Daugherty, M. G.

Gilbert W. MILLER to Rubye COPE Issued 8 Jul 1929 Rites 15 Jul 1929
                                          J. Paul Slayden, M. G.

John A. MILUM to Anna Belle MARTIN Issued 13 Jul 1929 Rites 20 Jul 1929
                                          E. D. Martin, M. G.

Ernest HICKEY to Cloie LOONEY Issued 15 Jul 1929 Rites 16 Jul 1929
                                          J. B. Dobbs, J. P.

J. J. HENNESSEE to Georgia NEWMAN Issued 19 Jul 1929 Rites 20 Jul 1929
                                          L. F. Daugherty, M. G.

Will LUNA to Thelma ROGERS Issued 27 Jul 1929 Rites 27 Jun 1929
                                          J. B. Dobbs, J. P.

Beecher CLARK to Myra SAFLEY Issued 30 Jul 1929 Rites 5 Aug 1929
                                          Irving Patton, J. P.

J. B. WATSON to Josie Mai RIGSBY Issued 1 Aug 1929 Rites 2 Aug 1929
                                          John F. Smithson

Eugene HUSSEY to Willie CAMPBELL Issued 3 Aug 1929 Rites 3 Aug 1929
                                          L. T. Lawrence, M. G.

E. M. WISEMAN to Lillian CANTRELL Issued 8 Aug 1929 Rites 8 Aug 1929
                                          F. L. Leeper, M. G.

Walter PARSLEY to Emma JONES Issued 9 Aug 1929 Rites 11 Aug 1929
                                          J. T. CASEY, M. G.

Herman RICHARDSON to Edna SCOTT Issued 14 Aug 1929 Rites 15 Aug 1929
                                          I, C. Roberts

A. O. PRATER to Irene WOODLEE Issued 22 Aug 1929 Rites 22 Aug 1929
                                          E. D. Martin, M. G.

James W. WHITTICE to Mary Evelyn RODDY Issued 7 Aug 1929 Rites 8 Sep 1929
                                          W. B. Woodlee, M. G.

Marcus L. HOBBS to SArah E. PERRY Issued 31 Aug 1929 Rites 31 Aug 1929
                                          J. L. Barnes, J. P.

Debs H. MANUS to Pearl BAIN Isseud 31 Aug 1929 Rites 2 Sep 1929
                                          D. P. Myers, J. P.

Carl BAIN to SALLIE CASE Issued 31 Aug 1929 Rites 2 Sep 1929
                                          D. P. Myers, J. P.

William RUTLEDGE to Maud DAVIS Issued 6 Sep 1929 Rites 6 Sep 1929
                                          J. T. Casey, M. G.

Frank GAGNON to Iva DODSON Issued 28 Jun 1929 Rites 2 Jul 1929
                                          V. D. Lusk, J. P.

Marvin Edward HUNT to Willow Dean KENDALL Issued 29 Jun 1929 Rites 18 Aug 1929
                                          L. T. Lawrence, M. G.

Charles CLENDENON to Minerva RHEA Issued 24 Jun 1929 Rites 4 Jun 1929
                                          Reece H. Rogers, M. G.

J. L. HILLIS to Hazel DODSON Issued 29 Jun 1929 Rites 11 Jul 1929
                                          D. P. Myers, J. P.

J. HOLLANDSWORTH to Mai PRIEST Issued 29 Jun 1929 Rites 29 Jun 1929
                                          J. E. Sanders, J. P.

Vernie LANCE to Marshie PETTS Issued 29 Jun 1929   Not Returned

Charles MOORE to Maud Ella ALLEY Issued 29 Jun 1929 Rites 11 Jul 1929
                                          P. A. Kirby, M. G.

Brown TURNER to Pearl FORD Issued 29 Jun 1929 Rites 27 Jul 1929
                                          W. T. Warren, J. P.

319 Issues in this book

Claud COLLINS to Bessie SWINDELL Issued 16 Nov 1929 Rites 16 nov 1929
J. B. Dobbs, J. P.

Dewey NUNLEY to Hallie SMITH Issued 16 nov 1929 Rites 16 Nov 1929
J. L. Bonner, J. P.

Roy (Ray) SHOCKLEY to Lexie DONNAHOE Issued 24 Nov 1929 Rites 24 Nov 1929
A. C. Parker, M. G.

Poindexter ALLISON to FArry E. LOCKE Issued 27 Nov 1929 Rites 28 Nov 1929
L. L. Lawrence, M. G.

Isaac GRAYSON (C) to Emma LINDSEY (C) Issued 28 Nov 1929 Rites 28 Nov 1929
L. C. Maple, M. G.

Vonso SAVAGE (C) to Mary Ella DURHAM (Col) Issued 29 Nov 1929 Rites 1 Dec 1929
E. F. Cunningham, J. P.

Oliver CATEN to Zena DELONG Issued 30 Nov 1929 Rites 30 Nov 1929
Fate Walker, J. P.

Will DELONG to HASSIE COPE Issued 30 nov 1929 Rites 30 Vov 1929
Fate WAlker, J. P.

Henry RAMSEY (C) to Anneah YOUNG (C) Issued 30 Nov 1929 Rites 1 Dec 1929
J. R. Gray, M. G.

Ned LEACH (C) to Pauline CROFT (C) Issued 2 Dec 1929 Rites 2 Dec 1929
J. E. SAnders, J. P.

WAlter ROGERS to Ida Mai CLENDENEN Issued 14 Dec 1929 Rites 2 Jan 1929
E. D. Martin, M. G.

Herbert/ BROWN, Jr. to Virginia RIVERS Issued 15 Dec 1929 Rites 15 Dec 1929
J. B. Dobbs, J. P.

Otis LAFFEVER to Beulah YOUNG Issued 16 Dec 1929 Rites 21 Dec 1929
Van McGee, J. P.

Howard T. MARTIN to Sadie J. ROBINSON Issued 16 Dec 1929 Rites 18 Dec 1929
J. R. Gray, M. G.

John BEASLEY (C) to Elizabeth HILL (C) Issued 16 Dec 1929 Rites 16 Dec 1929
Frank R. Davis, Jdg.

Jennings Bryan DuBOIS to Lucille VANN Issued 17 Dec 1929 Rites 21 Dec 1929
T. Q. MArtin, M. G.

Jonah PLEASANT (C) to Meda WILSON (C) Issued 17 Dec 1929 Rites 19 Dec 1929
W. H. Craven, M. G.

Lowell SANDERS to Hazel MARTIN Issued 19 Dec 1929 Rites 20 Dec 1929
E. R. Little, M. G.

Tom GRISSOM to Velma Pearl DUNLAP Issued 20 Dec 1929 Rites 21 Dec 1929
J. L. Smith, J. P.

Perry BROCK to BULAH DONEY Issued 6 Sep 1929 Rites 6 Sep 1929
I. N. Smoot, J. P.

Oliver DAVIS to Edna Mai CHRISTIAN Issued 10 Sep 1929 License not completed
other than marked "Not Solemnized".

Herman PRIEST to Dollie PITMAN Issued 14 Sep 1929 Rites 21 Sep 1929
J. B. Dobbs, J. P.

Calvin GLENN to Mollie FIELDS Issued 28 Sep 1929 Rites 28 Sep 1929
P. A. Kirby, M. G.

N. M. JACO to Ethel BATES Issued 29 Sep 1929 Rites 29 Sep 1929
F. L. Leeper, M. G.

Edward F. DORMAN to Lorna PRESTON Issued 29 Sep 1929 Rites 1 Oct 1929
L. T. Lawrence, M. G.

C. H. SMIDDIE to Amanda WOODLEE Issued 2 Oct 1929 Rites 2 Oct 1929
A. H. Huff, M. G.

Henry YORK to Bertha Mai McCOWAN Issued 5 Oct 1929 Rites 20 Oct 1929
E. F. Cunningham, J. P.

Condy RUTLEDGE to Beatrice DAVIS Issued 11 Oct 1929 Rites 13 Oct 1929
D. P. Myers, J. P.

J. L. CERTAIN to HASSIE Pearl BELL Issued 12 Oct 1929 Rites 12 Oct 1929
J. T. Cooly

Eugene GREEN to Carmen BROWN Issued 12 Oct 1929 Rites 12 Oct 1929
L. L. Mawrence, M. G.

Kellum CHILTON to Lula HUSSEY Issued 12 Oct 1929 Rites 16 Oct 1929
F. L. Leeper, M. G.

Fred SUMMERS to Bertha SHIRLEY Issued 26 Oct 1929 Rites 3 Nov 1929
J. N. Winnett, J. P.

Lee P. SMARTT to Dorthy HOBBS Issued 26 Oct 1929 Rites 27 Oct 1929
J. L. Barnes, J. P.

Johnnie HAWKINS to Zora JONES Issued 26 Oct 1929 Rites 26 Oct 1929
john Morton, M. G.

Lonnie HAWKINS to Alta NIXON Issued 26 Oct 1929 Rites 17 Nov 1929
A. H. Huff, M. G.

Frank STUBBLEFIELD to Lucill HASTON Issued 1 Nov 1929 Rites 3 Nov 1929
W. B. Snipes, M. G.

C. Grey ELKINS to Mae Louise HUFF Issued4 Nov 1929 Rites 7 Nov 1929
A. H. Huff, M. G.

Robert MARTIN (C) to MAGGIE MARTIN (C) Issued 7 Nov 1929 Rites 7 Nov 1929
J. S. NAnce, M. G.

J, W. AKEMAN to Jennie GRISSOM Issued 11 Nov 1929 Rites 11 Nov 1929
J. W. Cooley, M. G.

Roy W. SMITH to Jewell GILLEY Issued 21 Dec 1929 Rites 26 Dec 1929
A. Z. Holder, J. P.

C. C. VAnHOOSER to Roberta SMITH Issued 21 Dec 1929 Rites 22 Dec 1929
P. A. King, M. G.

Jesse HILLIS to Aley CARRICK Issued 23 Dec 1929 Rites 24   1929
A. H. Huff, M. G.

D. C. SWANGER to Minnie B. BRYAN Issued 23 Dec 1929 Rites 29 Dec 1929
Bruce L. Lyle, M. G.

Robert A. SMITH to MArgie L. HANES Issued 23 Dec 1929 Rites 24 Dec 1929
Bruce L. Lyle, M. G.

N. S. GRIZZLE to HAllie FUSTON Issued 23 Dec 1929 Rites 24 Dec 1929
J. B. Dobbs, J. P.

Sam WILSON to Willie EVANS Issued 24 Dec 1929 Rites 24 Dec 1929
J. B. Dobbs, J. P.

Herman LANCE to Nella MAi HULLETT Issued 24 Dec 1929 Rites 25 Dec 1929
J. N. Winnett, J. P.

C. L. CLENDENEN to Ina PANTER Issued 24 Dec 1929 Rites 24 Dec 1929
P. N. Moffitt, J. P.

A. L. JONES to Nettie Lee GRIBBLE Issued 25 Dec 1929 Rites 25 Dec 1929
J. B. Dobbs, J. P.

Willie LOCKE to Nellie BYRD Issued 28 Dec 1929 Rites 28 Dec 1929
Frank R. DAvis, Jdg.

Wilbur HUDGENS (C) to Annie Mai ROWAN (C) Issued 29 Dec 1929 Rites 29 Dec 1929
J. R. Gray, M. G.

JaMES Clarence BRADY to Eloise TUBB Issued 31 Dec 1929 rites 5 Jan 1930
Joe L. Netherland, M. G.

W. T. WARREN to Winnie STONE Issued 4 Jan 1930 Rites 4 JAn 1930
D. P. Myers, J. P.

Clyde HENNESSEE to Folssie BROWN Issued 11 Jan 1930 Rites 11 Jan 19.
P. A. Kirby, M. G.

Tom DUKE to Dee RECHARD Issued 11 JAn 1920 Rites 11 JAN 1930
W. B. Snipes, M. ?

Mont WINNARD to MArgie GREEN Issued 11 JAn 19.0 Rites 12 jAN 1930
G. W. Hinkley, J. P.

Sam ANDERSON to Mildred DURHAM Issued 11 Jan 1920 Rites 12 Jan 1930
J. B. Dobbs, MJ. P.

Curtis JUDD to Louise SULLINS Issued 14 Jan 1930 Rites 14 Jan 1930
Frank R. Davis, Jdg.

H. R. STEWART to Francis ROBINSON Issued 18 JAn 1930 Rites 18 JAn 1930
J. T. Casey, M. G.

Robert ARMSTRONG to Mary PEARSON Issued 19 Jan 1930 Rites 19 JAn 1930
D. P. Myers, J. P.

Cephus WEST to Willie MAi BELLE Issued 21 JAN 1930 Rites 21 Jan 1930
I. N. Smoot, J. P.

James ROGERS to Kate ROGERS Issued 22 Jan 1930 Rites 22 Jan 1930
R. S. LAmb, M. G.

JAmes CANTRELL to Myrtle CANTRELL Issued 25 Jan 1930 Rites 25 Jan 1930
Irving PAtton, J. P.

Robert BARNES to Pearl TATE Issued 25 Jan 1930 Rites 26 Jan 1930
B. F. Killian

Aubrey TUCKER to Mary DODLEY Issued 1 Feb 1930 Rites 2 Feb 1930
A. C. PArker, M. G.

RAymond BLUE to Lennie Lynn LOOPER Issued 1 Feb 1930 Rites 1 Feb 1930
I. N. Smoot, J. P.

LAcklan CANTRELL to VAllie MARTIN Issued 1 Feb 1930 Rites 1 Feb 1930
P. A. Kirby, M. G.

Joe QUICK to Eva CANTRELL Issued 2 Feb 1930 Rites 2 feb 1930
J. W. Cooley, M. G.

Bob BELL to Ann MILLER Issued 8 Feb 1930 Rites 8 Feb 1930
Claud Myers, M. G.

Jim RIVERS to Estine MASON Issued 9 Feb 1930 Rites 9 Feb 1930
J. S, NAnce, M. G.

L. J. PEARSALL to Amon PRATER Issued 9 Feb 1930 Rites 9 Feb 1930
A. H. Huff, M. G.

Charels LANE to Lena COTTEN Issued 11 Feb 1930 Rites 12 Feb 1930
L. C. LAne, J. P.

Garndville BLANKENSHIP to Malissa LOONEY Issued 12 Feb 1930 Rites 12 Feb 1930
P. A. Kirby, M. G.

DAn FERRELL to Martha BAIN Issued 14 Feb 1930 Rites 15 feb 1930
L. B. Moffitt, J. P.

Howard GOODMAN to Ola Mai GRAHAM Issued 15 Feb 1930 Rites 15 Feb 1930
Reece Rogers, M. G.

Bennett BOLTON to Gladys GRIFFITH Issued 17 feb 1930 Rites 17 Feb 1930
V. D. Lusk, J. P.

D. M. CLARK to Emma TALLANT Issued 20 Feb 1930 Rites 20 Feb 1930
W. V. D. Miller, J. P.

Vester HALL to Ollie RAINS Issued 20 Feb 1930 Rites 23 Feb 1930
E. F. Cunningham, J. P.

Otto PRATER to Flora BOULDIN Issued 1 Mar 1930 Rites 1 Mar 1930
I. C. Roberts, M. G.

Chas. C. STUBBLEFIELD to Rebeth J. LOOPER Issued 1 Mar 1930 Rites 4 Mar 1930
J. R. Gray, M. G.

James Reuben GARRETT to Ruby Lee LAMB Issued 3 Mar 1930 Rites 3 Mar 1930
A. H. Huff, M. G.

Elmer MORTON to Juanita STUBBLEFIELD Issued 8 Mar 1930 Rites 8 Mar 1930
J. R. Gray, M. G.

Johnnie MORTON to Willie GREEN Issued 15 Mar 1930 Rites 15 Mar 1930
Frank R. Davis, Jdg.

L. W. HUTCHISON to Vera STEWART Issued 15 Mar 1930 Rites 15 Mar 1930
E. H. Greenwell, M. G.

W. C. ADCOCK to Dorthy PEATH Issued 18 Mar 1930 Rites 18 Mar 1930
F. R. Davis, Jdg.

Clarence GIVENS to Odel HUDSON Issued 22 Mar 1930 Rites 22 Mar 1930
J. B. Dobbs, J. P.

George TAYLOR to Willis GEORGE Issued 22 Mar 1930 Rites 22 Mar 1930
J. B. Dobbs, J. P.

Milton HENEGAR to Gladys PERRY Issued 28 Mar 1930 Rites 29 Mar 1930
T. Q. Martin, M. G.

Clark TURNER to Nettie YOUNG Issued 29 Mar 1930 Rites 29 Mar 1930
I. N. Smoot, J. P.

J. D. GROSS to Nora PATTON Issued 1 Apr 1930 Rites 2 Apr 1930
J. L. Walker, J. P.

Clarence HIGGINBOTHAM to Hallie HILLIS Issued 4 Apr 1930 Rites 4 Apr 1930
D. P. Myers, J. P.

Ephriam BOBBITT to Mrs. D. W. A. MITCHELL Issued 17 Apr 1930 Rites 17 Apr 1930
Frank R. Davis, Jdg.

C. H. McVEY to Alice ELLIOTT Issued 19 Apr 1930 Rites 21 Apr 1930
Fate Walker, J. P.

G. C. NETTLES to Mai FIELDS Issued 19 Apr 1930 Rites 19 Apr 1930
Irving Patton, J. P.

Martin CURTIS to Myrtle DODSON Issued 19 Apr 1930 Rites 19 Apr 1930
P. N. Moffitt, J. P.

J. I. WALKER to Lela GOFF Issued 21 Apr 1930 Rites 21 Apr 1930
H. Rogers, M. G.

Leburn TURNER to Margie MELTON Issued 25 Apr 1930 Rites 27 Apr 1930
Richard Turner, M. G.

Will NEWBY to Eveline SPANGLER Issued 26 Apr 1930 Rites 26 apr 1930
C. R. Scott, J. P.

W. J. SPENCER to Elsie McCORMICK Issued 26 Apr 1930 Rites 26 Apr 1930
L. T. LAWRENCE, M. G.

W. A. RICHARDSON to Grace MOORE Issued 27 Apr 1930 Rites 27 Apr 1930
J. B. Dobbs, M. G.

J. MORGAN to Lorene HENNESSEE Issued 28 Apr 1930 Rites 4 May 1930
J. L. Smith, J. P.

B. J. MARTIN to Vera TEMPLETON Issued 2 May 1930 Rites 2 May 1930
A. H. Huff, M. G.

L. J. CHISAM to Nettie MORRIS Issued 3 May 1930 Riets 3 May 1920
L. T. Lawrence, M. G.

Roy VERBLE to Pearl NEAL Issued 12 May 1930 Riets 19 May 1930
P. A. Kirby, M. G.

Alex WILSON to MAggie ROLLINS Issued 22 May 1930 Rites 22 May 1930
J. D. Dobbs, J. P.

William DOUGLAS to Eula WEBB Issued 22 MAy 1930 Rites 22 May 1930
F. L. Kirby, J. P.

George ROBBINS to Willie ROGERS Issued 23 May 1930 Rites 23 May 1930
Frank R. Davis, Jdg.

Aaron MARBERRY to Dora MARTIN Issued 24 May 1930 Rites 24 May 1930
L. C. Maple, M. G.

Albert RICHARDSON to Willie PATRICK Issued 27 May 1930 Rites 27 May 1930
J. B. Dobbs, J. P.

Reuben TURNER to Flora TURNER Issued 29 May 1930 rites 31 May 1930
J. W. Cooley, M. G.

Gaines SHANNON to HAllie ROGERS Issued 31 May 1930 Rites 1 Jun 1930
Irving Patton, J. P.

T. C. STOKES to Lorene DURHAM Issued 31 May 1930 Riets 31 May 1930
J. S. NAnce, M. G.

Lawrence J. OTIS to Pauline Nelle ROBERTS Issued 4 jun 1930 Rites 11 Jun 1930
George Stoves, M. G.

Tom HUNTER to Florence MARTIN Issued 7 Jun 1930 Rites 7 Jun 1930
J. B. Dobbs, J. P.

Percy WILLIAMS to Lula Mai RAMSEY Issued 7 Jun 1930 Rites 7 Jun 1930
J. B. Dobbs, J. P.

GArner CLARK to Atena RAMSEY Issued 10 Jun 1930 Riets 10 jun 1930
R. M. Gleaves

W. R. NOAH to Gladys MASEY Issued 14 Jun 1930 Rites 14 Jun 1930 E. D. Martin, M. G.

J. Willis KING to Dovie Ann COPE Issued 14 jun 1930 Rites 15 jun 1930 T. Q. Martin, M. G.

C. R. THOMPSON to Lucill PAGE Issued 19 Jun 1930 Rites 19 Jun 1930 J. B. Dobbs, J. P.

Henry GOODWIN to Alice WALLACE Issued 21 jun 1930 Rites 22 Jun 1930 O. H. Wood, J. P.

Lofton SMARTT to Lela Mai VICKERS Issued 24 Jun 1930 Rites 24 jun 1930 W. B. Snipes, M. G.

Clifford COUCH to Mona HUDSON Issued 26 Jun 1930 Rites 28 Jun 1930 L. F. Daugherty, M, G.

W. H. MOORE to Georgia Meade HAYES Issued 3 jul 1930 Riets 3 Jul 1930 Reece H. Rogers, M. G.

Milton BROWN (C) to Gussie CLARK Issued 8 Jul 1930 Rites 8 Jul 1930 J. R. Gray, M. G.

J. E. FERRELL to Bessie STANLEY Issued 10 Jul 1930 Rites 10 Jul 1930 J. B. Dobbs, J. P.

L. E. HARRIS to Verbla SEAMON Issued 12 Jul 1930 Rites 12 jul 1930 A. H. Huff, M. G.

Harold MEDLEY to Minnie ADAMSON Issued 12 Jul 1930 Rites 12 jul 1930 J. N. Winnett, J. P.

KIRK MALONE to CAtherine RAMSEY Issued 12 Jul 1930 Rites 13 Jul 1930 Isaac Grizzle, J. P.

Hershel HITSON to Ollia COAKLEY Issued 17 Jul 1930 Rites 19 Jul 1930 W. H. Craven, M. G.

H. F. SCOTT to Sylva ROGERS Issued 18 Jul 1930 Not Returned

W. D. SNEED to Ruby M. HARRISON Issued 25 Jul 1930 Rites 25 Jul 1930 J. L. McAliley

Charles HILL (C) to Stella MARTIN (C) Issued 25 Jul 1930 Rites 25 jul 1930 E. F. Erwin, M. G.

L. D. PRITCHARD to Grace JACO Issued 25 Jul 1930 Rites 27 Jul 1930 T. Perry Brown, M. G.

R. L. TUCK to Anna MAy HUDSON Issued 2 Aug 1930 Rites 2 Aug 1930 J. N. Winnett, J. P.

Lindsay M. DAVIS to MAry Frances HUTCHINS Issued 6 Aug 1930 Rites 6 Aug 1930 Bruce L. LYLE, M. G.

George FOSTER to Alica HOLLAND Issued 11 Aug 1930 Rites 11 Aug 1930 A. H. Huff, M. G.

Oscar BONNER to Ella Mai CATHCART Issued 20 Aug 1930 Rites 21 Aug 1930 Reese H. Rogers, M. G.

Thaddis BATEMAN to Retha LUSK Issued 25 Aug 1930 Rites 25 Aug 1930 J. S. NAnce, M. G.

Herman BRAXTON to Corene SISSOM Isseud 27 Aug 1930 Rites 4 Sep 1930 L. H. Byles, J. P.

Henry SULLIVAN to Onna RHINEHOLZ (?) Issued 4 Sep 1930 Rites 4 Sep 1930 J. B. McAffee, J. P.

Joe McLEAN to Pearl TURNER Issued 6 Sep 1930 Rites 6 Sep 1930 Claud Myers, M. G.

G. R. TENPENNY to DAisy GRIFFITH Issued 11 Sep 1930 Rites 14 Sep 1930 A. Z. Holder, J. P.

J. E. CLARK to MArtha KELL Issued 15 Sep 1930 Rites 18 Sep 1930 n. B. Moffitt, M. G.

Jim McCORMICK to Maggie Lou GEORGE Issued 20 Sep 1930 Rites 20 Sep 1930 Fate Walker, J. P.

Hiram PELHAM, Jr. to Audie Lee COPPINGER Issued 20 Sep 1930 Rites 20 Sep 1930 E. W. Sutherlin, J. P.

Jim WHITTENBURG to Susie McBRIDE Issued 20 Sep 1930 Rites 20 Sep 1930 J. L. BArnes, J. P.

Dewey MATHIS to Velma MAi ROLLER Issued 23 Sep 1930 Rites 27 Sep 1930 W. F. Roach, J. P.

Tom HARRELL to Ruth HELTON Issued 25 Sep 1930 Rites 26 Sep 1930 J. A. Cunningham

Jeese Meredith CARMACK to Margarette COLVILLE Issued 26 Sep 1930 Rites 27 Sep 1930 L. T. Lawrence, M. G.

Parker DONEY to Lessie Ann PELHAM Issued 27 Sep 1930 Rites 27 Sep 1930 Bruce L. Lyle, M. G.

PAul T. SMITH to Beulah Mai SCOTT Issued 28 Sep 1930 Rites 28 Sep 1930 A. Z. Holder, J. P.

.hurman DUDLEY to Odine ALLISON Issued 30 Sep 1930 Rites 30 Sep 1930 Frank R. Davis, Jdg.

Leonard PASCAL to Evelyn JOHNSON Issued 4 Oct 1930 Rites 4 Oct 1930 Isaac Grizzle, J. P.

James D. RAMSEY to Josie STEMBRIDGE Issued 4 Oct 1930 Rites 4 Oct 1930 J. B. McAfee, J. P.

Smith BYARS to Willie Martha COPE Issued 21 Nov 1930 Rites 21 Nov 1930
Reese H. Rogers, M. G.

Alvie WINNARD to Agness ROGERS Issued19 Nov 1930 Rites 19 Nov 1930
Edgar Henegar, J. P.

Henry CURTIS to Wavie ROBERTS Issued 22 Nov 1930 Rites 22 Nov 1930
John Morton, M. G.

Ray DOVE to Mary McGEE Issued 24 Nov 1930 Rites 26 Nov 1930
W. M. Rowland, J. P.

Silas DOUGLAS to Mary E. BARNES Issued 24 Nov 1930 Rites 30 nov 1930
G. H. O'NEAL, M. G.

H. R. AVERY to Sallie COPE Issued 1 Dec 1930 Rites 7 Dec 1930
L. F. DAugherty, M. G.

Virgil CONALY to Clara BRAGG Issued 5 Dec 1930 Rites 5 Dec 1930
T. Q. Martin, M. G.

Jim HOBBS to May WILSON Issued 7 Dec 1930 Rites 7 Dec 1930
E. W. Sutherlin, J. P.

Unos HASTY to Eunice CHURCH Issued 13 Dec 1930 Rites 13 Dec 1930
Frank R. Davis, Jdg.

Willie HALL to Irene RAINS Issued 20 Dec 1930 Rites 21 dec 1930
G. B. J. Mitchell, J. P.

Walter GIBBS to Laura COX Issued 20 Dec 1930 Rites 20 Dec 1930
G. P. Brasier, J. P.

C. W. CANTRELL to Hazel ARLEDGE Issued 22 dec 1930 Rites 22 Dec 1930
T. Q. Martin, M. G.

Charles LOWE to Virgie GANN Issued 22 Dec 1930 Rites 28 Dec 1930
A. Z. Holder, J. P.

Stanley RAYBURN to Louise ROACH Issued 23 Dec 1930 Rites 23 Dec 1930
A. B. Moffitt, M. G.

Harvey PACK to Josie MERRITT Issued 24 dec 1930 Rites 24 Dec 1930
Frank R. Davis, Jdg.

W. H. TURNER to Vera GANN Issued 24 Dec 1930 Rites 24 Dec 1930
A. Z. Holder, J. P.

Bill HAYES to Delma CLARK Issued 25 Dec 1930 Rites 27 Dec 1930
N. P. McWhirter, J. P.

Overton ROGERS to Bessie PATTERSON Issued 21 Dec 1930 Rites 26 dec 1930
G. H. O'Neal, M. G.

Clyde SPENCER to Edith MULLIGAN Issued 26 Dec 1930 Rites 28 Dec 1930
T. Q. Martin, M. G.

Elmer HUMPHREY to Ila MOORE Issued 3 Oct 1930 Rites 5 Oct 1930
W. V. D. Miller, J. P.

H. T. DODSON to Daisy BYRD Issued 4 Oct 1930 Rites 5 Oct 1930
A. A. Flanders, M. G.

Charles BILBREY to Myrtle BATES Issued 5 Oct 1930 Rites 5 Oct 1930
F. L. Leeper, M. G.

E. KOONCE to Belle DURHAM Issued 11 Oct 1930 Rites 11 Oct 1930
A. A. Flander, M. G.

Albert SCHLAGETER to Mrs. Willie PATTON Issued 16 Oct 1930 Rites 16 Oct 1930
A. H. Huff, M. G.

Frank F. COUCH, Jr. to Mattie WEBB Issued 21 Oct 1930 Rites 26 Oct 1930
J. S. Dunlap, J. P.

Jesse PALMER to Vivian JENNINGS Issued 22 Oct 1930 Rites 25 Oct 1930
Reese H. Rogers, M. G.

Huston MOORE to Aline FITTS Issued 25 Oct 1930 Rites 25 Oct 1930
J. B. McAfee, J. P.

George SIMMONS to Hortense MARTIN Issued 27 Oct 1930 Rites 8 Nov 1930
N. P. McWhirter, J. P.

Tommie PETTY to Modie CALDWELL Issued 27 Oct 1930 Rites 29 Oct 1930
J. K. Martin, J. P.

Leon TOSH to Lillian SCOTT Issued 1 Nov 1930 Rites 1 Nov 1930
W. H. Byles, J. P.

Stroud CLANCY to Amie McMAHAN Issued 1 Nov 1930 Rites 1 Nov 1930
J. R. Stubblefiled, M.G.

Ed RANDOLPH to Betsey ODELL Issued 3 Nov 1930 Rites 3 Nov 1930
N. P. McWhirter, J. P.

Felix LIMBAUGH to Willie CANTRELL Issued 8 Nov 1930 Rites 8 Nov 1933
T. Q. Martin, M. G.

Vernon REED to Carrie PARKER Issued 8 Nov 1930   Not Solemnized

Robert SEALS to Lelia HIGGINBOtHAM Issued 14 Nov 1930 Rites 14 Nov 1930
V. D. Lusk, J.

McKinley ROMAN to Vanley B. MYERS Issued 15 Nov 1930 Rites 15 Nov 1930
J. R. Gray, M. G.

Cecil SMITH to Opal MEARS Issued 15 Nov 1930 Rites 16 Nov 1930
A. Z. Holder, J. P.

Preston MOORE to Ella HENNESSEE Issued 17 Nov 1930 Rites 17 Nov 1930
Edgar Henegar, J. P.

King COPE to Willie GRIBBLE Issued 27 Feb 1931 Rites 27 Feb 1931
Frank R. Davis, Jdg.

Theron MARTIN (C) to Beatrice STUBBLEFIELD (C) Issued 28 Feb 1931 Rites 1 Mar 1931
J. R. Gray, M. G.

Charles SMITH to Thelma Martin HUMPHREY Issued 20 Mar 1931 rites 20 Mar 1931
E. W. Sutherlin, J. P.

Lafayette SMITH to Ruby JOHNSON Issued 21 MAR 1931 Rites 26 Mar 1931
J. P. Bilbrey, J. P.

Grady PUGH to Lizzie PHILLIPS Issued 4 Apr 1931 Rites 5 Apr 1931
W. H. Moss, M. G.

L. C. C. WALLACE to SAllie COTTEN Issued 4 Apr 1931 Rites 5 Apr 1931
E. R. Little, M. G.

Albert WARREN to Genovia BASHAM Issued 4 Apr 1931 Rites 4 Apr 1931
W. B. Snipes, M. G.

Edgar HALE to Alma JOHNSON Issued 4 Apr 1931 Rites 4 Apr 1931
N. P. McWhirter, J. P.

Isaac SIOTTS to Mattie Pearl DODSON Issued 6 Apr 1931 Rites 6 Apr 1931
J. L. Barnes, J. P.

Ewell BILES (C) to Leora RAMSEY (C) Issued 6 Apr 1931 Rites 6 Apr 1931
Edgar Henegar, J. P.

Johnnie Alton FERRELL to Hazel DILL Issued 11 Apr 1931 Rites 11 Apr 1931
A. H. Huff, M. G.

Earl HUGHES to Mary E. COLINOT Issued 6 Apr 1931 Rites 18 Apr 1931
W. T. Warren, J. P.

Thomas ROBINSON (C) to Johnnie OFFICER (C) Issued 18 Apr 1931 Rites 18 Apr 1931
J. S. NAnce, M. G.

George SMARTT to Opal YOUNG Issued 25 Apr 1931 Rites 25 Apr 1931
W. H. Byles, J. P.

A. A. TURNER to Ethel STEMBRIDGE Issued 25 Apr 1931 Rites 25 Apr 1931
James K. Martin, J. P.

Altom WOMACK to Jewell GLENN Issued 2 May 1931 Rites 3 May 1931
A. J. Locke, J. P.

Elmer HALL to HAzel McMILLON Issued 2 MAy 1931 Rites 2 May 1931
R. H. HALL, M. G.

Odus UNDERHILL to Willie Mai STEMBRIDGE Issued 8 MAY 1931 Rites 10 May 1931
W. T. Watson, J. P.

Julius L. BAIRD to Lela Holland PAGE Issued 9 May 1931 Rites 10 MAy 1931
L. T. Lawrence, M. G.

Luther MARTIN to Lola COUCH Issued 26 Dec 1930 Rites 26 Dec 1930
J. B. McAfee, J. P.

Lonnie CHISAM to Clata DAVENPORT issued 27 Dec 1930 rites 27 Dec 1930
Reece Rogers, M. G.

George EITER to Notie CUMMINGS Issued 3 Jan 1931 Rites 3 Jan 1931
N. P. McWhirter, J. P.

R. E. JONES to Blanche DODSON Issued 3 Jan 1931 Rites 3 Jan 1931
L. T. Lawrence, M. G.

G. W. TODD to Betsy CATES Issued17 Jan 1931 Not Returned

Will CROUCH to Nettie RAYMOND Issued 17 Jan 1931 Rites 4 jan 1931
W. H. Craven, M. G.

Charles DUTTON to Glada SPURLOCK Issued 22 Jan 1931 Rites 22 jan 1931
J. B. McAfee, J. P.

RAymond WOMACK to Ila Mai REYNOLDS Issued 24 Jan 1931 Rites 24 jan 1931
Frank R. DAvis, Jdg.

J. T. STEWART to Mildred RAYBURN Issued 24 Jan 1931 Rites 25 Jan 1931
W. F. Roach, J. P.

Beecher WOODLEE to Pauline FULTS Issued 26 Jan 1931 Rites 26 JAn 1931
Frank R. Davis, Jdg.

Tom STUBBLEFIELD to May BUFFALO Issued 27 Jan 1931 Rites 27 JAn 1931
W. B. Snipes, M. G.

Rayford CAPLINGER to Martha Joe PRIEST Issued 28 JAn 1931 Rites 28 JAn 1931
F. L. Leeper, M. G.

Morgan SMITHSON to Stella YOUNG Issued 2 Feb 1931 Rites 2 feb 1931
Frank R. Davis, Jdg.

Lindsey HILLIS to Florence BAIN Issued 7 Feb 1931 Rites 7 Feb 1931
W. V. D. Miller, J. P.

Rhea Dibrell POTTER to Sarah Frances WINTON Issued 10 Feb 1931 Rites 13 Feb 1931
T. Q. Martin, M. G.

M. E. KELL to Delma REEDER Issued 11 Feb 1931 Rites 11 Feb 1931
FAte Walker, J. P.

H. S. HALE to Mammie DAVENPORT issued 16 Feb 1931 Rites 20 Feb 1931
G. B. J. Mitchell, J. P.

Lawrence HALE to Elsie Mai GREEN Issued 23 Feb 1931 Rites 24 Feb 1931
Wm. Rowland, J. P.

Jim OGLES to Effie Mai VANAITA Issued 24 Feb 1931 Rites 24 feb 1931
Frank R. Davis, Jdg.

J. E. ELKINS to Ova WARREN Issued 24 Feb 1931 Rites 24 Feb 1931
E. W. Sutherlin, J. P.

Ezra COLE to Pearl DEATON Issued 9 May 1931 Rites 10 May 1931
E. D. Martin, M. G.

H. C. FAulkner to Ardemia BLUE Issued 13 May 1931 Rites 13 May 1931
J. S. Nance, M, M.G

JAmes DAVIS to Flora HALL Issued 15 May 1931 Rites 15 May 1931
Fate Walker, J. P.

C. B. LORANCE to Myra SUMMERS Issued 16 May 1931 Rites 17 May 1931
P. A. Kirby, M. G.

John RAOCH to Helen Lou BROWN Issued 16 May 1931 Rites 17 May 1931
John Morton, M. G.

John GRIFFITH to Mrs. Edna BOYD Issued 22 May 1931 Rites 24 May 1931
D. R. Womack, J. P.

Lee BROWN to Carrie COMERS Issued 23 May 1931 Rites 24 May 1931
A. Z. Holder, J. P.

Cecil OVERTURFF to Susie LAWSON Issued 23 May 1931 Rites 23 May 1931
J. B. McAfee, J. P.

Booker SETTLES (C) to Ida Lee YORK (C) Issued 25 May 1931 Rites 25 May 1931
E. S. Bedford, M. G.

William HENDRICKS to Laura NOWLIN Issued 30 May 1931 Rites 30 May 1931
Edgar Henegar, J. P.

Jim BLUE to Leola DONAHUE Issued 30 May 1931 Rites 30 May 1931
J. S. Nance, M. G.

Thurman HALL to Mae EARL Issued 2 Jun 1931 Rites 2 Jun 1931
C. L. Webster

Beecher HUMPHREY to Velma Pearl FARLEY Issued 2 Jun 1931 Rites 7 Jun 1931
W. V. D. Miller, J. P.

Kenneth.H. COATES to Margrett PAGE Issued 5 Jun 1931 Rites 5 Jun 1931
P. A. Kirby, M. G.

Clifton MALONE to Reese SETTLES Issued 5 Jun 1931 Rites 5 jun 1931
E. S. Bedford, M. G.

Virgil GLENN to Ruby MITCHELL Issued 5 jun 1931 Rites 5 jun 1931
A. J. Locke, J. P.

Luther GRISSOM to Hilda Mai GINN Issued 13 Jun 1931 Rites 13 Jun 1931
A. H. Huff, M. G.

Aggie SULLIVAN to Connie LAWSON Issued 13 Jun 1931 Rites 13 Jun 1931
N. P. McWhirter, J. P.

Timothy M. WILLIAMS to Rose Anna STILES Issued 13 Jun 1931 Rites 13 Jun 1931
J. S. Nance, M. G.

Robert L. SMITHSON to Dolly NEWBY Issued 16 Jun 1931 Rites 16 jun 1931
Frank R. DAvis, JDG.

Leonard Glenn BONNER to Gladys DUNHAM Issued 19 Jun 1931 Rites 20 Jun 1931
A. B. Moffitt, M. G.

W. A. WOODLEE to Ollie PRATER Issued 20 Jun 1931 Rites 20 Jun 1931
Edgar Henegar, J. P.

W. F. PRESLEY to Mrs. N. B. CANTRELL Issued 20 Jun 1931 Rites 20 Jun 1931
J.A. Cunningham, M. G.

Olen LEAGE to Willie B. MARTIN Issued 20 Jun 1931 Rites 20 Jun 1931
Frank R. Davis, Jdg.

Earl J. CROSSLIN to Mary Lou DURHAM Issued 20 1931 Rites 20 Jun 1931
J. L. Mc Aliley

Richard STACEY to Wavie PANTER Issued 22 Jun 1931 Rites 22 Jun 1931
J. L. Barnes, J. P.

Dave WARD to Edith HENDRICKS Issued 22 Jun 1931 Rites 22 Jun 1931
Edgar Henegar, J. P.

J.W. FISH to Ceva RAYMON Issued 24 Jun 1931 Rites 24 Jun 1931
W. H. Jones

William BRACC to Alma White PASCHAL Issued 26 Jun 1931 Rites 26 Jun 1931
A. H. Huff, M. G.

William J. KIRK to Florence RUTHERFORD Issued 27 Jun 1931 Rites 27 Jun 1931
L. T. Lawrence, M. G.

W. K. ELDER to Willie McBROM Issued 30 Jun 1931 Rites 30 Jun 1931
J. B. McAfee, J. P.

Hillis EVANS to Eunice BRAY Issued 1 Jul 1931 Rites 2 Jul 1931
I. P. McGregor, J. P.

Allen GREEN to Octa MORTON Issued 3 Jul 1931 Rites 4 Jul 1931
P. A. Kirby, M. G.

Raymond SMARTT to Mattie ARGO Issued 10 Jul 1931   Not Returned

George SIMMONS to Hattie MYERS Issued 18 Jul 1931 Rites 19 Jul 1931
T. A. Richardson, M. G.

Herman FOSTER to Audrey Mai SIMONS Issued 18 Jul 1931 Rites 18 Jul 1931
A. H. Huff, M. G.

Will G. PHILLIPS to Lou SMITH Issued 25 Jul 1931 Rites 27 Jul 1931
W. W. Pullen

Enyol BRATCHER to Lela LAWSON Issued 4 Aug 1931 Rites 4 Aug 1931
Edgar Henegar, J. P.

Austin GLENN to Edna FISHER Issued 4 Aug 1931 Rites 4 Aug 1931
J. S. Dunlap, J. P.

Virgle TAYLOR to Louise WILSON Issued 5 Aug 1931 Rites 5 Aug 1931
John Morton, M. G.

John D. YOUNG to Dortha ANDERSON Issued 5 Aug 1931 Rites 15 Aug 1931
E. R. Little, M. G.

Delta DAVENPORT to Dovie BARRETT Issued 7 Aug 1931 Rites 9 Aug 1931
R. H. Hale, M. G.

Emmett CURTIS to Wilma TOWRY Issued 8 Aug 1931 Rites 8 Aug 1931
Isaac Grizzle, J. P.

Arthue SAVAGE (C) to Rhoda MOZY (C) Issued 12 Aug 1931 Rites 13 Aug 1931
J. S. Nance, M. G.

W. T. TURNER to Della ODINEAL Issued 15 Aug 1931 Rites 15 Aug 1931
C. L. Webster

Selmer CAMPBELL to Mazel GILBERT Issued 19 Aug 1931 Rites 19 Aug 1931
Reece H. Rogers, M. G.

D. L. Pack to Lula BEATY Issued 25 Aug 1931 Application not completed

Robert SAVAGE (C) to Pricilla HOWARD (C) Issued 28 Aug 1931 Rites 28 Aug 1931
N. B. Newsom

S. J. WANNAMAKER to Sadie Belle COPPINGER Issued 29 Aug 1931 Rites 30 Aug 1931
P. N. Moffitt, J. P.

Creed ARNOLD to Mrs. Laura Jean Leak BRADFORD Issued 1 Sep 1931 Rites 1 Sep
L. T. Lawrence, M. G.

Bill LAWSON to Ada COOKLEY Issued 2 Sep 1931 Rites 3 Sep 1931
W. H. Craven, M. G.

Ben GRISSOM to Louella SCOTT Issued 6 Sep 1931 Rites 9 Sep 1931
Charles Hillis, J. P.

James S. READY to Mary OGLE Issued 11 Sep 1931 Rites13 Sep 1931
W. M. Rowland, J. P.

Will SANDERS to Harriett WORLEY Issued 12 Sep 1931 Rites 12 Sep 1931
J. B. McAfee, J. P.

Thos. Emmett ANDES to Mildred Fay ALLISON Issued 12 Sep 1931 Rites 12 Sep 1931
Reece H. Rogers, M. G.

George BROWN to Wavue DILL Issued 19 Sep 1931 Not Returned

Thos. H. RHEA (C) to Mary Eliz SCOTT (C) Issued 22 Sep 1931 Rites 22 Spe 1931
J. S. NAnce, M. G.

Firm HULETT to Pearl YORK Issued 25 Sep 1931 Rites 25 Sep 1931
J. D. Vandergriff, M. G.

Herbery MILLER to Mary Ellen WILSON Issued 26 Sep 1931 Rites 27 Dec 1931
A. H. Huff, M. G
(Both from MASCOT, Th.)

W. C. YORK to Nettie ROACH Issued 26 Sep 1931 Rites 26 Sep 1931
A. B. Moffitt, M. G.

Sammie COPE to Pauline GOFF Issued 26 Sep 1931 Rites 27 Sep 1931
W. T. Watson, J. P.

Cooper HALE to Mollie TALANT Issued 1 Oct 1931 Rites 1 Oct 1931
L. A. Maxley, M. G.

James Thos. BOSTICK to Roberta CLARK Issued 7 Oct 1931 Rites 7 Oct 1931
W. W. Pullen

Grady AUSTIN to Elsie JONES Issued 9 Oct 1931 Rites 13 Oct 1931
W. T. Warren, J. P.

Joe WEBB to Clisty DAVIS Issued 10 Oct 1931 Rites 11 Oct 1931
Cass R. Womack, J. P.

Floyd SULLENS to Virgie DAVIS Issued 15 Oct 1931 Rites 15 Oct 1931
J. A. Cunningjam, J. P.

Harve TURNER to Dorsie Lee CORNELIUS Issued 17 Oct 1931 Rites 17 Oct 1931
Edgar Henegar

Joe Lawrence SIMONS to Mimmie Marie BUSEY Issued 17 Oct 1931 Rites 17 Oct 1931
A. Z. Holder, J. P.

C. G. STROUD to Ora Lee BAILEY Issued 21 Oct 1931 Rites 21 Oct 1931
T. Q. Martin, M. G.

Sherman LANCE to Mabel McKNIGHT Issued 22 Oct 1931 Rites 22 Oct 1931
G. B. J. Mitchell, J. P.

George JENNINGS to Alice PICKETT Issued 24 Oct 1931 Rites 25 Oct 1931
N. M. Hill, J. P.

Herbert KNIGHT to Willie Fay HOLDER Issued 24 Oct 1931 Rites 24 Oct 1931
W. T. WArren, J. P.

Claud HICKEY to Cathern Louise LUTRELL Issued 29 Oct 1931 Rites 29 Oct 1931
L. B. Moffitt, J. P.

Bruster BAIN to Ova May MULLICAN Issued 30 Oct 1931 Rites 31 Oct 1931
J. B. McAfee, J. P.

Eugene SCOTT to Minnie Bell MYERS Issued 30 oct 1931 Rites 30 Oct 1931
W. H. Byles, J. P.

Sam HASTON to Cleo YOUNG Issued 31 Oct 1931 Rites 1 Nov 1931
J. B. Moffitt, J. P.

Faulkner J. WOMACK to Mrs. Martha J. FULTS Issued 31 Oct 1931 Rites 31 Oct 1931
R. W. Smartt, Jdg.

Vernon CRIM to Virgie CANTRELL Issued 31 Oct 1931 Rites 2 Nov 1931
Frank R. Davis, Jdg.

George MULLICAN to Nannie CANTRELL Issued 24 Dec 1931 Rites 24 Dec 1931
J. B. Gribble

Steve HILL to Osle LASSITER Issued 24 Dec 1931 Rites 24 Dec 1931
T. Q. Martin, M. G.

Paul LORING to Leona WILCHER Issued 24 Dec 1931 Rites 25 Dec 1931
L. T. Lawrence, M. G.

JAmes RUTLEDGE to Audry MAi CARTWRIGHT Issued 25 Dec 1931 Rites 25 Dec 1931
J. L. Barnes, J. P.

Delbert BOREN to Willie HARPER Issued 26 Dec 1931 Rites 26 dec 1931
W. H. Craven, M. G.

Robert CRIPPS to Ella STANLEY Issued 26 Dec 1931 Rites 26 Dec 1931
J. B. McAfee, J. P.

Charles BONNER to Eugenia PHILLIPS Issued 28 dec 1931 Rites 28 Dec 1931
J. S. Nance, M. G.

J. E. PANTER to Evelyn CURTIS Issued 29 Dec 1931 Rites 29 Dec 1931
P. N. Moffitt, J. P.

Charles Lee TOWNSEND to Maggie CANTRELL Issued 2A Jan 1932 Rites 4 Jan 1932
J. B. Gribble, M. G.

G. G. WOODLEE to Ella NUNLEY Issued 9 Jan 1932 Rites 10 Jan 1932
W. B. Snipes, JM. G.

Shelton BRATTEN to Iona DRIVER Issued 9 JAn 1932 Rites 10 Jan 1932
H. J. Holcomb, J. P.

Bernard SIMPSON to DAisy SNIPES Issued 9 JAn 1932 Rites 9 Jan 1932
A. B. Moffitt, M. G.

Hugh MOFFITT to Louise CANTRELL Issued 16 Jan 1932 Rites 16 Jan 1932
T. Q. Martin, M. G.

Thomas J. MAYES to Minnie SHOCKLEY Issued 16 Jan 1932 Rites 16 Jan 1932
Reece H. Rogers, M. G.

Charles ARMSTRONG to Lila GLENN Issued 16 Jan 1932 Rites 16 Jun 1932
J. B. McAfee, J. P.

Albert GROSS to Jennie Belle ELKINS Issued 18 Jan 1932 Rites 18 Jan 1932
Frank R. DAvis, Jdg.

Theodore COPPINGER to Ezell WANNAMAKER Issued 18 JAn 1932 Rites 18 Jqn 1932
J. L. BArnes, J. P.

Henry Lee FANN to Novella CAMPBELL Issued 23 Jan 1932 Rites 23 JAn 1932
A. Z. Holder, M. G.

Bryan WOMACK to Mattie ELROD Issued 26 Jan 1932 Rites 26 jan 1932
JAM. K. MArtin, J. P.

Elmer C. GRŐCE to Nannie G. GRIFFITH Issued 2 Nov 1931 Rites 2 Nov 1931
Edgar Henegar, J. P.

Eugene POWELL to Eunice AUGHINBAUGH Issued 10 Nov 1931 Rites 11 Nov 1931
T. A. Richards

Luther ADCOCK to Lassie BROWN Issued 14 Nov 1931 Rites 14 Nov 1931
R. J. Tucker

Leo PATTON to Loretta CANTRELL Issued 19 Nov 1931 Rites 22 Nov 1931
Reece H. Rogers, M. G.

Christtian CURTIS to Ruby PICKETT Issued 21 Nov 1931 Not Returned

T. M. MORENO to Mammie St. JOHN Issued 23 Nov 1931 Rites 23 Nov 1931
T. Q. Martin, M. G.

C. H. BURKS to Etter DENNIS Issued 23 Nov 1931 Rites 26 Nov 1931
J. A. Cunningham, J. P.

Joe GILLENTINE to Alma ARLEDGE Issued 25 Nov 1931 Rites 25 Nov 1931
Reece H. Rogers, M. G.

Jesse R. DONEY to Novella KNOWLES Issued 26 Nov 1931 Rites 26 nov 1931
Frank R. Davis, Jdg.

Norman SMARTT to Dosie NUNLEY Issued 27 Nov 1931 Rites 27 Nov 1931
J. L. Barnes, J. P.

R. G. WRIGHT to MAry THOMAS Issued 28 Nov 1931 Rites 1 dec 1931
T. Q. Martin, M. G.

Raymond SCOTT to Lorene MITCHELL Issued 28 Nov 1931 Rites 28 Nov 1931
W. H. Byles, J. P.

Walter ERNSBERGER to Irene HULETT Issued 3 Dec 1931 Rites 3 Dec 1931
Frank R. Davis, Jdg.

Brown HENNESSEE to Jane McGEE Issued 5 Dec 1931 Rites 5 Dec 1931
J. L. Barnes, J. P.

E. L. HALE to Hazel McMILLEN Issued 10 Dec 1931 Rites 8 May 1932
R. W. Smartt, Jdg.

R. M. PARSLEY to Jessie SNIPES Issued 12 Dec 1931 Rites 13 Dec 1931
A. Z. Holder, J. P.

C. M. TURNER to Mary Lee LEATH Issued 18 Dec 1931 Rites 20 Dec 1931
N. P. McWhirter, J. P.

Robert HILLIS to Mae WOMACK Issued 18 Dec 1931 Rites 20 Dec 1931
E. D. MArtin, M. G.

Lester WEBSTER to Elsie DICKSON Issued 23 Dec 1931 Rites 24 dec 1931
Edgar Henegar, J. P.

Clifton LOCKRIDGE to Ethel Myra BREEDLOVE Issued 23 Dec 1931 Rites 23 Dec 1931
N. P. McWhirter, J. P.

Thomas E. MARTIN to Eva McCULLUM Isseud 26 JAn 1932 Rites 27 JAn 1932
T. A. Richards

Robert DODSON to Aline ROGERS Issued 30 JAn 1932 Rites 30 Jan 1932
dgar Henegar, J. P.

Harold NELMS to Mercedes RICHTER Issued 30 JAn 1932 Rites 30 Jan 1932
R. J. Tucker, M. G.

Frank McCORKLE to Virgia RANKHORN Issued 2 Feb 1932 Rites 3 Feb 1932
W. M. Rowland, J. P.

Thomas B. THAXTON to Frances COMER Issued 3 Feb 1932 Rites 4 Feb 1932
G. P. Brasier, J. P.

Clarence JONES to Alma NEAL Issued 4 Feb 1932 Rites 4 Feb 1932
Frank R. Davis, Jdg.

Aulton FULTS to Renda STARKEY Issued 5 Feb 1932 Rites 6 Feb 1932
J. T. Casey, M. G.

Clifford YOUNGBLOOD to Illilun SMOOT Issued 6 Feb 1932 Rites 7 Feb 1932
G. B. J. Mitchell, J. P.

Lorenza AKERS to Mary TANNER Issued 6 Feb 1932 Rites 6 Feb 1932
A. Z. Holder, J. P.

Lee GAZAWAY to Lillie THROWER Issued 8 Feb 1932 Rites 8 Feb 1932
N. P. McWhirter, J. P.

Leo HARDING to Ruby ROGERS Issued 11 Feb 1932 Rites 14 Feb 1932
W. B. Snipes, M. G.

Jewell LANCE to Anna Belle GRIFFITH Issued 13 Feb 1932 Rites 13 Feb 1932
A. Z. Holder, J. P.

JOnah BESS to Velma BOULDIN Issued 20 Feb 1932 Rites 20 Feb 1932
N. M. Hill, J. P.

Millard DIXSON to Ethel Mai MUNCEY Issued 20 Feb 1932 Rites 21 Feb 1932
J. T. Casey, M. G.

Wesley BROWNER to Eva JORDAN Issued 21 Feb 1932 Rites 21 Feb 1932
Edgar Henegar, J. P.

Ernest MAXWELL to Elizabeth YOUNG Issued 27 Feb 1932 Rites 27 Feb 1932
R. W. Smartt, Jdg.

J. D. VICKERS to Goldie SIMMONS Issued 1 MAr 1932 Rites 8 May 1932
G. B. J. Mitchell, J. P.

Fred HALE to Margie ACUFF Issued 3 Mar 1932 Rites 6 Mar 1932
Fate Walker, J.P.

John O'NEIL to Mable KING Issued 5 MAr 1932 Rites 5 Mar 1932
Frank R. Davis, Jdg.

Thomas HILL to Lillie Mai STUBBLEFIELD Issued 5 Mar 1932 Rites 5 Mar 1932
J. B. McAfee, J. P.

W. L. MILLER to Gertrude HUTCHINGS Issued 9 Mar 1932 Rites 10 Mar 1932
F. B. Worley

Bill RAY to Erline PRATER Issued 12 Mar 1932 Rites 12 Mar 1932
W. F. Presley

A. R. FISH to Mary L. DRIVER Issued 18 Mar 1932 Rites 20 Mar 1932
W. V. D. Miller, J. P.

Alex PRATER to Lauretta ALLEN Issued 19 Mar 1932 Rites 27 Mar 1932
T. Q. Martin, M. G.

Casto CARTER to Gladys DELONG Issued 21 Mar 1932 Rites 26 Mar 1932
N. P. McWhirter, J. P.

Claborne CURTIS to Seawillow HITCHCOCK Issued 26 Mar 1932 Rites 27 Mar 1932
E. D. Martin, M. G.

Earl WARE to Doty McCORMICK Issued 1 Apr 1932 Rites 1 Apr 1932
J. L. Barnes, J. P.

Brown DOAK to Wilma HOBBS Issued 2 Apr 1932 Rites 2 Apr 1932
J. L. Barnes, J. P.

Joe BLACK to Henretta HANCOCK Issued 4 Apr 1932 Rites 4 Apr 1932
E. S. Bedford, M. G.

Thurman ROGERS to Flora Mai ROGERS Issued 4 Apr 1932 Rites 6 Apr 1932
W. H. Byles, J.P.

Hoyt GRISSOM to Pauline WARE Issued 9 Apr 1932 Rites 9 Apr 1932
Chas. Hillis, J. P.

Otto CARTWRIGHT to Nora MULLICAN Issued 9 Apr 1932 Rites 9 Apr 1932
J. P. Bilbrey, J. P.

Lon STOTTS to Ona FULTS Issued 9 Apr 1932 Rites 9 Apr 1932
Frank R. Davis, Jdg.

William JOHNSON to Bernie GEORGE Issued 9 Apr 1932 Rites 9 Apr 1932
J. L. Walker, J. P.

Hubert MAXWELL to Mary ALLEN Issued 14 Apr 1932 Rites 16 Apr 1932
H. J. Holcomb, J. P.

Eugene LORANCE to Nettie SUMMERS Issued 20 Apr 1932 Rites 23 Apr 1932
G. B. J. Mitchell, J. P.

Otto RUSSELL to Cecil BRYANT Issued 22 Apr 1932 Rites 22 Apr 1932
Fate Walker, J. P.

W. L. HENDRICKS to MAudie TOLLIVER Issued 23 Apr 1932 Rites 23 Apr 1932
R. L. BAker

F. J. HENDLEY to Cornelia SMARTT Issued 30 Apr 1932 Rites 30 Apr 1932
L. T. LAwrence, M. G.

Kelly FISHER to Jedie BESS Issued 25 Jun 1932 Rites 25 Jun 1932
J. B. McAfee, J. P.

Gentry ROLLER to Gladys DRIVER Issued 28 jun 1932 Rites 28 Jun 1932
H. J. Holcomb, J. P.

Harrison BILES to Bertha ROBERTS Issued 29 Jun 1932 Rites 29 jun 1932
J. R. Gray, M. G.

JAck STARKEY to Kate DURHAM Issued 30 Jun 1932 Rites 30 jun1932
E. W. Sutherlin, J. P.

Hobart VAughn HALE to Mary Belle PACK Issued 30 Jun 1932 Rites 30 jun 1932
W.T.Presley, M. G.

Rayburn GREEN to Una Mai LEATHERWOOD Issued 2 Jul 1932 Rites 2 Jul 1932
E. D. Martin, M. G.

Thomas C. PRICE to Charles Kelly TATUM Issued 2 jul 1932 Rites 3 Jul 1932
R. W. Smartt, Jdg.

A. G. FERRELL to Nellie WISEMAN Issued 2 Jul 1932 Rites 9 Jul 1932
W. H. Craven, M. G.

FLauk MUNCY to Alice WHITTENBURG Issued 2 Jul 1932 Rites 3 Jul 1932
J. L. Barnes, J. P.

Lonnie PINEGAR to Reutha Mai SPARKMAN Issued 16 Jul 1932 Rites 22 jul 1932
L. T. Lawrence, J. P.

Grover FULTS to Maggie ROGERS Issued 22 Jul 1932 Rites 23 jul 1932
F. L. Kirby, J. P.

E. S. FOSTER to Nora WOAMCK Issued 23 Jul 1932 Rites 23 jul 1932
E. F. CAntrell, J. P.

Goebel JENNINGS to Ethel HILLIS Issued 23 Jul 1932 Rites 23 Jul 1932
Frank R. Davis, Jdg.

Brady PARKHURST to Anna Leora PHILLIPS Issued 27 Jul 1932 Rites 30 Jul 1932
W. T. Watson, J. P.

James STARKEY to Viola STEWART Issued 28 Jul 1932 Rites 28 jul 1932
R. J. Tucker, M. G.

Jonathan HENDRICKSON to Novella LAUDERMILK Issued 3 Aug 1932 Rites 3 Aug 1932
J. B. McAfee, J. P.

J. D. GREEN to Ruby MALONE Issued 6 Aug 1932 Rites 6 Aug 1932
R. J. Tucker, M. G.

Charles MADEWELL to Della CHRISTIAN Issued 8 Aug 1932 Rites 8 Aug 1932
S. J. RAmsey, J. P.

Sherman SOLOMON (C) to Sadie STARKEY (Col) Issued 15 Aug 1932 Rites 15 Aug 1932
E. W. Sutherlin, J. P.

B. N. SIMONS to Lula DURHAM Issued 30 Apr 1932 Rites 30 Apr 1932
J. B. Gribble, M. G.

Troy PUGH to Virginia GLENN Issued 30 Apr 1932 Rites 1 MAy 1932
T. A. Richards

Clarence PAGE to Mary Lee LATIMER Issued 2 MAy 1932 Rites 4 May 1932
Claud Myers, M. G.

Otis DYKES to Josie JONES Issued 7 May 1932 Rites 7 May 1932
Fate Walker, J. P.

Grover PELHAM to Lula TURNER Issued 17 May 1932 Rites 17 May 1932
G. P. Brasier, J. P.

Raymond EARLE to Myrtle ROGERS Issued 21 May 1932 Rites 21 May 1932
C. L. Webster, M. G.

C. R. FOSTER to Vesta REDMOND Isseud 21 May 1932 Rites 22 May 1932
J. K. Martin, J. P.

Wade MADEWELL to Grace BOYD Issued 21 MAy 1932 Rites 22 MAy 1932
Reece H. Rogers, M. G.

Billie BOULDIN to Gertrude HOBBS Issued 25 MAy 1932 Rites 25 MAy 1932
F. L. Kirby, J. P.

T. Emerson SIMPKINS to CAtherine JENNINGS Issued 27 May 1932 Rites 27 MAy 1932
T. Q. Martin, M. G.

Emmett MYERS to Sarah SHORT Issued 28 May 1932 Rites 28 MAy 1932
Frank R. Davis, Jdg.

Lowell McGEE to Delma HALE Issued 4 Jun 1932 Rites 4 jun 1932
J. B. McAfee, J. P.

Jack W. WILSON to Hazel BOYD Issued 6 Jun 1932 Rites 10 jun 1932
T. Q. Martin, M. G.

Hall TENPENNY to Mary Lee LOGUE Issued 10 Jun 1932 Rites 11 jun 1932
E. D. Martin, M. G.

R. H. SCHILD to Virginia CAIN Issued 11 Jun 1932 Rites 11 Jun 1932
T. Q. Martin, M. G.

Ransom TANNER to Jessie CAMPBELL Issued 11 Jun 1932 Jun 1932 Jun 1932
A. Z. Holder, J. P.

Hooper WATTS to Ollie Mai GRIBBLE Issued 18 Jun 1932 Rites 25 jun 1932
A. J. Locke, J. P.

Scott NELSON to Elizabeth HILLIS Issued 23 Jun 1932 Rites 23 Jun 1932
W. B. Snipes, M. G.

JAmes GORDY to Hassie MATHIS Issued 25 Jun 1932 Rites 25 jun 1932
J. B. McAfee, J. P.

Lerel HORTON to Ruth COMER Issued 25 Jun 1932 Rites 26 Jun 1932
T. Q. Martin, M. G.

Tom HALL to Florence WINTON Issued 16 Aug 1932 Rites 18 Aug 1932
   Isham Hunt, M. G.

James E. FREDERICK to Elizabeth LANSDEN Issued 26 Aug 1932 Rites 27 Aug 1932
   A. H. Huff, M. G.

Howard BUTCHER to Irene DODSON Issued 27 Aug 1932 Rites 27 Aug 1932
   O. B. Wiseman, J. P.

Lonnie JENNINGS to Carrie PALMER Issued 27 Aug 1932 Rites 27 Aug 1932
   O. B. Wiseman, J. P.

Sidney WILLIAMSON to Mary Belle ODINEAL Issued 3 Sep 1932 Rites 4 Sep 1932
   T. Q. Martin, M. G.

Jenery DELANEY to Ruth MUNCEY Issued 3 Sep 1932 rites 3 Sep 1932
   T. Q. Martin, M. G.

A. P. ADCOCK to Pearl WELLS Issued 9 Sep 1932
   Jas. K. Martin, J. P.

Alpha YOUNG, Jr. to HAzel WOAMCK Issued 10 Sep 1932
   J. R. Gray, M. G.

George HILLIS to Mary LANGFORD Issued 12 Sep 1932 Rites 12 Sep 1932
   Frank R. Davis, Jdg.

W. Z. WILSON to Lillian FREEZE Issued 13 Sep 1932 Rites 18 Sep 1932
   G. B. J. Mitchell, J. P.

Edley NEWMAN to Frances LOCKE Issued 16 Sep 1932 Rites 16 Sep 1932
   F. L. Leeper, M. G.

Layton HARRIS to Gladys Ray BAIN Issued 17 Sep 1932 Rites 17 Sep 1932
   N. P. McWhirter, J. P.

D. BELL to Mammie PARKER Issued 22 Sep 1932 Rites 2 Oct 1932
   W. F. Roach, J. P.

Polk ELDER to Ethel TAYLOR Issued 23 sep 1932   Not Returned

Otis MARTIN to Hazel GLENN Issued 24 Sep 1932 Rites 9 Oct 1932
   J. S. Dunlap, J. P.

Lytle KEATHLEY to Lula BRATCHER Issued 24 Sep 1932 Rites 24 Sep 1932
   A. J. Locke, J. P.

Clarence BUTCHER to Velma BOTTOMS Issued 24 Sep 1932 Rites 24 Sep 1932
   J. W. McCollum, J. P.

Frank DENBY to Mabel TURNER Issued 24 Sep 1932 Rites 24 Sep 1932
   C. L. Webster, M. G.

Porter LEE to Fannie SMITH Issued 26 Sep 1932 Rites 26 Sep 1932
   J. S. NAnce, M. G.

Leonard WILLIAMSON to Alma SIMONS Issued 27 Sep 1932 Rites 8 Oct 1932
   A. Z. Holder, J. P.

Foster JERNIGAN Helma MAi WELLS Issued 27 Sep 1932 Rites 27 Sep 1932
   G. B. J. Mitcehll, J. P.

Posey FLANNIGAN to PAuline PATRICK Issued 29 Sep 1932 Rites 29 sep 1932
   W. E. Johnson, M. G.

Rufus LANCE to Clara Belle REDMON Issued 30 Sep 1932 Rites 1 Oct 1932
   G. B. J. Mitchell, J. P.

Homer BOYD (C) to Lula Mai RAMSEY (C) Issued 5 Oct 1932 Rites 6 Oct 1932
   J. R. Gray,.M. G.

Dempsey ROLLER to Lizzie BOREN Issued 8 Oct 1932 Rites 8 Oct 1932
   C. R. Womack, J. P.

Denton ORRICK to Certie YOUNG Issued 8 Oct 1932 Rites 9 Oct 1932
   G. B. J. Mitchell, J. P.

H. H. PALMER to Mecca LAFEVER Issued 8 Oct 1932 Rites 8 Oct 1932
   Reece H. Rogers, M. G.

Charles MILLRANEY to Nivella HOLLAND Issued 15 Oct 1932 Rites 15 Oct 1932
   J. H. Mayo, J. P.

Kermit JONES to Margie LOTHAM Issued 15 Oct 1932 Rites 15 Oct 1932
   W. F. Presley, M. G.

Clabe JENNINGS to Emma NUNLEY Issued 15 Oct 1932 Rites 15 Oct 1932
   J. L. Barnes, J. P.

Benjamin LANCE to Maxine DAVIS Issued 15 Oct 1932 Rites 15 Oct 1932
   A. Z. Holder, J. P.

Roscoe HARMON to Bertie CANTRELL Issued 18 Oct 1932 Rites 18 Oct 1932
   J. H. Mayo, J. P.

Ace HOWARD to Ola WILSON Issued 19 Oct 1932 Rites 20 Oct 1932
   J. H. Mayo, J. P.

Max WINNINGHAM to Ruth Ann SMITH Issued 19 Oct 1932 Rites 19 oct 1932
   A. H. Huff, M. G.

MArlin MOSER to Ophia HUBBARD Issued 23 Oct 1932 Rites 23 Oct 1932
   J. H. Mayo. J. P.

Henry JONES to Della MOFFITT Issued 24 Oct 1932 Rites 24 Oct 1932
   C. H. Riddle, J. P.

James RAMSEY (C) to Bessie BLUE (C) Issued 26 Oct 1932 Rites 31 Oct 1932
   T. Q. Martin, M. G.

A. F. VAN HOOSER to Bettie THOMAS Issued 31 Oct 1932 Rites 1 Nov 1932
   R. W.Smartt, Jdg.

J. T. WARD to Ova CHRISTIAN Issued 5 Nov 1932 Rites 5 Nov 1932
   J. H. Mayo, J. P.

Book 17 - Warren County Marriages - Nov. 26 1932 to Apr. 27, 1935

Robert NEELEY to Beulah ROWLAND Issued 26 Nov 1932 Rites 3 Dec 1932
    Cass R. Womack, J, P,

Hugh CAGLE to Ruby Ethel YORK Issued 26 Nov 1932 Rites 26 Nov 1932
    J. H. Mayo, J. P.

W. T. LUSK to Annie FUSTON Issued 28 Nov 1932 Rites 28 Nov 1932
    J. S. Nance, M. G.

William BROWN to Gertrude CLENDENEN Issued 28 Nov 1932 Rites 28 Nov 1932
    Frank R. DAvis, Jdg.

Granville BURKS to Willie Lee BAIN Issued 2 Dec 1932 Rites 4 Dec 1932
    W. F. Roach, J, P.

John McBRIDE to MAry Elizabeth TURNER Issued 3 Dec 1932 Rites 3 Dec 1932
    C. H. Riddle, J. P.

ClarenceWARRICK to Beatrice GREEN Issued 3 Dec 1932 Rites 3 Dec 1932
    Alf T. Judkins, M, G.

John Edward WARREN to Alma Grace O'NEAL Issued 18 Dec 1932 Rites 18 Dec 1932
    T. Q. MaLLin, M. G.

E. L. BELL to Maie MULLICAN Issued 15 Dec 1932 Rites 17 Dec 1932-
    J. H. MAyo, J. P.

J. F. WOODLEE to Lillie HUTCHINS Issued 16 Dec 1932 Rites 24 Dec 1932
    Stewart J. Ramsey, J. P.

C. L. ACUFF to Ona Mai HENDRIXSON Issued 17 Dec 1932 Rites 17 Dec 1932
    irving Patton, J. P.

Wilson REED to Laverna FITTS Issued 21 Dec 1932 Rites 24 Dec 1932
    T. A. Richard, M. G.

Grady KNIGHT ti Lyda TUBBS Issued 21 Dec 1932 Rites 25 Dec 1932
    J. T. CASEY, M. G.

Jesse ARGO to Gladys BOULDIN Issued 22 Dec 1932 Rites 22 Dec 1932
    J. L. BArnes, J. P.

Gilbert TURNER to Irene DEADMAN Issued 22 Dec 1932 Rites 23 Dec 1932
    J. H. Mayo, J. P.

Gilbert MAXWELL to Lillie PUGH Issued 23 Dec 1932 Rites 24 Dec 1932
    T. A. Richard, M. G.

Kenneth SMITH to LARNELL WILSON Issued 24 Dec 1932 Rites 24 Dec 1932
    T. Q. MArtin, M. G.

Raden SAUNDERS to Juanita CUNNINGHAM Issued 24 Dec 1932 Rites 24 Dec 1932
    J. T. Caset, M. G.

Herman L. PONDER to Sarah VANATTA Issued 24 Dec 1932 Rites 24 Dec 1932
    T, A. Richard, m. G.

Odra MITCHELL to Nina TURNER Issued 9 Nov 1932 Rites 9 Nov 1932
    J. H. MAyo, J. P.

Joe AUGHINBAUGH to Thelma WISER Issued 12 Nov 1932 Rites 12 Nov 1932
    T. A. Richards, M. G.

E. G. SCOTT to Pauline RODGERS Issued 12 Nov 1932 Rites 12 Nov 1932
    J. E. Clark, M. G.

Richmond FARLESS, Jr. to Clara MAYO Issued 12 Nov 1932 Rites 12 Nov 1932
    J. H. MAyo, J. P.

Jim VICKERS to Dewey WOODS Issued 12 Nov 1932 Rites 13 Nov 1932
    A. Z. Holder, J. P.

Buford LOCKE to Bonnie RHEA Issued 14 Nov 1932 Rites 14 Nov 1932
    L. B. Moffitt, J. P.

Herman CANTRELL to Irene REDMON Issued 19 Nov 1932 Rites 20 nov 1932
    E. T. Cantrell. J. P.

J. H. HALEY to Erline BARNETT Issued 19 Nov 1932 Rites 20·Nov 1932
    J. L. Walker, J. P.

Virgle LOCKE to Wretha CANTRELL Issued 19 Nov 1932 Rites 20 nov 1932
    Wm. Rowland, J. P.

Hamby MARTIN to Rosa JONES Issued 24 Dec 1932 Rites 24 dec 1932
    J. S. Dunlap, J. P.

496 Marriages in this book

Toy BATES to HAZEL STARKEY Issued 26 Dec 1932 Rites 26 Dec 1932
Irving Patton, J. P.

Lonnie Ford JORDAN to Mary Lee EARLS Issued 26 Dec 1932 Rites 28 Dec 1932
L.,B. Moffitt, J. P.

Henry L. LINDNER to Myrtle UPCHURCH Issued 26 Dec 1932   Not Returned

DAlton BURKS to Thelma DENNIS Issued 30 Dec 1932 Rites 31 Dec 1932
J. E. CLARK, M. G.

C. E. SMITH to MAtilda WATLEY Issued"31 Dec 1932 Rites 31 Dec 1932
W. H. Craven, M. G.

Alton BARNES to Irene McGEE Issued 31 Dec 1932 Rites 31 Dec 1932
N. M. Hill, J. P.

W. L. CUNNINGHAM to Iva MAI McMURTRY Issued 31 DEC 1932. Rites 1 JAn 1933
A. H. Huff, M.,G.

Frank PAul JONES to HAzel Down BARBER Issued 7 JAn 1933 Rites 7 JAn 1933
W. T. Wilson, J. P.

Alvin COPE to Virgia ROLLER Issued 7 Jan 1933. Rites 7 Jan 1933.
J. W. Cooley, M. G.

Gilbert ROGERS to MAry CAMPBELL Issued 11 Jan 1933. Rites 12 Jan 1933
W. H. Byles, J. P.

Taylor RIGSBY to Melie HUTCHINS Rites 12 JAn 1933. Rites 12 Jan 1933.
Irving Patton, J. P.

RAy GILLETTE to Jewell BUMBALOUGH Issued 14 JAn 1933 Rites 14 JAn 1933
G. B. J. Mitchell, J. P.

E. S. BEDFORD to Clara WARE Issued 14 Jan 1933 Rites 17 Jan 1933
J. R. Gray, M. G.

Aubrey HUTCHINS to Lorene TURNER Issued 15 JAn 1933 Rites 15 JAn 1933
J. H. Mayo, J. P.

W. V. JONES to Naomi AUGHINBAUGH Issued 17 JAn 1933 Rites 21 JAn 1933
J. B. Gribble, M. G.

Otis SPENCER to Ruth TENPENNY Issued 21 Jan 1933 Rites 22 Jan 1933
J. T. Casey, J, G.

W. S. STANLY to Parlee MOORE Issued 27 JAn 1933 Rites 30 Jan 1933
W. T. Watson, J. P.

Haskell SMITH to Shelby GREEN Issued 28 JAN 1933 Rites 29 Jan 1933
T. Q. Martin, M. G.

Andrew PRESSLY to Tennie MAYNARD Issued 2 Feb 1933 Rites 2 Feb 1933
Irving Patton, J.

Bill DRAKE to Bessie RIGSBY Issued 10 Feb 1933 Rites 12 Feb 1933
Wm. Rowland, J. P.

George Everett REDD to Virginia Frances MOORE Issued 15 Feb 1933 Rites 17 Feb 1933
A. H. Huff, M. G.

JAMES D. BREWER to Mrs. L. L. HUGGINS Issued 15 Feb 1933 Rites 15 Feb 1933
Frank R. DAvis, Jdg.

Lee Denton ROSS to Mary Morford POTTER Issued 15 Feb 1933 Rites 18 Feb 1933
L. T. Lawrence, M. G.

R. H. WINNETT to Aathaline TRAVIS Issued 17 Feb 1933 Rites 18 Feb 1933
A. Z. Holder, J. P.

Aubrey GREEN to Syble CUNNINGHAM Issued18 Feb 1933 Rites 26 Feb 1933
J. W. McCollum, J. P.

Dave MILLER to Stella MADEWELL Issued 20 Feb 1933 Rites 20 Feb 1933
G. P. Brasier, J. P.

Woodrow SMOOT to Frances MORGAN Issued 22 Feb 1933 Rites 23 Feb 1933
A. Z. Holder, J. P.

Tolbert COPE to Ruby DENTON Issued 24 Feb 1933 Rites 26 Feb 1933
J. W. Cooley, J. P.

Thurman SCOTT to Emma KESEY Issued 1 MAr 1933 Rites 1 MAr 1933
J. L. BArnes, J. P.

Floyd YORK to Willie Mai SHERRELL Issued 3 Mar 1933 Rites 5 Mar 1933
J. D. Vandergriff

James A. BROWN to Lula GIBBS Issued 6 Mar 1933 Rites 6 Mar 1933
C. E. Hawkins, Jr.. M. G.

Percy BELL to Ida MORTON Issued 8 Mar 1933 rites 11 MAR 1933
john Morton, M. G.

RAy LOONEY to Cloa LOONEY Issued 10 Mar 1933 Rites 11 Mar 1933
Wm. Rowland, J. P.

MAson MOORE to Cleo McGEE Issued 11 Mar 1933 Rites 11 Mar 1933
J. H. MAyo, J. P.

John AKEMAN to Mary CRUSE Issued 18 Mar 1933 Rites 19 Mar 1933
V. D. Lusk, J. P.

Roy RAY to Cassie LATHOM Issued 18 Mar 1933 Rites 18 Mar 1933
J. H. Mayo, J. P.

Frank FORD to Mabel PATTERSON Issued 18 Mar 1933 Rites 19 Mar 1933
W. J. Carothers, M. G.

Roy CLENDENON to Sallie PEARSON Issued 22 Mar 1933 Rites 22 Mar 1933
E. D. MARTIN, M. G.

Henry VANDERGRIFF to Eloise SHERRELL Issued 7 Apr 1933 Rites 15 Apr 1933
J. E. Clark, M. G.?

Thurman HASTON to Velma GRISSOM Issued 7 Apr 1933 Rites 8 Apr 1933
A. H. Huff, M. G.

Eugene CRAVEN to Edith CRAWLEY Issued 11 Apr 1933 Rites 12 Apr 1933
W. F. Roach, J. P.

Samuel L. RICHARDSON to Gladys A. MEADORS Issues 11 Apr 1933 Not Returned

T. L. TUBB to Louise WILMORE Issued 15 Apr 1933 Rites 15 Apr 1933
A. Z. Holder, J. P.

Odie TALLEY to Clarice SCOTT Issued 17 Apr 1933 Rites 17 Apr 1933
Reece H. Rogers, M. G.

Loyd B. WALKER to Lela WATSON Issued 17 Apr 1933 Rites 17 Apr 1933
John Morton, M. G.

Elbert BELL to Walthan PARKER Issued 17 Apr 1933 Rites 19 Apr 1933
W. F. Roach, J. P.

J. G. TRAPP to Meda JOHNSON Issued 18 Apr 1933 Rites 18 Apr 1933
Frank R. Davis, jdg.

Frank SLAUGHTER to Velma JENNINGS Issued 21 Apr 1933 Not Returned

J. M. GEORGE to Hixie FOWLER Issued 22 Apr 1933 Rites 22 Apr 1933
FAte Walker, J. P.

Ike NUNLEY to Cora BOULDIN Issued 25 Apr 1933 Rites 26 Apr 1933
Reece H. Rogers, M. G.

Jim PACK to Ruby BEARD Issued 26 Apr 1933 Rites 26 Apr 1933
John Morton, M. G.

Ferman TURNER to Betty WILLOUGHBY Issued 27 Apr 1933 Rites 27 Apr 1933
I. D. Walker,

Robert L. LOVETT to MAud ROBERTS Issued 27 Apr 1933 Rites 27 Apr 1933
J. H. Mayo, J. P.

Frank OGLE to Elizabeth WISER Isseud 29 Apr 1933 Rites 29 Feb 1933
J. B. Gribble, M. G.

F. L. SULLIVAN to Mrs. A. L. HOBBS Issued 6 May 1933 Rites 7 May 1933
E. D. Martin, M. G.

Brown SIMPSON to Frances WOODLEE Issued 6 May 1933 Rites 11 May 1933
A. B. Moffitt, M. G.

Flaval PATTON to Ola Mai CUMMINGS Issued 11 May 1933 Rites 11 May 1933
E. D. Martin, M. G.

R. S. SCOTT to Leola CAGLE Issued 11 May 1933 Rites 12 May 1933
J. L. BArnes, J. P.

R. T. HOAWARD to Hassie Rella REED Issued 13 May 1933 Rites 13 May 1933
T. Q. Martin, M. G.

Chester KELSAY to Irena YOUNG Issued 13 May 1933 Rites 13 May 1933
T. A. Richard, M. G.

Hackett Ross POTTER to Sallie Serena CHRISTIAN 13 May 1933 Rites 13 May 1933
T. Q. Martin, M. G.

R. T. SKELTON to Edith JOHNSON Issued 19 May 1933 Rites 20 May 1933
W. J. CAruthers, M. G.

Haward GANN to opal HENDRIXSON Issued 20 May 1933
A. Z. Holder, J. P.

Grady TURNER to Verna WILSON Issued 20 May 1933
J. H. Mayo, J. P.

Radford M. REAMS to Clauretta M. HENNESSEE Issued 22 MAy 1933 Rites 22 May 1933
A. H. Huff, M. G.

Ernest HANKINS to Anna Louise HILL issued 22 MAy 1933 Rites 22 May 1933
Irving Patton, J. P.

Tom REYNOLDS to Margaret BLAYLOCK Issued 22 May 1933 Rites 24 May 1933
C. L. Webster

Moses Lee BEARD to Gertrude LAWS Issued 23 May 1933 Rites 23 May 1933
A. H. Huff, M. G.

Clifton WANNAMAKER to Juanita FOWLER Issued 24 May 1933 Rites 25 May 1933
J. L. Barnes, J. P.

Toy PITTMAN to Virgie JACO Issued 26 May 1933 Rites 27 May 1933
J. B. Gribble, M. G.

Fred PATTERSON to Juanita COPE Issued 29 May 1933 Rites 29 May 1933
Stewart J. Ramsey, J. P.

Grover L. HILLIS to Ada Vera HOLLAND Issued 30 May 1933 Rites 30 May 1933
J. H. Mayo, J. P.

DeWitt WOODMORE to Jennie Louise DAVIS Issued 1 Jun 1933 Rites 2 Jun 1933
C. E. HAwkins, M. G.

Clyde GREEN to Aline WOMACK Issued 3 Jun 1933 Rites 3 Jun 1933
E. D. Martin, M. G.

Forest WILSON to Alma BRATCHER Issued 3 Jun 1933 Rites 3 Jun 1933
Herbert Knight, J. P.

William THOMISON to Bettie BOUNDS Issued 3 Jun 1933 Rites 3 jun 1933
J. H. Mayo, J. P.

James LYONS to Ersa BOYD Issued 5 Jun 1933 Rites 10 Jun 1933
T. Q. MaLin, M. G.

RAymond RODDY to Maxine DUNLAP Issued 6 Jun 1933 Not Returned

Thomas WALKER to Henrietta S. BEARD Issued 7 Jun 1933 Rites 7 Jun 1933
J. H. Mayo, J. P.

Huberrt ELKINS to Eunice PACK Issued 7 Jun 1933 Rites 11 jun 1933
A. Z. Holder, J. P.

W. V. EVANS to Yvonne WARE Issued 9 Jun 1933 Rites 9 Jun 1933
I. P. McGregor, J. P.

Hayden SMITH to Lillian HIGGINS Issued 9 Jun 1933 Rites 9 Jun 1933
T. Q. Martin, M. G.

Homer SANDERS to Virginia PATTERSON Issued 9 Jun 1933 Rites 9 Jun 1933
A. H. Huff, M. G.

Oscar R. SMITH to Ruby L. FREEZE Issued 10 Jun 1933 Rites 10 Jun 1933
Elisha Henry, M. G.

J. H. YOUNGBLOOD to Estelle SMITH Issued 12 Jun 1933 Rites 12 Jun 1933
J. H. Mayo, J. P.

Archie M. WINFREE to Ida Belle BRAGG Issued 16 Jun 1933 Rites 17 jun 1933
Llewellyn T. Lawrence, M. G.

George WINTON (C) to Eva THOMAS (C) Issued 17 Jun 1933 Rites 24 Jun 1933
J. R. Stubblefield, M. G.

Ross STILES to Opal BOULDIN Issued 17 Jun 1933 Rites 17 jun 1933
J. H. Mayo, J. P.

Zollie POTTER to Carrie KING Issued 17 Jun 1933 Rites 17 jun 1933
R. W. Smartt, Jdg.

L. M. MUNCY to Margie STROUD Issued 17 Jun 1933 Rites 17 jun 1933
L. B. Moffitt, J. P.

Monroe FIELDS to Maggie KIRBY Issued 21 jun 1933 Rites 21 jun 1933
J. B. Gribble, M. G.

J. P. CLARK to Rosa WOMACK Issued 22 Jun 1933 Rites 23 Jun 1933
J. B. Gribble, M. G.

Houston GRIFFITH to Francis HALEY Issued 23 Jun 1933 Rites 24 Jun 1933
W. T. Watson, J. P.

Oren (JACK) DYER to Gracie FUSTON Issued 24 Jun 1933 Rites 24 jun 1933
Wm. E. Jojinson, M. G.

Jesse Howard HILL to Deskin MITCHELL Issued 24 Jun 1933 Rites 25 Jun 1933
L. T. LAWRENCE, M. G.

Dewey CAMPBELL to Myrl LAWS Issued 1 Jul 1933 Rites 1 Jul 1933
J. H. Mayo, J. P.

James C. BLANKS to Pearl GATHER Issued 8 Jul 1933 Rites 8 Jul 1933
A. Z. Holder, J. P.

Hollie WILCHER to Dora May NEWBY Issued 8 Jul 1933 Rites 8 Jul 1933
V. D. Lusk, J. P.

Tramble TURNER to Tula HOBBS Issued 11 Jul 1933 Rites 11 Jul 1933
T. Q. Martin, M. G.

John GREER to Myrtle LOVE Issued 12 Jul 1933 Rites 15 Jul 1933
J. H. Mayo, J. P.

Carlton LYLE to Eira MOORE Issued 3 Jul 1933 Rites 15 Jul 1933
L. T. Lawrence, M. G.

Thurman CURTIS to Alice NUNLY Issued 15 Jul 1933 rites 15 Jul 1933
Steve Smartt, M. G.

Leland MALCOMB to Virginia NELSON Issued 15 Jul 1933 Rites 15 Jul 1933
T. Q. Martin, M. G.

Robert McCORMICK to Ruby ROBERTS Issued 15 Jul 1933 Ret. 13 Aug 1933
Unexplained

Leland ARLEDGE to Pearl MITCHELL Issued 18 Jul 1933 Rites 19 Jul 1933
Herbert Knight, J. P.

Arnold DUNHAM to Rufine CURTIS Issued 22 Jul 1933 Rites 22 jul 1933
W. H. Craven, M. G.

Hackett O'NEAL to Lizzie SMITH Issued 22 Jul 1933 Rites 22 jul 1933
O. B. Wiseman, J. P.

J. L. SPARKMAN to Lela GIST Issued 24 Jul 1933 Rites 24 jul 1933
W. G. Keyt, M. G.

Truman BESS to Eunice DENNIS Issued 25 Jul 1933 Rites 25 jul 1933
T. A. Richards, M. G.

Noll TOSH to Bussie Mai ALLEN Issued 29 jul 1933 Rites 29 jul 1933
A. T. Judkins, M. G.

Joe McGREGOR (C) to Sallie MAi YORK (C) Issued 1 Aug 1933 Rites 1 Aug 1933
J. H. Mayo, J. P.

Roy SMITH to Irene SCOTT Issued 5 Aug 1933 Rites 5 Aug 1933
J. B. Gribble, M. G,

Orbary JONES to Pearlie PRATER Issued 5 Aug 1933 Rites 5 Aug 1933
Reece H. Rogers, M. G.

Nellis WOODS to Fannie LOOPER Issued 5 Aug 1933 Rites 6 Aug 1933
Irving Patton, J. P.

Alvie TEMPLETON to Odel KEITH Issued 5 Aug 1933 Rites 6 Aug 1933
A. H. Huff, M. G.

Richard E. MITCHELL to Anna McBRIDE Issued 6 Aug 1933 Rites 6 Aug 1933
A. H. Huff, M. G.

Omar McGIBONEY to Catherine HASTON Issued 7 Aug 1933 Rites 7 Aug 1933
A. T. Judkins, M.-G.

Vorgil OWENS to Ethel SPENCER Issued 12 Sep 1933 Rites 12 sep 1933
A. H. Huff, M. G.

J. R. COOPER to Willie ROACH Issued 13 Sep 1933 rites 13 Sep 1933
Reece H. Rogers, M. G.

Elmo SNYDER to Ethel ROLLINS Issued 16 Sep 1933 Rites 16 Sep 1933
Irving Patton, J. P.

Johnnie ROWLAND to Lillie B. LOONEY Issued 18 Sep 1933 Rites 18 Sep 1933
A. T. Judkins, M. G.

Thurman MARTIN to Hattie Mai BATES Issued 19 sep 1933 rites 19 Sep 1933
Frank R. Davis, Jdg.

John BESS to Bobbie KELLEY Issued 23 Sep 1933 rites 23 Sep 1933
C. E. HAwkins, M. G.

L. D. SPARKMAN to Gladys CHANDLEY Issued 23 Sep 1933 Rites 1 Oct 1933
Irving Patton, J. P.

Tom YOUNG to Lacy C. BREWINGTON Issued 23 Sep 1933 Rites 23 Sep 1933
L. T. Lawrence, M. G.

Aubry WANAMAKER to Helen GROSS Issued 23 sep 1933 Rites 24 sep 1933
J. L. BArnes, J. P.

W. W. WITTY to R. M. JONES Issued 26 Sep 1933 Rites 1 Oct 1933
G. B. J. Mitchell, J. P.

Lewis P. SMITH to PAuline BROWN Issued 28 Sep 1933 Rites 29 Sep 1933
C. E. HAWKINS, M. G.

J. O. MOORE to Grace POWELL Issued 29 Sep 1933 Rites 29 Sep 1933
L. T. LAwrence, M. G.

Horace J. KIMSEY to Blanche MORGAN Issued 30 Sep 1933 rites 14 oct 1933
J. R. Stubblefield, M. G.

Burchel KNOWLES to Virgil CANTRELL Issued 30 Sep 1933 rites 30 Sep 1933
A. H. Huff, M. G.

BArney SWAN to Celia Mai HENDRIX Issued 30 Sep 1933 rites 1 Oct 1933
A. Z. Holder, J. P.

J. E. STOKES to Louvina SMARTT Issued 2 Oct 1933 Rites 2 Oct 1933
L. B. Moffitt, J. P.

M. P. FRALEY to Bessie Lee TEMPLETON Issued 3 Oct 1933 Rites 4 Oct 1933
Irving Patton, J. P.

William CROUCH to Virgie Lee ROBINSON Issued 5 Oct 1933 Rites 5 Oct 1933
G. B. J. Mitchell, J. P.

Frank BELCHER to Violet McAFEE Issued 10 Oct 1933 Rites 10 Oct 1933
J. H. Mayo, J. P.

George DAVIS to Eliza ROBERTS Issued 11 Aug 1933 Rites 11 Aug 1933
Irving Patton, J. P.

Robert DAVIS to Lillie McDOWELL Issued 12 Aug 1933 Rites 12 Aug 1933
W. T. WArren, J. P.

George BONNER to Martha LEE Issued 14 Aug 1933 Rites 14 Aug 1933
J. S. NAnce, M. G.

Carl BRYMER to Cleo SIMONS   Dated 24 Aug 1933 - Not Issued

Creed WRIGHT to Alberta WILLIAMSON Issued 24 Aug 1933   VOIDED

Creed WRIGHT to Alberta WILLIAMSON Issued 24 Aug 1933 Rites 24 Aug 1933
Herbert Knight, J. P.

Hackett SEITLES to Bettie WALLING Issued 26 Aug 1933 Rites 26 aug 1933
J. S. NAnce, M. G.

Aubrey SIMONS to Anna Belle TODD Issued 2 Sep 1933 Rites 2 Sep 1933
T. Q. MArtin, M. G.

Clinton STONER to leida WANAMAKER Issued 2 Sep 1933 rites 3 Sep 1933
J. L. BArnes, J. P.

John PANTER to Lorene CURTIS Issued 5 Sep 1933 Rites 5 Sep 1933
J. L. BArnes, J. P.

J. V. EMERICK to Ella EMERICK Issued 5 Sep 1933 Rites 5 Sep 1933
J. H. MAyo, J. P.

Perry BYARS to Margia GRIFFITH Issued 6 Sep 1933 Rites 6 Sep 1933
T. Q. MArtin, M. G.

MArsheall YOUNGBLOOD to Alma BISHOP Issued 6 Sep 1933 Rites 6 Sep 1933
J. D. Jones, M. G.

Mahlon CAMPBELL to Bertha TODD Issued 7 Sep 1933 Rites 9 Sep 1933
A. B, Moffitt, M. G.

Henry BLAIR to Dovie YOUNGBLOOD Issued 7 Sep 1933 Rites 7 Sep 1933
J. Il. MAyo, J. P.

Richard MATHIS to Waldine EARLS Issued 7 Sep 1933 Rites 7 Sep 1933
A. Z. Holder, J. P.

Lawrecne HOOVER to Ila May REEDER Issued 9 Sep 1933 rites 10 Sep 1933
A. J. Locke, J. P.

Herman LOOPER (C) to Marie WOMACK (C) Issued 9 Sep 1933 Rites 9 Sep 1933
J. W. McCollum, J. P.

Roy GRIFFITH to Gertie FUSTON Issued 9 Sep 1933 rites 9 Sep 1933
R. W. Womack, Jdg.

Kelton PERRY to Lucile STUBBLEFIELD Issued 9 Sep 1933 Rites 9 Sep 1933
Reese H. Rogers, M. G.

Ellis BENSLEY to Alda WALLING Issued 11 Oct 1933 Rites 11 Oct 1933
J. W. GArdner, M. G.

James CALHOUN to Ione SPENCER Issued 18 oct 1933 Rites 20 oct 1933
C. R. Womack, J. P.

L. G. POLK to Rishia NEAL Issued 21 Oct 1933 Rites 27 Oct 1933
Foy E. Wallace, M. G.

Calhoun BOTTOMS to Evelyn CUNNINGHAM Issued 21 Oct 1933 Rites 21 oct 1933
I. P. McGregor, J. P.

G. W. DARNELL, Jr. to Alda KESEY issued 21 Oct 1933 Rites 21 oct 1933
J. O. McClardy, M. G.

Harold EVANS to Ersie PRIEST Issued 21 Oct 1933 Rites 21 oct 1933
I. P. McGregor, J. P.

Charles Meadows CLARK to Evelyn HOWARD Issued 23 Oct 1933 Rites 27 Oct 1933
T. Q. Martin, M. G.

Virgil THOMAS to Mollie Mai ANDERSON Issued 23 Oct 1933 Rites 23 Oct 1933
J. H. Mayo. J. P.

Elmer TANNER to Opal HOLLAND Issued 28 Oct 1933 Rites 28 Oct 1933
C. L. Webster, M. G.

J. KING to Anna E. FULTS Issued 28 Oct 1933 Rites 29 Oct 1933
Hubert Knight, J. P.

RAymond SWANGER to Ruth TRAVIS Issued 28 Oct 1933 Rites 28 Oct 1933
A. Z. Holder, J. P.

J. L. QUICK to Willie ARGO Issued 3 Nov 1933 Rites 4 Nov 1933
H. J. Holcomb, J. P.

Eugene HALEY to Essie MAi MASEY issued 4 Nov 1933 Rites 4 Nov 1933
G. B. J. Mitchell, J. P.

Barton WARE to Lorelle CAMPBELL Issued 4 Nov 1933 Rites 4 Nov 1933
J. H. Mayo, J. P.

Dave SMITH to MArie MORTON Issued 7 Nov 1933 Rites 7 Nov 1933
Alf T. Judkins, M. G.

Roy PARKER to Aline HERMAN Issued 8 Nov 1933 Rites 7 JAn 1934
H. J. Holcomb, J. P.

Johnnie MADEWELL to Ona Lee BOULDIN Issued 17 Nov 1933 Returned - Not Solemnized

J. B. CAPSHAW to Connie Avo HILLIS Issued 20 nov 1933 Rites 20 Nov 1933
I. P. McGregor, J. P.

Marcus HOBBS to Wilma CLENDENON Issued 21 Nov 1933 Rites 26 Nov 1933
C. H. Riddle, J. P.

RAy HALEY to Lucy NUNLY Issued 23 Nov 1933 Rites 23 Nov 1933
I. P. McGregor, J. P.

Joe NEWBY to Willie Ann HILLIS Issued 26 Nov 1933 Rites 26 Nov 1933
Frank R. Davis, Jdg.

Arnold HOBBS to Christine RACKLEY issued 29 Nov 1933 Rites 2 Dec 1933
E. W. Sutherlin, J. P.

Haskel WANAMAKER to Ethel BYARS Issued 29 Nov 1933 Rites 2 Dec 1933
J. L. BArnes, J. P.

Rayburn PRIEST to Frances OGLE Issued 1 Dec 1933 Rites 1 Dec 1933
Irving Patton, J. P.

Etheridge SMARTT to HAzel BEATY Issued 1 Dec 1933 Rites 3 Dec 1933
W. H. Byles, J. P.

Phillip STUBBLEFIELD to Edith RICHARDSON Issued 2 Dec 1933 Rites 3 Dee 1933
J. W. GArdner, M. G.

J. F. PENNINGTON to Flossie MEADOWS Issued 4 Dec 1933 Rites 4 Dec 1933
A. T. Judkins, M. G.

PAul DAVIS to Wilma LENTZ Issued 5 Dec 1933 Rites 6 Dec 1933
C. E. Hawkins, M. G.

William WALSH to Mrs. Nola CRIPPS Issued 5 Dec 1933 Rites 5 Dec 1933
T. A. Richards, M. G.

J. L. BISHOP to Jimmie LAYNE (?) Issued 9 Dec 1933 Rites 10 Dec 1933
A. Z. Holder, J. P.

O. T. CANNON to Lois SIMMONS Issued 9 Dec 1933 Rites 11 Dec 1933
Irving Patton, J. P.

Clifton SMITHSON to Pearl BATES Issued 22 Dec 1933 Rites 23 Dec 1933
G. B. J. Mitchell, J. P.

Howard GIVENS to Ethel REEVES Issued 22 Dec 1933 Rites 22 Dec 1933
J. H. Mayo, J. P.

John W. NEWBY to Lenda RAY Issued 22 Dec 1933 Rites 24 Dec 1933
E. D. Martin, M. G.

Claudie PAGE to Ruby PARKER issued 23 Dec 1933 Rites 24 Dec 1933
W. B. Snipes, M. G.

Comer JONES to Emma PRATER Issued 23 Dec 1933 Not Returned

Dorris JERNIGAN to Sarah LOWE Issued 23 Dec 1933 Not Returned

William DURHAM to Kittie POWELL Issued 23 Dec 1933 Rites 23 Dec 1933
A. Z. Holder, J. P.

A. G. POWELL to Daisy Ellen GLENN Issued 23 Dec 1933 Rites 23 Dec 1933
A. Z. Holder, J. P.

Oscar NUNLEY to Lucy YOUNG Issued 23 Dec 1933 Rites 23 Dec 1933
T. A. Richards, M. G.

Jack DOAK to Ruth ANDERSON Issued 24 Dec 1933 Rites 24 Dec 1933
J. H. Mayo, J. p.

Willie HENNESSEE (C) to Josie SPURLOC (C) Issued 26 Dec 1933 Rites 26 Dec 1933
J. H. Mayo, J. P.

Fred DAVIS to Lula BLAYLOCK Issued 26 dec 1933 Rites 26 Dec 1933
J. H. Mayo, J. P.

William Scott DAVIS to PAuline ROMANS Issued 30 Dec 1933 Rites 30 Dec 1933
J. W. McCollum, J. P.

C. M. SNIPES to Mary Elizabeth TITTSWORTH Issued 30 Dec 1933 Rites 1 Jan 1934
A. B. Moffitt, M. G.

Matt W. WARREN to Lula ADAMS Issued 30 Dec 1933 Rites 30 Jan 1934
W. H. Craven, M. G.

Gordon McMAHAN to Alberta ROWLAND Issued 10 Jan 1934 Rites 14 jan 1934
C. E. HAWKINS, M. G.

Clarence SELBY to Louida TAYS Issued 15 JAn 1934 Rites 15 JAn 1934
J. H. Mayo, J. P.

BArton WEBB to Josephine SMOOT Issued 16 JAN !(#$ Rites 16 JAn 1934
J. H. MAyo, J. P.

E. C. HAYES to Mollie McBRIDE Issued 19 JAn 1934 Rites 21 Jan 1934
N. P. McWhirter, J. P.

Marcus WOODLEE to Mamie WOODLEE Issued 20 JAn 1934 Rites 21 jan 1934
J. H. Mayo, J. P.

Russell TAYLOR to Magaline PINEGAR Issued 20 Jan 1934 Rites 20 JAn 1934
J. H. Mayo, J. P.

Alex WILSON to Nellie TURNER Issued 23 Jan 1934 Rites 23 jan 1934
T. A. Richards,.M. G.

J. L. MARTIN to Lola Mai KELLEY Issued 27 Jan 1934 Rites 27 Jan 1934
F. L. Leeper, M. G.

M. F. GULLEY to Hattie BONNER Issued 2 Feb 1934 Rites 3 Feb 1934
L. T. Lawrence, M. G.

A. G. GLENN to Grace PUGH Issued 2 Feb 1934 Rites 3 Feb 1934
T. A. Richards, M. G.

H. D. McCORMICK to Teallie BRADY Issued 3 Feb 1934 Rites 3 Feb 1934
J. L. Barnes, J. P.

Arthur SCOTT to Louise LEFTRICK Issued 3 Feb 1934 Rites 3 Feb 1934
T. Gene West, M. G.

Jim FARMER to MAry MERCER Issued 7 Feb 1934 Rites 7 Feb 1934
J. H. MAyo, J. P.

Woodrow BRADLEY to Pauline NOWLIN Issued 9 Feb 1934 Rites 9 Feb 1934
A. H. Huff, M. G.

Clarence BATES to Edna SCOTT Issued 14 Feb 1934 Rites 14 Feb 1934
W. H. Byles, J. P.

Clarence TURNER to Reba PITT Issued 17 Feb 1934 Rites 17 Feb 1934
E. D. Martin, M. G.

Cloy MULLICAN to MAry Ann OWENS Issued 22 Feb 1934 Rites 23 Feb 1934
A. Z. Holder, J. P.

Marvin MORGAN to Vera HODGE Issued 24 Feb 1934 Rites 24 Feb 1934
J. H. Mayo, J. P.

James M. HEWITT to Lura V. GRISSOM Issued 26 Feb 1934 Rites 26 Feb 1934
C. E. Hawkins, M. G.

Roy PINEGAR to Lola WEST Issued 3 Mar 1934 Rites 3 Mar 1934
J. T. CAsey, M. G.

Waletr HUGHES to Sarah BRYANT Issued 3 MAr 1934 Rites 3 Mar 1934
H. J. Holcomb, J. P.

D. J. WILLIS to Lucille STUBBLEFIELD Issued 5 Mar 1934 Rites 6 Mar 1934
C. E. Hawkins,. M. G.

Robert PATRICK to Ellen RAINS Issued 9 MAr 1934   Not Returned

Elisha RAOCH to Emma Lou McMAHAN Issued 15 Mar 1934 Rites 18 Mar 1934
C. H. Riddle, J. P.

George SCOTT to LAura MILLER Issued 21 MAr 1934 Rites 25 Mar 1934
S. P. McDowell, J. P.

WAymon COPE to Ermon HUNTER Issued 25 Mar 1934 Rites 26 Mar 1934
O. L. Green

H. D. SELF to Ethel ADAMSON Issued 26 Mar 1934 Rites 1 Apr 1934
H. J. Holcomb, J. P.

Joe SHOCKLEY to Eveline NORTHCUTT Issued 26 Mar 1934 Rites 26 Mar 1934
J. R. Stubblefield M. G.

Walter NUNLEY to JAmie Mai GREEN Issued 26 MAr 1934 Rites 26 Mar 1934
J. H. MAyo, J. P.

J. T. ARNOLD to Alda HOBBS Issued 28 Mar 1934 Rites 28 Mar 1934
T. Q. Martin, M. G.

Jewell WOMACK to June WRIGHT Issued 30·Mar 1934 Rites 30 Mar 1934
Frank R. Davis, jdg.

Alton McGEE to Gladys Lee FORD Issued 31 Mar 1934 Rites 1 Apr 1934
A. T. Judkins, M. G.

John Lewis ANDERSON to Zelma Irene BARNES Issued 31 Mar 1934 Rites 31 Mar 1934
C. E. HAwkins, M. G.

Elbert PACK to Tennie CANTRELL Issued 1 Apr 1934 Rites 1 Apr 1934
Irving Patton, J. P.

William A. SLATTON to Dorothy Ann VAUGHN Issued 2 Apr 1934 Rites 2 Apr 1934
J. H. Mayo, J. P.

R. L. DUNCAN to Ruby ADCOCK Issued 2 Apr 1934
Irving Patton, J. P.

Nathan CANTRELL to Cornelia CANTRELL Issued 6 Apr 1934 Rites 6 Apr 1934
T. Q. Martin, M. G.

Lonnie ALLEN to Evelyn HAMMOCK Issued 13 Apr 1934 Rites 13 Apr 1934
J. H. Mayo, J. P.

Woodrow BARNES to Lillie Maple ROGERS Issued 14 Apr 1934 Rites 14 Apr 1934
Frank R. Davis, Jdg.

A. H. HUTTLE (?) to Laura OVERTURFF Issued 14 Apr 1934 Rites 14 Apr 1934
J. H. Mayo, J. P.

Willie JOHNSON to Edna SCOTT Issued 21 Apr 1934 Rites 21 Apr 1934
S. P. McDonald

Herbert FOSTER to Della Irene MULLICAN Issued 26 Apr 1934 Rites 26 Apr 1934
J. W. Cooley, M. G.

John STIPES to Eugenia MITCHELL Issued 1 May 1934 Rites 5 May 1934
A. H. Huff, M. G.

John Roy BRAGG to Neva Melle CLARK Issued 4 May 1934 Rites 5 May 1934
T. Q. Martin, M. G.

Chester Lee MYERS to Lena Mai RUTLEDGE Issued 5 May 1934 Rites 13 May 1934
Irving Pattor, J. P.

Robert RIGSBY to Nettie WOMACK Issued 5 May 1934 Rites 6 May 1934
W. T. Watson, J. P.

Rufus WHITE to Palma GARDNER Issued 5 May 1934 Rites 5 May 1934
J. H. Mayo, J. P.

Don HASTINGS to Margarette LAWRENCE Issued 6 May 1934   Not Returned

Durward TOSH to HaDENA VAUGHN Issued 7 May 1934 Rites 7 May 1934
J. H. Mayo, J. P.

Earl HOLLAND to Metta WALKER Issued 7 May 1934 Rites 7 May 1934
J. H. Mayo, J. P.

Tim RANDOLPH to Annette PRIEST Issued 9 May 1934 Rites 9 May 1934
J. H. MAYO, J. P.

Charles PERRY to Virginia PERRY Issued 12 MAY 1934 Rites 12 May 1934
Stewart Ramsey, J. P.

J. .C. WARE to Nettie DENNIE Issued 12 May 1934 Rites 12 May 1934
A. T. Judkins, M. G.

G. P. COPE to Ellie GIBBS Issued 15 May 1934 Rites 15 May 1934
A. T. Judkins, M. G.

Ta.   MORGAN to Catherine FUGGITT Issued 15 May 1934 Rites 20 May 1934
E. R. Little, M. G.

A. L. GRIBBLE to Myra GRISSOM Issued 19 May 1934 Rites 19 May 1934
J. B. Gribble, M. G.

Walter S. DAVIS to Mai Belle WOOD Issued 19 May 1934 Rites 19 May 1934
J. Gene West, M. G.

A. W. GOLDEN to Flora Jane GRIZZELL Issued 23 May 1934 Rites 29 May 1934
T. Q. MARTIN, M. G.

Jim BLACK to Irene BASHAM Issued 24 May 1934 Rites 26 May 1934
W. B. Snipes, M. G.

J. W. ROARK to Licena ROBERTS Issued 25 May 1934 Rites 25 May 1934
Fate Walker, J. P.

B. F. HENEGAR to Alta HEATHERLY Issued 26 May 1934 Rites 3 Jun 1934
E. W. Sutherlin, J. P.

Harold NEIGHBORS to HASSIE Lee BARNES Issued 26 May 1934 Rites 26 May 1934
W. B. Snipes, M. G.

O. V. MOONEYHAM to Myrtle POLLARD Issued 29 May 1934 Rites 30 Jun 1934
J. W. McCollum, J. P.

Howard WILCHER to Hattie OGLE Issued 29 May 1934 Rites 30 May 1934
Irving Patton, J. P.

Hubert REYNOLDS to Margaretta CRICK : Issued 2 Jun 1934 Rites 2 Jun 1934
A. H. Huff, M. G. ·
crick

Oscar SPURLOCK to Nettie CUMMINGS Issued 2 Jun 1934 Rites 2 Jun 1934
W. M. Holder, M. G.

Roscoe FOUTCH to Etheline MAXWELL Issued 2 Jun 1934 Rites 2 Jun 1934
J. H. Mayo, J. P.

Frank SIMONS to Virgia CARRICK Issued 2 Jun 1934 Rites 3 Jun 1934
C. H. Riddle, J. P.

Ollis HUNTER to Ruby HIGGINBOTHAM Issued 5 Jun 1934 Rites 6 Jun 1934
J. H. Mayo, J. P.

Herman ROBINSON to Mattie CANTRELL Issued 7 Jun 1934 Rites 7 Jun 1934
J. H. Mayo, J. P.

Alvis A. JOHNSON to Sarah Ruth CUNNINGHAM Issued 8 Jun 1934 Rites 9 Jun 1934
L. T. Lawrence, M. G.

Albert DYKES to MArie McBRIDE Issued 9 Jun 1934 Rites 10 Jun 1934
N. P. McWhirter, J. P.

W. C. COOLEY (C) to Hassie MARTIN (C) Issued 5 Jul 1934 Rites 24 Jul 1934
T. Gene West, M. G.

Zollie POTTER to Julia PENDERGRASS issued 7 Jul 1934 Rites 7 Jul 1934
J. H. MAyo, J. P.

Jesse GREER to Beulah WILLIAMS Issued 7 Jul 1934 Rites 14 Jul 1934
J. H. Mayo, J. P.

Winton BROWN to Mary Etta COUCH Issued 11 Jul 1934 Rites 11 Jul 1934
T. Q. MArtin, M. G.

L. R. WINSTEAD to Mildred MURDOCK Issued 11 Jul 1934 Rites 11 Jul 1934
J. H. MAyo, J. P.

Oscar CAMPBELL to Ruby PARTON Issued 14 Jul 1934 Rites 14 Jul 1934
J. H. Mayo, J. P.

Oscar POWERS to Bessie Lee HODGE Issued 14 Jul 1934 Rites 14 Jul 1934
Irving Patton, J. P.

Farmer WILLIS to Ester PARSLEY Issued 17 Jul 1934 Rites 18 Jul 1934
Reece H. Rogers, M. G.

Charlie Clark St. JOHN to Lila JARRELL issued 21 Jul 1934 Rites 22 Jul 1934
W. H. Craven, M. G.

Oliver DUNCAN to Isabel DAVENPORT Issued 21 Jul 1934 Rites 21 Jul 1934
C. L. Webster, M. G.

Manuel GOODSON to Mandy Ester MOORE Issued21 Jul 1934 Rites 21 Jul 1934
J. H. Mayo, J. P.

George McGEEHEE (C) to Lillie ROBERTS (C) Issued 24 Jul 1934 Rites 24 Jul 1934
E. R. Stubblefield, M. G.

George ROSS to Mildred WOODS Issued 25 Jul 1934 Rites 25 Jul 1934
John Morton, M. G.

Clifton MALONE to Charlotte BONNER Issued 30 Jul 1934 Rites 30 Jul 1934
E. S. Bedford, M. G.

Reece ROBERTS to Alda SCOTT Issued 3 Aug 1934 Rites 3 Aug 1934
A. H. Huff, M. G.

Bill CANTRELL to Bertha GLENN Issued 4 Aug 1934 Rites 5 Aug 1934
E. F. CAntrell, J. P.

L. D. RAMSEY to Nadine WOMACK Issued 4 Aug 1934 Rites 5 Aug 1934
E. R. Little, M. G.

Firm GRIBBLE to Virginia DOUGLAS Issued 4 Aug 1934 Rites 4 Aug 1934
J. H. Mayo, J. P.

John RAYBURN to Stella BARNES Issued 10 Aug 1934 Rites 10 Aug 1934
C. E. HAWKINS, M. G.

Thomas M. APPLETON to Dorothy Lea COMER Issued 11 Jun 1934   Not Returned

Clarence MATTINGLY to Edith LANGFORD Issued 12 Jun 1934 Rites 12 Jun 1934
C. E. Hawkins, M. G.

L. M. BELL to Elsie ROBINSON Issued 16 Jun 1934 Rites 16 Jun 1934
Herbert Knight, J. P.

Buford MEADOWS to Margie WOODLEE Issued 16 Jun 1934 Rites 17 Jun 1934
C. H. Riddle, J. P.

Charles PINEGAR to Willie ROGERS Issued 18 Jun 1934 Rites 23 Jun 1934
W. B. Snipes, M. G.

DAvis Lee WARREN to Ruby CHISAM Issued 19 Jun 1934 Rites 19 Jun 1934
E. D. Martin, M. G.

Major J. CRAWLEY to Georgia Louise MEDLEY issued 19 Jun 1934 Rites 21 Jun 1934
W. F. Roach, J. P.

E. P. CALLAHAN to HATTIE Louise STUBBLEFIELD Issued 22 Jun 1934 Rites 23 Jun 1934
T. Q. Martin, M. G.

Howard JONES to Audry CARTER Issued 23 Jun 1934 Rites Jun 1934
Frank K. David, Jdg.

Thos. J. STUBBLEFIELD to Vivian Eliz. RAMSEY Issued 23 Jun 1934 Rites 24 Jun 1934
C. E. Hawkins, M. G.

J. D. GREEN to Mozell JUDKINS Issued 23 Jun 1934 Rites 23 Jun 1934
John Morton, M. G.

J. E. SULLIVAN to Lila PACK Issued 23 Jun 1934 Rites 23 Jun 1934
J. H. MAyo, J. P.

Alvin BEASLEY to Pauline CURTIS Issued 23 Jun 1934 Rites 30 Jun 1934
V. D. Lusk, J. P.

Robert E. BONNER to Lillian RAMSEY Issued 26 Jun 1934 Returned - Not Solemnized

Carl MORTON to Irene NEAL Issued 30 Jun 1934 Rites 30 Jun 1934
John Morton, M. G.

Lincoln MITCHELL to Ethel DUKE Issued 30 Jun 1934 Rites 30 Jun 1934
J. H. Mayo, J. P.

Thurman HALL to Pauline FREEZE Issued 30 Jun 1934 Rites 15 Jul 1934
G. B. J. Mitchell, J. P.

Thurman R. SWINDLE to Devona YOUNG Issued 3 Jul 1934 Rites 4 Jul 1934
Irving Patton, J. P.

Luther KEEL to Elizabeth RILES Issued 3 Jul 1934 Returned - Not Solemnized

Vernon BASHAM to lillian NORROD Issued 4 Jul 1934 Rites 4 jul 1934
W. B. Snipes, M. G.

George Lewis BROWN to KATIE V. BUCK Issued 11 Aug 1934 Rites 12 Aug 1934 S. P. McDonald, M. G.

Hoyt BRYSON to Frances BRATTEN Issued 11 Aug 1934 Rites 11 Aug 1934 C. E. HAWKINS, M. G.

William B. HENEGAR to Bettie BURCH Issued 13 Aug 1934 Rites 13 Aug 1934 Frank R. Davis, Jdg.

Hubert BEARD to Bessie GAYNESS Issued 13 Aug 1934 Rites 13 Aug 1934 J. H. Mayo, J. P.

France FULTS to MAry Belle ROWLAND Issued 14 Aug 1934 Rites 14 Aug 1934 P. N. Moffitt, J. P.

Z. W. HEATHERLY to lillie MAi RIDDLE Issued 22 Aug 1934 Rites 23 Aug 1934 E. T. Brazzell,

O. C. BARNES to Margie MULLICAN Issued 22 Aug 1934 Rites 26 Aug 1934 W. T. Warren, J. P.

William HIGGINBOTHAM to Rilla LAMB Issued 25 Aug 1934 Rites 25 Aug 1934 V. D. Lusk, J. P.

Charels McDOWELL to Willie Mai MUNCY Issued 25 Aug 1934 Rites 26 Aug 1934 Reece H. Rogers, M. G.

Ad HILL to Fannie BONNER Issued 28 Aug 1934 Rites 28 Aug 1934 E. S. Bedford, M. G.

Sam TINDLE to Josie DEATON Issued 31 Aug 1934 Rites 31 Aug 1934 Irving Patton, J. P.

John Y. TURNER to Mary GRAHAM Issued 1 Sep 1934 Not Returned

W. C. HENNESSEE to Delma RUSSELL Issued 1 Sep 1934 Rites 2 Sep 1934 FAte Walker, J. P.

Enoch TURNER to Mina WILSON Issued 1 Sep 1934 Rites 1 Sep 1934 E. W. Sutherlin, J. P.

Albert BYARS to edna Gladys BARNES Issued 5 Sep 1934 Rites 5 Sep 1934 T. Q. Martin, M. G.

Robert FISHER to Nora Lee BEATY Issued 7 Sep 1934 Rites 8 Sep 1934 W. E. GArner, M. G.

B. D. IRWIN to Ruby COLE Issued 12 Sep 1934 Rites 15 Sep 1934 Irving Patton, J. P.

Jewell ROLLER to Verdia D. HOLDER Issued 12 Sep 1934 Rites 16 Sep 1934 W. T. Warren, J. P.

Lester DOAK, Jr. to Louella BOULDIN Issued 15 Sep 1934 Rites 15 Sep 1934 J. H. Mayo, J. P.

Jack SIMONS to Eliza MITCHELL Issued 18 Sep 1934 Rites 18 Sep 1934 J. H. MAyo, J. P.

Lewis BROWN to Haura HARRIMAN Issued 19 Sep 1934 Rites 27 Sep 1934 C. L. Webster, M. G.

Phillip GROSCH to Bertha HICKERSON Issued 22 Sep 1934 Rites 22 Sep 1934 P. N. Moffitt, J. P.

Paul TAYLOR to Margie ELLIOTT Issued 22 Sep 1934 Rites 22 Sep 1934 R. F. KilliaN

Luke GILL to Alta MULLICAN Issued 22 Sep 1934 Rites 23 Sep 1934 E. T. CANTRELL, J. P.

Alfred BROOKS to Roselee JUDKINS Issued 24 Sep 1934 Rites 24 Sep 1934 Herbert Knight, J. P.

Wooten DUKE to Julia LEWIS Issued 24 Sep 1934 Rites 29 Sep 1934 J. H. Mayo, J. P.

Aubrey LAWSON to Mottie TURNER Issued 27 Sep 1934 Rites 13 Oct 1934 J. R. BAiley, M. G.

B. C. LUSK to Laura BOST Issued 29 Sep 1934 Rites 29 Sep 1934 Charles Hillis, J. P.

John W. RUCKER to Minnie Ruth CUNNINGHAM Issued 29 Sep 1934 Rites 29 Sep 1934 E. H. ijams

Lewis RAMSEY (C) to Elizabeth THOMAS (C) Issued 29 Sep 1934 Rites 29 Sep 1934 J. H. Mayo, J. P.

Andy HILLIS to Ela Ray WILSON Issued 29 Sep 1934 Not Returned

O. T. COMLEY, Jr. to Mildred HARDCASTLE Issued 2 Oct 1934 Rites 4 Oct 1934 C. E. HAWKINS, M. G.

Alva BROWN to Florence LOCKE Issued 4 Oct 1934 Rites 4 Oct 1934 J. H. Mayo, J. P.

Louie DODSON to Willie HOBBS Issued 5 Oct 19234 Rites 5 Oct 1934 L. T. Lawrecne, M. G.

Norville TITTSMORTH to Mary Eliz BLANKENSHIP Issued 11 Oct 1934 Rites 14 Oct 1934 J. S. Dunlap, J. P.

Marlin CROSSLIN to J. C. RAY Issued 20 Oct 1934 Rites 21 Oct 1934 A. H. Huff, M. G.

Curtis H. WILLIAMS to Mammie WEBB Issued 20 Oct 1934 Rites 4 Jul 1935 Elisha Henry, M. G.

Ottoway WEBB to Beatrice WINTON Issued 21 Oct 1934 Rites 21 Oct 1934 E. S. Bedford, M. G.

Clyde T. WHITE to Thelma EWTON Issued 22 Oct 1934 Rites 22 Oct 1934 J. H. Mayo, J. P.

Julius GRAY to Sammie RAMSEY Issued 24 Oct 1934 Rites 24 Oct 1934
J. H. Mayo, J. P.

George MASON (C) to Endie THOMAS Issued 27 Oct 1934 Rites 27 Oct 1934
J. H. Mayo. J. P.

Odis ROGERS to Rosa HINES Issued 31 Oct 1934 Rites 31 Oct 1934
R. W. Smartt, Jdg.

Harvey HOLLAND to Mary JOHNSON Issued 3 Nov 1934 Rites 13 Nov 1934
W. H. CraVEN, M. G.

Henry NORTHCUTT to Renma PELHAM Issued 5 Nov 1934 Rites 6 Nov 1934
A. Z. Holder, J. P.

MAlcolm HALEY to Roberta SMITH Issued 15 Nov 1934 Rites 15 Nov 1934
L. B. Moffitt, J. P.

Herman GOODMAN to Velma TOSH Issued 17 Nov 1934 Rites 17 Nov 1934
C. H. Riddle, J. P.

Herman BASHAM to Opal JONES Issued 17 Nov 1934 Rites 18 Nov 1934
R. H. Bonner, J. P.

Mark FOSTER to Lillian BROWN Issued 17 Nov 1934 Rites 17 Nov 1934
W. H. Craven, M. G.

W. E. BROWN to Mary ANDERSON Issued 18 Nov 1934 Rites 18 Nov 1934
C. E. Hawkins, M. G.

Frank KEITH to Lola THURMAN Issued 27 Nov 1934 Rites 2 Dec 1934
O. L. Green

Will SPARKMAN to Dovie Ada GREEN Issued 29 Nov 1934 Rites 30 nov 1934
J. K. Martin, J. P.

Eugene RHEAY to Leusie SMARTT Issued 1 Dec 1934 Rites 2 Dec 1934
E. D. Martin, M. G.

John Henry THURMAN to Rubby GILMER Issued 1 Dec 1934 Rites 1 Dec 1934
P. N. Moffitt, Jdg.

Charles E. ELKINS to Ardean THURMAN Issued 1 Dec 1934 Rites 1 dec 1934
P. N. Moffitt, Jdg.

Raden MUNCEY to Oma YOUNG Issued 7 Dec 1934 Rites 7 Dec 1934
J. H. MAyo, J. P.

Claud NORROD to Laura Mai YOUNG Issued 8 Dec 1934 Rites 9 Dec 1934
L. B. Moffitt, J. P.

Rsatus ALLEN to Georgia CHILDRESS Issued 8 Dec 1934 Rites 8 Dec 1934
A. H. Huff, M. G.

H. H. TITTSWORTH to Ellen WALLACE Issued 8 Dec 1934 Rites 30 Dec 1934
A. B. Moffitt, J. P.

S. T. GUEST, Jr. (C) to Janie FUSTON (C) Issued 8 Dec 1934 Rites (dec 1934
J. H. Huston, M. G.

Lebert RIGSBY to Lillie BOND Issued 10 Dec 1934 Rites 10 Dec 1934
A. T. Judkmins, M. G.

Edmund C. MILLER to Elizabeth BRATCHER Issued 13 Dec 1934 Rites 13 Dec 1934
A. Z. Holder, J. P.

Sidney PISTOLE to Ruth PARKER Issued 15 Dec 1934 Rites 15 Dec 1934
P. N. Moffitt, Jdg.

Kyle STILES to Ollie CANTRELL Issued 15 Dec 1934 Rites 15 Dec 1934
J. H. Mayo, J. P.

Valdus NUNLEY to Mary Lou RUSSELL Issued 17 dec 1934 Rites 20 Dec 1934
P.N. Moffitt, Jdg.

Lincoln BROWN to Evelyn MITCHELL Issued 18 Dec 1934 Rites 18 Dec 1934
P. N. Moffitt, Jdg.

Aubrey TAYLOR to Lora CANTRELL Issued 18 Dec 1934 Rites 18 Dec 1934
J. H. Mayo, J. P.

Fucman WARREN to Vera ROGERS Issued 19 Dec 1934 Rites 22 dec 1934
W. B. Snipes, M. G.

Brownie SMITH to Prudie SMITH Issued 22 Dec 1934 Rites 13 Jan 1935
Frank C. Watson, M. G.

Radford WALKER to Ollie Mai CURTIS Issued 29 Dec 1934 Rites 6 Jan 1935
Fate Walker, J. P.

Harold HALE to Roberta ROBERTS Issued 29 Dec 1934 Rites 31 Dec 1934
Irving Patton, J. P.

E. W. HITTSON to Josephine SWOAPE Issued 5 JAn 1935 Rites 5 Jan 1935
R. H. Bonner, J. P.

Floyd E. PENDLETON to Nola WOOD Issued 5 Jan 1935 Rites 6 Jan 1935
C. E. Hawkins, M. G.

C. L. WHITLOCK to Maud ALLEY Issued 10 JAn 1935 Rites 11 Jan 1935
Herbery Knight, J. P.

Nolen MULLICAN to Emma CANTRELL Issued 12 Jan 1935 Rites 13 JAn 1935
J. S. Dunlap, J. P.

Kelley B. POTTER to Hazel SMITH Issued 12 Jan 1935 Rites 12 Jan 1935
A. T. Judkins, M. G.

Walker BYARS to Drucilla PINEGAR Issued 12 Jan 1935 Rites 12 Jan 1935
W. B. Snipes, M. G.

C. C. CRAVEN to Mary Edith RICH Issued 14 Jan 1935 Rites 14 Jan 1935
T. Q. Martin, M. G.

Alton YORK to Ida DUNCAN Issued 17 JAn 1935 Rites 19 Jan 1935
J. E. Clark, M. G.

Lloyd THOMPKINS to Ethel RUST Issued 19 JAn 1935 Rites 19 JAn 1935
C. E. Hawkins, M. G.

Harold SIMONS to Mary JORDAN Issued 19 JAn 1935 Rites 19 Jan 1935
J. H. MAyo, J. P.

William CHILTON to Icie STARKEY Issued 19 Jan 1935 Rites 2 Feb 1935
P. N. Moffitt, Jdg.

Ed JOHNSON to Vera Lee VANN Issued 20 Jan 1935 Rites 27 Jan 1935
T. Q. Martin, M. G.

Frank HUDSON to Audrey BOULDIN Issued 21 JAn 1935 Rites 22 Jan 1935
V. D. Lusk, J. P.

Frank ALBRIGHT to Virginia HOBBS Issued 22 Jun 1935 Rites 22 Jan 1935
P. N. Moffitt, Jdg.

Daniel JARRELL to Bonnie ELROD Issued 25 Jan 1935 Rites 25 Jan 1935
T. Q. Martin, M. G.

Adam MOONEYHAM to Blanche WOODS Issued 25 Jan 1935 Rites 25 JAn 1935
J. H. Mayo, J. P.

Johnson HAMMONS to Maggie LISK Issued 26 Jan 1935 Rites 26 Jan 1935
L. B. Moffitt, J. P.

W. H. BURKS to Gladys DELANEY Issued 27 JIn 1935 Rites 27 Jan 1935
W. S. Wileman

Wm. Howard PRATER to Edwina PASSONS Issued 1 Feb 1935 Rites 1 Feb 1935
G. B. J. Mitchell, J. P.

A. W. CUNNINGHAM to Eva ROBERTS Issued 2 Feb 1935 Rites 6 Feb 1935
C. E. HAWKINS, M. G.

Henry Curtis WILLIAMSON to MARY M. DUTTON Issued 2 Feb 1935 Rites 6 Feb 1935
J. D. Vandergriff

Jesse CARR to Willette LEWIS Issued 6 Feb 1935 Rites 8 Feb 1935
Irving Patton, J. P.

Clarence JUDKINS to Bertha BENNETT Issued 8 Feb 1935 Rites 8 Feb 1935
O. L. Green

Arry YOUNGBLOOD to Almon WOOD Issued 9 Feb 1935 Rites 9 Feb 1935
E. W. Sutherlin, J. P.

Andrew L. MATTHEWS to Nannia A. ANDERSON Issued 16 Feb 1935 Rites 16 Feb 1935
T. Q. Martin, M. G.

A. R. MILLER to Zelda DAVIS Issued 16 Feb 1935 rites 16 Feb 1935
J. H. Mayo, J. P.

(Page #316 skipped
in numbering)

Charles CUNNINGHAM to Mona ANDERSON Issued 16 Feb 1935 Rites 16 Feb 1935
F. L. Kirby, J. P.

Elza DAVENPORT to Ella Mai ROGERS Issued 16 Feb 1935 Rites 16 Feb 1935
J. H. Mayo, J. P.

J. D. FUSTON to Clara SMITH Issued 22 Feb 1935 Rites 22 Feb 1935
J. H. Mayo, J. P.

Clint WILLIAMSON to Bessie Lou TITTSWORTH Issued 23 Feb 1935 Rites 24 Feb 1935
J. D. VAndergriff

W. T. JOHNSON to Lucinda M. FITTS Issued 23 Feb 1935 Rites 23 Feb 1935
W. S. Wileman, M. G.

Oscar TUTNER to Ella Mai HERMAN Issued 23 Feb 1935 Rites 23 Feb 1935
F. J. Winton, J. P.

E. L. TOSH to Pauline JARRELL Issued 23 Feb 1935 Rites 23 Feb 1935
E. W. Sutherlin, J. P.

Jewell WHITAKER to Minnie MOFFITT Issued 27 Feb 1935 Rites 27 Feb 1935
I. P. McGregor, J. P.

Albert PRATER to Bonnie PERRY Issued 1 Mar 1935 Rites 4 Mar 1935
J. H. Mayo, J. P.

Orval McCORMICK to Elizabeth JOHNSON Issued 2 Mar 1935 Rites 2 Mar 1935
A. H. Huff, M. G.

Floyd FLANDERS to Ophia GREEN Issued 2 Mar 1935 Rites 3 Mar 1935
E. T. Cantrell, J. P.

I. C. AKIN to Susie OVERTURFF Issued 12 MAr 1935 Rites 12 Mar 1935
J. H. Mayo, J. P.

S. C. HALE to Leona RAPER Issued 14 Mar 1935 Rites 14 Mar 1935
J. W. McCollum, J. P.

Gilbert MAXWELL to Lillie PUGH Issued 16 Mar 1935 Rites 16 Mar 1935
J. H. Mayo, J. P.

J. W. LOWRY to Esther LORANCE Issued 22 Mar 1935 Rites 22 Mar 1935
E. W. Sutherlin, J. P.

Harold OAKES to Pearl SWOOPE Issued 23 Mar 1935 Rites 23 Mar 1935
R. H. Bonner, J. P.

Robert WALLACE to Beulah TURNER Issued 30 MAr 1935 Rites 31 Mar 1935
A. Z. Holder, J. P.

John D. TUBB to Beatrice BELL Issued 4 Apr 1935 Rites 7 Apr 1935
A. Z. Holder, J. P.

Clessie TUBBS to Lila CANTRELL Issued 4 Apr 1935 Rites 14 Apr 1935
G. B. J. Mitcehll, J. P.

Robert G. OLIVER to Mary Eliz. DIXON Issued 6 Apr 1935 Rites 7 Apr 1935
T. Q. Martin, M. G.

Charles DENTON to Ruby CARR Issued 9 Apr 1935 Rites 14 Apr 1935
W. H. Craven, M. G.

Hollis BAIN to Alene CARTER Issued 18 Apr 1935 Rites 27 Apr 1935
J. S. Dunlap, J. P.

JAson CANTRELL to Lela PRATER Issued 20 Apr 1935 Rites 20 Apr 1935
P. N. Moffitt, Jdg.

F. B. BARRETT to Jetta Lee BELL Issued 20 Apr 1935 Rites 20 Apr 1935
A. Z. Holder, J. P.

V. P. JARRELL to Christien CARROLL Issued 20 Apr 1935 Rites 20 Apr 1935
P. N. Moffitt, Jdg.

HArold JACKSON to Irene JARRELL Issued 20 Apr 1935 Rites 10 May 1935
E. W. Sutherlin, J. P.

Garner JOHNSON to Willie Jo PEPPER Issued 20 Apr 1935 Rites 20 Apr 1935
J. H. Mayo, J. P.

J. T. MARTIN to Hazel WILLIAMSON Issued 23 Apr 1935 Rites 27 Apr 1935
Rouchen Horton, M. G.

Tom MARTIN to Emma L. NEWBY Issued 27 Apr 1935 Rites 27 Apr 1935
C. E. HAwkins, M. G.

457 marriages in this book

Book 18 - Warren County Marriages - May 1, 1935 to Jan 16, 1938

Fred GRIFFITH to Lou CANTRELL Issued 1 May 1935 Rites 1 May 1935
J. H. Mayo, J. P.

Woodrow MARTIN to Wavie GROVE Issued 4 May 1935 Rites 4 May 1935
V. D. Lusk, J. P.

G. G. CLARK to Emma CANTRELL Issued 4 May 1935 Rites 4 May 1935
T. Q. Martin, M. G.

Clark TURNER to Lida ADCOCK Issued 8 May 1935 Rites 15 May 1935
E. W. Sutherlin, J. P.

Northcutt THROWER to Mamie TANNER Issued 10 May 1935 Rites 10 May 1935
J. H. Mayo, J. P.

Billie THAXTON to Claudine LAWRENCE Issued 11 May 1935 Rites 11 May 1935
C., E. Hawkins, M. G.

Beecher HERRIMAN to Louise CUTTS Issued 11 May 1935 Rites 12 May 1935
C. L. Webster, M. G.

Firm ROBERTS, Jr. to Lucille SAFLEY Issued 20 May 1935 Rites 21 May 1935
A. T. Judkins, M. G.

Mack GRAHAM to Jennie BARRETT Issued 21 MAy 1935 Rites 26 May 1935
J. H. Mayo, J. P.

Carl SPAKES to Susie ODELL Issued 22 May £935 Rites 22 May 1935
Irving Patton, J. P.

Floyd SIMONS to Pearl CANTRELL Issued 24 May 1935 Rites 24 May 1935
J. B. Gribble, M. G.

C. V. MYERS to Jessie Ruth JACKSON Issued 27 May 1935 Rites 29 May 1935
Elisha Henry

Crockett UPCHURCH to Iva Nell DAVENPORT Issued 31 May 1935 Rites 1 Jun 1935
A. H. Huff, M. G.

Robert HUTCHINS to Vera WALKER Issued 31 May 1935 Rites 1 Jun 1935
C. H. Riddle, J. P.

Ulysses WOOD to Ruby RUTLEDGE Issued 1 Jun 1935 Rites 1 Jun 1935
E. D. Martin, M. G.

Claborn GROVE to Eloise CURTIS Issued 1 Jun 1935 Rites 2 Jun 1935
V. D. Lusk, J. P.

Jim D. HOLT to Ida BELL Issued 1 Jun 1935 Rites 1 Jun 1935
P. N. Moffitt, Jdg

Charles WARREN to Frances Ethel LANE Issued 1 Jun 1935 Rites 7 Jun 1935
W. H. Craven, M. G.

Cap HARPER to May BEARD Issued 3 Jun 1935 Rites 3 Jun 1935
W. H. Craven, M. G.

Harold McGEE to Pauline McMAHAN Issued 5 Jun 1935 Rites 5 Jun 1935
I. P. McGregor, J. P.

Joe Landon EVINS to Ann Roberta SMARTT Issued 7 Jun 1935 Rites 7 Jun 1935
T. A. Wiggington, M. G.

Arlis POTTER to Lucille BALES Issued 8 Jun 1935 Rites 8 Jun 1935
P. N. Moffitt, Jdg.

George TAYLOR to Emma SIMONS Issued 8 Jun 1935 Rites 8 Jun 1935
J. H. MAyo, J. P.

Clifford ADCOCK to Francis FERRELL Issued 11 Jun 1935 Rites 11 Jun 1935
C. R. Womack, J. P.

Herbert BATES to Etta SIMONS Issued 12 Jun 1935 Rites 12 Jun 1935
P. N. Moffitt, Jdg.

Hershel V. FISHER to Myrtle E. HUMPHREY Issued 13 Jun 1935 Rites 16 Jun 1935
A. H. Huff, M.G.

Robert ENKEMA to Carloyn KING Issued 14 Jun 1935 Rites 14 jun 1935
T. Q. Martin, M. G.

Wilkon BAKER to Elise TEMPLETON Issued 15 Jun 1935 Rites 15 Jun 1935
Irving Patton, J. P.

Wilburn ROBERTS to Erma BROWN Issued 15 Jun 1935 Rites 15 jun 1935
E. W. Sutherlin, J. P.

Owen CONASTER to Waldine HENNESSEE Issued 15 Jun 1935 Rites 15 Jun 1935
O. L. Green, M. G.

C. H. MITCHELL to Pearl FOSTER Issued 22 Jun 1935 Rites 22 Jun 1935
G. B. J. Mitchell, J. P.

Abe SIMONS to Olivene FULTS Issued 22 Jun 1935 Rites 22 Jun 1935
J. H. Mayo, J. P.

Cornell GOODWIN to Georgia STEWART Issued 22 Jun 1935 Rites 22 Jun 1935
Irving Patton, J. P.

Leo BRUCE to Louise ELROD Issued 28 Jun 1935 Rites 28 Jul 1935
Elisha Henry, M. G.

S. L. RIGNEY to Willene ORRICK Issued 29 Jun 1935 Rites 29 Jul 1935
C. H. Riddle, J. P.

Sherman DODSON to Ella Mai BREEDLOVE Issued 29 Jun 1935 Rites 29 Jun 1935
Elisha Henry, M. G.

Dow CAMPBELL to Lillie JENNINGS Issued 29 Jun 1935 Rites 29 Jun 1935
W. H. Craven, M. G.

Price SAIN to Gladys WHEELER Issued 29 Jun 1935 Rites 30 jun 1935
T. Q. Martin, M. G.

Jamie W. STEPP to Muriel EDMONDS Issued 29 Jun 1935 Rites 30 Jun 1935
BAiley Brooks

Lowell GRISSOM to Jessie Pearl WHITTENBURG Issued 1 Jul 1935 Rites 6 Jul 1935
J. H. MAyo, J. P.

Calvin HALL to Pauline RAINS Issued 1 Jul 1935 Rites 4 Jul 1935
H. J. Wilson, J. P.

Arthur TRAIL to Nita WHARTON Issued 2 Jul 1935 Rites 2 Jul 1935
P. N. Moffitt, Jdg.

Charles ROLLER to Virgia WILLIAMSON Issued 3 Jul 1935 Rites 3 Jul 1935
P. N. Moffitt, Jdg.

Jim MADEWELL to Murel Ross ARGO Issued 5 Jul 1935 Rites 7 Jul 1935
I. P. McGregor, J. P.

B.A. HENNESSEE to Crrie Belle CRIM Issued 6 Jul 1935 Rites 6 Jul 1935
A. T. Judkins, M. G.

G. T. ROACH to Mary HIGGINS Issued 10 Jul 1935 Rites 29 Jul 1935
Boyd D. Fanning

Charles CLENDENON to Katherine CURTIS Issued 10 Jul 1935 Rites 12 Jul 1935
E. D. Martin, M. G,

Davis DURHAM to Zenoba CANTRELL Issued 13 Jul 1935 Rites 13 Jul 1935
J. B. Gribble, M. G.

Sanford PUTNAM to May BURKHART Issued 13 Jul 1935 Rites 13 Jul 1935
T. Q. Martin, M. G.

John WHITE to Vernon McCOY Issued 13 Jul 1935 Rites 14 jul 1935
Irving Patton, J. P.

Claud MALONE to Rebecca MORRIS Issued 15 Jul 1935 Rites 16 Jul 1935
W. J. Thompson

Bill LANCE to Ada CAMPBELL Issued 19 Jul 1935 Rites 20 Jul 1935
A. Z. Holder, J. P.

Eugene RUTLEDGE to Iris McCORMICK Issued 20 Jul 1935 Rites 20 Jul 1935
C. M. Mongler

Willie Morton HUTCHINGS to Clara Mai ROBINSON Issued 20 Jul 1935 Rites 20 Jul
J. H. Mayo, J. P.

Lessie BOULDIN to Effie MYERS Issued 20 Jul 1935 Rites 20 Jul 1935
J. H. Mayo, J. P.

Harrison SAULTS (?) to Hassie SLIGER Issued 20 Jul 1935 Rites 20 Jul 1935
J. H. Mayo, J. P.

Richard LOWE to Viola JOHNSON Issued 21 jul 1935 Rites 21 Jul 1935
J. S. NArce, M. G.

Charles F. JONES to Mary Lucy JOHNSON Issued 22 Jul 1935 Rites 28 Jul 1935
A. H. Huff, M. G.

John LYLE to Belle WARD Issued Rites 25 Jul 1935
R. H. Hale, M. G.

Carlos VINSON to Myrtis HAGWOOD Issued 26 Jul 1935 Rites 26 jul 1935
Herbert Knight, J. P.

Jesse CURTIS to Edna MARTIN Issued 27 Jul 1935 Rites 27 Jul 1935
J. H. Mayo, J. P.

Lee McGEHEE to Mary WOOD Issued 27 Jul 1935 Rites 27 Jul 1935
R. H. Bonner, J. P.

Zollie DAVIS to Lola Mai MOONEYHAM Issued 1 Aug 1935 Rites 5 Aug 1935
Irvign Patton, J. P.

John R. DODD to Fannie WILSON Issued 2 Aug 1935 Rites 3 Aug 1935
H. J. Wilson, J. P.

Gentry BRATCHER to Ofellene HOLDER Issued 2 Aug 1935 Rites 7 Aug 1935
J. H. MAyo, J. P.

Bernice CHISAM to Bessie FERRELL Issued 3 Aug 1935 Rites 4 Aug 1935
W. M. ROwland, J. P.

Clarence BOGLE to May SMITHSON Issued 3 Aug 1935 Rites 3 Aug 1935
R. H. HAle

Palmer DAVENPORT to Eunice BELL Issued 3 Aug 1935 Rites 4 Aug 1935
G. B. J. Mitchell, J. P.

Willie Robert GANN to BeulahLAWS Issued 7 Aug 1935 Rites 10 Aug 1935
P. N. Moffitt, Jdg.

Jewell BRADY to Edna COPE Issued 10 Aug 1935 rites 10 Aug 1935
J. B. Gribble, M. G.

L. V. BRIXEY to Hazel HIGGINBOTHAM Issued 10 Aug 1935 rites 15 Aug 1935
J. H. Mayo, J. P.

Grover DONNELL to Doris SELF Issued 16 Aug 1935 Rites 19 Aug 1935
John Morton, M. G.

JACK BARRETT to Ottie Pearl LYLES Issued 19 Aug 1935 Rites 24 Aug 1935
W. T. Watson, J. P.

Haskell HITCHCOCK to Hassie DILLON Issued 20 Aug 1935 Rites 20 Aug 1935
J. H. Mayo, J. P.

Fred ALLEY to Violet HAWKINS Issued 20 Aug 1935 Rites 21 Aug 1935
J. H. Mayo, J. P.

Thomas Owen BRATCHER to Nina Mai PASSONS Issued 20 Aug 1935 Rites 20 Aug 1935
Berry Mitchell, J. P.

Jesse ROGERS to Clady DEBERRY Issued 29 Aug 1935 Rites 30 Aug 1935
A. Z. Holder, J. P.

Leroy D. C. FOX to Delma SHERRELL Issued 31 Aug 1935 Rites 1 Sep 1935
C. E. Hawkins, M. G.

Joe ALEXANDER to Myrtle DURHAM Issued 31 Aug 1935 Rites 31 Aug 1935
J. H. Mayo, J. P.

Jesse F. CONASTER to Ida Mai REED Issued 31 Aug 1935 Rites 31 Aug 1935
O. L. Green, M. G.

Charles LAFEVERS to Bernice WISER Issued 31 aug 1935 Rites 31 Aug 1935
O. L. Green, M. G.

Chas. Leslie PENDLETON to Lilly MUNCY Issued 31 Aug 1935 Rites 31 Aug 1935
C. E. Hawkins, M. G.

Silas JACO to Willie Mai WITT Issued 31 Aug 1935 Rites 1 Sep 1935
J. B. Gribble, M. G.

Arvil AUSTIN to Ora MAI HOLT Issued 5 Sep 1935 Rites 11 Sep 1935
R. W. Smartt, Jdg.

Carl HUDSON to Emma MASON Issued 7 Sep 1935 Rites 7 Sep 1935
P. N. Moffitt, Jdg.

Alfred BONNER (C) to Martha HUNTER (C) Issued 9 Sep 1935 Rites 9 Sep 1935
V. D. Lusk, J. P.

John FERRELL to Morning PRESLY .Issued 10 Sep 1935 Rites 10 Sep 1935
A. H. Huff, M. G.

Ernest MITCHELL to LORANCE Issued 14 Sep 1935 Rites 14 Sep 1935
P. N. Moffitt, Jdg.

Paul ADCOCK to Mildred GREEN Issued 14 Sep 1935 Rites 23 Sep 1935
H. C. Green

Dillard CARR to June DAVIS Issued 14 Sep 1935 Rites 15 Sep 1935
E. W. Sutherlin, J. P.

Isaac RICHARDSON to Anna BOULDIN Issued 14 Sep 1935 Rites 16 Sep 1935
J. H. Mayo, J. P.

Herman FARLESS to Delma HILLIS Issued 19 Sep 1935 Rites 19 Sep 1935
J. H. Mayo, J. P.

James R. MASON to Emma Louise WORTHINGTON Issued 24 Sep 1935 Rites 27 Sep 1935
A. R. Hill

Vernon STOKES to Jennie SMITH Issued 24 Sep 1935 Rites 24 Sep 1935
J. S. Nance, M. G.

Matt ROACH to Susie GESSLER issued 26 Sep 1935 Rites 27 Sep 1935
C. E. Hawkins. M. G.

Jesse L. BYARS to Juanita HENNESSEE Issued 28 Sep 1935 Rites 28 Sep 1935
J. H. Mayo, J. P.

Gentry GIBBS to Frances BYRD Issued 28 Sep 1935 Rites 28 Sep 1935
J. H. Mayo, J. P.

Wallace CARTER to Lillie MAi BROCK Issued 28 Sep 1935 Rites 6 Oct 1935
J. H. Mayo, J. P.

Haskell GRIFFITH to Bessie Lorene BLANKENSHIP Issued 28 Sep 1935 Rites 29 Sep
J. S. Dunlap, J. P.

H. B. HOBBS to Mary STOTTS Issued 30 Sep 1935 Rites 1 Oct 1935
Elisha Henry, M. G.

A. C. HINTON to Julia DUTTON Issued 1 Oct 1935 Rites 1 Oct 1935
J. H. Mayo, J. P.

Arthur MAY to Ellen HAWKS Issued 1 Oct 1935 Rites 1 Oct 1935
J. H. Mayo, J. P.

M. M. McBRIDE to Hassie BILES Issued 1 Oct 1935 Rites 2 Oct 1935
W. L. Peery

Willie SHELBY to MAi PHILLIPS Issued 5 Oct 1935 Rites 6 Oct 1935
J. H. MAyo, J. P.

JAmes E. JOHNSON to Evelyn QUINN Issued 5 Oct 1935 Rites 6 Oct 1935
A. H. Huff, M. G.

Paul MAYO to Grace RITCHEY Issued 6 Oct 1935 Rites 6 Oct 1935
J. H. Mayo, J. P.

Cecil NELSON to Louise NELSON Issued 9 Oct 1935 Rites 9 Oct 1935
J. H. Mayo, J. P.

Clark BOGLE to Inez GEORGE Issued 11 Oct 1935 Rites 11 Oct 1935
J. H. MAyo, J. P.

Walter HOOD to Verda ALEXANDER Issued 11 Oct 1935 Rites 11 Oct 1935
T. Q. Martin, M. G.

Charles CRAVEN to Pearl CRIM Issued 11 Oct 1935 Rites 13 Oct 1935
J. P. Bilbrey, J. P.

John WILLIAMSON to Opeholan JONES Issued 12 Oct 1935 Rites 12 Oct 1935
A. Z. Holder, J. P.

James JOHNSON to Adele RAPER Issued 12 Oct 1935 Rites 13 Oct 1935
Irving Patton, J. P.

Grady HALE to Jannie CANTRELL issued 16 Oct 1935 Rites 20 Oct 1935
A. H. Huff, M. G.

Haskell HOLDER to Mazel MELTON Issued 17 Oct 1935 Rites 18 Oct 1935
Herbert Knight, J. P.

Reece PASSONS to Eula THURMAN Issued 17 Oct 1935 Rites 19 Oct 1935
Herbert Knight, J. P.

Cecil OVERTURFF to Louise SCOTT issued 19 Oct 1935 Rites 19 Oct 1935
E. D. MArtin, M. G.

Lawrence BROWN to Margaret GRAYSON Issued 20 Oct 1935 Rites 20 Oct 1935
J. H. Mayo, J. P.

Johnnie BASHAM to Stella NEWBY Issued 21 Oct 1935 Rites 27 Oct 1935
W. B. Snipes, M. G.

G. D. McREYNOLDS to Eunice HITSON Issued 22 Oct 1935 Rites 6 Nov 1935
J. H. Mayo, J. P.

Frank PATRICK to Edna Louise MARTIN Issued 26 Oct 1935 Rites 26 Oct 1935
C. H. Riddle, J. P.

Zollie GIBBS to Willie ORRICK Issued 26 Oct 1935 Rites 31 Oct 1935
Fate Walker, J. P.

Everett BOULDIN to Louise WARREN Issued 2 nov 1935 Rites 2 nov 1935
Cark Dickson, M. G.

George HARDIN to Lucille SHIRLEY Issued 4 Nov 1935 Rites 4 Nov 1935
H. J. Wilson, J. P.

Alfred WILLAIMSON to Etheline JONES Issued 8 Nov 1935 Rites 9 Nov 1935
Herbert Knight, J. P.

Edward COOLEY to Ruth MARTIN Issued 8 Nov 1935 Rites 10 Nov 1935
A. H. Huff, M. G.

Thomas WARREN to Bessie Lee McLEAN Issued 9 Nov 1935 Rights 10 Nov 1935
Rouchen Horton, M. G.

Erby ADCOCK to Clara LAWSON Issued 9 Nov 1935 Rites 9 Nov 1935
P. N. Moffitt, Jdg.

George THOMAS to Clopie NORTHCUTT Issued 11 Nov 1935 Rites 11 Nov 1935
R. H. Bonner, J. P.

J. S. DUNLAP to Elizabeth LESLIE Issued 16 Nov 1935 Rites 16 Nov 1935
J. S. Dunlep, J. P.

Waymon HILLIS to Mary Perkins BRAGG Issued 18 Nov 1935 Rites 19 Nov 1935
T. Q. Martin, M. G.

James CARR to Emily YOUNGBLOOD Issued 21 Nov 1935 Rites 4 JAn 1936
E. W. Sutherlin, J. P.

Rayford FARLESS to Edna WILSON Issued 21 Nov 1935 Rites 21 Nov 1935
john L. Ferguson, B. D.

Mark WOODLEE to MArgie CLENDENON Issued 23 Nov 1935 Rites 23 Nov 1935
J. L. BArnes, . J.

Bob McCORMACK to Ruby Belle ROBERTS Issued 29 Nov 1935 Rites 29 Nov 1935
J. L. BArnes, J. P.

Clayborn POPE to Larrimoar BAKER Issued 24 Dec 1935 Rites 25 Dec 1935
J. B. Gribble, J. P.

Noel C. WOMACK to MAry Ruth KING Issued 24 Dec 1935 rites 25 Dec 1935
T. Q. Martin, M. G.

Thelda Lester CAMPBELL to HAzel PAuline TODD Issued 24 Dec 1935 Rites 24 Dec
J. H. Mayo, J. P.

Jimmie ROLLER to Zelma MITCHELL Issued 28 Dec 1935 Rites 5 Jan 1936
James K. Martin, J. P.

Lester PRIEST to Lela Mai GLENN Issued 30 Dec 1935 Rites 5 JAn 1936
J. W. McCollum, J. P.

C. Russell MURPHY to Pauline BRYANT Issued 3 Jan 1936 Rites 4 Jan 1936.
J. B. Leeper, M. G.

Z. T. SMARTT to Annie LAura SPURLOCK Issued 4 Jan 1936 Rites 6 Jan 1936
E. W. Sutherlin, J. P.

Lawrence HILLIS to Queenie Virgil MEADOWS Issued 7 Jan 1936 Rites 4 Feb 1936
P. N. Moffitt, Jdg.

Cliford FISHER to Mabel LANE Issued 14 Jan 1936 Rites 14 Jan 1936
J. S. Dunlap, J. P.

A. J. SMITH to Leo PINEAGR Issued 15 Jan 1935 Rites 15   1936
P. N. Moffitt, Jdg.

Lawrecne HOOVER to Stella FULTS Issued 12 Jan 1936 Rites 23 JAn 1936
CASS R. Womack, J. P.

J. W. DAVIS to Joda HENGHLEY Issued 24 Jan 1936 Rites 24 Jan 1936
J. H. MAyo, J. P.

George VAUGHN to Gertrude SIMONS Issued 24 Jan 1936 Rites 25 JAn 1936
P. N. Moffitt, Jdg.

Berbice HILLIS to Willie McMAHAN Issued 25 Jan 1936 Rites 25 Jan 1936
G. B. J. Mitchell, J. P.

Arthue COLE to Fannie Belle SCOTT Issued 28 Jan 1936 Rites 3 Feb 1936
DAn Perkins, M. G.

M. L. ADAMS to Edna TURNER Issued 1 Feb 1936 Rites 6 Feb 1936
F. J. Winton, J. P.

James M. SEVIER to Mary Eliz. WOMACK Issued 1 Feb 1936 Rites 2 Feb. 1936
T. Q. Martin, M. G.

E. J. BESS to Maxine BROWN Issued 8 Feb 1936 Rites 8 Feb 1936
W. L. Perry, M. G.

Robert GRIBBLE to Hazel MORGAN Issued 8 Feb 1936 Rites 8 Feb 1936
J. B. Gribble, M. G.

Edmond ROBERTS to Mamie FORD Issued 30 Nov 1935 Rites 30 Nov 1935
FAte Walker, J. P.

Clarence JOHNSON to MAggoleen MORGAN Issued 30 Nov 1935 Rites 30 Nov 1935
N. P. McWhirter, J. P.

Paul STEPHAN to Hazel THAXTON Issued 5 Dec 1935 rites 5 Dec 1935
T. Q. Martin, M. G.

Taft SUMMERS to Mildred LANCE Issued 14 Dec 1935 Rites 15 Dec 1935
G. B. J. Mitchell, J. P.

Raymond RODDEY to Treva HOBBS Issued 14 Dec 1935 Rites 14 Dec 1935
N. P. McWhirter, J. P.

Frank CHASTAIN to Delia HIGGINBOTHAM Issued 17 Dec 1935 Rites 22 Dec 1935
J. W. McCollum, J. P.

Everett GREEN to Mildred GARMON Issued 18 Dec 1935 Rites 25 Dec 1935
Hubert C. Green, M. G.

George MILSTEAD to Edith CURTIS Issued 18 Dec 1935 Rites 21 Dec 1935
T. Q. Martin, M.C.

Luther SMITH to Flora WALKER Issued 19 Dec 1935 Rites 23 Dec 1935
W. T. Warren, J. P.

Clint WILSON to Mary WILLIAMS Issued 21 Dec 1935   Not Returned

Clessie BRATCHER to Alma HAGEWOOD Issued 21 Dec 1935 Rites 24 Dec 1935
A. Z. Holder, J. P.

George ELLIOTT to MArgaret SNIPES   Issued 21 Dec 1935 Rites 21 Dec 1935
A. H. Huff, M. G.

Robert J. WEBB to Ruby GRISSOM Issued 21 Dec 1935 Rites 25 Dec 1935
J. S. Dunlap, J. P.

Howard TALLEY to Erra Belle FENNELL Issued 21 Dec 1935 Rites 25 Dec 1935
Hubert C. Green, M. G.

Glenn Austin BEATY to Hazel CAGLE Issued 23.Dec 1935 Rites 28 Dec 1935
W. B. Snipes, M. G.

Cecil BOTTOMS to Earleen CUNNINGHAM Issued 23 Dec 1935 Rites 24 dec 1935
I. P. McGregor, J. P.

Austin MADEWELL to Pauline COPPINGER Issued 23 Dec 1935 Rites 25 Dec 1935
F. M. Smartt, J. P.

Everett C. GREEN to Ellen CANTRELL Issued 23 Dec 1935 Rites 24 Dec 1935
J. S. Dunlap, J. P.

B. J. BURCH to Flora Lee LAWRENCE Issued 23 dec 1935 Rites 24 dec 1935
L. B. Moffitt, J. P.

Buck TURNER to Jessie Ruth TURNER Issued 23 Dec 1935 Rites 23 deq 1935
J. H. Mayo, J. P.

J. M. SCOTT to Florence CURTIS Issued 8 Feb 1936 Rites 9 Feb 1936
I. P. McGregor, J. P.

William HULETT to Nola WILSON Issued 10 Feb 1936 Rites 11 Feb 1936
H. J. Wilson, J. P.

I. P. DURHAM to Flora MAYNARD Issued 13 Feb 1936 Rites 15 Feb 1936
Carl Dickson, M. G.

Robert S. WOMACK to Nan Hampton SMARTT Issued 14 Feb 1936 Rites 16 Feb 1936
John L. Ferguson, M. G.

Houston BOND to Violet STONER Issued 15 Feb 1936 Rites 15 Feb 1936
A. T. Judkins, M. G.

Willie B. TURNER to Eunice HILL Issued 15 Feb 1936 Rites 16 Feb 1936
I. P. McGregor, J. P.

Edward WOODLEE to Ollie JONES Issued 15 Feb 1936 Rites 15 feb 1936
Rouchen HOrton, M. G.

Furman RIVERS to Ada SHAW Issued 18 Feb 1936 Rites 18 Feb 1936
J. H. MAyo, J. P.

W. P. MURPHY to Nettie JUDKINS Issued 20 Feb 1936 Rites 20 Feb 1936
J. T. Casey, M. G.

Johnson MITCHELL to Mollie STARKEY Issued 22 Feb 1936 Rites 23 Feb 1936
E. W. Sutherlin, J. P.

E. D. GOLDEN to MAggie CAMPBELL Issued 29 Feb 1936 VOIDED

JAmes CUTTS to Mildred FULTS Issued 29 Feb 1936 Rites 29 Feb 1936
A. T. Judkins, M. G.

Alton ROGERS to Lillie CARR issued 29 Feb 1936 rites 29 Feb 1936
E. W. Sutherlin, J. P.

Lloyd W. BOLES to Ola Mai SIMONS Issued 2 Mar 1936 rites 2 Mar 1936
J. W. Cooley, M. G.

Charlei SUTTON to Mattie CAMPBELL Issued 7 Mar 1936 Rites 7 Mar 1936
A. Z. Holder, J. P.

Goldie BOULDIN to Alene ALEXANDER Issued 7 Mar 1936 Rites 14 Mar 1936
I. P. McGregor, J. P.

Lester RICHARDSON to RAchel BOULDIN Issued 9 MAr 1936 Rites 15 Mar 1936
N. M. Hill, J. P.

Bill ASKEW to Deamie TANNER Issued 9 Mar 1936 Rites 9 Mar 1936
J. H. Mayo, J. P.

WArner JONES to Lucille BRYAN Issued 14 Mar 1936 Rites 15 Mar 1936
N. U. Allen, M. G.

Ivor RHEA to Mary Ellen SMARTT Issued 14 Mar 1936 Rites 14 Mar 1936
E. D. Martin, M. G.

Frank Ward to Hazel RAPER Issued 18 Mar 1936 Rites 18 Mar 1936
J. L. Walker, J. P.

Will MILRANEY to Thelma THOMISON Issued 23 Mar 1936 Rites 23 Mar 1936
P. N. Moffitt, Jdg.

David MULLICAN to Laura WALKER Issued 23 Mar 1936 Rites 23 Mar 1936
J. H. Mayo, J. P.

Estill WRIGHT to Bessie FUSTON Issued 25 Mar 1936 Rites 25 Mar 1936
J. B. Gribble, M. G.

Cooper SPARKMAN to Pearl Hill JONES Issued 28 Mar 1936 Rites 28 Mar 1936
A. T. Judkins, M. G.

J. W. COOPER to Theonia LAFEVER Issued 30 Mar 1936 Rites 31 Mar 1936
P. N. Moffitt, Jdg.

A. B. DAVIS to Rena JOHNSON Issued 1 Apr 1936 Rites 5 Apr 1936
J. W. McCollum, J. P.

Charles HOBBS to Ruby WOODLEE Issued 4 Apr 1936 Rites 5 Apr 1936
J. L. Barnes, J. P.

Willie MOORE to margie MUNCY Issued 16 Apr 1936 Rites 17 APr 1936
J. H. Mayo, J. P.

Charles KIRBY to Juanita WHITE Issued 18 Apr 1936 Rites 19 Apr 1936
J. H. Mayo, J. P.

Charlie DURHAM to Inez MYERS Issued 28 Apr 1936 Rites 28 Apr 1936
J. H. Mayo, J. P.

Charles M. TILFORD to A. D. WHEELER Issued 29 Apr 1936 Rites 3 May 1936
T. Q. Martin, M. G.

Millard HOLLAND to Roberta GANN Issued 2 May 1936 Rites 2 May 1936
J. L. Walker, J. P.

Marvin RHEA to Frances NORTHCUTT issued 2 May 1936 Rites 2 May 1936
J. L. Barnes, J. P.

Rexie WEST to Luleea ROBERTS Issued 1 May 1936 Rites 2 May 1936
Charles HIllis, J. P.

John SIMPSON to Minnie SUMMERS ISSued 4 May 1936 Rites 9 May 1936
Herbert Knight, J. P.

Lynnwood PARKER to KAtherine BAILEY Issued 4 May 1936 Rites 4 May 1936
P. N. Moffitt, Jdg.

C. H. DUKE to MAry Lou BURR Issued 7 May 1936 Rites 15 May 1936
J. L. Ferguson, M. G.

John Thomas TAYLOR to Cassie JOHNSON Issued 8 MAy 1936 Rites 23 May 1936
Irving Patton, J. P.

J. B. JENNINGS to Ola KILLIAN Issued 9 May 1936 Rites 9 May 1936
F. M. Smartt, J. P.

Arvin KIRBY to JUNE DAVIS Issued 9 May 1936 Rites 10 May 1936
J. F. Leeper, M. G.

Frank CANTRELL to Opal CLOSE Issued 16 May 1936 Rites 23 May 1936
James K. Martin, J. P.

Cecil A. SPECK to Nell MArie QUINN Issued 16 May 1936 Rites 17 May 1936
Richard Huff, M. G.

Barnes BAKER to Lorena JOHNSON Issued 18 May 1936 Rites 19 May 1936
J. H. Mayo, J. P.

Sidney CLARK to Virginia CANTRELL Issued 22 May 1936 Rites 23 May 1936
C. T. CAntrell, J. P.

Ernest COUCH to Lila MAi BASS Issued 23 May 1936 Rites 23 May 1936
J. H. MAyo, J. P.

Marvin Craig BARNES to Hazel Lee CHRISTIAN Issued 23 May 1936 Rites 24 May 1936
T. Q. Martin, M. G.

Kenneth R. KESEY to Willie Mai WARE. Issued 30 May 1936 Rites 31 may 1936
IsAAC Grizzle, J. P.

Robert ERVIN to MAry YOUNG Issued 1 Jun 1936 Rites 1 jun 1936
J. H. Mayo, J. P.

PAul HERNDON to Lois DENNIS Issued 2 jun 1936 Rites 6 Jun 1936
H. J. Wilson, J. P.

Arnold McDOWELL to Magnola FULTS Issued 6 Jun 1936 Rites 6 Jun 1936
J. T. Casey, M. G.

James C. ARGO to Jessie Ruth FREEZE Issued 6 Jun 1936 Rites 6 Jun 1936
E. W. Sutherlin, J. P.

Waymon LOWRY to Imogene POWELL Issued 6 Jun 1936 Rites 10 Jun 1936
E. W. Sutherlin, J. P.

Willard TALLEY to Catherine LOCKE Issued 6 Jun 1936 Rites 7 Jun 1936
R. H. Huff, M. G.

Clifford SEDORE to Hazel Va. HOLDER Issued 6 Jun 1936 VOIDED

Clyde CHRISTIAN to Eunice MOFFITT Issued 9 Jun 1936 Rites 9 Jun 1936
J. H. MAyo, J. P.

W. E. CANTRELL to Cathaleen DAVIS Issued 12 jun 1936 Rites 13 Jun 1936
T. Q. Martin, M. G.

Flavil LANCE to Louise JONES Issued 13 Jun 1936 Rites 14 jun 1936
G. B. J. Mitchell, J. P.

Jay HOBBS to LASSIE Emma CLENDENON Issued 13 Jun 1936 Rites 19 Jun 1936
J. H. Mayo, J. P.

Grady McBRIDE to Dasrine ELKINS Issued 13 Jun 1936 Rites 13 Jun 1936
J. H. Mayo, J. P.

A. R. FISH to Lizzie CANTRELL Issued 13 Jun 1936 Rites 17 Jun 1936
E. T. Cantrell, J. P.

Otis R. HALEY to Josephine M. STUBBLEFIELD Issued 13 Jun 1936 Rites 14 Jun 1936
J. T. Casey, M. G.

Hooper BOST to VAda PAGE Issued 13 Jun 1936 Rites 13 Jun 1936
P. N. Moffitt, J. P.

Ed EVANS to Catherine SAVAGE Issued 16 Jun 1936 Rites 17 Jun 1936
J. H. Houston, M. G.

Edgar CAMPBELL to Ruth WALLACE Issued 16 June 1936 Rites 16 Jun 1936
H. C. Green, M. G.

Jmaes N. DARNELL to Edith RIDDLE Issued 17 Jun 1936 Rites 23 jun 1936
J. Ridley Stroup., M. G.

Edward W. TURRENTINE to Ruth FLETCHER Issued 17 Jun 1936 Rites 17 Jun 1936
J. L. Ferguson, M. G.

Arthur TURNER to Clisty KEITH Issued 19 Jun 1936 Rites 20 jun 1936
J. B. Gribble, M. G.

DAvis BOULDIN to Louise FREEMAN Issued 20 Jun 1936 rites 20 jun 1936
O, C. Dickson, M. G.

Brown WILSON to Lottie HENDRICKS Issued 20 Jun 1936 Rites 20 jun 1936
H. J. Wilson, J. P.

Wm. F. ALMOND to Lillian Beatrice SPARKMAN Issued 20 Jun 1936 Rites 20 Jun 1936
Irving Patton, J. P.

Leonard TODD to Roberta ALEXANDER Issued 25 Jun 1936 Rites 25 Jun 1936
J. H. MAyo, J. P.

Wm. E. COOLEY to opal Louise ROLLER issued 26 jun 1936 Rites 27 Jun 1936
J. H. MAyo, J. P.

James A. SMITH to KAtherine Ruth BROOKS Issued 26 Jun 1936 Rites 27 Jun 1936
J. L. Ferguson, M. G.

Mose MARTIN to Minnie GUINN Issued 29 Jun 1936 Rites 30 Jun 1936
J. E. Witt, M. G.

L. M. LASATER to Emily KAtherine TAYLOR Issued 29 Jun 1936 Rites 29 Jun 1936
J. H. Mayo, J. P.

Will Howard CRIPPS to Bernie Lee SIMONS Issued 1 Jul 1936 Rites 1 Jul 1936
P. N. Moffitt, Jdg.

Henry Howard HALE to Helen Gladys MURPHY Issued 1 Jul 1936 Rites 1 Jul 1936
P. N. Moffitt, Jdg.

Zollie HENSLEY to JAnie WINNETT Issued 2 Jul 1936 Rites 2 Jul 1936
J. H. Mayo, J. P.

Willie THOMPSON to Azzelene MORGAN Issued 3 Jul 1936 Rites 4 Jul 1936
G. B. J. Mitchell, J. P.

Delbert COUCH to Mildred BARRETT Issued 3 Jul 1936 Rites 4 Jul 1936
J. H. MAyo, J. P.

D. C. PITMAN to Edith PARSLEY Issued 3 Jul 1936 Rites 4 Jul 1936
C. E. Simmons, M. G.

Royce COPE to Tommie STUBBLEFIELD Issued 4 Jul 1936 Rites 4 Jul 1936
A. T. Judkins, M. G.

Woodrow TAYLOR to Viva RIGNEY Issued 8 Jul 1936 Rites 8 Jul 1936
T. Q. Martin, M. G.

Brown PRATER to Elizabeth JORDAN Issued 11 Jul 1936 Rites 11 Jul.1936
Lawrence Reed, M. G.

Ernest MORGAN to Nona GRIBBLE Issued 11 Jul 1936 Rites 11 Jul 1936
Lawrence Reed, M. G.

Hayden LOWERY to Dororthy O. McMAHAN Issued 11 Jul 1936 Rites 11 Jul 1936
E. W. Sutherlin, J. P.

Forrest GENTRY to Pauline HOLT Issued 18 Jul 1936 Rites 18 Jul 1936
E. W. Sutherlin, J. P.

Luther KEEL (C) to Amelia PLEASANT (C) Issued 18 Jul 1936 Rites 19 Jul 1936
T. M. Tuggle, M. G.

Virgil Benton FOWLER to Mamie IVIE Issued 21 Jul 1936 Rites 21 Jul 1936
J. H. MAyo, J. P.

Haskell BILBREY (C) to Catherine RAMSEY (C) Issued 23 Jul 1936 Rites 23 Jul 1936
T. M. Tuggle, M.G.

Elbert MORGAN to Rose TITTSWORTH Issued 25 Jul 1936 Rites 2 Aug 1936
W. G. Mullican, M. G.

Wm. S. TALMAGE to Mildred McAFEE Issued 27 Jul 1936 Rites 27 Jul 1936
T. Q. Martin, M. G.

Jesse BRATCHER to Sarah SCOTT Issued 29 Jul 1936 Rites 29 Jul 1936
J. H. MAyo, J. P.

Golden D. THOMAS to Violet LESTER Issued 1 Aug 1936 Rites 1 Aug 1936
J. H. MAyo, J. P.

Willie LAEGUE to Minnie MARTIN Issued3 Aug 1936 Rites 3 Aug 1936
P. N. Moffitt, Jdg.

WArner MORRISON to Jerline SANDERS Issued 3 Aug 1936 Rites 3 Aug 1936
J. H. MAyo, J. P.

Clifford SEDORE to Hazel Virginia HOLDER Issued 4 Aug 1936 Rites 4 Aug 1936
Herbert Knight, J. P.

Elmer HAYES to Lillian LAFEVERS Issued 7 Aug 1936 Rites 7 Aug 1936
J. H. Mayo, J. P.

Bernard McAFEE to Clara McMAHAN Issued 7 Aug 1936 Rites 9 Aug 1936
E. Christian, M. G.

Aubrey DILLDINE to Gladys MARTIN Issued 8 Aug 1936 Rites 8 Aug 1936
J. H. Mayo, J. P.

Troy HILL to Thelma STILES Issued 8 Aug 1936 Rites 8 Aug 1936
J. H. MAyo, J. P.

Escal HILL to Irene LITTLE Issed 8 Aug 1936 Rites 9 Aug 1936
A. Z. Holder, J. P.

John A. FORD, Jr. to Helen Mai BARRINGER Issued 8 Aug 1936 Rites 9 Aug 1936
H. T. Richmond, M. G.

Clayton GENTRY to Evaline HOLT Issued 10 Aug 1936 Rites 11 Aug 1936
E. W. Sutherlin, J. P.

Shelton CANTRELL to Clara Belle MITCHELL Issued 11 Aug 1936 Rites 2 Sep 1936
I. J. Grizzle, J. P.

John D. FITZGERALD to Charlotte BROWN Issued 13 Aug 1936 Rites 13 Aug 1936
S. P. Pitman, M. G.

Jesse Frank CONASTER to Eva Dean EVANS Issued 14 Aug 1936 Rites 14 Aug 1936
J. P. Bilbrey, J. P.

Oney G. BROWN (C) to Sarah Eliz. RIVERS (C) Issued 14 Aug 1936 Rites 14 Aug 1936
J. H. Houston, M. G.

Leland Brown ARGO to Betty THOMISON Issued 15 Aug 1936 rites 15 Aug 1936
Isaac Grizzle, J. P.

Lester GOOCH to Idella CLARK Issued 15 Aug 1936 Rites 15 Aug 1936
John Morton, M.G.,

W. B. TAYLOR, Jr. to Bessie CANTRELL Issued 15 Aug 1936 Rites 15 Aug 1936
H. C. Glenn, M. G.

G. E. DRIVER to VAda PEDIGO Issued 15 Aug 1936 Rites 15 Aug 1936
J. H. Mayo, J. P.

Murphu Ray STEAKLEY to Mona JOHNSON Issued 15 Aug 1936 Rites 16 Aug 1936
N. P. McWhirter, J. P.

Thos. William BUNTLEY to MAry KAtherine MARSHALL Issued 20 Aug 1936 Rites 20 Aug 1936
W. S. Marshall, M. G.

Ural GUEST to Ora MACON Issued 21 Aug 1936 Rites 21 Aug 1936
E. W. Sutherlin, J. P.

Richard McGEE to Sallie PAuline NEWBY Issued 21 Aug 1936 Rites 22 Aug 1936
H. T. Richmond, M. G.

B. B. HILLIS to Anna Lou STINNETT Issued 22 Aug 1936 Rites 22 Aug 1936
J. H. Mayo, J. P.

JAMES O. MASEY to Their Mai DENIS (?) Issued 24 Aug 1936 Rites 24 Aug 1936
J. L. Ferguson, M. G.

Offa WILLIAMSON to Thelma RADER Issued 24 Aug 1936 Rites 24 Aug 1936
J. H. Mayo, J. P.

James DUNLAP to Ophalinn FISHER Issued 27 Aug 1936 Rites 30 Aug 1936
J. H. Mayo, J. P.

LAndus GOOCH to Mary Eliz. ALLEN Issued 29 Aug 1936 Rites 29 Aug 1936
H. C. Green, M. G.

Lawrence WALKER to Laurine HILL Issued 29 Aug 1936 Rites 29 Aug 1936
J. H. Mayo, J. P.

Isaac BROWN to Elizabeth DONELSON ISsued 2 Sep 1936 Rites 3 Sep 1936
J. H. Houston, M. G.

B. J. BESS to Iris BOULDIN Issued 3 Sep 1936 Rites 3 Sep 1936
J. H. Mayo, J. P.

Arthur HENDRICKS to Vera ORRICK Issued 4 Sep 1936 Rites 5 Sep 1936
H. J. Wilson, J. P.

Gilbert GRAYSON to Goldie Mai CARR Issued 4 Sep 1936 Rites 5 Sep 1936
P. N. Moffitt, J. P.

James L. HENNESSEE to Martha J. WOMACK Issued 5 Sep 1936 Rites 5 Sep 1936
A. T. Judkins, M. G.

Ernest BROWN to Annie WINTON Issued 5 Sep 1936 Rites 8 Sep 1936
W. E. Garner, M. G.

Fred MATHIS to Mildred BAILEY Issued 5 Sep 1936 Rites 8 Sep 1936
J. N. Winnett, J. P.

Willie ALLEN to MAGGIE McDANIEL Issued 5 Sep 1936 Rites Sep 1936
J. H. MAyo, J. P.

Lonnie MARKUM to Edna SNIPES Issued 5 Sep 1936 Rites 7 Sep 1936
A. B. Moffitt, M. G.

Aubrey Allen MARTIN to Ida Bell REDMON Issued 11 Sep 1936 Rites 16 Sep 1936
Cass R. Womack, J. P.

O. T. MILLER to Virginia HIBDON Issued 12 Sep 1936 rites 12 Sep 1936
J. H. MAyo, J. P.

Roosevelt LANCE to Elizabeth HALL Issued 12 Sep 1936 Rites 13 Sep 1936
H. C. Green, M. G.

George JENNINGS to Cora Mai HOBBS Issued 15 Spe 1936 rites 18 Sep 1936
J. L. Barnes, J. P.

Charlie HOLLAND to Frances HALL Issued 16 Sep 1936 Rites 16 Sep 1936
J. H. MAyo, J. P.

G. W. NEWBY to Oma Lee MASEY Issued 17 Sep 1936 Rites 17 Sep 1936
L. D. McDonald, M. G.

Charles L. HUDSON to Ruby McDOWELL Issued 17 Sep 1936 Rites 17 Sep 1936
J. L. MAyo, J. P.

Clarence MELTON to Nannie MCBRIDE Issued 18 Sep 1936 Rites 18 Sep 1936
Isaac Grizzle, J. P.

John Hugh CALDWELL to Vernie Sue SPRY Issued 19 Sep 1936 rites 19 Sep 1936
H. J. Wilson, J. P.

Frazier SWEETON to Beulah Lee BOWEN Issued 19 Sep 1936 rites 19 Sep 1936
F. L. Kirby, J. P.

Will HOLLAND (C) to Pearl THOMAS (C) Issued 19 Sep 1936 Rites 19 Sep 1936
H. E. Taylor, M. G.

Marcus PATRICK to Jessie V. MADEWELL Issued 21 Sep 1936 Rites 21 Sep 1936
J. P. Bilbrey, J. P.

JAmes TERRY to Lexie DONOUGHUE Issued 23 Sep 1936 Rites 25 Sep 1936
J. H. Mayo, J. P.

Lester MARTIN to Mildred HALEY Issued 25 Sep 1936 Rites 3 Oct 1936
Wm. T. Steele, M. G.

PAul SMITHSON to Maxine GILLENTINE Issued 25 Sep 1936 Voided

Bryan BOULDIN to Mary Etta FULTS Issued 26 Sep 1936 Rites 26 sep 1936
N. M. Hill, J. P.

George HALE to Martha RIGSBY Issued 26 Sep 1936 Rites 26 Sep 1936
F. J. Winton, J. P.

Thomas W. IAMES, Jr. to Emma L. FISK Issued 27 Sep 1936 Rites 27 Sep 1936
G. H. Powell, J. P.

Herman SUMMERS to Mary RICHARDSON Issued 28 Sep 1936 rites 2 Oct 1936
N. M. King, J. P.

George W. OLIVER to Frances M. ROGERS Issued 30 Sep 1936 rites 4 Oct 1936
T. Q. Martin, M. G.

Buford BROWN to L. Ann CUNNINGHAM Issued 30 Sep 1936 rites 30 Sep 1936
J. H. AMyo, J. P.

E. E. FREAR to Mamie Belle REYNOLDS Issued 1 Oct 1936 Rites 1 Oct 1936
J. H. MAyo, J. P.

Claud HICKEY to Mary Eliz. PRATER Issued 6 Oct 1936 Rites 6 Oct 1936
J. H. MAyo, J. P.

Charlie FLOYD to Fern LANIER Issued 7 Oct 1936 Rites 11 Oct 1936
N. O. allen, M. G.

Lester MILLS to Ella MAe BOREN Issued 8 Oct 1936 Rites 9 Oct 1936
W. S. Wilmore, M. G.

Eual SPARKMAN to Casteen NEAL Issued 10 Oct 1936 Rites 11 oct 1936
Irving Patton, J. P.

Willie GORE to Lou BEARD Issued 9 Nov 1936 Rites 9 Nov 1936 J. H. Mayo, J. P.

Walter VAN DE CAR to Wilma Virginia THATCH Issued 11 Nov 1936 Rites 11 Nov 1936 J. H. Mayo, J. P.

J. W. FREEZE to Lura Mai JARRELL Issued 14 Nov 1936 Rites 14 Nov 1936 P. N. Moffitt, Jdg.

Albert PLEASANT to Louise YORK Issued 14 Nov 1936 Rites 15 Nov 1936 R. G. Martin, J. P.

Hugh Donnell PARIS to Mary Lusk DAVIES Issued 14 Nov 1936 Rites 14 Nov 1936 T. Q. Martin, M. G.

George FERRELL to Laura PADGETT Issued 16 Nov 1936 Rites 17 Nov 1936 L. B. Moffitt, J. P.

J. A. CHAMBERS Jr. to Charlei Mai PARISH Issued 18 Nov 1936 Rites 18 Nov 1936 J. P. Bilbrey, J. P.

James E. BRANNAN to Juanita LEACH Issued 18 Nov 1936 Rites 18 Nov 1936 J. B. Gribble, M. G.

Willie Arnold TITSWORTH to Malinda LORANCE Issued 21 Nov 1936 Rites 21 Nov 1936 J. H. Mayo, J. lP.

Rascoe ARGO to Willie CARVER Issued 21 Nov 1936 Rites 21 Nov 1936 J. H. MAyo, J. P.

Arzie SIMMONS to Frances HANEY Issued 21 Nov 1936 Rites 22 Nov 1936 C. B. Cook, M. G.

Andrew JONES to Bulah WARREN Issued 23 Nov 1936 Rites 23 Nov 1936 T. Q. Martin, M. G.

Wilburn McDOWELL to Maggie BOTTOMS Issued 25 Nov 1936 Rites 26 Nov 1936 A. T. Judkins, M. G.

Billie STANLEY to Aline PEELER Issued 25 Nov 1936 Rites 29 Nov 1936 W. T. Warren, J. P.

Clayburn J. REED to Allace Eliz. BRYANT Issued 25 Nov 1936 Rites 26 Nov 1936 A. T. Judkins, M. G.

Tommy KING to Geneva GOOCH Issued 28 Nov 1936 Rites 28 Nov 1936 G. H. Powell, J. P.

Troy CRIPPS to Myrtle CRIPPS Issued 29 Nov 1936 Rites 29 Nov 1936 J. H. Mayo, J. P.

James W. ALLEN to Eula Mai CANTRELL Issued 1 Dec 1936 Rites 2 Dec 1936 J. T. Casey, M. G.

Henry HOLLAND to Estel HOLT Issued 4 Dec 1936 Rites 5 Dec 1936 J. T. CAsey, M. G.

Robert RICHARDSON to Edna BOULDIN Issued 10 Oct 1936 Rites 11 Oct 1936 A. E. Curtis, J. P.

Clarence RICHARDSON to Oma BOULDIN Issued 10 Oct 1936 Rites 10 Nov 1936 A. E. Curtis, J. P.

Roy SHOCKLEY to Mimmie Lee METLOCK Issued 10 Oct 1936 Rites 11 Oct 1936 J. H. Mayo, J. P.

J. B. WILLIAMS (C) to Bessie APPLE (C) Issued 10 Oct 1936 Rites 10 Oct 1936 J. H. Houston, M. G.

HAston JUDKINS to Zona YOUNG Issued 12 Oct 1936 Rites 14 Oct 1936 E. T. Cantrell, J. P.

Dallas RIDINER to Georgia LOWERY Issued 12 Oct 1936 Rites 12 Oct 1936 J. H. Mayo, J. P.

Raymond DUKE to Lee Arthur ARMSTRONG Issued 15 Oct 1936 Rites 16 Oct 1936 T. Q. Martin, M. G.

R. W. RICHARD to Berueze HOLLAND Issued 17 Oct 1936 rites 17 Oct 1936 J. H. Mayo, J. P.

Willis DILLON to Edna TAYLOR Issued 17 Oct 1936 Rites 17 Oct 1936 W. S. Wileman, M. G.

Virgil SMITH to Lucy PARSLEY Issued 24 Oct 1936 rites 28 Oct 1936 J. T. Casey, M. G.

Lloyd ELAM to Fannie Lou PITMAN Issued 24 Oct 1936 Rites 31 Oct 1936 H. J. Wilson, J. P.

George GILLIAM to Edith SCISSOM Issued 25 Oct 1936 Rites 26 Oct 1936 P. N. Moffitt, Jdg.

James NORTH to Sara TRIPP Issued 25 Oct 1936 Rites 26 oct 1936 P. N. Moffitt, Jdg.

William Allen WALKER to Fannie DAi NOBLITT Issued 29 Oct 1936 Rites 1 Nov 1936 T. Q. Martin, M. G.

Eugene GREEN to Bessie Lou TITSWORTH Issued 31 Oct 1936 Rites 1 Nov 1936 A. B. Moffitt, M. G.

Charlie S. McMILLEN to Mildred MELTON Issued 31 Oct 1936 Rites 7 Nov 1936 T. Q. MARTIN, M. G.

Cecil BALDWIN to Catherine DILLON Issued 4 Nov 1936 Rites 4 Nov 1936 G. H. Powell, J. P.

T. C. SELF to Geraldine WINFREE Issued 5 Nov 1936 Rites 5 Nov 1936 J. N. Winnett, J. P.

Earl PHILLIPS to Ruth PAGE Issued 5 Nov 1936 Rites 5 Nov 1936 G. H. Powell, J. P.

Buck JONES (C) to Elizabeth SAVAGE (C) Issued 7 Nov 1936 Rites 7 Nov 1936 T. M. Tuggle, M. G.

Ralph HIGGINBOTHAM to Ruth GOODMAN Issued 5 Dec 1936 Rites 5 Dec 1936
J. H. Mayo, J. P.

Willard BOULDIN to Martha Ann ROBERTS Issued 11 Dec 1936 Rites 11 Dec 1936
P. N. Moffitt, Jdg.

Howard JONES to LAura BARNES Issued 11 Dec 1936 Rites 12 Dec 1936
P. N. Moffitt, Jdg.

Virgil GENTRY to Geneva HAYES Issued 11 Dec 1936 Rites 13 Dec 1936
H. J. Wilson, J. P.

John F. MARTIN to Myrtle GRIBBLE Issued 14 Dec 1936 Rites 14 Dec 1936
E. D. Martin, M. G.

Norman L. SWINDELL to Myrtle ROBERTS Issued 16 Dec 1936 Rites 16 Dec 1936
F. J. Winton, J. P.

Ed JONES to Rasha WEBSTER Issued 16 Dec 1936 Rites 16 Dec 1936
J. H. Mayo, J. P.

George JONES to Kathleen HENNESSEE Issued 16 Dec 1936 Rites 20 Dec 1936
E. D. Martin, M. G.

George BOYD to Georgia Mai ZWINGLE Issued 19 Dec 1936 Rites 24 Dec 1936
Irving Patton, J. P.

Alton ROBERTS to Argie ROBERTS Issued 19 Dec 1936 Rites 19 Dec 1936
P. N. Moffitt, Jdg.

Odell PIKE to Lorene BYRD Issued 19 dec 1936 Rites 19 Dec 1936
E. D. Martin, M. G.

Charles F. BRYAN to Edith HILLIS Issued 19 Dec 1936 Rites 21 Dec 1936
C. B. Cook, M. G.

Clifford W. WILKERSON to Lora CRAIN Issued 19 Dec 1936 Rites 19 Dec 1936
J. H. Mayo, J. P.

J. R. GREEN to Martha JONES Issued 21 Dec 1936 Rites 24 Dec 1936
P. N. Moffitt, Jdg.

J. D. NUNLEY to Daisy MOORE Issued 22 Dec 1936 Rites 23 Dec 1936
John R. Safley, J. P.

Paul SMITHSON to Maxine GILLENTINE Issued 22 Dec 1936 Rites 22 Dec 1936
A. Z. Holder, J. P.

Whyte TENPENNY to Virginia TODD Issued 23 Dec 1936 Rites 24 Dec 1936
A. T. Judkins, M. G.

Lee DICKSON to Gertrude TURNER Issued 23 Dec 1936 Rites 25 Dec 1936
C. C. Dickson, M. G.

Clyde RAINS to Louise WRIGHT Issued 24 Dec 1936 Rites 24 Dec 1936
T. Q. Martin, M. G.

Chester JONES to Ruth WATSON Issued 24 Dec 1936 Rites 24 Dec 1936
J. N. Winnett, J. P.

Frank Duncan LUSK (C) to Rosena STARKEY (C) Issued 24 Dec 1936 Rites 24 ec 1936
E. S. WAllace, J. P.

Edward PEGG to Cynthia TEMPLETON Issued 24 Dec 1936 Rites 24 Dec 193
R. W. Smartt, Jdg.

Robert F. JONES to Rebecca MAI BELL Issued 24 dec 1936 Rites 24 Dec 1936
Lawrence Reed, M. G.

J. Delbert GREEN to Alma THOMAS Issued 24 Dec 1936 Rites 24 Dec 9136
H. C. Green, M. G.

Clarence GAITHER to Callie Mai MORGAN Issued 25 Dec 1936 Rites 25 Dec 1936
J. H. Mayo, J. P.

Thurman HILLIS to Sylvia HILLIS Issued 25 Dec 1936 Rites 25 Dec 1936
Fred Amacher, M. G.

Herbert HOBBS to Christine NORTHCUTT Issued 26 Dec 1936 Rites 26 Dec 1936
J. I. Patton, J. P.

William BRADY to Lona YOUNG Issued 28 Dec 1936 Rites 28 ec 1936
J. H. Mayo, J. P.

George RAINS to Zora Bell GRAHAM Issued 29 Dec 1936 Rites 29 Dec 1936
P. N. Moffitt, Jdg.

Joe Lane FINGER to Vivian JOHNSON Issued 29 Dec 1936 Rites 31 Dec 1936
J. W. Swann, M. G.

Arthur Lee MARTIN (C) to Ida Lee GRAYSON (C) Issued 31 Dec 1936 Rites 31 Dec
Irving Patton, J. P.

Fred ROBERTS to Mary Jane BAKER Issued 2 Jan 1937 Rites 4 Jan 1937
J. H. Mayo, J. P.

W. F. WINTON to Ethel WARE Issued 2 Jan 1936 Rites 2 JAn 1936
J. L. Barnes, J. P.

Dillard AUSTIN to Frances SUMMERS Issued 2 Jan 1937 Rites 2 Jan 1937
E. W. Sutherlin, J. P.

Delmer ATNIP to Ruby Brown HALL Issued 3 Jan 1937 Voided

Lloyd B. SMITH to PAralee BRASWELL Issued 14 JAN 1937 Rites 15 Jan 1937
W. T. Warren, J. P.

Will ETTER (C) to Annie Mai COPE Issued 21 Jan 1937 Rites 21 Jan 1937
L. C. Maple, M. G.

Leo CANTRELL to Nell LANE Issued 27 Jan 1937 Rites 27 Jan 1937
J. L. Barnes, J. P.

Jesse COPPINGER to Mable SAVAGE Issued 27 Mar 1937 Rites 27 Mar 1937
J. H. MAyo, J. P.

Frank WArren to Elliot FISHER Issued 27 Mar 1937 Rites 27 Mar 1937
W. M. Rowland, J. P.

Charles MILSTEAD to Gertrude ROBERTS Issued 27 Mar 1937 Rites 27 Mar 1937
J. L. BArnes, J. P.

Lester McGOWAN to Nellie WADE Issued 27 Mar 1937 Rites 27 MAr 1937
H. J. Wilson, J. P.

Joe B. COUCH to Martha E. HOLT Issued 28 Mar 1937 Rites 28 Mar 1937
O. L. Minks, M, G.

Martin HILLIS to Elmer SAVAGE Issued 29 Mar 1937 Rites 29 Mar 1937
J. H. MAyo, J. P.

Julius RIGSBY to Myrtle Mae SEALS Issued 3 Apr 1937 Rites 3 Apr 1937
Irving Patton, J. P.

Eugene SMITH to Eva TREECE Issued 6 Apr 1937 Rites 6 Apr 1937
J. D. Jones, M. G.

John KING to Hassie PERRY Issued 10 Apr 1937 Rites 10 Apr 1937
P. N. Moffitt, Jdg.

CArl WILLIAMSON to Bessie SMITH Issued 10 Apr 1937 Rites 10 Apr 1937
J. H. MAyo, J. P.

Eskell CLEMONS to Essie MALONE Issued 12 Apr 1937 Rites 12 Apr 1937
J. H. MAyo, J. P.

Willie B. MAYNARD to Flora DURHAM Issued 17 Apr 1937 Rites 17 Apr 1937
J. H. MAyo, J. P.

Homer KIRBY to Nannie HILLIS Issued 19 Apr 1937 Rites 19 Apr 1937
J. H. MAyo, J. P.

Charlie T. ETHRIDGE to Virginia BLUM Issued 19 Apr 1937 Rites 19 Apr 1937
J. H. MAyo, J. P.

Bethel MULLICAN to Myrtle VANAITA Issued 20 Apr 1937 Rites 20 Apr 1937
H. C. Green, M. G.

W. F. SANDERS to Mary LYNCH Issued 1 May 1937 Rites 1 May 1937
P. N. Moffitt, Jdg.

Charles D. COTTEN to Emma Lee ROLLER Issued 1 May 1937 Rites 2 May 1937
Jas. K. MArtin, J. P.

Roy FOSTER to Mary E. McGINNESS Issued 3 May 1937 Rites 3 May 1937
Jas. K. Martin, J. P.

Lloyd HOLT to Gladys TOBBITT Issued 7 May 1937 Rites 8 May 1937
J. N. Winnett, J. P.

Virgil HALL to Ora MITCHELL Issued 30 JAn 1937 Rites 30 Jn 1937
J. D. Jones, M. G.

Harry V. COPENHAVER to Bessie WILLIAMS Issued 1 Feb 1937 Rites 21 Feb 1937
J. A. Overholser

Meadows REED to Elsie GILBERT Issued 4 Feb 1937 Rites 4 Feb 1937
J. H. MAyO, J. P.

J. W. YOUNG to Leona McELROY Issued 6 Feb 1937 Rites 7 Feb 1937
J. N. Winnett, J. P.

J. P. HILL to Ollie KEATON Issued 9 Feb 9137 Rites 9 Feb 1937
E. D. Martin. M. G.

L. L. BUSEY to Lucille LAFEVER Issued 15 Feb 1937 Rites 15 feb 1937
J. N. Winnett,|J. P.

Ray TITTSWORTH to Gertrude GRIFFITH Issued 19 Feb 1937 Rites 20 Feb 1937
A. Z. Holder, J. P.

John W. BAKER to Helen MArie REEDER Issued 20 Feb 1937 Rites 20 Feb 1937
J. B. Gribble, M. G.

Frank L. FISHER to Elsie OWINGS Issued 20 Feb 1937 Rites 20 Feb 1937
O. L.Minks, M. G.

Jerry CRAIN to Beatrice GROVE Issued 20 Feb 1937 Rites 20 Feb 1937
A. E. Kell, J. P.

Collie GRIBBLE (C) to Jennie STARKEY (C) Issued 26 Feb 1937 Rites 28 Feb 1937
E. W. Sutherlin, J. P.

Cecil ADCOCK to Lela Mai HARDIN Issued 26 Feb 1937. Rites 26 Feb 1937
P. N. Moffitt, Jdg.

Phillip I. HITE to Louise Stone BERG Issued 1 MAr 1937 Rites 2 Mar 1937
Irving Patton, J. P.

Henry RAMSEY (C) to Belle LEFTRICK (C) Issued 6 Mar 1937 Rites 6 Mar 1937
J. H. Collier, M. G.

John MArion WILLIAMS to Wallie Elota GROSS Issued 6 Mar 1937 Rites 6 Mar 1937
T. Q. Martin, M. G.

Ervin TURNER to Cora Lee BROWN Issued 19 Mar 1937 Rites 19 Mar 1937
Walter HAncock

John DELON to PAuline BOULDIN Issued 20 Mar 1937 Rites 20 Mar 1937
J. D. Jones, M. G.

Powell MEASLES to Lee Vesta MAYFIELD Issued 25 Mar 1937 Rites 28 Mar 1937
J. A. Grissom, J. P.

Howard RIGSBY to Helen NEWBY Issued 26 Mar 1937 Rites 27 Mar 1937
H. F. Richmond, J. P.

William WARREN to Josie McGREGOR Issued 7 May 1937 Rites 7 May 1937 C. C. Dickson, M. G.

W. S. PAYNE to Tennie CANTRELL Issued 15 May 1937 Rites 15 May 1937 P. N. Moffitt, Jdg.

Delcy PRYOR to Luberta UNDERHILL Issued 15 MAy 1937 Rites 15 May 1937 P. N. Moffitt, Jdg.

Keck LYNN to Alice Marie SMARTT Issued 15 May 1937 Rites 15 May 1937 W. B. Snipes, M. G.

Robt. L. OFFICER (C) to Leona B. LUSK (C) Issued 17 May 1937 Rites 17 May 1937 J. H. MAyo, J. P.

Arthur FRAZIER to Marjorie MUNCY Issued 31 May 1937 Rites 31 May 1937 P. N. Moffitt, Jdg.

F. Z. POTTER to Martha HENNESSEE Issued 5 Jun 1937 Rites 5 Jun 1937 J. W. Cooley, M. G.

J. W. FLETCHER,JR. to Nettie Lucille SCOTT Issued 5 Jun 1937 Rites 5 Jun 1937 P. N. Moffitt, Jdg.

Charles BOULDIN to Lois MARTIN Issued 10 Jun 1937 Rites 12 Jun 1937 P. N. Moffitt, Jdg.

Eugene RINER to Mae TITTSWORTH Issued 12 Jun 1937 Rites 13 Jun 1937 A. B. Moffitt, M. G.

Charlie LATIMER to Allie WATSON Issued 16 Jun 1937 Rites 19 Jun 1937 J. H. Mayo, J. P.

Harold SAIN to Dorothy TRAMMELL Issued 21 Jun 1937 Rites 27 Jun 1937 W. J. McElroy, M. G.

William MALONE to Alma GRIFFITH Issued 23 Jun 1937 Rites 23 Jun 1937 Isaac Grizzle, J. P.

Jesse Aubra WOODLEE to Willie B. ROGERS Issued 25 Jun 1937 Rites 25 Jun 1937 T. Q. Martin, M. G.

Jesse Lee YORK to Ethel PERRY Issued 26 Jun 1937 Rites 26 Jun 1937 Charlie Simmons, M. G.

Ned KING (C) to Frances BROWN (C) Issued 26 Jun 1937 Rites 18 Jun 1937 A. B. Moffitt, M. G.

Levi BARNES to Annie Lee JONES Issued 3 Jul 1937 Rites 3 Jul 1937 J. H. Mayo, J. P.

Lester McCORMICK to Pauline BOULDIN Issued 3 Jul 1937 Rites 3 Jul 1937 P. N. Moffitt, Jdg.

Claud STEMBRIDGE to Maggie PARSLEY Issued 5 Jul 1937 Rites 5 Jul 1937 A. Z. Holder, J. P.

Woodrow RAMSEY to Eunice ROACH Issued 6 Jul 1937 Rites 6 Jul 1937 N. O. Allen, M. G.

JAmes A. TURNER to Martina DAVIS Issued 6 Jul 1937 Rites 6 Jul 1937 J. H. Mayo, J. P.

Elmer RIGSBY to Amanda DAVIS Issued 7 Jul 1937 Rites 7 Jul 1937 P. N. Moffitt, Jdg.

Remus BRYAN to Gerogina CUNNINGHAM Issued 10 Jul 1937 Rites 11 Jul 1937 N. O. Allen, M. G.

G. M. MILLER to Ada Irene HALEY Issued 10 Jul 1937 Rites 10 Jul 1937 P. N. Moffitt, Jdg.

Henry ROBERSON to Opal BOULDIN Issued 10 Jul 1937 Rites 10 Jul 1937 J. H. Mayo, J. P.

William Jewell MULLICAN to Arnella BRIXEY Issued 12 Jul 1937 Rites 12 Jul 1937 T. Q. Martin, M. G.

James Thos. WALKER to Linnie Belle KIRBY Issued 17 Jul 1937 Rites 17 Jul 1937 A. Z. Holder, J. P.

S. T. ROGERS to Maggie Lou MUNCY Issued 17 Jul 1937 Rites 17 Jul 1937 J. L. BArnes, J. P.

Herman SMITH to Ola LAMB Issued 17 Jul 1937 Rites 17 Jul 1937 William Davis, M. G.

Clayborn WILSON to Ona WILSON Issued 17 Jul 1937 Rites 17 Jul 1937 J. H. Mayo, J. P.

Clifford GRIBBLE to Alma PRATER Issued 20 Jul 1937 Rites 20 Jul 1937 J. B. Gribble, M. G.

Albert CUNNINGHAM to Agnes EARLS Issued 21 Jul 1937 Rites 21 Jul 1937 C. L. Webster, M. G.

Douglas HARLEY to Mrs. Vassie RAMSEY Issued 22 Jul 1937 Rites 22 jul 1937 J. H. MAyo, J. P.

HArlie CLENDENON to Etta Bell NUNLEY Issued 24 Jul 1937 Rites 24 Jul 1937 J. H. MAyo, J.·P.

Claud FULTS to Jesse TIPTON Issued 24 jul 1937 Rites 24 Jul 1937 J. L. BArnes, J. P.

Billie LACKEY to Gladys WITT Issued 27 Jul 1937 Rites 27 Jul 1937 P. N. Moffitt, Jdg.

Joe TEMPLETON to Alline JOHNSON Issued 30 Jul 1937 Rites 30 Jul 1937 Irving PAtton, J. P.

Robert PRATER to Ruth JACOBS Issued 30 Jul 1937 Rites 1 Aug 1937 A. Z. Holder, J. P.

Ira DUNCAN to Hallie WILBURN Issued 31 Jul 1937 Rites 31 Jul 1937
J. S. Dunlap, J. P.

W. M. CAMPBELL to Sallie MAI ROMANS Issued 31 Jul 1937 Rites 31 Jul 1937
Frank J. Winton, J. P.

John KESEY to ZADA MAi CURTIS Issued 31 Jul 1937 Rites 31 Jul 1937
John R. Safley, J. P.

Haskel GOFF to Bertha PATTERSON Issued 31 Jul 1937 Rites 1 Aug 1937
J. M. Campbell, J. P.

G. Berto ODINEAL to Eliza ALLEY Issued 31 Jul 1937 Rites 31 Jul 1937
J. H. MAyo, J. P.

J. T. PORTER to Willie Pearl GINN Issued 7 Aug 1937 Rites 7 Aug 1937
O. L. Minks, M. G.

Clifton WOOD to Emma Gene SMITH Issued 10 Aug 1937 Rites 10 Aug 1937
J. H. Mayo, J. P.

Fred SHOCKLEY (C) to SArah BREWINGTON (C) Issued 12 Aug 1937 Rites 14 Aug 1937
J. H. Mayo, J. P.

John L. BROWN (C) to Louverna MCFARLAND (C) Issued 14 Aug 1937 Rites 15 Aug 1937
J. H. Collier, M. G.

Luther DEADMAN to Stella TURNER Issued 14 Aug 1937 Rites 14 Aug 1937
T. Q. Martin, M. G.

Haskell KNIGHT to Hallie DUGGIN Issued 17 Aug 1937 Rites 18 Jul 1937
H. F. Richmond, J. P.

Thomas B. SPAIN to Evelyn Aurellia LONG Issued 18 Aug 1937 Rites 18 Jul 1937
C. B. Cook, M. G.

Alvin BESS to Beulah HILL Issued 20 Aug 1937 Rites 21 Aug 1937
J. H. Mayo, J. P.

J. J. TITTSWORTH to Willie C. CANTRELL Issued 21 Aug 1937 Rites 22 Jul 1937
O. E. Simmons, M. G.

Joe KIRBY to Hattie PATTERSON Issued 21 Aug 1937 Rites 21 Aug 1937
J. R. Safley, J. P.

Campbell R. CRADDOCK to Marjorie HOLCOMB Issued 23 Aug 1937 Rites 24 Aug 1937
T. Q. MArtin, M. G.

F. Adolphe TISSOT to Willie Mae BASHAM Issued 26 Aug 1937 Rites 28 Aug 1937
W. T. LAne, M. G.

Richard TURNER to Mattie PARISH Issued 27 Aug 1937 Rites 27 Aug 1937
Isaac Grizzle, J. P.

Raymond MILLS to Nancy REES Issued 28 Aug 1937 Rites 28 Aug 1937
A. J. VAN Wyk, M. G.

Sidney HOBBS to MAry Frances EATON Issued 28 Aug 1937 Rites 28 Aug 1937
J. H. Mayo, J. P.

Woodrow ALEXANDER to Maxine PALMER Issued 14 Sep 1937 rites 1 Sep 1937
J. H. Mayo, J. P.

Coy HALEY to Virginia McAFEE Issued 2 Sep 1937 Rites 3 Sep 1937
T. Q. Martin, M. G.

C. B. BRINKLEY to Ruby Velma BROWN Issued 4 Sep 1937 Rites 4 Sep 1937
J. H. Mayo, J. P.

Walter DUKE to Anna LOCKE Issued 4 Sep 1937 Rites 4 Sep 1937
J. H. Mayo, J. P.

Gordon TURNER to Zadia BYNUM Issued 6 Sep 1937 rites 6 Sep 1937
C. C. Dickson, M. G.

Roy Dave McBROOM to W. T. HENDRIXSON Issued 10 Sep 1937 Rites 10 sep 1937
T. Q. Martin, M. G.

J. F. KEEL to Eliz. Louise McCORMACK Issued 11 Sep 1937 Rites 11 sep 1937
J. R. SAfley, J. P.

GAines SCHROCK to Jennie LOCKE Issued 11 Sep 1937 Rites 12 Sep 1937
J. B. Gribble, M. G.

Elmer BANKER to DeALVA WINSTEAD Issued 17 Sep 1937 Rites 17 Sep 1937
J. H. Mayo, J. P.

S. H. DAVIS to Agnes ORRICK Issued 18 Sep 1937 Rites 18 Sep 1937
P. N. Moffitt, Jdg.

Delbert Brown LAPPIN to RAchel Louise BARNES Issued 23 Sep 1937 Rites 23 Sep 1937
J. H. Mayo, J. P.

Avery EVANS to Josephine SAVAGE Issued 25 Sep 1937 Rites 25 Sep 1937
I. P. McGregor, J. P.

Byron CLENDENON (C) to Mary McGREGORY (C) Issued 25 Sep 1937 Rites 25 Sep
J. R. Grady, M. G.

MAson GRISSOM to Mildred MATHENEY Issued 25 Sep 1937 Rites 26 Sep 1937
F. L. Kirby, J. P.

James SEALS to Gusty MOFFITT Issued 27 Sep 1937 Rites 27 Sep 1937
J. H. Mayo, J. P.

John G. TIDWELL (C) to Rena COPE (C) Issued 4 Oct 1937 Rites 6 Oct.1937
C. Curtis, M. G.

J. P. BRATCHER to Rosie COPE Issued 7 Oct 1937 Rites 10 10 Sep 1937
J. M. Campbell, J. P.

Alton F. VINSON to Jetta HOLDER Issued 15 Oct 1937   VOIDED

Freeman RAMSEY (C) to Rosetta SCOTT (C) Issued 16 Oct 1937 Rites 16 Oct 1937
G. T. Speaks, M. G.

W. R. DAVIS to Pearl Etta JONES Issued 16 Oct 1937 Rites 18 Oct 1937
I. J. Grizzle, J. P.

Kelton BOULDIN to Leona FINCHUM Issued 16 Oct 1937 rites 16 Oct 1937
A. E. Curtis, J. P.

Tom ROACH to Stella WOODLEE Issued 18 Oct 1937 Rites 23 Oct 1937
J. L. Barnes, J. P.

Thomas FULTS to Bernice STANLEY Issued 23 Oct 1937 Rites 23 Oct 1937
J. P. Bilbrey, J. JP.

JOHN C. SMOOT to Linde MABEL BELL Issued 23 Oct 1937 Rites 27 Oct 1937
C. B. Cook, M. G.

Leonard SEALS to DAisy CHRISTIAN ISsued 23 Oct 1937 Rites 23 Oct 1937
J. H. MAyo, J. P.

John HILDRETH, Jr. to Oleda VAUGHN Issued 27 Oct 1937 Rites 30 Oct 1937
H. F. Richmond, J. P.

Lillard VANDERGRIFF to Nora Frances PARKER Issued 29 Oct 1937 Rites 30 Oct 1937
J. H. MAyo, J. P.

Alex Martin HOLDER to Rachel GRIZZELL Issued 30 Oct 1937 Rites 31 Oct 1937
Irving Patton, J. P.

VAn McGEE to Mrs. Jessie WRIGHT Issued 30 Oct 1937 Rites 30 Oct 1937
J. H. MAyo, J. P.

Floyd LOWE to Mary Dell MASON Issued 30 Oct 1937 Rites 7 Nov 1937
N. O. Allen, M. G.

George GRISSOM to Clara Mae CALDWELL Issued 30 Oct 1937 Rites 6 Nov 1937
J. A. Grissom. J. P.

William N. BONNER (C) to Irene LEE (C) Issued 2 Nov 1937 Rites 2 Nov 1937
L. C. Maples, M. G.

Luther H. YOUNG to Pauline BOREN Issued 3 Nov 1937 Rites 6 Nov 1937
F. L. Kirby, J. P.

DAvid DURHAM to Zenolia CANTRELL Issued 3 Nov 1937 Rites 6 Nov 1937
A. Z. Holder, J. P.

Rayburn HENDERSON to Minnie BASHAM Issued 6 Nov 1937 Rites 6 Nov 1937
J. R. Grove, J. P.

James C. MCGEE to Fern CRAIN Issued 6 Nov 1937 Rites 6 Nov 1937
I. P. McGregor, J. P.

Curtis HENDERSON to Idell HENDERSON Issued 15 nov 1937 Rites 15 nov 1937
J. H. MAyo, J. P.

Leon RUSSELL to Anna Mae SMITH Issued Issued 20 Nov 1937 Rites 20 Nov 1937
J. H. MAyo, J. P.

Vel GILL to Bertie BING Issued 26 Nov 1937 Rites 26 Nov 1937
P. N. Moffitt, Jdg.

Roy HENNESSEE to Tennie Lee UPCHURCH Issued 27 Nov 1837 Rites 28 Nov 1937
E. R. Little, M. G.

F. H. HALE to Beatrict DAVIS Issued 30 Nov 1937   VOIDED

J. R. MEDLEN to Elsie Lucille AUSTIN Issued 30 Nov 1937 Rites 30 Nov 1937
P. N. Moffitt, Jdg.

Brown CAGLE to Maude Louise REED Issued 4 Dec 1937 Rites 4 Dec 1937
J. L. Barnes, J. P.

Obie WOOD to Lettie BELL Issued 4 Dec 1937 Rites 5 Dec 1937
C. H. Smithson, M. G.

Oscar Brown HARDING to SAllie Mason SNOW Issued 4 Dec 1937 Rites 4 Dec 1937
T. Q. Martin, M. G.

Cordell LEE to Enzie McCOY Issued 4 Dec 1937 Rites 25 Dec 1937
Irving Patton, J. P.

L. L. SCOTT to Anna Mai DAVY Issued 6 Dec 1937 Rites 6 Dec 1937
Irving Patton, J. P.

E. C. SMOOT to Louise BIGELOW Issued 9 Dec 1937 Rites 9 Dec 1937
H. F. Richmond, J. P.

William PERRY to Lucille WOMACK Issued 14 Dec 1937 Rites 15 Dec.1937
E. L. Knowles

Buford JACKSON to Rantha FLETCHER Issued15 Dec 1937 Rites 15 Dec 1937
J. H. Mayo, J. P.

L. H. REDMON to Mrs. Mary ADCOCK Issued 17 Dec 1937 Rites 24 Dec 1937
J. B. Gribble, M. G.

Henry JONES to Ada McREYNOLDS Issued 18 Dec 1937 Rites 18 Dec 1937
C. H. Riddle, J. P.

James H. RIGSBY to Agnes DAVENPORT Issued 18 Dec 1937 Rites 18 Dec 1937
E. W. Sutherlin, J. P.

Minnie Melvin MARRIS to Mona CRIM Issued 21 Dec 1937 Rites 21 Dec 1937
P. N. Moffitt, Jdg.

Frank HARPER to Ruby BEARD Issued 27 Dec 1937 Rites 22 Dec 1937
C. L. Webster, M. G.

R. B. MILLER to Margaret MOORE Issued 22 Dec 1937 Rites 22 Dec 1937
J. H. Mayo, J. P.

O. J. LYNN to Catherine GAFFIN Issued 22 Dec 1937 Rites 26 dec 1937
O. L. Minks, M. G.

I. D. ADCOCK to Magnolia HALEY Issued 22 Dec 1937 Rites 22 Dec 1937
    T. Q. Martin, M. G.

Woodrow THURMAN to Ruby BAILEY Issued 23 Dec 1937 Rites 23 Dec 1937
    W. T. Warren, J. P.

Quim C. BRYANT to Irene FELTY Issued 23 Dec 1937 Rites 23 Dec 1937
    T. Q. Martin, M. G.

Everett JONES to Estiel SMITH Issued 23 Dec 1937 Rites 23 Dec 1937
    A. Z. Holder, J. P.

Amon GLENN to Virginia ADCOCK Issued 23 Dec 1937 Rites 25 Dec 1937
    J. S. Dunlap, J. P.

H. C. AUSTIN to Virginia GEER Issued 23 Dec 1937 Rites 24 Dec 1937
    C. B. Cook, M. G.

Alvin DAVIS to Gladys ADCOCK Issued 24 Dec 1937 Rites 24 Dec 1937
    JAS. K. Martin, J. P.

H. H. NEAL to Wyona WHITLOCK Issued 24 Dec 1937 Rites 25 Dec 1937
    L. D. McDonald, M. G.

Clarence WORTHINGTON (C) to Annie Edna WALLING (C) Issued 24 Dec 1937 Rites 25 Dec
    R. G. Martin, Jr., J. P.

Alton COUCH to Minnie Mae JONES Issued 24 Dec 1937 Rites 25 Dec 1937
    E. R. Little, M. G.

Oda BOULDIN to Eliza McBRIDE Issued 24 Dec 1937 Rites 24 Dec 1937
    J. H. Mayo, J. P.

Gennett HALE to Mona FISHER Issued 24 Dec 1937 Rites 24 Dec 1937
    F. J. Winton, J. P.

M. R. WOODLEE to Pauline SCOTT Issued 24 Dec 1937 Rites 24 Dec 1937
    J. H. Mayo, J. P.

Aubrey WOMACK to Dora Emma SNOW Issued 27 Dec 1937 Rites 27 Dec 1937
    P. N. Moffitt, Jdg.

T. H. HALE to Beatrice DAVIS Issued 28 Dec 1937 Rites 28 Dec 1937
    J. H. Mayo, J. P.

Lee BRYAN to Bessie COUCH Issued 31 Dec 1937 Rites 31 Dec 1937
    J. H. MaYO, J. P.

Charlie WITT to Anna DOVE Issued 6 Jan 1938 Rites 6 Jan 1938
    J. H. Mayo, J. P.

Clyde NEWBY to Bessie EVANS Issued 11 Jan 1938 Rites 10 Feb 1938
    John Morton, M. G.

Cecil SMITH to Gracie WILLIAMSON Issued 13 Jan 1938 Rites 13 JAn 1938
    J. N. Winnett, J. P.

Elmore GRAVES to Virginia HARRIS Issued 15 Jan 1938 Rites 15 Jan 1938
    G. H. Powell, J. P.

John Edwin COOLEY to Roberta JUDKINS Issued 15 JAn 1938 Rites 15 Jan 1938
    I. J. Grizzle, J. P.

Herbert ROBERTS to Gracie Pearl O'NEAL Issued 16 Jan 1938 Rites 16 Jan 1938
    G. H. O'Neal, M. G.

584 marriages in this book

Book #19 - Warren County Marriages Jan. 29, 1938 to Jun 27, 1941

Clarence HARRIS to Beta Mae JORDAN Issued 39 Jan 1938 Rites 29 Jan 1938
T. Q. Martin, M. G.

P. A. Earls to Aggie HENDERSON Issued 2 Feb 1938 Rites 2 Feb 1938
J. H. Mayo, J. P.

Luther SMITH to Bessie COPE Issued 5 Feb 1938 Rites 5 Feb 1938
T. Q. Martin, M. G.

Arthue Everett LEONARD to Theodocia "LINDSAY Issued 6 Feb 1938 Rites 6 Feb 1938
C. B. Cook, M. G.

Tom C. TURNER to Opal GRISSOM Issued 9 Feb 1938 Rites 9 Feb 1938
J. T. Ferrell

Ed VINSON to Sarah Lucille BLACK Issued 12 Feb 1938 Rites 12 Feb 1938
T. Q. Martin, M. G.

A. Winton WALLING to Mary Madoline FARLEY Issued 16 Feb 1938 Rites 19 Feb 1938
J. L. Ferguson, M. G.

J. D. BARNES to Pauline HILLIS Issued 19 Feb 1938 Rites 19 Feb 1938
G. H. Powell, J. P.

Arthur Lee ROGERS to Margarite Leona EARLS Issued 23 Feb 1938 Rites 26 Feb 1938
C. L. Whiteaker, M. G.

E. H. ALLEN to Verna ALLEN Issued 24 Feb 1938 Rites 24 Feb 1938
E. R. Little, M. G.

Lester DODSON to Bessie Mae WITT Issued 28 Feb 1938 Rites 6 MAR 1938
J. A. Grissom, J. P.

True F. STEED to Alice SMITH Issued 28 Feb 1938 Rites 28 Feb 1938
A. Z. Holder, J. P.

Carl MORTON to Lorene FARMER Issued 4 Mar 1938 Rites 4 Mar 1938
E. L. Knowles

J. C. YOUNG to Anna Lee REYNOLDS Issued 4 Mar 1938 Rites 5 Mar 1938
E. W. Sutherlin, J. P.

Robert CHASTAIN to Cora Lee STEPHENS Issued 5 Mar 1938 Rites 5 Mar 1938
G. H. O'Neal, M. G.

Joseph HENNESSEE to Ruby PELHAM Issued 9 Mar 1938 Rites 9 Feb 1938
E. P. Cagle, M. G.

B. L. MURPHY to Maurine HOOPER Issued 10 Mar 1938 VOIDED

Malcomb G. SMITH to Arrie Mai TEMPLETON Issued 11 MAR 1938 Rites 11 Mar 1938
T. Q. Martin, M. G.

W. M. BROWN to Martha PENNINGTON Issued 14 Mar 1938 Rites 14 Mar 1938
J. H. Mayo, J. P.

Walter Anderson ROWLAND to Clara Bell ATNIP Issued 17 Mar 1938 Rites 9 Mar 1938
Jas. K. Martin, J. P.

EarL SHERMAN to Esther HAWKINS Issued 24 Mar 1938 Rites 24 Mar 1938
P. N. Moffitt, Jdg.

Asa DICKSON to Velma Louise McCORMACK Issued 1 Apr 1938 Rites 3 Apr 1938
E. R. Little, M. G.

Arthur Lee CASEY to Roberta ASKEW Issued 2 Apr 1938 Rites 2 Apr 1938
J. T. Casey, M. G.

William LAFEVERS to Christine STANLEY Issued 2 Apr 1938 Rites 2 Apr 1938
C. H. Riddle, J. P.

Barney HALE to Nora HOLLANDSWORTH Issued 4 Apr 1938 Rites 4 Apr 1938
J. H. Mayo, J. P.

Everett PEDIGO to Colysta PARSLEY Issued 4 Apr 1938 Rites 4 Apr 1938
J. M. Campbell, J. P.

Willie TAYLOR to Cornelia CHISAM Issued 7 Apr 1938 Rites 15 Apr 1938
J. D. Jones, M. G.

W. C. GAFFIN, Jr. to Mary Katherine STONE Issued 12 Apr 1938 Rites 17 Apr 1938
T. Q. Martin, M. G.

L. L. HAYES to Vennie Lou HUTCHINS Issued 15 Apr 1938 Rites 15 Apr 1938
P. N. Moffitt, Jdg.

Waymon KESEY to Frances ALLISON Issued 15 Apr 1938 Rites 15 Apr 1938
J. R. Safley, J. P.

Frank L. WOMACK to Ora Belle HUNTLEY Issued 15 Apr 1938 Rites 16 Apr 1938
T. Q. Martin, M. G.

EArl KEATON to Lucille HOLLANDSWORTH Issued 16 Apr 1938 Rites 17 Apr 1938
H. F. Richmond, J. P.

Clifford SNIPES to Evelyn MILLER Issued 16 Apr 1938 Rites 17 Apr 1938
W. E. Miller, M. G.

Mayo COPELAND to Evelyn MOFFITT Issued 16 Apr 1938 Rites 16 Apr 1938
E. W. Sutherlin, J. P.

F. S. WOODLEE to Janie HOBBS Issued 19 Apr 1938 Rites 19 Apr 1938
P. N. Moffitt, Jdg.

Albert A. JONES to Mary Evelyn CANTRELL Issued 20 Apr 1938 Rites 24 Apr 1938
R. H. HAle, M. G.

Lorn PANTER to Alma BOULDIN Issued 23 Apr 1938 Rites 23 Apr 1938
J. L. BArnes, J. P.

Jennings DUNLAP to Virginia ROWLETT Issued 28 Apr 1938 Rites 1 May 1938
J. A. Grissom, J. P.

Franklin Porter BLUE to Della Eliz. FLANDERS Issued 30 Apr 1938 Rites 30 Apr 1938. M. G.
T. Q. Martin. M. G.

Alvie BOGLE to Edith UMBARGER Issued 30 Apr 1938 Rites 1 May 1938
E. W. Sutherlin., J. P.

J. Brady McBRIDE to Annie Mae McGREGOR Issued 30 Apr 1938 Rites 1 May 1938
E. R. Knowles, M. G.

Merrell H. ETTER, Jr. (C) to Liny D. RAMSEY (C) Issued 5 May 1938 Rites 5 May 1938
Julius M. Hayden, M. G.

Walker BAKER (C) to Lethin SCOTT (C) Issued 9 May 1938 Returned - Not Solemnized

R. E. HODGES to Wavie DAVIS Issued 21 May 1938 Rites 22 May 1938
J. S. Dunlap, J. P.

Higgins RAMSEY to Evelyn PERRY issued 21 May 1938 Rites 21 May 1938
O. L. Minks, M. G.

R. E. WALKER to Letha HOLLANDSWORTH Issued 26 May 1938 Rites 26 May 1938
C. C. Dickson, M. G.

Thomas W. BURBAGE to Twella DAVIS Issued 28 May 1938 Rites 28 May 1938
Bill A. Jordan, M. G.

Vernice DOTSON to Mollie Fay NEWBY Issued 3 Jun 1938 Rites 4 Jun 1938
G. H. O'Neal, M. G.

Howard McGEE to Lucille MITCHELL Issued 3 Jun 1938 Rites 3 Jun 1938
O. L. Minks, M. G.

W. T. MOON to Pauline VANDERGRIFF Issued 4 Jun 1938 Rites 4 Jun 1938
J. S. Dunlap, J. P.

Arlin C. HILLIS to Beatrice WANAMAKER Issued 4 Jun 1938 Rites 4 Jun 1938
Bill A. Jordan, M. G.

Marion JACKSON to Mary YORK Issued 4 Jun 1938 Rites 4 Jun 1938
P. N. Moffitt, Jdg.

R. L. AINIP to Amelia WALKER Issued 4 Jun 1938 Rites 4 jun 1938
E. R. Little, M. G.

Alton F. VINSON to Jetta HOLDER Issued 8 Jun 1938 Rites 24 Aug 1938
J. H. Mayo, J. P.

Warren MASON to Vassie Lee WARREN Issued 11 Jun 1938 Rites 11 Jun 1938
Isaac Grizzle, J. P.

Elmer GRIFFITH to Georgia Lee GRIBBLE Issued 11 Jun 1938 Rites 11 Jun 1938
Isaac Grizzle, J. P.

Leo W. KLARR to Marie Shofner MEADOWS Issued 14 Jun 1938 Rites 20 Jun 1938
C. B. Cook, M. G.

Leo H. DAVIDSON to Louise J. ANDERSON Issued 17 Jun 1938 Rites 18 Jun 1938
C. B. Cook, M. G.

O. L. BRATCHER to Velma WOOD Issued 18 Jun 1938 Rites 19 Jun 1938
R. W. Smartt, Jdg.

John E. STEMBRIDGE to Cora E. FOSTER Issued 20 Jun 1938 Rites 20 Jun 1938
Jas. K. Martin, J. P.

H. C. DONAHUE to Josie BROWN (C) Issued 22 Jun 1938 Rites 22 Jun 1938
C. Curtis, M. G.

Joe R. STROUD to Jettie M. STROUD Issued 23 Jun 1938 Rites 23 Jun 1938
J. H. May, J. P.

Grady WOOD to Virginia LAFEVER Issued 25 Jun 1938 Rites 25 Jun 1938
T. Q. Martin, M. G.

H. B. ETTER (C) to Johnnie L. MARTIN (C) Issued 25 Jun 1938 Rites 25 Jun 1938
J. M. Hayden, M. G.

Edward MARTIN (C) to Letha SCOTT (C) Issued 27 Jun 1938 Rites 27 Jun 1938
J. R. Grady, M. G.

Walker HASTON to Hazel VAUGHN Issued 28 Jun 1938 Rites 28 Jun 1938
J. H. Mayo, J. P.

Charley FULIS to Irene MUNCEY Issued 2 Jul 1938 Rites 2 Jul 1938
W. B. Snipes, M. G.

Lyndon HILLIS to Wilda McGEE Issued 2 Jul 1938 Rites 3 Jul 1938
B. F. Killian, M. G.

Andy HILLIS to Minnie BOTTOMS Issued 4 Jul 1938 Rites 4 Jul 1938
Bill A. Jordan, M. G.

Edward KEITH to Marie CLEMONS Issued 9 Jul 1938 Rites 9 Jul 1938
J. H. Mayo, J. P.

Herman SUMMERS to Pearl ROGERS Issued 9 Jul 1938 Rites 9 Jul 1938
J. H. Mayo, J. P.

Frank C. BROWN (C) to Susie Amanda ROBERTS (C) Issued 14 Jul 1938 Rites 14 Jul 1938
J. H. Mayo, J. P.

Willie Lee BEARD to Jessie M. MEDLEY Issued 16 Jul 1938 Rites 16 Jul 1938
J. H. Mayo, J. P.

Fred FERRELL to Edna HENNESSEE Issued 18 Jul 1938 Rites 18 Jul 1938
J. H. Mayo, J. P.

Walter GLENN to Thelma STILES Issued 21 Jul 1938 Rites 21 Jul 1938
J. H. Mayo, J. P.

James L. DAVIS to Dulcie Irene TOBITT Issued 23 Jul 1938 Rites 24 Jul 1938
J. N. Winnett, J. P.

Lannie CLENDENON to Jadie PANTER Issued 29 Jul 1938 Rites 29 Jul 1938
E. D. Martin, M. G.

I. N. JOHNSON to Inez MILLER Issued 1 Aug 1938 Rites 1 Aug 1938
J. M. Campbell, J. P.

Strat HOLLAND to May PHILLIPS Issued 10 Aug 1938 Rites 10 Aug 1938
J. H. Mayo, J. P.

Ben ROWLAND to Bessie HUDSON Issued 11 Aug 1938 Rites 13 Aug 1938
L. B. Moffitt, J. P.

Alva Dean WARREN to Edna McREYNOLDS Issued 12 Aug 1938 Rites 14 Aug 1938
L. B. Moffitt, J. P.

Theodore HESTER to Alica PACK Issued 19 Aug 1938 Rites 19 Aug 1938
W. S. Wileman, M. G.

Bob Price HICKS to Mary Lou HUGHES Issued 24 Aug 1938 Rites 27 Aug 1938
J. N. Winnett, J. P.

Frank ROBINSON to Naomi WILSON Issued 27 Aug 1938 Rites 27 Aug 1938
E. H. Jones, M. G.

J. J. MORTON to Etta BOX Issued 27 Aug 1938 Rites 27 Aug 1938
C. C. Dickson, M. G.

Cecil JOHNSON to Lucil FUSTON Issued 27 Aug 1938 Rites 28 Aug 1938
J. S. Dunlap, J. P.

R. E. MARTIN to Sylvia WANAMAKER Issued 27 Aug 1938 Rites 27 Aug 1938
P. N. Moffitt, Jdg.

John STILES to PAuline SCOTT Issued 27 Aug 1938 Rites 27 Aug 1938
J. H. Mayo, J. P.

Wm. Martin PINKLEY to Ruth MANSFIELD Issued 3 Sep 1938 Rites 3 Sep 1938
T. Q. Martin, M. G,

Willie Arthur SMITH to Lelia SMITH Issued 9 Sep 1938 Rites 10 Sep 1938
J. N. Winnett, J. P.

George Herbert LANCE to Anna Bell LANCE Issued 10 Sep 1938 Rites 10 Sep 1938
A. Z. Holder, J. P.

Haley Brown MARTIN to Willie Mae CRAWLEY Issued 10 Sep 1938 Rites 10 Sep 1938
T. Q. Martin, M. G,

Marshall MUNCY to Eunice HILLIS Issued 12 Sep 1938 Rites 12 Sep 1938
J. H. MAyo, J. P.

Dillard JARRELL to Alice RIDDLE Issued 17 Sep 1938 Rites 17 Sep 1938
E. W. Sutherlin, J. P.

George B. WOMACK to Willie COUCH Issued 17 Sep 1938 Rites 17 Sep 1938
J. S. Dunlap, J. P.

J. C. WOMACK to Ada Virginia WARD Issued 19 Sep 1938 Rites 22 Sep 1938
R. H. Hale, M. G.

Thurman NUNLEY to Yolinda NUNLEY Issued 23 Sep 1938 Rites 24 Sep 1938
J. P. Bilbrey, J. P.

JAmes Herbert ALLEN to Ruby Mai MORGAN Issued 26 Sep 1938 Rites 26 Sep 1938
T. Q. Martin, M. G.

Joe LEE (C) to Mable DRAKE (C) Issued 1 Oct 1938 Rites 30 Oct 1938
J. M. HAyden, M. G.

B. F. YATES to Wilma FISHER Issued 1 Oct 1938 Rites 1 Oct 1938
O. L. Minks, M. G.

Hazelton B. FENNIMORE to Julia PENDERGRAFF Issued 3 Oct 1938 Rites 3 Oct 1938
A. E. Kell, J. P.

Shirley MAYNARD to Omah COLE Issued 4 Oct 1938 Rites 4 Oct 1938
J. H. Mayo, J. P.

R. P. HOLDER to Leota NEWBY Issued 7 Oct 1938 Rites 8 Oct 1938
E. II. Jones, M. C.

George CANTRELL, JR. to Elizabeth MALONE Issued 7 Oct 1938 Rites 7 Oct 1938
Isaac Grizzle, J. P.

Virgil DONALSON to Minnie Belle JONES Issued 8 Oct 1938 Rites 8 Oct 1938
W. S. Wileman, M. G.

Emerson PLEASANT to Elma CARR Issued 8 Oct 1938 Rites 9 Oct 1938
Irving Patton, J. P.

Paul TURNER to Willie Mae HOBBS Issued 8 Oct 1938 Rites 8 Oct 1938
C. C. Dickson, M. G.

Colonel WIMBERLY to Marie DUKE Issued 8 Oct 1938 Rites 9 Oct 1938
E. P. CAgle, M. G.

William L. SLATTON to Clytie SIMONS Issued 15 Oct 1938 Rites 16 Oct 1938
Bill A. Jordan, M. G.

Jim CLARK to May BOULDIN Issued 17 Oct 1938 Rites 17 Oct 1938
J. H. Mayo, J. P.

RAy PAYNE to Reba GRISSOM Issued 20 Oct 1938 Rites 21 Oct 1938
C. W. Cecil, M. G.

Waymon COPE (C) to Nona THOMAS (C) Issued 28 Oct 1938 Rites 28 Oct 1938
J. H. Mayo, J. P.

Clifton BURBAGE to Annie HOLLAND Issued 29 Oct 1938 Rites 30 Oct 1938
Bill A. Jordan, M. G.

Marvin BARRETT to Alma WOMACK Issued 27 Oct 1938 Rites 30 Oct 1938
Bill A. Jordan, M. G.

SAmuel E. PATRICK to Maxine DUNLAP Issued 31 Oct 1938 Rites 31 Oct 1938
J. H. Mayo, J. P.

Wesley B. WILLIAMS to MARGARET Ann WARREN Issued 1 Nov 1938 Rites 6 Nov 1938
Price Billingsley, M. G.

Willie Andrew WOODLEE to Velma KIDD Issued 17 Dec 1938 Rites 21 Dec 1938
E. D. Martin, M. G.

Phillip FARLESS to MArgie GANN Issued 17 Dec 1938 Rites 17 Dec 1938
J. H. Mayo, J. P.

Jesse SEAGLE to Clistine TURNER Issued 19 Dec 1938 Rites 19 Dec 1938
P. N. Moffitt, Jdg.

Charles A. HODGES to Vivian BESS Issued 20 Dec 1938 Rites 20 Dec 1938
J. H. Mayo, J. P.

Ray BROCK to Mollie Mae TALLANT Issued 21 Dec 1938 Rites 21 Dec 1938
J. H. MAyo, J. P.

Erby PAGE to Mildred ARGO issued 21 Dec 1938 Rites 24 Dec 1938
E. W. Sutherlin, J. P.

Brown WILLIAMS (C) to cathaleen MARBERRY (C) Issued 21 Dec 1938 Rites 21 Dec
H. E. Long, M. G.

Marvin WOMACK to Delma Ruth HASH Issued 22 Dec 1938 rites 23 Dec 1938
Irving Patton, J. P.

J. C. HALE to Elsie WINNETT Issued 23 Dec 1938 Rites 24 Dec 1938
J.A. Grissom, J. P.

Jesse ROGERS to Ollie KILLIAN Issued 23 Dec 1938 Rites 23 Dec 1938
J. L. BArnes, J. P.

Clifford CASEY to Iris BURKS Issued 23 Dec 1938 Rites 23 Dec 1938
R. W. Smartt, Jdg.

J. C. JACOBS to Christine MILLIGAN Issued 24 Dec 1938 Rites 25 Dec 1938
W. B. Snipes, M. G.

Ray PAGE to Rose Zetta RITCHEY Issued 24 Dec 1938 Rites 27 Dec 1938
C. C. Hinkle, M. G.

Emmett TASH to Stella KENNAMER Issued 24 Dec 1938 Rites 28 Dec 1938
R. H. Bonner, J. P.

Alvin PARKER to Lavonia WALKER issued 24 Dec 1938 Rites 24 Dec 1938
J. R. Grove, J. P.

Willard WHITE to PAuline SMITH Issued 24 Dec 1938 Rites 25 Dec 1938
J. A. Grissom, J. P.

H. E. WILLIAMS to Ruth BAILEY Issued 24 Dec 1938 Rites 25 Dec 1938
H. F. Richmond, J. P.

John L. DAVIDSON to Flora B. HALEY Issued 27 Dec 1938 Rites 27 Dec 1938
J. H. Mayo, J. P.

W. W. BLACKBURN to HAzel SHELTON Issued 27 Dec 1938 Rites 27 Dec 1938
C. C. Hinkle, M. G.

Charles L. KNOWLES to Dessie HICKS Issued 5 Nov 1938 Rites 5 Nov 1938
CASS R. Womack, J. P.

Bernard JACKSON to Louise STONE Issued 9 Nov 1938 Rites 9 Nov 1938
W. L. Perry, M. G.

Robert Lee CRAIG to Iola McDOWELL Issued 10 Nov 1938 Rites 10 Nov 1938
J. H. MAyo, J. P.

Lester UPCHURCH to Dorothy ALEXANDER Issued 10 Nov 1938 Rites 13 Nov 1938
W. M. Rowland, J. P.

Arthur SMITH (C) to Leola DONAHUE (C) Issued 15 Nov 1938 Rites 15 Nov 1938
J. S. Dunlap, J. P.

J. C. McDOWELL to Annie Mae STEVENS Issued 17 Nov 1938 Rites 17 Nov 1938
J. H. MAyo, J. P.

Joe B. COLVARD to Frances Sumner DEWS Issued 19 Nov 1938 Rites 23 Nov 1938
C. C. Dickson, M. G.

Jesse CLAYBURN to Rebecca KENNAMER Issued 19 Nov 1938 Rites 19 Nov 1938
H. J. Wilson, J. P.

Herman FOSTER (C) to Mary RYAN (C) Issued 19 Nov 1938 Rites 19 Nov 1938
C. Curtis, M. G.

Walter Edgar DYCUS to Nettie YOUNG Issued 20 Nov 1938 Rites 20 Nov 1938
C. E. Simmons, M. G.

Elzy PARKS to CArolyn ANDES Issued 26 Nov 1938 Rites 26 Nov 1938
G. H. O'Neal, M. G.

Murray PARISH to Hassie NUNLEY Issued 28 Nov 1938 Rites 28 Nov 1938
J. P. Bilbrey, J. P.

JAck HOBBS to Ruby JARRELL Issued 1 Dec 1938 Rites 3 Dec 1938
E. W. Sutherlin, J. P.

William Paul LYLE to Susie Mai MOORE Issued 3 Dec 1938 Rites 4 Dec 1938
J. F. Leeper, M. G.

Alonzo JOHNSON to Eva DODSON Issued 5 Dec 1938 Rites 6 Dec 1938
J. A. Grissom. J. P.

J. R. SAIN to Eva ROBERTS Issued 7 Dec 1938 Rites 10 Dec 1938
J. L. Barnes, J. P.

Quitman PRIEST to NAmie Lou CRAIG Issued 12 Dec 1938 Rites 12 Dec 1938
Irving Patton, J. P.

Goodloe St. JOHN to Pearl ELROD Issued 17 Dec 1938 Rites 17 Dec 1938
T. Q. Martin, M. G.

Willard VANDAGRIFF to Robbie PARKER Issued 17 dec 9138 Rites 22 Dec 1938
A. B. Moffitt, M. G.

Elvin CANTRELL to Velma PATTON Issued 17 Dec 1938 Rites 18 Dec 1938
J. R. Grove, J. P.

M. T. HILLIS to Laura MAI SIMPSON Issued 31 Dec 1938 Rites 31 Dec 1938
I. P. McGregor, J. P.

Grant L. GESSLER to Carrie B. JUSTICE Issued 31 Dec 1938 Rites 1 Jan 1939
T. Q. Martin, M. G.

Elmer GREEN to Dollie GREEN Issued 31 dec 1938 Rites 31 Dec 1938
E. T. CAntrell, J. P.

Auburn E. WOOD to Nell PATTERSON Issued 2 Jan 1939 Rites 2 JAn 1939
T. Q. Martin, M. G.

George W. BRONSON to Minnie KIRBY Issued 6 JAn 1939 Rites 6 Jan 1939
O. L. Minks, M. G.

Cleo Vernice SPARKMAN to Emma Frances SKILLINGS Issued 7 Jan 1939 Rites 7 JAn 1939
Jas. K. Martin, J. P.

Jess MASTERS to Myrtle HUSSEY Issued 14 Jan 1939 Rites 15 JAn 1939
W. B. Snipes, M. G.

Henry HOOSIER to Nannie Lee DICKSON Issued 20 JAn 1939 Rites 21 an 1939
J. H. Mayo, J. P.

Delphas FISHER to Mary Lou SAYLORS Issued 21 Jan 1939 Rites 21 Jan 1939
J. S. Dunlap, J. P.

Jim DENTON to Jessie McMAHAN Issued 23 JAN 1939 Rites 23 JAN 1939
Wm. O. Hall, M. G.

Leland O. CROSSLIN to Rebecca BATES Issued 24 jan 1939 Rites 4 Feb 1939
O. L. Minks, M. G.

Barnes BAKER to Eula KIRBY Issued 28 Jan 1939 Rites 28 Jan 1939
J. A. Grissom, J. P.

Alex NUNLEY to Ruth GREEN Issued 31 Jan 1939 Rites 31 Jan 1939
P. N. Moffitt, Jdg.

Rollie WOMACK to Cordie CANTRELL Issued 3 Feb 1939 Rites 4 Feb 1939
J. B. Gribble, M. G.

James Herbert BRUCE to Louise WILDER Issued 8 Feb 1939 Rites 9 Feb 1939
T. W. Mitchell, M. G.

Carl STONE to Georgia WHITTEMORE Issued 9 Feb 1939 Rites 9 Feb 1939
Isaac Grizzle, J. P.

Perry W. DUNHAM to Mary Agnes VANN Issued 15 Feb 1939 Rites 19 Feb 1939
T. Q. Martin, M. G.

Calvin E. SHEPPARD to Frances Hallie LEEPER Issued 24 Feb 1939 Rites 24 Feb
J. F. Leeper, M. G.

Lowell BARNES to Addie MADEWELL Issued 24 Feb 1939 Rites 25 Feb 1939
A. E. Curtis, J. P.

Vernon L. PASSONS to Bessie SWINDELL Issued 25 Feb 1939 Rites 25 Feb 1939
J. N. Winnett, J. P.

Fred MYERS to Julia May TANNER issued 11 Mar 1939 Rites 11 Mar 1939
C. C. Dickson, M. G.

Hervey SMITH to Peggy TILLMAN Issued 18 Mar 1939 Rites 18 Mar 1939
A. E. Curtis, J. P.

W. B. HILLIARD to Ella Lee CHRISTIAN Issued 13 Mar 1939 Rites 18 Mar 1939
J. H. Mayo, J. P.

Grady WILLIAMSON to Lena ORRICK Issued 22 Mar 1939 Rites 25 Mar 1939
H. T. Knight, J. P.

Paul W. CROOK to Ethel ROBINSON Issued 25 Mar 1939 Rites 25 Mar 1939
C. C. Hinkle, M. G.

Alvin COPE to Lois McDOWELL Issued 29 Mar 1939 Rites 29 Mar 1939
J. R. Grove, J. P.

G. L. STUBBLEFIELD to Mildred TEMPLETON Issued 3 Apr 1939 Rites 3 Apr 1939
J. F. Leeper, M. G.

James Thomas HILL to Olivia ROBERTS Issued 4 Apr 1939 Rites 4 Apr 1939
C. E. Curtis, M. G.

Francis PEARSALL to Lorene STONER Issued 4 Apr 1939 Rites 4 Apr 1939
J. P. Bilbrey, J. P.

Johnnie ELROD to Irene REDMOND Issued 6 Apr 1939 Rites 8 Apr 1939
J. H. Mayo, J. P.

Clarence ORRICK to Velma MORGAN Issued 6 Apr 1939 Rites 6 Apr 1939
J. N. Winnett, J. P.

Paul R. BROWN to Mebel LANE Issued 7 Apr 1939 Rites 8 Apr 1939
O. H. Lane, M. G.

Laton CUNNINGHAM to Ava Nelle UPCHURCH Issued 7 Apr 1939 Rites 8 Apr 1939
O. L. Minks, M. G.

Mack SPARKMAN to Ester MAe ROBERTS Issued 8 Apr 1939 Rites 8 Apr 1939
P. N. Moffitt, Jdg.

William J. KEENAN to Leatrice BRATCHER Issued 12 Apr 1939 Rites Apr 1939
W. T. WARren, J. P.

W. W. SHIELDS to Nellie Cleo TALBERT Issued 15 Apr 1939 Rites 16 Apr 1939
A. B. Moffitt, M. G.

R. B. BONNER to Alice SCOTT Issued 25 Apr 1939 Rites 25 Apr 1939
P. N. Moffitt, Jdg.

Clarence LEVERETT to Sallie MASSINGILL Issued 5 May 1939 Rites 5 May 1939
W. C. Byrd, M. G.

Richmond WILSON to Irene WISEMAN Issued 6 May 1939 Rites 6 May 1939
A. Z. Holder, J. P.

Vinson MAYFIELD to Cola June CUNNINGHAM Issued 12 May 1939 Rites 12 May 1939
A. E. Kell, J. P.

Luther BAIN to Lewta FULTS Issued 13 May 1939 Rites 13 May 1939
W. C. Byrd, M. G.

Clarence BROWN (C) to Rosa WILKERSON (C) Issued 13 May 1939 Rites 13 May 1939
J. H. MAyo, J. P.

James D. RYMER to ELa Ray WILSON Issued 15 May 1939 Rites 15 May 1939
O. L. Minks, M. G.

W. L. BURCH to Cora PARKER ISsued 19 May 1939 Rites 19 May 1939
A. Z. Holder, J. P.

A. Y. COPELAND to Lela GOFF Issued 20 May 1939 Rites 20 May 1939
J. R. BAiley, M. G.

Jim MALONE to Lela Mae BOREN Issued 20 May 1939 Rites 25 May 1939
F. L. Kirby, J. P.

Huel Eaton CUNNINGHAM to Lillian SAIN Issued 22 May 1939 Rites 1 Jun 1939
T. Q. Martin, M. G.

Clayborn KNOWLES to Helen CANTRELL Issued 23 May 1939 Rites 27 May 1939
James DAVENPORT, M. G.

Woodrow VAUGHN to Ernestine MOORE Issued 26 May 1939 Rites 27 May 1939
L. B. Moffitt, J. P.

Charles W. GWYN to Brownie BARRY Issued 26 May 1939 Rites 26 May 1939
T. Q. Martin, M. G.

Billy SHIPP to Audrey BAKER Issued 26 May 1939 Rites 27 May 1939
J. P. Bilbrey, J. P.

Fred McGEE to Bessie Smith THOMLSON Issued 27 May 1939 Rites 27 May 1939
T. Q. Martin, M. G.

John W. YOUNG to Lula Mai TOLBERT Issued 27 May 1939 Rites 27 May 1939
H. J. Wilson, J. P.

Kermit JONES to Evelyn TUBB Issued 2 Jun 1939 Rites 4 Jun 1939
J. H. MAyo, J. P.

Wiley HAYES to Lila HAYES Issued 3 Jun 1939 Rites 3 Jun 1939
P. N. Moffitt, Jdg.

William H. THOMAS to LaVern K. SELF Issued 3 jun 1939 Rites 3 Jun 1939
C. C. Hinkle, M. G.

George Everett MILLS to Georgia I. ELAM Issued 3 Jun 1939 Rites 3 Jun 1939
T. Q. Martin, M. G.

Herman B. FOSTER to Mary L. WARD Issued 3 Jun 1939 Rires 10 Jun 1939
Bill A. Jordan, M. G.

Howard GRIBBLE to Ola Mae BLAIR Issued 3 Jun 1939 Rites 3 Jun 1939
J. P. Bilbrey, J. P.

Robert CRABTREE to Reece DUNCAN Issued 5 Jun 1939 Rites 6 Jun 1939
G. T. Speaks, M. G.

Leonard CRAWLEY to Geneva HAYES issued 9 Jun 1939 Rites 11 Jun 1939
C. C. Hinkle, M. G.

Robert C. TAYLOR to Opal RIGSBY Issued q0 Jun 1939 Rites 10 Jun 1939
G. P. Brasier, J. P.

Henry BOYD to Rhea BRAGG Issued 10 Jun 1939 Rites 10 Jun 1939
T. Q. Martin, M. G.

Sam TAYLOR to Gertrude HOLT Issued 10 Jun 1939 Rites 10 Jun 1939
Irving Patton, J. P.

Edward L. HAMMONS to Va. Ruth STEWART Issued 12 Jun 1939 Rites 18 Jun 1939
N. O. Allen, M. G,.

W. C. PERRY to Ruby Irene STANLEY Issued 14 Jun 1939 Rites 14 Jun 1939
A. Z. Holder, J. P.

Clarence MAYFIELD to Velma TASH Issued 24 Jun 1939 Rites 26 Jun 1939
E. W. Sutherlin, J. P.

Alton COPE to Pearl McDOWELL Issued 26 Jun 1939 Rites 2 Jul 1939
J. H. Mayo, J. P.

Billy J. CASEY to MAry Sue CECIL Issued 12 Jul 1939 Rites 12 Jul 1939
J. T. Casey, M. G.

Hebern Earl BESS to Esther Lee BOULDIN Issued 15 Jul 1939 Rites 15 Jul 1939.
Bill A. Jordan, M. G.

Henry ERWIN to Gladys MERRIMAN Issued 18 Jul 1939 Rites 18 Jul 1939
A. J. Van Wyk, M. G.

Robert Rowland SPOON to Lucille ARMENTROUT Issued 21 Jul 1939 Rites 21 Jul 1939
J. H. Mayo, J. P.

Austin COPE to Frances JONES Issued 22 Jul 1939 Rites 22 jul 1939
J. M. Campbell, J. P.

V. J. THOMPSON to Nerene PAGE Issued 22 Jul 1939 Rites 22 Jul 1939
Dean Irwin, M. G,

Edward BOND to Dorothy MILLER Issued 22 Jul 1939 Rites 22 Jul 1939
J. H. Mayo, J. P.

George G. GAILEY to MAry NAdine CARLTON Issued 30 Jul 1939 Rites 5 Aug 1939
P. N. Moffitt, Jdg.

Marcus BRADY to Lucy Emma BARNES Issued 5 Aug 1939 Rites 5 Aug 1939
J. R. SAfley, J. P.

Porter VANHOOSER to Jewell McGREGOR Issued 5 Aug 1939 Rites 6 Aug 1939
W. P. Willis, J. P.

L.A. FAIRBANKS to Lena MEEKS Issued 9 Aug 1939 Rites 10 Aug 1939
P. N. Moffitt, Jdg.

Gilbert GUY to Ruth HIERS (?)Issued 10 Aug 1939 Rites 10 Aug 1939
A. E. Kell, J. P.

Willard KEENER to Flossie HALE Issued 11 Aug 1939 rites 11 Aug 1939
J. H. MAyo, J. P.

Robert Levoy HOLLAND to Louise DODD Issued 12 Aug 1939 Rites 12 Aug 1939
C. C. Dickson, M. G.

Newell M. COMER to Bertha Bell HASTING Issued 12 Aug 1939 Rites 13 Aug 1939
W. L. Peery, M. G.

Clarence ANDERSON to Lota Lee BUST Issued 12 Aug 1939 Rites 12 Aug 1939
Bill A. Jordan, M. G.

Joe GUNTER to Ruby MAi JONES Issued 17 Aug 1939 rites 20 Aug 1939
Herbert Knight, J. P.

Carl W. DICKSON to Clara Belle O'NEAL Issued 19 Aug 1939 Rites 20 Aug 1939
C. C. Dickson, M. G.

Carden KELLEY to Wilma SMITH Issued 19 Aug 1939 Rites 19 Aug 1939
J. R. Stubblefield, M. G.

Haward ROWE to Sallie BUCK Issued 19 Aug 1939 Rites 19 Aug 1939
J. H. MAyo, J. P.

William COX to Grace BUCK Issued 19 Aug 1939 Rites 19 Aug 1939
J. H. Mayo, J. P.

Henry LANCE to PAuline JONES Issued 22 Aug 1939 Rites 22 Aug 1939
J. N. Wimmett, J. P.

Jim RIVERS (C) to Hylia YORK (C) Issued 25 Aug 1939 Rites 27 Aug 1939
Ben BAtes, M. G.

Ernest MORGAN to Gladys Marie THOMPSON Issued 26 Aug 1939 Rites 26 Aug 1939
C. C. Dickson,M. G.

N. P. ROWLAND to Ina CUNNINGHAM Issued 26 Aug 1939 Rites 27 Aug 1939
J. S. Dunlap, J. P.

W. W. BRADLEY to Lurine Thrower CROSSLIN Issued 28 Aug 1939 Rites 28 Aug 1939
Isaac Grizzle, J. P.

Harold Lively JORDAN to Edna Earl STEVENSON Issued 28 Aug 1939 Rites 1 Sep
T. Q. Martin, M. G.

Elbert WOOD to Vivian BESS Issued 30 Aug 1939 Rites 30 Aug 1939
E. W. Sutherlin, J. P.

Sidney LOCKE to Jennie THAXTON Issued 2 Sep 1939 Rites 2 Sep 1939
W. L. Peery, M. G.

Theoplus GREEN to Beatrice RHEA Issued 2 Sep 1939 Rites 2 Sep 1939
J. L. Barnes, J. P.

Melvin HILLIS to Mildred Lee CLENDENON Issued 2 Sep 1939 Rites 2 Sep 1939
J. H. MAyo, J. P.

Alton J. SMITH to Edith ROBINSON Issued 2 Sep 1939 Rites 2 Sep 1939
bill A. Jordan, M. G.

Fountain M. BLANKENSHIP to Emma J. TINSLEY Issued 2 Sep 1939 Rites 3 Sep
T. Q. Martin, M. G.

James STROUD to Ruth DENTON Issued 5 Sep 1939 Rites 10 Sep 1939
G. P. Brasier, J.P.

George E. LAFEVER to Lucille THOMPSON Issued 7 Sep 1939 Rites 9 Sep 1939
T. Q. Martin. M. G.

Willie RACKLEY to Marie SMITHSON Issued 7 Sep 1939 Rites 9 Sep 1939
J. H. MAyo, J. P.

Ray HASTON to Clara NORROD Issued 9 Sep 1939 Rites 9 Sep 1939
J. P. Bilbrey, J. P.

J. T. HAYES to Lizzie BOND Issued 11 Sep 1939 Rites 23 Sep 1939
Jas. Davenport, M. G.

Floyd TURNER to Dollie PINEGAR Issued 13 Sep 1939 Rites 24 Aug. 1940
T. Q. Martin, M. G.

Lillard HEATHERLY to Lorine WILLIAMS Issued 14 Sep 1939 Rites 23 Sep 1939
H. J. Wilson, J. P.

E. M. SHEPHARD to Dorothy L. HEAD Issued 15 Sep 1939 Rites 15 Sep 1939
T. Q. Martin, M. G.

Leon BARNES to Jobyna WAKE Issued 23 Sep 1939 Rites 23 Sep 1939
J. H. Mayo, J. P.

Tommy JOHNSON to Velma Grace FULTS Issued 29 Sep 1939 Rites 30 Sep 1939
J. R. Ramsey, J. P.

John T. CHRISTIAN to Lorene DENTON Issued 30 Sep 1939 Rites 1 Oct 1939
W. J. McElroy, M. G.

H. G. WOMACK to Corrine CRADDOCK Issued 30 Sep 1939 Rites 30 Sep 1939
H. F. Richmond, J. P.

James GRISSOM to Dorothy Mae CLARK Issued 30 Sep 1939 Rites 30 Sep 1939
J. H. Mayo, J. P.

JAmes S. MOORE to Evelyn COLBERT Issued 3 Oct 1939 Rites 3 Oct 1939
J. H. Mayo, J. P.

M. T. HILLIS to Jessie NUNLEY Issued 6 Oct 1939 Rites 6 Oct 1939
Irving Patton, J. P.

Lloyd H. VANDAGRIFF to Edith V. WOMACK Issued 7 Oct 1939 Rites 7 Oct 1939
W. P. Willis, M. G.

Herbert Samuel PUGH to Leola RUCKER Issued 10 Oct 1939 Rites 10 Oct 1939
O. L. Minks, M; G.

Frank Lee to Martha R. WEBB Issued 18 Oct 1939 Rites 18 Oct 1939
C. C. Hinkle, M. G.

Alexander CAMPBELL to Bertie JONES Issued 21 Oct 1939 Rites 21 Oct 1939
W. T. Warren, J. P.

WAlter Allen BARNES to Lillie WEST Issued 28 Oct 1939 Rites 28 Oct 1939
Irving Patton, J. P.

James L. SIMPSON to Edith LAWS Issued 10 Nov 1939 Rites 19 Nov 1939
J. N. Winnett, J. P.

W. W. McCOY to Ethel TAYLOR Issued 13 Nov 1939 Rites 13 Nov 1939
A. Z. Holder, J. P.

Willie H. MATHIS to Beatrice CAMPBELL Issued 14 Nov 1939 Rites 14 Nov 1939
W. J. McElroy, M G.

Sutton BARNES to Pauline VICKERS Issued 18 Nov 1939 Rites 19 Nov 1939
A. E. Curtis, J. P.

Ernest CROWE to Inez KING Issued 18 Nov 1939 Rites 18 Nov 1939
A. E. Curtis, J. P.

Walter WEST to Clara Mae BARNES Issued18 Nov 1939 Rites 18 Nov 1939
P. N. Moffitt, Jdg.

Fred C. WILSON to Anna Lou BOULDIN Issued 18 Nov 1939 rites 23 Nov 1939
T. Q. Martin, M. G.

Dennis BROWN to Frances HUGHES Issued 20 Nov 1939 Rites 26 Nov 1939
C. C. Hinkle, M. G.

Ray W. HOLDER to Florence CANTRELL Issued 25 Nov 1939 Rites 25 Nov 1939
J. N. Winnett, J. P.

George B. ZECHMAN to Marie McGEE Issued 1 Dec 1939 Rites 9 Dec 1939
T. Q. Martin, M. G.

Lucian GAMBLE to Lois ARGO Issued 2 Dec 1939 Rites 2 Dec 1939
C. C. Hinkle, M. G.

Alford BONNER (C) to Annie BROWN (C) Issued 2 Dec 1939 Rites 2 Dec 1939
J. H. Mayo, J. P.

CArson CANTRELL to MAry Lee HALE Issued 2 Dec 1939 Rites 2 Dec 1939
W. J. Thompson, M. G.

Arlow LYTLE to Jewell STEAKLEY Issued 3 Dec 1939 Rites 3 Dec 1939
A. E. Curtis, J. P.

Owen HYDE to Nellie YOUNGBLOOD Issued 4 Dec 1939 Rites 4 Dec 1939
E. T. Brazzle, M. G.

James Elmer GREEN to Daisy HEATHERLY issued 9 Dec 1939 Rites 10 Dec 1939
W. J. McElroy, M. G.

J. M. HENDERSON to Cora HENDERSON Issued 9 Dec 1939 Rites 9 Dec 1939
J. H. Mayo, J. P.

Albert B. WILLIAMS to Virginia HENDERSON Issued 14 Dec 1939 Rites 16 Dec 1939
W. E. Miller, M. G.

Fermon DAVENPORT to Alice Frances WISER Issued 16 Dec 1939 Rites 16 Dec 1939
O. L. Minks, M. G.

Wallace CHRISTIAN to Mary Bettie CURTIS Issued 16 Dec 1939 Rites 16 Dec 1939
A. E. Curtis, J. P.

Edward BARNES to Kate GRISSOM Issued 16 Dec 1939 Rites 17 Dec 1939
Frank C. Curtis, J. P.

Brown MARTIN to Frances ROBINSON Issued 16 Dec 1939 Rites 20 Dec 1939
N. O. Allen, M. G.

George ROMANS to Minnie Lee BLANKS Issued 16 Dec 1939 Rites 16 Dec 1939
J. H. Mayo, J. P.

Isaiah DURHAM to Florence HART Issued 16 Dec 1939 Rites 16 Dec 1939
R. G. Martin, Jr., J. P.

Richard TURNER to Mary Frances HILDRETH Issued 16 Dec 1939 Rites 17 Dec 1939
J.W. Shaw, M. G.

Thomas DICKSON to Katherine DAVIS Issued 18 Dec 1939 Rites 24 Dec 1939
Bill A. Jordan, M. G.

Fred RITCHEY to Dollie KEATON Issued 19 Dec 1939 Rites 24 Dec 1939
J. M. Campbell, J. P.

Jesse LORANCE to Sylvia ADCOCK Issued 22 Dec 1939 Rites 22 Dec 1939
W. E. Miller, M. G.

Robert J. PAYNE to Mazel FORD Issued 23 Dec 1939 Rites 23 Dec 1939
W. L. Peery, M. G.

Louis DUNCAN to NAomi YOUNG Issued 23 Dec 1939 Rites 23 Dec 1939
A. E. Kell, J. P.

James E. HINES to Doshie PINEGAR Issued 23 Dec 1939 Rites 23 Dec 1939
J. H. Mayo, J. P.

James A. JENNINGS to Beulah WHITE Issued 23 Dec 1939 Rites 23 Dec 1939
E. P. Cagle, M. G.

Eugene N. ETTER to Mamie SUBLETTE Issued 23 Dec 1939 Rites 23 Dec 1939
T. Q. Martin, M. G.

Thomas J. SMITH, Jr. to Carman EVANS Issued 10 Feb 1940 Rites 10 Feb 1940
J. P. Bilbrey, J. P.

Everett L. GREEN to Naomi FUSTON Issued 14 Feb 1940 Rites 18 Feb 1940
E. T. Cantrell, J. P.

James E. LYNCH to Wilma GROVE Issued 16 Feb 1940 Rites 16 Feb 1940
J. H. Mayo, J. P.

CliftonPEDEN to Lorena GREEN Issued 19 Feb 1940 Rites 24 Feb 1940
O. L. Minks, M. G.

James BARNES to Osha LEE Issued 19 Feb 1940 Rites 19 Feb 1940
P. N. Moffitt, Jdg.

Clarence D. PATTON to Henrietta GOLDEN Issued 21 Feb 1940 Rites 24 Feb 1940
O. L. Minks, M. G.

Charles UNDERHILL to Daisy Pearl HOLDER Issued 27 Feb 1940 Rites 28 Feb 1940
W. B. Snipes, M. G.

J. E. WITT to Hester FORD Issued 28 Feb 1940 Rites 28 Feb 1940
E. D. Martin, M. G.

James C. JOHNSON to Mable M. FULTS Issued 2 Mar 1940 Rites 2 Mar 1940
J. R. Ramsey, J. P.

Jesse TURNER to Fanny Bell COX Issued 5 Mar 1940 rites 5 Mar 1940
C. H. Riddle, J. P.

John Henry KIZZORT to Nona LIPHAM Issued 5 Mar 1940 Rites 5 Mar 1940
C. H. Riddle, J. P.

Gilbert MARTIN to Ida Mae TASH Issued 9 Mar 1940 Rites 9 Mar 1940
J. T. Casey, M. G.

Charles CAPLINGER to Wilma TRAMEL Issued 12 Mar 1940 Rites 12 Mar 1940
Irving Patton, J. P.

George W. COMER, Jr. to Mary Avis WILSON Issued 16 Mar 1940 Rites 24 Mar 1940
A. J. Van Wyk, M. G.

James P. TURNER to Mary Rachel BOWMAN Issued 16 Mar 1940 Rites 18 Mar 1940
T. Q. Martin, M. G.

Eugene CARR (C) to Pearlie MCKINLEY (C) Issued 22 Mar 1940 Rites 21 Mar 1940
Irving Patton, J. P.

Wm. A. ROWLAND to Edith GREEN issued 22 Mar 1940 Rites 23 Mar 1940
J. S. Dunlap, J. P.

Edgar BREEDLOVE to Thelma RUTLEDGE Issued 23 Mar 1940 Rites 23 Mar 1940
R. H. Hale, M. G.

Kelly CRAWFORD to Blanche MINTON Issued 23 Mar 1940 Rites 23 Mar 1940
R. H. Hale, M. G.

Johnnie L. MADEWELL to Rilla A. VAUGHN Issued 23 Mar 1940 Rites 25 Mar 1940
J. H. Mayo, J. P.

Lynwood MICHAEL to Nora Lee STUBBLEFELD Issued 23 Dec 1939 Rites 23 Dec 1939
Bill A. Jordan, M. G.

J. R. GRIBBLE to Roberta HODGES Issued 23 Dec 1939 Rites 24 Dec 1939
T. Q. Martin, M. G.

Noble V. GRAHAM to Susie Ruth WOMACK Issued 26 Dec 1939 Rites 26 Dec 1939
T. Q. Martin, M. G.

Homer DIXSON to Edna CLEMONS Issued 26 dec 1939 Rites 26 dec 1939
J. H. MAyo, J. P.

J. W. CRAVEN to Sarah Mae MELTON Issued 27 Dec 1939 Rites 27 Dec 1939
E. W. Sutherlin, J. P.

Herbery L. HOKE to Mary E. RAMSEY Issued 29 Dec 1939 Rites 29 Dec 1939
T. Q. Martin, M. G.

Raymond NEWTON to Virginia OBERLE Issued 30 Dec 1939 Rites 30 Dec 1939
P. N. Moffitt, Jdg.

J. O. BAILEY to Mary SAIN Issued 9 Jan 1940 Rites 9 Jan 1940
T. Q. Martin, M. G.

Herbert L. MULLINS to Mary Agnes PRATER Issued 13 Jan 1940 Rites 14 Jan 1940
J. N. Winnett, J. P.

Lester ROGERS to Virginia Ruth GOOCH Issued 17 Jan 1940 Rites 17 Jan 1940
E. P. CAgle, M. G.

Wm. Albert HALE to Nelle SAFLEY Issued 18 Jan 1940 Rites 21 Jan 1940
O. L. Minks, M. G.

Howard CANTRELL to Roberta PARSLEY Issued 27 Jan 1940 Rites 27 Jan 1940
J. N. Winnett, J,.P.

P. D. CANNON (C) to Ada SUTTON (C) Issued 27 Jan 1940 Rites 28 JAN 1940
G. T. SPeaks, M. G.

Elmer GREEN to Annie Mae PACK Issued 27 JAn 1940 Rites 27 Jan 1940
J. Il. MAyo, J. P.

Harold JACO to MArgaret L. JACO Issued 31 Jan 1940 Rites 31 Jan 1940
J. H. Mayo, J. P.

A. J. DURHAM to Margie Mae TURNER Issued 3 Feb 1940 Rites 3 Feb 1940
J. W. ShAW, M. G.

Hurbert RAMSEY (C) to Virginia FUSTON (C) Issued 9 Feb 1940 Rites 10 Feb 1940
C. Curtis, M. G.

Howard KILGORE to Nettie MILLER Issued 10 Feb 1940 Rites 12 Feb 1940
J. M. Campbell, J. P.

Alvin BYARS to Delma SMITH Issued 10 Feb 1940 Rites 10 Feb 1940
J. H. Mayo, J. P.

J. N. Elkins to Rebecca FARLESS issued 25 Mar 1940 Rites 25 Mar 1940
P. N. Moffitt, Jdg.

Thomas R. YOUNG to Louise WILSON Issued 3 Apr 1940 Rites 3 Apr 1940
E. P. Cagle, M. G.

james M. IRWIN to Eleanor LANIER Issued 3 Apr 1940 Rites 5 Apr 1940
T. Q. Martin, M. G.

George Edward JORDAN to Edna M. BARRETT Issued 4 Apr 1940 Rites 6 Apr 1940
J. R. Bailey, M. G.

Tom ROWLAND to MAry GRISSOM Issued 4 Apr 1940 Rites 6 Apr 1940
J. B. Gribble, M. G.

J. D. JARRELL to Nellie NOBLES Issued 6 Apr 1940 ites 6 Apr 1940
J. M. Casey, M. G.

Gilbert J. WILLIAMS to Dixie BARRETT issued 6 Apr 1940 Rites 6 Apr 1940
T. Q. Martin, M. G.

Jerry ROBERTS to Martha ADCOCK Issued 8 Apr 1940 Rites 8 Apr 1940
J. B. Gribble, M. G.

Grady Howard FOSTER to Evaline PATTON Issued 9 Apr 1940 Rites 21 Apr 1940
W. J. Thompson

Elbert BELL to Josephine SMITH issued 12 Apr 1940 Rites 13 Apr 1940
J. H. Mayo, J. P.

Elmer PICKETT to Irene JOHNSON Issued 13 Apr 1940 Rites 13 Apr 1940
P. N. Moffitt, Jdg.

Ellis FULTS to Gladys FULTS Issued 13 Apr 1940 Rites 13 Apr 1940
W. B. Snipes, M. G.

Alvin GANN to Hazel HEATHERLY issued 13 Apr 1940 rites 14 Apr 1940
J. N. Winnett, J. P.

JAmes ATNIP to Ruth WEST Issued 13 Apr 1940 Rites 13 Apr 1940
C. R. Womack, J. P.

Fred SAIN to Christine McCORMICK Issued 24 Apr 1940 Rites 24 Apr 1940
J. R. Grove, J. P.

James U. WILSON to Willadean HALL Issued 27 Apr 1940 Rites 28 Feb 1940
J. H. MAyo, J. P.

Woodrow BYARS to Lele Mae SMITH Issued 3 May 1940 Rites 3 May 1940
J. H. Mayo, J. P.

E. L. ROMANS to Ruth Pearl SHALLMAN Issued 4 May 1940 Rites 4 May 1940
G. E. Brazell, M. G.

Clifton BOYD to Edith BENNETT Issued 4 May 1940 Rites 4 May 1940
J. H. Mayo, J. P.

Alonzo WOMACK (C) to MAria SOLOMON (C) Issued 6 May 1940 Rites 6 May 1940
S. J. Morgan, M. G.

Charles HILL (C) to Margaret SAVAGE (C) Issued 6 May 1940 Rites 7 May 1940
J. M. Hayden, M. G.

C. W. FRAZIER to Gibbie BREWER Issued 22 May 1940 Rites 22 May 1940
J. H. Mayo, J. P.

Russ RHEA to Ola KILLIAN Issued 25 May 1940 Rites 25 May 1940
F. C. Curtis, J. P.

James S. HILL to Ruby FULTS Issued 25 May 1940 Rites 25 May 1940
J. H. MAyo, J. P.

David AMOS EPPEHIMER to Margaret SIMONS Issued 28 May 1940 Rites 8 Jun 1940
A. J. VAn Wyk, M. G.

Rudolph ILLING to Harriet Fisher GREEK Issued 29 May 1940 Rites 1 Jun 1940
A. J. Van Wyk, M. G.

Alvie HITCHCOCK to Catherine McAFEE Issued 1 Jun 1940 Rites 2 Jun 1940
T. Q. Martin, M. G.

Foster TAYLOR to Edna POWELL Issued 1 Jun 1940 Rites 1 Jun 1940
J. L. Barnes, J. P.

T. C. HARDEN ot Alma CAPSHAW Issued 1 Jun 1940 Rites 1 Jun 1940
J. H. Mayo, J. P.

Thomas CHASTAIN to Dovie Starkey PEDIGO Issued 1 Jun 1940 Rites 1 Jun
Bill A. Jordan, M. G.

Clyde MELTON to Eula KENNEDY Issued 1 Jun 1940 Rites 1 Jun 1940
J. H. Mayo, J. P.

H. G. CHISAM to Rebecca McELROY Issued 1 Jun 1940 Rites 5 Jun 1940
W. H. Jones, M. G.

Homer B. HUGHES to Minnie Ruth CANTRELL Issued 5 Jun 1940 Rites 5 Jun 1940
E. D. Martin, M. G.

Orville H. MOORE to Grace COPE Issued 7 Jun 1940 Rites 12 Jun 1940
J. B. Gribble, M.G.

E. D. PISTOLE to Hazel Lee REED Issued 8 Jun 1940 Rites 8 Jun 1940
J. H. Mayo, J. P.

Odie William BROCK to Bessie Lou HODGE Issued 8 Jun 1940 Rites 8 Jun 1940
J. H. Mayo, J. P.

Doss A. MARTIN to Tennie SIMONS Issued 8 Jun 1940 Rites 8 Jun 1940
J. B. Gribble, M. G.

John DAVIS to Retha HILLIS Issued 12 Jun 1940 Rites 14 Jun 1940
W. G. Hawkins, M. G.

William ROUND, Jr. to Lera CHISAM Issued 12 Jun 1940 Rites 12 Jun 1940
J. H. Mayo, J. P.

Henry PERKINS (C) to Ella MAE CRISP (C) Issued 15 Jul 1940 Rites 13 Jul 1940
G. P. Brasier, J. P.

Harry D. LORANCE to Ruth CASEY issued 13 Jul 1940 Rites 21 jul 1940
J. T. Casey, M. G.

James W. DREWAR to Minnie JAne BAILEY Issued 13 Jul 1940 Rites 13 Jul 1940
J. H. Mayo, J. P.

Walter M. PHILLIPS to Helen Clara KENNEDY Issued 14 Jul 1940 Rites 21 Jul 1940
T. Q. Martin, M. G.

Arthur COONROD (C) to Freeda Mae PRICE (C) Issued 20 Jul 1940 Rites 21 Jul 1940
E. W. Sutherlin, J. P.

Hollis WINTON (C) to May BROWN (c) Issued 20 Jul 1940 Rites 20 Jul 1940
J. H. Mayo, J. P.

Archie B. BROWN (C) to Annie Mae THOMAS (C) Issued 22 Jul 1940 rites 22 Jul 1940
N. O. allen, M. G.

John R. ROLLINS to Eunice HIGGINS Issued 27 Jul 1940 Rites 28 Jul 1940
Irving Patton, J. P.

CArson MARTIN to Treva HOBBS Issued 28 Jul 1940 Rites 28 Jul 1940
J. H. Mayo, J. P.

Jesse G. ELROD to Tiney Lee GRIZZLE Issued 29 Jul 1940 Rites 29 Jul 1940
T. Q. Martin, M. G.

Thomas LAW to Lela Josephine CASEY Issued 1 Aug 1940 Rites 3 Aug 1940
O. L. Minks, M. G.

Norman Trail BOST to Flossie Beatrice WILMORE Issued 1 Aug 1940 Rites 1 Aug 1940
W. B. Snipes, M. G.

William CARDEN to Lena Louise JOHNSON Issued 2 Aug 1940 Rites 2 Aug 1940
J. H. Mayo, J. P.

T.L.COPPINGER to Amy Irene WIMBERLY Issued 3 Aug 1940 Rites 3 Aug 1940
J. L. Barnes, J. P.

Cecil THWEATT to Marjorie CALDWELL Issued 3 Aug 1940 Rites 3 Aug 1940
E. T. Cantrell, J. P.

Albert Lloyd ELROD to Bertha Louise BLAIR Issued 7 Aug 1940 Rites 17 Aug 1940
R. W. Smartt, Jdg.

Willaim WARD to Ada JONES Issued 9 Aug 1940 rites 9 Aug 1940
J. T. Casey, M. G.

John Wm. JORDAN to O'Fallen PINEGAR Issued 10 Aug 1940 Rites 10 Aug 1940
L. B. Moffitt, J. P.

Earl RIGSBY to MAmie SNIPES Issued 10 Aug 1940 Rites 10 Aug 1940
P. N. Moffitt, Jdg.

Russell A. FARLEY to Lottie TATE Issued 15 Jun 1940 Rites 15 Jun 1940
C. C. Hinkle, M. G.

J. A. FUSTON to Sophia DUNLAP Issued 15 Jun 1940 Rites 23 Jun 1940
E. T. Cantrell, J. P.

Albert BARNES to Pearl ELKINS Issued 17 Jun 1940 Rites 17 Jun 1940
F. J. Winton, J. P.

James E. JUDKINS to Mary Lou ADCOCK Issued 17 Jun 1940 Rites 22 Jun 1940
M. A. Clark, M. G.

Clifton CRIM to Estella DURHAM Issued 21 Jun 1940 Rites 22 Jun 1940
J. H. Mayo, J. P.

Willard A. GRISSOM to Louie Marie ROBERTS Issued 22 Jun 1940 Rites 22 Jun 1940
J. H. Mayo, J. P.

George Marion SPENCER to Lou Ella DENTON Issued 22 Jun 1940 Rites 22 Jun 1940
C. C. Hinkle, M. G.

Dan JONES to MArtha JAne FREED Issued 22 Jun 1940 Rites 22 Jun 1940
J. H. Mayo, J. P.

Manuel TALBERT to Lucile JOHNSON Issued 25 Jun 1940 Rites 25 Jun 1940
P. N. Moffitt, Jdg.

Estelle MYERS to Theresa TAFT Issued 27 Jun 1940 Tites 27 Jun 1940
M. A. Clark, M. G.

Foster HENDERSON to Mattie Lee SWOAPE Issued 29 Jun 1940 Rites 29 Jun 1940
P. N. Moffitt, Jdg.

James DURHAM to Nannie Lou CRIM Issued 29 Jun 1940 Rites 29 Jun 1940
C. C. Dickson, M. G.

JAson HOLDER to Alma PAGE Issued 2 Jul 1940 Rites 4 Jul 1940
H. T. Knight, J. P.

Wm. Butler SMITH to Marjorie Loretta JORDAN Issued 3 Jul 1940 Rites 4 Jul
A. B. Moffitt, M. G.

Audrey B. HILLIS to Willie SAVAGE Issued 6 Jul 1940 Rites 6 Jul 1940
P. N. Moffitt, Jdg.

Jack C. SMITH to Marjorie B. HENEGAR Issued 6 Jul 1940 Rites 7 Jul 1940
T. Q. Martin, M. G.

Charlie GLENN to Gladys MALONE Issued 10 jul 1940 Rites 10 Jul 1940
Irving Patton, J. P.

Rufus SIMMONS to Nettie Lee PENDLETON Issued 13 Jul 1940 Rites 13 Jul 1940
J. J. Morton, M. G.

Joyce ROBINSON to Gladys BELL issued 13 Jul 1940 Rites 13 Jul 1940
T. Q. Martin, M. G.

Scott BArton WALKER, Jr. to Virginia LEEPER Issued 14 Sep 1940 Rites 14 Sep 1940
C. C. Hinkle, M. G.

F. B. CROWNOVER to Maggie Irene NEWBY Issued 14 Sep 1940 Rites 14 Sep 1940
T. Q. Martin. M. G.

Butler CUTTS to Ella Mae ROGERS Issued 15 Sep 1940 Rites 16 sep 1940
R. W. Smartt, Jdg.

J. B. BROWN (C) to Mattielene HENDERSON (C) Issued 17 sep 1940 Rites 17 Sep 1940
N. O. Allen, M. G.

Raymond E. YOUNG to Barbara Louise HOLT Issued 17 Sep 1940 rites 17 Sep 1940
M. A. Cook, M. G.

Luther PRIEST to Mary KESEY issued 18 Sep 1940 Rites 18 Sep 1940
A. E. Qurtis, J. P.

Thos. J. GIVAN to MAry Eliz. MILES Issued 20 Sep 1940 Rites 2o Sep 1940
T. Q. Martin, M. G.

James R. WARREN to hattie Lou PINEGAR Issued 21 Sep 1940 Rites.26 Sep
Irving Patton, J. P.

Claud BLAYLOCK to Nannie Belle REYNOLDS Issued 21 Sep 1940 Rites 21 Sep 1940
J. H. Mayo, J. P.

Cap HARPER to Cora YORK Issued 26 Sep 1940 Rites 26 Sep 1940
A. J. Van Wyk, M.G.

I. J. PERRY to Mae BEARD Issued 27 Sep 1940 Rites 27 Sep 1940
J. H. Mayo, J. P.

John Wilson PARIS to Jessie Louise JORDAN Issued 27 Sep 1940 Rites 27 Sep
W. J. Thompson

Lillard NABORS to Edna KNIGHT Issued 28 Sep 1940 rites 28 Sep 1940
G. P. Brasier, J. P.

Floyd SMARTT, Jr. to Mary Frances HALE Issued 30 Sep 1940 Rites 30 Sep 1940
J. J. Morton, M. G.

Nolen SLAUGHTER to Thelma COPPINGER Issued 1 Oct 1940 rites 1 Oct 1940
P. N. Moffitt, Jdg.

William BASHAM to Geneva NUNLEY Issued 2 Oct 1940 Rites 5 Oct 1940
W. B. Snipes, M. G.

Wilmer T. SANDERS to Georgia WARREN Issued 3 Oct 1940 rites 7 Oct 1940
P. N. Moffitt, J. P.

Paul C. SOULSBY to Reba Dean BURNETTE Issued 4 Oct 1940 rites 4 Oct 1940
O. L. Minks, M. G.

C. K. GRISSOM to Anna WHITE Issued 4 Oct 1940 Rites 6 Oct 1940
E. S. Wallace, J. P.

J. F. CUNNINGHAM to Louise BELL Issued 10 Aug 1940 Rites 10 Aug 1940
J. K. CARR, M. G.

James RANDALL to Muriel HUTCHESON Issued 12 Aug 1940 Rites 12 Aug 1940
E. W. Sutherlin, J. P.

P. D. GRISSOM, Jr. to Dorothy COOPER Issued 13 Aug 1940 Rites 13 Aug 1940
W. M. Rowland, J. P.

Billy SWANN to Marie TURNER Issued 16 Aug 1940 Rites 17 Aug 1940
G. P. Brasier, J. P.

Albert SEXTON to Jodie JONES Issued 17 Aug 1940 rites 17 Aug 1940
J. H. mayo, J. P.

Andrew B. TURNER to Leta Mae CONASTER Issued 17 aug 1940 Not Returned

Grady TURNER to Frances BROWN Issued 17 Aug 1940 rites 18 AUG 1940
Bill A. Jordan, M. G.

L. L. MOFFITT to Annie Lucile CRAWFORD Issued 17 Aug 1940 Rites 17 Aug 1940
C. C. Hinkle, M. G.

Clyde M. REED to Eunice MArie HOBBS Issued 24 Aug 1940 Rites 24 Aug 1940
E. W. Sutherlin, J. P.

Walter ROBERTS to Elizabeth SMARTT Issued 24 Aug 1940 rites 24 Aug 1940
G. H. O'Neal, M. G.

Eugene HENNESSEE to JOhnie PITTS Issued 24 Aug 1940 rites 24 Aug 1940
J. J. Morton, M. G.

Gordon P. ADCOCK to Thelma Willene CANTRELL Issued 29 Aug 1940 Rites 29 Aug 1940
Irving Patton, J. P.

A. J. INGLE, Jr. to Eliz. Jane YAGER Issued 30 Aug 1940 rites 1 Sep 1940
A. J. Van Wyk, M. G.

Tommie CAGLE to Delma HALE Issued 31 Aug 1940
J. H. Mayo, J. P.

John A?IEL to Belle LORANCE Issued 31 Aug 1940 Rites 31 aug 1940
W. L. Peery, M? G.

Frank C. BYARS to Thelma Imogene TURNER Issued 31 Aug 1940 Rites 31 Aug 1940
J. H. Mayo, J. P.

Lewis G. THAXTON to Gradie D. CURTIS Issued 31 Aug 1940 Rites 13 Sep 1940
J. T. Caset, M. G.

Woodrow ?RANCE to Lina CHERRY Issued 7 Sep 1940 Rites 16 Sep 1940
J. N. Winnett, J. P.

E. H. ALL? to Susie CANTRELL Issued 10 Sep 1940 Rites 10 Sep 1940
W. G. Hawkins, M. G.

Jess Willar? JARRELL to Frances MArie YOUNG Issued 14 Sep 1940 Rites 14 Sep 1940
E. W. Sutherlin, M. G.

Moses Houston GAMBLE, Jr. to Mary Neal WILSON Issued 5 Oct 1940 Rites 5 Oct 1940 Richard Huff, M. G.

A. C. MEASLES to Magdalene GUY Issued 5 Oct 1940 Rites 6 Oct 1940 J. R. Grove, J. P.

Walter ROWLAND to Louise NELSON Issued 5 Oct 1940 Rites 5 Oct 1940 Irving Patton, J. P.

Cecil BRATCHER to Bobbie PARTON Issued 7 Oct 1940 Rites 7 Oct 1940 A. Z. Holder, J. P.

Geroge B. ROUTTE to Mary J. MORGAN issued 8 Oct 1940 Rites 8 Oct 1940 P. N. Moffitt, Jdg.

William M. FRAZIER to Carrie MULLICAN Issued 12 Oct 1940 Rites 12 Oct 1940 E. W. Sutherlin, J. P.

Carmack SELLARS to Alta CANTRELL Issued 12 Oct 1940 Rites 13 Oct 1940 E. D. Martin, M. G.

Willard MCBRIDE to Willie Marie OAKLEY Issued 12 Oct 1940 Rites 12 Oct 1940 W. E. Miller, M. G.

Elmer MARTIN (C) to Marjorie SAVAGE (C) Issued 15 Oct 1940 Rites 15 Oct 1940 C. Curtis, M. G.

Elam GREEN to Eva Pearl COPE Issued 18 Oct 1940 VOIDED

Zeb EDGE to Sallie GREEN Issued 19 Oct 1940 Rites 19 Oct 1940 A. J. Van Wyk, M. G.

Cecil MULLICAN to Betty TEETERS Issued 25 Oct 1940 Tites 25 Oct 1940 J. H. Mayo, J. P.

Doorwood CRIM to Arminta Lee Jones issued 2 Nov 1940 Rites 2 Nov 1940 J. H. Mayo, J. P.

W. L. HILLIS to Lela KANIPE Issued 9 Nov 1940 Rites 10 Nov 1940 Marion Thomison, M. G.

Louie ASKEW to Willie HERMAN Issued 16 Nov 1940 Rites 16 Nov 1940 C. C. Dickson, M. G.

Charlie CUTTS to Annie FARMER Issued 16 Nov 1940 Rites 16 Nov 1940 J. H. Mayo, J. P.

Harold PARROTT to Hazel BLUM Issued 20 Nov 1940 Rites 21 Nov 1940 Bill A. Jordan, M. G.

James Lewis JOHNSON to Mildred TALLEY SPARKMAN Issued 21 Nov 1940 Rites 23 Nov J. T. Casey, M. G.

Roland H. STEWART to Nealy KIRBY Issued 21 Nov 1940 Rites 21 Nov 1940 T. Q. Martin, M. G.

Cecil DAVENPORT to Audry Mae BURKS Issued 23 Nov 1940 Rites 23 Nov 1940 G. P. Brasier, J. P.

Albert HENDERSON to Elizabeth TURNER Issued 23 Nov 1940 Rites 24 Nov 1940 Horace Snipes, M. G.

William STRICK to Louise WOMACK Issued 25 Nov 1940 Rites 14 Dec 1940 T. Q. Martin, M. G.

Sam FRAKES to Lillian MERRITT Issued 25 Nov 1940 Rites 25 Nov 1940 J. P. Bilbrey, J. P.

John Oscar PRESSLEY to Wilma Rebecca DAVIS Issued 26 Nov 1940 Rites 26 Nov P. N. Moffitt, Jdg.

Alvie LYLE to Josephine TUCK Issued 29 Nov 1940 Rites 30 Nov 1940 J. J. Morton, M. G.

Jack L. TRAUX to Evelyn MINNIE MYERS Issued 3 Dec 1940 Rites 3 Dec 1940 J. P. Bilbrey, J. P.

James Lester BARRETT to Willie Beatrice JONES Issued 8 Dec 1940 Rites 9 Dec J. P. Bilbrey, J. P.

Herman W. DURHAM to Fannie M. MARSHALL Issued 13 Dec 1940 Rites 13 Dec 1940 J. H. Mayo, J. P.

Dessie Brown JONES to Pearl SPARKMAN Issued 14 Dec 1940 Rites 14 Dec 1940 E. S. Wallace, J. P.

James R. ROLLER to Ethel FARMER Issued 14 Dec 1940 Rites 14 Dec 1940 J. B. Gribble, M. G.

Charlie STEMBRIDGE to Margie SIMMONS Issued 18 Dec 1940 Rites 18 Dec 1940 J. H. Mayo, J. P.

Walter JUDKINS to Marie BARNES Issued 21 Dec 1940 Rites 22 Dec 1940 E. T. Cantrell, J. P.

Howard WAGNER to Iola BLANKENSHIP Issued 23 Dec 1940 Rites 23 Dec 1940 T. Q. Martin, M. G.

George HILDRETH to Ruth MULLICAN Issued 23 Dec 1940 Rites 23 Dec 1940 J. M. Campbell, J. P.

Charlie Price TURNER to Odie Pearl LYLE Issued 26 Dec 1940 Rites 27 Dec 1940 L. L. Morton, M. G.

JAmes C. FISHER to Johnnie Ruth PRATER Issued 26 Dec 1940 Rites 26 Dec 1940 G. P. Brasier, J. P.

Wm. W. EWING to Mildred Culley WILSON Issued 26 Dec 1940 Rites 29 Dec 1940 H. E. BAker, M. G.

R. L. ANDERSON to Mary Va. RAMSEY Issued 27 Dec 1940 Rites 28 Dec 1940 A. J. Van Wyk, M. G.

Sidney CRABTREE to Mildred MILLER Issued 27 Dec 1940 Rites 27 dec 1940 M. M. League, M. G.

Thomas OFFICER (C) to Georgia BROWN (C) Issued 28 Dec 1940 Rites 29 Dec 1940 Ben BAtes, M. G.

Woodrow ADCOCK to Coleen MAGGART Issued 28 Dec 1940 Rites 28 Dec 1940 J. H. Mayo, J. P.

John Pope GRIZZLE to Dorothy J. KENNAMER Issued 28 Dec 1940 Rites 28 Dec 1940 I. J. Grizzle, J. P.

Joe WOMACK to Tennie AINIP Issued 1 Jan 1941 Rites 1 Jan 1941 C. R. Womack, J. P.

Charlie Ray SMITH to Alice JONES Issued 31 Dec 1941 Rites 31 Dec 1941 J. H. MAyo, J. P.

Ernest HOLDER to Evelyn BRATCHER Issued 4 Jan 1941 Rites 4 Jan 1941 J. H. MAyo, J. P.

J. C. WINTON (C) to Carrie Lee GRAYSON (C) Issued 8 Jan 1941 Rites 8 Jan 1941 M. M. League, M. G.

George Byron BESS to Obelie COPE Issued 11 Jan 1941 Rites 11 Jan 1941 Bill A. Jordan, M. G.

Ferman SPENCER to Bessie LOCKE Issued 24 Jan 1941 Rites 24 Jan 1941 M. M. League, M. G.

BArt W. RAY to Alberta ASKEW Issued 24 jan 1941 Rites 24 Jan 1941 J. T. Casey, M. G.

Lawrence Wm. LOCKE to Zelma COPE Issued 27 JAn 1941 Rites 27 Jan 1941 M. M. League, Ml G.

John Z. SAYLORS to HAllie ARGO Issued 1 Feb 1941 Rites 1 Feb 1941 W. G. McDonough, Jdg.

Ed David LEE to Mary Ann SMITH Issued 1 Feb 1941 Rites 1 Feb 1941 Ben Bates, M. G.

Fred C. PARSLEY to Mary Ella WHITLOCK Issued 1 Feb 1941 Rites 2 Feb 1941 J. T. Casey, M. G.

Roy DUGGIN to Gertrude WILLIAMS Issued 14 Feb 1941 Rites 5 Feb 1941 J. N. Winnett, J. P.

Henry TAYLOR (C) to Henrietta HANCOCK (C) Issued 1 Feb 1941 Rites 1 Feb 1941 W. M. Taylor, M. G.

DAvid W. ARNOLD to Frances WOMACK Issued 2 Feb 1941 Rites 8 Feb 9141 T. Q. Martin, M. G.

Samuel Chester KEATON to Wilma Rebecca HIBDON Issued 2 Feb 1941 Rites 19 Feb Jas. K. Martin,J. P.

Tommy T. PERRY to MAry JONES Issued 8 Feb 1941 Rites 8 Feb 1941 I. P. McGregor, J. P.

Francis L. TEMPLETON to Rosa Lee SHARP Issued 13 Feb 1941 Rites 14 Feb 1941 J. B. Gribble, M. G.

Lem GIBBS to Emma RUTLEDGE Issued 15 Feb 1941 Rites 15 Feb 1941 Irving Patton, J. P.

Cecil PRATER to Frances SAIN Issued 15 Feb 1941 Rites 16 Feb 1941 T. Q. Maryin, M. G.

Wm. I. STEMBRIDGE to Vada Lee WRIGHT issued 15 Feb 1941 Rites 115 Feb 1941 H. T. Knight, J. P.

Virgil G. LATIMER to Alice VANDYGRIFF Issued 20 Feb 1941 Rites 20 Feb 1941 W. G. McDonough, Jdg.

Aldo BOYD to Minnie McCORMICK Issued 22 Feb 1941 Rites 22 Feb 1941 W. G. McDonough, Jdg.

Clyde SMITH to HAzel PARKER Issued 1 Mar 1941 Rites 1 Mar 1941 W. G. HAwkins, M. G.

Houston REED to Clara Mae PHILLIPS Issued 1 Mar 1941 Rites 1 Mar 1941 J. H. Mayo, J. P.

Thomas Edward SHAW to Edith Nell FARRAR Issued 7 Mar 1941 Rites 7 Mar 1941 P. N. Moffitt, Jdg.

Marion RUST to Beatrice CUNNINGHAM Issued 9 Mar 1941 Rites 9 Mar 1941 J. R. Ramsey

J. H. BISHOP to Myrtle REYNOLDS Issued 15 Mar 1941 Rites 16 Mar 1941 A. B. Moffitt, M. G.

Wayne CLARK to Laura CONNOR Issued 15 MAr 1941 Rites 15 Mar 1941 J. LAmbert Womack, M. G.

B. S. PRESCOTT to Levonia MELTON Issued 15 Mar 1941 Rites 15 Mar 1941 Harry Kutz, M. G.

R. B. ROGERS to Ruth AKINS Issued 19 Mar 1941 Rites 20 Mar 1941 J. R. Grove, J. P.

H. B. POWELL to Geneva CARLTON Issued 19 Mar 1941 Rites 19 Mar 1941 P. N. Moffitt, Jdg.

J. L. RAY to Orene STARNES Issued 21 Mar 1941 Rites 29 Mar 1941 A. B. Moffitt, M. G.

Glenn PRATER to Dean McDOWELL Issued 22 Mar 1941 Rites 22 Mar 1941 T. Q. Martin, M. G.

Howard TUBB to Melba NORTHCUTT Issued 22 Mar 1941 Rites 22 Mar 1941 J. N. Winnett, J. P.

Lloyd McRAY to Nettie E. DUKE Issued 22 Mar 1941 Rites 22 Mar 1941 Irving Patton, J. P.

Howrie KEEL to Gladys McBRIDE Issued 25 Mar 1941 Rites 25 Mar 1941
W. E. Miller, M. G.

John Everette CARTER to Sara Louise FARLEY Issued 1 Apr 1941 Rites 6 Apr 1941
H. E. Baker, M. G.

Clyde CHERRY to Laura Maye HAYNES Issued 5 Apr 1941 Rites 7 Apr 1941
H. E. BAker, M. G.

David F. RAY to Donnie Lee MOLLOY Issued 5 Apr 1941 Rites 12 Apr 1941
T. Q. Martin, M. G.

Walter B. HAAS to Cora TREECE Issued 12 Apr 1941 Rites 20 Apr 1941
C. P. Lillie, M. G.

James Edward STEM (C) to Katie P. BEDFORD (C) Issued 15 Apr 1941 Rites 15 Apr
W. G. McDonough, Jdg.

James T. BOTTOMS to Belle RUSSELL Issued 18 Apr 1941 Rites 18 Apr 1941
I. P. McGregor, J. P.

Clarence RASHAM to Ellen MUNSEY Issued 19 Apr 1941 Rites 19 Apr 1941
J. L. Barnes, J. P.

Brown RAMSEY (C) to Timmy PINCHEON (C) Issued 19 Apr 1941 Rites 19 Apr 1941
A. L. Guerard, M. G.

Virble TAYLOR to Myrtle KEITH Issued 21 Apr 1941 Rites 21 Apr 1941

Ray LORANCE to Lillian FREEZE Issued 24 Apr 1941 Rites 24 Apr 1941
E. L. Hudgens, M. G.

Lambert SMITHSON to Pearl BAILEY Issued 26 Apr 1941 Rites 26 Apr 1941
Willie Jenkins, M. G.

Wm. Thos. WOOD (C) to Josephine MARTIN (C) Issued 26 Apr 1941 VOIDED

Ernest CURTIS to Mary Eliz. SMITH Issued 30 Apr 1941 Rites 30 Apr 1941
J. P. Bilbrey, J. P.

Urville MARTIN to Mary F. CUNNINGHAM Issued 20 Apr 1941 Rites 3 May 1941
H. E. BAker, M. G.

John BARBEE to Josie NEAL Issued 1 May 1941 Rites 2 May 1941
C. R. Womack, J. P.

Lee Alvin O'NEAL to Mary Louise HOBBS Issued 3 May 1941 Rites 3 May 1941
C. L. Webster, M. G.

Arthur L. LORANCE to Irene GAITHER Issued 3 May 1941 Rites 3 May 1941
J. N. Winnett, J. P.

Edward NICHOLS to Alice WHITMAN Issued 3 May 1941 Rites 3 May 1941
C. F. Hudgens, M. G.

John WISER to Mamie REYNOLDS Issued 3 May 1941 Rites 3 May 1941
W. J. Thompson

Johnie Elisha REED to Audrey Lorene PHILLIPS Issued 3 May 1941 Rites 3 MAY 1941
W. G. McDonough, Jdg.

Malchus C. BAKER to Vera McCORMICK Issued 5 May 1941 Rites 5 May 1941
P. N. Moffitt, Jdg.

John PUCKETT to Mattie STALEY Issued 5 May 1941 Rites 5 May 1941
J. R. Bailey, M. G.

Wm. E. LUTRELL to Louise WOODLEE Issued 6 May 1941 Rites 10 May 1941
P. N. Moffitt, Jdg.

E. C. CANTRELL to Eula Mae ALLEN Issued 6 May 1941 Rites 7 May 1941
W. E. Miller, M. G.

JAmes C. SHOCKLEY (C) to Lillian NORTHCUTT (C) Issued 10 May 1941 Rites 11 May
Ben Bates, M. G.

Henry Clay JOHNSTON to Lula Mae IRWIN Issued 10 May 1941 Rites 10 May 1941
J. H. Mayo, J. P.

S. L.CORDELL to Georgia C. BRAGG Issued 12 May 1941 Rites 16 May 1941
T. Q. Martin, M. G.

Wm. Bruse TAYLOR to Hassie Pauline JONES Issued17 May 1941 Rites 17 Mat 1941
P. N. Moffitt, Jdg.

Robert J. SHERRER to Sue DANIELS Issued 17 May 1941 Rites 17 May 1941
T. Q. Martin, M. G.

Jmaes Manuel MASON to Juanita McMAHAN Issued 18 May 1941 Rites 18 May 1941
I. J. Grizzle, J. P.

Leonard Levi FREEZE to Fannie L. FARRAR Issued 23 May 1941 Rites 24 May 1941
E. W. Sutherlin, J. P.

Lonnie ROBERTS to Leona RUSSELL Issued 26 May 1941 Rites 26 May 1941
I. P. McGregor, J. P.

Armstrong SUMMERS to Robbie PATTERSON Issued 29 May 1941 Rites 31 May 1941
J. N. Winnett, J. P.

Joe WATSON to Jessie Mae KING Issued 31 May 1941 Rites 31 May 1941
W. G. McDonough, Jdg.

Thos. Edward GREEN to Mary Jane MULLICAN Issued 31 May 1941 Rites 4 Jun 1941
A. J. Van Wyk, M. G.

W. H. SMITH to Annie CARVER Issued 31 May 1941 Rites 31 May 1941
Harry Kutz, M. G.

Nick EPISCOPE to Millie ROTH Issued 1 Jun 1941 Rites 1 Jun 1941
J. H. Mayo, J. P.

Laster CHRISTIAN to Drucie ELLIOTT Issued 7 Jun 1941 Rites 7 Jun 1941
P. N. Moffitt, Jdg.

James Houston STILES to Winnie Mae BLANKS Issued 9 Jun 1941 Rites 14 Jun 1941
E. D. Martin, M. G.

Milton JONES to Joan COMER Issued 11 Jun 1941 Rites 15 jun 1941
H. E. BAker, M. G.

T. F. TOLBERT to Elsie Fay DENTON Issued 13 Jun 1941 Rites 14 Jun 1941
G. P. Bradier, J. P.

Finis MILLER (C) to Mary REASONOVER Issued 14 Jun 1941 Rites 14 Jun 1941
A. L. Guerald, M. G.

W. H. WELLS to Ella Louise CRAWLEY Issued 14 Jun 1941 Rites 15 Jun 1941
O. L. Minks, M. G.

Jerry CATEN to Lucille BROWN Issued 16 Jun 1941 Rites 16 Jun 1941
E. D. Martin, M. G.

David HENNINGER to Mary Myers McCOLLOCH Issued 19 Jun 1941 Rites 19 Jun 1941
H. E. BAker, M. G.

Richard DAVENPORT to Pauline COUCH Issued 20 Jun 1941 Rites 21 Jun 1941
Bill A. Jordan, M. G.

Oney BROWN (C) to Sadie MALONE (C) Issued 20 Jun 1941 Rites 20 Jun 1941
M. M.League, M. G.

Charlie McGARRAH to Julia MOORE Issued 21 Jun 1941 Rites 21 Jun 1941
W. G. McDonough, Jdg.

Eugene C. JONES to Georgia ANN MAXWELL Issued 23 jun 1941 Rites 23 Jun 1941
J. N. Winnett, J. P.

Isham PERRY to Helen Mae DICKEY Issued 24 Jun 1941 Rites 24 Jun 1941
P. N. Moffitt, Jdg.

Edward B. MOLLOY to Geraldine V. SAPP Issued 25 Jun 1941 Rites 29 Jun 1941
R. W. Smith, Jdg.

Frank WOODLEE (C) to Mary Lou YORK (C) Issued 27 Jun 1941 Rites 27 Jun 1941
W. G. McDonough, Jdg.

Clancy McQUIGG to Doris Ann LAWRENCE Issued 27 Jun 1941 Rites 27 Jun 1941
J. H. Mayo, J. P.

599 Marriages in this book

Book #20 - Warren County Marriages - Jun 28, 1941 to Oct 8, 1949

Frank E. DAVENPORT to Roberta TAYLOR Issued 28 Jun 1941 Rites 28 Jun 1941
A. Z. Holder, J. P.

Henry Earl PEPPER to Willie PERRY Issued 28 Jun 1941 Rites 28 Jun 1941
W. G. McDonough, Jdg.

Hoyte GOFF to Jewell STEAKLEY Issued 28 Jun 1941 Rites 28 Jun 1941
W. T. Warren, J. P.

Sterling LORANCE to Linnie ADAMS Issued 28 Jun 1941 Rites 29 Jun 1941
W. E. Miller, M. G.

William H. JACKSON to Irene HAMMONDS Issued 30 Jun 1941 Rites 30 Jun 1941
A. B. Moffitt, M. G.

Ed EVANS (C) to Shula SPURLOCK (C) Issued 30 Jun 1941 Rites 30 Jun 1941
M. M. League, M. G.

Grady R. FLETCHER to Nellie Irene CARR Issued 30 Jun 1941 Rites 30 Jun 1941
E. F. Hudgens, M. G.

Howard Bonner RAMSEY to Elizabeth MURPHY Issued 12 Jul 1941 Rites 12 Jul 1941
James R. Cope

Owen Marshall CROUCH to Mona Bell BUMBALOUGH Issued 14 Jul 1941 Rites 14 Jul
Irving Patton, J. P.

Robert G. SPARKMAN to Viola FANN Issued 18 Jul 1941 Rites 18 Jul 1941
Irving Patton, J. P.

Alfred GLENN to Laverne MARTIN Issued 19 Jul 1941 Rites 19 Jul 1941
C. E. Simmons, M. G.

Emmett WARREN to Elizabeth BREWER Issued 4 Aug 1941 Rites 4 Aug 1941
E. W. Sutherlin, J. P.

Marvin ANDERSON to Sudie Alene PACK Issued 4 Aug 1941 Rites 5 Aug 1941
C. R. Womack, J. P.

James Gordon ADCOCK to Malliory MAcon SLATTON Issued 22 Aug 1941 Rites 22 A g
A. Z. Holder, J. P.

C. B. DOUGLAS to Nannie REDMAN Issued 26 Aug 1941 Rites 26 Aug 1941
W. G. McDonough, Jdg.

A. L. GUERARD (C) to MAble Louise STOKES Issued 26 Aug 1941 Rites 27 Aug 1941
G. T. Speaks, M. G.

Lusk Edward WOODLEE to Emma Allison BROWN Issued 30 Aug 1941 Rites 30 Aug
W. E. Miller, M. G.

Hubert PENDERGRAPH to Jessie D. GRIBBLE Issued 30 Aug 1941 Rites 30 Aug 1941
A. J. Van Wyk, M. G.

Jesse G. EARLS, Jr. to Sue McGIBONEY Issued 4 Sep 1941 Rites 7 Sep 1942
T. Q. Martin, M. G.

Andrew Jackson DURHAM to Nora YOUNG Issued 6 Sep 1941 Rites 7 Sep 1941
HArry Kutz, M. G.

James Thos. WILKERSON to Anna Eliz. REEDER Issued 6 Sep 1941 Rites 7 Sep 1941
H. E. BAker, M. G.

Leland BOSWELL to Louise CLARK Issued 13 Sep 1941 Rites 14 Sep 1941
F. M. Dowell, Jr., M. G.

Walter GRIBBLE to Bennie Louise DAVIS Issued 15 Sep 1941 Rites 15 Sep 1941
Ben Bates, M. G.

Loyd Harrison FOSTER to Clydie CANTRELL Issued 18 Sep 1941 Rites 20 Sep 1941
J. K. Martin, J. P.

Homer Clee MOORE to MArgie Louise MASTERS Issued 20 Sep 1941 Rites 21 Sep 1941
W. E. Miller, M. G.

John James WALKER to Johnnie MASON Issued 24 Sep 1941 Rites 2 Oct 1941
T. Q. Martin, M. G.

Thos. Atlas BREWER to Dola V. SCRUGGS Issued 1 Oct 1941 Rites 1 Oct 1941
J. N. Winnett, J. P.

John Baptist ROBERTS to Marie MOONEY Issued11 Oct 1941 Rites 11 Oct 1941
I. P. McGregor, J. P.

Willie D. YORK to Christine FORD Issued 18 Oct 1941 Rites 18 Oct 1941
J. J. Morton, M. G.

Homer T. COATS to Mary Burton RAYBURN Issued 18 Oct 1941 Rites 18 Oct 1941
James Rayburn, M. G.

Maloney WOODLEE to Edna Lela MAYES Issued 18 Oct 1941 Rites 18 Oct 1941
P. N. Moffitt, Jdg.

George W. BUSEY to Gladys PRIEST Issued 20 Oct 1941 Rites 20 Oct 1941
P. N. Moffitt, Jdg.

Jim BROWN (C) to Ida KEELE (C) Issued 24 Oct 1941   Not Returned

J. M. FISHER to Lillie STEPHENS Issued 12 Nov 1941 Rites 12 Nov 1941
P. N. Moffitt, Jdg.

William J. STARKEY to Ada Lois BELL Issued 17 Nov 1941 Rites 23 Nov 1941
T. Q. Martin, M. G.

James Eugene HENNESSEE to Frankie Irene WILLIAMS Issued 21 Nov 1941 Rites 29 Nov
T. Q. Martin, M. G.

Amon RANDOLPH to Mrs. Flora Cobb Randolph Issued 24 Nov 1941 Rites 24 Nov.
P. N. Moffitt, JUg.

Barrett EVANS to Minnie Jo FOUTCH Issued 25 Nov 1941 Rites 25 Nov 1941
J. P. Bilbrey, J. P.

William Lee GREEN to Annie Pearl BURCH Issued 25 Nov 1941 Rites 25 Nov 1941
J. H. Mayo, J. P.

Dewey V. PELHAM to Ruthie Velma BRINKLEY Issued 1 Dec 1941 Rites 1 Dec 1941
A. B. Moffitt, M. G.

Clyde HALE to Georgia Laura SMITH Issued 13 Dec 1941 Rites 13 Dec 1941
J. P. Bilbrey, J. P.

Alton Claud SOUTHARD to Willene GRISSOM Issued 13 Dec 1941 Rites 20 Dec 1941
Granville Tyler, M. G.

Kermit TURNER to Tillaree WILLIAMSON Issued 16 ec 1941 Rites 20 ec 1941
P. N. Moffitt, Jdg.

J. W. SEIGENTHALER to Cornell McDOWELL Issued 20 Dec 1941 Rites 20 Dec 1941
H. E. Baker, M. G.

Noel H. WOMACK to MARGARET SAIN Issued 24 Dec 1941 Rites 24 Dec 1941
T. Q. Martin, M. G.

Davis Crissrow WISER to Ovalee SCOTT Issued 24 Dec 1941 Rites 24 Dec 1941
C. C. Dickson, M. G.

John Rolfe GOLDEN to Susie Mai CASE Issued 27 Dec 1941 Rites 30 Dec 1941
T. Q. Martin, M. G.

Joseph Taylor MARTIN to Audie Mae STIPE Issued 2 Jan 1942 Rites 2 Jan 1942
E. L. Smothers, M. G.

David C. BURWOOD to Betty PAuline CLENDENON Issued 10 JAn 1942 Rites 10 Jan 1942
T. Q. Martin, M. G.

Moses A. CANTRELL to Silverrie McCOY Issued 12 Jan 1942 Rites 24 Jan 1942
W. M. Wood, M. G.

James Y. FINLEY to Maurice HAWKINS Issued 17 Jan 1942 Rites 17 Jan 1942
W. G. Hawkins, M. G.

Marcus F. C. SMARTT to Elizabeth G. ETTER Issued 23 Jan 1942 Rites 23 Jan 1942
E. D. Martin, M. G.

Thomas Andrew LOCKE to M. Virginia NELSON Issued 27 Jan 1942 Rites 30 Jan 1942
F. U. Fields, M. G.

Wm. Burl TUCKER to Audrey CUNNINGHAM Issued 31 JAn 1942 Rites 31 Jan 1942
W. G. McDonough, Jdg.

Sidney ROGERS to Minnie Bell GANN Issued 2 Feb 1942 Rites 2 Feb 1942
W. G. McDonough, Jdg.

Walter WOMACK to Irene BOYD Issued 14 Feb 1942 Rites 21 Feb 1942
T. Q. Martin, M. G.

Robert Forrest SUMMERS to Grace V. WILLIAMS Issued20 Feb 1942 Rites 21 Feb 1942
J. K, CArr, M. G.

Louis S. DURHAM to Margaret Louise SMITH Issued 28 Feb 1942 Rites 28 Feb 1942
J. H. Mayo, J. P.

Willie Thos. HANKINS to Ruby Gordon MARTIN Issued 7 Mar 1942 Rites 7 Mar 1942
C. E. Simmons, M. G.

Paul OGLES to Martha STALLINGS Issued 7 Mar 1942 Rites 7 Mar 1942
A. J. Van Wyk, M. G.

Woodrow H. EAGAN to Dorothy Esther COATES Issued 7 Mar 1942 Rites 7 Mar 1942
J. H. Mayo, J. P.

Frank Houston HOWARD to Roy Mae HARDCASTLE Issued 10 Mar 1942 Rites 10 Mar 1942
T. Q. Martin, M. G.

Glenn Lewis ARGO to Marguerite WIMBERLY Issued 14 Mar 1942 Rites 14 Mar 1942
C. L. Webster, M. G.

J. T. HALE to Betty GUNTER Issued 19 Mar 1942 Rites 21 Mar 1942
R. H. Hale, M. G.

H. T. TARWATER to KAtherine POTTER Issued 21 Mar 1942 Rites 21 Mar 1942
T. G. Martin, M. G.

John Wyatt LEE to Dorothea Iva BOYD Issued 28 Mar 1942 Rites 2 Apr 1942
T. Q. Martin, M. G.

C. C. DICKSON to Nancy SCOTT Issued 4 Apr 1942 Rites 5 Apr 1942
John Morton, M. G.

Albert A. GONCE, Jr. to Janie Blanche SAIN Issued 15 Apr 1942 Rites 18 Apr 1942
HArold Sain, M. G.

Jesse Dredman ROBERTS to Annie Bettie BOULDIN Issued 18 Apr 1942 Rites 18 Apr
A. E. Curtis, J. P.

Clarence Cebert MYERS to Alva SMARTI. Issued 18 Apr 1942 Rites 18 Apr 1942
P. N. Moffitt, Jdg.

Chas. William BROWN to Juanita Faye WILLIAMS Issued 21 Apr 1942 Rites 21 Apr
W. E. Miller, M. G.

Elton DUNLAP to Thelma DOVE Issued 25 Apr 1942 Rites 25 Apr 1942
J. B. Gribble, M. G.

Wm. G. FELL to Mildred SMITH Issued 2 May 1942 Rites 9 May 1942
A. J. Van Wyk, M. G.

Thomas Monroe KELL to Virgie Willene McGEE Issued 8 May 1942 Rites 8 May 1942
J. M. Byrm, M. G.

Louie Thomas PURGASON to Thelma Mae GATEWOOD Issued 17 May 1942 Rites 17 May 1942
O. B. Johnson, M. G.

John Franklin PARSLEY to Glenna Edith IRONS Issued 22 May 1942 Rites 22 May 1942
J. T. Casey, M. G.

Erby SCOTT (C) to Maue M. MARTIN (C) Issued 22 May 1942 Rites 22 May 1942
G. T. Speaks, M. G.

Flavil TRAVIS to Edith CURRY Issued 23 May 1942 Rites 23 May 1942
W. J. McElroy, M. G.

Wm. T. DRUMRIGHT to Billie DENTON Issued 28 May 1942 Rites 30 May 1942
H. E. BAker, M. G.

John D. GORMAN to Georgia HILLIS Issued 2 Jun 1942 Rites 2 Jun 1942
W. G. McDonough, Jdg.

Edward Price SMITH to Leona GREEN Issued 20 Jun 1942 Rites 26 Jun 1942
A. E. Curtis, J. P.

Marion Thomas MULLICAN to Connie Cleo WILLIAMS Issued 25 Jun 1942 Rites 27 Jun
T. Q. Martin, M. G.

James Thos. TURNER to Alene CARTER Issued 26 Jun 1942 Rites 26 Jun 1942
T. Q. Martin, M. G.

Charles D. DIBRELL to Mary Clay LEIPER Issued 29 Jun 1942 Rites 30 Jun 1942
H. E. BAker, M. G.

Robert LANCE to Josephine FERRELL Issued 7 Jul 1942 Rites 7 Jul 1942
W. G. McDonough, Jdg.

James BOULDIN to Ruby CARTER Issued 10 Jul 1942 Rites 10 Jul 1942
P. N. Moffitt, Jdg.

Thomas J. NEWMAN to Billie Margaret MELTON Issued 11 Jul 1942 Rites 11 Jul 1942
P. N. Moffitt, Jdg.

Charlie GREEN to Sallie Carolyn VAUGHAN Issued 15 Aug 1942 Rites 15 Jun 1942
C. W. Cecil, M. G.

John Michael ADEN to Marie Ionah SCHWAB Issued 17 Aug 1942 Rites 18 Aug 1942
A. J. Van Wyk, M. G.

Eulous MARTIN (C) to Juanita STUBBLEFIELD (C) Issued 29 Aug 1942 Rites 29 Aug
A. L. Guerard, M. G.

Clifton PACK to Bobbie ADAMS Issued 5 Sep 1942 Rites 5 Sep 1942
J. J. Morotn, M. G.

J. O. DIXON, Jr. (C) to Mildred C. FIELDS Issued 8 Sep 1942 Rites 11 Sep
M. M. League, M. G.

Oliver DAVIS to Edna CHRISTIAN Issued 17 Sep 1942 Rites 17 Sep 1942
W. M. Wood, M. G.

Willis DILLON to Pauline WINNETT Issued 18 Sep 1942 Rites 19 Sep 1942
H.C. Wakefield, M. G.

Orley WEBB to Dorothy COWDEN Issued 19 Sep 1942 Rites 19 Sep 1942
E. L. Smothers, M. G.

Robert T. GHOLSON to Laura Mae HATCHER Issued 19 Sep 1942 Rites 19 Sep 1942
H. E. BAker, M. G.

Dennie N. GILL to Tennie SIMMONS Issued 26 Sep 1942 Rites 26 Sep 1942
T. Q. Martin, M. G.

Eli F. PIERCE to Pearl BAIN Issued 3 Oct 1942 Rites 3 Oct 1942
J. C. McGee, Jdg.

Robt. Hudson WOMACK to Mary Eliz. DUCKWORTH Issued 5 Oct 1942 Rites 8 Oct 1942
T. Q. Martin, M. G.

J. M. McDOUGAL to Myra MEARS Issued 5 Oct 1942 Rites 5 Oct 1942
J. C. McGee, Jdg.

Irving PATTON to Sallie Denton PATTON Issued 5 Oct 1942 Rites 5 Oct 1942
J. C. McGee, Jdg

Jasper BOREN to Lois Dawn BLAIR Issued 17 Oct 1942 Rites 18 Oct 1942
A. R. R. Mc Garven, M. G.

Robert MELTON to Thelma NELSON Issued 17 Oct 1942 Rites 17 Oct 1942
W. J. McElroy, M. G.

Paris BOTTOMS to Gladys HEATHERLY Issued 31 Oct 1942 Rites 31 Oct 1942
F. L. Kirby, J. P.

Elijah Hale JONES to Lillian Bailey GERWIG Issued 4 Nov 1942 Rites 4 Nov 1942
H. E. BAker, M. G.

Clinton MARTIN (C) to Christine MARTIN (C) Issued 9 Nov 1942 Rites 9 Nov 1942
J. C. McGee, Jdg

Audry CLARK to Perelene MORGAN Issued 14 Nov 1942 Rites 14 Nov 1942
J. C. McGee, Jdg.

Edward TEMPLETON to Emma Lee DAVIS Issued 16 Nov 1942 Rites 16 Nov 1942
J. C. McGee, Jdg.

Jacob F. SIMMONS, Jr. to Bernice DODSON Issued 20 Nov 1942 Rites 20 Nov 1942
H. E. BAker, M. G.

W. V. GLENN to Nora CANTRELL Issued 19 Nov 1942 Rites 19 Nov 1942
B. T. Grissom, J. P.

Leonard SMITH, Jr. to MArie BOYD Issued 21 Nov 1942 Rites 26 Nov 1942
T. J. Wagner, M. G.

Cyrus KEYT to Tennie UNDERWOOD Issued 27 Nov 1942 Rites 28 Nov 1942
J. C. McGee, Jdg

Otis REDMON to Dana SMITH Issued 5 Dec 1942 Rites 5 Dec 1942
J. C. McGee, Jdg.

Nicholas STANISH to Eva CONASTER Issued 21 Dec 1942 Rites 21 Dec 1942
J. C. McGee, Jdg.

Jesse J. MARTIN to Dorothy FREEMAN Issued 22 Dec 1942 Rites 22 dec 1942
J. P. Bilbrey, J. P.

Verl E. PETERSON to Mary KESEY Issued 23 dec 1942 Rites 23 Dec 1942
J. P. Bilbrey, J. P.

Frank HILLIS to Virginia PRATER Issued 23 Dec 1942 Rites 23 dec 1942
F. L. Kirby, J. P.

Norman BRUNDAGE to Ruth BRIXEY Issued 29 Dec 1942 Rites 29 Dec 1942
T. Q. Martin, M. G.

W Horace SWIPES to MArtha SCOTT Issued 30 Dec 1942 Rites 1 JAn 1943
W. B. Snipes, M. G.

Cleo E. JONES to PAULINE LANCE Issued 2 Jan 1943 Rites 2 Jan 1943
E. D. Martin, M. G.

Ernest C. WATTS to Ruth Mable ROMANS Issued 4 Jan 1943 Rites 4 Jan 1943
J. C. McGee, Jdg.

J. M. PINEGAR to MAry Jane LUNA Issued 7 Jan 1943 Rites 7 Jan 1943
J. C. McGee, Jdg.

Jerry K. CARTER to Henrietta WELCH Issued 9 JAn 1943 Rites 9 Jan 1943
H. E. BAker, M. G.

Everette L. McINTIRE to Coe LaJeaune ROYSTER Issued 23 Jan 1943 Rites 23 Jan 1943
H. E. BAker, M. G.

Wm. Thomas GARDNER to Paralee CANTRELL Issued 28 JAn 1943 Rites 28 Jan 1943
J. M. Byron, M. G.

Kenneth R. WRIGHT to Bernice HALEY issued 12 Feb 1943 Rites 12 Feb 1943
H. E. BAker, M. G.

Harden B. HUDSON to Maggie Hale WARREN Issued 16 Feb 1943 Rites 16 Feb 1943
F. J. Winton, J. P.

James Elbert GREENWOOD to Zella HUNTER Issued 19 Mar 1943 Rites 19 Mar 1943
J. C. McGee, Jdg.

Chas. J. CANTRELL to MAGGIE Allene McCORMICK Issued 20 Mar 1943 Rites 20 Mar
R. W. Smartt, Jdg.

Levi COPPINGER to Margaret PELHAM Issued 27 Mar 1943 Rites 27 Mar 1943
A. J. Van Wyk, M. G.

T. R. COLEMAN to Virginia BLANKS Issued 27 MAr 1943 Rites 28 Mar 1943
T. Q. Martin, M. G.

Thomas M. WHITESIDE to Estelle CECIL Issued 1 Apr 1943 Rites 1 Apr 1943
G. W. Cecil, M. G.

Homer O'Brien PEDIGO to Emma Lee ROLLER Issued 2 Apr 1943 Rites 2 Apr 1943
Frank Gilley, M. G.

Wm. H. PIERCE to Margaret SCHNEIDER Issued 6 Apr 1943 Rites 6 Apr 1943
J. C. McGee, Jdg.

Auburn Dale CASEY to Perrile BOGLE Issued 8 Apr 1943 Rites 12 Apr 1943
J. T. Casey, M. G.

Thomas P. CRISCO to Zola HATLEY Issued 8 Apr 1943 Rites 8 Apr 1943
E. L. Smothers, M. G.

Edward Douglas PARKER to Ertis GOLDMAN Issued 1 May 1943 Rites 1 May 1943 E. L. Smothers, M. G.

Edd GANN to Stella Ethelene SAVAGE Issued 13 May 1943 Rites 13 May 1943 J. N. Winnett, J. P.

Otha E. PAYNE to Faye LOCKE Issued 14 May 1943 Rites 15 May 1943 H. E. BAker, M. G.

Everett BROCK, Jr. to Jimmie WOMACK Issued 18 May 1943 Rites 19 May 1943 Granville Tyler, M. G.

Charlie CLENDENON to Leona CURTIS Issued 18 May 1943 Rites 18 May 1943 F. C. Curtis, J. P.

Harry C. DAVIS to Bessie E. WEBB Issued 25 May 1943 Rites 25 May 1943 J. C. McGee, Jdg.

Lonnie ADAMS to Ozell McCORMICK Issued 1 Jun 1943 Rites 1 Jun 1943 W. T. Warren, J. P.

Garnett BRIDGES, Jr. to Dorothy HILLIS Issued 4 Jun 1943 Rites 4 Jun 1943 H. E. BAker, M. G.

James EMBRY to Ina Lee HODGE Issued 5 Jun 1943 Rites 5 Jun 1943 Granville Tyler, M. G.

JAmes TRISLER to Georgia GILBERT Issued 11 Jun 1943 Rites 11 Jun 1943 J. C. McGee, Jdg.

John B. GUIDRY to Mary H. EATON Issued 11 Jun 1943 Rites 11 Jun 1943 F. J. Winton, J. P.

Daniel WEIRSMA to Esther SYDOW Issued 19 Jun 1943 Rites 19 Jun 1943 H. E. BAker, M. G.

John W. SHORTER to Marie BRATCHER Issued 19 Jun 1943 Rites 19 Jun 1943 H. E. BAker, M. G.

john H. McKINNEY to June Talbott ROCHESTER Issued 23 Jun 1943 Rites 23 Jun 1943 E. L. Smothers, M. G.

Sam H. SADLER to Margie WOMACK Issued 20 Jun 1943 Rites 30 Jun 1943 E. L. Smothers, M. G.

T. R. SPENCER to Donnie FERRELL Issued 2 Jul 1943 Rites 2 Jul 1943 F. S. Bentley, Jdg.

Norman D. PHILLIPS to Betty Jo HENEGAR Issued 7 Jul 1943 Rites 10 Jul 1943 E. L. Smothers, M. G.

John Walter TERRY (C) to Priscilla L. COPE (C) Issued 12 Jul 1943 Rites 12 Jul C. Curtis, M. G.

Forest GEYER to DArlene HARGRAVE Issued 17 Jul 1943 Rites 17 Jul 1943 Clinton Gribble, J. P.

Frank T. MAYOTTE to Janette WARRICK Issued 9 Apr 1943 Rites 13 Apr 1943 H. E. BAker, M. G.

Edward C. HAYES to Seible SCRIVNER Issued 10 Apr 1943 Rites 10 Apr 1943 E. L. Smothers, M. G.

Alfred L. STEMLER to Audrey Elaine HILLEGAS Issued 12 Apr 1943 Rites 12 Apr 1943 A. J. VAn Wyk, M. G.

Leroy E. WILLIS to Lucille CAVENDER Issued 15 Apr 1943 Rites 15 Apr 1943 W. M. Wood, M. G.

Clifford J. STORCH to Helen MARSH Issued 15 Apr 1943 Rites 15 Apr 1943 F. J. Winton, J. P.

Irving BERLIN to MARTHA ABBATICCHIO Issued 16 Apr 1943 Rites 16 Apr 1943 F. J. Winton, J. P.

Virgil W. GARRELS to Marie DENNY Issued 16 Apr 1943 Rites 16 Apr 1943 E. L. Smothers, M. G.

Russell WALKER to AllIEREE FOSTER Issued 16 Apr 1943 Rites 16 Apr 1943 J. P. Bilbrey, J. P.

Charles M. BYRD to Myrtle McLean WEBB Issued 16 Apr 1943 Rites 16 Apr 1943 E. L. Smothers, M. G.

Wallace D. CLAUSER to Rosalie McHENRY Issued 17 Apr 1943 Rites 17 Apr 1943 H. E. BAker, M. G.

Orville E. TANGER to Helen STROM Issued 17 Apr 1943 Rites 17 Apr 1943 F. Louis Grafton, Chap.

Clarence COLLETTE to Beatrice DAVIDSON Issued 17 Apr 1943 Rites 17 Apr 1943 T. Q. Martin, M. G.

Davis R. LYBROOK to Frances LYONS Issued 19 Apr 1943 Rites 23 Apr 1943 H.E. BAker, M. G.

Charles CASTLE to Nellie GIBSON Issued 19 Apr 1943 Rites 19 Apr 1943 T. Q. Martin, M. G.

Lyle L. PASCAL to Lavonne NICHOLS Issued 21 Apr 1943 Rites 21 Apr 1943 E. L. Smothers, M. G.

Wilson WOMACK to Dorothy GRIZZELL Issued 22 Apr 1943 Rites 24 Apr 1943 Granville Tyler, M. G.

JAmes R. ROGERS to Velma Edna JACOBS Issued 23 Apr 1943 Rites 23 Apr 1943 F. J. Winton, J. P.

Walter E. BRIGGS to Janet GRISWOLD Issued 23 Apr 1943 Rites 24 Apr 1943 F. J. Winton, J. P.

H. B. GEBHARTT to Ethelda Lane Issued 1 MAy 1943 Rites 1 May 1943 W. E. Miller, M. G.

Clarke RAYMOND to Vollie Belle HASTON Issued 18 Nov 1943 Rites 18 Nov 1943
T. Q. Martin, M. G.

Quim ROGERS to Avis GANN Issued 26 Nov 1943 Rites 26 Nov 1943
F. J. Winton, J. P.

Wm. E. FINE, Jr. to Eileen BREWER Issued 18 .ec 1943 Rites 18 Dec 1943
J. B. Spurlock, M. G.

Clarence Wm. McCARTY to Dorothy Hayden DAVIS Issued 19 Dec 1943 Rites 19 Dec
J. B. Spurlock, M. G.

Wm. G. NECHANICKY to Carroll WOMACK Issued 22 Dec 1943 Rites 22 Dec 1943
James RAyburn, M. G.

Harry Cecil KARNES to Gladys FREEMAN Issued 22 Dec 1943 Rites 23 Dec 1943
T. Q. Martin, M. G.

Robert GREEN to Cansady VAUGHN Issued 24 Dec 1943 Rites 24 Dec 1943
C. W. Cecil, M. G.

Herbert D. HUGHES to Mary Sue SMARTT Issued 28 Dec 1943 Rites 28 Dec 1943
J. C. McGee, Jdg.

Frank MUNCEY to Henry Etta RACKLEY Issued 1 Jan 1944 Rites 1 Jan 1944
Frank Bentley, Jdg.

John Lewis STILES to Mildred Imogene MARTIN Issued 8 JAn 1944 Rites 10 Jan 1944
J. T. Casey, M. G.

Wm. H. SMITH to Laurine DAVIS Issued 11 Jan 1944 Rites 11 Jan 1944
J. B. Spurlock, M. G.

Sidney MEAGER to HAzel MArie LEUDY Issued 25 Jan 1944 Rites 25 Jan 1944
F. J. Winton, J. P.

Fred Murray SAIN to Zada Bell BOULDIN Issued 27 Jan 1944 Rites 27 Jan 1944
Frank Bentley, Jdg.

Escal DOYD to Pearl PANTER Issued 2 Feb 1944 Rites 2 Feb 1944
F. C. Curtis, J. P.

Powell WALLACE to Ella Mildred BRYANT Issued 7 Feb 1944 Rites 7 Feb 1944
J. Cole, M. G.

Elmer Walter HODGES to Bertha Lee FULTS Issued 12 Feb 1944 Rites 12 Feb 1944
R. W. Smartt, Jdg.

Allen Lewis STAMPE to Helen Elaine BAILEY Issued 17 Feb 1944 Rites 17 Feb 1944
J. C. McGee, Jdg

William HAMILTON to Alda ADELL SAVAGE Issued 28 Feb 1944 Rites 28 Feb 1944
F. J. Winton, J. P.

Noble Douglas RHEA to Virginia Jo SMITH Issued 1 Mat 1944 Rites 5 Mar 1944
R. H. Bonner, J. P.

Joe SHOCKLEY (C) to Manilla LUSK (C) Issued 24 Jul 1943 Rites 30 Jul 1943
F. J. Winton, J. P.

Jimmie GRIBBLE to Martha THWEATT Issued 22 Jul 1943 Rites 29 Jul 1943
J. P. Bilbrey, J. P.

Emma LEWIS to Lillian MOORE Issued 31 Jul 1943 Rites 31 Jul 1943
E. L. Smothers, M. G.

Beecher McCOLLUM to Flora SPARKMAN Issued 4 Aug 1943 Rites 4 Aug 9143
I. J. Grizzell, J. P.

Sherman HUDSON to Maude WADE Issued 7 Aug 1943 Rites 7 Aug 1943
J. C. McGee, Jdg.

Paul E. SAGE to Maxine GEORGE issued 14 Aug 1943 Rites 14 Aug 1943
W. H. Owen, M. G.

Will JORDAN to Lillian HALE Issued 21 Aug 1943 Rites 21 Aug 1943
Frank Bentley, Jdg.

Julius WEISSMAN to Enzena GREENE Issued 23 Aug 1943 Rites 28 Aug 1943
H. B. Hunt, M. C.

John Henry PINEGAR to Malissa BLANKENSHIP Issued 28 Aug 1943 Rites 28 Aug 1943
J. P. Bilbrey, J. P.

Raymond GRISSOM to Thelma GREEN Issued 31 Aug 1943 Rites 31 aug 1943
Granville Tyler, M. G.

JAmes Herman STILES to Grace F. FARMER Issued 3 Sep 1943 Rites 3 Sep 1943
H. E. Baker, M. G.

John Albert THOMAS to Floena CUMMINGS Issued 14 Sep 1943 Rites 14 Sep 1943
Frank Bnetley, Jdg.

Elbert L. LOVETT to Willie Mae TERRY Issued 18 Sep 1943 Rites 18 Sep 1943
Frank Bentley, Jdg.

Wm. O. McCORMACK to Millie Frances BOREN Issued 23 Oct 1943 Rites 23 Oct 1943
J. C. McGee, Jdg.

Luther NEWBY to Lizzie ELROD Issued 30 Oct 1943 Rites 31 Oct 1943
M. E. Rhodes, Jr.

Claud EARLS to Mabel NEWMAN Issued 1 Nov 1943 Rites 2 Nov 1943
Tallman Boyd, J. P.

Alonzo SHOOPMAN to Violet FRANKLIN Issued 6 Nov 1943 Rites 6 Nov 1943
J. B. Spurlock, M. G.

Donald WALTON to Mildred POTTER Issued 6 Nov 1943 Rites 7 Nov 1943
M. KURFEES Pullias, M. G.

DAvid E. SNIDER to Ruth L. FARMER Issued 13 Nov 1943 Rites 13 Nov 1943
J. C. McGee, Jdg.

Cecil MULLICAN to Sarah Ann RIGSBY Issued 16 Nov 1943 Rites 18 Nov 1943
Frank Bentley, Jdg.

Willie A. CANTRELL to Eula CHISAM Issued 14 Mar 1944 Rites 1 Apr 1944
J. C. McGee, Jdg.

Marion A. BOULDIN to Ruby PERRY Issued 2 Mar 1944 Rites 2 Mar 1944
F. C. Curtis, J. P.

Andy M. McCLURG to Olga MAY COMER Issued 10 Mar 1944 Rites 10 Mar 1944
F. S. Bentley, Jdg.

Joe B. MAXWELL to Mattie Lee HENNESSEE issued 10 Mar 1944 Rites 12 Mar 1944
C. H. Riddle, J. P.

Edgar W. WALLING, Jr. to Mary Eliz. WOMACK Issued 15 Mar 1943 Rites 16 Mar 1943
D. M. Carhart, M. G.

Kenneth COLLIER to Clara E. McGREGOR Issued 21 Mar 1944 Rites 25 Mar 1944
T. Q. Martin, M. G.

Miley C. BELL to Louella HALEY issued 25 Mar 1944 Rites 26 Mar 1944
H. J. Wilson, J. P.

Wm. B. BRANDON to Billie West BALDWIN Isued 6 Apr 1944 Rites 9 Apr 1944
B. H. Brandon, M. G.

James Estill PEPPER to Wilma L. WISEMAN Issued 6 Apr 1944 Rites 9 Apr 1944
W. H. Owen, M. G.

Grover MCMINN to Frieda HIMMELBERGER Issued 15 Apr 1944 Rites 15 Apr 1944
J. B. Spurlock, M. G.

Robert D. TARR to Dorothy BLANKENSHIP Issued 18 Apr 1944 Rites 19 Apr 1944
E. L. Smotherman, M. G.

Oscar CANTRELL to Myrtle PRATER Issued 22 Apr 1944 Rites 22 Apr 1944
F. S. Bentley, Jdg.

James RUSSELL to Roberta BLANKS Issued 22 Apr 1944 Rites 22 Apr 1944
F. L. Kirby, J. P.

Ira HALE to Evelyn YATES Issued 6 May 1944 Rites 6 May 1944
F. S. Bentley, Jdg.

Bill WILLIAMS to Edrie HUDSON Issued 30 MAy 1944 Rites 3 Jun 1944
J. B. Spurlock, M. G.

Charles LANCE to Stella Mae WOMACK issued 3 Jun 1944 Rites 3 Jun 1944
W. E. Miller, M. G.

Marshall COPELAND to Juanita BELL Issued 14 Jun 1944 rites 16 Jun 1944
W. E. Miller, M. G.

Enoch James AINIP to Ruby Lee WALKER Issued 16 Jun 1944 Rites 17 Jun 1944
J. C. McGee, Jdg.

Roy Clayton BATTLES to Ollie Lee McGEE Issued 21 Jun 1944 Rites 21 Jun 1944
J. C. McGee, Jdg.

Burger MOFFITT to Pauline McCormick Issued 23 Jun 1944 Rites 23 Jun 1944
F. S. Bentley, Jdg.

T. H. HUSSEY to Nettie Ray LYLES Issued 15 Jul 1944 Rites 16 Jul 1944
T. J. Carrick, M. G.

Charlie Robert ROMANS to Nellie Mai CRIM Issued 18 Jul 1944 Rites 18 Jul 1944
F. S. Bentley, Jdg.

Isaac BYARS to Evelyn BOYD Issued 22 Jul 1944 Rites 23 Jul 1944
T. Q. Martin, M. G.

Hobart V. MASSEY, Jr. to Queen Otelia CURTIS Issued 26 Jul 1944 Rites 27 Jul
T. Q. Martin, M. G.

James M. DODD to Della GRIFFIN Issued 28 Jul 1944 Rites 28 Jul 1944
R. L. Whitlock, M. G.

Jim R. MOORE to Lessie JOHNSON Issued 8 Aug 1944 Rites 8 Aug 1944
W. E. Miller, M. G.

Robert Avery BOYD to Bobbie G. TURNER Issued 15 Aug 1944 Rites 19 Aug 1944
Abe Curtis, J. P.

Orvel Earl WEBB to Emma Pearl HOLT Issued 2 Sep 1944 Rites 2 Sep 1944
J. C. McGee, Jdg.

Paul WARD to Wilma Jean MARTIN Issued 9 Sep 1944 Rites 9 Sep 1944
E. S. WAllace, J. P.

Earl POND, SR. to Clara HENDRICKSON Issued 9 Sep 1944 Rites 10 Sep 1944
W. J. Thompson, M. G.

Elbert Lee MASON to Ida Mae PRICE Issued 11 Sep 1944 Rites 11 Sep 1944
F. S. Bentley, Jdg.

Lonnie GREEN to Novella YOUNG Issued 27 Sep 1944 rites 27 Sep 1944
J. C. McGee, Jdg.

James Edward WOODLEE (C) to Emma J. WOODARD (C) Issued 30 Sep 1944 Rites 1 Oct
J. E. Turner, M. G.

Olyn M. TAYLOR to Juaanita GILBERT Issued 14 Oct 1944 Rites 14 Oct 1944
J. B. Spurlock, M. G.

Earl ARLEDGE to Mae SMITH Issued 24 Oct 1944 Rites 25 Oct 1944
H. V. Massey, M. G.

Wm. S. WOMACK to Frances EVINS Issued 26 Oct 1944 Returned - Not Solemnized

John Jacob WARREN to Irene CRAVEN Issued 3 Nov 1944 Rites 3 Nov 1944
T. Q. Martin, M. G.

Oliver BROWN (C) to Maggie Elnora HOPKINS (C) Issued 4 Nov 1944 Rites 4 Nov
J. E. Turner, M. G.

James WARE to Martha E. HILLIS Issued 4 Nov 1944 Rites 4 Nov 1944—
Frank Gilley, M. G.

George W. TEMPLETON to Novella HOLLAND Issued 24 Mar 1945 Rites 31 Mar 1945
F. S. Bentley, Jdg.

George H. O'NEAL to Lorena SEAMONS Issued 1 Mar 1945 Rites 1 Mar 1945
M. Kurfees Pullias, M. G.

Charlie HENDERSON to Mary CLAYBOURNE Issued 31 Mar 1945 Rites 31 Mar 1945
J. R. Grove, J. P.

Herbert HOLT to Mary Eliz. BROWN Issued 7 Apr 1945 Rites 7 Apr 1945
F. S. Bentley, Jdg.

Ezra A. MILLER to Bennie Mae WARD Issued 19 May 1945 Rites 19 May 1945
F. S. Bentley, Jdg.

Robert Lee BROWN to Wilma Opal JOINES Issued 21 MAY 1945 Rites 21 may 1945
T. Q. Martin, M. G.

James R. KEEFAUVER to Sarah QUINN Issued 4 Jun 1945 Rites 5 Jun 1945
E. L. Smothers, M. G.

John JAmes DUCK to Betty Jean GRIBBLE Issued 18 Jun 1945 Rites 18 Jun 1945
E. L. Smothers, M. G.

Herbert Randall HAYES to Robbie Jean MITCHELL Issued 19 Jun 1945 Rites 19 Jun
E. T. Brazzle, J. P.

Verble NABORS to Brownie PRATER Issued 20 Jun 1945 Rites 23 Jun 1945
H. B. Hunt, M. G.

James A. ROGERS to Sarah Ann SMITH Issued 23 Jun 1945 Rites 24 Jun 1945
Granvile Tyler, M. G.

Bill PRATER to Lela Mai STONER Issued 29 Jun 1945 Rites 1 Jul 1945
T. Q. Martin, M. G.

Edd L. JONES to Mary WATSON Issued 3 Jul 1945 Rites 4 Jul 1945
J. N. Winnett, J. P.

Herman L. SHOCKLEY to Bertha L. MARTIN Issued 5 Jul 1945 Rites 5 Jul 1945
J. C. McGee, Jdg.

Jim Alta HUGHES to Mazel Lee THOMAS Issued 21 Jun 1945 Rites 22 Jun 1945
Chas. T. Powell, M. G.

Glenn BYARS to Ola Mae GILLENTINE Issued 30 Jul 1945 Rites 30 Jul 1945
J. C. McGee, Jdg.

Pleas TAYLOR to Martha FRAZIER Issued 25 Aug 1945 Rites 27 Aug 1945
R. W. Smartt, Jdg.

Geo. Edward MELTON to Mary Eliz. HILL Issued 29 Aug 1945 Rites 29 Aug 1945
F. J. Winton, J. P.

Arrie C. HOLLAND to Bessie BURCH Issued 8 Sep 1945 Rites 8 Sep 1945
F. S. Bentley, Jdg.

Ira Thomas WARE to Betty RAYMON Issued 17 Sep 1945 Rites 17 Sep 1945
Abe Qurtis, J. P.

Erbie RIGSBY to Robie TALLANT Issued 8 Nov 1944 Rites 8 Nov 1944
W. M. Rowland, J. P.

Robt. Melvin MEADOWS to Daisy Ruth DENNIS Issued 11 Nov 1944 Rites 11 Nov 1944
Theodore Hanner, J. P.

Claud JONES to Virgil CANTRELL Issued 15 Nov 1944 Rites 15 Nov 1944
J. C. McGee, Jdg.

Howard GREENE to Alma CAMPBELL Issued 15 Nov 1944 Rites 18 Nov 1944
H. C. Green, M. G.

Lindsey E. MASON to Bessie Lee WOMACK Issued 15 Nov 1944 Rites 15 Nov 1944
R. W. Smartt, Jdg.

Joe Beecher MITCHELL (C) to Margret PINCHON (C) Issued 24 Nov 1944 Rites 24 Nov
A. L. Guerard, M. G.

Paul WILCOX to Rowena SPARKMAN Issued 8 Dec 1944 Rites 8 Dec 1944
J. C. McGee, Jdg.

Clayton L. DYKES to Mable L. MILNER Issued 13 Dec 1944 Rites 14 Dec 1944
J. C. McCcc, Jdg.

John O'NEAL to Julia FULTS Issued 16 Dec 1944 Rites 16 Dec 1944
J. C. McGee, Jdg.

Grady Wm. MULLICAN to Carrie DUGGIN Issued 19 Dec 1944 Rites 19 Dec 1944
J. N. Winnett, J. P.

Orvil B. WISEMAN to Beatrice McGEE Issued 20 Dec 1944 Rites 24 Dec 1944
J. T. Casey, M. G.

William H. HOLLIS to Wavie RAINS Issued 20 Dec 1944 Rites 20 Dec 1944
T. Q. Martin, M. G.

Floyd NUNLEY to Ella STEMBRIDGE Issued 28 Dec 1944 Rites 28 Dec 1944
J. C. McGee, Jdg.

Werdell HARRISON to Evelyn TUCK Issued 30 Dec 1944 Rites 30 Dec 1944
H. B. Hunt, M. G.

Fred C. PARKER to Anna SMITH Issued 26 Jan 1945 Rites 26 Jan 1945
I. J. Grizzle, J. P.

Jesse A. DIXON to Latha M. FULTS Issued 3 Feb 1945 Rites 3 Feb 1945
F. S. Bentley, Jdg.

T. C. McGEE to Eula SMITHSON Issued 14 Feb 1945 Rites 14 Feb 1945
J. C. MCGee, Jdg.

James C. HARVEY to Aleen TATE Issued 21 Feb 1945 Rites 21 Feb 1945
E. L. Smothers, M. G.

John H. FERRELL to Dorothy GUNNELS Issued 27 Feb 1945 Rites 27 Feb 1945
R. W. Smartt, Jdg.

Ernest E. LaFOLLETTE to Dell Zell TALLEY Issued 22 Sep 1945 Rites 22 Sep 1945
J. C. McGee, Jdg.

Milton MILLER to Lucille BOREN Issued 29 Sep 1945 Rites 29 Sep 1945
E. L. Smothers, M. G..

Robert V. TERRY to Sara Eliz. CANTRELL Issued 20 Oct 1945 Rites 21 Oct 1945
J. B. Spurlock, M. G.

Kurley MYERS to Lucille MILLER Issued 20 Oct 1945 Riets 21 Oct 1945
J. D. Jones, M. G.

Joe Thomas RAMSEY (C) to Lola SHEPPARD (C) Issued 2 Nov 1945 Rites 2 Nov 1945
J. C. McGee, Jdg.

Leonard Woodrow GLENN to Mildred Inez GRIBBLE Issued 7 Nov 1945 Rites 10 Nov
G. H. O'Neal, M. G.

Raymond Earl LIBEY to Jimmie Loreda PORTERFIELD Issued 7 Nov 1945 Rites 8 Nov
E. L. Smothers, M. G.

Bennett LAMKIN to Ellen ROGERS Issued 8 Nov 1945 Rites 8 Nov 1945
Thos. F. Harrison

Earl C. SMITH to Christine CALDWELL Issued 9 Nov 1945 Rites Nov 1945
F. S. Bentley, Jdg.

Quim C. SMITH to Ona Lee ROBERTS Issued 10 Nov 1945 Rites 10 Nov 1945
J. C. McGee, Jdg.

Wm. Davis COX to Annie Gladys HOLLIS Issued 10 Nov 1945 Rites 10 Nov 1945
Allen Phy, M. G.

Elmer WILSON to Margaret SOUTHARD Issued 28 Nov 1945 Rites 28 Nov 1945
Allen Phy, M. G.

Eugene H. BOOHER to Joyce SMITH Issued 30 Nov 1945 Rites 30 Nov 1945
E. L. Smothers, M. G.

Willard SIMONS to Hazel Lee GUNTER issued 8 Dec 1945 Rites 8 Dec 1945
J. C. McGee, Jdg.

Walter Parker HARDING to Beatrice BAKER Issued 10 Dec 1945 Rites 11 Dec 1945
T. Q. Martin, M. G.

Euclid HITCHCOCK to Mary M. SHACKELFORD Issued 14 Dec 1945 Rites 14 Dec 1945
W. H. Huddleston, M. G.

Harris Edward GRAHAM to Ethel O. FARMER Issued 15 Dec 1945 Rites 15 Dec 1945
J. C.McGee, Jdg.

Thurman HOOPER to Jammye ALLEN Issued 17 Dec 1945 Rites 17 Dec 1945
J. C. McGee, Jdg.

John T. MARTIN to Gladys Mae FREEMAN Issued 20 Dec 1945 Rites 20 Dec 1945
J. C. McGee, Jdg.

Wm. M. OSMENT to Nancy VINSON Issued 21 Dec 1945 Rites Dec 1945
Allen Phy, M. G.

Thomas O. PARKER to Velma Ray PAGE Issued 22 Dec 1945 Rites 24 Dec 1945
I. J. Grizzell, J. P.

Carl DUNCAN to Opal BUMBALOUGH Issued 22 Dec 1945 Rites 24 Dec 1945
J. B. Spurlock, M. G.

Charlie Harris EARLS to Annie Leta HOLT Issued 22 Dec 1945 Not Returned
E. L. Smothers, M. G.

John Lee SMITH to Frances HILL Issued 24 dec 1945 Rites 24 dec 1945
D. M. Carhart, M. G.

JohnHenry WHITTIER to Margaret D. DANCE Issued 26 dec 1945 Rites 26 dec 1945
J. B. Spurlock, M. G.

George W. Miller to Irene GRIBBLE Issued 2 Jan 1946 Rites 2 Jan 1946
F. J. Winton, J. P.

Donald E. CAROTHERS to Audrey Lee SANDERS Issued 5 Jan 1946 Rites 9 JAn 1946
T. Q. Martin, M. G.

RAy BYARS to Walene MARTIN Issued 11 Jan 1946 Rites 12 Jan 1946
T. Q. Martin, M. G.

Lonnie HILL to Audrey COPE Issued 12 Jan 1946 Rites 12 JAn 1946
E. L. Smothers, M. G.

Kelly MARTIN to Ila Mae CROWE Issued 17 Jan 1946 Rites 17 Jan 1946
Fred Walker, M. G.

James BEARD to Roberta SMITH Issued 26 Jan 1946 Rites 27 JAn 1946
J. R. Grove, J. P.

Alvin MARTIN (C) to Eddie KEEL (C) Issued 26 Jan 1946 Rites 27 Jan 1946
Ben Bates, M. G.

Chas. Thomas BARLOW to Georgeia Mae CARTWRIGHT Issued 26 Jan 1946 Rites 26 Jan
Harold B. Bowe, Jr., M. G.

Floyd K. PAGE to Era E. DAVIDSON Issued 30 Jan 1946 Rites 2 Feb 1946
F. S. Bentley, Jdg.

Carl NEWBY to Lucille PERRY Issued 8 Feb 1946 Rites 10 Feb 1946
Allen Phy, M. G.

Herman SHELTON o Virginia BLUE Issued 9 Feb 1946 Rites 14 Feb 1946
J. C. McGee, Jdg.

Tommie H. DIXON to Dora BONNER Issued 13 Feb 1946 rites 14 feb 1946
C. C. Dickson, M. G.

Robert PAYNE to Ruth GUNTER Issued 15 Feb 1946 Rites 16 Feb 1946
J. C. McGee, Jdg.

John Franklin HILLIS to Edna Lee PARRISH Issued 16 Feb 1946 Rites 21 Feb 1946
F. S. Bentley, Jdg.

Robert CAGLE to Shirley DAVIS Issued 1 Mar 1946 Rites 3 Mar 1946
J. B. Spurlock, M. G.

Niles Thoams MCGEE to Bessie Lee MITCHELL issued 16 Feb 1946 Rites 16 Feb 1946
J. C. McGee, Jdg.

George Huston THAXTON to Daisy Lee BUNCH Issued 16 Feb 1946 Rites 16 Feb
J. R. Grove, J. P.

Robert ROWAN (C) to Mary Ann SMITH (C) Issued 1 mar 1946 Rites 2 Mar 1946
G. T. Speaks, M. G.

France FULTS to Martha M. FULTS Issued 2 Mar 1946 Rites 2 Mar 1946
J. C. McGee, Jdg.

Norman E. DURAIN to Waudene PORTERFIELD Issued 15 Mar 1946 Rites 17 Mar 1946
E. L. Smothers, M. G.

PAul H. OFFICER (C) to Mildred E. YORK (C) Issued 18 Mar 1946 Rites 18 MAr 1946
J. E. Turner, M. G.

J. D. NUNLEY to Lillie Mae McBRIDE Issued 5 Apr 1946 Rites 5 Apr 1946
J. T. Casey, M. G.

George MYERS to Irene ROLLINS Issued 1 Apr 1946 Rites 10 Apr 1946
R. W. Smartt, Jdg.

Phillip B. MOFFITT to Nina HALEY Issued 10 Apr 1946 Rites 11 Apr 1946
J. B. Spurlock, M.G.

Isaac Randle JONES to Mary Helen WOMACK Issued 16 Apr 1946 Rites 17 Apr 1946
E. L. Smothers, M. G.

Chas. Edward CANTRELL to Beatrice HALE Issued 20 Apr 1946 Rites 27 Apr 1946
R. H. HALe, M. G.

Jos. Tillman ALLEN to Bobbie V. STONE Issued 22 Apr 1946 Rites 22 Apr 1946
C. M. Gleaves, M. G.

Thurman DRIVER to Edna GREEN Issued 29 Apr 1946 Rites 29 Apr 1946
J. C. McGee, Jdg.

Clifford A. KINGSBURY to May Cannon SMITH Issued 4 May 1946 Rites 5 May
J. B. Spurlock, M. G.

Marion Thomas WARD to Winona P. MARTIN Issued 9 May 1946 Rites 9 May
J. C. McGee, Jdg.

Chas. Clifford RAINS to Louella McGEE Issued 10 May 1946 Rites 10 May 1946
J. C. Sandusky, M. G.

Benton W. LOGAN to Sylvia BORNSTEIN Issued 11 May 1946 Rites 11 May 1946
J. C. McGee, Jdg.

Brown Ramsey MOORE to Ethel DUGAN Issued 22 May 1946 Rites 25 May 1946
Fred Walker, M. G.

Elijah Rhea to Hazle Florine JONES Issued 25 May 1946 Rites 25 MAy 1946
Albert A. Lance, M. G.

Thomas A. HENDRICKSON to Evelyn L. BRYAN Issued 31 May 1946 1946 Rites 8 Jun 1946
W. J. Thompson, M. G.

Walter STEELE to Alice CARR Issued 1 Jun 1946 Rites 1 Jun 1946
J. C. McGee, Jdg.

Herbert C. KELLY to Agnes ELMORE Issued 3 Jun 1946 Rites 6 Jun 1946
J. E. Turner, M. G.

Lloyd SMITH to Wanda EVANS Issued 10 Jun 1946 Rites 15 Jun 1946
E. L. Smothers, M. G.

Jmaes Clayton ADCOCK to Dorothy Cathaleen GREEN Issued 14 Jun 1946 Rites 14 Jun 1946
T. Q. Martin, M. G.

Chas. Julius PRATER to Alice G. ARMENTROUT Issued 15 Jun 1946 Rites 15 Jun 1946
T. Q. Martin, M. G.

John Paul SLAYDEN to Sara Jean COLVILLE Issued 17 Jun 1946 Rites 20 Jun 1946
E. H. Hoover, M. G.

Cecil Bee GILLEY to Carolyn B. CROWE Issued 19 Jun 1946 Rites 20 Jun 1946
F. L. Smothers, M. G.

Urby Franklin HINES to Mary Etta HILLIS Issued 22 Jun 1946 Rites 22 Jun 1946
F. S. Bentley, Jdg.

Willie HAWKINS to Edna Mae HOLLAND Issued 22 Jun 1946 Rites 22 Jun 1946
F. S. Bentley, Jdg.

Leland A. NORRIS, Jr. to Dora Hayden HENEGAR Issued 28 Jun 1946 Rites 30 Jun 1946
T. Q. Martin, M. G.

Eugene H. POLLARD to Wavie B. TEETERS Issued 29 Jun 1946 Rites 29 Jun 1946
F. S. Bentley, Jdg.

Charles L. SMITH to Dorotha Jo EVANS Issued 2 Jul 1946 Rites 4 Jul 1946
E. L. Smothers, M. G.

Wm. M. KEELING to Nancy Jane HASTON Issued 9 Jul 1946 Rites 29 Sep 1946
Allen Phy, M. G.

Wm. J. TAYLOR to Jessie Ruth TAYLOR Issued 10 Jul 1946 Rites 10 Jul 1946
J. B. Spurlock, M. G.

Enoch WILLIAMS to Joanna MADDUX Issued 30 Jul 1946 rites 31 Jul 1946
J. C. McGee, Jdg.

Eudeen WEBB to Helen PIRTLE Issued 30 Jul 1946 Rites 3 Aug 1946
J. B. Spurlock, M. G.

Robert K. JORDAN to Mary DELANEY Issued 31 Jul 1946 Rites 2 Aug 1946
T. Q. Martin, M. G.

Joe HOLDER to Willie B. FULTS Issued 8 Aug 1946 Rites 10 Aug 1946
H. M. Hunt, M. G.

James M. REDMON to Crystal BROWN Issued 9 Aug 1946 Rites 10 Aug 1946 J. C. McGee, Jdg.

James Robt. HOOPER to Ora BARNES Issued 17 Aug 1946 Rites 17 Aug 1946 J. C. McGee, Jdg.

Lloyd BATES to Hattie SOUTHARD issued 17 Aug 1946 Rites 17 Aug 1946 W. J. thompson, M. G.

George SIMMONS to John Ann MELTON Issued 21 Aug 1946 Rites 22 Aug 1946 J. B. Spurlock, M. G.

Alton BARNES to William KILLIAN Issued 23 Aug 1946 Rites 23 Aug 1946 J. C. McGee, Jdg.

John L. BOULDIN to Juanita JONES Issued 30 Aug 1946 Rites 31 Aug 1946 D. P. Myers, J. P.

Edwin C. HAMMER to Virginia SLATTON Issued 4 Sep 1946 Rites 6 Sep 1946 T. Q. Martin, M. G.

Carl F. SOUTHARD to Annie Mae SAIN Issued 6 Sep 1946 Rites 7 Sep 1946 Albert A. Gonce, M. G.

Lloyd M. GEORGE to Margie Dee SMITH Issued 7 Sep 1946 Rites 7 Sep 1946 J. N. Winnett, J. P.

Andy Landon WAGNER to Nita MARTIN Issued 9 Sep 1946 Rites 11 Sep 1946 Allen PHY, M. G.

Lee Roy BARRETT to Violet Va. STARKEY Issued 14 Sep 1946 rites 14 Sep 1946 J. C. McGee, Jdg.

Fount Ezekial PITTS, Jr. to Jonnie Bailey HALEY Issued 18 Sep 1946 Rites 22 Sep W. H. Owens, M. G.

Robert C. HOLLANDSWORTH to Irene Jessie BONNER Issued 21 Sep 1946 Rites 21 Feb E. T. Brazzell, M. G.

Robt. Howard BRAN to Florence Helen RICH Issued 27 Sep 1946 Rites 27 Sep 1946 J. Vernon Rich, M. G.

Essel E. HARTBARGER to Lois Mason RICH Issued 27 Sep 1946 Rites 27 Sep 1946 J. Vernon Rich, M. G.

Edward CAMPBELL to Pauline KIRBY Issued 28 Sep 1946 rites 28 Sep 1946 W. H. Owens, M. G.

Howard E. LOCKE to Jo Ruth MULLICAN Issued 4 Oct 1946 Rites 13 Oct 1946 Granville Tyler, M. G.

T. R. NUNLEY to Lorene CLARK Issued 12 Oct 1946 rites 12 Oct 1946 J. C. McGee, Jdg.

Marvin E. KELL to Thelma NEAL Issued 18 Oct 1946 Rites 19 Oct 1946 E. L. Smothers, M. G.

Wilburn E. WILSON to Nora Mae TAYLOR Issued 19 Oct 1946 Rites 19 Oct J. T. Casey, M. G.

Ellis D. MALONE to Edith McLEMORE Issued 20 Oct 1946 Rites 20 Oct 1946 E. L. Smothers, M. G.

Herbert Algot JOHNSON to Drucie Mae BOREN Issued 31 Oct 1946 Rites 31 Oct 1946 T. Q. Martin, M. G.

John Edward MEADOWS to Edna PASSONS Issued 15 Nov 1946 VOIDED

John Denis MULLICAN to Bernita HIGGINBOTHAM Issued 23 Nov 1946 Rites 23 Nov E. L. Smothers, M. G.

Fred LOCKE (C) to Maggie M. WOOD (C) Issued 30 Nov 1946 Rites 2 Dec 1946 J. C. McGee, Jdg.

Everett WALLING to Tomy J. SAIN Issued 9 Dec 1946 Rites 10 Dec 1946 W. H. Owen, M. G.

Fred E. JORDAN to Helen ROGERS Issued 9 Dec 1946 Rites 9 Dec 1946 F. S. Bentley, Jdg.

A. J. SMITH, Jr. to Clemma Grace MYERS Issued 14 dec 1946 Rites 14 dec 1946 T. Q. Martin, M. G.

Wm. Robert HORTON to Billie Roy REEDER Issued 14 Dec 1946 Rites 22 Dec 1946 W. H. Moss, M. G.

Roy Lee PAGE to Oneida DONALDSON ISsued 16 Dec 1946 Rites 21 Dec 1946 I. J. Grizzell, J. P.

Wm. Thomas GARDNER to Ona Ann HAVRON Issued 19 Dec 1946 Rites 19 Dec 1946 J. C. Sandusky, M. G.

James A. SMITH to Charlene MAYES Issued 21 Dec 1946 Rites 24 Dec 1946 T. Q. Martin, M. G.

Richard E. SOLOMON (C) to Ernestine LOCKE (C) Issued 21 Dec 1946 Rites 24 Dec Ben Bates, M. G,

Bill E. HENDRIXSON to Josephine DAVIS Issued 24 Dec 1946 rites 28 Dec 1946 W. H. Moss, M. G.

Emmett TURNER to Mary WILLIAMS Issued 28 Dec 1946 Rites 30 Dec 1946 J. C. McGee, M. G.

Alton CANTRELL to Ruth ROBINSON Issued 2 JAn 1947 Rites 3 JAn 1947 H. M. RAndall, M. G.

Will JORDAN to Frances Rita HOBBS Issued 4 Jan 1947 Rites 4 Jan 1947 F. S. Bentley, Jdg.

Frank C. MARTIN to Helen P. WEST Issued 18 JAN 1947 Rites 18 Jan 1947 E. L. Smothers, M. G.

Wm. Lawrence MARTIN (C) to Nannie B. RAMSEY (C) Issued 25 Jan 1947 Rites 25 Jan
W. R. Smith, M.G.

Max BURNSTINE to Josephine BURNSTINE Issued 25 JAn 1947 Rites 26 Jan 1947
T. Q. Martin, M. G.

George Henry TREECE to MAude BLACK Issued 28 Jan 1947 Rites 30 Jan 1947
R. W. Smartt, Jdg.

JAmes Elbert RUTLEDGE to Charity Pearl BOULDIN Issued 1 Feb 1947 Rites 1 Feb
D. P. Myers, J. P.

Ray KINSLOW to Willie Curtis PARTIN Issued 7 Feb 1947 Rites 14 Feb 1947
Allen Phy, M. G.

Fred C. BILES to Josephine STUBBLEFIELD Issued 21 Feb 1947 Rites 21 Feb
E. L. Smothers, M. G.

Henry Webb JONES to Vivial CHASTAIN Issued 22 Feb 1947 Rites 8 Mar 1947
E. L. Smothers, M. G.

Billy Akers MULLICAN to Dorothy Grey JONES Issued 24 Feb 1947 Rites 28 Feb 1947
Granville Tyler, M. G.

Tom G. NORTHCUTT to Susie Pearl REYNOLDS Issued 7 Mar 1947 Rites 9 Mar 1947
D. P. Myers, J. P.

Charlie Hershel TURNER to Roberta CRAWLEY Issued 8 Mar 1947 Rites 8 Mar 1947
E. L. Smothers, M. G.

Lester Cordell FRANKS to Era Mae WEBB Issued 22 Mar 1947 Rites 22 Mar 1947
Allen Phy, M. G.

Clayton Neal GRIBBLE to Betty June DOVE Issued 26 Mar 1947 Rites 29 Mar 1947
Wymer Wiser

Clifton SHARPE, Jr. to FAy SIMONS Issued 29 Mar 1947 Rites 29 Mar 1947
H. M. Randall, M. G.

Leveorn HALE to Margaret R. TAYLOR Issued 29 Mar 1947 Rites 5 Apr 1947
J. V. Jones, M. G.

Charles SMITH, Jr. to Beatrice STILES Issued 4 Apr 1947 Rites 5 Apr 1947
Allen Phy, M. G.

Phillip EARHART to Katheryn M. BROWN Issued 11 Apr 1947 Rites12 Apr 1947
T. J. Wagner, M. G.

James Riichard McMILLEN to Eula M. HOWARD Isseud 13 Apr 1947 Rites 13 Apr 1947
C. S. McMillen, M. G.

JAmes Lewis HENEGAR to LAurine MITCHELL Issued 21 Apr 1947 Rites 21 Apr 1947
G. T. Speaks, M. G.

William Van GLENN to Martha JONES Issued 19 Apr 1947 Rites 19 Apr 1947
E. R. Lattle, M. G.

Claude M. SWINNEY to Bernice SMITH Issued 1 May 1947 Rites 1 MAY 1947
E. L. Smothers, M. G.

Willard YORK to Adredia LUNA Issued 1 May 1947 Rites 4 May 1947
E. L. Smothers, M. G.

Wm. Henry CATHCART to Melba C. CLENDENON Issued 16 May 1947 Rites 17 May 1947
Luke GIBBS, M. G.

Buford HUNTER (C) to Helen L. WOODS (C) Issued 19 May 1947 Riets 23 May 1947
A. L. Guerard, M. G.

Almous RAMAGE to Nina PRATER Issued 23 May 1947 Rites 24 May 1947
J. C. McGee, Jdg.

Alfred H. BOYD to Willie Boyd Issued 24 May 1947 Rites 24 May 1947
J. C. McGee, Jdg.

Clarence E. SAFLEY to Elsie HILLIS Issued 21 May 1947 Riets 1 Jun 1947
J. C. McGee, Jdg.

James E. BROWN to Beulah Mae NESTER Issued 2 Jun 1947 Rites 2 Jun 1947
H. H. Scullins, M. G.

Robert D. FAIRBANKS to Grace GARRETSON Issued 2 Jun 1947 Rites 4 Jun 1947
W. H. Moss, M. G.

Charles B. LAWRENCE to Ella Mae WOODS Issued 11 Jun 1947 Rites 12 Jun 1947
D. M. CARHART, M. G.

HArold Brown MAYFIELD to Dorothy E. PARSLEY Issued 13 Jun 1947 Rites 14 Jun 1947
E. L. Smothers, M. G.

Douglas W. MOYERS to Nettie A. WALLING Issued 13 Jun 1947 Rites 16 Jun 1947
W. H. Moss, M. G.

Jim Houston KILLIAN to Lyda Kate CHRISTIAN Issued 13 Jun 1947 Rites 14 Jun 1947
C. F. Southard

George Leonard GRAYSON (C) to Edwina BLACK Issued 14 Jun 1947 Rites 14 Jun
W. R. Smith

Franklin J. WOODLEE (C) to Eulos M. WOODS Issued 21 Jun 1947 Rites 21 Jun 1947
W. R. Smith, M. G.

Earl Ray GREEN to Ethel Louise BOREN Issued 27 Jun 1947 Rites 28 Jun 1947
Clinton Gribble, J. P.

Winfred Doyle PRATER to Lennie Mae TALBERT Issued 28 Jun 1947 Rites 28 Jun 1947
Oris W. RAy, M. G.

John Wesley WARD, Jr. to Virgie Mae SIMONS Issued 28 Jun 1947 Rites 28 Jun 1947
J. C. McGee, Jdg.

Thomas GRAYSON (C) to Dorothy WOMACK (C) Issued 30 Jun 1947 Rites 30 Jun 1947
J. C. McGee, Jdg.

William O. ROMANS to Lucile BUTCHER issued 3 Jul 1947 Rites 3 Jul 1947
J. C. McGee, Jdg.

Willie R. BATES C() to Vera Lucille MARTIN (C) Issued 10 Jul 1947 Rites 1 Sep
W. R.Smith

Wm. L. MAKEPEACE to Emil Fay CARNEY Issued 12 Jul 1947 Rites 12 Jul 1947
W. H. Moss, M. G.

Charlie F. CAmPBELL to Dorothy J. CAMPBELL Issued 12 Jul 1947 Rites 12 Jul 1947
R. W. Smartt, Jdg.

Charles WARREN to Mary C. HIGGINBOTHAM Issued 15 Jul 1947 rites 19 Jul 1947
Harold B. Bowe, M. G.

Gordon D. TURNER to Ethel Carolyn MOSSER Issued 19 Jul 1947 Rites 16 Jul 1947
J. C. Sandusky

Paul M. SARAZEN, Jr. to Jo Carmen PATTON Issued 25 Jul 1947 Rites 26 Jul 1947
Allen Phy, M. G.

Paul D. MATHENEY to Audrey Dean MARTIN Issued 26 Jul 1947 Rites 26 Jul 1947
E. L. Smothers, M. G.

Wm. B. MOODY to Bonnie Kate STANTON Issued 29 Jul 1947 Rites 3 Aug 1947
T. Emerson Wortham

Charels Austin JONES to Mildred I. BOYD Issued 30 Jul 1947 Rites 3 Aug 1947
W. H. Owens, M. G.

James Wayne WALL to Barbara V. CANTRELL Issued 14 Aug 1947 Rites 7 Sep 1947
A. A. Gonce, M. G.

Elijah S. SCOTT to Mollie RAY Issued 26 Aug 1947 rites 26 Aug 1947
Frank Watson, M. G.

John W. PEARSON to Audrene LAWRENCE Issued 26 Aug 1947 Rites 8 Sep 1947
C. H. Woodroof, M. G.

Edward Henry BRAEGER (?) to Lillie WILLIAMSON Issued 6 Sep 1947 Rites 6 Sep 1947
W. H. Moss, M. G.

Jas. Aubrey COOLEY to Dorothy Jo BYRD Issued 8 Sep 1947 rites 8 Sep 1947
E. L. Smothers, M. G.

Geo. E. DAVIS to Will Eva JONES Issued 13 sep 1947 Rites 13 Sep 1947
J. C. McGee, Jdg

Fred P. DAVENPORT to Clydene BARNETT Issued 20 Sep 1947 Rites 21 Sep 1947
E. D. Martin, M. G.

C. Preston WILLIAMS to Lillian PRATER Issued 26 Sep 1947 rites 27 Sep 1947
Allen Phy, M. G.

Floyd MYERS to Mel TURNER Issued 2 Oct 1947 Rites 2 Oct 1947
F. J. Winton, J. P.

David GRAYSON (C) to Mary WOODS (C) Issued 14 Oct 1947 Rites 14 Oct 1947
W. R. Smith, M. G.

Stanley MANKOS to Edna MEASLES Issued 16 Oct 1947 Rites 16 Oct 1947
J. C. McGee, Jdg.

Alfred BLAIR to Donnie Lee McCORMICK Issued 18 Oct 1947 Rites 18 Oct 1947
O. W. Ray, M. G.

Wm. F. WOMACK to Nora DUNLAP Issued 22 Oct 1947 Rites 26 Oct 1947
Allen Phy, M. G.

Hardy COPE, Jr. (C) to Ruth GRAYSON Issued 21 Oct 1947 Rites 25 Oct 1947
W. R. Smith

Hollis SIMMONS to Dorothy DELONG Issued 25 Oct 1947 rites 25|Oct 1947
J. C. McGee, Jdg.

Tarlton MARTIN (C) to Earline B. BROWN (C) Issued 27 Oct 1947 rites 2 Nov 1947
W. R. SMITH

Winston DRIVER to Dorothy Jean POWELL Issued 1 Nov 1947 Rites 8 Nov 1947
A. A. Gonce, M. G.

Willard MARCROM to Winnie Fay COMER Issued 3 Nov 1947 rites 3 Nov 1947
W. P. Willis, M. G.

John Paul DAVIS to Mary Ruth McMAHAN Issued 21 Nov 1947 Rites 23 Nov 1947
W. P. Willis

Robert Lee HASTON to Juanita BOULDIN Issued 22 Nov 1947 Rites 26 Nov 1947
Allen Phy, M. G.

Junior GREEN to Wilma CURTIS Issued 22 Nov 1947 Rites 22 Nov 1947
J. C. McGee, Jdg.

Shirley MADEWELL to Goldie PRIEST Issued 22 Nov 1947 Rites 29 Nov 1947
J. C. McGee, Jdg.

Phillip D. GRISSOM, SR. to Edna Jane KELL Issued 22 Nov 1947 Rites 29 Nov 1947
D. P. Myers, J. P.

Jas. Darwin WISEMAN to Martha J. KELL Issued 22 Nov 1947 rites 27 Nov 1947
James B. Dotson, M. G.

Henry Bradford WALKER to Virginia Mullican STEELE Issued 24 Nov 1947 Rites 27 Nov
Allen Phy, M. G.

Wm. Thos. KING (C) to Queen Ester GRAYSON (C) Issued 28 Nov 1947 Rites 28 Nov
W. R. Smith

Edgar Lloyd BLACK to Johnnie Sue PHIFER Issued 12 dec 1947 rites 13 Dec 1947
E. L. Smothers, M. G.

Chas. Franklin RAY to Beatrice EUBANK Issued 20 dec 9147 Rites 23 Dec 1947
E. L. Smothers, M. G.

James Henry BREEDLOVE to Sallie B. HUTCHINS Issued 22 dec 1947 rites 22 dec 1947
F. J. Winton, J. P.

Robert H. BARRY to Mary Frances SMARTT Issued 23 Dec 1947 Rites 27 Dec 1947
D. M. Carhart, M. G.

Wiley MARTIN (C) to Betty MILLER (C) Issued 26 Jan 1948 Rites 26 Jan 1948
J. C. McGee, Jdg.

Tom C. GRISSOM to Hassie Lee McCORMICK Issued 8 Jan 1948 Rites 11 Jan 1948
E. L. Smothers, M. G.

Walker F. MULLICAN to Ruth V. MELTON Issued 21 Jan 1948 Rites 23 Jan 1948
E. L. Smothers, M. G.

James C. PARSLEY to Eva Eliz. CANTRELL Issued 24 Jan 1948 Rites 24 JAN !($*
J. C. McGee, Jdg.

Joseph F. EVANS to Minnie Ethel ROBINSON Issued 24 Jan 1948 Rites 25 Jan 1948
H. M. Randall, M. G.

Hesper A. REYNOLDS to Andrea SMITH Issued 20 Feb 1948 Rites 20 Feb 1948
D. P. Myers, J. P.

Carl F. DUKE to Mildred P. STILES Issued 21 Feb 1948 Rites 21 Feb 1948
W. H. Owen, M. G.

Emil PRIEMER to Anna Marie YOUNG Issued 28 Feb 1948 Rites 28 Feb 1948
E. L. Smothers, M. G.

Kenneth BAILEY to Dorothy STAFFORD Issued 3 Mar 1948 Rites 7 Mar 1948
Jesse R. Bailey, M. G.

Eugene FULTS to Ilda Jones BARNES Issued 13 Mar 1948 Rites 13 Mar 1948
J. C. McGee, Jdg.

James Howard DAVIS to Melba Jean SMITH Issued 19 Mar 1948 Rites 24 Mar 1948
W. H. Moss, M. G.

Charlie GLENN to Myrtle MYERS Issued 3 Apr 1948 Rites 3 Apr 1948
E. R. Little, M. G.

James B. BROWN to Rose Carrie DANIELSON Issued 6 Apr 1948 Rites 9 Apr 1948
W. H. Owen, M. G.

James Adron MARTIN to Blanche E. DANIELSON Issued 7 Apr 1948 Rites 9 Apr 1948
W. H. Owen, M. G.

R. Carl HITCHCOCK to Mildred K. HALE Issued 9 Apr 1948 Rites 10 Apr 1948
E. L. Smothers, M. G.

John E. WOODARD (C) to Margaret ADKINS (C) Issued 17 Apr 1948 Rites 17 Apr 1948
W. R. Smith, M. G.

L. V. CURTIS (C) to Georgea M. MILLER (C) Issued 24 Apr 1948 Rites 1 May 1948
W. C. Bolden, M. G.

Taylor B. CAMPBELL to Gladys L. SCOTT Issued 27 Apr 1948 Rites 1 May 1948
W. J. Thompson, M. G.

Joseph M. ENGLAND to Reba McGEE Issued 15 May 1948 Rites 15 May 1948
J. C. McGee, Jdg.

Melvin E. GILLETTE to Dorothy J. DAVENPORT Issued 26 May 1948 Rites 27 May 1948
E. L. Smothers, M. G.

Logan HERRIMAN to Edith CANTRELL Issued 4 Jun 1948 Rites 5 Jun 1948
Allen Phy, M. G.

William H. CLARK to Geraldine WALLING Issued 21 Jun 1948 Rites 22 Jun 1948
W. H. Owens, M. G.

Eric W. BERRY, Jr. to Ennys S. GWYNN (C) Issued 25 Jun 1948 Rites 26 Jun 1948
J. E. Turner, M. G.

Harold PENDERGRAPH to Mazel DUNCAN Issued 3 Jul 1948 Rites 3 Jul 1948
J. C. McGee, Jdg.

Clayton E. JUDKINS to Treva I. PAYNE Issued 10 Jul 1948 Rites 17 Jul 1948
A. A. Gonce, M. G.

Robert W. SIMS to Lilliam W. MARTIN Issued 10 Jul 1948 Rites 15 Jul 1948
D. M. Carhart, M. G.

Roy Burmal BLANKENSHIP to Emily P. WALKER Issued 13 Aug 1948 Rites 20 Aug 1948
E. L. Smothers, M. G.

Howard B. WALKER to Eugenia BOTTOMS Issued 21 Aug 1948 Rites 23 Aug 1948
Harold Bowe, M. G.

Harold C. DEDMAN to Bobbye Jean GRISWOLD Issued 21 Aug 1948 Rites 29 Aug 1948
B. C. Alexander, M. G.

F. Richard PORTER to Ada G. LYLE Issued 23 Aug 1948 Rites 27 Aug 1948
E. L. Smothers, M. G.

Herman B. ARGO to Betty F. POWELL Issued 27 Aug 1948 Rites 27 Aug 1948
J. N. Winnett, J. P.

Robert RACKLEY, Jr. to Ruby P. TITTSWORTH Issued 28 Aug 1948 Rites 28 Sep 1948
J. C. McGee, Jdg.

Wheeler K. McGREGOR, Jr. to Frankie M. SIMONS Issued 31 Aug 1948 Rites 3 Sep
A. A. Gonce, M. G.

JAmes E. HARRIS to Peggy CHRISTIAN Issued 3 Sep 1948 Rites 3 Sep 1948
W. H. Owen, M. G.

Lee Allen LIVELY to Ethel Cook LIVELY Issued 15 Sep 1948 Rites 18 Sep 1948
Allen Phy, M. G.

Clarence A. MOORE to Sara F. HENEGAR Issued 17 Sep 1948 Rites 18 Sep 1948
Allen Phy, M. G.

Andrew RACKOWSKI to Hilda C. BOOTH Issued 18 Sep 1948 Rites 18 Sep 1948
J. W. Dempster, Jdg.

Charles E. LOWDER, Jr. to Mary Evelyn MYERS Issued 27 Sep 1948 Rites 17 Oct W. H. Moss, M. G.

Erby SCOTT (C) to Maude M. MARTIN (C) Issued 6 Oct 1948 Rites 19 Oct 1948 J. C. McGee, Jdg.

Gerald G. ODOM to Ophylene Odom Issued 11 Oct 1948 Rites 11 Oct 1948 F. L. Watson. M. G.

Emmitt DODSON to Edna Ann PASSONS Issued 16 Oct 1948 Rites 16 Oct 1948 W. H. Moss, M. G.

Govie L. TAYLOR to Edna FERRELL Issued 16 Oct 1948 Rites 16 Oct 1948 Otto Cartwright, J. P.

George MARTIN (C) to Lillie Mae HENEGAR (C) Issued 23 Oct 1948 Rites 23 Oct 1948 J. C. McGee, Jdg.

Paul HENDRIXSON to Lynn Opal SCOTT Issued 5 Nov 1948 Rites 5 Nov 1948 Vestal Chaffin, M. G.

Gerald Gross BOYD to Mary Helen LENTZ Issued 12 Nov 1948 Rites 12 Nov 1948 Allen Phy, M. G.

Ivan D. GILLEY to Mary Lois GREEN Issued 20 Nov 1948 Rites 21 Nov 1948 E. L. Smothers, M. G.

Jess Walter BENNETT to Thelma V. DUNLAP Issued 26 Nov 1948 Rites 27 Nov E. L. Smothers, M. G.

Elmer C. GRIFFITH to Alice A. WILLARD Issued 1 Dec 1948 Rites 8 Dec 1948 W. H. Moss, M. G.

Edwin F. HENDRICKSON to Edna E. CHRISTIAN Issued 3 Dec 1948 Rites 5 Dec 1948 Allen Phy, M. G.

Lawrence E. HYATT to Edna HILLIS Issued 23 Dec 1948 Rites 24 Dec 1948 W. J. Thompson, M. G.

J. W. ANDERSON to Joan DICKEY Issued 31 Dec 1948 Rites 1 Jan 1949 Granville Tyler, M. G.

Willie BESS to Willie ROZZELL Issued 7 Jan 1949 Rites 7 JAn 1949 W. H. Moss, M. G.

Billy Webb GILLEY to Elva Jean HASTON Issued 12 Jan 1949 Rites 14 Jan 1949 E. L. Smothers, M. G.

Billie E. RIGSBY to Dorothy J. ELAM Issued 21 Jan 1949 Rites 21 Jan 1949 R. W. Whitlock, M. G.

Hugh L. JONES to Nettie HARDING Issued 28 Jan 1949 Rites 7 Feb 1949 J. M. Prater, J. P.

Tom BOWLING (C) to Cora LOCKE (C) Issued 28 an 1949 Rites 29 Jan 1949 G. T. Speaks, M. G.

E. Eugene GRIBBLE to Mary F. GILLEY issued 12 Feb 1949 Rites 14 Feb 1949 E. L. Smotherman, M. G.

Jerry J. THURLOW to Jessie Lee HASH Issued 17 Feb 1949 Rites 18 Feb 1949 D. A. Ensor, M. G.

Columbus TALLEY to Roxie TENPENNY Issued 23 Feb 1949 Rites 23 Feb 1949 C. C. Dickson. M. G.

Wm. Wade SLATTON to Mildred M. BOYD Issued 24 Feb 1949 Rites 25 Feb 1949 Joe Netherland, M. G.

Clifford L. HILL to Naomi C. SIMONS Issued 24 Feb 1949 Rites 24 Feb 1949 Allen Phy, M. G.

Edwin C. DOBBINS to Minnie A. DEATON Issued 26 Feb 1949 Rites 26 Feb 1949 Peter F. DAVITT, M. G.

Robert G. ROBINSON to Betty Jo NEAL Issued 2 Mar 1949 Rites 5 Mar 1949 R. C. Reid, M. G.

Eric M. CAMPBELL to Pearl CHESNEY Issued 2 Mar 1949 Rites 4 Mar 1949 W. H. Moss, M. G.

Frank PADGETT to Ova D. JUDKINS Issued 26 Mar 1949 Rites 26 Mar 1949 Felix Cantrell

Charles D. DAVIS to Mollie B. PATTERSON Issued 7 Apr 1949 rites 7 Apr 1949 H. O. Kutz, M. G.

Chas. Joel ROGERS to Anna Mae ELDRIDGE Issued 15 Apr 1949 Rites 16 Apr 1949 Gordon Browning, Gov.-State ofTh..

James PINEGAR to Anna J. DUNCAN Issued 16 Apr 1949 Rites 16 Apr 1949 C. C. Dickson, M. G.

Morris L. DAVENPORT to Wilma O. CATES Issued 30 Apr 1949 Rites 30 Apr 1949 E. L. Smothers, M. G.

Floyd LUSK (C) to Carrie ROWAN (C) Issued 6 May 1949 Rites 6 May 1949 J. C. McGee, Jdg.

Woodrow W. ST. JOHN to Emogene BOULDIN Issued 7 May 1949 Rites 7 May 1949 T. R. Pitman, M. G.

Eubert MARTIN to Ollie NORTHCUTT Issued 7 May 1949 Rites 8 May 1949 Rufe Higgins, M. G.

Cowan ROBERTS (C) to Arizona GRAYSON (C) Issued 7 May 1949 Rites 8 May 1949 P. F. Davitt, M. G.

Alton MULLICAN to Nettie I. JUDKINS Issued 21 May 1949 Rites 22 May 1949 Claud Turner, J. P.

Lennie B. RUSSELL to Ora M. CRAIG Issued 11 Jun 1949 Rites 11 Jun 1949 J. C. McGee, Jdg.

James Noel GREEN to Pearl MORTON Issued 29 Aug 1949 Rites 29 Aug 1949 W. H. Jones, M. G.

Bernard Richard LOONEY to Mary Lou BONNER Issued 2 Sep 1949 Rites 2 Sep 1949 J. Edward Wolven, M. G.

Leonard E. McBRIDE to Lela M. BILBREY Issued 2 Sep 1949 Rites 3 Sep 1949 E.L. Smothers, M. G.

Hubert D. SULLIVAN to Mary Jo DeFORD Issued 6 Sep 1949 Rites 12 Sep 1949 James H. Elder, M. G.

James R. TANNER to Marion E. FREEMAN Issued 10 Sep 1949 Rites 10 Sep 1949 J. C. McGee, Jdg.

Haskell L. CANTRELL to Elfreda ROBINSON Issued 10 sep 1949 Rites 10 Sep 1949 J. R. Bailey, M. G.

Alvin H. ROLLER to Elatia CRAWLEY Issued 14 Sep 1949 Rites 14 Sep 1949 J. E. Doyle, M. G.

Edwin B. KIRBY to Rebecca WOODLEE Issued 16 Sep 1949 Rites 16 Sep 1949 Allen Phy, M. G.

Thomas McDOWELL to Martha ROBERTS Issued 16 Sep 1949 Rites 17 Sep 1949 K. P. Reeder, J. P.

David M. BRADY to Ellen Eliz. SIMMONS Issued 24 Sep 1949 Rites 28 Sep 1949 R. C. REID

Omer N. RIGSBY to Wanda Jo BRAXTON Issued 23 Sep 1949 Rites 23 Sep 1949 H. M. Randall, M. G.

George E. BAIN to Rose Omega CANTRELL Issued 28 Sep 1949 Rites 28 Sep 1949 Felix Cantrell, M. G.

James Van JOWERS, Jr. to Agnes L. BRYAN Issued 1 Oct 1949 Rites 1 Oct 1949 E. L. Smothers, M. G.

Willard Frank POWELL to Edna E. WATSON Issued 6 Oct 1949 Rites 6 Oct 1949 F. L. Watson, M. G.

Murray HARDING to Vivian Mae RUTLEDGE Issued 8 Oct 1949 Rites 8 Oct 1949 E. O.Lee, M. G.

Elmus YOUNG to Evelyn DUGAN Issued 8 Oct 1949 Rites 8 Oct 1949 E. L. Smothers, M. G.

594 marriages in this book

Elcain BROWN (C) to Helen Louise MARTIN (C) Issued 22 Jun 1949 Rites 2 Jul F. S. Sutton, M. G.

Ray BROCK to Ruby MORTON Issued 25 Jun 1949 Rites 25 Jun 1949 J. B. Dotson, M. G.

Morris H. HOGAN to Gertrude DIXON Issued 2 Jul 1949 Rites 3 Jul 1949 R. T. Harding, J. P.

Gerald C. REID to Trutha M. HOWELL Issued 2 Jul 1949 Rites 3 Jul 1949 R. C. Reid, M. G.

Wm. Henry SIMMONS to Gertrude B. CROWLEY Issued 9 Jul 1949 Rites 9 Jul H. M. Randall, M. G.

Julius BOWDOIN, Jr. to Juanita RICHARDSON Issued 9 Jul 1949 Rites 9 Jul C. C. Dickson, M. G.

Roby J. HOWARD, Jr. to Dorothy E. GUNN Issued 13 Jul 1949 Rites 17 Jul 1949 W. H. Moss, M. G.

Jack R. DELONG to Elaie Jean HALE Issued 22 Jul 1949 Rites 22 Jul 1949 J. C. McGee, Jdg.

David HENRY to Elsie Lou ROBINSON Issued 23 jul 1949 Rites 23 Jul 1949 J. H. Netherland, M. G.

Quim G. POWELL to Ruby PURSLEY Issued 1 Jul 1949 Rites 1 Jul 1949 T. D. Killian, J. P.

Dallas L. SAVAGE (C) to Clara NORTHCUTT (C) Issued 1 Aug 1949 Rites1 Aug Ben Bates, M. G.

John T. R. DILLON, Jr. to Ann BADGER Issued 3 Aug 1949 Rites 6 Aug 1949 W. H. Moss, M. G.

Donald C. LOGUE to Grace G. BROWN Issued 6 Aug 1949 Rites 19 Aug 1949 J. R. Bailey, M. G.

Paul KERR to Frances G. PEAY Issued 10 Aug 1949 Rites 10 Aug 1994 J. W. Dempster, Jdg.

Forest Clark CANTRELL to Geraldine RADER Issued 13 Aug 1949 rites 15 Aug E. L. Smothers, M. G.

A. Leird WOODLEE to Dorothy J. NELMS Issued 18 Aug 1949 Rites 20 Aug 1949 M. O. Nelms, M. G.

Andy HENNESSEE to Kate HILLIS Issued 20 Aug 1949 Rites 20 Aug 1949 Otto Cartwright, J. P.

O. C. PANTER to Evelyn GULICK Issued 24 Aug 1949 Rites 24 Aug 1949 E. D. Martin, M. G.

Herman BRAXTON to Nettie Pearl ROGERS Issued 26 Aug 1994 Rites 28 Aug 1949 R. H. Bonner, J. P.

Onzy BROWN (C) to Pauline McKINLEY (C) Issued 15 Oct 1949 Rites 16 Oct 1949
F. S. Sutton, M. G.

Edgar Ray HUDGENS to Mary Sue POWELL Issued 4 Nov 1949 Rites 4 Nov 1949
W. H. Moss, M. G.

Isaac Van HALEY to Sarah Ella McAFEE issued 4 Nov 1949 rites 6 nov 1949
R. W. Smartt, Jdg

John W. ROACH to Lillian F. NICKS, Issued 5 Nov 1949 Rites 5 Nov 1949
Allen Phy, M. G.

John Malcolm CROTHERS to Eva L. COPE Issued 5 Nov 1849 Rites 22 Nov 1949
J. P. Sanders, M. G.

J. Fred WHITTENBURG to Mary Lorene HOBBS Issued 9 Nov 1949 Rites 12 Nov 1949
W. H. Moss, M. G.

Wm. Benton FARISS to Jean McCLAIN Issued 12 Nov 1949 Not Returned

William M. KEENER to MAry Jo MILLS Issued 19 Nov 1949 Rites 19 Nov 1949
E. O. Lee, M. G.

Edward L. WALKER to Frances WEBB Issued 19 Nov 1949 Rites 23 Nov 1949
W. H. Owens, M. G.

Robert R. DANIEL to Lillian NELMS Issued 22 Nov 1949 Rites 24 Nov 1949
W. H. Moss, M. G.

Wm. H. SMARTT, Jr. to Billie Sue DOWNS Issued 22 Nov 1949 Rites 24 Nov 1949
M. Kurfees PULLIAS, M. G.

John RRayford DAVIS to Hannah E. GREENE Issued 23 Nov 1949 Rites 24 Nov 1949
Vestal Chaggin, M. G.

Hoyt B. FITTS to Mary Louella MOFFITT Issued 23 Nov 1949 Rites 23 Nov 1949
E. L. Smothers, M. G.

Thomas V. BEARD to Willie Rowland SIMONS Issued 25 Nov 1949 Rites 25 Nov 1949
R. W. Smartt, Jdg.

G. W. WALKER to Dossie PRIEST Issued 26 Nov 1949 Rites 26 Nov 1949
J. C. McGee, Jdg.

William McCARVER to Julia HOPKINS Issued 26 Nov 1949 Rites 26 Nov 1949
H. M. Randall, M.G.

EMMETT BASHAM to Elsie P. HOLLANDSWORTH Issued 26 Nov 1949 Rites 26 Nov 1949
H. M. RAndall, M. G.

Lee M. WILLIAMS to Mildred A. TEAL Issued 26 Nov 1949 Rites 26 Nov 1949
Rufe Higgins, M. G.

Virgil RAINS to Macon OSMENT Issued 3 Dec 1949 Rites 3 Dec 1949
G. A. Lovel, J. P.

Robert L. McREYNOLDS (C) to Johnnie B. VAUGHN (C) Issued 6 Dec 1949 Rites 6 Dec 1949
F. S. Sutton, M. G.

Harold S. BROWN (C) to Carrie E. BOULDIN Issued 10 Dec 1949 Rites 10 Dec 1949
T. R. Pitman, M. G.

Joe Vacy BROWN to Elsie May BROWN Issued 15 Dec 1949 Rites 20 Dec 1949
Geddes Ormon, M. G.

Charles P. ELAM to Irma Ruth HARRELL Issued 19 Dec 1949 rites 19 Dec 1949
Allen HArdison

Hugh L. JONES to Maude Myrtle JONES Issued 22 Dec 1949 Rites 22 Dec 1949
T. F. Gilley, M. G.

Thomas E. BETCHEL to Aileen JORDAN Issued 22 Dec 1949 Rites 22 éec 1949
Jas. B. Dotson. M. G.

Robert H. MEADOR to Mildred FARLESS Issued 22 Dec 1949 Rites 27 Dec 1949
E. L. Smothers, M. G.

James Paul JONES to Georgia Mae HALE Issued 23 Dec 1949 Rites 24 Dec 1949
T. D. Killian, J. P.

J.C. Deskin BOULDIN to Betty J. RANKHORN Issued 23 Dec 1949 rites 23 Dec 1949
W. M. Johnson, J. P.

Kenneth S. YOUNG to Vernie B. BICKFORD Issued 23 Dec 1949 Rites 23 Dec 1949
Earnest Lee

Melvin B. ADCOCK to Mary Lou REDMAN Issued 23 Dec 1949 Rites 25 Dec 1949
H. O. Kutz, M. G.

Wm. HARGWOOD, Jr. (C) to Edith L. BATES (C) Issued 23 Dec 1949 Rites 25 Dec 1949
Ben Bates, M. G.

J. L. SMITH to Emma Gladys RHEA Issued 24 dec 1949 Rites 24 Dec 1949
R. W. Smartt, Jdg.

Randolph RAMSEY (C) to Ocenia OFFICER (C) Issued 27 Dec 1949 rites 27 Dec 1949
Ben Bates, M. G.

Vernon BASHAM to Jeanne Lewis HASKER Issued 30 Dec 1949 Rites 30 Dec 1949
J. C. McGee, Jdg.

Comer Losson PRATER to Reba Inez CANTRELL Issued 31 Dec 1949 rites 8 Jan 1950
W. H. Owen, M. G.

Claude C. DAVIS to Bessie H. MAYNARD Issued 3 Jan 1950 Rites 7 JAn 1950
J. C. McGee, Jdg.

Clyde W. RAMSEY (C) to SARAH J. SMITH (C) Issued 4 jan 1949 Rites 7 JAn 1949
B. M. Sutton

Paul E. REEDER toMildred L. HAWKINS Issued 7 Jan 1950 Not Returned

Wilburn L. NORROD to Dorothy E. CHAMBERS Issued 11 Jan 1950 Rites 14 Jan 1950
W. H. Owen, M.G.

Johnnie W. GROVE to Betty S. THURMAN Issued 12 jan 1949 Rites 12 Jan 1949 JaS. B. Dotson, M. G.

Ray Arthue PERKINS to Clyda E. FERRELL Issued 15 JAn 1950 Rites 13 jan 1950 J. Edward Wolvan, M. G.

Edward RAMSEY, Jr. (C) to Annie Ruth RAMSEY (C) Issued 13 Jan 1950 Rites 15 Jan Calvin Donnell, M. G.

Gerald E. DODSON to Edith BROCK Issued 18 Jan 1950 Rites 18 JAn 1950 R. W. Smarttm Jdg.

Woodrow Wilson PACK to Gladys M. MYERS Issued 24 Jan 1950 Rites 24 Jan 1950 R. W. Smartt, Jdg.

Franklin B. STONER to Daisy MOORE Issued 24 Jan 1950 Rites 24 Jan 1950 Robert Hobbs, J. P.

H. D. GRISSOM to Ocie Mai JONES Issued 28 Jan 1950 Rites 28 jan 1950 Robert Hobbs, J. P.

Walter J. ROGERS, Jr. to MARY Corrine GROVE Issued 28 Jan 1950 Rites 4 Feb 1950 B. W. Ramsey, M. G.

Hugh WISEMAN to Virginia M. BOULDIN Issued 28 Jan 1950 Rites 28 Jan 1950 Harry Amstutz, M. G.

George H. POWELL, Jr. to Patsy Sue PHILLIPS Issued 31 jan 1950 Rites 4 Feb 1950 Lewis Savage, M. G.

Frank A. ABNEY to Archie Belle ABNEY Issued 2 Feb 1950 Rites 2 Feb 1950 W. H. Moss, M. G.

Wallace NELSON to Ida Willene McGEE Issued 4 Feb 1950 Rites 4 Feb 1950 Rufe higgins, M. G.

Malcolm YORK to Jean Marie HANSEL Issued 6 Feb 1950 Rites 6 Feb 1950 W. J. McElroy, M. G.

Walter A. PHILLIPS to Bertha P. GARNER Issued 8 Feb 1950 rites 21 Feb 1950 Allen Ohy, M. G.

Robert W. WOODHURST to Geneva G. SAIN Issued 11 Feb 1950 rites 11 Feb 1950 E. L. Smothers, M. G.

Royce B. LUNA to Eliza J. TALLEY Issued 13 Feb 1950 Rites 13 feb 1950 K. P. Reeder, J. P.

RAlph M. TODD to Edith W. SULLENS Issued 13 feb 1950 Rites 19 feb 1950 Billy NICKS, M. G.

Wm. C. BARNHILL (C) to Georgia SAVAGE (C) Issued 15 feb 1950 Rites 19 feb 1950 F. S. Sutton

JAmes Toy JOHNSON to Catherine L. WOODS Issued 17 feb 1950 Rites 18 Feb 1950 J. E. Doyle

Boyd Elmer ATNIP to Emogene HOOPER Issued 24 Feb 1950 Not Retuened

Grady LOCKE (C) to Agness MOORE (C) Issued 25 Feb 1950 Rites 25 Feb 1950 J. W. Dempster, Jdg.

Billy Ray WEBB to Murial Dean WILSON Issued 3 Mar 1950 Rites 3 Mar 1950 E. L. Smothers, M. G.

Alvin MARTIN to Rena L. TEETERS IssueD $ Mar 1950 Rites 4 Mar 1950 Geddes Orman, M. G.

Wesley RIGGS to Bettie MORTON Issued 4 Mar 1950 Rites 4 Mar 1950 W. H. Moss, M. G.

Charles E. ROWAN (C) to Minnie L. HENNESSEE (C) Issued 7 Mar 1950 Rites 7 MAR F. S. Sutton, M. G.

Sam ROGERS, Jr. to Virginia CANTRELL Issued 11 Mar 1950 Rites 11 Mar 1950 Felix Cantrell

Sam H. ODOM to Florence E. ODOM Issued 12 Mar 1950 Rites 12 Mar 1950 W. H. Moss, M. G.

Earl HARRIS to Willie Mae LIVELY Issued 17 Mar 1950 Rites 18 Mar 1950 W. H. Moss, M. G.

Haskel WAGNER to Rebecca CALDWELL Issued 18 Mar 1950 Rites 18 Mar 1950 W. H. Atwell, Jdg.

Charles E. TALLEY to Doris K. CANTRELL Issued 18 Mar 1950 Rites 18 Mar 1950 Allen Phy, M. G.

JAMES Titus WEST to Ruby GAY Issued 25 Mar 1950 Riyes 29 Mar 1950 J. C. McGee, Jdg.

John H. POTTER to Elnora HARVEY Issued 28 Mar 1950 Rites 28 Mar 1950 Tallman Boyd, J. P.

Ernest P. TURNER to Sarah Irene ADCOCK Issued 1 Apr 1950 Rites 1 Apr 1950 J. W. Dempster, Jdg.

A. T. HALE, Jr. to Helen R. FISHER Issued 1 Apr 1950 Rites 1 Apr 1950 J. W. Dempster, Jdg.

Willie A. SMITH (C) to Bertha HOPKINS Issued 15 Apr 1950 Rites 15 Apr 1950 W. C. Bolden,

Ray A. TURNER to Georgia M. OGLE Issued 15 Apr 1950 Rites 15 Apr 1950 H. O. Kutz, M. G.

George MASSENGILL to Ruby GAYNESS Issued 21 Apr 1950 Rites 21 Apr 1950 L. H. Barnes, J. P.

James F. STARNES to Evelyn SMITH Issued 24 Apr 1950 Rites 25 Apr 1950 Allen Phy, M. G.

Robert C. SMITH to Christine BLAIR Issued 29 Apr 1950 Rites 29 Apr 1950 F. L. Watson, M. G.

Wm. J. PASCAL to Marie LOCKHART Issued 4 MAy 1950 Rites 5 May 1950
J. W. Dempster, Jdg.

Wm. E. BYARS to Beatrice LEE Issued 13 May 1950 Rites 14 May 1950
E. L. Smothers, M. G.

Joe Willis PRYOR to Joy HALE Issued 15 May 1950 rites 15 May 1950
Rufe Higgins, M. G.

Sammie E. SCOTT to Myrtle V. JACKSON Issued 20 May 1950 Rites 20 May 1950
J.C. McGee, Jdg.

J. C. HOLT to Juanita HARRELL Issued 27 May 1950 Rites 27 May 1950
R. W. Whitlock, M. G.

John D. GREENE to DAphne COPE Issued 1 Jun 1950 Rites 1 Jun 1950
E. L. Smothers, M. G.

Osmond KING to Betty Jean TEETERS Issued 2 Jun 1950 Rites 2 Jun 1950
R. W. Smartt, Jdg.

A. J. Webb to Maymie St. JOHN Issued 3 Jun 1950 Rites 3 Jun 1950
W. J. McElroy, M. G.

Wilson CALDWELL to Pearl ELLIOTT Issued 3 Jun 1950 Rites 8 Jun 1950
H. O. Kutz, M. G.

George W. MORGAN to Martha A. TEMPLETON Issued 20 Jun 1950 rites 23 jun 1950
Rufe Higgins, M. G.

Wm. Lee BLAIR to Ida Lee POWELL Issued 21 Jun 1950 Rites 23 jun 1950
J. R. Bailey, M. G.

James Robt. DEARMAN to Heloise RAMSEY Issued22 Jun 1950 Rites 23 Jun 1950
Rufus Underwood, M. G.

Lester CAMPBELL to Mary TURNBO Issued 23 Jun 1950 rites 23 jun 1950
J. W. Dempster, Jdg.

Jonah C. NUNLEY to Margaret WOLF Issued 24 jum 1950 Rites 24 jun 1950
Robert Hobbs, J. P.

Edward MITCHELL to Bobbie Jo SMARTT Issued 24 jun 1950 Rites 24 jun 1950
W. H. Owen, M. G.

H. L. STILES, Jr. to Mary F. CAMPBELL Issued 24 Jun 1950 Rites 1 Jul 1950
J. R. Bailey, M. G.

Kenneth C. ALLEN to Naomi LOWE Issued 27 Jun 1950 Rites 8 Jul 1950
W. H. Owen, M. G.

Ray Earl MOORE to Dorothy FIELDS Issued 29 Jun 1950 Rites 29 Jun 1950
J. B. Dotson, M. G.

Melvin E. EVANS to Elyese YOUNG Issued 30 jun 1950 Rites 30 Jun 1950
E. L. Smothers, M. G.

Charlie MEDLEN to Sarah Edith DAVIS Issued 1 jul 1950 Rites 2 Jul 1950
W. H. Moss, M. g.

John H. KRICKEL to Mary Ann BROWN Issued 8 Jul 1950 Rites 23 Jul 1950
J. I. McDonough, M. G.

Jasper B. HILL to Gladys R. BARNES Issued 11 Jul 1950 Rites 11 Jul 1950
E. L. Smothers, M. G.

Wm. Thomas BELL to Virginia A. WHITE Issued 22 Jul 1950 rites 22 Jul 1950
J. W. Dempster, Jdg.

J. C. McCORMICK to Hazel RAY Issued 22 Jul 1950 rites 22 Jul 1950
T. D. Killian, J. P.

Frank BOULDIN to Hazel LEDBETTER Issued 27 Jul 1950 Rites 27 Jul 1950
A. E. Curtis, J. P.

Shelton OSMENT to Sara MASON Issued 28 Jul 1950 Rites 28 Jul 1950
Geddes Orman, M. G.

Virble Ray SPENCER to Ruth CHARLES Issued 28 Jul 1950 Rites 28 jul 1950
W. H. Moss, M. G.

Max Leroy CALKIN to Mae Dell POWELL Issued 1 Aug 1950 Rites 2 Aug 1950
W. H. Moss, M. G.

Edward E. LEWIS to Jimmie K. OFFICER Issued 5 Aug 1950 Rites 6 Aug 1950
Geddes Orman, M. G.

JAs. Robt. VANATTA to Grace A. McDANIEL Issued 5 Aug 1950 Rites 5 Aug 1950
R. W. Smartt, Jdg.

Clarence Allen McGEE to Sylvia WIRT Issued 6 Aug 1950 Rites 6 Aug 1950
W. H. Moss, M. G.

Boyd RIGSBY to Gleda WILSON Issued 9 Aug 1950 Rites 9 Aug 1950
R. W. Whitlock, M. G.

Jas. PRESTON CONLEY to Willie L. BURKS Issued 12 Aug 1950 Rites 16 Aug 1950
J. M. Prater, J. P.

Clayton F. SPINDLER to Blanche WARREN Issued 12 Aug 1950 Rites 20 Aug 1950
J. Edward Wolven, M. G.

John C. WHITLOCK to Doris Belle GOLDEN Issued 16 Aug 1950 Rites 17 Aug 1950
W. H. Owen, M. G.

Willie BEARD to Jessie M. BEARD Issued 26 Aug 1950 Rites 27 Aug 1950
A. E. Curtis, J. P.

B. H. WRIGHT to Delores STUBBLEFIELD Issued 27 Aug 1950 Rites 2 Sep 1950
Allen Hardison, M. G.

Edward N. YAGER III to J. Josephine RUSSELL Issued 31 Aug 1950 Rites 1 Sep
E. L. Smothers, M. G.

Joe Dillon SCOGGINS to Frances KNOWLES Issued 19 Oct 1950 Rites 19 oct 1950 W. T. Warren, Jdg.

James L. HILLIS to Frances Coleen SMITH Issued 20 Oct 1950 Rites 20 oct 1950 T. J. Carrick, M. G.

Jessie F. TURNER to Clata G. PENDLETON Issued 21 Oct 1950 Rites 21 Oct 1950 Herbert Perry, M. G.

Wade MADEWELL to Callie PEARSON Issued 28 Oct 1950 Rites 28 Oct 1950 Vestal Chaffin, M. G.

Hubert A. DILLON to Fay MULLICAN Issued 7 Nov 1950 rites 8 Nov 1950 Allen Phy, M. G.

S. H. DODD to Mattie SMITH Issued 13 Nov 1950 Rites 13 Nov 1950 H. M. Randall, M. G.

Charles J. LOUVERN to Edith SAVAGE Issued 14 Nov 1950 Rites 14 Nov 1950 T. R. Pitman, M. G.

C. L. McGEE to Lucille BROWN Issued 15 Nov 1950 Rites 15 Nov 1950 W. T. WArren, Jdg.

Joe Fred SMITH to Betty Ruth BRAXTON Issued 16 Nov 1950 Rites 17 Nov 1950 H. J. Ditter, M. G.

Thomas MILSTEAD to Eona YORK Issued 18 Nov 1950 Rites 18 Nov 1950 E. D. Martin, M.G.

Wade JACKSON to Sara Dean MAGNESS Issued 20 Nov 1950 Rites 21 Nov 1950 R. L. Benton, M. G.

J. P. SANDERS to Tommye ELDRIDGE Issued 21 Nov 1950 Rites 23 Nov 1950 R. L. Benton, M. G.

Alvin BESS to Beulah BESS Issued 23 Nov 1950 Rites 23 Nov 1950 L. L. Scott, J. P.

John Thos. PAINE to Edna V. SPARKMAN Issued 22 Nov 1950 Rites 22 Nov 1950 C. E. Simmons, M. G.

Willie J. YOUNG to Lucille CRIM Issued 25 Nov 1950 Rites 26 Nov 1950 W. H. Lewis, M. G.

Charles H. CANTRELL to Beatrice STRATTON Issued 7 Dec 1950 Rites 7 Dec 1950 W. T. Warren, Jdg.

A. M. SUTTON to Irene GRANDSTAFF Issued 9 Dec 1950 Rites 9 Dec 1950 Allen Phy, M. G.

Robert A. C. HILLIS, Jr. to Leona Pearl MARTIN   License Issued 9 Dec 1950 and Rites 9 Dec 1950 - Chattanooga, Tennessee - Carl Giers, M. G.

James L. SPANGLER to Hallene WHITLOCK Issued 13 Dec 1950 Rites 14 Dec 1950 W. H. Owen, M. G.

A. J. WINTON, Jr. to Cathern Ellen SEARS Issued 1 Sep 1950 Rites 3 Sep 1950 Mayhew Peery, M. G.

Verble E. CANTRELL to Suzanne LEFEBURE Issued 1 Sep 1950 Rites 2 Sep 1950 E. L. Smothers, M. G.

Arsey W. WOMACK to Betty Jo CANTRELL Issued 1 Sep 1950 Rites 2 Sep 1950 Vestal Chaffin, M. G.

HAckett Jr. POTTER to Ora A. HARVEY Issued 1 Sep 1950 rites 1 sep 1950 J. B. Dotson, M. G.

Clark Edward SMITH to Imogene HAYES Issued 9 Sep 1950 Rites 9 Sep 1950 W. T. Warren, Jdg.

Bobbie COPPINGER to Julia RISNER Issued 11 sep 1950 rites 11 Sep 1950 W. H. Moss, M. G.

Robert PARSLEY, Jr. to Dimple DAVIS Issued 13 Sep 1950 rites 16 Sep 1950 J. E. Doyle, M. G.

L. S. ROWLAND to Bess Horton STACY Issued 14 sep 1950 rites 14 sep 1950 W. G. Hawjins, M. G.

H. Clarence MOORE, Jr. to Annalee HALL Issued 16 sep 1950 Rites 16 Sep 1950 W. T. WArren, Jdg.

James F. EVANS to Elnora YOUNG Issued 16 Sep 1950 Rites 16 Sep 1950 E. L. Smothers, M. G.

Ray MOORE to Betty Sue MOLLOY Issued 25 Sep 1950 Rites 24 Sep 1950 Allen Phy, M. G.

Colonel E. ROACH to Beuna V. RAMSEY Issued 25 Sep 1950 Rites 5 Oct 1950 P. A. Kirby, M. G.

Thomas RUTLEDGE to Edith C. CORBITT Issued 30 Sep 1950 Rites 30 Sep 1950 W. T. Warren, Jdg.

Martin SCOTT to Grace MOORE Issued 30 Sep 1950 Rites 30 Sep 1950 Rufe Higgins, M. G.

Carlos H. JERDEN to Carmine CHEERS Issued 30 Sep 1950 Rites 11 Oct 1950 E. L. Smothers, M. G.

E. Lionel FORD to Bobbie ROLLER Issued 7 Oct 1950 Rites 7 Oct 1950 J. W. Dempster, Jdg.

Edwin W. BEARD to Louise KING Issued 7 Oct 1950 Rites 7 Oct 1950 W. T. Warren, Jdg.

J. L. BOULDIN to Georgia Fay STILES Issued 11 Oct 1950 rites 11 Oct 1950 Rufe Higgins, M. G.

Wm. Benton FARRIS to Joan McCLAIN Issued 14 Oct 1950 Rites 14 Oct 1950 C. L. Webster, M. G.

Wesley Lee SAVAGE to Agnes IRWIN Issued 14 Oct 1950 Rites 15 Oct 1950 J. C. Johnson, M. G.

Herbert D, DODD to Mary E. SPENCER Issued 16 Dec 1950 Rites 16 Dec 1950
J. R. BAiley, M. G.

Orville H. JONES to Ruby Nell PEDIGO Issued 26 Dec 1950 Rites 16 Dec 1950
J. R. BAiley, M. G.

Charles E. DAVIS to Gloria MARCROM Issued 20 dec 1950 Rites 24 dec 1950
J. R. BAiley, M. G.

Jerry D. MORRIS to Jacqueline WOMACK Issued 22 Dec 1950 Rites 24 Dec 1950
Ira North, M. G,

Robert L. WEBB to Mary O. BROCK Issued 23 Dec 1950 Rites 24 Dec 1950
T. F. Gilley, M. G.

Fred Robt. MORTON to Caroline REYNOLDS Issued 23 Dec 1950 Rites 26 Dec 1950
Geddes Orman, M. G.

Ray WATSON to Lula BILLINGS Issued 23 Dec 1950 Rites 23 Dec 1950
Thos. J. Carrick, M. G.

Harris Clark JACOBS, Jr. to Gladys HENRY Issued 29 Dec 1950 Rites 31 Dec 1950
P. A. Kirby, M. G.

163 marriages in the portion
of Book # 21

- 420 -

Bird 94

Birt 63

Bishop 48,87,103,198,302,305,378

Bize 67

Black 2,13,47c,152,169,182,222,23+c,25+c, 262,289,309,351,402,403,405

Blackburn 85,86,112,359

Blackney 101

Blackwell 146

Blair 4,61,70,89,100,101,123,132,156,169, 173,194,197,201,218,228,302,352,372,387,405, 415,416

Blake 68

Blakely 191

Blankenship 37,57,98,133,168,178,184,201, 218,238,302,362,372,387,405,415,416

Blanks 20,38,53,129,143,162,179,202,219,248, 255,265,266,267,300,336,381,388,393

Blaylcok 299,306,374

Blocher 186

Block 202

Bloomberry 215,252

Blount 262

Blue 12,27,53,102,191,273,282,293c,353,398

Bluhm-Blum 35,137,264,342,375

Boaz 51,56

Bobbitt 274

Bogle 91,204,208,323,325,353,388

Boles 149,169,184,237,329

Boley 212

Bolin 4,32

Boling 47c

Bolt 95,128,215,216

Bolton 273

Bomar 23

Bond (s) 58,105,158,188,194,226,315,329, 362,364

Bondreau 113

Bonner 3,7c,23,25,35c,44,46,49c,50, 52,54,65,70,72,78,80.98,103,107c,109c, 112,120,124,125c,147,155,158c,170,173, 181,183,184,197,203c,222,245c,246,253, 260,277,283,287,302,306,310,311,312, 326c,347c,360,365c,398,401,411

Bonnie 140

Booher 149,172,397

Booth 407

Boren 1,42,72,83,94,100,101,113,134, 137,143,184,229,221,233,242,287,293, 335,347,361,387,391,397,401A,403

Bornstein 399

Bosson 250

Bost 24,74,75,93,101,103,113,122,128, 135,137,153,164,169,170,172,174,178, 191,313,332,363,372

Bostick 56,124,285

Boswell 383

Bottoms 11,50,60,73,108,110,122,148, 150,152,164,170,183,184, 221,228,237,238,251,292,304,327,338, 354,379,387,407

Boulden-Bouldin 6,25,41c,57,66,68, 78,110,136,152,154,163c,190,199,209, 210,227,239,252,253,254,257,274,288, 290,295,298,300,304,312,317,322,324, 326,329,332,335,336,337,339,341,343, 344,347,349,352,356,362,365,385,386, 392,393,401,402,405,409,413,413c,414, 427,418

Bounds 107,129,136,299

Bowdoin 238,410

Bowen 40,336

Bowerman 175

Bowman 63,153,368

Bowling 408c

Boyd 6,12,23,27,40,104,108,111,112,120, 123,127,131,135,144,148,158,169,170, 175,177,181,182,204,210,213,217,227, 256,264,282,290,293,299,339,362,369, 378,384,385,387,392,394,403,404,408,409

Boyde 81

Box 355

Brackney 101

Braden 137

Bradford 4,11c,1fc,58,66,263,284

Bradley 130,256,306,363

Bradshaw 172

Brady 30,65,96,113,132,145,191,200,221,229, 235,236,257,272,306,323,340,362,411

Braeger 404

Bragg 113,161,170c,179,198,243,179,183,300, 308,326,362,380

Bran 401

Branch 250

Brandon 393

Brannon 338

Brantley 102,177

Brasher 228

Braswell 106,131,223,340

Bratcher 2,43,45,49,52,58,67,68,79,86,97,111, 128,130,131,132,154,170,175,188,190,195,208, 216,217,224,229,222,252,254,283,292,299,315, 323,327,331,346,354,360,375,377,390

Bratten-Bratton 192,229,241,243,250,261, 287,312

Brawley 184

Braxton 25,185,223,277,410,411,419

Bray 283

Brazelton 76

Breedlove 25,185,223,277,410,411,419

Brenceloy. 17

Brewer 31,42,81,90,103,125,126,132,141,221, 247,265,267,297,370,382,383,392

Brewington 17+c,303,345

Bridges 390

Brien 141

Briggs 389

Bright 34,64,79,109,154,156,260

Brinkley 346,384

Brittian 49

Britton 55c

Brixey 14,19,178,182,323,344,388

Brock 141c,236,240,270,325,390, 410,414,420

Bronson 359

Brooks 80,313,332

Broudon 233

Brown 1,3,6c,10,11c,14,16c17, 17c,22,23,25c,32,37,38,39,44,44c,46c, 47c,54,60,64,65,68c,70,72,73,74,76,79, 84,86,87,90,91,91c,93,97,99,100,100c, 101,104,105,105c,107,120,121,132,138c, 14+c,146,153,155,161,163c,166,166,171c, 180,182c183,187,188,19c,193c,199,199c,20c, 20c,201,205,206,209,21c,217c,219,226, 245,246,247,249,250c,252,260,261,264c, 270,271,272,276,282,284,286,295,297, 303,311,312,313,314,315,321,326,328, 33c,335,336,341,34c,345c,346,351,35c, 360,36c,365,365c,37c,373,374,377c, 381,38c,382,383c,385,39c,396,401, 400,403,405c,406,410,41c,412,413, 413c,417,419

Browner 288

Broyles 243,246,256,257

Bruce 59,321,359

Brundage 388

Bruster 4c,89c

Bryan-Bryen 37,41,54,71,158, 184,215,225,272,329,339,344, 349,400,411

Bryant 14,24,27,87,156,157,198,199, 208,264,289,307,328,338,349,392

Brymer 137c,302

Bryson 152,199,246,312

Buchan 9

Buck 312,363

Buffalo 280

Buckner 11,71,184

Bullard 147

Bullen 188

Bumbalough 205,258,296,382,398

Bunch 399

Buntley 334

Burch 34,50,57,66,105,132,138,139,190, 193,213,216,237,240,243,248,312,327, 361,383,396

Combs 1

Comer (s) 14,36,65,66,69,96,110,187,213,
26c,288,290,310,363,368,381,393,405

Conaly 279

Conaster 262,321,334,373,387

Conger 202

Conlin 113,137

Conley 26

Connell 12

Conrad 372

Conrod 144c

Cooley 122,140,225,242,310,326,332,350,404

Cook 104,157,180,181,259,284

Cookley 284

Coonrod 72,8c,214c,372c

Cooper 20,31c,32,32c,35,37,55,57,76,101,138,
151,164,177,197,201,217c,303,330,373

Cope 1c,12c,15,17c,42,43,48c,52,54,71,81,85c,
88,93,93c,95,98c,101c,109,110,122,122c,140,
141,147,148,157c,160c,164c,166,171,178,179,
189,195,200,210,211c,216,217,224,230,233,235,
237c,242c,243,246c,251c,252,259,269,271,272,
276,279,281,285,296,297,299,307,309,323,333,
340c,346,346c,351,356c,360,362,370,375,377,
390,398,405c,412,416

Copehart 17,37,64,197

Copeland 79,352,361,393

Copenhaver 341

Coppinger 26c,40,47,61,63,71,72,74,102,106,
112,142,144,148,163,170,180,207,216,224,250,
252,256,262,277,284,287,327,342,372,374,388,418

Coppie 152

Corbitt 418

Cordell 11,129,211,380

Corder 172

Core 183

Corley 239

Cornelius 285

Cornwell 262

Cotten-Cot on 2,5,14,24,36,83,101,143,
172,195,209,256,260,273,342

Cothern 65

Couch 17,21c52,73,79,146,161,162,172,
182,191,206,227,267,276,277,280,311,331,
333,342,349,355,381

Cowan 16,48c

Cowden 386

Cowley 313

Cox 48,243,252,261,267,279,363,368,397

Crabtree 261,362,376

Craddock 32,345,364

Cragg 170

Craig 225,357,409

Crain 45,51,54,75,76,96,108,113,121,
124,145,150,152,163,173,177,196,211,250,
260,339,341,347

Crane 96,153

Craven 20,38,65,125,169,257,259,298,
315,325,367,399

Crawford 1,3,46,82,113,129,141,160,174,
188,191,197,212,267,368,373

Crawley 17,26,72,81,94,97,98,124,173,
203,206,210,215,298,310,355,362,381,
402,411

Crick 204,309

Crim 19,39,44,48,51,71,101,103,133,138,
145,154,165,172,198,225,243,261,285,322,
325,348,371,375,394,412

Cripps 46c,124,131,205,215,230,287,
305,332,338

Crisco 388

Crisp 17,19,89,100,242c,372c

Crittendon 42,50,57

..kett 63c

Croft 271c

Crook 360

Crossen 91

Crosslin 266,283,313,359,363

Crouch 3,9,17,22,65,74,81,92,97,103,
107,109,113,124,126,176,181,184,230,234,
239,253,257,280,303,382

Crowe 3,37,39,51,180,198,254,255,266,
365,398,400

Crothers 412

Crowley 410

Cruise-Cruse 99,173,297

Crutcher 4c

Cubbins 123,134

Cullen 81

Culveyhouse 46

Cummings 13,35,47c,48,60,62,68,75,78,98,108,
154,168,175,177,197c,198c,221,262,280,298,
309,391

Cunningham 10,15,49,73,74,83,86,88,92,107,
109,110,113,124,126,136,139,142,149,153,156,
160,166,167,175,176,177,178,179,191,193,209,
213,217,230,249,252,295,296,297,304,309,313,
317,318,327,336,344,360,361,363,378,379,384

Curby 79

Curl 88

Curtis 1,15,31,38,45,48,58,70,78,96,99,100,
137,141,148,149,154,159,173,180,183,184,185,
188,191,193,196,201,203,210,242,260,262,274,
279,284,286,287,289,301,302,310,315,322,323,
327,329,345,365,373,379,390,394,405,406c

Cutts 53,215,233,320,329

- D -

Dance 398

Daniel (s) 84,91,380,412

Danielson 406

Darling 4

Damron 240

Darnell 23,31,83,104,174,193,212,234,
235,304,332

Daugherty 11,88,94

Davenport 7,8,9,22,42,43,53,68,78,82,95,100,
102,149,158,160,166,178,182,198,204,209,222,
225,238,241,246,252,264,280,284,311,318,320,
323,348,356,375,381,382,404,407,409

Davey 60

Davidson 7,139,142,353,358,389,398

Davies 338

Davis 8,10,13,16,17,20,24,27,29,31,32,32c,34,
38,42,51,53,62,67,71,84,87,88,90,104,107,110,
121,123,127,128,130,132,133,133c,141,147,148,
150,151,153,156,164,169,173,174,175,179,181,

Cont'd - Next Column

Davis (Cont'd) 182,183,186,187,193-200,
201,203,212,214,221,222,235,239,240,
246,247,249,252,255,265,266,267,269,
270,276,282,285,293,299,302,305,305,
307,317,323,324,328,330,331,344,346,
347,348,349,353,366,370,376,383,386,
387,390,392,299,401A,404,405,406,409,
412,413,417,418,420

Davy 348

Dawson 5,36

Day 4

Deadman-Dedman 186,295,345,407

Deakins 120

Dean 170c

Dearman-Dearmond 212,214c416

Deaton 282,312,409

Deberry 5,7,17,43,45,93,97,109,111,
113,153,323

DeFord 102,411

DeGroat 148

Dehle 222

Delaney 59,143,192,240,292,317,400

Delon-Delong 108,134,157,189,246,
256,261,271,289,341,405,410

Delzell 147

Denby 172,392

Denham 170

Dennie 308

Dennis 156,206,209,240,249,266,286,
296,301,331,335,395

Denny 389

Dentis 255

Denton 26,37,54,55,65,81,86,107,125,
130,141,169,177,178,195,199,224,237,
240,257,297,357,359,364,371,381,386

Devins 207c

Deweese 106,160

Dewey 93

Dewitt 215

Dews 238,257

Dial 19

Dibrell 386

Dickey 255c,381,406

Harpole 253

Harrell 183,186,209,260,277,413,416

Harriman 313

Harris 9,16,101c152,178,186,188,245, 245c,276,292,350,351,407,415

Harrison 17,37,67,68,129,168,215, 233,235,276,395

Hart-Hartt 132,138,225,366

Hartbarger 401

Harter 49

Harvey 395,415,418

Harwell 2,36

Hash 40,66,106,137,145,148,149,160,184, 188,194,210,226,230,255,358,409

Hasker 413

Hasky 279

Hastings 10,215,308,363

Haston 104,189,219,252,262,263,270, 285,298,301,354,364,392,400,405,408

Hatcher 386

Hatfield 14,241

Hatley 388

Havron 189,401A

Hawk 233,266

Hawks 325

Hawkins 1,27,30,32,131,231,232,270, 323,352,384,400,413

Hayes 23,31,47,52,59,60,63,70,157, 177,182,208,212,254,276,279,306,334, 339,352,361,362,364,396,418

Hayhurst 222

Haynes 49,51,379

Head 364

Heard 15c

Hearse 224

Heatherly 309,312,364,366,369,387

Hefner 187

Helen 237

Helton 167,266,277

Hench 1

Haley 36,64,80,86,87,88,102,109,111,139,142, 185,204,211,217,226,259,294,300,304,314,332, 336,346,349,358,388,393,399,410,412

Hallum 151

Hall 5,105,165,221,273,279,281,282,292,310, 322,335,340,341,369,418

Halterman 52,147,152,159

Hamby 2

Hamilton 23,67,68,70,73,125c,222, 224,226,392

Hamily 5

Hammer 3,78,139,146,152,208,248,401

Harmock. 308

Harmond.(s) 5,18c,46,46c,189,382

Harmon(s) 95m145c,146,161,176,187,207,232, 317,362

Hamrick 12,134,227

Hancock 128,219,289,377c

Handley 33c

Hanes 79,272

Haney 258,338

Hanley 255

Hankins 9,34,41,78,79,101,105,240,384

Hannah 183

Hansel 414

Hardcastle 15,62,82,83,313,385

Hardin 139,341

Harding 64c,159,168,187,223,224c,243, 248,288,348,397,408,411

Hardy 15

Hargett 196

Hargis 174,250,258

Hargrave 390

Hagwood 413c

Harkness 351

Harley 344

Harlow 82

Harmon 11,28,44,293

Harper 43,243,263,287,320,348,374

Gramling 142

Granderson 49c

Grandey 130

Grandstaff 54,213,419

Grannison 14c

Graves 55,129,350

Gravison 250c

Gray 136,160,314

Grayson 2c,11c,32c,164c,178,179c,196c,198c, 196c,249,263,263c,264c,271c,326,335,340c,377c, 403c,404c,405c,409c

Gregg 366

Greek 22,137,157,370

Green 2,4,7,10,12,16,18c,19,21,24, 26,27,29,34,37,38,41,42,43,45,47, 49,51,53,54,56,59,62,64,65,68,71, 75,76,78,79,80,82,83,84,85,86,88c,89, 90,91,93,99,102,103,111,112,121,130, 131,137,139,143,145,146,147,150,152, 154,155,157,158,159,160,162,165,169, 170,171,177,180,183,188,192,193,200, 203,208,209,210,213,215,226,234,235, 236,238,239,241,247,248,249,251,253, 260,270,272,274,280,283,291,295,296, 297,299,301,311,307,310,314,318,324, 327,339,340,359,364,366,367,368,375, 380,383,386,391,392,394,395,399,400, 403,405,408,411,412,416

Greenwood 388

Greer 38,62,183,254

Gribble 3,4,9c,11,14,17,21,27,29,33,33c, 35,47,48c62c67,69,73,75,84,85c86,90,94,99, 102,109,110c,112,120,122,133,141,145,146, 147,149,156,162,168,169,175,178,187,190c, 202,208,209,213,218,223c,233,234,239,242,264, 272,281,290,309,311,328,333,339,341c,344, 353,352,367,382,383,391,396,397,398,402,409

Griff 24

Griffie 250

Griffin-Griffen 134,142,146,176,178, 202,213,260,394

Griffith 28,50,59,98,155,159,160,175,189,231, 242,254,266,267,273,277,282,286,288,300,302, 320,325,341,343,353,408

Griffy 201

Grimes 95,146,173

Grimmett 136

Grissom 3,22,31,34,60,61,65,72,77,78, 88,94,122,131,167,168,178,185,193,200, 205,221,235,240,253,270,271,282,284, 289,298,307,309,322,327,346,347,351, 356,364,366,369,371,373,374,384,391, 405,406,414

Griswold 58c,235,389,407

Grizzell-Grizzle 2,21,60,63,67, 104,154,200,232,272,309,347,. 372,377,389

Groce 286

Grosch 313

Gross 59c,63,76,135,140,143,155,181, 202,253,274,287,303,341

Grove(s) 12,16,21,86,88,106, 130,141,142,148,187,188,219, 239.246.256.258.324.341.368.414

Guerard 382c

Guest 12c,17c191c,197c,315c

Guinn 332

Guirdy 390

Gulick-Gullick 231,240

Gulley 41,84,90c,220,306

Gum 195,410

Gunnels 395

Gunter 363,385,397,398

Guthrie 18

Guy 224,363,375

Gwyn(n) 100c,135,158,187c,257, 361,407c

- H -

Haas 379

Hagewood 254,327

Hagwood 323

Hailey 18

Hale 37,87,111,123,140,142,147,151, 153,162,163,167,189,190,196,198,200, 202,205,206,208,225,237,242,265,267, 280,281,285,286,288,290,291,315,318, 325,332,336,348,349,352,358,363,365, 367,373,374,384,385,391,393,399,402, 406,410,413,415,416

Padgett 257,338,409

Paine 29,131,227c,229,250,419

Palmer 2,70,71,73,75,99,278,292,293,346

Panter-Painter-Paynter 28,48,55,127,165,
205,207,241,243,257,272,283,287,302,352,354,
392,410

Paris 18,28,41,44,65,89,97c,102,104,154,194,
276,229,222,238,359,374,398

Parish-Parrish 16,338,345

Parker 5,11,14,19,20,24,30,40,41,56,61,70,73,
75,79,88,90,-91,99,103,104,140,175,176,184,
186,195,199,202,222,223,245,249,252,265,
278,292,298,304,305,315,330,347,357,358,361,
378,390,395,398

Parkhurst 250,291

Parks 140,192,231263,351

Parrott 375

Parsley 27,49,53,65,68,85,90,91,109,113,135,
206,211,232,238,248,269,286,311,333,33,343,
352,367,377,385,403,406,418

Parson 218,250

Patton-Partin 106,125,311,375,402

Pascal-Paschal 277,283,389,416

Passons 44,102,105,107,109,131,145,152,207,
227,255,317,323,325,360,401A,408

Patent 15

Patrick 24,41,46,53,58,63,66,93,95,109,124,
131,143,211,229,230,247,275,293,307,326,336,356

Patterson 1c,12,21,22,-25,28,36,49,51,60,71,
80,125,133,148,162,1992c,204,205,215,220,221,223,
225,226,238,248,250,279,307,345,359,380,409

Patton 30,53,68,85,86,110,123,140,143,152163,
165,174,187,191,194,219,228,250,274,278,298,
357,368,369,387,404

Paty 4

Payne 66,67,103,109,151,216,224,343,366,390,
398,407

Peak 9,36

Pearsall 5,20,70,93,97,113,163,183,273,360

Pearson 17,36,70,179,202,211,214,224,234,273,
297,404,419

Peath 274

Peay 410

Peden 3,47,53,56,64,71,80,81,98,127,144,
173,176,106,210,215,368

Pedigo 127,130,167,173,185,200,202,222,
226,334,352,370,388,420

Peeler 87,157,338

Pegg 83,340

Pelham 65,84,89,135,169,171,181,197,
229,233,243, 248,277,290,314,351,
384,388

Pendergrass 45,66,103,311,356

Pendergraph 382,407

Pendleton 84,97,159,161,169,171,220,
315,324,371,419

Penn 19

Pennington 14,63,73,87,94,96,149c,150,
162,163,168,172,178,183,213,266,305,351

Pepper 3,6,88,96,99,105,157,193c,199,
206,234,240,258,319,382,393

Peren-Perren 168,196

Perkins 36,41,113,372c,414

Perrigen 233

Perry 9,13,15,42,51,60,67,72,75,80,81,
91,104,134,145,150,167,168,172,174,190,
194,201,205,212,219,226,239,241,249,250,
261,269,274,332,318,342,343,348,353,
362,274,377,381

Persinger 156

Peterson 387

Pettit-Pettitt 10,23,207

Petts 268

Petty 278

Peyton 55

Phelps 5c,40,83,89,98,122,130,
175,188,257

Phifer 108,170,249,252,405

Phillips 23,44,61,68,73,80,93,100,158,
180,186,190,198,265,266,281,283,287,291,
325,337,355,372,378,380,390,414

Philpot 181,220

Pickett 259,285,286,369

Pierce 386,388

Pigg 14

Pike 96,319

Pincheaon 379c,395c

Pinegar 6,21,80,128,130,137,167,181,198,240,
242,291,306,307,310,315,328,364,366,372,374,
388,391,409

Pinkerton 126c

Pinkley 355

Pinklin 151

Pippin 200

Pipkin 75

Pirtle 137,400

Pistole 75,218,266,315,370

Pitman 240,255,269,299,335,337

Pitt(s) 130,307,373,401

Pleasant 3c,210c,261c,271c,333,338,356

Plumlee 77

Plyant 46,56

Poe 219

Pointer 87

Pollard 49,153,170,309,400

Pond 394

Ponder 231,295

Pope 10,22,45,240,328

Porter 108,345,407

Porterfield-Poterfield 48,54,64,68,176
397,399

Potter 10,40,71,89,94,123,134,143,144,155,
167,177,241,243,247,280,297,299,330,311,315,
321,343,385,391,415,418

Powell 7,17,20,28,78,98,135,150,183,184,194,
198,207,218,223,224,262,286,303,305,331,370,
378,405,407,410,411,412,414,416,417

Powers 229,231,311

Prater 18,62,66,82,92,95,98,100,176c,192,193,
214,243,246,257,263,266,269,273,274,283,289,
301,317,318,319,333,336,344,367,376,378,389,
393,396,400,403,404,413

Prather 171

Pratt 96

Prescott 378

Presley-Pressley 39,283,296,304,376

Preston 124,189,214,247,270,417

Price 11c,76,135c,167,291,372c,394

Priemer 406

Priest 2,39,48,51,54,58,77,112,
184,187,208,231,239,269,280,304,
305,308,328,357,374,383,405,412

Prime 227c

Pritchard 227,276

Pritchett 21c,60c

Pryor 148,155,201,343,365,416

Puckett 158,175,380

Pugh 66,136,281,290,295,306,318

Purgason 385

Purser 148

Pursley 410

Puterbaugh 1,51

Putnam 322

- Q -

Qualls 103,109

Quick 33,36,124,146,215,222,273,304

Quinn 325,331,336

- R -

Rackley 188,305,392,407

Rackowski 407

Rader 335,410

Raines-Rains 14c,22,28,47C,49,71,80,
107,111,130,178,248,273,279,307,322,
339,340,395,399,412

Ramage 403

Ramsey 2c,8,11c,14,15c,20-24c,29c,30c,
46,46c,48c,51c,55,82,83,98,107c,112c,
14c,147,151,151c,15c,162,174,196c,
204,216c,21c,21b,218c,223,226c,231,
233,233c,237,240c,246c,253c,25c,266,
271c,275,276,277,281c,293c,310,311,
(Ramsey - Cont'd, Next Page)

Smiddie 270

Smith 4,9,11c,13,16,17,18,19c,21,21c,
22,24c,25,26,27,28,29,30,34,36,37,39,
40,41,43,46,47,47c,48,52,54c,50,61,62,
62c,64,65,67,68,69,73,74,75,76,77c,79,
83,85,85c,91,99,102,103,105,108,109,
111,112,124,125,126,127,128,13,132,
133,137,138c,144,146,147,150,150c,
152c,153,156,165,167,169,175,176,182c,
185,187c,188,189c,192,192c,193,194,196,
197,198,200,201,201c,203,20c,206,210,
215,219,224,225,227,229,231,234c,235,
235,239,246,247,252,254,257,259,263c,
264,271,277,278,281,283,292,293,
295,296,300,301,303,304,314,315,318,
324,327,332,337,340,342,344,345,347,
349,351,355,357c,358,360,363,364,
384,385,386,387,392,394,395,396,397,
398,399,39c,400,401,401A,402,403,406,
413,413,415,415c,418,419

Smithson 19,78,146,176,182,194,203,
212,217,230,280,282,305,323,328,335,
339,364,379,395

Smittie 237

Smoot 25c,31,35,37,46,60,78,86,91,97,
104,123,130,134,137,144,200,204,260,
221,297,305,347,348

Smooty 288

Smotherman 99

Snider, Snyder 17,265,303,391

Snelling 148c

Snipe (s) 22,23,26,41,44,45,81,103,108,123,
160,169,186,235,251,286,287,306,327,335,352,
372,388

Snodgrass 26c

Snead-Sneed 161,276

Snow 349

Solomon 45c,101c,249c,291c,370,401tc

Soulsley 374

Southard 384,397,401

Sims-Simms 97,,126,131,152,162,164,
189c,407 - 15,61,225,254

Simmons 1,35,50,56,132,152,157,168,
170,174,181,208,215,217,229,230,234,
236,237,240,278,283,288,302,305,338,
370,371,376,387,401,405,410,411

Simons 2,4,33,38,60,64,105,127,160,
162,179,192,195,196,202,203,208,212,
219,227,234,239,247,264,283,285,290,
292,302,309,312,317,320,321,328,329,
332,356,370,386,397,402,403,407,409,
412

Simpkins 290

Simpson 13,25,34,46,70,92,108,123,
160,185,222,233,267c,287,298,330,359,
365

Simrell 23

Singleton 183

Sisk 223

Sissom 21,41,106,277

Skelton 299

Skilling 359

Slatten-Slatton 15,24,35c,28,35,42,
112,134,189,197,241,251,308,356,382,
401,409

Slaughter 47,49,56,60,63,74,84,104,
298,374

Slayden 400

Sliger 84,92,322

Sloan 220

Smallman 1

Smartt 3,13,16c,17c,19c,22c,23c,24,24c,
29,32,33,38,39,40,41,42,52,56,58,59c,
63,64c,65,68,72,73c,75,95,96,97m68c,100,
106,109,127,134,151,161,163,164,171c,
173,174,175c,180,181,186,187,187c,189c,
19c,201,203,204,207,210,212c,223,224,
229,237,251,256,260,261,264c266,270,
276,281,283,286,289,303,305,314,321,
328,329,343,373,374,384,385,392,406,
412,416

Sattin 23

Saults 322

Savage 6c,11c,15c,17,21c,29c,37c,38,43c,
65c,71,72c,76,92,111,142c,143,152,183c,
19c,19c,202c,223c,240,247c,252c,256c,271c,
284c,332,337c,342,
346,370c,371,375c,390,410c,414c,418,418

Satlors 256,359,377

Schalgeter 278

Schild 290

Schmitz 61

Schneider 388

Schrock 137,203,225,238,260,364

Schwab 386

Scissom 337

Scoggins 419

Scott 21c,23,35,48,50,52,55,56,60,62,
75,80,82,84,89,97c,111,124c,147,148,
148c,156,165,170,173,176,177,180,
193,194,205,207,215,220,222c,226,235,
235,236,237,238,245,252,253,257,260c,261,
263,265,269,276,277,278,284,284c,285,286,294,
297,298,301,306,307,308,311,326,328,329,333,
343,346c,348,349,353c,35c,355,360,384,385,
385c,388,404,406,408c,416,418

Scriviner 389

Scrugg (s) 171,216,383

Scurlock 188

Seagle 358

Seal 141

Seale 342,346,347

Seals 194,197,228,278

Seamon (s) 199,219,276,396

Sears 418

Sedberry 126

Sedore 331,333

Seip 173

Seitz 4c

Selby 306

Selby 306

Self 166,194,210,218,220,307,323,337,361

Sellars 88,90,152,168,180,375

Sells 139

Semones 94

Seneker 112

Settle (s) 189c,282,282c,302

Sevier 328

Sexton 373

SHackleford 397

Shadow 112

Shallman 369

Shannon 6,162,275

Sharp-Sharpe 378,402

Shaw 83,242c,329,379

Shawver 38,102

Shelby 325

Shelton 107,110,132,358,398

Shephard Shepherd 359,364,397c

Sherer 380

Sherman 352

Sherrell 12,67,73,134,193,194,219,
231,232,234,238,263,297,324

Shields 55,105,129,132,169,259,
360

Shirley 23,30,42,55,81,159,179,
188,211,267,270,326

Shoal 135

Shockley 82,102,164c,167c,250c,271,
287,307,337,345c,380c,391c,396

Shoopman 351

Shores 14c

Short 290

Shorter 390

Showers 248

Shugars 162c

Suster 112

Sigenthaler 394

Sillaway - Silloway 25,256

Weirsma 390

Weissman 391

Welch 178,267,388

Wells 292,293,381

Werber 185

West 70,85,91,99,151,158,206,229,267,273,
307,330,365,369,401A,415

Westphal 63

Wharton 322

Wheeling 245

Wherry 222c

Wheeler 18,36,50,152,188,197,206,321,330

Whitaker 65,66,232

White 30,67c,73,108,122,152,160,164,173,181,
19tc,205,214,217c,219,221c,239,246,259c,308,
313,322,330,358,366,374,417

Whiteaker 52,73,82,122,143,174,232,

Whiteside 388

Whitlock 46,51,68,87,105,127,138,155,157,159,
185,188,194,200,219,243,315,349,377,417,419

Whitlow 224c

Whitman 3,156,240,379

Whitson 52,175

Whittemore 359

Whittenbury 142,144,155,159,221,277,291,
32,412

Whittice 269

Whittier 398

Whitworth 174

Wiant 225

Wilburn 7c,345

Wilcher 8,65,155,214,219,287,300,309

Wilcox 149,395

Wilder 359

Wiley 28

Wilkerson 339,361c,383

Wilkinson 144

Willard 408

Williams 5,15,16,18,25,28,31,44,44c,
45,50,51,57,65,75,76,84,94,99,100,
104,105c,110,163c,168,175,184,189,
202,204,206,207,213,234,238,250,275,
282,311,313,327,332c,341,356,358,358c,
364,366,369,377,383,384,384,386,393,
400,401A,404,412

Williamson 33,65,85,93,109,124,127,
142,194,227,232,262,292,302,317,318,
319,322,325,342,349,384,404

Willis 12c,15,31,110,128,191,307,311,
389

Willett 30

Willoughby 298

Wilmore 298,372

Wilcher, Wilsher 18

Wilson 3,4c,14,18,24,28,35,37,42,47,
49,51c,60,61,66,81c,83,86,87,88,91c,
92,93,93c,97,99,102,103,106,109,125c,
126,127,135,139,142,143,147,149,151,
153,161,166,171,177,
179,184,211,230,233,238,239,241,245,253,
261,267,271c,272,275,279,284,290,293,295,
299,306,312,313,323,327,329,332,344,
355,360,361,365,368,369,375,376,397,
401A,415,417

Wimberly 99,101,111,124,170,
242,356,372,385

Windham 238

Windom 90c

Windsor 247

Winfree-Winfrey 82,134,135,192,
300,357

Winnard 162,272,279

Winnett 1,10,24,85,159,205,242,267,
297,332,358,386

Winningham 293

Winstead 177,207,311,346

Winston 122c

Winton 16,53,59,70,110c,148c,157,
191,262,280,292,300c,313,335,340,37tc,
37tc,414

Wires 205

Wirt 417

Wiseiner 22

Wiseman 3,31,53,59,90,126,138,218,269,291,
360,393,395,405,414

Wiser 294,298,324,356,380,384

Witt 44,50,150,324,344,349,351,368

Witty 216,303

Wollard 252

Womack 2,11,18,26,27,35,42,45,50,52,55,58,
62,64,74,76,78,80,83,85,86,90,94,100,105, "
106,108,110,123c,124,126,127,128,129c,132,135c,
136,138,142,143,145,146,147,148,150c,153,155c,
163,165,166,167,178,185,188,190,197,204,217,
221,221,229,243,248,249,250,258,259,260,262,
267,280,281,285,286,287,291,292,299,300,30tc,
307,308,311,325,329335,348,349,352,355,356,
358,359,364,365,367,37tc,376,377,384,387,389,
390,392,393,394,395,399,403c,405,418,420

Wood (s) 8c,13,20,26,40,45,47c54,57,63,
63c,66,69,70,71,93c,95c,113,123,124c,125,125c,
127,133,113c,134,138c,147,151,152c,153,158,
163,166,189,19tc,195,209,210,213c,214,217,
222,226,226c,227,227c,236,238,241,248,253,259,
264c,294,301,309,311,315,317,320,323,345,348,
354,359,363,379c,401Ac,403,403c,40tc,414

Woodard 11,11c,64,77c,394c,406c

Woodhurst 414

Woodlee 2c,10c,18c,32,32c,63c,70,77c,81c,
96,107,108c,128,134,136,163,171,172c,180c,
191,192,199,203,207,210,220,228,238,241,258,
260,267,270,280,283,287,295,296c,306,310,326,
329,330,343,347,349,352,358,380,38tc,382,383,
39tc,403c,410,411

Woodmore 299

woodside 217,232

Woody 86

Wooten 55,60c,109,112,139,176,201,219c

Worley 14,16,26,157,186,284

Worthington 1,27c,28c,80,140c,324,349c

Wright 13,45,62,76,87,89,90,97,99,128,132,
144,181,202,203,207,210,217,225,236,256,286,
302,307,339,347,378,388,417

Wrightman 46,196

- Y -

Yager 71,373,417

Yergan 94

Yates 160,196,356,393

York 102c,113,126,129,133c,140c,142c,
146,150,151,152c,163,164,171c,180,201c,
205,212c,216,229,240,264c,270,282c,284,
285,295,297,301,317,338,343,353,363c,
414,419

Young 73,85,89c,111,125,135,140,141,
145,161,166,171,173,189,198,202,204,
207,219,221,226,228,232,242,253,257,
263,271,271c,274,280,281,284,285,288,
292,293,299,303,305,310,314,331,337,
340,341,347,351,357,361,366,369,373,
374,383,394,406,411,413,416,418,419

Youngblood 74,95,102,158,167,192,219,
243,248,288,300,302,317,326,366

- Z -

Zechman 365

Zwingle 4,13,91,130,148,164,339